358

THE NEW POETRY

THE MACMILLAN COMPANY
NEW YORK · BOSTON · CHICAGO · DALLAS
ATLANTA · SAN FRANCISCO

MACMILLAN & CO., Limited
LONDON · BOMBAY · CALCUTTA
MELBOURNE

THE MACMILLAN COMPANY
OF CANADA, Limited
TORONTO

THE NEW POETRY

AN ANTHOLOGY

OF TWENTIETH-CENTURY VERSE
IN ENGLISH

EDITED BY

HARRIET MONROE

EDITOR OF POETRY: A MAGAZINE OF VERSE

AND

ALICE CORBIN HENDERSON

NEW EDITION

REVISED AND ENLARGED BY H. M.
WITH BIOGRAPHICAL AND CRITICAL NOTES

87
BIP

Grangers

NEW YORK

THE MACMILLAN COMPANY

1937

Set up and electrotyped. Published February, 1917. New and
Enlarged edition, April, 1923. Reprinted, November, 1925;
May, 1926. Reissued June, 1926; June, 1927. New edition revised
and reset, September, 1932 ; November, 1934; January, 1936 ;
June, 1936 ; April, November, 1937.

ACKNOWLEDGMENTS

D. Appleton & Co.: For poems from *The Wind in the Corn and Other Poems,* by Edith Wyatt.

Albert & Charles Boni: For poems from *Tulips and Chimneys,* by E. E. Cummings.

Boni & Liveright: For a poem from *Introducing Irony,* by Maxwell Bodenheim; and for poems from *Personæ: The Collected Poems of Ezra Pound.*

Brandt & Brandt: As agents for Conrad Aiken (one poem), Stephen Vincent Benét (three poems), and Edna St. Vincent Millay (six poems).

Brentano's: For poems from *Color of Water,* by Marjorie Meeker.

B. J. Brimmer Co.: For poems from *The Poems of Seumas O'Sullivan.*

Nicholas L. Brown: For poems from *Sonnets from the Patagonian,* by Donald Evans; and from *Blood of Things,* by Alfred Kreymborg.

Jonathan Cape & Harrison Smith: For poems from *Blue Juniata,* by Malcolm Cowley.

The Century Co.: For poems from *Songs for the New Age,* by James Oppenheim: and from *Challenge,* by Louis Untermeyer.

Covici, Friede, Inc.: For poems from *Toward Equilibrium,* by Polly Chase Boyden; and from *Chelsea Rooming House,* by Horace Gregory.

Coward, McCann, Inc.: For poems from *Songs of the Coast-dwellers,* by Constance Lindsay Skinner.

John Day Co.: For poems from *High Falcon,* by Léonie Adams.

Dial Press: For poems from *XLI Poems,* by E. E. Cummings; and from *Observations,* by Marianne Moore.

Dodd, Mead & Co.: For poems from *Curtains* and *Walkers,* by Hazel Hall.

George H. Doran Co.: For poems from *Candles That Burn* and *Vigils,* by Aline Kilmer; from *Trees and Other Poems,* by Joyce Kilmer; and from *Kensington Gardens,* by Humbert Wolfe.

Doubleday, Doran & Co.: For poems from *Intellectual Things,* by Stanley J. Kunitz.

Duffield & Co.: For poems from *Flashlights,* by Mary Aldis.

E. P. Dutton & Co.: For poems from *Cry of Time,* by Hazel Hall; from *Eidola,* by Frederic Manning; and from *The Old Huntsman, Counter-attack,* and *Picture-show,* by Siegfried Sassoon.

Faber & Faber: For a poem from *Ecliptic,* by Joseph Gordon Macleod.

Farrar & Rinehart: For poems from *White April,* by Lizette Woodworth Reese.

The Four Seas Co.: For poems from *The House of Dust,* by Conrad Aiken; from *Images,* by Richard Aldington; from *Morning, Noon and Night,* by Glenn Ward Dresbach; from *Collected Poems,* by Yone Noguchi; and from *Al que Quiere* and *Sour Grapes,* by William Carlos Williams.

Harcourt, Brace & Co.: For poems from *Apples Here in My Basket,* by Helen Hoyt; from *The Noise That Time Makes,* by Merrill Moore; from *Smoke and Steel,* by Carl Sandburg; from *Once in a Blue Moon,* by Marion Strobel; from *The New Adam,* by Louis Untermeyer; from *The Contemplative Quarry and The Man with a Hammer,* by Anna Wickham; from *The Unknown Goddess,* by Humbert Wolfe; and from *Nets to Catch the Wind,* by Elinor Wylie.

Harper & Bros.: For poems from *Cyclops' Eyes,* and *Sunrise Trumpets,* by Joseph Auslander; from *Color* and *Copper Sun,* by Countee Cullen; from *Outcrop,* by Abbie Huston Evans; and from *Sea-drinking Cities,* by Josephine Pinckney.

v

Henry Holt & Co.: For poems from *Wild Earth and Other Poems*, by Padraic Colum; from *Wilderness Songs*, by Grace Hazard Conkling; from *Hymen*, by H. D.; from *The Listeners*, *Motley*, and *Collected Poems*, by Walter de la Mare; from *A Boy's Will*, *North of Boston*, *A Mountain Interval*, *West-running Brook*, and *New Hampshire*, by Robert Frost; from *Chicago Poems* and *Cornhuskers*, by Carl Sandburg; from *Many Many Moons*, *Slow Smoke*, and *Wings against the Moon*, by Lew Sarett; from *Poems*, by the late Edward Thomas; and from *The Factories and Other Lyrics*, by Margaret Widdemer.

The Houghton Mifflin Co.: For poems from *Afternoons of April*, by Grace Hazard Conkling; from *Sea Garden*, by H. D.; from *Poems 1908–1919*, by John Drinkwater; from *Irradiations* and *Goblins and Pagodas*, by John Gould Fletcher; from *A Dome of Many-colored Glass*, *Sword Blades and Poppy Seed*, *Pictures of the Floating World*, and *Legends*, by Amy Lowell; from *Streets in the Moon* and *New Found Land*, by Archibald MacLeish; from *Long Leash*, by Jessica Nelson North; from *The Sister of the Wind*, by Grace Fallow Norton; from *The Singing Man* and *Harvest Moon*, by the late Josephine Preston Peabody; from *Gold Coast Customs*, by Edith Sitwell; and from *Lost City*, by Marion Strobel.

B. W. Huebsch, Inc.: See the Viking Press.

Mitchell Kennerley: For poems from *Interpretations*, by Zoë Akins; from *Sonnets of a Portrait Painter*, and *The Man on a Hilltop*, by Arthur Davison Ficke; from *The Jew to Jesus and Other Poems*, by Florence Kiper Frank; from *Renascence and Other Poems*, and *Second April*, by Edna St. Vincent Millay; from *Man-song*, and *The Quest*, by John G. Neihardt; and from *The Pilgrimage*, by Yone Noguchi.

Alfred A. Knopf: For poems from *Punch the Immortal Liar*, by Conrad Aiken; from *The New World*, *Grenstone Poems*, *The Beloved Stranger*, *A Canticle of Pan*, and *Indian Earth*, by Witter Bynner; from *April Twilights and Other Poems*, by Willa Cather; from *Flying Fish* and *Witch*, by Grace Hazard Conkling; from *Verse*, by the late Adelaide Crapsey; from *Poems*, by T. S. Eliot; from *Fine Clothes to the Jew*, by Langston Hughes; from *Asphalt and Other Poems*, by Orrick Johns; from *Mushrooms*, by Alfred Kreymborg; from *Lustra with Earlier Poems*, by Ezra Pound; from *Chills and Fever*, and *Two Gentlemen in Bonds*, by John Crowe Ransom; from *A Woman of Thirty*, by Marjorie Allen Seiffert; from *Troy Park* and *Bucolic Comedies*, by Edith Sitwell; from *Fiddler's Farewell*, by Leonora Speyer; from *Harmonium*, by Wallace Stevens; from *Profiles from China*, *Body and Raiment*, and *Leaves in Windy Weather*, by Eunice Tietjens; from *In American* and *Finders*, by John V. A. Weaver; from *Black Armour*, *Trivial Breath*, and *Angels and Earthly Creatures*, by Elinor Wylie.

John Lane Co. (now Dodd, Mead & Co.): For poems from *Collected Poems*, by the late Rupert Brooke; and from *On Heaven and Poems Written on Active Service*, by Ford Madox (Hueffer) Ford.

Horace Liveright: For poems from *Machinery*, by MacKnight Black; from *The Bridge* and *White Buildings*, by Hart Crane, from *Roan Stallion*, by Robinson Jeffers; and from *The White Rooster* and *God Beguiled*, by George O'Neil.

Robert McBride & Co.: For a poem from *Body of This Death*, by Louise Bogan.

Minton, Balch & Co.: For a poem from *Mr. Pope and Other Poems*, by Allen Tate.

Edwin Valentine Mitchell: For poems from *New Poems and Old*, by Muriel Stuart.

Moffat, Yard & Co.: For poems from *Poems*, by Haniel Long.

Pagan Publishing Co.: For poems from *Minna and Myself*, by Maxwell Bodenheim.

Norman Remington & Co.: For poems from *Spicewood*, and *Wild Cherry*, by Lizette Woodworth Reese.

A. M. Robertson: For poems from *Beyond the Breakers*, and *Sails and Mirage*, by George Sterling.

Charles Scribner's Sons: For poems from *Charnel Rose*, *John Deth*, and *Selected Poems*, by Conrad Aiken; from *Dark Summer*, by Louise Bogan; from *Poems*, by

Alice Meynell; from *The Children of the Night*, and *The Town down the River*, by Edwin Arlington Robinson; from *Ballads of a Singing Bowl* and *The King with Three Faces*, by Marjorie Allen Seiffert; from *Poems*, by the late Alan Seeger; and from *The Bright Doom*, by John Hall Wheelock.

Thomas Seltzer (now Albert & Charles Boni): For poems from *For Eager Lovers*, by Genevieve Taggard.

Ralph Fletcher Seymour: For poems from *The Spinning Woman of the Sky* and *Red Earth*, by Alice Corbin; and from *Faces and Open Doors*, and *New Lyrics and a Few Old Ones*, by Agnes Lee.

Frank Shay: For poems from *This Morning*, by Hildegarde Flanner; and from *Figs and Thistles*, by Edna St. Vincent Millay.

Sherman, French & Co.: For poems from *The Beloved Adventure* and *Love and Liberation*, by John Hall Wheelock; and from *In Vivid Gardens*, by the late Marguerite Wilkinson.

Frederick A. Stokes & Co.: For poems from *Poems by a Little Girl*, by Hilda Conkling; from *Ardors and Endurances*, by Robert Nichols; and from *Collected Poems*, by the late Padraic Pearse.

The Viking Press (formerly B. W. Huebsch, Inc.): For poems from *Mid-American Chants*, by Sherwood Anderson; from *Boy in the Wind* and *The Flowering Stone*, by George Dillon; from *God's Trombones*, by James Weldon Johnson; from *Chamber Music*, by James Joyce; from *Amores* and *Look! We Have Come Through*, by D. H. Lawrence; from *Two Lives*, by William Ellery Leonard; from *Poems*, by Wilfred Owen; from *The Ghetto and Other Poems*, by Lola Ridge; from *Under the Tree*, by Elizabeth Madox Roberts; from *Dreams out of Darkness*, by Jean Starr Untermeyer; and from *The Hesitant Heart* and *This Delicate Love*, by Winifred Welles.

Monroe Wheeler: For poems from *The Living Frieze*, by Mark Turbyfill; from *The Bitterns*, by Glenway Wescott; and from *The Immobile Wind*, by Yvor Winters.

Yale University Press: For poem from *The Falconer of God*, by William Rose Benét.

To the following magazines also we express our thanks for poems not yet included in books:

The New Republic, for a poem by William Rose Benét, one by Harold Lewis Cook, and one by Marion Strobel.

Poetry: A Magazine of Verse, for poems by Mary Austin, Emanuel Carnevali, Harold Lewis Cook, H. L. Davis, Louise Driscoll, Helen Dudley, Fenton Johnson, Maurice Lesemann, Max Michelson, Elder Olson, Patrick Orr, Ernest Rhys, Frances Shaw, Ajan Syrian, the late Allen Upward, Morton Dauwen Zabel, and Marya Zaturensky.

To a few poets who control their own copyrights wholly or in part, and have been very generous in lending their poems to this anthology, we wish to express our special thanks. These are: Mary Austin, Stephen Vincent Benét, Howard McKinley Corning, Glenn Ward Dresbach, T. S. Eliot, William Closson Emory, Ford Madox Ford, Agnes Lee, Maurice Lesemann, Edna St. Vincent Millay, Yone Noguchi, Ezra Pound, the late John Reed, Charles Reznikoff, and Humbert Wolfe.

We acknowledge with thanks also the courtesy of the following poets, who have permitted the use of poems from books published by The Macmillan Company: the late Gladys Cromwell, Hildegarde Flanner, John Gould Fletcher, Wilfrid Gibson, the late Thomas Hardy, DuBose Heyward, Ralph Hodgson, Muna Lee, the late Vachel Lindsay, John Masefield, Edgar Lee Masters, the late Charlotte Mew, Harriet Monroe, Edwin Arlington Robinson, James Stephens, Rabindranath Tagore, Sara Teasdale, Ridgely Torrence, and William Butler Yeats.

TABLE OF CONTENTS

INTRODUCTION

In preparing this third edition, this second revision, of The New Poetry, *the editor finds little to add to the introductions of the two previous editions. The years between 1923 and 1931 have been rich in new personalities, and in new work by poets represented in the previous editions. These we have tried to exhibit by liberal inclusions; the reader will find new names and new poems to enrich his knowledge of present tendencies in the art. And to make room for these, a few names are omitted of poets whose literary interests have turned from the creation of poetry to novels, plays or critical work, or who have become absorbed in other pursuits.*

The present tendencies are almost as numerous as the individual poets who illustrate them. Radical experiment has led a few poets into extremes of insurgence—represented in transition (*now renewing after suspension*), Blues, Pagany, Front, Left *and other organs. Meanwhile poets more conservative have continued to use traditional rhymed forms—especially the sonnet, though often taking liberties with it; and some of the imagists and other revolutionists of 1912 and later have drifted into their company. Critics who love labels have created a "metaphysical school" for certain followers, more or less remote, of Donne, Vaughan, Herbert and other seventeenth-century poets of the speculative mind.*

On the whole, the modern poets are individualists, which is perhaps the healthiest tendency of all; and such group affiliations as they confess rarely prove binding. In this anthology we present them as individuals, connected only by the alphabetical chain which, with delightful unconcern, neighbors Edgar Lee Masters with Charlotte Mew and Winifred Welles with John V. A. Weaver. And by way of preface, to suggest the foundations and the structural progress of twentieth-century poetry, the editor reprints below her introductions to the two previous editions of this book.

From the original edition of 1917:

During the last few years there has been a remarkable renascence of poetry in both America and England, and an equally extraordinary revival of public interest in the art.

The editors of this anthology wish to present in convenient form representative work of the poets who are today creating what is commonly called "the new poetry"—a phrase no doubt rash and most imperfectly descriptive, since the new in art is always the elder old, but one difficult to replace with any form of words more exact. Much newspaper controversy, and a number of special magazines, testify to the demand for such a book; also many letters to the editors of *Poetry* asking for information—letters not only from individual lovers of the art, but also from college professors and literary clubs or groups, who have begun to feel that the poetry of today is a vital force no longer to be ignored. Indeed, many critics feel that poetry is coming nearer than either the novel or the drama to the actual life of our time. The magazine *Poetry*, ever since its foundation in October, 1912, has encouraged this new spirit in the art, and the anthology is a further effort on the part of its editors to present the new spirit to the public.

What is the new poetry? and wherein does it differ from the old? The difference is not in mere details of form, for much poetry infused with the new spirit conforms to the old measures and rhyme-schemes. It is not merely in diction, though the truly modern poet rejects the so-called "poetic" shifts of language—the *deems*, *'neaths*, *forsooths*, etc., the inversions and high-sounding rotundities, familiar to his predecessors: all the rhetorical excesses through which most Victorian poetry now seems "over-appareled," as a speaker at a *Poetry* dinner—a lawyer, not a poet—put it in pointing out what the new movement is aiming at. These things are important, but the difference goes deeper than details of form, strikes through them to fundamental integrities.

The new poetry strives for a concrete and immediate realization of life; it would discard the theory, the abstraction, the remoteness, found in all classics not of the first order. It is less vague, less verbose, less eloquent, than most poetry of the Victorian period and much work of earlier periods. It has set before itself an ideal of absolute simplicity and sincerity—an ideal which implies an individual, unstereotyped diction; and an individual, unstereotyped rhythm. Thus inspired, it becomes intensive rather than diffuse. It looks out more eagerly than in; it becomes objective. The term "exteriority" has been applied to it, but this is incomplete. In presenting the concrete object or the concrete environment, whether these be beautiful or ugly, it seeks to give more precisely the emotion arising from them, and thus widens immeasurably the scope of the art.

All this implies no disrespect for tradition. The poets of today do not discard tradition because they follow the speech of today rather than that of Shakespeare's time, or strive for organic rhythm rather than use a mold which has been perfected by others. On the contrary, they follow the great tradition when they seek a vehicle suited to their own epoch and their own creative mood, and resolutely reject all others.

Great poetry has always been written in the language of contemporary speech, and its theme, even when legendary, has always borne a direct relation with contemporary thought, contemporary imaginative and spiritual life. It is this direct relation which the more progressive modern poets are trying to restore. In this effort they discard not only archaic diction but also the shop-worn subjects of past history or legend, which have been through the centuries a treasure-trove for the second-rate.

This effort at modern speech, simplicity of form, and authentic vitality of theme, is leading our poets to question the authority of the accepted laws of English verse, and to study other languages, ancient and modern, in the effort to find out what poetry really is. It is a strange fact that, in the common prejudice of cultivated people during the four centuries from just before 1400 to just before 1800, nothing was accepted as poetry in English that did not walk in the iambic measure. Bits of Elizabethan song and of Dryden's two musical odes, both beating four-time instead of the iambic three, were outlandish intrusions too slight to count. To write English poetry, a man must measure his paces according to the iambic foot-rule; and he must mark off his lines with rhymes, or at least marshal them in the pentameter movement of blank verse.

The first protest against this prejudice, which long usage had hardened into law, came in the persons of four or five great poets—Burns, Coleridge, Keats, Shelley, Byron—who puzzled the ears of their generation with anapæsts and other four-time measures, and who carried into their work a certain immediacy of feeling and imagery—a certain modern passion of life—which even Cowper, Thompson and a few others of their time, though they had written of things around them, had scarcely attained. Quarterly critics and London moralists blinked and gasped, but at last the bars had to go down for these great radicals. And before long the extreme virtuosity of Swinburne had widened still further the musical range of the English language.

By the time Whitman appeared, the ear of the average reader —that formidable person—was attuned to anapæsts, dactyls, choriambics, sapphics, rhymed or unrhymed. He could not call them by name, but he was docile to all possible intricacies of pattern in any closely woven metrical scheme. But Whitman gave him a new shock. Here was a so-called poet who discarded all traditional patterns, and wove a carpet of his own. Once more the conservatives protested: was this poetry? and, if so, why? If poetry was not founded on the long-accepted metrical laws, then how could they distinguish it from prose, and thus keep the labels and catalogues in order? What was Whitman's alleged poetry but a kind of freakish prose, invented to set forth a dangerous anarchistic philosophy?

It would take too long to analyze the large rhythms of Whitman's free verse; but the mere fact that he wrote free verse and called it poetry, and that other poets—men like Rossetti, Swinburne, Symonds, even the reluctant Emerson—seemed to agree that it was poetry, this fact alone was, in the opinion of the conservatives, a challenge to four centuries of English poets. And this challenge, repeated by later poets, compels us to inquire briefly into the origins of English poetry, in the effort to get behind and underneath the instinctive prejudice that English poetry, to be poetry, must conform to prescribed metres.

Chaucer, great genius that he was, an aristocrat by birth and breeding, and a democrat by feeling and sympathy— Chaucer may have had it in his power to turn the whole stream of English poetry into either the French or the Anglo-Saxon channel. Knowing and loving the old French epics better than the Norse sagas, he naturally chose the French channel, and he was so great and so beloved that his world followed him. Thus there was no longer any question—the iambic measure and rhyme, both dear to the French-trained ears of England's Norman masters, became fixed as the standard type of poetic form.

But it was possibly a toss-up—the scale hung almost even in that formative fourteenth century. If Chaucer's contemporary Langland—the great democrat, revolutionist, mystic—had had Chaucer's authority and universal sympathy, English poetry might have followed his example instead of Chaucer's; and Shakespeare, Milton and the rest might have been impelled by common practice to use—or modify—the curious, heavy, alliterative measure of *Piers Ploughman*, which now sounds so strange to our ears:

> In a somer seson,
> When softe was the sonne,
> I shoop me into shroudes
> As I a sheep weere;
> In habite as an heremite
> Unholy of werkes,
> Wente wide in this world
> Wondres to here.

Though we must rejoice that Chaucer prevailed with his French forms, Langland reminds us that poetry—even English poetry—is older than rhyme, older than the iambic measure, older than all the metrical patterns which now seem so much a part of it. If our criticism is to have any value, it must insist upon the obvious truth that poetry existed before the English language began to form itself out of the débris of other tongues, and that it now exists in forms of great beauty among many far-away peoples who never heard of our special rules.

Perhaps the first of these disturbing influences from afar to be felt in modern English poetry was the Celtic renascence, the wonderful revival of interest in Old Irish song, which became manifest in translations and adaptations of the ancient Gaelic lyrics and epics, made by W. B. Yeats, Lady Gregory, Douglas Hyde and others.

This influence was most powerful because it came to us directly, not at second-hand, through the English work of two poets of genius, Synge and Yeats. These great men, fortified and inspired by the simplicity and clarity of primitive Celtic song, had little patience with the "over-apparelled" art of Tennyson and his imitators. They found it stiffened by rhetoric, by a too conscious morality leading to pulpit eloquence, and by second-hand bookish inspirations; and its movement they found hampered, thwarted of freedom, by a too slavish acceptance of ready-made schemes of metre and rhyme. The surprises and irregularities, found in all great art because they are inherent in human feeling, were being ruled out of English poetry, which consequently was stiffening into forms too fixed and becoming more and more remote from life. As Mr. Yeats said in Chicago:

"We were weary of all this. We wanted to get rid not only of rhetoric but of poetic diction. We tried to strip away everything that was artificial, to get a style like speech, as simple as the simplest prose, like a cry of the heart."

It is scarcely too much to say that "the new poetry"—if we may be allowed the phrase—began with these two great Irish masters. Think what a contrast to even the simplest lyrics of Tennyson the pattern of their songs presents, and what a contrast their direct outright human feeling presents to the somewhat culture-developed optimism of Browning, and the science-inspired pessimism of Arnold. Compared with these Irishmen the best of their predecessors seem literary. This statement does not imply any measure of ultimate values, for it is still too early to estimate them. One may, for example, believe Synge to be the greatest poet-playwright in English since Shakespeare, and one of the great poets of the world; but a few more decades must pass before such ranking can have authority.

At the same time other currents were influencing progressive minds toward even greater freedom of form. Strangely enough, Whitman's influence was felt first in France. It reached England, and finally America, indirectly from Paris, where the poets, stimulated by translations of the great American, especially Bazalgette's, and by the ever-adventurous quality of French scholarship, have been experimenting with free verse ever since

Mallarmé. The great Irish poets felt the French influence—it was part of the education which made them realize that English poetry had become narrow, rigid, and insular. Yeats has held usually, though never slavishly, to rhyme and a certain regularity of metrical form—in which, however, he makes his own tunes; but Synge wrote his plays in that wide borderland between prose and verse, in a form which, whatever one calls it, is essentially poetry, for it has passion, glamour, magic, rhythm, and glorious imaginative life.

This borderland between prose and verse is being explored now as never before in English; except, perhaps in the King James translation of the Bible. The modern "vers-libertines," as they have been wittily called, are doing pioneer work in an heroic effort to get rid of obstacles that have hampered the poet and separated him from his audience. They are trying to make the modern manifestations of poetry less a matter of rules and formulæ, and more a thing of the spirit, and of organic as against imposed rhythm. In this enthusiastic labor they are following not only a strong inward impulse, not only the love of freedom which Chaucer followed—and Spenser and Shakespeare, Shelley and Coleridge and all the masters—but they are moved also by influences from afar. They have studied the French *symbolistes* of the 'nineties, and the most recent Parisian *vers-libristes*. Moreover, some of them have listened to the pure lyricism of the Provençal troubadours, have examined the more elaborate mechanism of early Italian sonneteers and canzonists, have read Greek poetry from a new angle of vision; and last, but perhaps most important of all, have bowed to winds from the East.

In the nineteenth century the western world—the western esthetic world—discovered the orient. Someone has said that when Perry knocked at the gates of Japan, these opened, not to let us in, but to let the Japanese out. Japanese graphic art, especially, began almost at once to kindle progressive minds. Whistler, of course, was the first great creative artist to feel the influence of their instinct for balance and proportion, for subtle harmonies of color and line, for the integrity of beauty in art as opposed to the moralizing and sentimental tendencies which had been intruding more and more.

Poetry was slower than the graphic arts to feel the oriental influence, because of the barrier of language. But European scholarship had long dabbled with Indian, Persian and Sanskrit literatures, and Fitzgerald even won over the crowd to some remote suspicion of their beauty by meeting Omar halfway, and making a great poem out of the marriage, not only of two minds, but of two literary traditions. Then a few airs from Japan blew in—a few translations of *hokku* and other forms—which showed the stark simplicity and crystal clarity of the art among Japanese poets. And of late the search has gone further: we begin to discover a whole royal line of Chinese poets of a thousand or more years ago; and we are trying to search out the secrets of their delicate and beautiful art. The task is difficult, because our poets, ignorant of Chinese, have to get at these masters through the literal translations of scholars. But even by this round-about way, poets like Allen Upward, Ezra Pound, Helen Waddell and a few others, give us something of the rare flavor, the special exquisite perfume, of the original. And of late the Indian influence has been emphasized by the great Bengali poet and sage, Rabindranath Tagore, whose mastery of English makes him a poet in two languages.

This oriental influence is to be welcomed because it flows from deep original streams of poetic art. We should not be afraid to learn from it; and in much of the work of the imagists, and other radical groups, we find a more or less conscious, and more or less effective, yielding to that influence. We find something of the oriental directness of vision and simplicity of diction, also now and then a hint of the unobtrusive oriental perfection of form and delicacy of feeling.

All these influences, which tend to make the art of poetry, especially poetry in English, less provincial, more cosmopolitan, are by no means a defiance of the classic tradition. On the contrary, they are an endeavor to return to it at its great original sources, and to sweep away artificial laws—the *obiter dicta* of secondary minds—which have encumbered it. There is more of the great authentic classic tradition, for example, in the *Spoon River Anthology* than in the *Idylls of the King, Balaustian's Adventure*, and *Sohrab and Rustum* combined. And the free rhythms of Whitman, Mallarmé, Pound, Sandburg and others, in their inspired passages, are more truly in line with the biblical, the Greek, the Anglo-Saxon, and even the Shakespearean tradition, than all the exact iambics of Dryden and Pope, the patterned alexandrines of Racine, or the closely woven metrics of Tennyson and Swinburne.

Whither the new movement is leading no one can tell with exactness, nor which of its present manifestations in England and America will prove permanently valuable. But we may be sure that the movement is toward greater freedom of spirit and form, and a more enlightened recognition of the international scope, the cosmopolitanism, of the great art of poetry, of which the English language, proud as its record is, offers but a single phase. As part of such movement, even the most extravagant experiments, the most radical innovations, are valuable, for the moment at least, as an assault against prejudice. And some of the radicals of today will be, no doubt, the masters of tomorrow—a phenomenon common in the history of the arts.

———

From the revised edition of 1923, and applying equally to the present edition:

The first edition of *The New Poetry* was prepared in 1916, and published the following February. The present edition aims simply to add to that collection of twentieth-century verse in English the most significant work of the period which has passed since the book first appeared.

In considering the make-up of this edition, the editors have been compelled to put aside two temptations. The first was the temptation to disregard certain limitations mentioned in the introduction to the first edition—limitations drawn by time and death—in order to trace the beginnings of the modern movement wherever the quest might lead.

It might have led us even to Blake. Obviously it would have led us to Whitman, though we might legitimately have refrained from quoting so great a master, so ancestral a revolutionist. But we should have been compelled to represent generously such nineteenth-century moderns as Emily Dickinson, Gerard Hopkins and Stephen Crane; to acknowledge the new austerities practiced by the Celtic group of poets during the 'nineties; to admit a deviation from the Victorian tone and manner in a few poets of the closing century, like Robert Bridges, Wilfred Blunt, and the Shropshire Lad (A. E. Housman); to pay tribute to Rudyard Kipling's easy fling in modern balladry, and to his incisive directness in certain later poems; and possibly even to point out wherein some of the Victorians, especially Robert Browning and Christina Rossetti, were prophetic of change in certain poems. Also we should have had to revoke our omission of such twentieth-century poets now "enshrined by death" as Synge and Moody and Riley—the first a modern triumphantly, but greater as playwright than as lyrist; the others leading toward the more recent groups in certain aspects of their art.

We were tempted especially by three nineteenth-century poets who were unfairly obscure in their day and who really belong in "the new movement." Two of them were singularly reticent—both Emily Dickinson and Gerard Hopkins waited for posthumous publication. But the former achieved a vivid directness and compactness worthy of the imagists, as well as a very personal technique which searched for hidden, rather than obvious, delicacies of assonance and rhythm; as in many poems like this one on despair:

> The difference between despair
> And fear, is like the one
> Between the instant of a wreck
> And when the wreck has been!
>
> The mind is smooth—no motion—
> Contented as the eye
> Upon the forehead of a bust,
> That knows it cannot see.

And this poem shows the intensity of her spiritual life:

> There is a solitude of space,
> A solitude of sea,
> A solitude of death; but these
> Society shall be
> Compared with that profounder site,
> That polar privacy,
> A Soul admitted to Itself:
> Finite Infinity.

Hopkins, in his Jesuit seclusion, worked out a deeply original metric pattern, capable of exquisitely rich, subtle and flexible modulations, though always thoroughly controlled. In certain poems he presented an impressionistic rush of splendor, a veritable tumble of gorgeous colors and sounds, as different from Swinburne's smooth expansive patterns as Tschaikowsky is different from Chopin. One poem would carry conviction of the essential modernness of this priest who could ring adjectives like a chime of bells in such lines as—

> Tatter-tassel-tangled and dingle-a-dangled
> Dandy-hung dainty head.

We quote a passage from *The Leaden Echo*, a maiden's plaint, to show his luxuriant style and his "terrible immediacy of utterance":

How to keep—is there any any, is there none such, nowhere
    known some, bow or brooch or braid or brace, lace, latch or
    catch or key to keep
Back beauty, keep it, beauty, beauty, beauty, . . . from van-
    ishing away?
Oh, is there no frowning of these wrinkles, ranked wrinkles deep,
Down? no waving-off of these most mournful messengers, still
    messengers, sad and stealing messengers of grey?
No, there's none, there's none—oh no, there's none!
Nor can you long be, what you now are, called fair—
Do what you may do, what, do what you may,
And wisdom is early to despair:
Be beginning; since, no, nothing can be done
To keep at bay
Age and age's evils—hoar hair,
Ruck and wrinkle, drooping, dying, death's worst, winding
    sheets, tombs and worms and tumbling to decay;
So be beginning, be beginning to despair.
Oh there's none—no no no, there's none:
Be beginning to despair, to despair,
Despair, despair, despair, despair.

And here is the beautiful sonnet, *God's Grandeur:*

The world is charged with grandeur of God.
It will flame out, like shining from shook foil;

It gathers to a greatness, like the ooze of oil
Crushed. Why do men then now not reck his rod?
Generations have trod, have trod, have trod;
And all is seared with trade; bleared, smeared with toil;
And wears man's smudge and shares man's smell: the soil
Is bare now, nor can foot feel, being shod.

And, for all this, nature is never spent—
There lives the dearest freshness deep down things;
And though the last lights off the black West went,
Oh, morning, at the brown brink eastward, springs:
Because the Holy Ghost over the bent
World broods with warm breast and with—ah!—bright wings.

   The modern mood of Stephen Crane was perhaps more militant. Taking a hint possibly from Yone Noguchi, he printed during the later 'nineties two books of free-verse poems which challenged the established metrical order and were not without influence in beginning a new fashion. Most of them sound a bit sententious today; the best is the passionately ironic *War is Kind:*

Do not weep, maiden, for war is kind.
Because your lover threw wild hands toward the sky
And the affrighted steed ran on alone,
Do not weep.
War is kind.

Hoarse booming drums of the regiment,
Little souls who thirst for fight—
These men were born to drill and die.
The unexplained glory flies above them;
Great is the battle-god, great—and his kingdom
A field where a thousand corpses lie.

Do not weep, babe, for war is kind.
Because your father tumbled in the yellow trenches,
Raged at his breast, gulped and died,
Do not weep.
War is kind.

Swift blazing flag of the regiment,
Eagle with crest of red and gold,
These men were born to drill and die.

Point for them the virtue of slaughter,
Make plain to them the excellence of killing,
And a field where a thousand corpses lie.

Mother whose heart hung humble as a button
On the bright splendid shroud of your son,
Do not weep.
War is kind.

Synge's few poems have influenced "the movement," by their
hard simplicity, toward a more direct attack and a more vital
imaginative speech. Still more his plays, by the marvellous
lyricism of their rhythmic dialogue, derived from the speech-
rhythms of a primitive people, have taught many lessons to
modern poets. Probably this great Irishman has ended forever
the long reign of Elizabethan blank verse in English dramatic
poetry; and has given aid and comfort to all the groups of
present-day poets who are trying to study anew the rhythmic
bases and resources of the language.

But we need not repeat what was said of the Celtic group and
of other influences in the original introduction to this volume.
By the time Synge died, in 1909, Edwin Arlington Robinson
had published two or three books of stringent poems; in 1909
Ezra Pound's *Personæ* appeared in London, and three years
later the establishment of *Poetry* in Chicago gave an organ to
the poets who were separating from the old tradition. By introducing the imagists and such other independents as Carl
Sandburg and D. H. Lawrence and Vachel Lindsay, by presenting foreign poets like Rabindranath Tagore and Charles
Vildrac, besides many in translation, and by encouraging an
experimental spirit and certain new austerities of technique,
the magazine exerted a definite influence.

The second temptation which we have resisted urged us to include translations; especially some of the translations from the
Chinese which scholar-poets like Arthur Waley, Ezra Pound,
Amy Lowell and Witter Bynner, usually with the aid of collab-
orators, have published during the past five years—translations
which have had an important and far-reaching influence toward
simplicity, directness, condensation, and other virtues now
much prized. The inclusion of two Pound-Fenellosa paraphrases

from Li Po in the first edition seemed to constitute a precedent
which the editors were much inclined to follow.

But again they would have been led too far. Since 1917 the
search in China's treasury of poetry has brought forth numerous
volumes of absorbing interest. But, after all, these Chinese poets
lived long ago; and if their recent presentation and quaint modernness of spirit entitle them to a place in a twentieth-century
anthology, why should not Persia and India be searched as
well, and ancient Greece and Rome, and modern Europe—all
the fifteen or more literatures represented in *Poetry* by recent
translations? Versions from the Greek by H. D. and Richard
Aldington and F. S. Flint, from the Provençal by Ezra Pound,
from the modern French by a number of poets, from the Russian and other Slavic tongues by Deutsch-Yarmolinsky and
P. Selver, from the American aboriginal by Frank Gordon,
Mary Austin, Natalie Curtis Burlin and others—all these, as
well as the Chinese, have had an incalculable influence in breaking down provincial barriers which had tended to confine English
poets within too narrow bounds of artistic technique and motive.
They have assisted greatly in the broadening process now so
manifest in the art, in making poetry in the English language
more cosmopolitan and more representative of the age.

Thus the very number and excellence of important and suggestive translations have made it impossible to include them.
The editors were compelled to decide that if the volume was to
represent adequately the best work of twentieth-century poets
of the English-speaking nations, it would be necessary to confine its new inclusions strictly to this field.

One other detail of editorial policy, or taste, should perhaps
be touched upon.

In reading the poetry of the past ten years, we have become
conscious of increasing divergences between the English product
and that of the United States. This is, no doubt, inevitable and
desirable; and it may be both inevitable and desirable—at least
it is natural—that an anthology prepared in this country should
follow with the greater sympathy the American path in this
divergence.

But certain conclusions have been forced upon the editors
for which they were not quite prepared. The first is the wide

range and variety of modern American poetry. At last it begins to be continental in scope; to express the immense differences of climate, landscape, and racial and cultural environment, in this majestically vast and bewilderingly mixed nation. Compared with this variety and spaciousness, so to speak, most of the recent English poetry seems cribbed, cabined and confined in scope and range, and monotonous in feeling and style. Whole groups of poets in the mother country are occupied with English rural life—not wild nature, but nature possessed and civilized: a pleasing subject, but so long and competently handled for two hundred years as to become easily tiresome to an outsider unless presented with such rare freshness as only two or three of these pastoral poets attain.

A young English poet said in a recent letter:

"It is a question of race-vitality. Most American writers have a sense of life which cannot but impress any impartial English reader. I don't mean any shouting or screaming about modern wonders or modern beauty, I mean an inner force to the poem which is not found in English verse."

As American poetry ceases to be colonial, much British poetry seems, by comparison, provincial. The point was stated precisely, not long ago, by Mrs. Padraic Colum, in her review of a certain English novel in *The Freeman:*

"If books like this make all American books seem crude, even the crudest American book makes this seem insular; for despite the paucity of emotion, something of the bigness of this vast continent, with its immense spaces and its conglomeration of races, is in all recent American writings. The bigness, perhaps, crushes and dwarfs the people; but it is something which, when it becomes articulate in literature, will make American writing so different from English that one can hardly feel there is much the American can learn from English writing except its old aristocratic discipline."

The divergence of background and feeling will mean, of course, increasing divergence of critical attitude. In 1921 Mr. J. C. Squire, editor of the London *Mercury* and a well-known Georgian poet, asserted the general English attitude by including not a single American poet among the forty-six British in his anthology *Selections from Modern Poets.* The present editors, wondering at this insular exclusiveness, and at many of the book's inclusions as well, become aware that they represent a different world. Their world, unlike Mr. Squire's, contains numerous poets of the other nation. If the proportion of these is smaller than certain critics may demand, we can only reply that it presents justly our opinion of the relative importance and significance of the two groups. Every editor feels, and must necessarily reveal, certain unconscious sympathies and predilections; it is better, then, to reveal them quite frankly, without extenuation or apology. There is increasing evidence that Americans are beginning to give a direct and independent rating to the art of their contemporary fellow-countrymen. In particular they begin to appreciate their poets' offering; to admit that, as M. Jean Catel said two years ago in the *Mercure de France:*

"*Il est, je crois, évident que la poésie moderne d'Angleterre balbutie, ou—que les amis de Kipling me pardonnent—fait du ' jazz-band'. Il est, pour moi du moins, aussi évident que les Etats-Unis éntrent résolument dans l'Assemblée des Muses avec une merveilleuse offrande de poésie.*"

Of course the final verdict is not yet in; indeed, cannot be delivered for many years. Meantime, we offer this collection to the public as a presentation of one phase of contemporary opinion.

H. M.

NOTE. *A word about the typography of this volume. No rigid system of lineation, indentation, etc., has been imposed upon the poets who very kindly lend us their work. For example, sonnets are printed with or without indented lines according to the individual preference of the poet; also other rhymed forms, such as quatrains rhyming alternately; as well as various forms of free verse. Punctuation and spelling are more uniform, although a certain liberty has been conceded in words like* gray *or* grey, *the color of which seems to vary with the spelling, and in the use of dots, dashes, commas, colons, etc. Also a few poets, especially E. E. Cummings, require the use of their own individual systems of punctuation, capitalization, etc.*

THE NEW POETRY

Léonie Adams

SEND FORTH THE HIGH FALCON

Send forth the high falcon flying after the mind
To topple it from its cold cloud;
The beak of the falcon to pierce it till it fall
Where the simple heart is bowed.
Oh in wild innocence it rides
The rare ungovernable element,
But once it sways to terror and descent
The marches of the wind are its abyss,
No wind staying it upward of the breast.
Let mind be proud for this,
And ignorant from what fabulous cause it dropt,
And with how learned a gesture the unschooled heart
Shall lull both terror and innocence to rest.

THE LAMENT OF QUARRY

The hunter of huntsmen bred,
That looked on his quarry slain,
The lament of quarry made:
"Would you had your beauty again!
Light and lovely its part,
Stepping on velvet feet.
It is heavy in my heart.

"A sweet and wild decoy all night in sleep
I set lest any rove;
Snares I planted subtle and deep;
It was no guile, but love.
The gentle entered without fright
And bent upon the hunter's look
Their eyes of delicate light.

I

"Of my father's father I got a proud steed,
And a barb of my father I took—
O cunning barb of which you bleed—
But a white hind gave me suck.
For I was cradled in hardihood,
But a mild doe, but the hind pity,
With strangeness thinned my blood.

"Fierce and beauteous the hawk,
But where is the natureless creature,
That has confusion for his part?
To the greyhound his fleet foot,
To the moorhen her light wing,
And the waste track of beauty to the heart."

THE RIVER IN THE MEADOWS

Crystal parting the meads,
A boat drifted up it like a swan.
Tranquil, lovely, its bright front to the waters,
A slow swan is gone.

Full waters, O flowing silver,
Pure, level with the clover,
It will stain drowning a star,
With the moon it will brim over.

Running through lands dewy and shorn,
Cattle stoop at its brink,
And every fawny-colored throat
Will sway its bells and drink.

I saw a boat sailing the river
With a tranced gait. It seemed
Loosed by a spell from its moorings,
Or a thing the helmsman dreamed.

They said it would carry no traveller,
But the vessel would go down
If a heart were heavy-winged
Or the bosom it dwelt in stone.

THE MOUNT

No, I have tempered haste,
The joyous traveller said,
The steed has passed me now
Whose hurrying hooves I fled.
My spectre rides thereon,
I learned what mount he has,
Upon what summers fed,
And wept to know again,
Beneath the saddle swung,
Treasure for whose great theft
This breast was wrung.
His bridle bells sang out,
I could not tell their chime,
So brilliantly he rings,
But called his name as Time.
His bin was morning light,
Those straws which gild his bed
Are of the fallen West.
Although green lands consume
Beneath their burning tread,
In everlasting bright
His hooves have rest.

THE FIGUREHEAD

This that is washed with weed and pebblestone
Curved once a dolphin's length before the prow,
And I who read the land to which we bore
In its grave eyes, question my idol now,
What cold and marvelous fancy it may keep,
Since the salt terror swept us from our course,
Or if a wisdom later than the storm,
For old green ocean's tinctured it so deep;
And with some reason to me on this strand
The waves, the ceremonial waves have come
And stooped their barbaric heads, and all spread out
Their lovely arms before them, and are gone,
Leaving their murderous tribute on the sand.

Conrad Aiken

MORNING SONG FROM *SENLIN*

It is morning, Senlin says, and in the morning
When the light drips through the shutters like the dew,
I arise, I face the sunrise,
And do the things my fathers learned to do.
Stars in the purple dusk above the rooftops
Pale in a saffron mist and seem to die,
And I myself on a swiftly tilting planet
Stand before a glass and tie my tie.

Vine-leaves tap my window,
Dew-drops sing to the garden stones;
The robin chirps in the chinaberry tree,
Repeating three clear tones.

It is morning. I stand by the mirror
And tie my tie once more.
While waves far off in a pale rose twilight
Crash on a white sand shore.
I stand by a mirror and comb my hair:
How small and white my face!
The green earth tilts through a. sphere of air
And bathes in a flame of space.

There are houses hanging above the stars
And stars hung under a sea . . .
And a sun far off in a shell of silence
Dapples my walls for me . . .

It is morning, Senlin says, and in the morning
Should I not pause in the light to remember God?
Upright and firm I stand on a star unstable—
He is immense and lonely as a cloud.
I will dedicate this moment before my mirror
To him alone, for him I will comb my hair.
Accept these humble offerings, cloud of silence!
I will think of you as I descend the stair.

Vine-leaves tap my window,
The snail-track shines on the stones;
Dew-drops flash from the chinaberry tree
Repeating two clear tones.

It is morning, I awake from a bed of silence,
Shining I rise from the starless waters of sleep.
The walls are about me still as in the evening,
I am the same, and the same name still I keep.
The earth revolves with me, yet makes no motion,
The stars pale silently in a coral sky.
In a whistling void I stand before my mirror,
Unconcerned, and tie my tie.

There are horses neighing on far-off hills
Tossing their long white manes,
And mountains flash in the rose-white dusk,
Their shoulders black with rains . . .
It is morning. I stand by the mirror
And surprise my soul once more;
The blue air rushes above my ceiling,
There are suns beneath my floor . . .

It is morning, Senlin says, I ascend from darkness
And depart on the winds of space for I know not where.
My watch is wound, a key is in my pocket,
And the sky is darkened as I descend the stair.
There are shadows across the windows, clouds in heaven,
And a god among the stars; and I will go
Thinking of him as I might think of daybreak
And humming a tune I know. . . .

Vine-leaves tap at the window,
Dew-drops sing to the garden stones,
The robin chirps in the chinaberry tree
Repeating three clear tones.

PORTRAIT OF ONE DEAD

This is the house. On one side there is darkness,
On one side there is light.
Into the darkness you may lift your lanterns—
Oh, any number—it will still be night.
And here are echoing stairs to lead you downward
To long sonorous halls.
And here is spring forever at these windows,
With roses on the walls.

This is her room. On one side there is music—
On one side not a sound.
At one step she could move from love to silence,
Feel myriad darkness coiling round.
And here are balconies from which she heard you,
Your steady footsteps on the stair.
And here the glass in which she saw your shadow
As she unbound her hair.

Here is the room—with ghostly walls dissolving—
The twilight room in which she called you "lover";
And the floorless room in which she called you "friend".
So many times, in doubt, she ran between them!—
Through windy corridors of darkening end.

Here she could stand with one dim light above her,
And hear far music, like a sea in caverns,
Murmur away at hollowed walls of stone.
And here, in a roofless room where it was raining,
She bore the patient sorrow of rain alone.

Your words were walls which suddenly froze around her.
Your words were windows—large enough for moonlight,
Too small to let her through.
Your letters—fragrant cloisters faint with music.
The music that assuaged her there was you.

How many times she heard your step ascending,
Yet never saw your face!
She heard them turn again, ring slowly fainter,
Till silence swept the place.

Why had you gone? . . . The door, perhaps, mistaken . . .
You would go elsewhere. The deep walls were shaken.

A certain rose-leaf, sent without intention,
Became, with time, a woven web of fire—
She wore it, and was warm.
A certain hurried glance, let fall at parting,
Became, with time, the flashings of a storm.

Yet there was nothing asked, no hint to tell you
Of secret idols carved in secret chambers
From all you did and said.
Nothing was done, until at last she knew you.
Nothing was known, till, somehow, she was dead.

How did she die? You say she died of poison.
Simple and swift. And much to be regretted.
You did not see her pass
So many thousand times from light to darkness,
Pausing so many times before her glass.

You did not see how many times she hurried
To lean from certain windows, vainly hoping,
Passionate still for beauty, remembered spring.
You did not know how long she clung to music,
You did not hear her sing.

Did she, then, make the choice, and step out bravely
From sound to silence—close, herself, those windows?
Or was it true, instead,
That darkness moved—for once—and so possessed her? . . .
We'll never know, you say, for she is dead.

PUNCH: THE IMMORTAL LIAR

*He imagines that his puppet has a dark dream and hears
voices.*

First Voice
> Pave the sky with stars for Punch!
> And snare in flowers a moon for him—
> With white rose-trees and apple-trees,
> And cherubim and seraphim!

Second Voice

Look! he comes! how tall he is!
A crown of fire is on his head;
The sky unrolls before his feet,
Green mountains fear his tread.

The meteors now like dolphins dive
Into the white wave of the sky;
Blue moons and stars around him sing,
And suns triumphant cry!

Third Voice

Build a house of gold for Punch,
Of gold without and silk within;
With floors of glass—and let there be
For ever there a silver din

Of music's many instruments
In slow and low amazement heard:
In every window-niche a cage,
In every cage a singing bird.

Build it in a kingdom far
In a forest green and deep;
Where no tears nor sorrows are,
But only song and sleep.

There to the noise of wind in trees
And many rivers winding down,
Let him forget the cares of earth
And nod a kingly crown!

Fourth Voice

Like a tower of brass is Punch,
And great and stately is his pace;
There is no other as tall as he—
None with so fair a face.

Fall down, fall down, you kings of men—
Fall down before him! This is he
For whom the moon pursues her ghost
And demons bend the knee.

Woe unto you, you miscreants
Who dare the lightnings of his eyes!
His hand, how strong! His wrath, how just!
His brow, how white and wise!

Fifth Voice

Solomon, clown, put by your crown;
And Judas, break your tree:
Seal up your tomb and burn your cross,
Jesus of Galilee!

For here walks one who makes you seem
But atoms that creep in grass:
You are the pageant of his dream,
And he will bid you pass.

Let Rome go over the earth in gold
With trumpets harshly blown!
For here comes one whose splendor burns
More gloriously, alone.

Heliogabalus, laugh your last!
Queen Sappho, lie you down!
Punch the immortal shakes the seas
And takes the sun for crown.

PRELUDE

I

Winter for a moment takes the mind; the snow
Falls past the arclight; icicles guard a wall,
The wind moans through a crack in the window,
A keen sparkle of frost is on the sill.
Only for a moment; as spring too might engage it,
With a single crocus in the loam, or a pair of birds;
Or summer with hot grass; or autumn with a yellow leaf.
Winter is there, outside, is here in me:
Drapes the planets with snows, deepens the ice on the moon,
Darkens the darkness that was already darkness.
The mind too has its snows, its slippery paths,
Walls bayoneted with ice, leaves ice-encased.

Here is the in-drawn room to which you return
When the wind blows from Arcturus: here is the fire
At which you warm your hands and glaze your eyes;
The piano, on which you touch the cold treble;
Five notes like breaking icicles; and then silence.

II

The alarm clock ticks, the pulse keeps time with it,
Night and the mind are full of sounds. I walk
From the fireplace, with its imaginary fire,
To the window, with its imaginary view.
Darkness, and snow ticking the window: silence,
And the knocking of chains on a motor-car, the tolling
Of a bronze bell, dedicated to Christ.
And then the uprush of angelic wings, the beating
Of wings demonic, from the abyss of the mind:
The darkness filled with a feathery whistling, wings
Numberless as the flakes of angelic snow,
The deep void swarming with wings and sound of wings.
The winnowing of chaos, the aliveness
Of depth and depth and depth dedicated to death.

III

Here are the bickerings of the inconsequential,
The chatterings of the ridiculous, the iterations
Of the meaningless. Memory, like a juggler,
Tosses its colored balls into the light, and again
Receives them into darkness. Here is the absurd,
Grinning like an idiot, and the omnivorous quotidian,
Which will have its day. A handful of coins,
Tickets, items from the news, a soiled handkerchief,
A letter to be answered, notice of a telephone call,
The petal of a flower in a volume of Shakespeare,
The program of a concert. The photograph, too,
Propped on the mantel, and beneath it a dry rosebud;
The laundry bill, matches, an ash-tray, Utamaro's
Pearl-fishers. And the rug, on which are still the crumbs
Of yesterday's feast. These are the void, the night,
And the angelic wings that make it sound.

IV

What is the flower? It is not a sigh of color,
Suspiration of purple, sibilation of saffron,
Nor aureate exhalation from the tomb.
Yet it is these because you think of these,
An emanation of emanations, fragile
As light, or glisten, or gleam, or coruscation,
Creature of brightness, and as brightness brief.
What is the frost? it is not the sparkle of death,
The flash of time's wing, seeds of eternity:
Yet it is these because you think of these.
And you, because you think of these, are both
Frost and flower, the bright ambiguous syllable
Of which the meaning is both no and yes.

V

Here is the tragic, the distorting mirror
In which your gesture becomes grandiose;
Tears form and fall from your magnificent eyes,
The brow is noble, and the mouth is God's.
Here is the God who seeks his mother, Chaos—
Confusion seeking solution, and life seeking death.
Here is the rose that woos the icicle; the icicle
That woos the rose. Here is the silence of silences
Which dreams of becoming a sound, and the sound
Which will perfect itself in silence. And all
These things are only the uprush from the void,
The wings angelic and demonic, the sound of the abyss
Dedicated to death. And this is you.

Zoë Akins

THE TRAGEDIENNE

A storm is riding on the tide;
Grey is the day and grey the tide,
Far-off the sea-gulls wheel and cry—
A storm draws near upon the tide.

A city lifts its minarets
To winds that from the desert sweep;
And prisoned Arab women weep
Below the domes and minarets.

Upon a hill in Thessaly
Stand broken columns in a line
About a cold forgotten shrine,
Beneath a moon in Thessaly.
But in the world there is no place
So desolate as your tragic face.

I AM THE WIND

I am the wind that wavers,
   You are the certain land;
I am the shadow that passes
   Over the sand.

I am the leaf that quivers,
   You the unshaken tree;
You are the stars that are steadfast,
   I am the sea.

You are the light eternal—
   Like a torch I shall die.
You are the surge of deep music,
   I but a cry!

THE WANDERER

The ships are lying in the bay,
   The gulls are swinging round their spars;
My soul as eagerly as they
   Desires the margin of the stars.

So much do I love wandering,
   So much I love the sea and sky,
That it will be a piteous thing
   In one small grave to lie.

Richard Aldington

THE POPLAR

Why do you always stand there shivering
Between the white stream and the road?

The people pass through the dust
On bicycles, in carts, in motor-cars;

The wagoners go by at dawn;
The lovers walk on the grass path at night.

Stir from your roots—walk, poplar!
You are more beautiful than they are.

I know that the white wind loves you,
Is always kissing you and turning up
The white lining of your green petticoat.
The sky darts through you like blue rain,
And the grey rain drips on your flanks
And loves you.
And I have seen the moon
Slip his silver penny into your pocket
As you straightened your hair;
And the white mist curling and hesitating
Like a bashful lover about your knees.

I know you, poplar;
I have watched you since I was ten.
But if you had a little real love,
A little strength,
You would leave your nonchalant idle lovers
And go walking down the white road
Behind the wagoners.

There are beautiful beeches
Down beyond the hill.
Will you always stand there shivering?

LESBIA

Grow weary if you will, let me be sad.
Use no more speech now;
Let the silence spread gold hair above us,
Fold on delicate fold.
Use no more speech—
You had the ivory of my life to carve. . . .
And Picus of Mirandola is dead;
And all the gods they dreamed and fabled of,
Hermes, and Thoth and Bêl are rotten now,
Rotten and dank.

And through it all I see your pale Greek face;
Tenderness
Makes me eager as a little child to love you,
You morsel left half-cold on Cæsar's plate.

IMAGES

I

Like a gondola of green scented fruits
Drifting along the dank canals at Venice,
You, O exquisite one,
Have entered into my desolate city.

II

The blue smoke leaps
Like swirling clouds of birds vanishing.
So my love leaps forth toward you,
Vanishes and is renewed.

III

A rose-yellow moon in a pale sky
When the sunset is faint vermilion
In the mist among the tree-boughs,
Art thou to me, my beloved.

IV

A young beech-tree on the edge of a forest
Stands still in the evening,
Yet shudders through all its leaves in the light air
And seems to fear the stars:
So are you still, and so tremble.

V

The red deer are high on the mountain,
They are beyond the last pine-trees.
And my desires have run with them.

VI

The flower which the wind has shaken
Is soon filled again with rain;
So does my heart fill slowly with tears,
O Foam-driver, Wind-of-the-vineyards,
Until you return.

CHORICOS

The ancient songs
Pass deathward mournfully.

Cold lips that sing no more, and withered wreaths,
Regretful eyes, and drooping breasts and wings—
Symbols of ancient songs
Mournfully passing
Down to the great white surges,
Watched of none
Save the frail sea-birds
And the lithe pale girls,
Daughters of Okeanos.

And the songs pass
From the green land
Which lies upon the waves as a leaf
On the flowers of hyacinth;
And they pass from the waters,
The manifold winds and the dim moon.

And they come,
Silently winging through soft Kimmerian dusk,
To the quiet level lands
That she keeps for us all,
That she wrought for us all for sleep
In the silver days of the earth's dawning—
Proserpina, daughter of Zeus.

And we turn from the Kyprian's breasts,
And we turn from thee,
Phoibos Apollon,
And we turn from the music of old
And the hills that we loved and the meads,
And we turn from the fiery day,
And the lips that were over-sweet;
For silently
Brushing the fields with red-shod feet,
With purple robe
Searing the grass as with a sudden flame,
Death,
Thou hast come upon us.

And of all the ancient songs
Passing to the swallow-blue halls
By the dark streams of Persephone,
This only remains:
That in the end we turn to thee,
Death,
We turn to thee, singing
One last song.

O Death,
Thou art an healing wind
That blowest over white flowers
A-tremble with dew.
Thou art a wind flowing
Over far leagues of lonely sea.
Thou art the dusk and the fragrance;
Thou art the lips of love mournfully smiling;

Thou art the sad peace of one
Satiate with old desires.
Thou art the silence of beauty;
And we look no more for the morning,
We yearn no more for the sun,
Since with thy white hands,
Death,
Thou crownest us with the pallid chaplets,
The slim colorless poppies
Which in thy garden alone
Softly thou gatherest.

And silently,
And with slow feet approaching,
And with bowed head and unlit eyes,
We kneel before thee.
And thou, leaning toward us,
Caressingly layest upon us
Flowers from thy thin cold hands;
And, smiling as a chaste woman
Knowing love in her heart,
Thou sealest our eyes,
And the illimitable quietude
Comes gently upon us.

Mary Aldis

WHEN YOU COME

"There was a girl with him for a time. She took him to her room when he was desolate and warmed him and took care of him. One day he could not find her. For many weeks he walked constantly in that locality in search of her."—From *Life of Francis Thompson.*

When you come tonight
To our small room
You will look and listen—
I shall not be there.

You will cry out your dismay
To the unheeding gods;
You will wait and look and listen—
I shall not be there.

There is a part of you I love
More than your hands in mine at rest;
There is a part of you I love
More than your lips upon my breast.

There is a part of you I wound
Even in my caress;
There is a part of you withheld
I may not possess.

There is a part of you I hate—
Your need of me
When you would be alone,
Alone and free.

When you come tonight
To our small room
You will look and listen—
I shall not be there.

FLASH–LIGHTS

I

Candles toppling sideways in tomato-cans
Sputter and sizzle at head and foot.
The gaudy patterns of a patch-work quilt
Lie smooth and straight
Save where upswelling over a silent shape.
A man in high boots stirs something on a rusty stove
Round and round and round,
As a new cry like a bleating lamb's
Pierces his brain.
After a time the man busies himself

With hammer and nails and rough-hewn lumber,
But fears to strike a blow.
Outside the moonlight sleeps white upon the plain
And the bark of a coyote shrills across the night.

II

A smell of musk
Comes to him pungently through the darkness.
On the screen
Scenes from foreign lands,
Released by the censor,
Shimmer in cool black and white
Historic information.
He shifts his seat sideways, sideways—
A seeking hand creeps to another hand,
And a leaping flame
Illuminates the historic information.

III

Within the room, sounds of weeping
Low and hushed:
Without, a man, beautiful with the beauty
Of young strength,
Holds pitifully to the handle of the door.
He hiccoughs and turns away,
While a hand-organ plays,
"The hours I spend with thee, dear heart."

Sherwood Anderson

SONG OF INDUSTRIAL AMERICA

They tell themselves so many little lies, my beloved. Now wait,
little one—we can't sing. We are standing in a crowd, by a
bridge, in the West. Hear the voices. Turn around. Let's
go home—I am tired. They tell themselves so many little
lies.

You remember, in the night we arose. We were young. There
was smoke in the passage and you laughed. Was it good—
that black smoke? Look away—to the streams and the
lake. We're alive. See my hand, how it trembles on the
rail.

Here is song, here in America, here now, in our time. Now wait.
I'll go to the train—I'll not swing off into tunes. I'm all
right—I just want to talk.
You watch my hand on the rail of this bridge. I press down.
The blood goes down, there. That steadies me; it makes
me all right.
Now here is how it's going to come—the song, I mean. I've
watched things, men and faces. I know.
First there are the broken things, myself and the others. I
don't mind that—I'm gone, shot to pieces. I'm part of the
scheme—I'm the broken end of a song myself. We are all
that, here in the West, here in Chicago. Tongues clatter
against teeth. There's nothing but shrill screams and a
rattle. That had to be—it's a part of the scheme.

Souls, dry souls, rattle around.
Winter of song. Winter of song.

Now, faint little voices do lift up. They are swept away in the
void—that's true enough. It had to be so from the very
first.
Pshaw, I'm steady enough—let me alone. Keokuk, Tennessee,
Michigan, Chicago, Kalamazoo—don't the names in this
country make you fairly drunk? We'll stand by this brown
stream for hours. I'll not be swept away—watch my hand,
how steady it is. To catch this song and sing it would do
much, make much clear.
Come close to me, warm little thing. It is night—I am cold.
When I was a boy in my village here in the West, I always
knew all the old men. How sweet they were—quite biblical
too—makers of wagons and harness and plows, sailors and
soldiers and pioneers. We got Walt and Abraham out of
that lot.

Then a change came.

> *Drifting along. Drifting along.*
> *Winter of song. Winter of song.*

You know my city, Chicago triumphant—factories and marts
and the roar of machines—horrible, terrible, ugly and brutal.
It crushed things down and down. Nobody wanted to hurt.
They didn't want to hurt me or you. They were caught
themselves. I know the old men here—millionaires. I've
always known old men all my life. I'm old myself. You
would never guess how old I am.

Can a singer arise and sing in this smoke and grime? Can he
keep his throat clear? Can his courage survive?
I'll tell you what it is—now you be still. To hell with you. I'm
an old empty barrel floating in the stream—that's what I
am. You stand away—I've come to life. My arms lift up—
I begin to swim.
Hell and damnation—turn me loose! The floods come on. That
isn't the roar of the trains at all. It's the flood—the terrible, horrible flood turned loose.

> *Winter of song. Winter of song.*
> *Carried along. Carried along.*

Now, in the midst of the broken waters of my civilization,
rhythm begins. Clear above the flood I raise my ringing
voice. In the disorder and darkness of the night, in the
wind and the washing waves, I shout to my brothers—
lost in the flood.
Little faint beginnings of things—old things dead, sweet old
things—a life lived in Chicago, in the West, in the whirl
of industrial America.

God knows you might have become something else—just like me.
You might have made soft little tunes, written cynical little
ditties, eh? Why the devil didn't you make some money
and own an automobile?
Do you believe? Now listen—I do. Say, you—now listen!
Do you believe the hand of God reached down to me in the

flood? I do. 'Twas like a streak of fire along my back. That's a lie, of course. The face of God looked down at me, over the rim of the world.

Don't you see we are all a part of something, here in the West? We're trying to break through. I'm a song myself, the broken end of a song myself.

We have to sing, you see, here in the darkness. All men have to sing—poor broken things. We have to sing here in the darkness in the roaring flood. We have to find each other. Have you courage tonight for a song? Lift your voices. Come.

CHICAGO

I am mature, a man child, in America, in the West, in the great valley of the Mississippi. My head arises above the cornfields. I stand up among the new corn.

I am a child, a confused child in a confused world. There are no clothes made that fit me. The minds of men cannot clothe me. Great projects arise within me. I have a brain, and it is cunning and shrewd.

I want leisure to become beautiful, but there is no leisure. Men should bathe me with prayers and with weeping, but there are no men.

Now—from now—from today I shall do deeds of fiery meaning. Songs shall arise in my throat and hurt me.

I am a little thing, a tiny little thing on the vast prairies. I know nothing. My mouth is dirty. I cannot tell what I want. My feet are sunk in the black swampy land, but I am a lover. I love life. In the end love shall save me.

The days are long—it rains—it snows. I am an old man. I am sweeping the ground where my grave shall be.

Look upon me, my beloved, my lover who does not come. I am raw and bleeding, a new thing in a new world. I run swiftly o'er bare fields. Listen—there is the sound of the tramp-

ing of many feet. Life is dying in me. I am old and palsied.
I am just at the beginning of my life.

Do you not see that I am old, O my beloved? Do you not
understand that I cannot sing, that my songs choke me?
Do you not see that I am so young I cannot find the word
in the confusion of words?

EVENING SONG

Back of Chicago the open fields—were you ever there?
Trains coming toward you out of the West—
Streaks of light on the long grey plains? Many a song—
Aching to sing.

I've got a grey and ragged brother in my breast—
That's a fact.

Back of Chicago the open fields—were you ever there?
Trains going from you into the West—
Clouds of dust on the long grey plains.
Long trains go West, too—in the silence.
Always the song—
Waiting to sing.

AMERICAN SPRING SONG

In the spring, when winds blew and farmers were plowing fields,
It came into my mind to be glad because of my brutality.

Along a street I went and over a bridge.
I went through many streets in my city and over many bridges.
Men and women I struck with my fists, and my hands began to
      bleed.

Under a bridge I crawled, and stood trembling with joy
At the river's edge.
Because it was spring and soft sunlight came through the cracks
      of the bridge,
I tried to understand myself.

Out of the mud at the river's edge I molded myself a god—
A grotesque little god with a twisted face,
A god for myself and my men.

You see now, brother, how it was.

I was a man with clothes made by a Jewish tailor;
Cunningly wrought clothes, made for a nameless one.
I wore a white collar and someone had given me a jeweled pin
To wear at my throat.
That amused and hurt me too.

No one knew that I knelt in the mud beneath the bridge
In the city of Chicago.

You see I am whispering my secret to you.

I want you to believe in my insanity and to understand that I
    love God—
That's what I want.

And then, you see, it was spring,
And soft sunlight came through the cracks of the bridge.
I had been long alone in a strange place where no gods came.

Creep, men, and kiss the twisted face of my mud god.
I'll not hit you with my bleeding fists—
I'm a twisted God myself.

It is spring and love has come to me.
Love has come to me and to my men.

Joseph Auslander

ENIGMA

The swallowed thud of cattle shouldering through
Cool translucent distances of dew;
The blue dawn like a shell warmed by their lowing;
The patter of pigeon-feet on the roof; the rooster crowing;
The tepid interval when pale birds cheep
Beneath their wings; the flutter muffled with sleep;

Crickets on dripping planks; the delighted noises of things that
    creep
In subterranean softness: things too small for a name
Moving through private tunnels down to their instant of
    flame . . .
Strange, how beautiful these things are; how these
Things are still beautiful; strange
That our sweet flesh falters, knows ghastly change—
And these things are still beautiful under the hawk-dark trees!

REVENANTS

Must it be always so whenever rain
Rattles a little on the window sill,
That I shall hear at ledge and window pane
The poplar tapping her golden nails—until
The ghosts creep back again?

Is there no peace for you, ghost after ghost?
I ripped you bleeding forth and watched you go
Staring at me sideways with the most
Haggard look. . . . Is there no quiet, no
Sleep, you prowling host?

Why do you breathe like thugs who spring a lock,
Forcing the window of a dream? What wealth
Stuffs this autumnal heart that you should knock
So furtively? Why stand upon your stealth?
Gag the whirring clock?

Enter me decently as you would the door
Not of a harlot but a friend, and break
My lonely crust with me: I have no more,
Nothing that the paltriest thief would take.
My key lies on the floor.

When you have done with me, go as you came,
Erect and unabashed; and tell my dear
Indelible lady that I am the same,
And that she has no longer need to fear
The poor noise of my name.

ELEGY

Fled is the swiftness of all the white-footed ones
Who had a great cry in them and the wrath of speed:
They are no more among us: they and their sons
Are dead indeed.

So the river mews twist in long loops over the river,
Wheeling and shifting with the wind's and the tide's shift,
And pass in a black night—and nothing is left but a shiver
To show they were swift.

Whenever I hear a gull's throat throb in a fog,
Watch the owl's velvet swoop, the high hawk's lonely paces,
I think on the heels of him who lies like a log
And his friends under the turf and the rain creeping down on
    their faces.

And my heart goes sick and the hell in my heart could break
To the edge of my eyes for the mates I shall not be knowing
Anywhere now, though the ice booms loud in the lake
And the geese honk north again and the heron's going.

Mary Austin

THE EAGLE'S SONG

Said the Eagle:
        When my time came
        I was astonished
        To find that there was death;
        I felt cold sinking within me.

        Alas, my home—
        Shall I leave it?
        All-beholding mountains,
        From your snowy stations
        Shall I see my house no more?

North I went,
Leaning on the wind:
Through the forest resounded
The cry of the wounded doe.

East I went,
Seeking
Where the white-hot dawn
Treads on the trail of morning blueness:
The wind brought me
The smell of death in my nostrils.

South I went,
Looking
For the place where there is no death:
I heard singing,
The sound of wailing for the dead.

West I went,
On the world-encompassing water:
Death's trail was before me.

People, O people,
It must be that we shall leave this pleasant earth.
Therefore let us make songs together,
Let us make a twine of songs.
With them we shall bind the Spirit
Fast to the middle heaven—
There at least it shall roam no more.
The white way of souls—
There at least it shall roam no more.
The white way of souls,
There shall be our home.

SOUNDS

There is a sound of going
    in the tops of the mulberry trees,
The sound of a last breath.

In the cottonwoods also,
And the willow-leafed poplars
That a week ago were flame-pointed,
A sound as of bent blades clashing rustily.

There is a sound of going in the chamise
The sound of a besom sweeping, sweeping,
A sound of unconsidered things
Scurrying to brief corners of oblivion.

But with the spruce trees it is not so,
Nor with the balsam firs by the water borders.
A staying sound,
As of roots that strain but loose not
From the rock crevices.

I will go up to the evergreen pines,
To the blue spruces around Eagle Rock
And hearten myself with the sound of the star-built firs.

DROUTH

The drouth has taken the land!

On Mogollon the herd-grass breaks in white tinder,
The Gila shows its bones, the Mimbres
Is a dried sinew on a shank too long unburied.

Over on Kaibab the black-tail
Browse on the bitter brush and the hemlock branches.
The round-horned elk have passed over
By Wolf-creek Pass, to the lean ranges of Three Rivers.
Of the deer, there is nothing left worth the chut of an arrow.

Around Tsotsil the buzzards are making a merry-go-round;
The rack-boned cattle
With their heads toward the stopped water-courses
Are ringed with menacing shadows:
Nothing fattens now but the carrion kind.

Down all the dark bajadas the hot wind has raped
The thousand-belled maguey, and the white ladies—
The dasylirion—who used to bow there and curtsey,
Scattering scent from their laces.
There's never a leaf-bird hops in the straked corn;
Never a flick, in the one-leaved pines, of the piñonero;
Nor a magpie, bringing the junipers
White on its midnight wings, the footsteps of morning.
And dr-r-y, dr-r-y, dr-r-y churrs the night hawk.

This year six hundred Papagoes,
Who were once good cattle-owners,
Will be working the mines at Ajo.

On Moencopie a thousand flocks, unshepherded,
Will hear, for the voice of the herder,
The hunting cry of Mokiach, my lord Puma.
Dry farmers in Estancia, leaving their locked homesteads,
Are doubly shamed as they go, by the imploring
Stark arms of their orchards.
There is no weather sign watched now
By the citizens of small towns
Like the tightening lines around the lips of their bankers.

Truly, drouth has taken the land!

Joseph Warren Beach

RUE BONAPARTE

You that but seek your modest rolls and coffee,
When you have passed the bar, and have saluted
Its watchful madam, then pray enter softly
The inner chamber, even as one who treads
The haunts of mating birds, and watch discreetly
Over your paper's edge. There in the corner,
Obscure, ensconced behind the uncovered table,
A man and woman keep their silent tryst.
Outside the morning floods the pavement sweetly;

Yonder aloft a maid throws back the shutters;
The hucksters utter modulated cries
As wistful as some old pathetic ballad.
Within, the brooding lovers, unaware,
Sit quiet hand in hand, or in low whispers
Communicate a more articulate love.
Sometimes she plays with strings and, gently leaning
Against his shoulder, shows him childish tricks.
She has not touched the glass of milk before her,
Her breakfast and the price of their admittance.
She has a look devoted and confiding
And might be pretty were not life so hard.
But he, gaunt as his rusty bicycle
That stands against the table, and with features
So drawn and stark, has only futile strength.
The love they cherish in this stolen meeting
Through all the day that follows makes her sweeter,
And him perhaps it only leaves more bitter.
But you that have not love at all, old men
That warm your fingers by this fire, discreetly
Play out your morning game of dominoes.

THE VIEW AT GUNDERSON'S

Sitting in his rocker waiting for your tea,
Gazing from his window, this is what you see:

A cat that snaps at flies; a track leading down
By log-built shanties gray and brown;

The corner of a barn, and tangled lines of fence
Of rough-hewn pickets standing dense;

The ghost of a tree on a dull wet day;
And the blanket fog where lies the bay.

But when he's seen the last of you,
Sitting in his rocker, what's *his* view?

(For there he sits, day in, day out,
Nursing his leg—and his dreams, no doubt.)

The snow-slide up behind the *gaard;*
The farm beside old Trondjem *fjord;*

Daughters seven with their cold blue eyes,
And the great pine where his father lies;

The boat that brought him over the sea;
And the toothless woman who makes his tea.

(Their picture, framed on the rough log wall,
Proves she had teeth when he was tall.)

He sees the balsam thick on the hill,
And all he's cleared with a stubborn will.

And last he sees the full-grown son
For whom he hoards what he has won.

You saw little worth the strife:
What he sees is one man's life.

Stephen Vincent Benét

INVOCATION

(The first third of the opening poem in John Brown's Body)

American muse, whose strong and diverse heart
So many men have tried to understand
But only made it smaller with their art,
Because you are as various as your land,

As mountainous-deep, as flowered with blue rivers,
Thirsty with deserts, buried under snows,
As native as the shape of Navajo quivers,
And native, too, as the sea-voyaged rose.

Swift runner, never captured or subdued,
Seven-branched elk beside the mountain stream,
That half a hundred hunters have pursued
But never matched their bullets with the dream,

Where the great huntsmen failed, I set my sorry
And mortal snare for your immortal quarry.

You are the buffalo-ghost, the broncho-ghost
With dollar-silver in your saddle-horn,
The cowboys riding in from Painted Post,
The Indian arrow in the Indian corn.

And you are the clipped velvet of the lawns
Where Shropshire grows from Massachusetts sods,
The grey Maine rocks, and the war-painted dawns
That break above the Garden of the Gods;

The prairie-schooners crawling toward the ore,
And the cheap car parked by the station-door.

Where the skyscrapers lift their foggy plumes
Of stranded smoke out of a stony mouth
You are that high stone and its arrogant fumes,
And you are the ruined gardens in the South,

And bleak New England farms, so winter-white
Even their roofs look lonely, and the deep
The middle grainland where the wind of night
Is like all blind earth sighing in her sleep:

A friend, an enemy, a sacred hag
With two tied oceans in her medicine-bag.

They tried to fit you with an English song
And clip your speech into the English tale.
But even from the first the words went wrong,
The catbird pecked away the nightingale.

The homesick men begot high-cheekboned things
Whose wit was whittled with a different sound,
And Thames and all the rivers of the kings
Ran into Mississippi and were drowned.

They planted England with a stubborn trust,
But the cleft dust was never English dust.

Stepchild of every exile from content
And all the disavouched, hard-bitten pack
Shipped overseas to steal a continent
With neither shirts nor honor to their back:

Pimping grandee and rump-faced regicide,
Apple-cheeked younkers from a windmill-square,
Puritans stubborn as the nails of Pride,
Rakes from Versailles and thieves from County Clare,

The black-robed priests who broke their hearts in vain
To make you God and France or God and Spain.

These were your lovers in your buckskin-youth.
And each one married with a dream so proud
He never knew it could not be the truth
And that he coupled with a girl of cloud.

And now to see you is more difficult yet
Except as an immensity of wheel
Made up of wheels, oiled with inhuman sweat
And glittering with the heat of ladled steel.

All these you are, and each is partly you,
And none is false, and none is wholly true.

JOHN BROWN'S PRAYER

Omnipotent and steadfast God,
Who, in Thy mercy, hath
Upheaved in me Jehovah's rod
And his chastising Wrath,

For fifty-nine unsparing years
Thy Grace hath worked apart
To mold a man of iron tears
With a bullet for a heart.

Yet, since this body may be weak
With all it has to bear,
Once more, before Thy thunders speak,
Almighty, hear my prayer.

I saw Thee when Thou did display
The black man and his lord
To bid me free the one, and slay
The other with the sword.

I heard Thee when Thou bade me spurn
Destruction from my hand,
And, though all Kansas bleed and burn,
It was at Thy command.

I hear the rolling of the wheels,
The chariots of war!
I hear the breaking of the seals
And the opening of the door!

The glorious beasts with many eyes
Exult before the Crowned.
The buried saints arise, arise
Like incense from the ground!

Before them march the martyr-kings,
In bloody sunsets drest—
O Kansas, bleeding Kansas,
You will not let me rest!

I hear your sighing corn again,
I smell your prairie-sky,
And I remember five dead men
By Pottawattomie.

Lord God, it was a work of Thine,
And how might I refrain?
But Kansas, bleeding Kansas,
I hear her in her pain.

Her corn is rustling in the ground,
An arrow in my flesh.
And all night long I stanch a wound
That ever bleeds afresh.

Get up, get up, my hardy sons,
From this time forth we are
No longer men, but pikes and guns
In God's advancing war.

And if we live, we free the slave,
And if we die, we die.
But God has digged His saints a grave
Beyond the western sky.

Oh, fairer than the bugle-call
Its walls of jasper shine!
And Joshua's sword is on the wall
With space beside for mine.

And should the Philistine defend
His strength against our blows,
The God who doth not spare His friend,
Will not forget His foes.

AMERICAN NAMES

I have fallen in love with American names,
The sharp gaunt names that never get fat,
The snakeskin-titles of mining-claims,
The plumed war-bonnet of Medicine Hat,
Tucson and Deadwood and Lost Mule Flat.

Seine and Piave are silver spoons,
But the spoonbowl-metal is thin and worn,
There are English counties like hunting-tunes
Played on the keys of a postboy's horn,
But I will remember where I was born.

I will remember Carquinez Straits,
Little French Lick and Lundy's Lane,
The Yankee ships and the Yankee dates
And the bullet-towns of Calamity Jane.
I will remember Skunktown Plain.

I will fall in love with a Salem tree
And a rawhide quirt from Santa Cruz,
I will get me a bottle of Boston sea
And a blue-gum nigger to sing me blues.
I am tired of loving a foreign muse.

Rue des Martyrs and Bleeding-Heart-Yard,
Senlis, Pisa, and Blindman's Oast,
It is a magic ghost you guard;
But I am sick for a newer ghost—
Harrisburg, Spartanburg, Painted Post.

Henry and John were never so,
And Henry and John were always right?
Granted, but when it was time to go
And the tea and the laurels had stood all night,
Did they never watch for Nantucket Light?

I shall not rest quiet in Montparnasse.
I shall not lie easy in Winchelsea.
You may bury my body in Sussex grass,
You may bury my tongue at Champmédy.
I shall not be there. I shall rise and pass.
Bury my heart at Wounded Knee.

William Rose Benét

THE FALCONER OF GOD

I flung my soul to the air like a falcon flying.
I said: "Wait on, wait on, while I ride below!
    I shall start a heron soon
    In the marsh beneath the moon—
A strange white heron rising with silver on its wings.
       Rising and crying
     Wordless, wondrous things;
    The secret of the stars, of the world's heart-strings
    The answer to their woe.
Then stoop thou upon him, and grip and hold him so!"

My wild soul waited on as falcons hover.
I beat the reedy fens as I trampled past.
    I heard the mournful loon
    In the marsh beneath the moon.

And then, with feathery thunder, the bird of my desire
          Broke from the cover
          Flashing silver fire.
High up among the stars I saw his pinions spire.
          The pale clouds gazed aghast
As my falcon stooped upon him, and gripped and held him fast.

My soul dropped through the air—with heavenly plunder?—
Gripping the dazzling bird my dreaming knew?
          Nay! but a piteous freight,
          A dark and heavy weight
Despoiled of silver plumage, its voice forever stilled—
          All of the wonder
          Gone that ever filled
Its guise with glory. O bird that I have killed,
          How brilliantly you flew
Across my rapturous vision when first I dreamed of you!

Yet I fling my soul on high with new endeavor,
And I ride the world below with a joyful mind.
          I shall start a heron soon
          In the marsh beneath the moon—
A wondrous silver heron its inner darkness fledges!
          I beat forever
          The fens and the sedges.
The pledge is still the same—for all disastrous pledges,
          All hopes resigned!
My soul still flies above me for the quarry it shall find!

                    "WILD PHILOMELA"

          The step to silence taken,
          More far than star from star;
          The air still shaken
          Where you are,

          Where you burn with your branding,
          Lift to your light,
          Nourish understanding
          Of our night.

Is it understanding,
Or mere brute grieving—
The senses demanding,
Or believing.

Does it matter, does it matter,
In the void left behind,
Where the heart writhes to flatter
The mind?

Sudden, in desolation,
Where you were not, you grew.
Light filled creation,
Followed you.

From cruelty then or kindness
In escape you were away.
Utter blindness
Canceled day.

Bronze hair, the throat of one flying,
Level eyes scourging fear,
Singular laughter, eloquent crying—
You were here;

Yet, midway of Spartan duty,
Stood clear, facing the dawn
Of terrible ultimate beauty—
And are gone.

Some will praise you, some doubt you;
Most will say and nothing tell.
To live without you
Is their hell.

Glittering utterly bright,
Fabulous valor unforgot—
Oh, once more the Light! The Night
Knew it not.

MacKnight Black

ROCK, BE MY DREAM

Rock, be my dream—
Immense stillness of rock curved under the land.
Dark stone ripened on the sun-core of the world
Be the sphere of my peace.
The flame that fore-ran your deep strength
Has fathered my blood, and built wholeness within me.
Under the loam of my thought, broken with passing harvests,
Rock, be my dream, a burning fulfilled.

STRUCTURAL IRON WORKERS

What love do these men give their women
That is like the love they spend
On this iron harlot
With the sky between her breasts?

What kisses
Like the red sting of rivets
Have they left on any lips?

You will not find
The full fruit of their loins
In any daughters, any sons—
But lift your gaze and stare long
Toward the sky's edge.

NIGHT EXPRESS

Twice welcome, disrupter of stillness!
Once for your steel onward leap to assault the horizon,
And again for your rush
That tears clean through a mind's desolation.

Flowing into stillness and night, it is gone;
And the near stars are unshaken again;

39

The sides of the dark lean together,
And my thought is healed over from the cleft of this passing
As though I had seen the universe plunge, terrific in space,
And forgotten it then.

BESIDE A BALANCE–WHEEL

I watch the great spokes of this wheel
Club stillness with a might that churned the new stars,
And find the same labor under my breast;
I see the strokes fall and swirl away, soundless, impalpable,
On the wings of clean motion that father my pride.
This I shall remember when darkness comes to drown me at last;
I shall remember a rhythm deeper than blood; I shall hope
To enter the earth like a blow, and sweep clear in a flight.

Maxwell Bodenheim

THE REAR–PORCHES OF AN APARTMENT–BUILDING

A sky that has never known sun, moon or stars,
A sky that is like a dead kind face,
Would have the color of your eyes,
O servant-girl, singing of pear-trees in the sun,
And scraping the yellow fruit you once picked
When your lavender-white eyes were alive. . . .
On the porch above you are two women,
Whose faces have the color of brown earth that has never felt
    rain.
The still wet basins of ponds that have been drained
Are their eyes.
They knit gray rosettes and nibble cakes. . . .
And on the top porch are three children
Gravely kissing each others' foreheads—
And an ample nurse with a huge red fan. . . .

The passing of the afternoon to them
Is but the lengthening of blue-black shadows on brick walls.

THE INTERNE

Oh, the agony of having too much power!
In my passive palm are hundreds of lives.
Strange alchemy!—they drain my blood:
My heart becomes iron; my brain copper; my eyes silver; my
lips brass.
Merely by twitching a supple finger, I twirl lives from me—
strong-winged,
Or fluttering and broken.
They are my children, I am their mother and father.
I watch them live and die.

THE OLD JEW

No fawn-tinged hospital pajamas could cheat him of his aus-
terity,
Which tamed even the doctors with its pure fire.
They examined him; made him bow to them:
Massive altars were they, at whose swollen feet grovelled a
worshiper.
Then they laughed, half in scorn of him; and there came a
miracle:
The little man was above them at a bound.
His austerity, like an irresistible sledge-hammer, drove them
lower and lower:
They dwindled while he soared.

THE MINER

Those on the top say they know you, Earth—they are liars.
You are my father, and the silence I work in is my mother.
Only the son knows his father.
We are alike—sweaty, inarticulate of soul, bending under thick
knowledge.
I drink and shout with my brothers when above you—
Like most children we soon forget the parents of our souls.
But you avidly grip us again—we pay for the little noise of life
we steal.

TO AN ENEMY

I despise my friends more than you.
I would have known myself, but they stood before the mirrors
And painted on them images of the virtues I craved.
You came with sharpest chisel, scraping away the false
    paint.
Then I knew and detested myself, but not you:
For glimpses of you in the glasses you uncovered
Showed me the virtues whose images you destroyed.

TO A DISCARDED STEEL RAIL

Straight strength pitched into the surliness of the ditch,
A soul you have—strength has always delicate secret reasons.
Your soul is a dull question.
I do not care for your strength, but for your stiff smile at
    Time—
A smile which men call rust.

LOVE

You seemed a caryatid melting
Into the wind-blown dark blue temple of the sky.
But you bent down as I came closer, breaking the image.
When I passed, you raised your head
And blew the little feather of a smile upon me.
I caught it on open lips and blew it back.
And in that moment we loved,
Although you stood still waiting for your lover.
And I walked on to my love.

SONGS TO A WOMAN

I

You are like startled song-wings against my heart
Which flutters like a harp-string wounded
By too much quivering music.

You cover me with a blue dream-robe
Whose silk ripples out like imaged water. . . .
Amd when, for a moment, you leave,
I am a black sky awaiting its moon.

II

If I could be moon-light scattered out
Over the blowing dark-blue hair
Of kneeling flowing crystal breezes
Breathing a litany of pale odors;
If I could be moonlight scattered out
Over the whispers meeting in your heart,
The marriage of our souls would be
No more complete than now.

DEATH

I shall walk down the road.
I shall turn and feel upon my feet
The kisses of Death, like scented rain.
For Death is a black slave with little silver birds
Perched in a sleeping wreath upon his head.
He will tell me, his voice like jewels
Dropped into a satin bag,
How he has tip-toed after me down the road,
His heart made a dark whirlpool with longing for me.
Then he will graze me with his hands
And I shall be one of the sleeping silver birds
Between the cold waves of his hair, as he tip-toes on.

IMPULSIVE DIALOGUE

Poet. Will you, like other men,
    Offer me indigo indignities?
Undertaker. Indigo indignities!
    The words are like a mermaid and a saint
    Doubting each other's existence with a kiss.
Poet. The words of most men kiss
    With satiated familiarity.

Indigo is dark and vehement,
But one word in place of two
Angers barmaids and critics.

Undertaker. Straining after originality,
You argue with its ghost!
A simple beauty, like morning
Harnessed by a wide sparkle
And plodding into the hearts of men,
Cannot reach your frantic juggling.

Poet. I can appreciate
The spontaneous redundancy of nature
Without the aid of an echo
From men who lack her impersonal size.

Undertaker. The sweeping purchase of an evening
By an army of stars;
The bold incoherence of love;
The peaceful mountain-roads of friendship—
These things evade your dexterous epigrams!

Poet. A statue, polished and large,
Dominates when it stands alone.
Placed in a huge profusion of statutes,
Its outlines become humiliated.
Simplicity demands one gesture
And men give it endless thousands.
Complexity wanders through a forest,
Glimpsing details in the gloom.

Undertaker. I do not crave the dainty pleasure
Of chasing ghosts in a forest!
Nor do I care to pluck
Exaggerated mushrooms in the gloom.
I have lost myself on roads
Crossed by tossing hosts of men.
Pain and anger have scorched our slow feet:
Peace has washed our foreheads.

Poet. Futility, massive and endless,
Captures a stumbling grandeur
Embalmed in history.
In my forest you could see this
From a distance, and lose

Your limited intolerance.
Simplicity and subtlety
At different times are backgrounds for each other,
Changing with the position of our eyes. . . .
Death will burn your eyes
With his taciturn complexity.
Undertaker. Death will strike your eyes
With his wild simplicity!
Poet. Words are soldiers of fortune
Hired by different ideas
To provide an importance for life.
But within the glens of silence
They meet in secret peace. . . .
Undertaker, do you make of death
A puffing wretch forever pursued
By duplicates of vanquished forms?
Or do you make him a sneering king
Brushing flies from his bloodless cheeks?
Do you see him as an unappeased brooding
Walking over the dust of men?
Do you make him an eager giant
Discovering and blending into his consciousness
The tiny parts of his limitless mind?
Undertaker. Death and I do not know each other.
I am the stolid janitor
Who cleans the litter he has left
And claims a fancied payment.
Poet. Come to my fantastic forest
And you will not need to rise
From simple labors, asking death
For final wages.

Louise Bogan

THE CROSSED APPLE

I've come to give you fruit from out my orchard,
Of wide report.
I have trees there that bear me many apples
Of every sort:

Clear, streaked; red and russet; green and golden;
Sour and sweet.
This apple's from a tree yet unbeholden,
Where two kinds meet—

So that this side is red without a dapple,
And this side's hue
Is clear and snowy. It's a lovely apple.
It is for you.

Within are five black pips as big as peas,
As you will find,
Potent to breed you five great apple trees
Of varying kind:

To breed you wood for fire, leaves for shade,
Apples for sauce.
Oh, this is a good apple for a maid,
It is a cross,

Fine on the finer, so the flesh is tight,
And grained like silk.
Sweet Burning gave the red side, and the white
Is Meadow Milk.

Eat it; and you will taste more than the fruit:
The blossom, too,
The sun, the air, the darkness at the root,
The rain, the dew,

The earth we come to and the time we flee,
The fire and the breast.
I claim the white part, maiden, that's for me.
You take the rest.

OLD COUNTRYSIDE

Beyond the hour we counted rain that fell
On the slant shutter, all has come to proof.
The summer thunder, like a wooden bell,
Rang in the storm above the mansard roof,

And mirrors cast the cloudy day along
The attic floor; wind made the clapboards creak.
You braced against the wall to make it strong,
A shell against your cheek.

Long since, we pulled brown oak-leaves to the ground
In a winter of dry trees; we heard the cock
Shout its unplaceable cry, the axe's sound
Delay a moment after the axe's stroke.

Far back we saw, in the stillest of the year,
The scrawled vine shudder, and the rose-branch show
Red to the thorns, and, sharp as sight can bear,
The thin hound's body arched against the snow.

CASSANDRA

To me, one silly task is like another.
I bare the shambling tricks of lust and pride.
This flesh will never give a child its mother;
Song, like a wing, tears through my breast, my side,
And madness chooses out my voice again,
Again. I am the chosen no hand saves:
The shrieking heaven lifted over men,
Not the dumb earth, wherein they set their graves.

SONG

Love me because I am lost;
Love me that I am undone.
That is brave—no man has wished it,
Not one.

Be strong to look on my heart
As others look on my face.
Love me—I tell you that it is a ravaged
Terrible place.

SONG FOR A SLIGHT VOICE

If ever I render back your heart,
So long to me delight and plunder,
It will be bound with the firm strings
That men have built the viol under.

Your stubborn piteous heart, that bent
To be the place where music stood,
Upon some shaken instrument
Stained with the dark of resinous blood,

Will find its place, beyond denial,
Will hear the dance—oh, be most sure—
Laid on the curved wood of the viol
Or on the struck tambour.

THE ROMANTIC

Admit the ruse to fix and name her chaste
With those who sleep the spring through, one and one,
Cool nights, when the laurel builds up, without haste,
Its precise flower, like a pentagon.

In her obedient breast, all that ran free
You thought to bind, like echoes in a shell.
At the year's end, you promised, it would be
The unstrung leaves, and not her heart, that fell.

So the year broke and vanished on the screen
You cast about her; summer went to haws.
This, by your leave, is what she should have been—
Another man will tell you what she was.

THE MARK

Where should he seek, to go away
That shadow will not point him down?
The spear of dark in the strong day
Beyond the upright body thrown,
Marking no epoch but its own.

Loosed only when, at noon and night,
The body is the shadow's prison.
The pivot swings into the light;
The center left, the shadow risen
To range out into time's long treason.

Stand pinned to sight, while now, unbidden,
The apple loosens, not at call,
Falls to the field, and lies there hidden—-
Another and another fall
And lie there hidden, in spite of all

The diagram of whirling shade,
The visible, that thinks to spin
Forever webs that time has made
Though momently time wears them thin
And all at length are gathered in.

COME BREAK WITH TIME

Come, break with time,
You who were lorded
By a clock's chime
So ill afforded.
If time is allayed
Be not afraid.

I shall break, if I will.
Break, since you must.
Time has its fill,
Sated with dust.
Long the clock's hand
Burned like a brand.

Take the rocks' speed
And earth's heavy measure.
Let buried seed
Drain out time's pleasure,
Take time's decrees.
Come, cruel ease.

Gordon Bottomley

NIGHT AND MORNING SONGS

MY MOON

My moon was lit in an hour of lilies;
The apple-trees seemed older than ever.
It rose from matted trees that sever
The oats from the meadow, and woke the fillies
That reared in dew and gleamed with dew
And ran like water and shadow, and cried.
It moistened and veiled the oats yet new,
And seemed to drip long drops of the tide,
Of the mother-sea so lately left.
Feathers of flower were each bereft
Of color and stem, and floated low;
Another lily opened then
And lost a little gold-dust; but when
The lime-boughs lifted there seemed to go
Some life of the moon, like breath that moves
Or parting glances that flutter and strain—
A ghost with hands the color of doves
And feet the color of rain.

ELEGIAC MOOD

From song and dream for ever gone
Are Helen, Helen of Troy,
And Cleopatra made to look upon,
And many a daring boy—
Young Faust and Sigurd and Hippolytus:

They are twice dead and we must find
Great ladies yet unblemished by the mind,
Heroes and acts not cold for us
In amber or spirits of too many words.
Ay, these are murdered by much thinking on.
I hanker even for new shapes of swords,
More different sins, and raptures not yet done.
Yet, as I wait on marvels, such a bird
As maybe Sigurd heard—
A thrush—alighting with a little run
Out-tops the daisies as it passes
And peeps bright-eyed above the grasses.

DAWN

A thrush is tapping a stone
With a snail-shell in its beak;
A small bird hangs from a cherry
Until the stem shall break.
No waking song has begun,
And yet birds chatter and hurry
And throng in the elm's gloom
Because an owl goes home.

Polly Chase Boyden

FORM

The wide amorphous sea,
The unassembled arches of the trees,
Divergent clouds, irregular mountains—we
Perceive no grace in these.
We thread the protean forest mute and blind,
And in our vehemence and pride we find
No meaning in its multiform mobility.

Water may flow and autumn leaves may burn,
Winds sweep the firmament! We feel no loss

When quiet comes again and we may turn
To forms long fixed in stagnant symmetry:
Turn to Orion or the Southern Cross,
Or to the mesa's static unity,
Or to the sculptured elegance of stone
Perceived in planes that taper rhythmically
To a volcano's cone.

And when our eyes confront a city sky,
We find the same sure equilibrium
In slender tracery of tower or spire,
In marble pillar or in blazoned dome:
A pause imposed on matter to defy
The endless flux of water, wind and fire.

We find it, fugitive and delicate,
In figurines of jade and alabaster,
In concentrated shapes of ivory,
In lacquer work and bronze. It is delight to hold,
Curving within a palm, the luminous arc
Of bracelet, coin or ring
Wrought tenderly in gold.

Too well we know
That even stone
Will finally merge in all-consuming light . . .
That form is only a blurred overtone
Arrested for a moment of delight.

Too well we know! . . .
But still the flight
Of line imprisoned in an urn or vase
Supplies the sense of bright unbounded curves
Inviolate in space.
Contour perceived unites our scattered nerves,
Assailed on every side by loud negation.

Completed form is a swift consummation,
A moment's apprehension of the whole.
Because our hearts reject
The implication of oblivion,

We build our tabernacles and erect
Fair sanctuaries underneath the sun
Wherein to find
Brief answer to the doom we know must fall
From the ascendant rampart of the mind.

HANDS ON A CARD-TABLE

A woman's hands with polished finger-nail,
Creeping like puffy spiders on green baize,
Clicking the cards down softly as she plays.
Plump pampered hands!—too lifeless to assail
The keys Cecilia pressed, or glean the frail
Ripe wheat that Ruth's hands gleaned. Forlorn I gaze
On hands of card-crazed women—how to praise,
How glorify the dullness of their tale?

Better for hands to swing the singing loom
The Lady of Shalott turned pensively;
Or hold the gilded book in a convent room
With sad Francesca, listening to the sea;
Or pluck the idle fruit which sealed the doom
Of lily-fingered lost Persephone.

Rupert Brooke

RETROSPECT

In your arms was still delight,
Quiet as a street at night;
And thoughts of you, I do remember,
Were green leaves in a darkened chamber,
Were dark clouds in a moonless sky.
Love, in you, went passing by,
Penetrative, remote, and rare,
Like a bird in the wide air;
And, as the bird, it left no trace
In the heaven of your face.

In your stupidity I found
The sweet hush after a sweet sound.
All about you was the light
That dims the graying end of night;
Desire was the unrisen sun,
Joy the day not yet begun,
With tree whispering to tree,
Without wind, quietly.
Wisdom slept within your hair,
And Long-suffering was there,
And, in the flowing of your dress,
Undiscerning Tenderness.
And when you thought, it seemed to me,
Infinitely, and like a sea,
About the slight world you had known
Your vast unconsciousness was thrown. . . .

O haven without wave or tide!
Silence, in which all songs have died!
Holy book, where hearts are still!
And home at length under the hill!
O mother quiet, breasts of peace,
Where love itself would faint and cease!
O infinite deep I never knew,
I would come back, come back to you;
Find you, as a pool unstirred,
Kneel down by you, and never a word;
Lay my head, and nothing said,
In your hands, ungarlanded.
And a long watch you would keep;
And I should sleep, and I should sleep!

NINETEEN-FOURTEEN

I—PEACE

Now, God be thanked who has matched us with his hour,
   And caught our youth, and wakened us from sleeping!
With hand made sure, clear eye, and sharpened power,
   To turn, as swimmers into cleanness leaping,

Glad from a world grown old and cold and weary;
  Leave the sick hearts that honor could not move,
And half-men, and their dirty songs and dreary,
  And all the little emptiness of love!
Oh! we, who have known shame, we have found release there,
  Where there's no ill, no grief, but sleep has mending,
    Naught broken save this body, lost but breath;
Nothing to shake the laughing heart's long peace there,
  But only agony, and that has ending;
    And the worst friend and enemy is but Death.

II—SAFETY

Dear! of all happy in the hour, most blest
  He who has found our hid security,
Assured in the dark tides of the world that rest,
  And heard our word, "Who is so safe as we?"
We have found safety with all things undying—
  The winds, and morning, tears of men and mirth,
The deep night, and birds singing, and clouds flying,
  And sleep, and freedom, and the autumnal earth.
We have built a house that is not for Time's throwing.
  We have gained a peace unshaken by pain forever.
War knows no power. Safe shall be my going,
  Secretly armed against all Death's endeavor;
Safe though all safety's lost; safe where men fall;
And if these poor limbs die, safest of all.

III—THE DEAD

Blow out, you bugles, over the rich dead!
  There's none of these so lonely and poor of old,
  But, dying, has made us rarer gifts than gold.
These laid the world away; poured out the red
Sweet wine of youth; gave up the years to be
  Of work and joy, and that unhoped serene
  That men call age; and those who would have been
Their sons they gave, their immortality.
Blow, bugles, blow! They brought us, for our dearth,
  Holiness, lacked so long, and Love, and Pain.

Honor has come back, as a king, to earth,
And paid his subjects with a royal wage;
  And Nobleness walks in our ways again;
And we have come into our heritage.

IV—THE DEAD

These hearts were woven of human joys and cares,
  Washed marvellously with sorrow, swift to mirth.
The years had given them kindness. Dawn was theirs,
  And sunset, and the colors of the earth.
These had seen movement, and heard music; known
  Slumber and waking; loved, gone proudly friended;
Felt the quick stir of wonder; sat alone;
  Touched flowers and furs and cheeks. All this is ended.
There are waters blown by changing winds to laughter
And lit by the rich skies, all day. And after,
  Frost, with a gesture, stays the waves that dance,
And wandering loveliness. He leaves a white
  Unbroken glory, a gathered radiance,
A width, a shining peace, under the night.

V—SOLDIER

If I should die, think only this of me:
  That there's some corner of a foreign field
That is for ever England. There shall be
  In that rich earth a richer dust concealed;
A dust whom England bore, shaped, made aware,
  Gave once her flowers to love, her ways to roam,
A body of England's, breathing English air,
  Washed by the rivers, blest by suns of home.
And think, this heart, all evil shed away,
  A pulse in the eternal mind, no less
    Gives somewhere back the thoughts by England given;
Her sights and sounds; dreams happy as her day;
  And laughter, learnt of friends; and gentleness,
    In hearts at peace, under an English heaven.

Witter Bynner

GRASS-TOPS

What bird are you in the grass-tops?
  Your poise is enough of an answer,
With your wing-tips like up-curving fingers
  Of the slow-moving hands of a dancer—

And what is so nameless as beauty,
  Which poets, who give it a name,
Are only unnaming forever?—
  Content, though it go, that it came.

DREAM

I had returned from dreaming—
When there came the look of you,
And I could not tell after that;
And the sound of you
And I could not tell;
And at last the touch of you
And I could tell then less than ever;
Though I silvered and fell
As at the very mountain-brim
Of dream.

For how could the motion of a shadow in a field
Be a person?
Or the flash of an oriole-wing
Be a smile?
Or the turn of a leaf on a stream
Be a hand?
Or a bright breath of sun
Be lips?

I can reach out and out—and nothing will be there;
None of these things are true.
All of them are dreams—
There are neither streams
Nor leaves nor orioles nor you.

57

TO CELIA

CONSUMMATION

There was a strangeness on your lips,
  Lips that had been so sure;
You still were mine but in eclipse,
  Beside me but obscure.

There was a cloud upon your heart;
  For, Celia, where you lay,
Death, come to break your life apart,
  Had led your love away.

Through the cold distance of your eyes
  You could no longer see.
But when you died, you heard me rise
  And followed suddenly.

And close beside me, looking down
  As I did on the dead,
You made of time a wedding-gown,
  Of space a marriage-bed.

I took, in you, death for a wife,
  You married death in me,
Singing, "There is no other life,
  No other God than we!"

NIGHT

Celia, when you bid me
  Good-morning, I awake
Quick again on your account,
  Eager for your sake.

Yet at morning, or at noon
  In the clearest light,
Is there any voice as near
  As your voice at night?

Or has anyone alive
Ever come and said
Anything as intimate
As you are saying, dead?

DURING A CHORALE BY CESAR FRANCK

In an old chamber softly lit
  We heard the Chorale played,
And where you sat, an exquisite
Image of life and lover of it,
  Death sang a serenade.

I know now, Celia, what you heard,
  And why you turned and smiled.
It was the white wings of a bird
Offering flight, and you were stirred
  Like an adventurous child.

Death sang: "Oh, lie upon your bier,
  Uplift your countenance!"
Death bade me be your cavalier,
Called me to march and shed no tear,
  But sing to you and dance.

And when you followed, lured and led
  By those mysterious wings,
And when I heard that you were dead,
I could not weep. I sang instead,
  As a true lover sings.

Today a room is softly lit;
  I hear the Chorale played.
And where you come, an exquisite
Image of death and lover of it,
  Life sings a serenade.

SONGS ASCENDING

Love has been sung a thousand ways—
    So let it be;
The songs ascending in your praise
Through all my days
    Are three.

Your cloud-white body first I sing;
    Your love was heaven's blue,
And I, a bird, flew carolling
In ring on ring
    Of you.

Your nearness is the second song;
    When God began to be,
And bound you strongly, right or wrong,
With his own thong,
    To me.

But oh, the song, eternal, high
    That tops these two!—
You live forever, you who die;
I am not I
    But you.

GRIEVE NOT FOR BEAUTY

Almost the body leads the laggard soul; bidding it see
The beauty of surrender, the tranquillity
Of fusion with the earth. The body turns to dust
Not only by a sudden whelming thrust
Or at the end of a corrupting calm,
But oftentimes anticipates, and entering flowers and trees
Upon a hillside or along the brink
Of streams, encounters instances
Of its eventual enterprise:
Inhabits the enclosing clay,
In rhapsody is caught away
In a great tide
Of beauty, to abide

Translated through the night and day
Of time, and by the anointing balm
Of earth to outgrow decay.

Hark in the wind—the word of silent lips!
Look where some subtle throat, that once had wakened lust,
Lies clear and lovely now, a silver link
Of change and peace!
Hollows and willows and a river-bed,
Anemones and clouds,
Raindrops and tender distances
Above, beneath,
Inherit and bequeath
Our far-begotten beauty. We are wed
With many kindred who were seeming dead.
Only the delicate woven shrouds
Are vanished, beauty thrown aside
To honor and uncover
A deeper beauty—as the veil that slips
Breathless away between a lover
And his bride.

So, by the body, may the soul surmise
The beauty of surrender, the tranquillity
Of fusion: when, set free
From semblance of mortality,
Yielding its dust the richer to endue
A common avenue
Of earth for other souls to journey through,
It shall put on in purer guise
The mutual beauty of its destiny.
And who shall fear for his identity,
And who shall cling to the poor privacy
Of incompleteness, when the end explains
That what pride forfeits, beauty gains!
Therefore, O spirit, as a runner strips
Upon a windy afternoon,
Be unencumbered of what troubles you—
Arise with grace
And greatly go, the wind upon your face!

Grieve not for the invisible transported brow
On which like leaves the dark hair grew;
Nor for the lips of laughter that are now
Laughing inaudibly in sun and dew;
Nor for the limbs that, fallen low
And seeming faint and slow,
Shall alter and renew
Their shape and hue
Like birches white before the moon,
Or a young apple-tree
In spring, or the round sea;
And shall pursue
More ways of swiftness than the swallow dips
Among . . . and find more winds than ever blew
The straining sails of unimpeded ships!

. . . .

For never beauty dies
That lived. Nightly the skies
Assemble stars, the light of many eyes,
And daily brood on the communal breath—
Which we call death.

CHAPALA POEMS

CALENDAR

Why should I know or care what month it is?
An Aztec calendar was made long since.
What year was it? What century? What matter,
Except that stone became symmetrical?
If I watch the time, some of my friends will die,
If I watch the time, I shall surely die myself.
Let me then gather all my friends about me
And carve an endless moment out of stone.

MONTEZUMA

The sunset was a crown of spiked flame—
"Come, put me on if you can!" and no one could.
Even the mountain turned away its head

From coronation, wore but an ashen summit.
Suddenly Montezuma rose again,
Forgot that his young heart was full of dust
And, setting on his brow the level turquoise,
Walked with flamingo feathers down the world.

ASLEEP

In a pool of shadow floating on the sand
And cool to lean asleep in it like a fish,
The boatman lies, shirt drawn away by earth
From the brown middle, hands under head, legs
Dreaming of death. And close to him as a weed
Is to a fish, his hat is sleeping too.
How intimate he is with the good earth!—
As if, long buried, he were still alive
Among the many other mounds of sand.

THE WEB

I am caught in an iridescent spider-web,
One end of it attached to a pepper-tree
And the other to a weed on Tunapec.
Why should I break the pattern of the world?
Better to swing so delicately caught
Than to have my eyes put out in hollow flame.
I flutter my wings awhile and then subside,
Till a shadow shall find me in the evening wind.

Joseph Campbell

AT HARVEST

Earth travails,
Like a woman come to her time.

The swaying corn-haulms
In the heavy places of the field
Cry to be gathered.
Apples redden, and drop from their rods.

Out of their sheath of prickly leaves
The marrows creep, fat and white.
The blue pallor of ripeness
Comes on the fruit of the vine.

Fecund and still fecund
After æons of bearing:
Not old, not dry, not wearied out;
But fresh as when the unseen Right Hand
First moved on Brí,
And the candle of day was set,
And dew fell from the stars' feet,
And cloths of greenness covered thee.

Let me kiss thy breasts:
I am thy son and lover.

Womb-fellow am I of the sunburnt wheat,
Friendly gossip of the mearings;
Womb-fellow of the dark and sweet-scented apple;
Womb-fellow of the gourd and of the grape:
Like begotten, like born.

And yet,
Without a lover's knowledge of thy secrets
I would walk the ridges of the hills,
Kindless and desolate.

What is the storm-driven moon to me,
Seed of another father?
What the flooding of the well of dawn?
What the hollow, red with rowan fire?
What the king-fern?
What the belled heath?
What the spread of heron's wing,
Or glint of spar,
Caught from the pit
Of a deserted quarry?

Let me kiss thy breasts:
I am thy son and lover.

ON WAKING

Sleep, gray brother of death,
Has touched me,
And passed on.

I arise, facing the east—
Golden termon
From which light,
Signed with dew and fire,
Dances.

Hail, essence, hail!
Fill the windows of my soul
With beauty:
Pierce and renew my bones:
Pour knowledge into my heart
As water
From a quenchless spring.

Cualann is bright before thee.
Its rocks melt and swim:
The secret they have kept
From the ancient nights of darkness
Flies like a bird.
What mourns?
Cualann's secret flying,
A lost voice
In lonely fields.

What rejoices?
My song lifted praising thee.

Praise! Praise! Praise!
Praise out of tubas, whose bronze
Is the unyoked strength of bulls;
Praise upon harps, whose strings
Are the light movements of birds;
Praise of leaf, praise of blossom,
Praise of the red human clay;

Praise of grass,
Fire-woven veil of the temple;
Praise of the shapes of clouds;
Praise of the shadows of wells;
Praise of worms, of fetal things,
And of the things in time's thought
Not yet begotten:
To thee, queller of sleep,
Looser of the snare of death.

THE OLD WOMAN

As a white candle
    In a holy place,
So is the beauty
    Of an aged face.

As the spent radiance
    Of the winter sun,
So is a woman
    With her travail done.

Her brood gone from her,
    And her thoughts as still
As the waters
    Under a ruined mill.

Nancy Campbell

THE APPLE-TREE

I saw the archangels in my apple-tree last night,
I saw them like great birds in the starlight—
Purple and burning blue, crimson and shining white.

And each to each they tossed an apple to and fro,
And once I heard their laughter gay and low;
And yet I felt no wonder that it should be so.

But when the apple came one time to Michael's lap
I heard him say: "The mysteries that enwrap
The earth and fill the heavens can be read here, mayhap."

Then Gabriel spoke: "I praise the deed, the hidden thing."
" The beauty of the blossom of the spring
I praise," cried Raphael. Uriel: "The wise leaves I sing."

And Michael: "I will praise the fruit, perfected, round,
Full of the love of God, herein being bound
His mercies gathered from the sun and rain and ground."

So sang they till a small wind through the branches stirred,
And spoke of coming dawn; and at its word
Each fled away to heaven, winged like a bird.

THE MONKEY

I saw you hunched and shivering on the stones,
The bleak wind piercing to your fragile bones,
Your shabby scarlet all inadequate:
A little ape that had such human eyes
They seemed to hide behind their miseries—
Their dumb and hopeless bowing down to fate—
Some puzzled wonder. Was your monkey soul
Sickening with memories of gorgeous days,
Of tropic playfellows and forest ways,
Where, agile, you could swing from bole to bole
In an enchanted twilight with great flowers
For stars; or on a bough the long night hours
Sit out in rows, and chatter at the moon?
Shuffling you went, your tiny chilly hand
Outstretched for what you did not understand;
Your puckered mournful face begging a boon
That but enslaved you more. They who passed by
Said nothing sorrowful; gave laugh or stare,
Unheeding that the little antic there
Played in the gutter such a tragedy.

Emanuel Carnevali

IN THIS HOTEL

The headwaiter says:
"Nice day today!"
He smiles sentimentally.
The headwaiter says:
"It will rain today!"
He frowns gracefully.
Those are the greetings, every morning,
To every old lady,
And every old gent,
And every old rogue,
And every young couple—
To every guest.

And I, who do not sleep, who wait and watch for the dawn,
One day I would come down to the world.
I would have a trumpet as powerful as the wind,
And I would trumpet out to the world
The splendid commonplace:
"Nice day today!"
And another day I would cry out in despair,
"It will rain today!"
For every old lady,
And every old gent,
And every old rogue,
And every young couple—
Are they not guests in this hotel,
Where the ceiling is the sky
And the floor is the earth,
And the rooms are the houses?

But I, I—this wretched, tired thing—
May I ask for a job
As headwaiter
Of this hotel?

SERMON

Chao-Mong-Mu freely laid his hands over the sky:
You do not know how to lay your hands over the breasts of
   your beloved.

Chao-Mong-Mu made the tree dance at his will:
You do not know how to hug a rough tree and say "darling" to it.

Chao-Mong-Mu magnificently ran a shaft of sunlight to smash
   against the treetops:
You walk carefully, carefully, and fend off the sunlight with your
   grey clothes, although you're very poor.

Chao-Mong-Mu painted a sky that was a pink-fleshed vase; then
   he became a very small thing and hid in the vase:
You build yourselves immense houses to live in, and you are
   afraid even there.

INVOCATION TO DEATH

Let me
Close my eyes tight.
Still my arms,
Let me be.
Then, come.
Let me be utterly alone:
Do not let the awful understanding that comes with
The thought of Death
Bother me.

Your love was not strong enough to hold me.

Death takes things away:
I have them here in my hands,
The rags.

I do not understand the cosmic humor
That lets foolish impossibilities, like me, live.

I have made a mess of it,
But I am no debtor.

It's the yearning of a nervous man,
The yearning for peace,
The curiosity for a word:
Forever.

If She would only come quietly,
Like a lady—
The first lady and the last.

Just not to hear any longer
The noise swelling from the morning streets,
Nor the two desperate sparrows chirruping;
Just not to fear any longer
The landlady.

Willa Cather

THE PALATINE

In the "Dark Ages"

"Have you been with the king to Rome,
　　Brother, big brother?"
"I've been there and I've come home.
　　Back to your play, little brother."

"Oh, how high is Cæsar's house,
　　Brother, big brother?"
"Goats about the doorways browse;
Night-hawks nest in the burnt roof-tree.
Home of the wild bird and home of the bee,
A thousand chambers of marble lie
Wide to the sun and the wind and the sky.
Poppies we find amongst our wheat
Grow on Cæsar's banquet seat.
Cattle crop and neat-herds drowse
On the floors of Cæsar's house."

"But what has become of Cæsar's gold,
　　Brother, big brother?"

"The times are bad and the world is old—
Who knows the where of the Cæsar's gold?
Night comes black o'er the Cæsar's hill;
The wells are deep and the tales are ill;
Fireflies gleam in the damp and mold—
All that is left of the Cæsar's gold.
        Back to your play, little brother."

"What has become of the Cæsar's men,
        Brother, big brother?"
"Dogs in the kennel and wolf in the den
Howl for the fate of the Cæsar's men,
Slain in Asia, slain in Gaul,
By Dacian border and Persian wall.
Rhineland orchard and Danube fen
Fatten their roots on Cæsar's men."

"Why is the world so sad and wide,
        Brother, big brother?"
"Saxon boys by their fields that bide
Need not know if the world is wide.
Climb no mountain but Shere-end Hill,
Cross no water but goes to mill.
Ox in the stable and cow in the byre,
Smell of the wood-smoke and sleep by the fire;
Sun-up in seed time—a likely lad
Hurts not his head that the world is sad.
        Back to your play, little brother."

SPANISH JOHNNY

The old West, the old time,
    The old wind singing through
The red, red grass a thousand miles—
    And, Spanish Johnny, you!
He'd sit beside the water ditch
    When all his herd was in,
And never mind a child, but sing
    To his mandolin.

The big stars, the blue night,
    The moon-enchanted lane;
The olive man who never spoke,
    But sang the songs of Spain.
His speech with men was wicked talk—
    To hear it was a sin;
But those were golden things he said
    To his mandolin.

The gold songs, the gold stars,
    The world so golden then;
And the hand so tender to a child—
    Had killed so many men.
He died a hard death long ago
    Before the Road came in—
The night before he swung, he sang
    To his mandolin.

Padraic Colum

POLONIUS AND THE BALLAD-SINGERS

A gaunt-built woman and her son-in-law—
A broad-faced fellow, with such flesh as shows
Nothing but easy nature—and his wife,
The woman's daughter, who spills all her talk
Out of a wide mouth, but who has eyes as gray
As Connemara, where the mountain-ash
Shows berries red indeed: they enter now—
Our country singers!

"Sing, my good woman, sing us some romance
That has been round your chimney-nooks so long
'Tis nearly native; something blown here
And since made racy—like yon tree, I might say,
Native by influence if not by species,
Shaped by our winds. You understand, I think?"

"I'll sing the song, sir."

> *Tonight you see my face—*
> *Maybe nevermore you'll gaze*
> *On the one that for you left his friends and kin;*
> *For by the hard commands*
> *Of the lord that rules these lands*
> *On a ship I'll be borne from Cruckaunfinn!*
>
> *Oh, you know your beauty bright*
> *Has made him think delight*
> *More than from any fair one he will gain;*
> *Oh, you know that all his will*
> *Strains and strives around you till*
> *As the hawk upon his hand you are as tame!*
>
> *Then she to him replied:*
> *I'll no longer you deny,*
> *And I'll let you have the pleasure of my charms;*
> *For tonight I'll be your bride,*
> *And whatever may betide*
> *It's we will lie in one another's arms!*

"You should not sing
With body doubled up and face aside.
There is a climax here—'It's we will lie'—
Hem—passionate! And what does your daughter sing?"

"A song I like when I do climb bare hills—
'Tis all about a hawk."

> *No bird that sits on rock or bough*
> *Has such a front as thine;*
> *No king that has made war his trade*
> *Such conquest in his eyne!*
> *I mark thee rock-like on the rock*
> *Where none can see a shape.*
> *I climb, but thou dost climb with wings,*
> *And like a wish escape,*
> *She said—*
> *And like a wish escape!*

No maid that kissed his bonny mouth
Of another mouth was glad;
Such pride was in our chieftain's eyes,
Such countenance he had!
But since they made him fly the rocks,
Thou, creature, art my quest.
Then lift me with thy steady eyes—
If then to tear my breast,
She said,
If then to tear my breast!

"The songs they have
Are the last relics of the feudal world:
Women will keep them—byzants, doubloons,
When men will take up songs that are as new
As dollar bills. What song have you, young man?"

"A song my father had, sir. It was sent him
From across the sea, and there was a letter with it,
Asking my father to put it to a tune
And sing it all roads. He did that, in troth;
And five pounds of tobacco were sent with the song
To fore-reward him. I'll sing it for you now—
The Baltimore Exile."

The house I was bred in—ah, does it remain
Low walls and loose thatch standing lone in the rain,
With the clay of the walls coming through with its stain,
Like the blackbird's left nest in the briar!

Does a child there give heed to the song of the lark,
As it lifts and it drops till the fall of the dark,
When the heavy-foot kine trudge home from the paurk,
Or do none but the red-shank now listen?

The sloe-bush, I know, grows close to the well,
And its long-lasting blossoms are there, I can tell,
When the kid that was yeaned when the first ones befell
Can jump to the ditch that they grow on!

But there's silence on all. Then do none ever pass
On the way to the fair or the pattern or mass
Do the gray-coated lads drive the ball through the grass
  And speed to the sweep of the hurl?

O youths of my land! Then will no Bolivar
Ever muster your ranks for delivering war
Will your hopes become fixed and beam like a star
  Will they pass like the mists from your fields?

The swan and the swallows, the cuckoo and crake,
May visit my land and find hillside and lake.
And I send my song. I'll not see her awake—
  I'm too old a bird to uncage now!

"Silver's but lead in exchange for songs,
But take it and spend it."

"We will. And may we meet your honor's like
Every day's end."

"A tune is more lasting than the voice of the birds."

"A song is more lasting than the riches of the world."

A DROVER

To Meath of the pastures,
  From wet hills by the sea,
Through Leitrim and Longford,
  Go my cattle and me.

I hear in the darkness
  Their slipping and breathing—
I name them the byways
  They're to pass without heeding;

Then the wet winding roads,
  Brown bogs with black water;
And my thoughts on white ships,
  And the King o' Spain's daughter.

O farmer, strong farmer!—
  You can spend at the fair;
But your face you must turn
  To your crops and your care.

And soldiers, red soldiers!—
  You've seen many lands;
But you walk two by two,
  And by captain's commands.

Oh, the smell of the beasts,
  The wet wind in the morn;
And the proud and hard earth
  Never broken for corn!

And the crowds at the fair,
  The herds loosened and blind,
Loud words and dark faces
  And the wild blood behind!

(O strong men, with your best
  I would strive breast to breast—
I could quiet your herds
  With my words, with my words.)

I will bring you, my kine,
  Where there's grass to the knee;
But you'll think of scant croppings
  Harsh with salt of the sea.

AN OLD WOMAN OF THE ROADS

Oh, to have a little house!
  To own the hearth and stool and all!
The heaped-up sods upon the fire,
  The pile of turf against the wall!

To have a clock with weights and chains,
  And pendulum swinging up and down!
A dresser filled with shining delph,
  Speckled and white and blue and brown!

I could be busy all the day
 Clearing and sweeping hearth and floor,
And fixing on their shelf again
 My white and blue and speckled store!

I could be quiet there at night
 Beside the fire and by myself,
Sure of a bed and loth to leave
 The ticking clock and the shining delph!

Och! but I'm weary of mist and dark,
 And roads where there's never a house nor bush;
And tired I am of bog and road,
 And the crying wind and the lonesome hush!

And I am praying to God on high,
 And I am praying Him night and day,
For a little house—a house of my own—
 Out of the wind's and the rain's way.

THE WILD ASS

The Wild Ass lounges, legs struck out
 In vagrom unconcern:
The tombs of Achæmedian kings
 Are for those hooves to spurn.

And all of rugged Tartary
 Lies with him on the ground,
The Tartary that knows no awe,
 That has nor ban nor bound.

The wild horse from the herd is plucked
 To bear a saddle's weight;
The boar is one keeps covert, and
 The wolf runs with a mate;

But he's the solitary of space,
 Curbless and unbeguiled,
The only being that bears a heart
 Not recreant to the wild.

THE SEA BIRD TO THE WAVE

On and on,
O white brother!
Thunder does not daunt thee!
How thou movest!
By thine impulse—
With no wing!
Fairest thing
The wide sea shows me!
On and on,
O white brother!
Art thou gone!

Grace Hazard Conkling

REFUGEES

Belgium—1914

"Mother, the poplars cross the moon;
  The road runs on, so white and far
We shall not reach the city soon:
  Oh, tell me where we are!"

"Have patience, patience, little son,
  And we shall find the way again:
(God show me the untraveled one!
  God give me rest from men!)"

"Mother, you did not tell me why
  You hurried so to come away.
I saw big soldiers riding by;
  I should have liked to stay."

"Hush, little man, and I will sing
  Just like a soldier, if I can—
They have a song for everything.
  Listen, my little man!"

"This is the soldiers' marching song:
   We'll play this is the village street—"
"Yes, but this road is very long,
   And stones have hurt my feet."

"Nay, little pilgrim, up with you!
   And yonder field shall be the town.
I'll show you how the soldiers do
   Who travel up and down.

"They march and sing and march again,
   Not minding all the stones and dust:
They go (God grant me rest from men!)
   Forward, because they must."

"Mother, I want to go to sleep."
   "No darling! Here is bread to eat!
(O God, if thou couldst let me weep,
   Or heal my broken feet!)"

"THE LITTLE ROSE IS DUST, MY DEAR"

The little rose is dust, my dear;
   The elfin wind is gone
That sang a song of silver words
   And cooled our hearts with dawn.

And what is left to hope, my dear,
   Or what is left to say?
The rose, the little wind and you
   Have gone so far away.

GUADALUPE

No matter how you love me,
   You cannot keep me home.
Along the airy lane of bells
   Beyond the peacock dome,

I know the way to travel,
    And I shall go at will—
Where the stone sails await the wind
    Upon the holy hill.

The mariners who made them,
    They have been long away:
But when a wind from Heaven blows,
    They will come back some day;

And I shall hear them singing
    And watch the stone sails fill,
Till the white city like a ship
    Moves out across the hill.

PYTHON

A lithe beautiful fear
    Thrusts through the parted canes.
I should have known it near.
    By the blind blood in my veins.

Here is one way of death,
    Though with no threat for me.
Now I have caught my breath,
    Now that my brain can see,

Amber pours over the ground,
    Darkness of amber too;
Blue of the gulf profound,
    Superb and bitter blue

Sharp on the lacquered black.
    Gold-corniced groping head,
Bold-swerving diamond back,
    Why wish such beauty dead?

Why thwart such will to live?
    Better to think twice.
It is I who am fugitive
    From Paradise.

MOUNTAINS

Mountains are good to look upon,
  But do not look too long.
They are made of granite. They will break your heart,
  They will break your song.

The thing to look upon is water
  Where the currents change.
It is like you; it has a mournful beauty
  Wandering and strange.

From the west it rolls a darkness under,
  And thick stars from the south.
If you hunger, there are stars drowned in deep water
  Enough for your mouth.

Hilda Conkling

A LITTLE GIRL'S SONGS

Rosy plum-tree, think of me
When Spring comes down the world.

TIRED

Sparkle up, little tired flower
Leaning in the grass!
Did you find the rain of night
Too heavy to hold?

WATER

The world turns softly
Not to spill its lakes and rivers.
The water is held in its arms,
And the sky is held in the water.
What is water,
That pours silver
And can hold the sky?

THUNDER SHOWER

The dark cloud raged:
Gone was the morning light.
The big drops darted down,
The storm stood tall on the rose-trees;
And the bees that were getting honey
Out of wet roses,
The hiding bees would not come out of the flowers
Into the rain.

MORNING

There is a brook I must hear
Before I go to sleep.
There is a birch-tree I must visit
Every night of clearness.
I have to do some dreaming,
I have to listen a great deal,
Before light comes back
By a silver arrow of cloud,
And I rub my eyes and say,
    It must be morning on this hill!

POPLARS

The poplars bow forward and back;
They are like a fan waving very softly.
They tremble,
For they love the wind in their feathery branches.
They love to look down at the shallows,
    At the mermaids
    On the sandy shore.
They love to look into morning's face
    Cool in the water.

SNOW-FLAKE SONG

Snow-flakes come in fleets
Like ships over the sea.
The moon shines down on the crusty snow;

The stars make the sky sparkle like gold-fish in a glassy bowl.
Bluebirds are gone now,
But they left their song behind them.
The moon seems to say,
  It is time for summer when the birds come back
  To pick up their lonesome songs.

POEMS

See the fur coats go by!
The morning is like the inside of a snow-apple.
I will curl myself cushion-shape
On the window-seat;
I will read poems by snow-light.
If I cannot understand them so,
I will turn them upside down
And read them by the red candles
Of garden brambles.

MY MIND AND I

We are friends,
My mind and I . . .
Yet sometimes we cannot understand each other,
As though a cloud had gone over the sun,
Or the pool all blind with trees
Had forgotten the sky.

LILACS

After lilacs come out,
The air loves to flow about them
The way water in wood-streams
Flows and loves and wanders.
I think the wind has a sadness
Lifting other leaves, other sprays . . .
I think the wind is a little selfish
About lilacs when they flower.

BUTTERFLY

As I walked through my garden
I saw a butterfly light on a flower.
His wings were pink and purple.
He spoke a small word; it was *Follow!*
"I cannot follow"
I told him,
"I have to go the opposite way."

I AM

I am willowy boughs
For coolness;
I am goldfinch wings
For darkness;
I am a little grape
Thinking of September,
I am a very small violet
Thinking of May.

Harold Lewis Cook

STARLIGHT

Starlight through the curve of space
Falls an age and does not tire,
Falls and knows not where it falls,
A curve of undiminished fire.

No interstellar cold may stay
These atoms in their arc of flight—
Their radiant geometry,
The mathematics of the night.

They see far off the burning suns,
The furious wash of tides that shake
The whirling nebulæ, that twist
A moon's orbit till it break.

And, while it plunges, there is born
The eye wherein, as in a well
This light will dive and cleave its way
To the dark brain where it must dwell

And beat against its ivory walls—
A fragment of a universe,
A shining prisoner whose name
The jailer cannot even rehearse.

This is a stranger house than ever
A thousand million years away
Opened to release the light
That ends incarcerate in clay.

Here in matrix bedded lie
Quintessential suns; the bold
Enormous mountains; snows and seas
Housed in a skull a hand may hold.

As fruit sleeps in the seed they sleep
Till memory, like a wind of spring,
Breathe but a moment, then they burst
Their husk of bone and rise and sing.

And bloom, each in the needful place,
Till, the wind over, they are led
Back to the granaries whence they came,
Hid in the storehouse of the head.

There in their sleep they dream and build
For man such towers as look upon
The wheel of heaven turning from
Oblivion to oblivion.

MAN

Man, twisted so with loves and hates,
In crooked mirrors contemplates
The autumnal ecstasies of leaves,
The beatings of a wing, the seas.

With mind he thinks his own he preaches,
Times oceans to his pulse, and teaches
Thunders to shudder in a string.

In the wide world everything
He knots into his flesh with words,
And cannot loose again. In cords
Of rhyme he thinks to capture motion,
And in a syllable's commotion
Entangle Death.

           He never dreams
That the full land, the hills, the streams
Possess him, not he them: for they
Encompass him and take their way
Along his bones, and cruelly start
Fires in the valleys of his heart,
Weight in his brain, ready to spring
To a moment of remembering.

And when he writes how dawn is sweet,
Or water cool under his feet,
Not he, but they, do write it down.

Oh, man is but the world's clown,
And any blade of dewy grass,
Trees shimmering in the sun like glass,
Can bring him to a dance, or tears.
A dark cloud can, around his ears,
Bring philosophic roofs to dust.
And dust itself so conquers man
That he lies last where he began.

COWARD

The fable of white sea
And thundering air
Is a pictured terror
He would not dare.

The fable of white peaks
Tearing the sky
Is a nightmare of dark dream
He dare not try.

The words of two in love,
Or two in hate,
Forge too strong a poem
To meditate.

All these stories seem
Too fierce by far
To one who hardly dares
Look on a star.

Repelled and frightened, he,
By the ache of the moon—
What will he do when he sees
Death walk at noon?

FUGUE

Were you and I to play this fugue again,
Piano and violin, and the rain outside,
The gulf between us would be spanned, and then
I could walk over to you and confide
That other melody my heart was playing
While you and I were fluently playing this.
I should not know very well what I was saying,
But there would be some words you could not miss.
And if I said, "I love you," you would know—
Because you are so beautiful and rare—
Why I must open my heart to you and show
To you the unwritten music hidden there.
Then, reading my heart, "A lovely phrase," you'd say,
And with your strong hands lift your bow and play.

Alice Corbin

O WORLD

O world that changes under my hand,
　　O brown world, bitter and bright,
And full of hidden recesses
　　Of love and light—

O world, what use would there be to me
　　Of power beyond power
To change, or establish new balance,
　　To build, or deflower?

O world, what use would there be?
　　Had I the Creator's fire,
I could not build you nearer
　　To my heart's desire!

TWO VOICES

There is a country full of wine
And liquor of the sun,
Where sap is running all the year,
And spring is never done,
Where all is good as it is fair,
And love and will are one.
Old age may never come there,
But ever in today
The people talk as in a dream
And laugh slow time away.

But would you stay as now you are,
Or as a year ago?
Oh, not as then, for then how small
The wisdom we did owe!
Or if forever as today,
How little we could know!

Then welcome age, and fear not sorrow;
Today's no better than tomorrow.
Or yesterday that flies.
By the low light in your eyes,
By the love that in me lies,
I know we grow more lovely
Growing wise.

LOVE ME AT LAST

Love me at last, or if you will not,
    Leave me;
Hard words could never, as these half-words,
    Grieve me:
Love me at last—or leave me.

Love me at last, or let the last word uttered
    Be but your own;
Love me, or leave me—as a cloud, a vapor,
    Or a bird flown.
Love me at last—I am but sliding water
    Over a stone.

HUMORESQUE

To some the fat gods
Give money,
To some love;

But the gods have given me
Money a n d love:

Not t o o m u c h money,
Nor q u i t e e n o u g h love!

To some the fat gods
Give money,
To some love.

ONE CITY ONLY

One city only, of all I have lived in,
And one house of that city, belong to me. . . .
I remember the mellow light of afternoon
Slanting across brick buildings on the waterfront,
And small boats at rest on the floating tide,
And larger boats at rest in the near-by harbor;
And I know the tidal smell, and the smell of mud,
Uncovering oyster flats, and the brown bare toes of small negroes
With the mud oozing between them;
And the little figures leaping from log to log,
And the white children playing among them—
I remember how I played among them.
And I remember the recessed windows of the gloomy halls
In the darkness of decaying grandeur,
The feel of cool linen in the cavernous bed,
And the window curtain swaying gently
In the night air;
All the half-hushed noises of the street
In the southern town,
And the thrill of life—
Like a hand in the dark
With its felt, indeterminate meaning:
I remember that I knew there the stirring of passion,
Fear, and the knowledge of sin,
Tragedy, laughter, death. . . .

And I remember, too, on a dead Sunday afternoon
In the twilight,
When there was no one else in the house,
My self suddenly separated itself
And left me alone,
So that the world lay about me, lifeless.
I could not touch it, or feel it, or see it;
Yet I was there.
The sensation lingers:
Only the most vital threads
Hold me at all to living . . .

Yet I only live truly when I think of that house;
Only enter then into being.

One city only of all I have lived in,
And one house of that city, belong to me.

APPARITIONS

I

A thin gray shadow on the edge of thought
Hiding its wounds:
These are the wounds of sorrow—
It was my hand that made them;
And this gray shadow that resembles you
Is my own heart, weeping . . .
You sleep quietly beneath the shade
Of willows in the South.

II

When the cold dawn stood above the house-tops,
Too late I remembered the cry
In the night of a wild bird flying
Through the rain-filled sky.

THE POOL

Do you remember the dark pool at Nîmes,
The pool that had no bottom?
Shadowed by Druids ere the Romans came—
Dark, still, with little bubbles rising
So quietly level with its rim of stone
That one stood shuddering with the breathless fear
Of one short step?

My little sister stood beside the pool
As dark as that of Nîmes.
I saw her white face as she took the plunge;
I could not follow her, although I tried.
The silver bubbles circled to the brink.
And then the water parted:

With dream-white face my little sister rose
Dripping from that dark pool, and took the hands
Outstretched to meet her.
I may not speak to her of all she's seen;
She may not speak to me of all she knows,
Because her words mean nothing:
She chooses them
As one to whom our language is quite strange,
As children make queer words with lettered blocks
Before they know the way. . . .

My little sister stood beside the pool—
I could not plunge in with her, though I tried.

MUSIC

The ancient songs
Pass deathward mournfully.
R. A.

The old songs
Die.
Yes, the old songs die.
Cold lips that sang them,
Cold lips that sang them—
The old songs die,
And the lips that sang them
Are only a pinch of dust.

I saw in Pamplona
In a musty museum—
I saw in Pamplona
In a buff-colored museum—
I saw in Pamplona
A memorial
Of the dead violinist;
I saw in Pamplona
A memorial
Of Pablo Sarasate.

Dust was inch-deep on the cases,
Dust on the stick-pins and satins,

Dust on the badges and orders,
On the wreath from the oak of Guernica!

The old songs
Die—
And the lips that sang them.
Wreaths, withered and dusty,
Cuff-buttons with royal insignia,
These, in a musty museum,
Are all that is left of Sarasate.

WHAT DIM ARCADIAN PASTURES

What dim Arcadian pastures
   Have I known
That suddenly, out of nothing,
   A wind is blown,
Lifting a veil and a darkness,
   Showing a purple sea—
And under your hair the faun's eyes
   Look out on me?

NODES

The endless foolish merriment of stars
   Beside the pale cold sorrow of the moon,
Is like the wayward noises of the world
   Beside my heart's uplifted silent tune.

The little broken glitter of the waves
   Beside the golden sun's intense white blaze,
Is like the idle chatter of the crowd
   Beside my heart's unwearied song of praise.

The sun and all the planets in the sky
   Beside the sacred wonder of dim space,
Are notes upon a broken tarnished lute
   That God will some day mend and put in place.

And space, beside the little secret joy
   Of God that sings forever in the clay,

Is smaller than the dust we can not see,
   That yet dies not, till time and space decay.

And as the foolish merriment of stars
   Beside the cold pale sorrow of the moon,
My little song, my little joy, my praise,
   Beside God's ancient everlasting rune.

IN THE DESERT

I have seen you, O king of the dead,
More beautiful than sunlight.

Your kiss is like quicksilver;
But I turned my face aside
Lest you should touch my lips.

In the field with the flowers
You stood darkly.

My knees trembled, and I knew
That no other joy would be like this.

But the warm field, and the sunlight,
And the few years of my girlhood,
Came before me, and I cried,
Not yet!
Not yet, O dark lover!

You were patient.
             ·—I know you will come again.

I have seen you, O king of the dead,
More beautiful than sunlight.

SAND PAINTINGS

The dawn breeze
Loosens the leaves
Of the trees;
The wide sky quivers
With awakened birds.

Two blue runners
Come from the east;
One has a scarf of silver,
One flings pine-boughs
Across the sky.

Noon-day stretched
In gigantic slumber—
Red copper cliffs
Rigid in sunlight.

An old man stoops
For a forgotten fagot—
Forehead of bronze
Between white locks
Bound with a rag of scarlet.

Where one door stands open,
The female moon
Beckons to darkness
And disappears.

ON THE ACEQUIA MADRE

Death has come to visit us today.
He is such a distinguished visitor
Everyone is overcome by his presence—
"Will you not sit down—take a chair?"

But Death stands in the doorway, waiting to depart;
He lingers like a breath in the curtains.
The whole neighborhood comes to do him honor—
Women in black shawls and men in black sombreros
Sitting motionless against white-washed walls;
And the old man with the grey stubby beard,
To whom death came,
Is stunned into silence.
Death is such a distinguished visitor,
Making even old flesh important.

But who now, I wonder, will take the old horse to pasture?

JUAN QUINTANA

The goat-herd follows his flock
　　Over the sandy plain,
And the goats nibble the rabbit-bush
　　Acrid with desert rain.

Old Juan Quintana's coat
　　Is a faded purple blue,
And his hat is a warm plum-brown,
　　And his trousers a tawny hue.

He is sunburnt like the hills,
　　And his eyes have a strange goat-look;
And when I came on him alone,
　　He suddenly quivered and shook.

Out in the hills all day
　　The trees do funny things—
And a horse shaped like a man
　　Rose up from the ground on wings.

And a burro came and stood
　　With a cross, and preached to the flock,
While old Quintana sat
　　As cold as ice on a rock.

And sometimes the mountains move,
　　And the mesa turns about;
And Juan Quintana thinks he's lost,
　　Till a neighbor hears him shout.

And they say with a little laugh
　　That he isn't quite right, up here;
And they'll have to get a *muchacho*
　　To help with the flock next year.

UNA ANCIANA MEXICANA

I've seen her pass with eyes upon the road—
An old bent woman in a bronze black shawl,
With skin as dried and wrinkled as a mummy's,

As brown as a cigar-box, and her voice
Like the low vibrant strings of a guitar.
And I have fancied from the girls about
What she was at their age, what they will be
When they are old as she. But now she sits
And smokes away each night till dawn comes round,
Thinking, beside the piñons' flame, of days
Long past and gone, when she was young—content
To be no longer young, her epic done:

For a woman has work and much to do,
And it's good at the last to know it's through,
And still have time to sit alone,
To have some time you can call your own.
It's good at the last to know your mind
And travel the paths that you traveled blind,
To see each turn and even make
Trips in the byways you did not take—
But that, *por Dios*, is over and done,
It's pleasanter now in the way we've come.
It's good to smoke, and none to say
What's to be done on the coming day,
No mouths to feed or coat to mend,
And none to call till the last long end.
Though one have sons and friends of one's own,
It's better at last to live alone.
For a man must think of soil to break,
And a woman's heart may fret and ache;
But when she is young she must curb her pride,
And her heart is tamed for the child at her side.
But when she is old her thoughts may go
Wherever they will, and none to know.
And night is the time to think and dream,
And not to get up with the dawn's first gleam;
Night is the time to laugh or weep,
And when dawn comes it is time to sleep . . .

When it's all over and there's none to care,
I mean to be like her and take my share

Of comfort when the long day's done,
And smoke away the nights, and see the sun
Far off, a shriveled orange in a sky gone black,
Through eyes that open inward and look back.

A SONG FROM OLD SPAIN

What song of mine will live?
On whose lips will the words be sung
Long years after I am forgotten—
A name blown between the hills
Where some goat-herd
Remembers my love and passion?

He will sing of your beauty and my love;
Though it may be in another tongue,
To a strange tune,
In a country beyond the seas—
A seed blown by the wind—
He will sing of our love and passion.

Howard McKinley Corning

THE MOUNTAIN IN THE SKY

Was it the wind they followed?
     Their feet were battered by stones.

Or a far voice that halloaed?
     The desert hardened their bones.

          The creak of leather, the grind
          Of ox-cart wheels, the despair
          Of trails that led them to find
          What wasn't there.

          Sage . . . and a splash of red
          Where the day sank into the sand;
          And the living camped with the dead,
          West, toward their promised land.

Days . . . and the trails endured;
Nights . . . and these sturdy hearts
Slept with their wills inured
Under their weary carts.

Days . . . and low in the west
Glimmered a drift of snow
Shot with fire at the crest,
And lit with their own dream's glow!

They marched . . . and westward the drift,
A handspan out of the sage,
Assumed and commenced to lift
Over their pilgrimage.

Westward . . . what once was a mote
White in the eye became
A passionate song in the throat—
While the proud heart breaks aflame.

For always the dream burns first,
Whether poet or pioneer;
And the mountain that rose out of thirst
Has completed a hemisphere.

RAINBOW LANDS

Winter has no cold teeth to crumble these:
The painted desert and the rainbow tower.
These are the changeless principalities,
The walls of wonder and the dreamer's dower.
I have rejected cities to go free
A season where the trails lift toward the sky,
Bedding my campfires by old masonry.
The lean cold does not find me where I lie.

And though by times I think how beds are white
In rooms I frequented, and how sweet food
Assailed the tongue, and comfort in the night,
I find, for being more the man, the good
Clean earth propitiates; the rich blood sings.
See how the morning rides on painted wings!

GREEN COUNCILLORS

Here in this windy place
Where mountains heave their floors,
Leaving low trails, I face
Green councillors.

And though from hearing tissues
Of heaven weave and spin
Among dark boughs, the issues
Of knowledge begin,

It is not sky that nurtures
The branches of my heart,
Nor the wind's bird whose measures
My own impart,

But earth, whose nervous message,
Soaring in solitude,
Finds in these green ones passage
To sting my blood.

SONG TO SAY A FAREWELL

Some evening, when the forest is a mist
Of green that is not green but moonlight sifting,
And the gaunt wolf howls far off, and the light lifting
Of branches troubles the hemlock, I shall twist
An alder sapling from the foaming river,
Measure the moon's arc on Nehalem's shoulder,
And through the light-lit waters, from boulder to boulder,
I'll follow the world's roll on its long endeavor.

I'll race, the wind's voice reedy in my ears,
The owl and chipmunk at the night's cool doors
Talking to silence—through the iron starkness
Of trees that split the stars—climb, till the floors
Of space are lifted and the sea appears;
And there leap out into the taking darkness.

Malcolm Cowley

TOWERS OF SONG

To A. T.

Out of an empty sky, the dust of hours:
a word was spoken and a folk obeyed;
an island uttered incandescent towers,
like frozen simultaneous hymns to Trade.

Here, in a lonely multitude of powers,
thrones, dominations, celestial cavalcade,
they rise
        —proclaiming sea and sky are ours,
and yours, O man, the shadow of our shade.

Or did a poet crazed with dignity
rear them upon an island to prolong
his furious contempt for sky and sea?

To what emaciated hands belong
these index fingers of infinity?

O towers of intolerable song!

THE LADY FROM HARLEM
In Memory of Florence Mills

The fetish-woman crossed the stage,
her limbs convulsed with yellow magic.
Art is the gratuitous
shiver that makes the shimmy tragic.
Obeah, obeah, wailed the saxophones.

Though orchestras play Dixie Dreams,
never in Dixie field was picked
the gun-cotton that swells your breast,
explodes, and leaves me derelict
amid the wreckage of your smile,

floating over the parterre.
Your sudden fingers touched my wrist.
Tell me, did Madam Walker do your hair
before she died in Tarrytown
among her butlers, footmen, chefs?

Throned on a tomb of brass you reign
between the bass and treble clefs.

THE FLOWER IN THE SEA

To H. H. C.

Jesus I saw, crossing Times Square
with John the Baptist, and they bade me stop;
their hands touched mine:

visions from the belly of a bottle.

The sea, white, white,
the flower in the sea,
the white fire glowing in the flower,
and sea and fire and flower one,
the world is one, falsehood and truth
one, morning and midnight, flesh and vision
one.

I fled along the avenues of night
interminably, and One pursued,

my bruised arms in His arms nursed,
my breast against His wounded breast,
my head limp against His shoulder.

THE URN

Wanderers outside the gates, in hollow
landscapes without memory, we carry
each of us an urn of native soil,
of not impalpable dust a double handful

carelessly gathered (was it garden mold,
or wood-soil fresh with hemlock needles, pine

and princess pine, this little earth we bore
in secret, vainly, over the frontier?)

A parcel of the soil not wide enough
or firm enough to build a dwelling on,
or deep enough to dig a grave, but cool
and sweet enough to sink the nostrils in
and find the smell of home, or in the ears
rumors of home like oceans in a shell.

Hart Crane

TO BROOKLYN BRIDGE

How many dawns, chill from his rippling rest
The seagull's wings shall dip and pivot him,
Shedding white rings of tumult, building high
Over the chained bay waters Liberty—

Then, with inviolate curve, forsake our eyes
As apparitional as sails that cross
Some page of figures to be filed away;
—Till elevators drop us from our day. . . .

I think of cinemas, panoramic sleights
With multitudes bent toward some flashing scene
Never disclosed, but hastened to again,
Foretold to other eyes on the same screen;

And Thee, across the harbor, silver-paced
As though the sun took step of thee, yet left
Some motion ever unspent in thy stride—
Implicitly thy freedom staying thee!

Out of some subway scuttle, cell or loft
A bedlamite speeds to thy parapets,
Tilting there momently, shrill shirt ballooning,
A jest falls from the speechless caravan.

Down Wall, from girder into street noon leaks,
A rip-tooth of the sky's acetylene.

All afternoon the cloud-flown derricks turn.
Thy cables breathe the North Atlantic still.

And obscure as that heaven of the Jews,
Thy guerdon . . . accolade thou dost bestow
Of anonymity time cannot raise:
Vibrant reprieve and pardon thou dost show.

O harp and altar, of the fury fused,
(How could mere toil align thy choiring strings!)
Terrific threshold of the prophet's pledge,
Prayer of pariah, and the lover's cry—

Again the traffic lights that skim thy swift
Unfractioned idiom, immaculate sigh of stars,
Beading thy path—condense eternity:
And we have seen night lifted in thine arms.

Under thy shadow by the piers I waited;
Only in darkness is thy shadow clear.
The City's fiery parcels all undone,
Already snow submerges an iron year. . . .

O sleepless as the river under thee,
Vaulting the sea, the prairies' dreaming sod,
Unto us lowliest sometime sweep, descend
And of the curveship lend a myth to God.

REPOSE OF RIVERS

The willows carried a slow sound,
A sarabande the wind mowed on the mead.
I could never remember
That seething steady leveling of the marshes
Till age had brought me to the sea.

Flags, weeds. And remembrance of steep alcoves
Where cypresses shared the noon's
Tyranny; they drew me into Hades almost.
And mammoth turtles climbing sulphur dreams
Yielded, while sun-silt rippled them
Asunder . . .

How much I would have bartered!—the black gorge
And all the singular nestings in the hills
Where beavers learn stitch and tooth.
The pond I entered once and quickly fled—
I remember now its singing willow rim.

And finally, in that memory all things nurse;
After the city that I finally passed
With scalding unguents spread and smoking darts
The monsoon cut across the delta
At gulf gates. . . . There, beyond the dykes

I heard wind flaking sapphire, like this summer,
And willows could not hold more steady sound.

VOYAGE

—And yet this great wink of eternity,
Of rimless floods, unfettered leewardings,
Samite sheeted and processioned where
Her undinal vast belly moonward bends,
Laughing the wrapt inflections of our love;

Take this Sea, whose diapason knells
On scrolls of silver snowy sentences,
The sceptred terror of whose sessions rends
As her demeanors motion well or ill,
All but the pieties of lovers' hands.

And onward, as bells of San Salvador
Salute the crocus lustres of the stars,
In these poinsettia meadows of her tides—
Adagios of islands, O my Prodigal,
Complete the dark confessions her veins spell.

Mark how her turning shoulders wind the hours,
And hasten while her penniless rich palms
Pass superscription of bent foam and wave—
Hasten, while they are true—sleep, death, desire,
Close round one instant in one floating flower.

Bind us in time, O Seasons clear, and awe.
O minstrel galleons of Carib fire,
Bequeath us to no earthly shore until
Is answered in the vortex of our grave
The seal's wide spindrift gaze toward paradise.

CUTTY SARK

> *"O the navies old and oaken,*
> *O the Temeraire no more!"*
> MELVILLE

I met a man in South Street, tall—
a nervous shark-tooth swung on his chain.
His eyes pressed through green glass
—green glasses or bar lights made them
so—
   shine—
      green—
         eyes—
stepped out—forgot to look at you
or left you several blocks away—

in the nickel-in-the-slot piano jogged
Stamboul Nights—weaving somebody's nickel—sang—
   O Stamboul Rose—dreams weave the rose!

       Murmurs of Leviathan he spoke,
         and rum was Plato in our heads . . .

"It's *S. S. Ala*—Antwerp—now remember kid
to put me out at three—she sails on time.
I'm not much good at time any more—keep
weak-eyed watches sometimes snooze—" his bony hands
got to beating time. . . . "A whaler once—
I ought to keep time and get over it—I'm a
Democrat—I know what time it is—no
I don't want to know what time it is—that
damned white Arctic killed my time. . . .

   O Stamboul Rose—drums weave—

"I ran a donkey engine down there on the Canal
in Panama—got tired of that—
then Yucatan selling kitchen-ware—beads—
have you seen Popocatepetl—birdless mouth
with ashes sifting down—?
                              And then the coast again. . . ."

>   *Rose of Stamboul O coral queen—*
>   *teased remnants of the skeletons of cities—*
>   *and galleries, galleries of watergutted lava*
>   *snarling stone—green—drums—drown—*

Sing!

"—That spiracle!" he shot a finger out the door. . . .
"Oh life's a geyser—beautiful—my lungs—
No I can't live on land—!"

I saw the frontiers gleaming of his mind;
or are there frontiers—running sands sometimes
running sands—somewhere—sands running. . . .
Or they may start some white machine that sings.
Then you may laugh and dance the axletree—
steel—silver—kick the traces—and know—

>   *ATLANTIS ROSE drums wreathe the rose,*
>   *the star floats burning in a lake of tears*
>   *and sleep another thousand—*

                                        interminably
long since somebody's nickel—stopped—playing—

A wind worried those wicker-neat lapels, the
swinging summer entrances to cooler hells. . . .
Outside a wharf-truck nearly ran him down
—he lunged up Bowery way while the dawn
was putting the Statue of Liberty out—that
torch of hers you know—

I started walking home across the Bridge. . . .
.   .   .   .

Blithe Yankee vanities, turreted sprites, winged
British repartees, skilful savage sea-girls

that bloomed in the spring—heave, weave
those white designs the trade winds drive. . . .

Sweet opium and tea, yo-ho!
Pennies for porpoises that bank the keel!
Fins whip the breeze around Japan!

Bright skysails ticketing the Line, wink round the Horn to
Frisco, Melbourne. . . .
                           Pennants, parabolas—
clipper dreams indelible and ranging,
baronial white on lucky blue
                           perennial-*Cutty*-trophied-*Sark!*

Thermopylæ, Black Prince, Flying Cloud through Sunda
—scarfed of foam, their bellies veered green esplanades
locked in wind-humors, ran their eastings down;

    at Java Head freshened the nip
    (sweet opium and tea)
    and turned and left us on the lee. . . .

Buntlines tusseling (91 days, 20 hours and anchored!)
                    Rainbow, Leander
(last trip a tragedy)—where can you be
Nimbus? and you rivals two—

            a long tack keeping—
                              Tæping?
                              Ariel?

Adelaide Crapsey

CINQUAINS

NOVEMBER NIGHT

Listen.
With faint dry sound,
Like steps of passing ghosts,
The leaves, frost-crisp'd, break from the trees
And fall.

TRIAD

These be
Three silent things:
The falling snow . . . the hour
Before the dawn . . . the mouth of one
Just dead.

SUSANNA AND THE ELDERS

"Why do
You thus devise
Evil against her?" "For that
She is beautiful, delicate;
Therefore."

THE GUARDED WOUND

If it
Were lighter touch
Than petal of flower resting
On grass, oh still too heavy it were,
Too heavy!

THE WARNING

Just now,
Out of the strange
Still dusk . . . as strange, as still . . .
A white moth flew. Why am I grown
So cold?

FATE DEFIED

As it
Were tissue of silver,
I'll wear, O fate, thy grey,
And go mistily radiant, clad
Like the moon.

THE PLEDGE

White doves of Cytherea, by your quest
Across the blue Heaven's bluest highest air,
And by your certain homing to Love's breast,
Still to be true and ever true—I swear.

EXPENSES

Little my lacking fortunes show
For this to eat and that to wear;
Yet laughing, Soul, and gaily go!
An obol pays the Stygian fare.

ADVENTURE

Sun and wind and beat of sea,
Great lands stretching endlessly . . .
Where be bonds to bind the free?
All the world was made for me!

DIRGE

Never the nightingale,
  O my dear,
Never again the lark
  Thou wilt hear;
Though dusk and the morning still
Tap at thy window-sill,
Though ever love call and call,
Thou wilt not hear at all,
  My dear, my dear.

SONG

I make my shroud, but no one knows—
So shimmering fine it is and fair,
With stitches set in even rows.
I make my shroud, but no one knows.

In door-way where the lilac blows,
Humming a little wandering air,
I make my shroud and no one knows,
So shimmering fine it is and fair.

THE LONELY DEATH

In the cold I will rise, I will bathe
In waters of ice; myself
Will shiver, and shrive myself,
Alone in the dawn, and anoint
Forehead and feet and hands;
I will shutter the windows from light,
I will place in their sockets the four
Tall candles and set them a-flame
In the grey of the dawn; and myself
Will lay myself straight in my bed,
And draw the sheet under my chin.

Gladys Cromwell

THE CROWNING GIFT

I have had courage to accuse;
And a fine wit that could upbraid;
And a nice cunning that could bruise;
And a shrewd wisdom, unafraid
Of what weak mortals fear to lose.

I have had virtue to despise
The sophistry of pious fools;
I have had firmness to chastise;
And intellect to make me rules,
To estimate and exorcise.

I have had knowledge to be true;
My faith could obstacles remove.
But now, by failure taught anew,
I would have courage now to love,
And lay aside the strength I knew.

FOLDED POWER

Sorrow can wait,
For there is magic in the calm estate
Of grief; lo, where the dust complies
Wisdom lies.

Sorrow can rest
Indifferent, with her head upon her breast;
Idle and hushed, guarded from fears;
Content with tears.

Sorrow can bide
With sealèd lids and hands unoccupied.
Sorrow can fold her latent might,
Dwelling with night.

But Sorrow will rise
From her dream of sombre and hushed eternities.
Lifting a child, she will softly move
With a mother's love.

She will softly rise.
Her embrace the dying will recognize,
Lifting them gently through strange delight
To a clearer light.

THE MOULD

No doubt this active will,
So bravely steeped in sun,
This will has vanquished Death
And foiled oblivion.

But this indifferent clay,
This fine experienced hand,
So quiet, and these thoughts
That all unfinished stand,

Feel death as though it were
A shadowy caress;
And win and wear a frail
Archaic wistfulness.

RENEWAL

Can this be love men yield me in return
For what I do? I hold a strange belief
That love is not a tribute, nor a leaf
Of laurel, nor a wage the soul can earn
By any kind of doing. The concern
Of love is need, and love is the spare sheaf
We glean from pain—the fruit of patient grief.
Can this be love men yield me? Nay. I spurn
Their recompense who could so long refrain
From giving. I myself will grant the gift
And prove what loving is. I'll finer sift
My sorrow, make new songs distilled from pain;
Above this hour of bitterness I'll lift
My spirit up and taste my grief again!

Countee Cullen

YET DO I MARVEL

I doubt not God is good, well-meaning, kind,
    And did He stoop to quibble could tell why
The little buried mole continues blind,
    Why flesh that mirrors Him must some day die;
Make plain the reason tortured Tantalus
    Is baited by the ficklefruit, declare
If merely brute caprice dooms Sisyphus
    To struggle up a never-ending stair.
Inscrutable His ways are, and immune
To catechism by a mind too strewn
    With petty cares to slightly understand
    What awful brain compels His awful hand.
Yet do I marvel at this curious thing:
To make a poet black and bid him sing.

A SONG OF PRAISE

For one who praised his lady's being fair

You have not heard my love's dark throat,
  Slow-fluting like a reed,
Release the perfect golden note
  She caged there for my need.

Her walk is like the replica
  Of some barbaric dance
Wherein the soul of Africa
  Is winged with arrogance.

And yet so light she steps across
  The ways her sure feet pass,
She does not dent the smoothest moss
  Or bend the thinnest grass.

My love is dark as yours is fair,
  Yet lovelier I hold her
Than listless maids with pallid hair,
  And blood that's thin and colder.

You-proud-and-to-be-pitied one,
  Gaze on her and despair;
Then seal your lips until the sun
  Discovers one as fair.

THE WIND BLOWETH WHERE IT LISTETH

"Live like the wind," he said, "unfettered,
  And love me while you can;
And when you will, and can be bettered,
  Go to the better man.

For you'll grow weary, maybe, sleeping
  So long a time with me:
Like this there'll be no cause for weeping—
  The wind is always free."

"Go when you please," he would be saying,
   His mouth hard on her own:
That's why she stayed and loved the staying,
   Contented to the bone.

And now he's dust, and him but twenty,
   Frost that was like a flame.
Her kisses on the head death bent, he
   Gave answer to his name.

And now he's dust and with dust lying
   In sullen arrogance:
Death found it hard, for all his trying,
   To shatter such a lance.

She laid him out as fine as any
   That had a priest and ring;
She never spared a silver penny
   For cost of anything.

E. E. Cummings

SONNET

O Thou to whom the musical white spring

offers her lily inextinguishable,
taught by thy tremulous grace bravely to fling

Implacable death's mysteriously sable
robe from her redolent shoulders,
                   Thou from whose
feet reincarnate song suddenly leaping
flameflung, mounts, inimitably to lose
herself where the wet stars softly are keeping

their exquisite dreams—O Love! upon thy dim
shrine of intangible commemoration,
(from whose faint close as some grave languorous hymn
pledged to illimitable dissipation
unhurried clouds of incense fleetly roll)

i spill my bright incalculable soul.

ORIENTALE

I

i spoke to thee
with a smile and thou didst not
answer
thy mouth is as
a chord of crimson music
                              Come hither—
O thou, is life not a smile?

i spoke to thee with
a song and thou
didst not listen
thine eyes are as a vase
of divine silence
                              Come hither—
O thou, is life not a song?

i spoke
to thee with a soul, and thou didst not wonder
thy face is as a dream locked
in white fragrance.
                              Come hither—

O thou, is life not love?

i speak to
thee with a sword
and thou art silent
thy breast is as a tomb
softer than flowers
                              Come hither—
O thou, is love not death?

III

my love
thy hair is one kingdom
    the king whereof is darkness
thy forehead is a flight of flowers

thy head is a quick forest
  filled with sleeping birds
thy breasts are swarms of white bees
  upon the bough of thy body
thy body to me is April
in whose armpits is the approach of spring

thy thighs are white horses yoked to a chariot of kings
they are the striking of a good minstrel
between them is always a pleasant song

my love
thy head is a casket
  of the cool jewel of thy mind
the hair of thy head is one warrior
  innocent of defeat
thy hair upon thy shoulders is an army
  with victory and with trumpets
thy legs are the trees of dreaming
whose fruit is the very eatage of forgetfulness

thy lips are satraps in scarlet
  in whose kiss is the combining of kings
thy wrists
are holy
  which are the keepers of the keys of thy blood
thy feet upon thy ankles are flowers in vases
  of silver

in thy beauty is the dilemma of flutes

  thy eyes are the betrayal
of bells comprehended through incense

CHANSON INNOCENTE

in just—
Spring   when the world is mud-
luscious, the little
lame balloon-man

whistles   far   and wee.

And eddieandbill come
running from marbles and
piracies and it's
spring,

when the world is puddle-wonderful

the queer
old balloon-man whistles
far   and   wee.
And bettyandisbel come dancing
from hop-scotch and jump-rope, and

it's
spring,
and
        the
            goat-footed
balloon-man whistles
far
and
wee.

SONNET

and what were roses. Perfume? for i do
forget . . . or mere music mounting unsurely
twilight
          but here were some more maturely
childish, more beautiful almost than you.

Yet if not flower, tell me softly who

be these haunters of dreams always demurely
halfsmiling from cool faces, moving purely
with muted step, yet somewhat proudly too—

are they not ladies, ladies of my dreams
justly touching roses their fingers whitely
live by?
          or better,
                    queens, queens laughing lightly
crowned with far colors,
                    thinking very much
of nothing and whom dawn loves most to touch

wishing by willows, bending upon streams?

SONNET

Realities Series

when thou hast taken thy last applause, and when
the final curtain strikes the world away,
leaving to shadowy silence and dismay
that stage which shall not know thy smile again,
lingering a little while i see thee then
ponder the tinsel part they let thee play;
i see the large lips livid, the face grey,
and silent smileless eyes of Magdalen.
The lights have laughed their last; without, the street
darkling awaiteth her whose feet have trod
the silly souls of men to golden dust:
she pauses on the lintel of defeat,
her heart breaks in a smile—and she is Lust. . . .

mine also, little painted poem of god

H. D.

HERMES OF THE WAYS

I

The hard sand breaks,
And the grains of it
Are clear as wine.

Far off over the leagues of it,
The wind,
Playing on wide shore,
Piles little ridges,
And the great waves
Break over it.

But more than the many-foamed ways
Of the sea,
I know him
Of the triple path-ways,
Hermes,
Who awaits.

Dubious,
Facing three ways,
Welcoming wayfarers,
He whom the sea-orchard
Shelters from the west,
From the east
Weathers sea-wind;
Fronts the great dunes.

Wind rushes
Over the dunes,
And the coarse salt-crusted grass
Answers.

Heu,
It whips round my ankles!

II

Small is
This white stream,
Flowing below ground
From the poplar-shaded hill;
But the water is sweet.

Apples on the small trees
Are hard,
Too small,
Too late ripened
By a desperate sun
That struggles through sea-mist.
The boughs of the trees
Are twisted
By many bafflings;
Twisted are
The small-leafed boughs.

But the shadow of them
Is not the shadow of the mast-head
Nor of the torn sails.

Hermes, Hermes,
The great sea foamed,
Gnashed its teeth about me;
But you have waited,
Where sea-grass tangles with
Shore-grass.

ORCHARD

I saw the first pear
As it fell.
The honey-seeking, golden-banded,
The yellow swarm,
Was not more fleet than I,
(Spare us from loveliness!)
And I fell prostrate,
Crying,

"You have flayed us with your blossoms;
Spare us the beauty
Of fruit-trees!"

The honey-seeking
Paused not;
The air thundered their song,
And I alone was prostrate.

O rough-hewn
God of the orchard,
I bring you an offering;
Do you, alone unbeautiful
Son of the god,
Spare us from loveliness.

These fallen hazel-nuts,
Stripped late of their green sheaths;
Grapes, red-purple,
Their berries
Dripping with wine;
Pomegranates already broken,
And shrunken figs,
And quinces untouched,
I bring you as offering.

THE POOL

Are you alive?
I touch you—
You quiver like a sea-fish.
I cover you with my net.
What are you, banded one?

OREAD

Whirl up, sea—
Whirl your pointed pines.
Splash your great pines
On our rocks.
Hurl your green over us—
Cover us with your pools of fir.

THE GARDEN

I

You are clear,
O rose, cut in rock;
Hard as the descent of hail.

I could scrape the color
From the petals,
Like spilt dye from a rock.

If I could break you
I could break a tree.

If I could stir
I could break a tree—
I could break you.

II

O wind, rend open the heat,
Cut apart the heat,
Rend it to tatters.

Fruit cannot drop
Through this thick air;
Fruit cannot fall into heat
That presses up and blunts
The points of pears,
And rounds the grapes.

Cut the heat:
Plough through it,
Turning it on either side
Of your path.

MOONRISE

Will you glimmer on the sea?
Will you fling your spear-head
On the shore?
What note shall we pitch?

We have a song,
On the bank we share our arrows—
The loosed string tells our note:

O flight,
Bring her swiftly to our song.
She is great,
We measure her by the pine-trees.

THE SHRINE

"She watches over the sea"

I

Are your rocks shelter for ships?
Have you sent galleys from your beach?
Are you graded, a safe crescent,
Where the tide lifts them back to port?
Are you full and sweet,
Tempting the quiet
To depart in their trading ships?

Nay, you are great, fierce, evil—
You are the land-blight.
You have tempted men,
But they perished on your cliffs.
Your lights are but dank shoals—
Slate and pebble and wet shells
And sea-weed fastened to the rocks.

It was evil—evil
When they found you,
When the quiet men looked at you.
They sought a headland
Shaded with ledge of cliff
From the wind-blast.

But you—you are unsheltered,
Cut with the weight of wind.
You shudder when it strikes,
Then lift, swelled with the blast.

You sink as the tide sinks,
You shrill under hail, and sound
Thunder when thunder sounds.

You are useless:
When the tides swirl
Your boulders cut and wreck
The staggering ships.

II

You are useless,
O grave, O beautiful.
The landsmen tell it—I have heard—
You are useless.

And the wind sounds with this,
And the sea,
Where rollers shot with blue
Cut under deeper blue.

Oh, but stay tender, enchanted
Where wave-lengths cut you
Apart from all the rest;
For we have found you,
We watch the splendor of you,
We thread throat on throat of freesia
For your shelf.

You are not forgot,
O plunder of lilies,
Honey is not more sweet
Than the salt stretch of your beach.

III

Stay—stay—
But terror has caught us now.
We passed the men in ships,
We dared deeper than the fisher-folk;
And you strike us with terror,
O bright shaft.

Flame passes under us
And sparks that unknot the flesh—
Sorrow, splitting bone from bone;
Splendors thwart our eyes,
And rifts in the splendor—
Sparks and scattered light.

Many warned of this,
Men said:
"There are wrecks on the fore-beach,
Wind will beat your ship,
There is no shelter in that headland;
It is useless waste, that edge,
That front of rock—
Sea-gulls clang beyond the breakers,
None venture to that spot."

IV

But hail—
As the tide slackens,
As the wind beats out,
We hail this shore—
We sing to you,
Spirit between the headlands
And the further rocks.

Though oak-beams split,
Though boats and seamen flounder,
And the strait grind sand with sand
And cut boulders to sand and drift—

Your eyes have pardoned our faults,
Your hands have touched us;
You have leaned forward a little
And the waves can never thrust us back
From the splendor of your ragged coast.

HESPERIDES

FRAGMENT XXXVI

> *I know not what to do:*
> *My mind is divided.*
> SAPPHO

I know not what to do—
My mind is reft.
Is song's gift best?
Is love's gift loveliest?
I know not what to do,
Now sleep has pressed
Weight on your eyelids.

Shall I break your rest,
Devouring, eager?
Is love's gift best?
Nay, song's the loveliest.
Yet, were you lost,
What rapture could I take from song?—
What song were left?

I know not what to do:
To turn and slake
The rage that burns,
With my breath burn
And trouble your cool breath—
So shall I turn and take
Snow in my arms,
(Is love's gift best?)

Yet flake on flake
Of snow were comfortless,
Did you lie wondering,
Wakened yet unawake.

Shall I turn and take
Comfortless snow within my arms,
Press lips to lips that answer not,
Press lips to flesh
That shudders not nor breaks?

Is love's gift best?—
Shall I turn and slake
All the wild longing?
Oh, I am eager for you!
As the Pleiads shake
White light in whiter water,
So shall I take you?

My mind is quite divided;
My minds hesitate,
So perfect matched
I know not what to do.
Each strives with each:
As two white wrestlers,
Standing for a match,
Ready to turn and clutch,
Yet never shake
Muscle or nerve or tendon;
So my mind waits
To grapple with my mind—
Yet I am quiet,
I would seem at rest.

I know not what to do.
Strain upon strain,
Sound surging upon sound,
Makes my brain blind;
As a wave line may wait to fall,
Yet waiting for its falling
Still the wind may take,
From off its crest,
White flake on flake of foam,
That rises
Seeming to dart and pulse
And rend the light,
So my mind hesitates
Above the passion
Quivering yet to break,
So my mind hesitates above my mind
Listening to song's delight.

I know not what to do.
Will the sound break,
Rending the night
With rift on rift of rose
And scattered light?
Will the sound break at last
As the wave hesitant,
Or will the whole night pass
And I lie listening awake?

AT BAIA

I should have thought
In a dream you would have brought
Some lovely perilous thing:
Orchids piled in a great sheath,
As who would say, in a dream,
"I send you this,
Who left the blue veins
Of your throat unkissed."

Why was it that your hands,
That never took mine—
Your hands that I could see
Drift over the orchid heads
So carefully;
Your hands, so fragile, sure to lift
So gently, the fragile flower stuff—
Ah, ah, how was it

You never sent, in a dream
The very form, the very scent,
Not heavy, not sensuous,
But perilous—perilous!—
Of orchids, piled in a great sheath,
And folded underneath on a bright scroll,
Some word:

Flower sent to flower;
For white hands the lesser white,
Less lovely, of flower leaf.

Or,

Lover to lover—no kiss,
No touch, but forever and ever this!

H. L. Davis

PROUD RIDERS

We rode hard, and brought the cattle from brushy springs,
From heavy dying thickets, leaves wet as snow;
From high places, white-grassed, and dry in the wind;
Draws where the quaken-asps were yellow and white,
And the leaves spun and spun like money spinning.
We poured them out on the trail, and rode for town.

Men in the fields leaned forward in the wind,
Stood in the stubble and watched the cattle passing.
The wind bowed all, the stubble shook like a shirt.
We threw the reins by the yellow and black fields, and rode,
And came, riding together, into the town
Which is by the gray bridge, where the alders are—
The white-barked alder trees dropping big leaves,
Yellow and black, into the cold black water.
Children, little cold boys, watched after us—
The freezing wind flapped their clothes like windmill paddles.
Down the flat frosty road we crowded the herd:
High stepped the horses for us, proud riders in autumn.

RUNNING VINES

Look up, you loose-haired women in the field,
From work, and thoughtless picking at the ground.
Cease for a little: pay me a little heed.

It is early: the red leaves of the blackberry vines
Are hoar with frosty dew, the ground's still wet,

There is vapor over toward the summer fallow.
And you three make a garden, being put by—
Since you are too old for love you make a garden?

It is love with me, and not these dark red frosty leaves
The vines of which you root for garden-space.
You will be concerned, you three used up and set by:
I could speak of the red vines, of pastures, of young trees;
And you would dibble at love as you do the vine-roots.

It is early, but before your backs be warmed,
And before all this dew be cleared and shed,
I shall be half among your hearts with speech:
Love, and my sorrow, the disastrous passages,
So that you'll cease all gardening, dangle dark red
Vines in your hands not knowing it, and whisper.

They forget me for a little pride of old time.

IN THE FIELD

The young grass burnt up, so hot the air was:
And I was lying by her knee, near the cool low
Spring branch, in sight of the green shining meadow.
How red her mouth was, how fine her hair, and so cool;
Her hair was cool as the ground; I thought how red
Her mouth was, and wondered at her white wrists.
Another would have meddled, not have let me lie;
Another would have laughed when I put in items her beauty,
But she was still, like any scene or the sky.

Her red mouth, her wrists so white. "This is cool blood,
And it is deep, since it colors your mouth only.
I wonder and wonder at you—do you seem best
Playing with your hand in the dirt, like any dumb person?
For then you are like a black river-bird at rest;
Or like a poet sitting on the stairs among
The people like yours, and talking familiarly with them.
I wonder at you moreover because of your people,
Whose daughters should not seem sweet, yet you seem to me

Pleasanter to touch than are the light breast feathers
Of a bird: and your heart plays lowers, more like wind.
It is pleasure to lie by your knee here in the fields."

I say yet, the white alders and the willows' switching,
And the weaving of thin graceful weeds, pleased me more
Than to own pastures: because of her beauty. But say
Nothing like "Come away," because her people
Work with her now where about cold low springs the smoke
From waters at morning stains the cold air all day.

THE SPIRIT

In the early spring, the fattening young weeds
Appear, all green, their veins stretched, amongst their dead.
And every sand-hill, with its bundle of willow
And young green riding the sand, is my pleasant walk.
The river, every rock there, and the wind
Molding cold waves, have seen a spirit by day
Which I would see; and now that my heart's a poor hired one
Which owns no favor or love, but did awhile,
I walk my pleasant walks. Where the new dark red
Willows feather in sand against the sky,
I make out a spirit sitting by the new grass:
The sun shines yellow on the hair, and a wind blows
That would melt snow, but her face calls it on.
And her hands are quiet in her red sleeves all day.
"All my pleasure begins when you come to this place."
"I am sorry for it, spirit, yet I most wished it;
Has my heart commanding shamed me to your eyes?"
"Never in life shall these eyes see you shamed.
I half live, like a stalk, but no girl orders me."

MY STEP-GRANDFATHER

My step-grandfather sat during the noon spell
Against the wild crabapple tree, by the vines.
Flies about the high hot fern played, or fell
To his beard, or upon the big vein of his hand.

With their playing he seemed helpless and old, in a land
Where new stumps, piles of green brush, fresh-burnt pines,
Were young and stubborn. He mentioned the old times
As if he thought of this: "I have marched, and run
Over the old hills, old plowed land, with my gun
Bumping furrows—oh, years old. But in this new place
There is nothing I know. I ride a strange colt."

"You know old times, and have seen some big man's face:
Out of the old times, what do you remember most?"
"General Lee. Once they called us out in a cold
Plowed field, to parade for him. He was old with frost.
I remember our style of dress; my dead friends last long,
(I would have thought longer); and there were peaked women
Who watched us march, and joked with us as they were trimming
The green shoots of wild roses to eat. But these with me
Lack what the other has—they are not so strong.
And lost battles?—I would be prouder starving in rain
And beaten and running every day, with General Lee,
Than fat and warm, winning under another man."

Alone presently, I laid myself face down
To avoid seeing the field; and thought of how the book
Describes Esther; and imagined how that queen might look,
Preferred for beauty, in her old fields red and brown.
"I am like my step-grandfather," I thought, "and could
Follow whatever I love, blind and bold;
Or go hungry and in great shame, and, for a cause, be proud."
And I came to work, sad to see him so old.

THE OLD ARE SLEEPY

A slow spring between two wheat-fields. High on the hill
In the straight weeds the men walk sizing the wheat,
Sweating through dry soft ground where wild sunflowers are.
The wind blows dust in the faces of these old men,
And dust is all over their faces as they ride down,
As they ride toward the poplars about the distant house.

Do I not know? They will watch the green willows between
These very fields; rest a day or two, mend roads
Against the harvesting of this high grain; and sleep,
The old men have seen it and are content with it,
Content among the women, and all content—
Women who lie uneasy at night against them.

I know of this, and of the mouth of music which said,
"A small spring between the wheat-fields." I know the low hair
And the beauty in which music is, as slow rain
Is in the willows when they dip over like hands.
I know her of whom you are proud, that before their sleep
They also behold her proudly—a distant spring's beauty.

Is this the distant spring's beauty? For in the rain
It shall be changed, and the willows about it be darkened.
The old men have put the hills in foal; yet past
Sundown, and until the morning the headed wheat
Finds me, and I feel her mouth and low hair.
Cry for their pride in her, when you lie by them at night!

THE VALLEY HARVEST

Honey in the horn! I brought my horse from the water
And from the white grove of tall alders over the spring,
And brought him past a row of high hollyhocks
Which flew and tore their flowers thin as his mane.
And women there watched, with hair blown over their mouths;
Yet in watching the oat field they were quiet as the spring.

"Are the hollyhocks full bloomed? It is harvest then.
The hay falls like sand falling in a high wind
When the weeds blow and fly—but steady the sand falls.
It is harvest, harvest, and honey in the horn.
I would like to go out, in a few days, through the stubble field,
And to all the springs—yours too we have known for years—
And to the bearing vines, and clean the berries from them."

Call, women!—why do you stand if not for your pride's sake?

But the women would neither call to me nor speak,
Nor to any man not mowing during their harvest.
They watched with their hair blowing, near the stalks,
In the row of red hollyhocks.
                              Quiet as the spring.
What is by the spring? A bird, and a few old leaves.

BY THE RIVER

I see a white river-bird, and I see the women
Among the weeds, the light of their dresses between
Quick willow leaves; and I see that there the wind
Comes like a bird from the river, and blows their dresses.
Today their pleasure's among willows and high cold weeds
Where the flood bred pale snapdragons in the shade.

I lie in the high grass by the spring at their door
And hear them across the white stubble of their own field's
Edge: along the willows in the sand where the reaper
Has never been driven, they go. It was the flood margin.
At the flood margin which they feared their pleasure is;
Their white dresses fly where the water felt at the young grain.

It seems they are silent, looking at the white bird.
"Does it follow us here?" And one, looking to the sky: "No,
There is nothing now till spring to be anxious for;
They are through reaping, the grain is gone, and two seasons
Are to come before spring comes: so enjoy the day."
They come pleasantly through high weeds, old foam in the
    branches.

Walter de la Mare

THE LISTENERS

"Is there anybody there?" said the Traveller,
    Knocking on the moonlit door;
And his horse in the silence champed the grasses
    Of the forest's ferny floor;

And a bird flew up out of the turret,
  Above the Traveller's head;
And he smote upon the door again a second time;
  "Is there anybody there?" he said.
But no one descended to the Traveller;
  No head from the leaf-fringed sill
Leaned over and looked into his grey eyes,
  Where he stood perplexed and still.
But only a host of phantom listeners
  That dwelt in the lone house then
Stood listening in the quiet of the moonlight
  To that voice from the world of men:
Stood thronging the faint moonbeams on the dark stair,
  That goes down to the empty hall,
Hearkening in an air stirred and shaken
  By the lonely Traveller's call.
And he felt in his heart their strangeness,
  Their stillness answering his cry,
While his horse moved, cropping the dark turf,
  'Neath the starred and leafy sky;
For he suddenly smote on the door, even
  Louder, and lifted his head:
"Tell them I came, and no one answered,
  That I kept my word," he said.
Never the least stir made the listeners,
  Though every word he spake
Fell echoing through the shadowiness of the still house
  From the one man left awake:
Ay, they heard his foot upon the stirrup,
  . And the sound of iron on stone,
And how the silence surged softly backward,
  When the plunging hoofs were gone.

AN EPITAPH

Here lies a most beautiful lady:
Light of step and heart was she;
I think she was the most beautiful lady
That ever was in the West Country.

But beauty vanishes; beauty passes;
However rare—rare it be;
And when I crumble, who will remember
This lady of the West Country?

WHEN THE ROSE IS FADED

When the rose is faded,
  Memory may still dwell on
Her beauty shadowed,
  And the sweet smell gone.

That vanishing loveliness,
  That burdening breath,
No bond of life hath then,
  Nor grief of death.

'Tis the immortal thought
  Whose passion still
Makes of the changing
  The unchangeable.

Oh, thus thy beauty,
  Loveliest on earth to me,
Dark with no sorrow, shines
  And burns, with thee.

THE LITTLE SALAMANDER

To Margot

When I go free,
I think 'twill be
A night of stars and snow,
And the wild fires of frost shall light
My footsteps as I go;
Nobody—nobody will be there
With groping touch, or sight,
To see me in my bush of hair
Dance burning through the night.

THE LINNET

Upon this leafy bush
  With thorns and roses in it,
Flutters a thing of light,
  A twittering linnet.
And all the throbbing world
  Of dew and sun and air
By this small parcel of life
  Is made more fair;
As if each bramble-spray
  And mounded gold-wreathed furze,
Harebell and little thyme,
  Were only hers;
As if this beauty and grace
  Did to one bird belong,
And at a flutter of wing
  Might vanish in song.

ALL THAT'S PAST

Very old are the woods;
  And the buds that break
Out of the brier's boughs,
  When March winds wake,
So old with their beauty are—
  Oh, no man knows
Through what wild centuries
  Roves back the rose.

Very old are the brooks;
  And the rills that rise
Where snow sleeps cold beneath
  The azure skies
Sing such a history
  Of come and gone
Their every drop is as wise
  As Solomon.

Very old are we men;
　　Our dreams are tales
Told in dim Eden
　　By Eve's nightingales.
We wake and whisper awhile,
　　But, the day gone by,
Silence and sleep like fields
　　Of amaranth lie.

George Dillon

WHAT ARTIFICE

What artifice against foul time
So difficult, I often cry,
As this I make of air and rhyme?
Oh, any other! I reply.
Yes, any house on any site
Sacred to eagles or to doves,
If a man builds it in delight
And terror, for the one he loves.

The thing his passionate hands devise
His mind reviews with cold despair:
Likely as not a storm will rise
And hurl it down, for all his care;
Likely as not when he has done
And pulled away the props and ropes,
His dear will wed another one.
He knows. But while he builds he hopes.

Warm youth with only time to fear
That brings you potions for your pain,
If you come here, and tarry here,
I shall as good as live again.
May you find here, desirous youth,
That wild and deathless fugitive
Whom I have followed—for in truth,
Living with her I long to live.

You waders through the weeds and flowers,
Come rest within my house of words—
And you who toil at loftier towers
Round which the planets play like birds,
And you who fell upon your knees
And heard the roofs of fortune fall.
A house of song will stand for these,
I daresay, if it stands at all.

If it should tumble, let it go.
Give back the ground to wordless things.
When wondering children want to know
What ruin is this beset by wings,
Tell them no matter: something made
In haste and ignorance—as it were
A house where Beauty never stayed.
But tell them it was made for her.

FALL OF STARS

The snow came down like stars tonight
Over the city silently.
The air, like a great glittering tree,
Bloomed noiselessly with light.

I thought, it is the snow I see
Like stars. And it was long ago
That ever I saw the stars like snow.

And I thought of a boy, a long time dead,
Who dreamed such beauty out of pain
That music moved within his brain,
And the stars stormed about his head.

His ghost is like the wind, I said,
That cries into the crystal gloom,
And wanders where the white clouds blow.

And I shall hear his song, I know,
Wherever the boughs of silence bloom
With snow like stars or stars like snow.

SERENADER

I have no thing that is mine sure
To give you, I am born so poor.

Whatever I have was given me:
The earth, the air, the sun, the sea.

If I have anything to give
Made surely of the life I live,
It is a song that I have made.

Now in your keeping it is laid.

EN ROUTE

Companioned by long loneliness
I go to meet my true mistress.

With loneliness too large to suffer
You go to meet your true lover.

Mistress or lover, Death must be
Vouchsafed our certain constancy.

Yet since we go one journey, and
Go toward a terribly dark land,
Let us go therefore hand in hand.

If out of loneliness we kiss,
Our honor is not hurt by this.

THE HOURS OF THE DAY

The city stirred about me softly and distant.
Its iron voice flew upward into the air.
All day I wondered that I walked and listened
As if in freedom there—

And wondered how love so led me and removed me:
My breath coming deep and glad, for she had drawn it,
My eyes being wild with pride because she loved me;
My heart being shielded with her beauty upon it.

TO LOSERS

Let loneliness be mute. Accuse
Only the wind for what you lose.
Only the wind has ever known
Where anything you lost has gone.
It is the wind whose breath shall come
To quench tall-flaming trees and numb
The narrow bones of birds. It is
The wind whose dissipating kiss
Disbands the soft-assembled rose.
It is the wordless wind that knows
Where every kind of beauty goes.

And if you lose love in the end
Say it was taken by the wind.

ADDRESS TO THE DOOMED
Sonnets I, III & X

Say it is life that matters. Say the bone
And flesh that blazoned it are but a book
Mislaid, forgotten, and the meaning known.
I will believe, but I have lived to look
On the cold body of the beautiful dead,
White and immobile as the moon in air—
The imperious heart being strangely quieted,
And the proud spirit flown I know not where.
Say it is earth again. Let it be hid
In ruined leaves. Account it as the dust
That quarrels not with doom and never did,
And reckon me among the quick who must.
Yet would I sleep tonight at the rose's root,
Seeing what Time has trampled underfoot.

I see how the forgetful earth replies,
Though plundered yearly, to the year's warm humor,
And leads new life, to stand with innocent eyes,
Unwarned, unweaned, upon the sill of summer.
I see her trust and her betrayal clearly—

The beaks of shivering birds put up to beg,
The hawthorn bloom upon the branch too early,
The snake unwinding from the stolen egg.
Yet since the heart's dismay were but a shadow
Weightless on earth as of a flying wing,
Or autumn leaf upon a flowering meadow
Caught in the quick machinery of spring—
Let the doomed brave be born and slapped to breath:
I take these tidings to my master Death.

Remember, though the telescope extend
Few manifestoes Time may not efface
When earth has wandered to her freezing end
And left no footprint on the paths of space,
How of all living creatures you alone
Surmise exclusion from the secret plan—
You, with the cipher cut into your own
Most unimaginable substance, Man.
Afraid! Afraid! Yet the bright skies you fear
Were black as doom, were but the want of skies,
Were nothing at all until you happened here,
Bearing the little lanterns of your eyes.
In the first gathering of the ultimate frost
Remember this, and let the world be lost.

Glenn Ward Dresbach

SONGS OF THE PLAINS

I

I saw a grown girl coming down
    The field with water for the men.
Her hair fell golden in the wind—
    She stopped and bound it up again.

Her thin dress by the wind was pressed
    (Was it in passion or in play?)
Against the full growth of her breast. . . .
    The men looked up. She looked away.

II

You saw me staring at the girl
    And then you stared at me.
Why did you come so close, and kiss
    My lips so passionately?
I would not have you quite so young
    Or quite so shy as she!

III

A gypsy passed me with a song
    Where men went out to sow,
And he went down the winding road
    Where the maples grow.

And still his song came back to me
    When he was far away:
"The Flask holds but a pint of wine—
    Tomorrow is Today!

"My love has made a tent for me
    From stars above the hill—
Go break your heart, and build yourself
    A stone house, if you will!"

IV

I would build myself a house
    On this mountain-top today,
Not to shun the world, or feel
    It was shutting me away,
But that I might come at times
    Little things had baffled me,
And look out, at set of sun,
    On immensity.

THE LITTLE SPRING FLOWS CLEAR AGAIN

The little spring flows clear again
    While I stand watching close to see
What clouded it. If wings were here
    To splash the silver merrily
They flew before I came too near.

And if a fawn had rubbed its nose,
   Thrust deep in silver running cool,
Upon the bottom of the spring,
   It heard me wading in the pool
Of shadow where the thrushes sing.

The little spring flows clear again,
   But now is clouded in my mind
The flight of wings that went away—
   And something that I came to find
Was loveliness afraid to stay.

EARLY MORNING IN A GLADE

A fawn sleeps in the glade.
   Its velvet sides will show
Patterns the daisies made,
   When it turns to go.

A bird awakes by the springs.
   Its song tosses seven
Late stars on dripping wings
   From these pools to heaven.

I shall time the turn of a leaf
   From green to silver, the sway
Of grass with dew, and as brief
   Is the time I shall stay.

John Drinkwater

SUNRISE ON RYDAL WATER

To E. de S.

Come down at dawn from windless hills
   Into the valley of the lake,
Where yet a larger quiet fills
   The hour, and mist and water make

With rocks and reeds and island boughs
  One silence and one element,
Where wonder goes surely as once
    It went
      By Galilean prows.

Moveless the water and the mist,
  Moveless the secret air above;
Hushed, as upon some happy tryst,
  The poised expectancy of love;
What spirit is it that adores
  What mighty presence yet unseen?
What consummation works apace
  Between
    These rapt enchanted shores?

Never did virgin beauty wake
  Devouter to the bridal feast
Than moves this hour upon the lake
  In adoration to the east.
Here is the bride a god may know,
  The primal will, the young consent,
Till surely upon the appointed mood
  Intent
    The god shall leap—and lo,

Over the lake's end strikes the sun—
  White flameless fire; some purity
Thrilling the mist, a splendor won
  Out of the world's heart. Let there be
Thoughts, and atonements, and desires;
  Proud limbs, and undeliberate tongue;
Where now we move with mortal care
  Among
    Immortal dews and fires.

So the old mating goes apace,
  Wind with the sea, and blood with thought,
Lover with lover; and the grace
  Of understanding comes unsought

When stars into the twilight steer,
  Or thrushes build among the may,
Or wonder moves between the hills,
  And day
    Comes up on Rydal mere.

RECIPROCITY

I do not think that skies and meadows are
Moral, or that the fixture of a star
Comes of a quiet spirit, or that trees
Have wisdom in their windless silences.
Yet these are things invested in my mood
With constancy, and peace, and fortitude;
That in my troubled season I can cry
Upon the wide composure of the sky,
And envy fields, and wish that I might be
As little daunted as a star or tree.

INVOCATION

As pools beneath stone arches take
  Darkly within their deeps again
Shapes of the flowing stone, and make
  Stories anew of passing men,

So let the living thoughts that keep,
  Morning and evening, in their kind,
Eternal change in height and deep,
  Be mirrored in my happy mind.

Beat, world, upon this heart, be loud
  Your marvel chanted in my blood.
Come forth, O sun, through cloud on cloud
  To shine upon my stubborn mood.

Great hills that fold above the sea,
  Ecstatic airs and sparkling skies,
Sing out your words to master me—
  Make me immoderately wise.

Louise Driscoll

THE METAL CHECKS

[*The scene is a bare room, with two shaded windows at the back, and a fireplace between them with a fire burning low. The room contains a few plain chairs, and a rough wooden table on which are piled many small wooden trays.* THE COUNTER, *who is Death, sits at the table. He wears a loose gray robe, and his face is partly concealed by a gray veil.* THE BEARER *is the World, that bears the burden of War. He wears a soiled robe of brown and green and he carries on his back a gunny-bag filled with the little metal disks that have been used for the identification of the slain common soldiers.*]

The Bearer

      Here is a sack, a gunny sack,
        A heavy sack I bring.
      Here is toll of many a soul—
        But not the soul of a king.

      This is the toll of common men,
        Who lived in the common way;
      Lived upon bread and wine and love,
        In the light of the common day.

      This is the toll of working men,
        Blood and brawn and brain.
      Who shall render us again
        The worth of all the slain?

The Counter

      Pour them out on the table here.
        C l i c k e t y—c l i c k e t y—c l a c k!
      For every button a man went out,
      And who shall call him back?
        C l i c k e t y—c l i c k e t y—c l a c k!
      One—two—three—four—
        Every disk a soul!
      Three score—four score—
      So many boys went out to war.

Pick up that one that fell on the floor—
   Didn't you see it roll?
That was a man a month ago.
This was a man. Row upon row—
Pile them in tens and count them so.

The Bearer
   I have an empty sack.
     It is not large. Would you have said
   That I could carry on my back
     So great an army—and all dead?

[*As* THE COUNTER *speaks* THE BEARER *lays the sack over his arm
   and helps count.*]

The Counter
   Put a hundred in each tray—
   We can tally them best that way.
   Careful—do you understand
   You have ten men in your hand?
   There's another fallen—there—
   Under that chair.

[THE BEARER *finds it and restores it.*]
   That was a man a month ago;
   He could see and feel and know.
   Then, into his throat there sped
   A bit of lead.
   Blood was salt in his mouth; he fell
   And lay amid the battle wreck.
   Nothing was left but this metal check—
   And a wife and child, perhaps.

[THE BEARER *finds the bag on his arm troublesome. He holds it up,
   inspecting it.*]

The Bearer
   What can one do with a thing like this?
   Neither of life nor death it is!
   For the dead serve not, though it served the dead.
   The wounds it carried were wide and red,
   Yet they stained it not. Can a man put food,

Potatoes or wheat, or even wood
That is kind and burns with a flame to warm
Living men who are comforted—
In a thing that has served so many dead?
There is no thrift in a graveyard dress,
It's been shroud for too many men.
I'll burn it and let the dead bless.

[*He crosses himself and throws it into the fire. He watches it burn.*
THE COUNTER *continues to pile up the metal checks, and drop
them by hundreds into the trays which he piles one upon
another.* THE BEARER *turns from the fire and speaks more
slowly than before. He indicates the metal checks.*]

Would not the blood of these make a great sea
For men to sail their ships on? It may be
No fish would swim in it, and the foul smell
Would make the sailors sick. Perhaps in Hell
There's some such lake for men who rush to war
Prating of glory, and upon the shore
Will stand the wives and children and old men
Bereft, to drive them back again
When they seek haven. Some such thing
I thought the while I bore it on my back
And heard the metal pieces clattering.

The Counter

Four score—five score—
These and as many more.
Forward—march!—into the tray!
No bugles blow today,
No captains lead the way;
But mothers and wives,
Fathers, sisters, little sons,
Count the cost
Of the lost;
And we count the unlived lives,
The forever unborn ones
Who might have been your sons.

The Bearer

      Could not the hands of these rebuild
      That which has been destroyed?
      Oh, the poor hands! that once were strong and filled
      With implements of labor whereby they
      Served home and country through the peaceful day.
      When those who made the war stand face to face
      With these slain soldiers in that unknown place
      Whither the dead go, what will be the word
      By dead lips spoken and by dead ears heard?
      Will souls say King or Kaiser? Will souls prate
      Of earthly glory in that new estate?

The Counter

      One hundred thousand—
      One hundred and fifty thousand—
      Two hundred—

The Bearer

      Can this check plough?
        Can it sow? can it reap?
      Can we arouse it?
        Is it asleep?

      Can it hear when a child cries?—
        Comfort a wife?
      This little metal disk
        Stands for a life.

      Can this check build,
        Laying stone upon stone?
      Once it was warm flesh
        Folded on bone.

      Sinew and muscle firm,
        Look at it—can
      This little metal check
        Stand for a man?

The Counter

      One—two—three—four—

Helen Dudley

TO ONE UNKNOWN

I have seen the proudest stars
    That wander on through space,
Even the sun and moon,
    But not your face.

I have heard the violin,
    The winds and waves rejoice
In endless minstrelsy,
    Yet not your voice.

I have touched the trillium,
    Pale flower of the land,
Coral, anemone,
    And not your hand.

I have kissed the shining feet
    Of Twilight lover-wise,
Opened the gates of Dawn—
    Oh, not your eyes!

I have dreamed unwonted things,
    Visions that witches brew,
Spoken with images,
    Never with you.

SONG

A few more windy days
Must come and go their ways,
And we will walk,
My love and I,
Beneath the amber-dripping boughs.
Then on the stars we'll tread,
On purple stars and red,
And wonder why,
The while we talk,
Men sing so much of broken vows.

T. S. Eliot

THE LOVE SONG OF J. ALFRED PRUFROCK

S'io credesse che mia risposta fosse
A persona che mai tornasse al mondo,
Questa fiamma staria senza piu scosse.
Ma periocche giammai di questo fondo
Non torno vivo alcun, s'i'odo il vero,
Senza tema d'infamia ti rispondo.

Let us go then, you and I,
When the evening is spread out against the sky
Like a patient etherized upon a table;
Let us go, through certain half-deserted streets,
The muttering retreats
Of restless nights in one-night cheap hotels
And sawdust restaurants with oyster-shells:
Streets that follow like a tedious argument
Of insidious intent
To lead you to an overwhelming question. . . .
Oh, do not ask, "What is it?"
Let us go and make our visit.

In the room the women come and go
Talking of Michelangelo.

The yellow fog that rubs its back upon the window-panes,
The yellow smoke that rubs its muzzle on the window-panes
Licked its tongue into the corners of the evening,
Lingered upon the pools that stand in drains,
Let fall upon its back the soot that falls from chimneys,
Slipped by the terrace, make a sudden leap,
And seeing that it was a soft October night,
Curled once about the house, and fell asleep.

And indeed there will be time
For the yellow smoke that slides along the street,
Rubbing its back upon the window-panes;
There will be time, there will be time

To prepare a face to meet the faces that you meet;
There will be time to murder and create,
And time for all the works and days of hands
That live and drop a question on your plate;
Time for you and time for me,
And time yet for a hundred indecisions,
And for a hundred visions and revisions,
Before the taking of a toast and tea.

In the room the women come and go
Talking of Michelangelo.

And indeed there will be time
To wonder, "Do I dare?" and, "Do I dare?"
Time to turn back and descend the stair,
With a bald spot in the middle of my hair—
(They will say: "How his hair is growing thin!")
My morning coat, my collar mounting firmly to the chin,
My necktie rich and modest, but asserted by a simple pin—
(They will say: "But how his arms and legs are thin!")
Do I dare
Disturb the universe?
In a minute there is time
For decisions and revisions which a minute will reverse.

For I have known them all already, known them all:
Have known the evenings, mornings, afternoons,
I have measured out my life with coffee spoons;
I know the voices dying with a dying fall
Beneath the music from a farther room.
  So how should I presume?

And I have known the eyes already, known them all—
The eyes that fix you in a formulated phrase,
And when I am formulated, sprawling on a pin,
When I am pinned and wriggling on the wall,
Then how should I begin
To spit out all the butt-ends of my days and ways?
  And how should I presume?

And I have known the arms already, known them all—
Arms that are braceleted and white and bare
(But in the lamplight, downed with light brown hair!)
Is it perfume from a dress
That makes me so digress?
Arms that lie along a table, or wrap about a shawl.
   And should I then presume?
   And how should I begin?

. . . .

Shall I say, I have gone at dusk through narrow streets
And watched the smoke that rises from the pipes
Of lonely men in shirt-sleeves, leaning out of windows? . . .

I should have been a pair of ragged claws
Scuttling across the floors of silent seas.

. . . .

And the afternoon, the evening, sleeps so peacefully
Smoothed by long fingers,
Asleep . . . tired . . . or it malingers,
Stretched on the floor, here beside you and me.
Should I, after tea and cakes and ices,
Have the strength to force the moment to its crisis?
But though I have wept and fasted, wept and prayed,
Though I have seen my head (grown slightly bald) brought in
    upon a platter,
I am no prophet—and here's no great matter;
I have seen the moment of my greatness flicker,
And I have seen the eternal Footman hold my coat, and snicker,
And in short, I was afraid.

And would it have been worth it, after all,
After the cups, the marmalade, the tea,
Among the porcelain, among some talk of you and me,
Would it have been worth while
To have bitten off the matter with a smile,
To have squeezed the universe into a ball
To roll it toward some overwhelming question,
To say: "I am Lazarus, come from the dead,

Come back to tell you all, I shall tell you all "—
If one, settling a pillow by her head,
   Should say: "That is not what I meant at all;
   That is not it, at all."

And would it have been worth it, after all,
Would it have been worth while,
After the sunsets and the dooryards and the sprinkled streets,
After the novels, after the teacups, after the skirts that trail
    along the floor—
And this, and so much more?—
It is impossible to say just what I mean!
But as if a magic lantern threw the nerves in patterns on a screen:
Would it have been worth while
If one, settling a pillow or throwing off a shawl,
And turning toward the window, should say:
   "That is not it at all,
That is not what I meant, at all."

     .   .   .   .

No! I am not Prince Hamlet, nor was meant to be;
Am an attendant lord, one that will do
To swell a progress, start a scene or two,
Advise the prince; no doubt, an easy tool,
Deferential, glad to be of use,
Politic, cautious, and meticulous;
Full of high sentence, but a bit obtuse;
At times, indeed, almost ridiculous—
Almost, at times, the Fool.

I grow old . . . I grow old . . .
I shall wear the bottoms of my trousers rolled.

Shall I part my hair behind? Do I dare to eat a peach?
I shall wear white flannel trousers, and walk upon the beach.
I have heard the mermaids singing, each to each.

I do not think that they will sing to me.

I have seen them riding seaward on the waves,
Combing the white hair of the waves blown back
When the wind blows the water white and black.

We have lingered in the chambers of the sea
By sea-girls wreathed with seaweed red and brown
Till human voices wake us, and we drown.

PORTRAIT OF A LADY

I

Among the smoke and fog of a December afternoon
You have the scene arrange itself—as it will seem to do—
With "I have saved this afternoon for you";
And four wax candles in the darkened room,
Four rings of light upon the ceiling overhead:
An atmosphere of Juliet's tomb
Prepared for all the things to be said, or left unsaid.

We have been, let us say, to hear the latest Pole
Transmit the Preludes, through his hair and finger-tips.
"So intimate, this Chopin, that I think his soul
Should be resurrected only among friends—
Some two or three, who will not touch the bloom
That is rubbed and questioned in the concert room."

And so the conversation slips
Among velleities and carefully caught regrets,
Through attenuated tones of violins
Mingled with remote cornets,
And begins:
"You do not know how much they mean to me, my friends;
And how, how rare and strange it is, to find,
In a life composed so much, so much of odds and ends—
(For indeed I do not love it . . . you knew? you are not blind!
How keen you are!)
To find a friend who has these qualities,
Who has, and gives
Those qualities upon which friendship lives:
How much it means that I say this to you—
Without these friendships—life, what *cauchemar!*"

Among the windings of the violins,
And the ariettes
Of cracked cornets,
Inside my brain a dull tom-tom begins
Absurdly hammering a prelude of its own—
Capricious monotone
That is at least one definite "false note."
Let us take the air, in a tobacco trance,
Admire the monuments,
Discuss the late events,
Correct our watches by the public clocks;
Then sit for half an hour and drink our bocks.

II

Now that lilacs are in bloom
She has a bowl of lilacs in her room
And twists one in her fingers while she talks.
"Ah my friend, you do not know, you do not know
What life is, you who hold it in your hands—"
(Slowly twisting the lilac stalks);
"You let it flow from you, you let it flow,
And youth is cruel, and has no remorse,
And smiles at situations which it cannot see."

I smile, of course,
And go on drinking tea.
"Yet with these April sunsets, that somehow recall
My buried life, and Paris in the spring,
I feel immeasurably at peace, and find the world
To be wonderful and youthful, after all."

The voice returns like the insistent out-of-tune
Of a broken violin on an August afternoon:
"I am always sure that you understand
My feelings, always sure that you feel,
Sure that across the gulf you reach your hand.

"You are invulnerable, you have no Achilles' heel.
You will go on, and when you have prevailed
You can say, 'At this point many a one has failed.'

But what have I, but what have I, my friend,
To give you, what can you receive from me?
Only the friendship and the sympathy
Of one about to reach her journey's end.

"I shall sit here, serving tea to friends . . ."

I take my hat: how can I make a cowardly amends
For what she has said to me?

You will see me any morning in the park
Reading the comics and the sporting page.
Particularly I remark
An English countess goes upon the stage,
A Greek was murdered at a Polish dance,
Another bank defaulter has confessed.
I keep my countenance,
I remain self-possessed
Except when a street piano, mechanical and tired,
Reiterates some worn-out common song,
With the smell of hyacinths across the garden
Recalling things that other people have desired.
Are these ideas right or wrong?

III

The October night comes down. Returning as before,
Except for a slight sensation of being ill at ease,
I mount the stairs and turn the handle of the door
And feel as if I had mounted on my hands and knees.

"And so you are going abroad; and when do you return?
But that's a useless question.
You hardly know when you are coming back,
You will find so much to learn."
My smile falls heavily among the bric-a-brac.

"Perhaps you can write to me."
My self-possession flares up for a second;
This is as I had reckoned.
"I have been wondering frequently of late
(But our beginnings never know our ends!)

Why we have not developed into friends."
I feel like one who smiles, and turning shall remark
Suddenly, his expression in a glass.
My self-possession gutters; we are really in the dark.

"For everybody said so, all our friends,
They all were sure our feelings would relate
So closely! I myself can hardly understand.
We must leave it now to fate.
You will write, at any rate.
Perhaps it is not too late.
I shall sit here, serving tea to friends."

And I must borrow every changing shape
To find expression . . . dance, dance
Like a dancing bear,
Cry like a parrot, chatter like an ape.
Let us take the air, in a tobacco trance . . .

Well! and what if she should die some afternoon,
Afternoon gray and smoky, evening yellow and rose;
Should die and leave me sitting pen in hand
With the smoke coming down above the house-tops;
Doubtful, for quite a while
Not knowing what to feel, or if I understand,
Or whether wise or foolish, tardy or too soon. . . .
Would she not have the advantage, after all?
This music is successful with a "dying fall"
Now that we talk of dying—
And should I have the right to smile?

LA FIGLIA CHE PIANGE

Stand on the highest pavement of the stair—
Lean on a garden urn—
Weave, weave, weave the sunlight in your hair—
Clasp your flowers to you with a pained surprise—
Fling them to the ground and turn
With a fugitive resentment in your eyes:
But weave, weave the sunlight in your hair.

So I would have had him leave,
So I would have had her stand and grieve,
So he would have left
As the soul leaves the body torn and bruised,
As the mind deserts the body it has used.
I should find
Some way incomparably light and deft,
Some way we both should understand,
Simple and faithless as a smile and shake of the hand.

She turned away, but with the autumn weather
Compelled my imagination many days—
Many days and many hours:
Her hair over her arms and her arms full of flowers—
And I wonder how they should have been together!
I should have lost a gesture and a pose.
Sometimes these cogitations still amaze
The troubled midnight and the noon's repose.

SWEENEY AMONG THE NIGHTINGALES

Apeneck Sweeney spreads his knees,
Letting his arms hang down to laugh;
The zebra stripes along his jaw
Swelling to maculate giraffe.

The circles of the stormy moon
Slide westward toward the River Plate.
Death and the Raven drift above,
And Sweeney guards the horned gate.

Gloomy Orion and the Dog
Are veiled; and hushed the shrunken seas.
The person in the Spanish cape
Tries to sit on Sweeney's knees;

Slips and pulls the table-cloth,
Overturns a coffee-cup.
Reorganized upon the floor,
She yawns and draws a stocking up.

The silent man in mocha brown
Sprawls at the window-sill, and gapes,
The waiter brings in oranges
Bananas, figs and hot-house grapes.

The silent vertebrate in brown
Contracts and concentrates, withdraws;
Rachel *née* Rabinovitch
Tears at the grapes with murderous paws.

She and the lady in the cape
Are suspect, thought to be in league;
Therefore the man with heavy eyes
Declines the gambit, shows fatigue,

Leaves the room and reappears
Outside the window, leaning in.
Branches of wistaria
Circumscribe a golden grin.

The host with someone indistinct
Converse at the door apart.
The nightingales are singing near
The Convent of the Sacred Heart;

And sang within the bloody wood
When Agamemnon cried aloud;
And let their liquid droppings fall
To stain the stiff dishonored shroud.

WHISPERS OF IMMORTALITY

Webster was much possessed by death
And saw the skull beneath the skin;
And breastless creatures under ground
Leaned backward with a lipless grin.

Daffodil bulbs instead of balls
Stared from the sockets of the eyes!
He knew that thought clings round dead limbs
Tightening its lusts and luxuries.

Donne, I suppose, was such another
Who found no substitute for sense;
To seize and clutch and penetrate,
Expert beyond experience.

He knew the anguish of the marrow,
The ague of the skeleton;
No contact possible to flesh
Allayed the fever of the bone.

.   .   .   .

Grishkin is nice: her Russian eye
Is underlined for emphasis;
Uncorseted, her friendly bust
Gives promise of pneumatic bliss.

The couched Brazilian jaguar
Compels the scampering marmoset
With subtle effuence of cat:
Grishkin has a maisonette.

The sleek Brazilian jaguar
Does not, in its arboreal gloom,
Distil so rank a feline smell
As Grishkin in a drawing-room.

And even the Abstract Entities
Circumambulate her charm;
But our lot crawls between dry ribs
To keep our metaphysics warm.

MARINA

Quis hic locus, quæ regio, quæ mundi plaga?

What seas what shores what grey rocks and what islands
What water lapping the bow
And scent of pine and the woodthrush singing through the fog
What images return
O my daughter.

Those who sharpen the tooth of the dog, meaning
Death
Those who glitter with the glory of the hummingbird, meaning
Death
Those who sit in the stye of contentment, meaning
Death
Those who suffer the ecstasy of the animals, meaning
Death

Are become unsubstantial, reduced by a wind,
A breath of pine, and the woodsong fog
By this grace dissolved in place

What is this face, less clear and clearer
The pulse in the arm, less strong and stronger—
Given or lent? more distant than stars and nearer than the
      eye
Whispers and small laughter between leaves and hurrying feet
Under sleep, where all the waters meet.

Bowsprit cracked with ice and paint cracked with heat.
I made this, I have forgotten
And remember.
The rigging weak and the canvas rotten
Between one June and another September.
Made this unknowing, half conscious, unknown, my own.
The garboard strake leaks, the seams need caulking.
This form, this face, this life
Living to live in a world of time beyond me; let me
Resign my life for this life, my speech for that unspoken,
The awakened, lips parted, the hope, the new ships.

What seas what shores what granite islands towards my timbers
And woodthrush calling through the fog
My daughter.

William Closson Emory

BE STILL

Always remembering always remembering
deep in the well the spring bubbles
slowly but always
remembering talking to you and me
inconsequential things Jim's marriage
the high rent of apartments
the symphony last night and
the scandal in the papers always
remembering how the air fluttered and whined
shaking the body fear was a quick fever
springing from the ambush of the mind
like a ravenous beast tearing the trembling nerves
and the feet moved like slow clouds always
remembering looking quiet and peaceful
with the brain torn and quivering
spilled on the green turf the eyes starkstaring
and a twitch of the graying body always
remembering as if set with concrete the
angular planes of thought projecting
through the normal periphery always
remembering the monstrous red-eyed rats
beside the ragged ghostly columns of Vailly watching
in the terrifying moonlight
the lonely walkers while the shells screamed
put your arms around me love this is
a fragrant pleasant flesh so quick it
can be limp and nauseous not now the guns but always
remembering how the sky shook red-gashed all night
and the steel death was a gray rain splashing fire
the liquid slosh of the gas shells warbling
like ill-omened birds and the sudden
ripping fingers in the throat choking always
remembering father why do you sit in bed like that
you frighten me be still my child be still it's
nothing but a dream nothing but a dream

Abbie Huston Evans

THE MINERAL COLLECTION

I always knew the Ural Mountains glowed
And burned inside with emeralds and gold,
Copper in clefts, and platinum in rifts
Like tamped-in tinfoil; now my eyes have seen
Splinters from that great beam that braces Asia.
Here in the dark, awake, I see again
Rock out of Mexico, Siam, Peru,
Thrace, Arizona, and the Isle of Malta;
Rock out of Chile burning fiercely, furred
With copper-blue like a kingfisher's feather:
Rock out of Greece, imperishable blue,
Cool blue of the Argives, lined with green of the sea;
Delicate rock of India lightly dyed
With milky azure, peach, and apricot;
Rock out of Maine, the ice-like tourmaline
In shattered spars, pencils of frigid rose
And chill black-green, of waters most dilute:
All these the bright credentials of dark workings,
Compulsions, interminglings, strangest love,
Knittings and couplings known but to the atom.

The thought of those bright fragments wrenched from darkness—
Of cinnebar, and slabs of malachite,
And crusts of amethyst—dazzles me still,
And raises me on my elbow in the dark.
Recalling topaz split and opal fractured
I tingle—great is life retired in stone!
Great is that obstinate impulsion launched
Against the opposition of the dust,
Whereof are we: we, and the red-cup moss,
The blowing tree, the boulder, and the fly
In amber under water; quick and slow
Braided in one, one indeterminate life
Riddling the dust. Show me one mote inert!

JONES'S PASTURE

Now is earth visibly gone over to spirit.
Bushes are more than bushes in this light.
Low sun, rolled cloud, and mile-long shadows cast,
Wild freshness, sharpened air, bathed sight, bare being,
Invade this old and all but empty pasture.
Seeing this ground under on-coming night
Lit by the colored sun down-rolling, dusk
Behind each reddened bush (and more than dusk),
I am back at the beginning, out of dust, in dew.
This, this is Dawn; this is primeval dew,
Death all to be, man unbegotten, life
Dazzling fire-naked over the face of the earth,
Licking up dust like stubble, without smoke.

FIRST CONCERNS

Better go outdoors now, shut the door on trouble,
Lest if I stay indoors life should bend me double;
Care hides in house corners, but has little use
For a hummock pasture full of sun-burnt spruce.

It is high time I found out one or two things; whether
Lambkill is blooming like a flowerier heather;
Whether after all this rain green-white bells are set
Thick on high bush blueberry like wild mignonette.

Better stub my feet on roots, let the bronze-green fly
Sun itself upon my hand imperturbably;
Through the blazing mica grains by a road well known
Watch the small red spider running down the stone.

MOONRISE

Seeing the great moon rising
On the edge of night,
Over quiet country
Shedding light;

Seeing the full moon rising
Haloed and slow,
Over darkened country
Shedding glow;

In silence and shadow
Tongued and long
I hear my heart, smitten,
Sound like a gong:

"*Solitary!*" "*Endless!*"
"*Transitory!*"
"*Flood-swept!*"—Thus my heart
To the moon's glory.

I see the moon in heaven
Like an orange haw;
I see the lighted lamp
That Shelley saw;

Small things in the grass pipe
At that amazing glare,
And Awe and Wonder, feathered,
Pass me on air.

THE TRUE LOVER

This is the naked unsurmountable truth:
Two shall not ever meet.
In spite of passion and the dream of youth,
Two still are two, discrete.

Take for your lover the importunate earth,
You shall achieve desire.
In that great meeting is no hint of dearth,
The tinder is the fire.

IN CONCLUSION

If I could live year-round upon this hill
I should be wiser, but I could not prove
Even then some things I know: say what you will,
The sweet-fern leans against the log for love.

Beyond the reach of argument with me
Is the purple on the shingles of the shed
That kindles as the sun sinks. When I see
Mist fill the lowlands as I go to bed,

I know I am through with cleverness, I know
That earth's great pulse ignores it: though it run
It cannot overtake that logic slow,
Uncontroverted, making nine fields one.

Donald Evans

IN THE VICES

Gay and audacious crime glints in his eyes;
And his mad talk, raping the commonplace,
Gleefully runs a devil-praising race,
And none can ever follow where he flies.
He streaks himself with vices tenderly;
He cradles sin, and with a figleaf fan
Taps his green cat, watching a bored sun span
The wasted minutes to eternity.

Once I took up his trail along the dark,
Wishful to track him to the witches' flame,
To see the bubbling of the sneer and snare.
The way led through a fragrant starlit park,
And soon upon a harlot's house I came—
Within I found him playing at solitaire!

EN MONOCLE

Born with a monocle he stares at life,
And sends his soul on pensive promenades;
He pays a high price for discarded gods,
And then regilds them to renew their strife.
His calm moustache points to the ironies,
And a faun-colored laugh sucks in the night,
Full of the riant mists that turn to white
In brief lost battles with banalities.

Masters are makeshifts, and a path to tread
For blue pumps that are ardent for the air;
Features are fixtures when the face is fled,
And we are left the husks of tarnished hair;
But he is one who lusts uncomforted
To kiss the naked phrase quite unaware.

IN THE GENTLEMANLY INTEREST

Piccadilly

He polished snubs till they were regnant art,
Curling their shameless toilets round the hour.
Each lay upon his lips an exquisite flower
Subtly malign and poisoned for its part.
The path of victims was no wanton plan—
He had bowed his head in sorrow at his birth,
For he had said long ere he came to earth
That it was no place for a gentleman.

But always a heart-scald lurked behind the screen,
And somehow he missed the ultimate degrees.
He saw a beggar at the daylight's fall,
And then he rose and robed him for the scene;
And when they called him cad he found release—
He knew he had used the finest snub of all.

EPICEDE

Wistfully shimmering, shamelessly wise and weak,
He lives in pawn, pledging a battered name;
He loves his failures as one might love fame,
And listens for the ghost years as they speak.
A fragrance bright and broken clasps his head,
And wildwood airs sing a frayed interlude;
While cloaked he comes in a new attitude
To play gravedigger, if the word be said.

He swore he would be glad and only glad,
And turned to Broadway for the peace of God.
He found it at the bottom of the glass;
For where the dregs lay it was less than sad,
And 'mid the murmur when the dance was trod
He heard the echo of a genius pass.

Arthur Davison Ficke

MEETING

Gray-robed Wanderer in sleep . . . Wanderer . . .
You also move among
Those silent halls
Dim on the shore of the unsailèd deep?
And your footfalls, yours also, Wanderer,
Faint through those twilight corridors have rung?

Of late my eyes have seen . . . Wanderer . . .
Amid the shadows' gloom
Of that sleep-girdled place
I should have known such joy could not have been—
To see your face: and yet, Wanderer,
What hopes seem vain beneath the night in bloom?

Wearily I awake . . . Wanderer . . .
Your look of old despair,
Like a dying star,

In morning vanishes. But for all memories' sake,
Though you are far—tonight, O Wanderer,
Tonight come, though in silence, to the shadows there . . .

AMONG SHADOWS

In halls of sleep you wandered by,
This time so indistinguishably
I cannot remember aught of it,
Save that I know last night we met.
I know it by the cloudy thrill
That in my heart is quivering still;
And sense of loveliness forgot
Teases my fancy out of thought.
Though with the night the vision wanes,
Its haunting presence still may last—
As odor of flowers faint remains
In halls where late a queen has passed.

PORTRAIT OF AN OLD WOMAN

She limps with halting painful pace,
    Stops, wavers, and creeps on again;
Peers up with dim and questioning face
    Void of desire or doubt or pain.

Her cheeks hang gray in waxen folds
    Wherein there stirs no blood at all.
A hand like bundled cornstalks holds
    The tatters of a faded shawl.

Where was a breast, sunk bones she clasps;
    A knot jerks where were woman-hips;
A ropy throat sends writhing gasps
    Up to the tight line of her lips.

Here strong the city's pomp is poured . . .
    She stands, unhuman, bleak, aghast:
An empty temple of the Lord
    From which the jocund Lord has passed.

He has builded him another house,
   Whenceforth his flame, renewed and bright,
Shines stark upon these weathered brows
   Abandoned to the final night.

I AM WEARY OF BEING BITTER

I am weary of being bitter and weary of being wise,
   And the armor and the mask of these fall from me, after long.
I would go where the islands sleep, or where the sea-dawns rise,
   And lose my bitter wisdom in the wisdom of a song.

There are magics in melodies, unknown of the sages;
   The powers of purest wonder on fragile wings go by.
Doubtless out of the silence of dumb preceding ages
   Song woke the chaos-world—and light swept the sky.

All that we know is idle; idle is all we cherish;
   Idle the will that takes loads that proclaim it strong.
For the knowledge, the strength, the burden—all shall perish:
   One thing only endures, one thing only—song.

FROM *SONNETS OF A PORTRAIT PAINTER*

I am in love with high far-seeing places
That look on plains half sunlight and half storm,
In love with hours when from the circling faces
Veils pass, and laughing fellowship glows warm.
You who look on me with grave eyes where rapture
And April love of living burn confessed—
The gods are good! the world lies free to capture!
Life has no walls—oh, take me to your breast!
Take me—be with me for a moment's span!
I am in love with all unveilèd faces.
I seek the wonder at the heart of man;
I would go up to the far-seeing places.
While youth is ours, turn toward me for a space
The marvel of your rapture-lighted face!

There are strange shadows fostered of the moon,
More numerous than the clear-cut shade of day. . . .
Go forth, when all the leaves whisper of June,
Into the dusk of swooping bats at play;
Or go into that late November dusk
When hills take on the noble lines of death,
And on the air the faint astringent musk
Of rotting leaves pours vaguely troubling breath.
Then shall you see shadows whereof the sun
Knows nothing—aye, a thousand shadows there
Shall leap and flicker and stir and stay and run,
Like petrels of the changing foul or fair;
Like ghosts of twilight, of the moon, of him
Whose homeland lies past each horizon's rim. . . .

LIKE HIM WHOSE SPIRIT

Like him whose spirit in the blaze of noon
Still keeps the memory of one secret star
That in the dusk of a remembered June
Thrilled the strange hour with beauty from afar—
And perilous spells of twilight snare his heart,
And wistful moods his common thoughts subdue,
And life seethes by him utterly apart—
Last night I dreamed, today I dream, of you.
Gleams downward strike; bright bubbles upward hover
Through the charmed air; far sea-winds cool my brow.
Invisible lips tell me I shall discover
Today a temple, a mystery, a vow . . .
The cycle rounds: only the false seems true.
Last night I dreamed, today I dream, of you.

THREE SONNETS

PERSPECTIVE OF CO-ORDINATION

The circles never fully round, but change
In spiral gropings—not, as on a wall,
Flat-patterned, but back into space they fall,

In depth on depth of indeterminate range.
Where they begin may be here at my hand
Or there far lost beyond the search of eye;
And though I sit, desperately rapt, and try
To trace round-round the line, and understand
The sequence, the relation, the black-art
Of their continuance, hoping to find good
At least some logic of part-joined-to-part,
I judge the task one of too mad a mood:
And prophecy throws its shadow on my heart,
And Time's last sunset flames along my blood.

WORLD BEYOND WORLD

Two mirrors, face to face, is all I need
To build a mazy universe for my mind
Where world grows out of world. I dizzily find
Solace in endless planes that there recede.
The fifth plane-world, soft-shimmering through the glass—
Surely it has a light more bland than ours.
And in the far ninth hides a whirl of powers
Unknown to our dull senses. I would pass
Down the long vista, pausing now and then
To taste the flavor of each separate sphere,
And with each vast perspective cool my eye.
Whom should I meet there? Never living men!
What should I love there? Nothing I hold dear!
What would the end be? Endless as am I!

LEAF-MOVEMENT

From its thin branch high in the autumn wind
The yellow leaf now sails in upward flight;
Hovers at top-slope; then, a whirling bright
Eddy of motion, sinks. The storm behind
With gusts and veering tyrannies would uphold
Even as it downward beats this gorgeous thing
Which like an angel's lost and shattered wing
Against the grey sky sweeps its broken gold.

Another eddy, desperate or in mirth,
Brings it to rest here on the crackled earth
Where men can see it better than on the bough.
What quite preposterous irony of wind's-will
Touches it where it lies, golden and still,
And once more lifts it vainly heavenward now!

Hildegarde Flanner

THIS MORNING

After the emotion of rain
The mist parts across the morning
Like the smile of one
Who has laughed in sleep
And cannot remember why.

The damp road companions my feet
And is a friend to every step.
Above me winter goldfinches
Cling like fruit
To the delighted birch-trees;
And the studious earth,
Thinking what flowers to speak in next,
Moves restlessly with small wise birds,
Who read the tucks in the moss,
The symbols on the beetle-wings,
And the comedies on pink and yellow pebbles
Which I am too tall to see.

BIRDS

Beloved, the black swans of my eyes
Are loosed to your behest,
And must I still keep caged from you
The white swans of my breast?

My hands, like slender pigeons,
Flutter the whole day through.

Did you not know the little things
Home unto you?

My lips, like slim canaries,
Sing when I hear you speak.
Beloved, bend and stroke once more
The finches of my cheek.

COMMUNION

I have spoken with the dead;
From the silence of my bed
I have heard them in the night.
Their voices are as white
As altar candles. Their voices are as gold as wheat,
And clustered in the dark their words are sweet
As ripened fruit. Their voices are the color of dim rain
Over grass where spring has lain.
Their speaking is an orchard of delight.
I have heard them in the night;
Their lips bloomed into heavy song
That hung like bells above me. You are wrong
Who say the dead lie still:
I heard them sing until
The cup of silence fell in two and lay
Broken by beauty of what dead men say.

There is no loveliness I cannot see.
There is no wall too stern for me.
There is no door that can withstand
The lifted symbol of my hand.

I know an ancient shibboleth:
I pass, for I have talked with Death!

PACIFIC WINTER

The quietly sipping rain that sucks the rose
Dangles from a cloud and then is gone.
The mists bow low and falling prone disclose
Towers and cities made of violet stone.

The air with one quick flash is lit within
And every flower is limpid on her stem
And crystal bushes shudder and begin
To disengage their rainbows gem from gem.
The trees look downward from green galleries
And view the garden with a plumy nod,
While I in vain with dim and spinning eyes
Run to outrun the presence of a god
Who paused an instant here and left behind
His fugitive cameo upon my mind.

SONNETS IN QUAKER LANGUAGE

Thee sets a bell to swinging in my soul,
And though the sound is nebulous and dark,
Yet musical my thought unto its toll,
And seldom is my hush! and loud my hark!
Thee knows that in response continual
My heart is all ways resonant to thee,
Yet with how dim a sound antiphonal,
Like a lost wind that blows beneath the sea.
Can thee resolve confusion of my tears
Into a single silence of desire?
Can thee, when singing has gone cold with fears,
Put on more music and put on more fire?
If so, then I am cloister to a bell
That utters advent of a miracle.

When thee is weary of the earth and all
The summers of a printed calendar;
When thee would hinder the continual
Arrival of tomorrow as before;
When both thy heart and spirit are as stone,
Gone rigid and grown terrible in thee;
When life seems preterit and death alone
The only creature left—thee come to me.
There will be slumber for thee in my heart,
When I have smiled at thee and dimmed the candles,

And toward dawn as darkness falls apart
We will arise to hunt in dewy sandals
The pale wild deer that has a lacy horn
And lives on hidden manna and star corn.

John Gould Fletcher

IRRADIATIONS

I

Over the roof-tops race the shadows of clouds:
Like horses the shadows of clouds charge down the street.

Whirlpools of purple and gold,
Winds from the mountains of cinnabar,
Lacquered mandarin moments, palanquins swaying and balanc-
    ing
Amid the vermilion pavilions, against the jade balustrades;
Glint of the glittering winds of dragon-flies in the light;
Silver filaments, golden flakes settling downwards;
Rippling, quivering flutters; repulse and surrender,
The sun broidered upon the rain,
The rain rustling with the sun.

Over the roof-tops race the shadows of clouds:
Like horses the shadows of clouds charge down the street.

II

O seeded grass, you army of little men
Crawling up the long slope with quivering quick blades of steel:
You who storm millions of graves, tiny green tentacles of Earth,
Interlace yourselves tightly over my heart
And do not let me go:
For I would lie here for ever and watch with one eye
The pilgrimaging ants in your dull savage jungles,
While with the other I see the stiff lines of the slope
Break in mid-air, a wave surprisingly arrested;
And above them, wavering, dancing, bodiless, colorless, unreal,
The long thin lazy fingers of the heat.

III

Not noisily, but solemnly and pale,
In a meditative ecstasy, you entered life,
As performing some strange rite, to which you alone held the
    clue.
Child, life did not give rude strength to you;
From the beginning you would seem to have thrown away,
As something cold and cumbersome, that armor men use against
    death.
You would perhaps look on him face to face and so learn the
    secret
Whether that face wears oftenest a smile or no.
Strange, old and silent being, there is something
Infinitely vast in your intense tininess:
I think you could point out with a smile some curious star
Far off in the heavens, which no man has seen before.

IV

The morning is clean and blue, and the wind blows up the clouds:
Now my thoughts, gathered from afar,
Once again in their patched armor, with rusty plumes and
    blunted swords,
Move out to war.

Smoking our morning pipes we shall ride two and two
Through the woods.
For our old cause keeps us together,
And our hatred is so precious not death or defeat can break it.

God willing, we shall this day meet that old enemy
Who has given us so many a good beating.
Thank God, we have a cause worth fighting for,
And a cause worth losing, and a good song to sing!

ARIZONA POEMS

MEXICAN QUARTER

By an alley lined with tumble-down shacks,
And street-lamps askew, half-sputtering,

Feebly glimmering on gutters choked with filth, and dogs
Scratching their mangy backs:
Half-naked children are running about,
Women puff cigarettes in black doorways,
Crickets are crying;
Men slouch sullenly
Into the shadows.
Behind a hedge of cactus,
The smell of a dead horse
Mingles with the smell of tamales frying.

And a girl in a black lace shawl
Sits in a rickety chair by the square of unglazed window,
And sees the explosion of the stars
Fiercely poised on the velvet sky.
And she seems humming to herself:
"Stars, if I could reach you
(You are so very clear that it seems as if I could reach you),
I would give you all to the Madonna's image
On the gray plastered altar behind the paper flowers,
So that Juan would come back to me,
And we could live again those lazy burning hours,
Forgetting the tap of my fan and my sharp words.
And I would only keep four of you—
Those two blue-white ones overhead
To put in my ears,
And those two orange ones yonder
To fasten on my shoe-buckles."

A little farther along the street
A man squats stringing a brown guitar.
The smoke of his cigarette curls round his hair,
And he too is humming, but other words:
"Think not that at your window I wait.
New love is better, the old is turned to hate.
Fate! Fate! All things pass away;
Life is forever, youth is but for a day.
Love again if you may,
Before the golden moons are blown out of the sky
And the crickets die.

Babylon and Samarkand
Are mud walls in a waste of sand."

RAIN IN THE STREET

The huge red-buttressed mesa over yonder
Is merely a far-off temple where the sleepy sun is burning
Its altar fires of pinyon and toyon for the day.

The old priests sleep, white-shrouded;
Their pottery whistles lie beside them, the prayer-sticks closely
    feathered.
On every mummied face there glows a smile.

The sun is rolling slowly
Beneath the sluggish folds of the sky-serpents,
Coiling, uncoiling, blue-black, sparked with fires.

The old dead priests
Feel in the thin dried earth that is heaped about them,
Above the smell of scorching, oozing pinyon,
The acrid smell of rain.

And now the showers
Surround the mesa like a troop of silver dancers:
Shaking their rattles, stamping, chanting, roaring,
Whirling, extinguishing the last red wisp of light.

THE BLUE SYMPHONY

I

The darkness rolls upward.
The thick darkness carries with it
Rain and a ravel of cloud.
The sun comes forth upon earth.

Palely the dawn
Leaves me facing timidly
Old gardens sunken:
And in the gardens is water.

Sombre wreck—autumnal leaves;
Shadowy roofs
In the blue mist,
And a willow-branch that is broken.

O old pagodas of my soul, how you glittered across green trees!

Blue and cool:
Blue, tremulously,
Blow faint puffs of smoke
Across sombre pools.
The damp green smell of rotted wood;
And a heron that cries from out the water.

II

Through the upland meadows
I go alone.
For I dreamed of someone last night
Who is waiting for me.

Flower and blossom, tell me, do you know of her?

Have the rocks hidden her voice?
They are very blue and still.

Long upward road that is leading me,
Light-hearted I quit you,
For the long loose ripples of the meadow-grass
Invite me to dance upon them.

Quivering grass,
Daintily poised
For her foot's tripping.

O blown clouds, could I only race up like you!
Oh, the last slopes that are sun-drenched and steep!

Look, the sky!
Across black valleys
Rise blue-white aloft
Jagged unwrinkled mountains, ranges of death.

Solitude. Silence.

III

One chuckles by the brook for me:
One rages under the stone.
One makes a spout of his mouth,
One whispers—one is gone.

One over there on the water
Spreads cold ripples
For me
Enticingly.

The vast dark trees
Flow like blue veils
Of tears
Into the water.

Sour sprites,
Moaning and chuckling,
What have you hidden from me?

"In the palace of the blue stone she lies forever
Bound hand and foot."

Was it the wind
That rattled the reeds together?

Dry reeds,
A faint shiver in the grasses.

IV

On the left hand there is a temple:
And a palace on the right-hand side.
Foot-passengers in scarlet
Pass over the glittering tide.

Under the bridge
The old river flows
Low and monotonous
Day after day.

I have heard and have seen
All the news that has been:
Autumn's gold and Spring's green!

Now in my palace
I see foot-passengers
Crossing the river,
Pilgrims of autumn
In the afternoons.

Lotus pools;
Petals in the water:
These are my dreams.

For me silks are outspread.
I take my ease, unthinking.

V

And now the lowest pine-branch
Is drawn across the disk of the sun.
Old friends who will forget me soon,
I must go on
Towards those blue death-mountains
I have forgot so long.

In the marsh grasses
There lies forever
My last treasure,
With the hopes of my heart.

The ice is glazing over;
Torn lanterns flutter,
On the leaves is snow.

In the frosty evening
Toll the old bell for me
Once, in the sleepy temple.

Perhaps my soul will hear.

After glow:
Before the stars peep
I shall creep out into darkness.

DOWN THE MISSISSIPPI

EMBARKATION

Dull masses of dense green,
The forests range their sombre platforms.
Between them silently, like a spirit,
The river finds its own mysterious path.

Loosely the river sways out, backward, forward,
Always fretting the outer side;
Shunning the invisible focus of each crescent,
Seeking to spread into shining loops over fields:

Like an enormous serpent, dilating, uncoiling,
Displaying a broad scaly back of earth-smeared gold;
Swaying out sinuously between the dull motionless forests,
As molten metal might glide down the lip of a vase of dark
    bronze.

HEAT

As if the sun had trodden down the sky,
Until no more it holds air for us, but only humid vapor,
The heat, pressing upon earth with irresistible languor,
Turns all the solid forest into half-liquid smudge.

The heavy clouds, like cargo-boats, strain slowly up against its
    current;
And the flickering of the heat haze is like the churning of ten
    thousand paddles
Against the heavy horizon, pale blue and utterly windless,
Whereon the sun hangs motionless, a brassy disk of flame.

FULL MOON

Flinging its arc of silver bubbles, quickly shifts the moon
From side to side of us as we go down its path;
I sit on the deck at midnight, and watch it slipping and
    sliding,
Under my tilted chair, like a thin film of spilt water.

It is weaving a river of light to take the place of this river—
A river where we shall drift all night, then come to rest in its
    shallows.
And then I shall wake from my drowsiness and look down from
    some dim tree-top
Over white lakes of cotton, like moon-fields on every side.

THE MOON'S ORCHESTRA

When the moon lights up
Its dull red camp-fire through the trees;
And floats out, like a white balloon,
Into the blue cup of the night, borne by a casual breeze;
The moon-orchestra then begins to stir:
Jiggle of fiddles commence their crazy dance in the darkness;
Crickets churr
Against the stark reiteration of the rusty flutes which frogs
Puff at from rotted logs
In the swamp.
And the moon begins her dance of frozen pomp
Over the lightly quivering floor of the flat and mournful
    river.
Her white feet slightly twist and swirl—
She is a mad girl
In an old unlit ball-room,
Whose walls, half-guessed-at through the gloom,
Are hung with the rusty crape of stark black cypresses,
Which show, through gaps and tatters, red stains half hidden
    away.

THE STEVEDORES

Frieze of warm bronze that glides with cat-like movements
Over the gang-plank poised and yet awaiting—
The sinewy thudding rhythms of forty shuffling feet
Falling like muffled drum-beats on the stillness:

> *Oh, roll the cotton down—*
> *Roll, roll, the cotton down!*
> *From the further side of Jordan,*
> *Oh, roll the cotton down!*

And the river waits,
The river listens,
Chuckling with little banjo-notes that break with a plop on the
    stillness.
And by the low dark shed that holds the heavy freights,
Two lonely cypress trees stand up and point with stiffened fingers
Far southward where a single chimney stands aloof in the sky.

NIGHT LANDING

After the whistle's roar has bellowed and shuddered,
Shaking the sleeping town and the somnolent river,
The deep-toned floating of the pilot's bell
Suddenly warns the engines.

They pause like heart-beats that abruptly stop:
The shore glides to us, in a wide low curve.

And then—supreme revelation of the river—
The tackle is loosed, the long gang-plank swings outwards;
And poised at the end of it, half naked beneath the search-light,
A blue-black negro with gleaming teeth waits for his chance to
    leap.

THE SILENCE

There is a silence which I carry about with me always—
A silence perpetual, for it is self-created;
A silence of heat, of water, of unchecked fruitfulness,
Through which each year the heavy harvests bloom, and burst,
    and fall.

Deep, matted green silence of my South,
Often, within the push and the scorn of great cities,
I have seen that mile-wide waste of water swaying out to you,
And on its current glimmering I am going to the sea.

There is a silence I have achieved—I have walked beyond its
    threshold.
I know it is without horizons, boundless, fathomless, perfect.
And some day maybe, far away,
I shall curl up in it at last and sleep an endless sleep.

F. S. Flint

LONDON

London, my beautiful,
It is not the sunset
Nor the pale green sky
Shimmering through the curtain
Of the silver birch,
Nor the quietness;
It is not the hopping
Of the little birds
Upon the lawn,
Nor the darkness
Stealing over all things
That moves me.

But as the moon creeps slowly
Over the tree-tops
Among the stars,
I think of her
And the glow her passing
Sheds on men.

London, my beautiful,
I will climb
Into the branches
To the moonlit tree-tops,
That my blood may be cooled
By the wind.

THE SWAN

Under the lily shadow
And the gold
And the blue and mauve
That the whin and the lilac
Pour down on the water,
The fishes quiver.

Over the green cold leaves
And the rippled silver
And the tarnished copper
Of its neck and beak,
Toward the deep black water
Beneath the arches,
The swan floats slowly.

Into the dark of the arch the swan floats,
And the black depth of my sorrow
Bears a white rose of flame.

IN THE GARDEN

The grass is beneath my head;
And I gaze
At the thronging stars
In the aisles of night.

They fall . . . they fall. . . .
I am overwhelmed,
And afraid.

Each little leaf of the aspen
Is caressed by the wind,
And each is crying.

And the perfume
Of invisible roses
Deepens the anguish.

Let a strong mesh of roots
Feed the crimson of roses
Upon my heart;
And then fold over the hollow
Where all the pain was.

Ford Madox Ford

WINTER–NIGHT SONG

My dearest dear, my honey love;
My brown-eyed squirrel, my soft dove:
All tiny furred and feathered things
Have long curled up and furled up their wings.

The taxi-lamps and street lights too
Grow dim along Fifth Avenue,
And in the doorways of the shops
Slumber the dawn-awaiting cops.

A thousand miles of frozen lands
Do veil our eyes and part our hands.
We've sundered, we have burnt our ships;
A thousand miles do part our lips.

The sirens calling from the Sound
Taunt me across the icy ground,
The cold sea-sirens of the main, taunting:
"Ye never shall, ye twain,
Set sail to sail the world around,
And round and round and round again."

But not King George nor Genghis Khan
Could keep my squirrel from her man,
Nor Solomon's broad-winged Efreets
Bar to my dove these Greenwich streets,

Who, betwixt the winds and down the night,
A thousand miles doth take her flight,
And who invisible doth creep
Through the interstices of sleep.

My window's wide, my door's ajar;
I'll hear your coming from afar—
Oh tiny, tiny best, O best
In all the world from West to West.

Before the stars at dawn depart,
Quick, quick, your home is on my heart.

You are my strength, you are my peace;
My sustenance and my increase;
You are my thought and you do bind
The convolutions of my mind.

You are my eyes and what I see,
And you the blossom of my tree;
You are my rhythm and my tune
And you my lily buds of June.

You are my sleep, in you I wake,
And you my thirst, my thirst do slake.
You are my hunger and my meat,
My honey hair, my nimble feet.

And your voice speaks when I rehearse
The form and content of this verse.

But when night falls, ah then you prove
My brown-eyed squirrel, my soft dove:
My dearest dear,
My honey love.

FOOTSLOGGERS

I

What is love of one's land? . . .
    I don't know very well.
It is something that sleeps
For a year, for a day,
For a month—something that keeps
Very hidden and quiet and still,
And then takes
The quiet heart like a wave,
The quiet brain like a spell,
The quiet will
Like a tornado; and that shakes
The whole of the soul.

II

It is omnipotent like love;
It is deep and quiet as the grave,
And it awakes
Like a flame, like a madness,
Like the great passion of your life.
The cold keenness of a tempered knife,
The great gladness of a wedding day,
The austerity of monks who wake to pray
In the dim light
Who pray
In the darkling grove:
All these and a great belief in what we deem right,
Creeping upon us like the overwhelming sand
Driven by a December gale,
Make up the love of one's land.

.   .   .   .

L'ENVOI

What is love of one's land?
    Ah, we know very well
It is something that sleeps for a year, for a day,
For a month; something that keeps
Very hidden and quiet and still,
And then takes
The quiet heart like a wave,
The quiet brain like a spell,
The quiet will
Like a tornado, and that shakes
The whole being and soul . . .
Aye, the whole of the soul.

Moireen Fox

LIADAIN TO CURITHIR

Liadain and Curithir were two poets who lived in Ireland in the seventh century. They fell in love, but while Curithir was absent making preparations for their marriage, Liadain, for some unexplained reason, took the vows of a nun. Curithir in despair became a monk. At first they continued to see each other, but when this led to the breaking of their vows, Curithir left Liadain to spend his life in penance and thus save his soul.

I

If I had known how narrow a prison is love,
Never would I have given the width of the skies
In return for thy kiss, O Curithir, thou my grief!

If I had known love's poverty, I would have given
Duns and forests and ploughlands and begged my bread:
For now I have lost the earth and the stars and my soul.

If I had known the strength of love, I would have laid
The ridge of the world in ashes to stay his feet:
I would have cried on a stronger lord—on Death.

II

I, that was wont to pass by all unmoved
As the long ridge of the tide sweeps to the shore,
Am broken at last on the crags of a pitiless love.

I, who was wont to see men pale at my glance,
Like the quivering grass am shaken beneath thine eyes;
At thy touch my spirit is captive, my will is lost.

I would darken the sun and moon to break from thy love,
I would shatter the world to win thee again to my side.
O aching madness of love! Have the dead repose?
Or wilt thou tear my heart in the close-shut grave?

III

I have done with blame, I have risen from the cold earth,
Where night and day my forehead has known the clay.
With faltering steps I have passed out to the sun.

Now in the sight of all I stand, that all may know
(For I myself will praise thee and prove their words)
How great was thy wisdom in turning away from me.

Who that has drunken wine will keep the lees?
Who that has slain a man wait for revenge?
Who that has had his desire of a woman will stay?

Farewell, O Curithir, let thy soul be saved!
I have not found a thing that is dearer to thee.
In the eyes of God is it priceless? Who can say!

My soul is a thing of little worth unto God:
Of less worth unto thee, O Curithir, than my love.
And unto me so small I flung it beneath thy feet.

IV

If the dark earth hold a Power that is not God
I pray it to bind up memory lest I die.

There was a day when Curithir loved me, now it is gone.
It was I that sundered his love from me, I myself;
Or it was God who struck me with madness and mocked.

If the dark earth hold a Power that is not God
I pray it to hide me forever away from His face.

V

All things are outworn now—grief is dead,
And passion has fallen from me like a withered leaf.
Little it were to me now though Curithir were beside me:
Though he should pass I would not turn my head.
My heart is like a stone in my body.
All I have grasped I loose again from my hands.

Florence Kiper Frank

THE JEW TO JESUS

O man of my own people, I alone
Among these alien ones can know thy face,
I who have felt the kinship of our race
Burn in me as I sit where they intone
Thy praises—those who, striving to make known
A God for sacrifice, have missed the grace
Of thy sweet human meaning in its place,
Thou who art of our blood-bond and our own.

Are we not sharers of thy Passion? Yea,
In spirit-anguish closely by thy side
We have drained the bitter cup and, tortured, felt
With thee the bruising of each heavy welt.
In every land is our Gethsemane—
A thousand times have we been crucified.

THE MOVIES

She knows a cheap release
    From worry and from pain—
The cowboys spur their horses
    Over the unending plain.

The tenement rooms are small;
    Their walls press on the brain.
Oh, the dip of the galloping horses
    On the limitless wind-swept plain!

SLEEP THE MOTHER

Sleep, the mother,
Has taken her over.
She has slipped from my arms
Into the arms of this other,
Who has touched her softly,
Who has flushed her with dreaming.

This is not the same
Sleep who gathers men
Heavy with labor,
Women drugged with pleasure.
This is the mother
Of little children only,
Moving as a wind
From white spaces,
Flushing their faces
With a soft flame, holily;
To whom the mothers of the earth
Give up their children
Joyously, with a clean gladness,
With only a little sadness,
Such as hurts mothers
For their mortality.
For they remember also,
Remembering swiftly,
Death too is a mother!

But now her lashes curl delicately,
The blue veins of her eyelids
Show sweetly in the soft skin,
Her red mouth droops slowly. . . .

Hovering over
The child she is holding
Is Sleep, the white mother,
With arms enfolding!

Robert Frost

MENDING WALL

Something there is that doesn't love a wall,
That sends the frozen ground-swell under it,
And spills the upper boulders in the sun;
And makes gaps even two can pass abreast.
The work of hunters is another thing:
I have come after them and made repair

Where they have left not one stone on stone,
But they would have the rabbit out of hiding,
To please the yelping dogs. The gaps I mean,
No one has seen them made or heard them made,
But at spring mending-time we find them there.
I let my neighbor know beyond the hill;
And on a day we meet to walk the line
And set the wall between us once again.
We keep the wall between us as we go—
To each the boulders that have fallen to each.
And some are loaves and some so nearly balls
We have to use a spell to make them balance:
"Stay where you are until our backs are turned!"
We wear our fingers rough with handling them.
Oh, just another kind of out-door game,
One on a side—it comes to little more.
There where it is we do not need the wall:
He is all pine and I am apple orchard.
My apple trees will never get across
And eat the cones under his pines, I tell him.
He only says, "Good fences make good neighbors."
Spring is the mischief in me, and I wonder
If I could put a notion in his head:
"Why do they make good neighbors? Isn't it
Where there are cows? But here there are no cows.
Before I build a wall I'd ask to know
What I was walling in or walling out,
And to whom I was like to give offence.
Something there is that doesn't love a wall,
That wants it down." I could say "Elves" to him,
But it's not elves exactly, and I'd rather
He said it for himself. I see him there
Bringing a stone grasped firmly by the top
In each hand, like an old-stone savage armed.
He moves in darkness as it seems to me,
Not of woods only and the shade of trees.
He will not go behind his father's saying,
And he likes having thought of it so well
He says again, "Good fences make good neighbors."

AFTER APPLE-PICKING

My long two-pointed ladder's sticking through a tree
Toward heaven still,
And there's a barrel that I didn't fill
Beside it, and there may be two or three
Apples I didn't pick upon some bough.
But I am done with apple-picking now.
Essence of winter sleep is on the night,
The scent of apples: I am drowsing off.
I cannot rub the strangeness from my sight
I got from looking through a pane of glass
I skimmed this morning from the drinking trough
And held against the world of hoary grass.
It melted, and I let it fall and break.
But I was well
Upon my way to sleep before it fell,
And I could tell
What form my dreaming was about to take.
Magnified apples appear and disappear,
Stem end and blossom end,
And every fleck of russet showing clear.
My instep arch not only keeps the ache,
It keeps the pressure of a ladder-round.
I feel the ladder sway as the boughs bend.
And I keep hearing from the cellar bin
The rumbling sound
Of load on load of apples coming in.
For I have had too much
Of apple-picking: I am overtired
Of the great harvest I myself desired.
There were ten thousand thousand fruit to touch,
Cherish in hand, lift down, and not let fall.
For all
That struck the earth,
No matter if not bruised or spiked with stubble,
Went surely to the cider-apple heap
As of no worth.
One can see what will trouble

This sleep of mine, whatever sleep it is.
Were he not gone,
The woodchuck could say whether it's like his
Long sleep, as I describe its coming on,
Or just some human sleep.

MY NOVEMBER GUEST

My Sorrow, when she's here with me,
   Thinks these dark days of autumn rain
Are beautiful as days can be.
She loves the bare, the withered tree;
   She walks the sodden pasture lane.

Her pleasure will not let me stay.
   She talks and I am fain to list:
She's glad the birds are gone away,
She's glad her simple worsted grey
   Is silver now with clinging mist.

The desolate deserted trees,
   The faded earth, the heavy sky—
The beauties she so truly sees—
She thinks I have no eye for these,
   And vexes me for reason why.

Not yesterday I learned to know
   The love of bare November days
Before the coming of the snow;
But it were vain to tell her so,
   And they are better for her praise.

MOWING

There was never a sound beside the wood but one,
And that was my long scythe whispering to the ground.
What was it it whispered? I knew not well myself;
Perhaps it was something about the heat of the sun,
Something, perhaps, about the lack of sound—
And that was why it whispered and did not speak.

It was no dream of the gift of idle hours,
Or easy gold at the hand of fay or elf:
Anything more than the truth would have seemed too weak
To the earnest love that laid the swale in rows—
Not without feeble-pointed spikes of flowers
(Pale orchises)—and scared a bright green snake.
The fact is the sweetest dream that labor knows.
My long scythe whispered and left the hay to make.

STORM FEAR

When the wind works against us in the dark,
And pelts with snow
The lower chamber window on the east,
And whispers with a sort of stifled bark,
The beast,
"Come out! Come out!"—
It costs no inward struggle not to go,
Ah, no!
I count our strength,
Two and a child,
Those of us not asleep subdued to mark
How the cold creeps as the fire dies at length—
How drifts are piled,
Dooryard and road ungraded,
Till even the comforting barn grows far away;
And my heart owns a doubt
Whether 'tis in us to arise with day
And save ourselves unaided.

GOING FOR WATER

The well was dry beside the door,
    And so we went with pail and can
Across the fields behind the house
    To seek the brook if still it ran;

Not loth to have excuse to go,
    Because the autumn eve was fair

(Though chill) because the fields were ours,
    And by the brook our woods were there.

We ran as if to meet the moon
    That slowly dawned behind the trees—
The barren boughs without the leaves,
    Without the birds, without the breeze.

But once within the wood, we paused
    Like gnomes that hid us from the moon,
Ready to run to hiding new
    With laughter when she found us soon.

Each laid on other a staying hand
    To listen ere we dared to look,
And in the hush we joined to make
    We heard—we knew we heard—the brook.

A note as from a single place,
    A slender tinkling fall that made
Now drops that floated on the pool
    Like pearls, and now a silver blade.

THE CODE

There were three in the meadow by the brook,
Gathering up windrows, piling cocks of hay,
With an eye always lifted toward the west,
Where an irregular sun-bordered cloud
Darkly advanced with a perpetual dagger
Flickering across its bosom. Suddenly
One helper, thrusting pitchfork in the ground,
Marched himself off the field and home. One stayed.
The town-bred farmer failed to understand.
"What is there wrong?"
                                "Something you just now said."
"What did I say?"
                                "About our taking pains."

"To cock the hay?—because it's going to shower?
I said that nearly half an hour ago.
I said it to myself as much as you."

"You didn't know. But James is one big fool.
He thought you meant to find fault with his work.
That's what the average farmer would have meant.
James would take time, of course, to chew it over
Before he acted; he's just got round to act."

"He *is* a fool if that's the way he takes me."

"Don't let it bother you. You've found out something.
The hand that knows his business won't be told
To do work faster or better—those two things.
I'm as particular as anyone:
Most likely I'd have served you just the same.
But I know you don't understand our ways.
You were just talking what was in your mind,
What was in all our minds, and you weren't hinting.
Tell you a story of what happened once.
I was up here in Salem, at a man's
Named Sanders, with a gang of four or five,
Doing the haying. No one liked the boss.
He was one of the kind sports call a spider,
All wiry arms and legs that spread out wavy
From a humped body nigh as big's a biscuit.
But work!—that man could work, especially
If by so doing he could get more work
Out of his hired help. I'm not denying
He was hard on himself: I couldn't find
That he kept any hours—not for himself.
Day-light and lantern-light were one of him:
I've heard him pounding in the barn all night.
But what he liked was someone to encourage;
Them that he couldn't lead he'd get behind
And drive, the way you can, you know, in mowing—
Keep at their heels and threaten to mow their legs off.
I'd seen about enough of his bulling tricks—
We call that bulling. I'd been watching him.
So when he paired off with me in the hayfield
To load the load, thinks I, look out for trouble!
I built the load and topped it off; old Sanders
Combed it down with the rake and says, 'O. K.'

Everything went well till we reached the barn
With a big catch to empty in a bay.
You understand that meant the easy job
For the man up on top of throwing down
The hay and rolling it off wholesale,
Where on a mow it would have been slow lifting.
You wouldn't think a fellow'd need much urging
Under these circumstances, would you now?
But the old fool seizes his fork in both hands,
And looking up bewhiskered out of the pit,
Shouts like an army captain. 'Let her come!'
Thinks I, d'ye mean it? 'What was that you said?'
I asked out loud, so's there'd be no mistake.
'Did you say, let her come?' 'Yes, let her come.'
He said it over, but he said it softer.
Never you say a thing like that to a man,
Not if he values what he is. God, I'd as soon
Murdered him as left out his middle name.
I'd built the load and knew just where to find it.
Two or three forkfuls I picked lightly round for,
Like meditating, and then I just dug in
And dumped the rackful on him in ten lots.
I looked over the side once in the dust
And caught sight of him treading-water-like,
Keeping his head above. 'Damn ye,' I says,
'That gets ye!' He squeaked like a squeezed rat.

That was the last I saw or heard of him.
I cleaned the rack and drove out to cool off.
As I sat mopping the hayseed from my neck,
And sort of waiting to be asked about it,
One of the boys sings out, 'Where's the old man?'
'I left him in the barn, under the hay.
If ye want him ye can go and dig him out.'
They realized, from the way I swobbed my neck
More than was needed, something must be up.
They headed for the barn—I stayed where I was.
They told me afterward: First they forked hay,
A lot of it, out into the barn floor.

Nothing! They listened for him. Not a rustle!
I guess they thought I'd spiked him in the temple
Before I buried him, or I couldn't have managed.
They excavated more. 'Go keep his wife
Out of the barn.'
             Some one looked in a window;
And curse me, if he wasn't in the kitchen,
Slumped way down in a chair, with both his feet
Stuck in the oven, the hottest day that summer.
He looked so clean disgusted from behind
There was no one that dared to stir him up
Or let him know that he was being looked at.
Apparently I hadn't buried him
(I may have knocked him down); but my just trying
To bury him had hurt his dignity.
He had gone to the house so's not to meet me.
He kept away from us all afternoon.
We tended to his hay. We saw him out
After a while picking peas in his garden:
He couldn't keep away from doing something."

"Weren't you relieved to find he wasn't dead?"

"No!—and yet I don't know—it's hard to say.
I went about to kill him fair enough."

"You took an awkward way. Did he discharge you?"

"Discharge me? No! He knew I did just right." . . .

A HILLSIDE THAW

To think to know the country, and not know
The hillside on the day the sun lets go
Ten million silver lizards out of snow.
As often as I've seen it done before,
I can't pretend to tell the way it's done.
It looks as if some magic of the sun
Lifted the rug that bred them on the floor,
And the light breaking on them made them run.

But if I thought to stop the wet stampede,
And caught one silver lizard by the tail,
And put my foot on one without avail,
And threw myself wet-elbowed and wet-kneed
In front of twenty others' wriggling speed—
In the confusion of them all aglitter,
And birds that joined in the excited fun
By doubling and redoubling song and twitter—
I have no doubt I'd end by holding none.
It takes the moon for this. The sun's a wizard,
By all I tell; but so's the moon a witch.
From the high west she makes a gentle cast,
And suddenly, without a jerk or twitch,
She has her spell on every single lizard.
I fancied, when I looked at eight o'clock,
The swarm still ran and scuttled just as fast.
The moon was waiting for her chill effect.
I looked at ten: the swarm was turned to rock
In every life-like posture of the swarm,
Transfixed on mountain slopes almost erect;
Across each other and side by side they lay.
The spell that so could hold them as they were
Was wrought through trees without a breach of storm
To make a leaf, if there had been one, stir.
It was the moon's. She held them until day,
One lizard at the end of every ray.
The thought of my attempting such a stay!

AN OLD MAN'S WINTER NIGHT

All out-of-doors looked darkly in at him
Through the thin frost, almost in separate stars,
That gathers on the pane in empty rooms.
What kept his eyes from giving back the gaze
Was the lamp tilted near them in his hand.
What kept him from remembering what it was
That brought him to that creaking room was age.
He stood with barrels round him—at a loss;

And having scared the cellar under him
In clomping there, he scared it once again
In clomping off; and scared the outer night,
Which has its sounds, familiar, like the roar
Of trees and crack of branches—common things,
But nothing so like beating on a box.
A light he was to no one but himself
Where now he sat, concerned with he knew what;
A quiet light, and then not even that.
He consigned to the moon, such as she was,
So late-arising, to the broken moon—
As better than the sun in any case
For such a charge—his snow upon the roof,
His icicles along the wall to keep;
And slept. The log that shifted with a jolt
Once in the stove, disturbed him and he shifted,
And eased his heavy breathing; but still slept.
One aged man—one man—can't fill a house,
A farm, a countryside; or if he can,
It's thus he does it of a winter night.

FIRE AND ICE

Some say the world will end in fire;
Some say in ice.
From what I've tasted of desire
I hold with those who favor fire.
But if it had to perish twice,
I think I know enough of hate
To know that for destruction ice
Is also great
And would suffice.

THE AIM WAS SONG

Before man came to blow it right
   The wind once blew itself untaught,
And did its loudest day and night
   In any rough place where it caught.

Man came to tell it what was wrong:
  It hadn't found the place to blow;
It blew too hard—the aim was song.
  And listen—how it ought to go!

He took a little in his mouth,
  And held it long enough for north
To be converted into south,
  And then by measure blew it forth.

By measure. It was word and note,
  The wind the wind had meant to be—
A little through the lips and throat.
  The aim was song—the wind could see.

THE HILL WIFE

LONELINESS

Her Word

One ought not to have to care
  So much as you and I
Care when the birds come round the house
  To seem to say good-bye;

Or care so much when they come back
  With whatever it is they sing;
The truth being we are as much
  Too glad for the one thing

As we are too sad for the other here—
  With birds that fill their breasts
But with each other and themselves,
  And their built or driven nests.

HOUSE FEAR

Always—I tell you this they learned—
Always at night when they returned
To the lonely house from far away

To lamps unlighted and fire gone gray,
They learned to rattle the lock and key
To give whatever might chance to be
Warning and time to be off in flight:
And preferring the out- to the in-door night,
They learned to leave the house-door wide
Until they had lit the lamp inside.

THE SMILE

Her Word

I didn't like the way he went away.
That smile!—it never came of being gay.
Still he smiled—did you see him?—I was sure!
Perhaps because we gave him only bread
And the wretch knew from that that we were poor.
Perhaps because he let us give instead
Of seizing from us as he might have seized.
Perhaps he mocked at us for being wed,
Or being very young (and he was pleased
To have a vision of us old and dead).
I wonder how far down the road he's got.
He's watching from the woods as like as not.

THE OFT-REPEATED DREAM

She had no saying dark enough
    For the dark pine that kept
Forever trying the window-latch
    Of the room where they slept.

The tireless but ineffectual hands
    That with every futile pass
Made the great tree seem as a little bird
    Before the mystery of glass!

It never had been inside the room,
    And only one of the two
Was afraid in an oft-repeated dream
    Of what the tree might do.

THE IMPULSE

It was too lonely for her there,
    And too wild;
And since there were but two of them
    And no child,

And work was little in the house,
    She was free,
And followed where he furrowed field,
    Or felled tree.

She rested on a log and tossed
    The fresh chips,
With a song only to herself
    On her lips.

And once she went to break a bough
    Of black alder.
She strayed so far she scarcely heard
    When he called her—

And didn't answer—didn't speak—
    Or return.
She stood, and then she ran and hid
    In the fern.

He never found her, though he looked
    Everywhere,
And he asked at her mother's house
    Was she there.

Sudden and swift and light as that—
    The ties gave,
And he learned of finalities
    Besides the grave.

ON LOOKING UP BY CHANCE AT
THE CONSTELLATIONS

You'll wait a long, long time for anything much
To happen in heaven beyond the floats of cloud
And the Northern Lights that run like tingling nerves.
The sun and moon get crossed, but they never touch,
Nor strike out fire from each other, nor crash out loud.
The planets seem to interfere in their curves.
But nothing ever happens, no harm is done.
We may as well go patiently on with our life,
And look elsewhere than to stars and moon and sun
For the shocks and changes we need to keep us sane.
It is true the longest drouth will end in rain,
The longest peace in China will end in strife.
Still it wouldn't reward the watcher to stay awake
In hopes of seeing the calm of heaven break
On his particular time and personal sight.
That calm seems certainly safe to last tonight.

ONCE BY THE PACIFIC

The shattered water made a misty din.
Great waves looked over others coming in,
And thought of doing something to the shore
That water never did to land before.
The clouds were low and hairy in the skies,
Like locks blown forward in the gleam of eyes.
You could not tell, and yet it looked as if
The shore was lucky in being backed by cliff,
The cliff in being backed by continent;
It looked as if a night of dark intent
Was coming, and not only a night, an age.
Someone had better be prepared for rage.
There would be more than ocean-water broken
Before God's last *Put out the Light* was spoken.

ACQUAINTED WITH THE NIGHT

I have been one acquainted with the night.
I have walked out in rain—and back in rain.
I have outwalked the furthest city light.

I have looked down the saddest city lane.
I have passed by the watchman on his beat
And dropped my eyes, unwilling to explain.

I have stood still and stopped the sound of feet
When far away an interrupted cry
Came over houses from another street,

But not to call me back or say goodbye;
And further still at an unearthly height,
One luminary clock against the sky

Proclaimed the time was neither wrong nor right.
I have been one acquainted with the night.

STOPPING BY WOODS ON A SNOWY EVENING

Whose woods these are I think I know.
His house is in the village, though;
He will not see me stopping here
To watch his woods fill up with snow.

My little horse must think it queer
To stop without a farmhouse near
Between the woods and frozen lake
The darkest evening of the year.

He gives his harness bells a shake
To ask if there is some mistake.
The only other sounds the sweep
Of easy winds and downy flake.

The woods are lovely, dark and deep.
But I have promises to keep,
And miles to go before I sleep—
And miles to go before I sleep.

Wilfrid Wilson Gibson

COLOR

A blue-black Nubian plucking oranges
At Jaffa by a sea of malachite,
In red tarboosh, green sash, and flowing white
Burnous—among the shadowy memories
That haunt me yet by these bleak northern seas
He lives forever in my eyes' delight,
Bizarre, superb in young immortal might—
A god of old barbaric mysteries.

Maybe he lived a life of lies and lust,
Maybe his bones are now but scattered dust;
Yet for a moment he was life supreme
Exultant and unchallenged: and my rhyme
Would set him safely out of reach of time
In that old heaven where things are what they seem.

OBLIVION

Near the great pyramid, unshadowed, white,
With apex piercing the white noon-day blaze,
Swathed in white robes beneath the blinding rays,
Lie sleeping Bedouins drenched in white-hot light.
About them, searing to the tingling sight,
Swims the white dazzle of the desert ways
Where the sense shudders, witless and adaze,
In a white void with neither depth nor height.

Within the black core of the pyramid,
Beneath the weight of sunless centuries,
Lapt in dead night King Cheops lies asleep:
Yet, in the darkness of his chamber hid,
He knows no black oblivion more deep
Than the blind white oblivion of noon skies.

TENANTS

Suddenly, out of dark and leafy ways,
We came upon the little house asleep
In cold blind stillness, shadowless and deep,
In the white magic of the full moon-blaze:
Strangers without the gate, we stood agaze,
Fearful to break that quiet, and to creep
Into the house that had been ours to keep
Through a long year of happy nights and days.

So unfamiliar in the white moon-gleam,
So old and ghostly like a house of dream
It seemed, that over us there stole the dread
That even as we watched it, side by side,
The ghosts of lovers, who had lived and died
Within its walls, were sleeping in our bed.

ON HAMPSTEAD HEATH

Against the green flame of the hawthorn-tree,
His scarlet tunic burns;
And livelier than the green sap's mantling glee
The spring fire tingles through him headily
As quivering he turns

And stammers out the old amazing tale
Of youth and April weather;
While she, with half-breathed jests that, sobbing, fail,
Sits, tight-lipped, quaking, eager-eyed and pale
Beneath her purple feather.

BATTLE

THE GOING

He's gone.
I do not understand.
I only know
That as he turned to go

And waved his hand,
In his young eyes a sudden glory shone:
And I was dazzled by a sunset glow,
And he was gone.

HIT

Out of the sparkling sea
I drew my tingling body clear, and lay
On a low ledge the livelong summer day,
Basking, and watching lazily
White sails in Falmouth Bay.
My body seemed to burn
Salt in the sun that drenched it through and through,
Till every particle glowed clean and new
And slowly seemed to turn
To lucent amber in a world of blue . . .

I felt a sudden wrench—
A trickle of warm blood—
And found that I was sprawling in the mud
Among the dead men in the trench.

THE HOUSEWIFE

She must go back, she said,
Because she'd not had time to make the bed—
We'd hurried her away
So roughly . . . and for all that we could say,
She broke from us, and passed
Into the night, shells falling thick and fast.

HILL-BORN

I sometimes wonder if it's really true
I ever knew
Another life
Than this unending strife
With unseen enemies in lowland mud;
And wonder if my blood

Thrilled ever to the tune
Of clean winds blowing through an April noon
Mile after sunny mile
On the green ridges of the Windy Gile.

THE FEAR

I do not fear to die
'Neath the open sky,
To meet death in the fight
Face to face, upright.

But when at last we creep
Into a hole to sleep,
I tremble, cold with dread,
Lest I wake up dead.

Horace Gregory

PRISONER'S SONG

Oh, Mary's lovelier than anything that grows
out of spring trees that stir
April when my mind goes
around and over her.

I love her more than skies bright with the wind and sun,
and all my thoughts arise
to travel, one by one,
into her lips and eyes.

She shuts me in her; she holds all my blood and brain
under her lock and key.
Christ, I'm jail in again—
she'll never let me free!

Sometimes, my blind dreams float far—like a wanderer
I go away, remote;
then I return to her
with panic in my throat.

INTERIOR: THE SUBURBS

There is no rest for the mind
in a small house. It moves, looking for God,
with a mysterious eye fixed on the bed,
into a cracked egg at breakfast,
looking for glory in an arm-chair,
or simply noting the facts of life
in a fly asleep on the ceiling.

The mind, sunk in quiet places,
(like old heroes) sleeps no more,
but walks abroad in a slouch hat
performing adultery at violent street corners;
then, trembling, returns,
sadly directs its mysterious eye
into a coffee-cup. There is no rest—
for there are many miles to walk in the small house,
traveling past the same chairs, the same tables,
the same glassy portraits on the walls,
flowing into darkness.

There is no victory in the mind,
but desperate valor,
shattering the four walls,
disintegrating human love,
until the iron-lidded mysterious eye
(lowered carefully with the frail body
under churchyard gardens)
stares upward, luminous, inevitable,
piercing solar magnitudes
on a fine morning.

UNLESS I AM CAREFUL

Unless I am careful,
night will come into me
before I know the quick sun
has fallen through the sky

and into the earth
and into the sea.

Night caught in me,
never to leave me
where streets go by
filled with stark lights
and metal noise of cats
small and terrible,
where none dare to go
unless they are careful . . .

Sometimes I know
That night was always in me,
turning with broad white rays
under the moon,
reaching through long green days
before my birth-time
where things made sharp noise
with the dark around them:
and it was terrible,
high as steel towers
built upon tall rock
in the black hours
when drunken men work
with the night in them
(they poised and careful!)

With the night in me,
I shall go into it
deeper than rocks are,
deeper than where the worms
follow Eurydice,
deeper than anyone;
dead as King Œdipus
who walked without the sun,
deeper than blood of war
plunged through the earth,
deeper than bones of us

plucked from our ancestors,
now grown infallible . . .

Unless I am careful,
all night within me
shall fill with the naked eyes
torn from King Œdipus,
there with the rolling head
of ripened Jocasta,
rolling where branches swing
from an oak tree. . . .

And I will step aside
from rails of iron
(where poised and high in air,
men talk to steel cranes
that rise and stride
over the far streets)—
then shall I fall from them
who sing my requiem,
deeper than songs are,
unless I am careful
                    now
                        careful!

Hazel Hall

TWO SEWING

The wind is sewing with needles of rain;
With shining needles of rain
It stitches into the thin
Cloth of earth—in,
In, in, in.
Oh, the wind has often sewed with me!—
One, two, three.

Spring must have fine things
To wear, like other springs.
Of silken green the grass must be
Embroidered. *One and two and three.*
Then every crocus must be made
So subtly as to seem afraid
Of lifting color from the ground;
And after crocuses the round
Heads of tulips, and all the fair
Intricate garb that Spring will wear.
The wind must sew with needles of rain,
With shining needles of rain
Stitching into the thin
Cloth of earth—in,
In, in, in—
For all the springs of futurity.
One, two, three.

INSTRUCTION

My hands that guide a needle
In their turn are led
Relentlessly and deftly,
As a needle leads a thread.

Other hands are teaching
My needle; when I sew
I feel the cool thin fingers
Of hands I do not know.

They urge my needle onward;
They smooth my seams, until
The worry of my stitches
Smothers in their skill.

All the tired women,
Who sewed their lives away,
Speak in my deft fingers
As I sew today.

MY NEEDLE SAYS

My needle says: Don't be young,
Holding visions in your eyes,
Tasting laughter on your tongue!
Be very old and very wise,
And sew a good seam up and down
In white cloth, red cloth, blue and brown.

My needle says: What is youth
But eyes drunken with the sun,
Seeing farther than the truth;
Lips that call, hands that shun
The many seams they have to do
In white cloth, red cloth, brown and blue!

ONE BY ONE

One by one, one by one,
Stitches of the hours run
Through the fine seams of the day;
Till like a garment it is done
    And laid away.

One by one the days go by,
And suns climb up and down the sky;
One by one their seams are run—
As Time's untiring fingers ply,
    And life is done.

HUNGER

I have known life's hunger,
Though by other name;
It has been dream and singing,
Faith and the whip of shame.

Not until I listened
To sounds of a world swept by,
Did I learn to hear my own heart
And hear all life in its cry.

Not until the hunger
Of all the world was blown
Like a wind against my window,
Could I name my own.

And I have learned that only
This is not proved vain:
Hunger by which a world is fed
As I am fed by pain.

ON THE STREET

Often I watch the walkers on the street.
A sea-bird does not lift its sinuous wing
To share the grey wind's wide adventuring
With grace more marvelous than moving feet.
Feet young or wide, defiant and discreet,
With an amazing ease balance and swing,
As in each footstep's even echoing
The slow triumph of time is made complete.

And sometimes I forget what time has told,
Hearing beneath the thud of feet a sound
Articulate as the silence of the sea.
I hear the furtive effort on the ground
Of those who strive to find and struggle to hold
The meaning of their own identity.

SUBMERGENCE

The only loneliness is the wind's,
The only sorrow is the sea's.
Why must a heart ache all life long
To learn such simple truths as these?

Lonely hours burn out like candles,
And sorrow is a leaf swept by;
But the wind is lonely forever and forever,
And the sea must hush an eternal cry.

ADMONITION BEFORE GRIEF

Let the night weep on your hand;
Let the night's tears, dark and fine,
Slip down your fingers; understand
This grief is neither yours nor mine.

There is a reason for the night.
Why weep for dark so luminous
That it is only tempered light?
Rather the night must weep for us.

Reach out your fingers to the cold
Blackness of space before tomorrow.
Lift up your hand, and night will hold
And cool it with its lovely sorrow.

Thomas Hardy

SHE HEARS THE STORM

There was a time in former years—
    While my roof-tree was his—
When I should have been distressed by fears
    At such a night as this.

I should have murmured anxiously,
    "The pricking rain strikes cold;
His road is bare of hedge or tree,
    And he is getting old."

But now the fitful chimney-roar,
    The drone of Thorncombe trees,
The Froom in flood upon the moor,
    The mud of Mellstock Leaze,

The candle slanting sooty wick'd,
    The thuds upon the thatch,
The eaves-drops on the window flicked,
    The clacking garden-hatch,

And what they mean to wayfarers,
    I scarcely heed or mind;
He has won that storm-tight roof of hers
    Which Earth grants all her kind.

THE VOICE

Woman much missed, how you call to me, call to me,
    Saying that now you are not as you were
When you had changed from the one who was all to me,
    But as at first, when our day was fair.

Can it be you that I hear? Let me view you then,
    Standing as when I drew near to the town
Where you would wait for me: yes, as I knew you then,
    Even to the original air-blue gown!

Or is it only the breeze, in its listlessness
    Travelling across the wet mead to me here,
You being ever consigned to existlessness,
    Heard no more again far or near?

Thus I; faltering forward,
    Leaves around me falling,
Wind oozing thin through the thorn from norward
    And the woman calling.

IN THE MOONLIGHT

"O lonely workman, standing there
In a dream, why do you stare and stare
At her grave, as no other grave there were?

"If your great gaunt eyes so importune
Her soul by the shine of this corpse-cold moon,
Maybe you'll raise her phantom soon!"

"Why, fool, it is what I would rather see
Than all the living folk there be;
But alas, there is no such joy for me!"

"Ah—she was one you loved, no doubt,
Through good and evil, through rain and drought,
And when she passed, all your sun went out?"

"Nay: she was the woman I did not love,
Whom all the others were ranked above,
Whom during her life I thought nothing of."

THE MAN HE KILLED

"Had he and I but met
    By some old ancient inn,
We should have sat us down to wet
    Right many a nipperkin!

"But ranged as infantry,
    And staring face to face,
I shot at him as he at me,
    And killed him in his place.

"I shot him dead because—
    Because he was my foe,
Just so: my foe of course he was;
    That's clear enough; although

"He thought he'd 'list, perhaps,
    Off-hand like—just as I;
Was out of work, had sold his traps—
    No other reason why.

"Yes; quaint and curious war is!
    You shoot a fellow down
You'd treat if met where any bar is,
    Or help to half-a-crown."

IN TIME OF "THE BREAKING OF NATIONS"

Only a man harrowing clods
    In a slow silent walk,
With an old horse that stumbles and nods
    Half asleep as they stalk.

Only thin smoke without flame
    From the heaps of couch-grass;
Yet this will go on the same
    Though dynasties pass.

Yonder a maid and her wight
    Come whispering by;
War's annals will cloud into night
    Ere their story die.

THE TWO HOUSES

In the heart of night,
    When farers were not near,
The left house said to the house on the right,
"I have marked your rise, O smart newcomer here!"

The other replied:
    "Newcomer here I am,
Hence stronger than you with your cracked old hide,
Loose casements, wormy beams, and doors that jam.

"Modern my wood,
    My hangings fair of hue;
While my windows open as they should
And water-pipes thread all my chambers through.

"Your gear is grey,
    Your face wears furrows untold."
"Yours might," said the other, " if you held, brother,
The Presences from aforetime that I hold.

"You have not known
    Men's lives, deaths, toils, and teens;
You are but a heap of stick and stone:
A new house has no sense of the have-beens.

"Void as a drum
    You stand: I am packed with these;
Though, strangely, living dwellers who come
See not the phantoms all my substance sees.

"Visible in the morning
  Stand they, when dawn crawls in;
  Visible at night; yet hint or warning
Of these thin elbowers few of the inmates win.

  "Babes new brought forth
    Obsess my rooms; straight-stretched
  Lank corpses, ere outborne to earth;
Yea, throng they as when first from the void upfetched!

  "Dancers and singers
    Throb in me now as once;
  Rich-noted throats and gossamered flingers
Of heels; the learned in love-lore, and the dunce,

  "Note here within
    The bridgroom and the bride,
  Who smile and greet their friends and kin,
And down my stairs depart for tracts untried.

  "Where such in be,
    A dwelling's character
  Takes theirs, and a vague semblancy
To them in all its limbs and light and atmosphere.

  "Yet the blind folk,
    My tenants, who come and go
  In the flesh mid these, with souls unwoke,
Of such sylph-like surrounders do not know."

  "Will the day come,"
    Said the new-built, awestruck, faint,
  "When I shall lodge shades dim and dumb,
And with such spectral guests become acquaint?"

  "That will it, boy;
    Such shades will people thee,
  Each in his misery, irk, or joy,
And print on thee their presences as on me!"

DuBose Heyward

THE MOUNTAIN WOMAN

Among the sullen peaks she stood at bay
And paid life's hard account from her small store.
Knowing the code of mountain wives, she bore
The burden of the days without a sigh;
And, sharp against the somber winter sky,
I saw her drive her steers afield each day.

Hers was the hand that sunk the furrows deep
Across the rocky, grudging southern slope.
At first youth left her face, and later hope;
Yet through each mocking spring and barren fall,
She reared her lusty brood, and gave them all
That gladder wives and mothers love to keep.

And when the sheriff shot her eldest son
Beside his still, so well she knew her part,
She gave no healing tears to ease her heart;
But took the blow upstanding, with her eyes
As drear and bitter as the winter skies.
Seeing her then, I thought that she had won.

But yesterday her man returned too soon
And found her tending, with a reverent touch,
One scarlet bloom; and, having drunk too much,
He snatched its flame and quenched it in the dirt.
Then, like a creature with a mortal hurt,
She fell, and wept away the afternoon.

A YOKE OF STEERS

A heave of mighty shoulders to the yoke,
Square patient heads, and flaring sweep of horn;
The darkness swirling down beneath their feet
Where sleeping valleys stir and feel the dawn;
Uncouth and primal, on and up they sway,
Taking the summit in a drench of day.

The night-winds volley upward bitter-sweet,
And the dew shatters to a rainbow spray
Under the slow-moving cloven feet.

There is a power here that grips the mind—
A force repressed and inarticulate,
Slow as the swing of centuries, as blind
As Destiny, and as deliberate.

They will arrive in their appointed hour
Unhurried by the goad of lesser wills,
Bearing vast burdens on.
                    They are the great
Unconquerable spirit of these hills.

Ralph Hodgson

EVE

Eve, with her basket, was
Deep in the bells and grass,
Wading in bells and grass
Up to her knees,
Picking a dish of sweet
Berries and plums to eat,
Down in the bells and grass
Under the trees.

Mute as a mouse in a
Corner the cobra lay,
Curled round a bough of the
Cinnamon tall . . .
Now to get even and
Humble proud heaven and
Now was the moment or
Never at all.

"Eva!" Each syllable
Light as a flower fell,

"Eva!" he whispered the
Wondering maid,
Soft as a bubble sung
Out of a linnet's lung,
Soft and most silverly
"Eva!" he said.

Picture that orchard sprite,
Eve, with her body white,
Supple and smooth to her
Slim finger tips,
Wondering, listening,
Listening, wondering,
Eve with a berry
Half-way to her lips.

Oh had our simple Eve
Seen through the make-believe!
Had she but known the
Pretender he was!
Out of the boughs he came,
Whispering still her name,
Tumbling in twenty rings
Into the grass.

Here was the strangest pair
In the world anywhere,
Eve in the bells and grass
Kneeling, and he
Telling his story low . . .
Singing birds saw them go
Down the dark path to
The Blasphemous Tree.

Oh what a clatter when
Titmouse and Jenny Wren
Saw him successful and
Taking his leave!
How the birds rated him,
How they all hated him!

How they all pitied
Poor motherless Eve!

Picture her crying
Outside in the lane,
Eve, with no dish of sweet
Berries and plums to eat,
Haunting the gate of the
Orchard in vain . . .
Picture the lewd delight
Under the hill tonight—
"Eva!" the toast goes round,
"Eva!" again.

TIME, YOU OLD GIPSY MAN

Time, you old gipsy man,
    Will you not stay,
Put up your caravan
    Just for one day?

All things I'll give you
Will you be my guest,
Bells for your jennet
Of silver the best,
Goldsmiths shall beat you
A great golden ring,
Peacocks shall bow to you,
Little boys sing,
Oh, and sweet girls will
Festoon you with may,
Time, you old gipsy,
Why hasten away?
Last week in Babylon,
Last night in Rome,
Morning, and in the crush
Under Paul's dome;
You tighten your rein,
Only a moment,

And off once again—
Off to some city
Now blind in the womb,
Off to another
Ere that's in the tomb.

Time, you old gipsy man,
    Will you not stay,
Put up your caravan
    Just for one day?

THE MYSTERY

He came and took me by the hand
    Up to a red rose tree,
He kept His meaning to Himself
    But gave a rose to me.

I did not pray Him to lay bare
    The mystery to me;
Enough the rose was Heaven to smell,
    And His own face to see.

STUPIDITY STREET

I saw with open eyes
    Singing birds sweet
Sold in the shops
    For the people to eat,
Sold in the shops of
    Stupidity Street.

I saw in vision
    The worm in the wheat,
And in the shops nothing
    For people to eat;
Nothing for sale in
    Stupidity Street.

Helen Hoyt

ELLIS PARK

Little park that I pass through,
I carry off a piece of you
Every morning hurrying down
To my work-day in the town;
Carry you for country there
To make the city ways more fair.
I take your trees,
And your breeze,
Your greenness,
Your cleanness,
Some of your shade, some of your sky,
Some of your calm as I go by;
Your flowers to trim
The pavements grim;
Your space for room in the jostled street,
And grass for carpet to my feet;
Your fountains take and sweet bird calls
To sing me from my office walls.
All that I can see
I carry off with me.
But you never miss my theft,
So much treasure you have left.
As I find you, fresh at morning,
So I find you, home returning—
Nothing lacking from your grace.
All your riches wait in place
For me to borrow
On the morrow.

Do you hear this praise of you,
Little park that I pass through?

THE NEW-BORN

I have heard them in the night—
The cry of their fear,
Because there is no light,
Because they do not hear
Familiar sounds and feel the familiar arm,
And they awake alone.
Yet they have never known
Danger or harm.
What is their dread?—
This dark about their bed?
But they are so lately come
Out of the dark womb
Where they were safely kept.
That blackness was good;
And the silence of that solitude
Wherein they slept
Was kind.
Where did they find
Knowledge of death?
Caution of darkness and cold?
These—of the little, new breath—
Have they a prudence so old?

RAIN AT NIGHT

Are you awake? Do you hear the rain?
How rushingly it strikes upon the ground,
And on the roof, and the wet window-pane!
Sometimes I think it is a comfortable sound,
Making us feel how safe and snug we are:
Closing us off in this dark, away from the dark outside.
The rest of the world seems dim tonight, mysterious and far.
Oh, there is no world left! Only darkness, darkness stretching
    wide,
And full of the blind rain's immeasurable fall!

How nothing must we seem unto this ancient thing!
How nothing unto the earth—and we so small!
Oh, wake, wake!—do you not feel my hands cling?
One day it will be raining as it rains tonight; the same wind
    blow—
Raining and blowing on this house wherein we lie: but you and
    I—
We shall not hear, we shall not ever know.
O love, I had forgot that we must die.

THE LOVER SINGS OF A GARDEN

Oh, beautiful are the flowers of your garden,
The flowers of your garden are fair:
Blue flowers of your eyes
And dusk flower of your hair;
Dew flower of your mouth
And peony-budded breasts,
And the flower of the curve of your hand
Where my hand rests.

SINCE I HAVE FELT THE SENSE OF DEATH

Since I have felt the sense of death,
Since I have borne its dread, its fear—
Oh, how my life has grown more dear
Since I have felt the sense of death!
Sorrows are good, and cares are small,
Since I have known the loss of all.

Since I have felt the sense of death,
And death forever at my side—
Oh, how the world has opened wide
Since I have felt the sense of death!
My hours are jewels that I spend,
For I have seen the hours end.

Since I have felt the sense of death,
Since I have looked on that black night—
My inmost brain is fierce with light

Since I have felt the sense of death.
O dark, that made my eyes to see!
O death, that gave my life to me!

HAPPINESS BETRAYS ME

Happiness betrays me—
Happiness slays me!

Sorrow was kind and loneliness was my sweet companion,
Denial gave me good gifts.
Now freedom is a bondage upon me.
And smoothness slackens my feet.
I will find my way back to the thorns;
I will find my way back again to the good thorns and steepness.

Happiness betrays me—
Happiness slays me.

MEMORY

I can remember our sorrow, I can remember our laughter;
I know that surely we kissed and cried and ate together;
I remember our places and games, and plans we had—
The little house and how all came to naught—
Remember well:
But I cannot remember our love,
I cannot remember our love.

ARCHES

Under the high-arching bridge
The shadow arch
Bends itself,
Curved
Down into the water;
And lies in the water
As motionless
As the arch above it is motionless:
Masonry of the dusk.

THE STONE-AGE SEA

Never has ship sailed on that sea
Nor ray of tower shone on it;
Motionless, without desire or memory,
Like a great languorous sea of stone it lies.
And as these ledges of rock on which they sit—
So stony, so unseeing—are the eyes
Of this strange folk who from the naked shore
Look ever beyond them to the aged face
Of the waters. One with the hoar
Mighty boulders they seem, one with the deep:
These the first beings of the first rude race
Of time. Their hearts are still locked asleep
So lately from the gray marble were they torn:
And all the multitudes of the world are yet unborn.

Langston Hughes

HARD LUCK

When hard luck overtakes you
Nothin' for you to do.
When hard luck overtakes you
Nothin' for you to do.
Gather up yo' fine clothes
An' sell 'em to de Jew.

Jew takes yo' fine clothes,
Gives you a dollar an' a half.
Jew takes yo' fine clothes,
Gives you a dollar an' a half.
Go to de bootleg's,
Git some gin to make you laugh.

If I was a mule I'd
Git me a waggon to haul.

If I was a mule I'd
Git me a waggon to haul.
I'm so low-down I
Ain't even got a stall.

FEET O' JESUS

At de feet o' Jesus,
Sorrow like a sea.
Lordy, let yo' mercy
Come drifting down on me.

At de feet o' Jesus,
At yo' feet I stand.
O, ma little Jesus,
Please reach out yo' hand.

FIRE

Fire,
Fire, Lord!
Fire gonna burn ma soul!

I ain't been good,
I ain't been clean,—
I been stinkin', low-down, mean.

Fire,
Fire, Lord!
Fire gonna burn ma soul!

Tell me, brother,
Do you believe
If you wanta go to heaben
Got to moan an' grieve?

Fire,
Fire, Lord!
Fire gonna burn ma soul!

I been stealin',
Been tellin' lies,
Had more women
Than Pharaoh had wives.

Fire,
Fire, Lord!
Fire gonna burn ma soul!
I means Fire, Lord!
Fire gonna burn ma soul.

Robinson Jeffers

NIGHT

The ebb slips from the rock, the sunken
Tide-rocks lift streaming shoulders
Out of the slack, the slow west
Sombering its torch; a ship's light
Shows faintly, far out,
Over the weight of the prone ocean
On the low cloud.

Over the dark mountain, over the dark pinewood,
Down the long dark valley along the shrunken river,
Returns the splendor without rays, the shining of shadow,
Peace-bringer, the matrix of all shining and quieter of shining.
Where the shore widens on the bay she opens dark wings
And the ocean accepts her glory. O soul worshipful of her
You like the ocean have grave depths where she dwells always,
And the film of waves above that takes the sun takes also
Her, with more love. The sun-lovers have a blond favorite,
A father of lights and noises, wars, weeping and laughter,
Hot labor, lust and delight and the other blemishes. Quietness
Flows from her deeper fountain; and he will die; and she is
    immortal.

Far off from here the slender
Flocks of the mountain forest

Move among stems like towers
Of the old redwoods to the stream,
No twig crackling; dip shy
Wild muzzles into the mountain water
Among the dark ferns.

O passionately at peace you, being secure, will pardon
The blasphemies of glowworms, the lamp in my tower, the
  fretfulness
Of cities, the crescents of the planets, the pride of the stars.
This August night in a rift of cloud Antares reddens,
The great one, the ancient torch, a lord among lost children,
The earth's orbit doubled would not girdle his greatness, one fire
Globed, out of grasp of the mind enormous; but to you O Night
What—not a spark? What flicker of a spark in the faint far
  glimmer
Of a lost fire dying in the desert, dim coals of a sand-pit the
  Bedouins
Wandered from at dawn . . . Ah singing prayer to what gulfs
  tempted
Suddenly are you more lost? To us the near-hand mountain
Be a measure of height, the tide-worn cliff at the sea-gate a
  measure of continuance.

The tide, moving the night's
Vastness with lonely voices,
Turns, the deep dark-shining
Pacific leans on the land,
Feeling his cold strength
To the outmost margins: you Night will resume
The stars in your time.

O passionately at peace, when will that tide draw shoreward?
Truly the spouting fountains of light, Antares, Arcturus,
Tire of their flow, they sing one song but they think silence.
The striding winter giant Orion shines, and dreams darkness.
And life, the flicker of men and moths and the wolf on the hill,
Though furious for continuance, passionately feeding, passion-
  ately
Remaking itself upon its mates, remembers deep inward

The calm mother, the quietness of the womb and the egg,
The primal and the latter silences: dear Night, it is memory
Prophesies, prophecy that remembers, the charm of the dark.
And I and my people, we are willing to love the four-score years
Heartily; but as a sailor loves the sea, when the helm is for
    harbor.

Have men's minds changed,
Or the rock hidden in the deep of the waters of the soul
Broken the surface? A few centuries
Gone by, none dared not to people
The darkness beyond the stars with harps and habitations.
But now, dear is the truth. Life is grown sweeter and lonelier,
And death is no evil.

JOY

Though joy is better than sorrow joy is not great;
Peace is great, strength is great.
Not for joy the stars burn, not for joy the vulture
Spreads her gray sails on the air
Over the mountain; not for joy the worn mountain
Stands, while years like water
Trench his long sides. "I am neither mountain nor bird
Nor star; and I seek joy."
The weakness of your breed: yet at length quietness
Will cover wistful eyes.

HURT HAWKS

I

The broken pillar of the wing jags from the clotted shoulder,
The wing trails like a banner in defeat.
No more to use the sky forever, but live with famine
And pain a few days: cat nor coyote
Will shorten the week of waiting for death, there is game with-
    out talons.
He stands under the oak-bush and waits

The lame feet of salvation; at night he remembers freedom
And flies in a dream, the dawns ruin it.
He is strong, and pain is worse to the strong, incapacity is
worse.
The curs of the day come and torment him
At distance; no one but death the redeemer will humble that
head,
The intrepid readiness, the terrible eyes.
The wild God of the world is sometimes merciful to those
That ask mercy, not often to the arrogant.
You do not know him, you communal people, or you have for-
gotten him.
Intemperate and savage, the hawk remembers him;
Beautiful and wild, the hawks, and men that are dying, remem-
ber him.

II

I'd sooner, except the penalties, kill a man than a hawk; but
the great redtail
Had nothing left but unable misery
From the bone too shattered for mending, the wing that trailed
under his talons when he moved.
We had fed him six weeks, I gave him freedom.
He wandered over the foreland hill and returned in the evening,
asking for death—
Not like a beggar, still eyed with the old
Implacable arrogance. I gave him the lead gift in the twilight.
What fell was relaxed,
Owl-downy, soft feminine feathers.   But what
Soared: the fierce rush: the night-herons by the flooded river
cried fear at its rising
Before it was quite unsheathed from reality.

SHINE, PERISHING REPUBLIC

While this America settles in the mold of its vulgarity, heavily
thickening to empire,
And protest, only a bubble in the molten mass, pops and sighs
out, and the mass hardens,

I sadly smiling remember that the flower fades to make fruit,
    the fruit rots to make earth.
Out of the mother; and through the spring exultances, ripeness
    and decadence; and home to the mother.

You making haste haste on decay: not blameworthy; life is good,
    be it stubbornly long or suddenly
A mortal splendor: meteors are not needed less than mountains:
    shine, perishing republic.

But for my children, I would have them keep their distance from
    the thickening center; corruption
Never has been compulsory, when the cities lie at the monster's
    feet there are left the mountains.

And boys, be in nothing so moderate as in love of man, a clever
    servant, insufferable master.
There is the trap that catches noblest spirits, that caught—they
    say—God, when he walked on earth.

Orrick Johns

LITTLE THINGS

There's nothing very beautiful and nothing very gay
About the rush of faces in the town by day,
But a light tan cow in a pale green mead,
That is very beautiful, beautiful indeed.
And the soft March wind, and the low March mist
Are better than kisses in a dark street kissed.
The fragrance of the forest when it wakes at dawn,
The fragrance of a trim green village lawn,
The hearing of the murmur of the rain at play—
These things are beautiful, beautiful as day!
And I shan't stand waiting for love or scorn
When the feast is laid for a day new-born. . . .
Oh, better let the little things I loved when little
Return when the heart finds the great things brittle;
And better is a temple made of bark and thong
Than a tall stone temple that may stand too long.

THE TREE TOAD

A tiny bell the tree-toad has
I wonder if he knows
The charm it is to hear him
Ringing as he goes.

He can't have gone the journeys
He tells me to go on,
Here in the darkness
Of the cool cropped lawn.

He cannot know the thrill
Of the soft spring wind,
Or the wonder, when you walk,
What will come behind.

He hasn't seen the places
I'd break my heart to win,
Nor heard the city calling
When the cold comes in.

He sings away contented
And doesn't leave his tree.
But he sets my blood a-going
Where his song will never be.

THE INTERPRETER

In the very early morning, when the light was low,
She got all together and she went like snow—
Like snow in the springtime on a sunny hill;
And we were only frightened and can't think still.

We can't think quite that the katydids and frogs,
And the little crying chickens and the little grunting hogs,
And the other living things that she spoke for to us
Have nothing more to tell her since it happened thus.

She never is around for anyone to touch,
But of ecstasy and longing she knew too much. . . .
And always when anyone has time to call his own
She will come and be beside him as quiet as a stone.

WILD PLUM

They are unholy who are born
    To love wild plum at night,
Who once have passed it on a road
    Glimmering and white.

It is as though the darkness had
    Speech of silver words,
Or as though a cloud of stars
    Perched like ghostly birds.

They are unpitied from their birth
    And homeless in men's sight,
Who love, better than the earth,
    Wild plum at night.

THE ANSWER

"Crying cranes and wheeling crows—
    I'll remember them," she said;
"And I will be your own, God knows,
    And the sin be on my head.

"I will be your own and glad;
    Lovers would be fools to care
How a thing is good or bad
    When the sky is everywhere.

"I will be your own," she said,
    "Because your voice is like the rain,
And your kiss is wine and bread,
    Better than my father's grain."

So I took her where she spoke,
  Breasts of snow and burning mouth . . .
Crying cranes and drifting smoke
  And the blackbirds wheeling south.

THE DOOR

Love is a proud and gentle thing, a better thing to own
Than all of the wide impossible stars over the heavens blown,
And the little gifts her hand gives are careless given or taken,
And though the whole great world break, the heart of her is not
    shaken.

Love is a viol in the wind, a viol never stilled,
And mine of all is the surest that ever God has willed.
I shall speak to her though she goes before me into the grave,
And though I drown in the sea, herself shall come upon a wave.
And the things that love gives after shall be as they were before,
For life is only a small house . . . and love is an open door.

Fenton Johnson

THREE NEGRO SPIRITUALS

THE LOST LOVE

Oh, where has my honey gone?
  Fly away, my Jubal, fly away!
Oh, where have they laid her bones?
  Fly away, my Jubal, fly away!
Conjure woman shake her head,
  Preacher dumb and master sad.
      Nobody knows!
      Nobody knows!

Why the tears that drop all night?
  Fly away, my Jubal, fly away!
Why the heart that burns like fire?
  Fly away, my Jubal, fly away!

Angel close the Book of Life,
Moon goes down and stars grow cold.
Nobody knows!
Nobody knows!

WHO IS THAT A-WALKING IN THE CORN?

Who is that a-walking in the corn?
I have looked to East and looked to West
But nowhere could I find Him who walks
Master's cornfield in the morning.

Who is that a-walking in the corn?
Is it Joshua, the son of Nun?—
Or King David come to fight the giant
Near the cornfield in the morning?

Who is that a-walking in the corn?
Is it Peter jangling Heaven's keys?—
Or old Gabriel come to blow his horn
Near the cornfield in the morning?

Who is that a-walking in the corn?
I have looked to East and looked to West
But nowhere could I find Him who walks
Master's cornfield in the morning.

THE LONELY MOTHER

Oh, my mother's moaning by the river,
My poor mother's moaning by the river,
For her son who walks the earth in sorrow.
Long my mother's moaned beside the river,
And her tears have filled an angel's pitcher:
"Lord of Heaven, bring to me my honey,
Bring to me the darling of my bosom,
For a lonely mother by the river."

Cease, O mother, moaning by the river;
Cease, good mother, moaning by the river.

I have seen the star of Michael shining,
Michael shining at the Gates of Morning.
Row, O mighty angel, down the twilight,
Row until I find a lonely woman,
Swaying long beneath a tree of cypress,
Swaying for her son who walks in sorrow.

James Weldon Johnson

THE CREATION

And God stepped out on space,
And he looked around and said:
I'm lonely—
I'll make me a world.

And far as the eye of God could see
Darkness covered everything,
Blacker than a hundred midnights
Down in a cypress swamp.

Then God smiled,
And the light broke,
And the darkness rolled up on one side,
And the light stood shining on the other,
And God said: That's good!

Then God reached out and took the light in his hands,
And God rolled the light around in his hands
Until he made the sun;
And he set that sun a-blazing in the heavens.
And the light that was left from making the sun
God gathered it up in a shining ball
And flung it against the darkness,
Spangling the night with the moon and stars.
Then down between
The darkness and the light
He hurled the world;
And God said: That's good!

Then God himself stepped down—
And the sun was on his right hand,
And the moon was on his left;
The stars were clustered about his head,
And the earth was under his feet.
And God walked, and where he trod
His footsteps hollowed the valleys out
And bulged the mountains up.

Then he stopped and looked and saw
That the earth was hot and barren.
So God stepped over to the edge of the world
And he spat out the seven seas—
He batted his eyes, and the lightnings flashed—
He clapped his hands, and the thunders rolled—
And the waters above the earth came down,
The cooling waters came down.

Then the green grass sprouted,
And the little red flowers blossomed,
The pine tree pointed his finger to the sky,
And the oak spread out his arms,
The lakes cuddled down in the hollows of the ground,
And the rivers ran down to the sea;
And God smiled again,
And the rainbow appeared,
And curled itself around his shoulder.

Then God raised his arm and he waved his hand
Over the sea and over the land,
And he said: Bring forth! Bring forth!
And quicker than God could drop his hand,
Fishes and fowls
And beasts and birds
Swam the rivers and the seas,
Roamed the forests and the woods,
And split the air with their wings.
And God said: That's good.

Then God walked around,
And God looked around

On all that he had made.
He looked at his sun,
And he looked at his moon,
And he looked at his little stars;
He looked on his world
With all its living things,
And God said: I'm lonely still.

Then God sat down—
On the side of a hill where he could think;
By a deep, wide river he sat down;
With his head in his hands,
God thought and thought,
Till he thought: I'll make me a man!

Up from the bed of the river
God scooped the clay;
And by the bank of the river
He kneeled him down;
And there the great God Almighty
Who lit the sun and fixed it in the sky,
Who flung the stars to the most far corner of the night,
Who rounded the earth in the middle of his hand;
This Great God,
Like a mammy bending over her baby,
Kneeled down in the dust
Toiling over a lump of clay
Till he shaped it in his own image;

Then into it he blew the breath of life,
And man became a living soul.
Amen. Amen.

James Joyce

SIMPLES

*O bella, bionda
sei come l'onda*

Of cool sweet dew and radiance mild
The moon a web of silence weaves
In the still garden where a child
Gathers the simple salad leaves.

A moon-dew stars her hanging hair,
And moonlight touches her young brow;
And, gathering, she sings an air:
"Fair as the wave is, fair art thou."

Be mine, I pray, a waxen ear
To shield me from her childish croon;
And mine a shielded heart to her
Who gathers simples of the moon.

SHE WEEPS OVER RAHOON

Rain on Rahoon falls softly, softly falling
Where my dark lover lies.
Sad is his voice that calls me, sadly calling
At grey moonrise.

Love, hear thou
How desolate the heart is, ever calling,
Ever unanswered—and the dark rain falling
Then as now.

Dark too our hearts, O love, shall lie, and cold
As his sad heart has lain
Under the moon-grey nettles, the black mold
And muttering rain.

ON THE BEACH AT FONTANA

Wind whines and whines the shingle;
The crazy pier-stakes groan;
A senile sea numbers each single
Slime-silvered stone.

From whining wind and colder
Grey sea I wrap him warm,
And touch his fine-boned boyish shoulder
And trembling arm.

Around us fear, descending,
Darkness of fear above;
And in my heart how sweet unending
Ache of love.

ALONE

The moon's soft golden meshes make
All night a veil;
The shore-lamps in the sleeping lake
Laburnum tendrils trail.

The sly reeds whisper in the night
A name—her name;
And all my soul is a delight,
A swoon of shame.

ALL DAY I HEAR

All day I hear the noise of waters
    Making moan,
Sad as the sea-bird is when, going
    Forth alone,
He hears the winds cry to the waters'
    Monotone.

The grey winds, the cold winds are blowing
    Where I go.

I hear the noise of many waters
    Far below.
All day, all night, I hear them flowing
    To and fro.

Aline Kilmer

MY MIRROR

There is a mirror in my room
Less like a mirror than a tomb,
There are so many ghosts that pass
Across the surface of the glass.

When in the morning I arise
With circles round my tired eyes,
Seeking the glass to brush my hair,
My mother's mother meets me there.

If in the middle of the day
I happen to go by that way,
I see a smile I used to know—
My mother, twenty years ago.

But when I rise by candlelight
To feed my baby in the night,
Then whitely in the glass I see
My dead child's face look out at me.

I SHALL NOT BE AFRAID

I shall not be afraid any more,
    Either by night or day.
What would it profit me to be afraid
    With you away?

Now I am brave. In the dark night alone
    All through the house I go,

Locking the doors and making windows fast
 When sharp winds blow.

For there is only sorrow in my heart;
 There is no room for fear.
But how I wish I were afraid again,
 My dear, my dear!

ONE SHALL BE TAKEN AND THE OTHER LEFT

There is no Rachel any more,
And so it does not really matter.
Leah alone is left, and she
Goes her own way inscrutably.
Soft-eyed she goes, content to scatter
Fine sand along a barren shore
Where there was sand enough before;
Or from a well that has no water
Raising a futile pitcher up
Lifts to her lips an empty cup.
Now she is Laban's only daughter—
There is no Rachel any more.

FOR ALL LADIES OF SHALOTT

The web flew out and floated wide:
 Poor lady!—I was with her then.
She gathered up her piteous pride,
 But she could never weave again.

The mirror cracked from side to side;
 I saw its silver shadows go:
"The curse has come on me!" she cried.
 Poor lady!—I had told her so.

She was so proud, she would not hide;
 She only laughed and tried to sing.
But singing, in her song she died;
 She did not profit anything.

THE HEART KNOWETH ITS OWN BITTERNESS

The heart knoweth? If this be true indeed,
  Then the thing that I bear in my bosom is not a heart,
For it knows no more than a hollow whispering reed
    That answers to every wind.
  I am sick of the thing. I think we had better part.

My heart would come to any piper's calling—
  A fool in motley that dances for any king;
But my body knows, and its tears unbidden falling
    Say that my heart has sinned.
  You would have my heart? You may. I am sick of the thing.

Joyce Kilmer

TREES

I think that I shall never see
A poem lovely as a tree:

A tree whose hungry mouth is pressed
Against the earth's sweet flowing breast;

A tree that looks to God all day,
And lifts her leafy arms to pray;

A tree that may in summer wear
A nest of robins in her hair,

Upon whose bosom snow has lain,
Who intimately lives with rain.

Poems are made by fools like me,
But only God can make a tree.

EASTER

The air is like a butterfly
  With frail blue wings.
The happy earth looks at the sky
  And sings.

POETS

Vain is the chiming of forgotten bells
  That the wind sways above a ruined shrine.
Vainer his voice in whom no longer dwells
  Hunger that craves immortal Bread and Wine.

Light songs we breathe that perish with our breath
  Out of our lips that have not kissed the rod.
They shall not live who have not tasted death;
  They only sing who are struck dumb by God.

Alfred Kreymborg

AMERICA

Up and down he goes,
With terrible reckless strides,
Flaunting great lamps
With joyous swings—
One to the East
And one to the West!
And flaunting two words
In a thunderous call
That thrills the hearts of all enemies:
All, One; All, One; All, One; All, One.
Beware that queer, wild, wonderful boy
And his playground—don't go near!
All, One; All, One; All, One; All, One;
Up and down he goes.

OLD MANUSCRIPT

The sky
Is that beautiful old parchment
In which the sun
And the moon
Keep their diary.
To read it all,
One must be a linguist
More learned than Father Wisdom;
And a visionary
More clairvoyant than Mother Dream.
But to feel it
One must be an apostle:
One who is more than intimate
In having been, always,
The only confidant—
Like the earth
Or the sea.

CÉZANNE

Our door was shut to the noon-day heat—
We could not see him.
We might not have heard him either—
Resting, dozing, dreaming pleasantly.
But his step was tremendous—
Are mountains on the march?

He was no man who passed;
But a great faithful horse
Dragging a load
Up the hill.

PARASITE

Good woman,
Don't love the man.
Love yourself,

As you have done so exquisitely before.
Like that tortoise-shell cat of yours
Washing away the flies; or are they fleas?
You've hurt him again?
Good!
Do it often.
No,
He'll love you the more—
Always.
Remember how he forgave you the last time,
And how he loved you in the forgiving.
Give him an adventure in godhood
And the higher moralities.
Hurt him again.
Fine!

PASTS

Science
Drove his plough—
So straight,
So strong,
So true—
Deep and far
Into the past,
And turned it topsy-turvy.
Now
We are frantically busy,
With all of our many hands,
Sowing the next past.

DIRGE

She came—
That wistful child—
On her way to red,
Deep red:
She came—

And they tried to tell him
She was Dawn.

She went—
That listless thing—
On her way to black,
Deep black:
She went—
And they tried to tell him
She was Night.

INDIAN SKY

The old squaw
Is one
With the old stone behind her.
Both have squatted there—
Ask mesa
Or mountain how long?
The bowl she holds—
Clay shawl of her art,
Clay ritual of her faith—
Is one
With the thought of the past,
And one with the now;
Though dim, a little old, strange.
The earth holds her
As she holds the bowl—
Ask kiva
Or shrine how much longer?
No titan,
No destroyer,
No future thought,
Can part
Earth and this woman,
Woman and bowl:
The same shawl
Wraps them around.

Stanley J. Kunitz

CHANGE

Dissolving in the chemic vat
Of time, man (gristle and fat),
Corrupting on a rock in space
That crumbles, lifts his impermanent face
To watch the stars, his brain locked tight
Against the tall revolving night.
Yet is he neither here nor there
Because the mind moves everywhere;
And he is neither now nor then
Because tomorrow comes again
Foreshadowed, and the ragged wing
Of yesterday's remembering
Cuts sharply the immediate moon.
Nor is he always: late and soon
Becoming, never being, till
Becoming is a being still.

Here, Now, and Always, man would be
Inviolate eternally:
This is his spirit's trinity.

VERY TREE

Forget the tube of bark,
Alliterative leaves,
Tenacious like a hand,
Gnarled rootage in the dark
Interior of land.

Bright incidental bird
Whose melody is fanned
Among the bundled sheaves,
Wild spool of the winding word,
Reject; and let there be
Only tree.

Earth's absolute arithmetic
Of being is not in the flowering stick
Filled with the sperm of sun,
But in a figure seen
By second eyes when we close
Slow petals of the brain
At evening like a rose.

Colors pour in and out:
Here is a timeless structure wrought
Like the candelabrum of pure thought,
Stripped of green root and leaf,
Getting no seed to sprout,
Yet lovely, lovely,
God's Very Tree,
Form of whose intense inner life
Abstractly branches to attain
What glory, Tree, what pain?

SOUL'S ADVENTURE

I heard the centuries tick slowly,
Earth's pulse equivocate. O Lord,
Gigantic silence strikes: Thy holy
And undeniable Word.

This is the bitter promised day
When, dragging wings, I leave behind
A faun-like head upon a tray,
Spear buried in the mind.

Now I must tread the starry wrack
And penetrate the burning sea.
Iscariot, I may come back,
But do not wait for me.

IN A STRANGE HOUSE

The memory of time is here imprisoned
In these walls, not fluent time that moves
Upon the flood, but time already reasoned
And undone of its quick eyes and loves.

We who are strangers in this finished house
Have slept with noiseless shadows, and we lie
Astonished in our chambers lest we rouse
The sleeping moments with an awful cry.

The dead would murder action. Oh I know
Their subtle ways. They separate with fear
The fiery lips of thought. And I shall go
By silent lanes and leave you timeless here.

MENS CREATRIX

Brain, be ice,
A frozen bowl of thought,
Pure radius of the marble eye
That is time's central spot:
In cold eternal calm
Chasten the trembling thigh.

Brain, brain:
Be fever's sepulcher,
Entomb the noise of frightened blood,
That I may strictly hear
The truthful pulse of beauty
Beyond this evil good.

Mental womb,
Intelligence of tight
Precision: He comes, the sudden Lord,
A rhythmic Spike of Light,
To cleave you with that spike:
Himself, His flowing Word.

Strike, O Poem, Strike!

FOR THE WORD IS FLESH

O ruined father dead, long sweetly rotten
Under the dial, the time-dissolving urn,
Beware a second perishing, forgotten;
Heap fallen leaves of memory to burn
On the slippery rock, the black eroding heart,
Before the wedged frost splits it clean apart.

The nude hand drops no sacramental flower
Of blood among the tough upthrusting weeds.
Senior, in this commemorative hour,
What shall the quick commemorate, what deeds
Ephemeral, what dazzling words that flare
Like rockets from the mouth to burst in air?

Of hypochondriacs that gnawed their seasons
In search of proofs, Lessius found twenty-two
Fine arguments, Tolet gave sixty reasons
Why souls survive. And what are they to you?
And, father, what to me, who cannot blur
The crystal brain with fantasies of Er,

Remembering such factual spikes as pierce
The supplicating palms, and by the sea
Remembering the eyes I hear the fierce
Wild cry of Jesus on the holy tree,
Yet have of you no syllable to keep,
Only the deep rock crumbling in the deep.

Observe the wisdom of the Florentine
Who, feeling death upon him, scribbled fast
To make revision of a deathbed scene,
Gloating that he was accurate at last.
Let sons learn from their lipless fathers how
Man enters hell without a golden bough.

D. H. Lawrence

A WOMAN AND HER DEAD HUSBAND

Ah, stern cold man,
How can you lie so relentless hard
While I wash you with weeping water!
Ah, face carved hard and cold,
You have been like this, on your guard
Against me, since death began.

You masquerader!
How can you shame to act this part
Of unswerving indifference to me?
It is not you; why disguise yourself
Against me, to break my heart,
You evader?

You've a warm mouth,
A good warm mouth always sooner to soften
Even than your sudden eyes.
Ah cruel, to keep your mouth
Relentless, however often
I kiss it in drouth.

You are not he.
Who are you, lying in his place on the bed,
And rigid and indifferent to me?
His mouth, though he laughed or sulked,
Was always warm and red
And good to me.

And his eyes could see
The white moon hang like a breast revealed
By the slipping shawl of stars,
Could see the small stars tremble
As the heart beneath did wield
Systole, diastole.

And he showed it me
So, when he made his love to me;
And his brows like rocks on the sea jut out,
And his eyes were deep like the sea
With shadow, and he looked at me
Till I sank in him like the sea,
Awfully.

Oh, he was multiform—
Which then was he among the manifold?
The gay, the sorrowful, the seer?
I have loved a rich race of men in one—
But not this, this never-warm
Metal-cold—!

Ah masquerader!
With your steel face white-enamelled,
Were you he, after all, and I never
Saw you or felt you in kissing?
—Yet sometimes my heart was trammelled
With fear, evader!

Then was it you
After all—this cold, hard man?
—Ah no, look up at me,
Tell me it isn't true,
That you're only frightening me!

You will not stir,
Nor hear me, not a sound.
—Then it was you—
And all this time you were
Like this when I lived with you.

It is not true,
I am frightened, I am frightened of you
And of everything.
O God!—God too
Has deceived me in everything,
In everything.

FIREFLIES IN THE CORN

A woman taunts her lover:
Look at the little darlings in the corn!
The rye is taller than you, who think yourself
So high and mighty: look how its heads are borne
Dark and proud on the sky, like a number of knights
Passing with spears and pennants and manly scorn.

And always likely! Oh, if I could ride
With my head held high-serene against the sky,
Do you think I'd have a creature like you at my side
With your gloom and your doubt that you love me?
    O darling rye,
How I adore you for your simple pride!

And those bright fireflies wafting in between
And over the swaying cornstalks, just above
All their dark-feathered helmets, like little green
Stars come low and wandering here for love
Of this dark earth, and wandering all serene!

How I adore you, you happy things, you dears,
Riding the air and carrying all the time
Your little lanterns behind you! It cheers
My heart to see you settling and trying to climb
The cornstalks, tipping with fire their spears.

All over the corn's dim motion, against the blue
Dark sky of night, the wandering glitter, the swarm
Of questing brilliant things—you joy, you true
Spirit of careless joy! Ah, how I warm
My poor and perished soul at the joy of you!

The man answers and she mocks:
You're a fool, woman. I love you, and you know I do!
    —Lord, take his love away, it makes him whine.
And I give you everything that you want me to.
    —Lord, dear Lord, do you think he ever *can* shine?

GREEN

The dawn was apple-green,
The sky was green wine held up in the sun,
The moon was a golden petal between.

She opened her eyes, and green
They shone, clear like flowers undone
For the first time, now for the first time seen.

GRIEF

The darkness steals the forms of all the queens.
But oh, the palms of her two black hands are red!
It is Death I fear so much, it is not the dead—
Not this gray book, but the red and bloody scenes.

The lamps are white like snowdrops in the grass;
The town is like a churchyard, all so still
And gray, now night is here: nor will
Another torn red sunset come to pass.

And so I sit and turn the book of gray,
Feeling the shadows like a blind man reading,
All fearful lest I find some next word bleeding.
Nay, take my painted missal book away.

SERVICE OF ALL THE DEAD

Between the avenue of cypresses
All in their scarlet capes and surplices
Of linen, go the chaunting choristers,
The priests in gold and black, the villagers.

And all along the path to the cemetery
The round dark heads of men crowd silently;
And black-scarfed faces of women-folk wistfully
Watch at the banner of death, and the mystery.

And at the foot of a grave a father stands
With sunken head, and forgotten folded hands;
And at the foot of a grave a mother kneels
With pale shut face, nor neither hears nor feels

The coming of the chaunting choristers
Between the avenue of cypresses,
The silence of the many villagers,
The candle-flames beside the surplices.

NOSTALGIA

The waning moon looks upward, this grey night
Sheers round the heavens in one smooth curve
Of easy sailing. Odd red wicks serve
To show where the ships at sea move out of sight.

This place is palpable me, for here I was born
Of this self-same darkness. Yet the shadowy house below
Is out of bounds, and only the old ghosts know
I have come—they whimper about me, welcome and mourn.

My father suddenly died in the harvesting corn,
And the place is no longer ours. Watching, I hear
No sound from the strangers; the place is dark, and fear
Opens my eyes till the roots of my vision seem torn.

Can I go nearer, never towards the door?
The ghosts and I, we mourn together, and shrink
In the shadow of the cart-shed—hovering on the brink
For ever, to enter the homestead no more.

Is it irrevocable? Can I really not go
Through the open yard-way? Can I not pass the sheds
And through to the mowie? Only the dead in their beds
Can know the fearful anguish that this is so.

I kiss the stones. I kiss the moss on the wall,
And wish I could pass impregnate into the place.
I wish I could take it all in a last embrace.
I wish with my heart I could crush it, perish it all.

A BABY ASLEEP AFTER PAIN

As a drenched drowned bee
Hangs numb and heavy from a bending flower,
So clings to me
My baby, her brown hair brushed with wet tears
And laid against her cheek;
Her soft white legs hanging heavily over my arm,
Swinging heavily to my movement as I walk.
My sleeping baby hangs upon my life,
Like a burden she hangs on me.
She has always seemed so light,
But now she is wet with tears and numb with pain.
Even her floating hair sinks heavily,
Reaching downwards;
As the wings of a drenched drowned bee
Are a heaviness, and a weariness.

MOONRISE

And who has seen the moon, who has not seen
Her rise from out the chamber of the deep
Flushed and grand and naked, as from the chamber
Of finished bridegroom, seen her rise and throw
Confession of delight upon the wave,
Littering the waves with her own superscription
Of bliss, till all her lambent beauty shakes toward us
Spread out and known at last: and we are sure
That beauty is a thing beyond the grave,
That perfect, bright experience never falls
To nothingness, and time will dim the moon
Sooner than our full consummation here
In this odd life will tarnish or pass away.

TOMMIES IN THE TRAIN

The sun shines.
The coltsfoot flowers along the railway banks

Shine flat like coin which Zeus, in thanks,
Showers on our lines.

A steeple
In purplish elms; daffodils
Sparkle beneath; luminous hills
Beyond—but no people.

England—O Danaë
To this spring of cosmic gold
Which falls on your lap of mold!
What then are we?

What are we—
Clay-colored, who roll in fatigue
As the train runs league after league
From our destiny?

Some hand is over my face,
Some dark hand. Peeping through the fingers,
I see a world that lingers
Behind, yet keeps pace.

Always, as I peep
Through the fingers that cover my face,
Something seems falling from place,
Seems to roll down the steep.

Is it the train,
That falls like a meteorite
Backward in space, to alight
Never again?

Or is it the illusory world,
That falls from reality
As we look? Or are we
Like a thunderbolt hurled?

One or another
We are lost, since we fall apart
Forever, forever depart
From each other.

RESURRECTION

Now all the hosts are marching to the grave;
The hosts are leaping from the edge of life
In a cascade of souls to sorrowful death.

And I am just awakened from the tomb;
And whither they are going, I have been
In timelessness laid by, in noiseless death.

Now like a crocus in the autumn time,
My soul comes lambent from the endless night
Of death—a cyclamen, a crocus flower
Of windy autumn when the winds all sweep
The hosts away to death, where heap on heap
The dead are burning in the funeral wind.

Now, like a strange light breaking from the ground,
I venture from the halls of shadowy death—
A frail white gleam of resurrection.

I know where they are going, all the lives
That whirl and sweep like anxious leaves away
To have no rest save in the utter night
Of noiseless death; I know it well—
The death they will attain to, where they go—
I, who have been, and now am risen again.

Now like a cyclamen, a crocus flower
In autumn, like to a messenger come back
From embassy in death, I issue forth
Amid the autumn rushing red about
The bitter world, amid the smoke
From burning fires of many smoldering lives,
All bitter and corroding to the grave.

If they would listen, I could tell them now
The secret of the noiseless utter grave,
The secret in the blind mouth of the worm.
But on they go, like leaves within a wind,
Scarlet and crimson and a rust of blood,
Into the utter dark: they cannot hear.

So like a cyclamen, a crocus flower
I lift my inextinguishable flame
Of immortality into the world,
Of resurrection from the endless grave,
Of sweet returning from the sleep of death.

And still against the dark and violent wind,
Against the scarlet and against the red
And blood-brown flux of lives that sweep their way
In hosts towards the everlasting night,
I lift my little pure and lambent flame,
Unquenchable of wind or hosts of death,
Or storms of tears, or rage, or blackening rain
Of full despair, I lift my tender flame
Of pure and lambent hostage from the dead—
Ambassador from halls of noiseless death,
He who returns again from out the tomb
Dressed in the grace of immortality,
A fragile stranger in the flux of lives
That pour cascade-like down the blackening wind
Of sheer oblivion.

Now like a cyclamen, a crocus flower
In putrid autumn issuing through the fall
Of lives, I speak to all who cannot hear;
I turn towards the bitter blackening wind,
I speak aloud to fleeting hosts of red
And crimson and the blood-brown heaps of slain,
Just as a cyclamen or crocus flower
Calls to the autumn, *Resurrection!*
I speak with a vain mouth.

Yet is uplifted in me the pure beam
Of immortality to kindle up
Another spring of yet another year,
Folded as yet: and all the fallen leaves
Sweep on to bitter, to corrosive death
Against me, yet they cannot make extinct
The perfect lambent flame which still goes up,
A tender gleam of immortality,

To start the glory of another year,
Another epoch in another year,
Another triumph on the face of earth,
Another race, another speech among
The multitudinous people unfused,
Unborn and unproduced, yet to be born.

Agnes Lee

MOTHERHOOD

Mary, the Christ long slain, passed silently,
Following the children joyously astir
Under the cedrus and the olive-tree,
Pausing to let their laughter float to her.
Each voice an echo of a voice more dear,
She saw a little Christ in every face.

Then came another woman gliding near
To watch the tender life that filled the place.
And Mary sought the woman's hand and spoke:
"I know thee not, yet know thy memory tossed
With all a thousand dreams their eyes evoke
Who bring to thee a child beloved and lost."

"I too have rocked my Lovely One—
And He was fair!
He was more luminous than the sun,
And like its rays through amber was
His sun-bright hair.
Still I can see it shine and shine."
"Even so," the woman said, "was mine."

"His ways were ever darling ways"—
And Mary smiled—
"So soft, so clinging! All our days
Were jewels strung on cords of love.
My Little Child!

My vanished star! My music fled!"
"Even so was mine," the woman said.

And Mary whispered: "Tell me, thou,
Of thine." And she:
"Oh, mine was rosy as a bough
Blooming with roses, and his eyes
Had lights of the sea!
His balmy fingers left a thrill
Deep in my breast that warms me still."

Then she gazed down some wilder, darker hour,
And said—when Mary questioned, knowing not,
"Who art thou, mother of so sweet a son?"—
"I am the mother of Iscariot."

A STATUE IN A GARDEN

I was a goddess ere the marble found me.
　　Wind, wind, delay not—
Waft my spirit where the laurel crowned me!
　　Will the wind stay not?

Then tarry, tarry, listen, little swallow!
　　An old glory feeds me—
I lay upon the bosom of Apollo!
　　Not a bird heeds me.

For here the days are alien. Oh, to waken
　　Mine, mine, with calling!
But on my shoulders bare, like hopes forsaken,
　　The dead leaves are falling.

The sky is gray and full of unshed weeping
　　As dim down the garden
I wait and watch the early autumn sweeping,
　　The stalks fade and harden.

The souls of all the flowers afar have rallied.
　　The trees, gaunt, appalling,
Attest the gloom, and on my shoulders pallid
　　The dead leaves are falling.

THE TOWER

Now that the tower is standing,
Stone upon stone in flower,
What of its soul—the master,
The maker of the tower?

Walking in mist of evening
Humbly amid the crowd
Beside the wide way's traffic,
Thoughtful perhaps, and bowed,

And pondering some failure
That shook his earlier days,
What exaltation waits him,
When upward he shall gaze

And see in sudden outline,
Mysterious and high,
Beauty, his own creation,
Imposed against the sky!

SHAKESPEARE

Because, the singer of an age, he sang
The passions of the ages,
It was humanity itself that leaped
To life upon his pages.

He told no single being's tale—he forced
All beings to his pen.
And when he made a man to walk the street
Forth walked a million men.

ENEMIES

For many and many a year
A sordid grudge we bore,
But now when he comes down the street
He lingers at my door.

For time is closing in,
And age forgives its debts
When family falls away like mist.
And memory forgets.

Now as we sit and talk
Under the mulberry tree
The only friend I have in life
Is my old enemy.

A LONELY MAN

It's lonely in lodgings above the street
When dusk slows down the day's long laboring,
With only a nod to a lad on the stair,
And neither kith nor kin to be neighboring.

It must be good to go out of a house
With the soft goodbye of your loved one spoken,
And a windowful of little faces
Smiling you off as you wave in token.

It must be good to come back to a house,
And hear the joy, the welcoming shout of it.
It must be good to have anyone care
If you come into a house or go out of it.

AN OLD WOMAN WITH FLOWERS

I like to see the eager-faced old woman
    Walking at sunset down the city street.
Always she holds against her heart with fervor
    Her sprays of meadow-sweet.

She passes daily, and I never see her
    Without the flowers she gathers to her so.
I do not know how destiny softens, hardens
    The ways her feet must go,

Nor what her eyes forever are beholding
  Beyond the sordid walls and grimy towers;
Nor what against her agèd heart she presses,
  Pressing the meadow flowers.

MRS. MALOOLY

Mrs. Malooly has gone to her rest,
Who scrubbed Manhattan's marble aisles.
She has forgotten, forgotten, forgotten
The mop and broom
And the patterned tiles.

Mrs. Malooly has gone to her rest
In the smooth-dug loam, to a rest so deep
She has forgotten, forgotten, forgotten
The unmade bed
And the whiskey sleep.

THE SWEEPER

Frail, wistful guardian of the broom,
  The dwelling's drudge and stay,
Whom destiny gave a single task—
  To keep the dust away!—

Sweep off the floor and polish the chair.
  It will not always last:
Some day, for all your arms can do,
  The dust will hold you fast.

THE ILEX TREE

What spirit touched the faded lambrequin,
And slept? The doorway's lintel, ambered, rosed
With age, overlooks a stunted ilex tree
Grown in the middle path. Its branches guard

The house in silence, or with green dark gesture
Spreading protection, whisper pleadingly:
"The past is asleep behind the lambrequin.
Do not go in. The door is closed."

NUMBERS

In all they brood,
The inexorable!
Out of primeval shadow have they stood
In judgment over all.
They brook not, these,
Earth's gainsay, nor the sea's,
Arbiters of our more, our less,
Our nothingness.

Apart, a few,
They merge, divide;
Or, gathering in multitudes anew,
Spread forth in armies.
Their ancient law
Still rules the world,
Bids science halt or dare,
Bids art beware.

Fact's own they are;
Yet, counselling dream,
Bright wings for thought's invasion of a star,
Fins for the diver's gleam,
Unerring eyes
To pierce the hidden skies,
Unerring feet to enter
The rock's dark center.

With lamps upheld,
Austere and strong
They wait behind the Muses. Sun-impelled
Apollo never outruns
Their fleet throng.
They guard a million suns—

Mindful to mold a sapling's grace,
A lily's face.

They forge the curse
Of ways unlit.
They are the heartbreak of the universe.
They are the joy of it.
Unseeing we pass
Their pattern in the grass.
But we are theirs, and they defy
Eternity.

Muna Lee

A SONG OF HAPPINESS

So many folk are happy folk—
  The feathered folk and furred;
And many a kindly glance I've had,
  And many a brisk bright word,
From squirrel and from gray fieldmouse,
  From cardinal and blackbird.

It's only folk within the wood
  Can know my happiness.
I did not tell my secret,
  But I heard the robins guess;
Even the golden minnow knows
  Beneath the water-cress.

A WOMAN'S SONG

This is my wrong to you, O man that I love—
  I who had all to give
And would have held back naught thereof,
  I whom love taught to live,

When you asked for a loaf of my baking,
  And a bit of blossomy spray,
Gave only these for your taking,
  And hid the rest away.

MELILOT

Behind the house is the millet plot,
And past the millet, the stile;
And then a hill where melilot
Grows with wild camomile.

There was a youth who bade me goodby
Where the hill rises to meet the sky.
I think my heart broke; but I have forgot
All but the scent of the white melilot.

DIRGE

Though you should whisper
   Of what made her weep,
She would not hear you—
   She is asleep.

Though you should taunt her
   With ancient heart-break,
She would not listen—
   She is awake.

Passion would find her
   Too cold for dishonor.
Candles beside her,
   Roses upon her!

SONNETS

It were easiest to say: "The moon and lake
Made wizardry—how could we see aright?
That was a world unreal in silver light,
And we were lovers for the moment's sake.
It was youth spoke in us, quick to mistake
Earth-lamp for dawn, the mirage for true sight;
Hailing a hill-crest as the long-sought height;
Swearing such oaths as honors us to break."

That were far easiest: then no regret
Could chill a heart grown happy to forget,
Nor touch a soul that sophistries sufficed.
There was a man once, in a hall of trial,
Thrice before cock-crow uttered such denial—
And knows forever that he denied the Christ.

Along my ways of life you never came—
You would be alien to the paths I take.
These orchards never reddened for your sake,
This larkspur never rustled with your name.
Startled alike by sound and sudden flame,
Swept centerward like clouds when tempests break,
We knew such unity as storms may make
Before returning calm shows earth the same.

I am not I who came back to old ways—
Not I, but what a dream has made of me,
Beyond earth's power to alter or undo.
And if I must walk quietly all my days,
As once I walked, content that this should be,
God must remake the world, or me, or you!

William Ellery Leonard

INDIAN SUMMER
After completing a book for one now dead

(*O earth-and-autumn of the setting sun,*
She is not by, to know my task is done!)
In the brown grasses slanting with the wind,
Lone as a lad whose dog's no longer near,
Lone as a mother whose only child has sinned,
Lone on the loved hill. . . . And below me here
The thistle-down in tremulous atmosphere
Along red clusters of the sumach streams;
The shrivelled stalks of goldenrod are sere,
And crisp and white their flashing old racemes.
(. . . forever . . . forever . . . forever . . .)

This is the lonely season of the year,
This is the season of our lonely dreams.

(O earth-and-autumn of the setting sun,
   She is not by, to know my task is done!)
The corn-shocks westward on the stubble plain
Show like an Indian village of dead days;
The long smoke trails behind the crawling train,
And floats atop the distant woods ablaze
With orange, crimson, purple. The low haze
Dims the scarped bluffs above the inland sea,
Whose wide and slanty waters in cold glaze
Await yon full moon on the night-to-be.
(. . . far . . . and far . . . and far . . .)
These are the solemn horizons of man's ways,
These the horizons of solemn thought to me.

(O earth-and-autumn of the setting sun,
   She is not by, to know my task is done!)
And this the hill she visited, as friend;
And this the hill she lingered on, as bride—
Down in the yellow valley is the end:
They laid her . . . in no evening autumn tide . . .
Under fresh flowers of that May morn, beside
The queens and cave-women of ancient earth.

This is the hill . . . and over my city's towers
Across the world from sunset, yonder in air,
Shines, through its scaffoldings, a civic dome
Of piled masonry, which shall be ours
To give, completed, to our children there . . .
And yonder far roof of my abandoned home
Shall house new laughter . . . Yet I tried . . . I tried . .
And, ever wistful of the doom to come,
I built her many a fire for love . . . for mirth . . .
(When snows were falling on our oaks outside,
Dear, many a winter fire upon the hearth . . .)
(. . . farewell . . . farewell . . . farewell . . .)
We dare not think too long on those who died,
While still so many yet must come to birth.

Maurice Lesemann

SHEEP HERDERS

You too, of course, have counted sheep
Trying to put yourself to sleep?
If you should ever come to hate
That simple harmless opiate
And ask a subtler one instead,
More potent for a pounding head
Than mere monotony of number,
Try this formula for slumber:

Imagine men who earn their bread
By counting sheep, who for the sake
Of counting sheep must keep awake,
(Lie long and quiet in your bed)
Men who through endless lonely days
Follow the herd from crest to crest,
Yet scarcely dare to drop their gaze,
(Lie long and still) who cannot rest
From seeing sheep, who look across
Whole hills moving as if the moss
Moved on a stone.
                              Lie still. Suppose
That you yourself were one of those.

Think yourself slowly south and west
Across the night. . . . They will be there,
Mexicans mostly, scattered far
Through Texas, underneath the glow
Of moonlight in New Mexico,
Folded darkly under the shadow
Of mountain peaks in Colorado . . .
Twinkling fires . . . the men and sheep
Huddled among the hills for sleep.

Small wonder if they stare about
At dawn and think the country strange.

So many days they have been out,
So many nights upon the range,
It's easy for the hills to change
Places. When you've looked so long
At sheep, and listened to the song
Of wind filled with the stupid cries
Of sheep, and watched along the sky's
Glimmering rim for sheep you've lost—
You're living in your sleep almost;
You see such things without surprise.

Small wonder if at times the older
Gaunter men stare at a bowlder
As if the stone wore wool; or follow
Gray chamisa down a hollow
(Gray bushes that the wind stirred)
As if they'd wandered from the herd.
Small wonder, when they hear the beat
Of warm bells mingling with the bleat
Of lambs so long, long in the heat,
If the bright air becomes alive
And drones with noise, if the loud sun
Sends swarming from its brazen hive
Great luminous bees across the noon.

(They'd never tell you there were bees,
But in a country of no trees,
Where the noon sky's a blazing bell,
You'll understand what a frail shell
Preserves a brain's precarious night
From being shattered by the light.)
Sometimes a stranger on the trail
Will catch them in so deep a drowse,
So stupefied with sheep, they'll rouse
Long after they have heard his hail,
Or hearing, raise bewildered brows.

Shut as they are behind a curtain,
You'll understand why they're uncertain

Whether one man they vaguely eye
Trudging naked toward the sky
Appears before them in broad day,
Or while they're turned some other way.

He passes by without a sound,
Leaving behind him on the ground
Blood of his feet from the sharp stone.
His pale flesh bears the livid mark
Of lashes that have torn the skin.
His bloodshot eyes are deep within.
His bearded face is strangely dark
And meagre, strangely like their own.
They cross themselves when he is gone.

. . . Dusk is a kinder light, and softer.
After they munch their beans and bread
They'd raise their throats in raucous laughter,
Only that all their shouts would seem
Drowned in the enormous stream
Of air that's flying overhead.
They stretch for sleep. . . . But even then,
Even asleep, they can't begin
To ease the drowsiness they're in.
It would take more than human sleep
To ease that drowsiness of sheep.
All night they have to hear the thud
Of tiny hoofbeats in their blood,
All night they have to feel the wool
Crowding softly on the skull,
Pushing it downward, till they wake
Wildly for breath before it break. . . .

They stir uneasy in their bed.
Stars wheel across from range to range,
Covering silently with light
The troubled dreamers down below.
They are as simple and as mad,
They are as fabulous and strange,

As those who kept their flocks by night
On hills of Asia long ago.

Think of them slowly one by one
Till you are wakened by the sun.

RANCHERS

They went off on the buckboard in the rain,
The children in the straw. I didn't know
Which one of the long roads they'd have to go,
But I saw them just as plain.

For anywhere they chose to turn the horses
There'd be the same gray miles of tableland,
The same rank smell of sage, the same wet sand
In the windy watercourses.

And anywhere in time there'd be red hills
Rising, raw rock against the rain. I saw
The plunge and splash across a lonely draw,
The long slow climb with red mud on the thills.

And somewhere, in good time, I knew they'd pass
As if in secret from the road they travelled,
To follow out like a thread of rope unravelled
Some faint mark in the grass,

And come to a gate, perhaps where a stray steer
Breathed in the dusk, or slipped on the wet stone there;
And come to a house. . . . I knew they'd be alone there
Most of the year.

The earth would slowly change where they had stepped,
The air would fill up softly with the sound
Of teams, voices . . . I thought the red hills must have slept
Until they woke the ground.

I thought no words could make, on anybody's mouth,
As true an image as their hills would keep of them,
Where on our world spread westward like a cloth
They worked a homely hem.

CITY ASLEEP

When my gray city wavers from her sleep,
And dawn slips in like news from foreign lands,
Sometimes for one amazing moment I keep
Dark knowledge of her that no one understands:

How all about this room, where the slow, sweet
Night odors flow, her body reaches far
With trees and towers, waiting, dim street by street,
Till soon, far out beneath a failing star

Her million atomies of men must pass
Minutely out of sleep to work her will,
Toward some strange end of ruin and wild grass,
Molding her plains into a flowery hill.

LOST

The light was gone, and there wasn't a sound
But the roar of wind through the pines and firs.
I came to a clearing at last and found
That I'd lost my way in the universe.

It wasn't alone that I'd lost my way
In the timber land I was plunging through.
Somehow I'd circled and lost the lay
Of the sky; there wasn't a star I knew.

The wind lashed down at the wintry grass,
And the dark was scattered high and far
With glints of fire and dust of glass.
I stared in panic to find a star

That burned familiar in its place.
It seemed the earth had strayed for once,
And now was running amuck through space
Among a swarm of hostile suns.

Then, like a name thrown suddenly out,
Perseus appeared, and low in the trees

Lyra, and then as if with a shout
Orion came, and the Pleiades,

And all the others, score on score.
Again the galaxy was right,
The planet in place, and I once more
Was a man on the earth, at home in the night.

NOCTIFLORA

I favor most in flowers the shyest ones,
And, most of these, the nebulæ of heaven.
I count their pale corollas lovelier
Than trilliums' even.

And though a trillium or a twin-flower bends
In ways that are more winsome to the mind,
And a blown harebell, rooted in a stone,
Comes nearer humankind,

I choose, instead, the flowers I cannot cull;
I turn a lens on starry evenings
Toward buds of fire, that break so slow they seem
Imperishable things.

I've known enough of fragile heads that lift
With something so like hope above the stem,
And shrink with something so like fear when frost
First blackens them;

I give my thought to hardier asters now.
When earth's last autumn dresses her for doom
And all the fields are lost—still, lavishly
The skies will bloom.

When hoary night has laid all flower heads
Of earth to sleep, that cold unearthly rose,
The great Orion-cloud, will still as now
Gravely unclose.

The spiral whorl beyond Triangulum
Will none the less because no eyes behold—
Fresh as with globes of dew bright-glittering—
Unwind its gold.

Ages will rush, and still no petal fall;
Calm will enfold each vastly burning flower;
And when a thousand years at length achieve
The thousandth power,

Somewhere a wide night-orchis will uncurl
Out of her involuted violet core
One star, will thrust up glowing from the dusk
One stamen more.

No love or care can force these blossomings;
Nor can the whitening over of one world
Retard what's curled there, crowding on the sheath
To be uncurled.

Vachel Lindsay

GENERAL WILLIAM BOOTH ENTERS INTO HEAVEN

To be sung to the tune of THE BLOOD OF THE LAMB
with indicated instruments

Booth led boldly with his big bass drum.
  Are you washed in the blood of the Lamb?
The saints smiled gravely, and they said, "He's come."
  Are you washed in the blood of the Lamb?   *Bass drums*
Walking lepers followed, rank on rank,
Lurching bravos from the ditches dank,
Drabs from the alleyways and drug-fiends pale—
Minds still passion-ridden, soul-powers frail!
Vermin-eaten saints with moldy breath
Unwashed legions with the ways of death—
  Are you washed in the blood of the Lamb?

Every slum had sent its half-a-score
The round world over—Booth had groaned for more.
Every banner that the wide world flies
Bloomed with glory and transcendent dyes.
Big-voiced lasses made their banjos bang!   *Banjos*
Tranced, fanatical, they shrieked and sang,
  Are you washed in the blood of the Lamb?
Hallelujah! It was queer to see
Bull-necked convicts with that land make free!
Loons with bazoos blowing blare, blare, blare—
On, on upward through the golden air.
  Are you washed in the blood of the Lamb?

Booth died blind, and still by faith he trod,
Eyes still dazzled by the ways of God.   *Bass drums*
Booth led boldly and he looked the chief: *slower and*
Eagle countenance in sharp relief,   *softer*
Beard a-flying, air of high command
Unabated in that holy land.

Jesus came from out the Court-House door,
Stretched his hands above the passing poor.
Booth saw not, but led his queer ones there   *Flutes*
Round and round the mighty Court-House square.
Yet in an instant all that blear review
Marched on spotless, clad in raiment new.
The lame were straightened, withered limbs uncurled
And blind eyes opened on a new sweet world.

Drabs and vixens in a flash made whole!   *Bass drums*
Gone was the weasel-head, the snout, the jowl;   *louder and*
Sages and sibyls now, and athletes clean,   *faster*
Rulers of empires, and of forests green!
The hosts were sandalled and their wings were fire—
  Are you washed in the blood of the Lamb?
But their noise played havoc with the angel-choir.   *Grand*
  Are you washed in the blood of the Lamb?   *chorus*
                                                             tambourines
Oh, shout Salvation! it was good to see   *—all instru-*
Kings and princes by the Lamb set free.   *ments in full*
The banjos rattled, and the tambourines   *blast*
Jing-jing-jingled in the hands of queens!

And when Booth halted by the curb for prayer
He saw his Master through the flag-filled air.
Christ came gently with a robe and crown *Reverently*
For Booth the soldier while the throng knelt down. *sung—no instruments*
He saw King Jesus—they were face to face,
And he knelt a-weeping in that holy place.
    Are you washed in the blood of the Lamb?

THE CONGO

A Study of the Negro Race

I—THEIR BASIC SAVAGERY

Fat black bucks in a wine-barrel room,
Barrel-house kings, with feet unstable,
Sagged and reeled and pounded on the table, *A deep rolling bass*
Pounded on the table,
Beat an empty barrel with the handle of a broom,
Hard as they were able,
Boom, boom, Boom,
With a silk umbrella and the handle of a broom,
Boomlay, boomlay, boomlay, Boom.
Then I had religion, Then I had a vision.
I could not turn from their revel in derision.
Then I saw the Congo, creeping through the black, *More deliberate.*
Cutting through the jungle with a golden track. *Solemnly chanted*
Then along that river bank
A thousand miles
Tattooed cannibals danced in files;
Then I heard the boom of the blood-lust song
And a thigh-bone beating on a tin-pan gong.
And "blood!" screamed the whistles and the fifes of the *A rapidly piling climax of speed*
    warriors, *max of speed*
"Blood!" screamed the skull-faced, lean witch-doctors; *and racket*
"Whirl ye the deadly voo-doo rattle,
Harry the uplands,
Steal all the cattle,
Rattle-rattle, rattle-rattle,
Bing!
Boomlay, boomlay, boomlay, Boom!"

A roaring, epic, rag-time tune
From the mouth of the Congo
To the Mountains of the Moon.
Death is an Elephant,
Torch-eyed and horrible,
Foam-flanked and terrible.
Boom, steal the pygmies,
Boom, kill the Arabs,
Boom, kill the white men,
Hoo, Hoo, Hoo.
Listen to the yell of Leopold's ghost
Burning in Hell for his hand-maimed host.
Hear how the demons chuckle and yell
Cutting his hands off down in Hell.
Listen to the creepy proclamation,
Blown through the lairs of the forest-nation,
Blown past the white-ants' hill of clay,
Blown past the marsh where the butterflies play:—
"Be careful what you do,
Or Mumbo-Jumbo, God of the Congo,
And all of the other
Gods of the Congo,
Mumbo-Jumbo will hoo-doo you,
Mumbo-Jumbo will hoo-doo you,
Mumbo-Jumbo will hoo-doo you."

With a philosophic pause

Shrilly and with a heavily accented metre

Like the wind in the chimney

All the O sounds very golden. Heavy accents very heavy. Light accents very light. Last line whispered

II—THEIR IRREPRESSIBLE HIGH SPIRITS

Wild crap-shooters with a whoop and a call
Danced the juba in their gambling-hall,
And laughed fit to kill, and shook the town,
And guyed the policemen and laughed them down
With a boomlay, boomlay, boomlay, Boom.
Then I saw the Congo creeping through the
    black,
Cutting through the jungle with a golden track.
A negro fairyland swung into view,
A minstrel river
Where dreams come true.

Rather shrill and high

Read exactly as in first section. Lay emphasis on the delicate ideas. Keep as light-footed as possible

The ebony palace soared on high
Through the blossoming trees to the evening sky.
The inlaid porches and casements shone
With gold and ivory and elephant-bone.
And the black crowd laughed till their sides were sore
At the baboon butler in the agate door,
And the well-known tunes of the parrot band
That trilled on the bushes of that magic land.

A troop of skull-faced witch-men came   *With pom-*
Through the agate doorway in suits of flame—   *posity*
Yea, long-tailed coats with a gold-leaf crust
And hats that were covered with diamond-dust.
And the crowd in the court gave a whoop and a call
And danced the juba from wall to wall.
But the witch-men suddenly stilled the throng   *With a great*
With a stern cold glare, and a stern old song: *deliberation*
        and ghostli-
"Mumbo-Jumbo will hoo-doo you." . . .   *ness*

Just then from the doorway, as fat as shotes   *With over-*
        whelming as-
Came the cake-walk princes in their long red coats,   *surance, good*
        cheer, and
Canes with a brilliant lacquer shine,   *pomp*
And tall silk hats that were red as wine.
And they pranced with their butterfly partners there,   *With grow-*
        ing speed
Coal-black maidens with pearls in their hair,   *and sharply*
        marked
Knee-skirts trimmed with the jassamine sweet,   *dance-*
And bells on their ankles and little black feet.   *rhythm*
And the couples railed at the chant and the frown
Of the witch-men lean, and laughed them down.
(Oh, rare was the revel, and well worth while
That made those glowering witch-men smile.)

The cake-walk royalty then began
To walk for a cake that was tall as a man
To the tune of "Boomlay, boomlay, Boom,"
While the witch-men laughed, with a sinister air,   *With a touch*
        of negro dia-
And sang with the scalawags prancing there: *lect, and as*
        rapidly as
"Walk with care, walk with care,   *possible to-*
Or Mumbo-Jumbo, god of the Congo,   *ward the end*

And all of the other
Gods of the Congo,
Mumbo-Jumbo will hoo-doo you.
Beware, beware, walk with care,
Boomlay, boomlay, boomlay, boom,
Boomlay, boomlay, boomlay, boom,
Boomlay, boomlay, boomlay, boom,
Boomlay, boomlay, boomlay,
Boom."

Oh, rare was the revel, and well worth while
That made those glowering witch-men smile.

Slow philosophic calm

III—THE HOPE OF THEIR RELIGION

A good old negro in the slums of the town
Preached at a sister for her velvet gown.
Howled at a brother for his low-down ways,
His prowling, guzzling, sneak-thief days.
Beat on the Bible till he wore it out
Starting the jubilee revival shout.
And some had visions, as they stood on chairs,
And sang of Jacob, and the golden stairs.
And they all repented, a thousand strong,
From their stupor and savagery and sin and wrong,
And slammed with their hymn-books till they shook the
    room
With "Glory, glory, glory,"
And Boom, boom, Boom."
Then I saw the Congo, creeping through the black,
Cutting through the jungle with a golden track.
And the gray sky opened like a new-rent veil
And showed the apostles with their coats of mail.
In bright white steel they were seated round,
And their fire-eyes watched where the Congo wound.
And the twelve Apostles, from their thrones on high,
Thrilled all the forest with their heavenly cry:
"Mumbo-Jumbo will die in the jungle;
Never again will he hoo-doo you,
Never again will he hoo-doo you."

*Heavy bass.
With a literal
imitation of
camp-meeting racket
and trance*

*Exactly as in
the first section. Begin
with terror
and power,
end with joy*

*Sung to the
tune of
"Hark ten
thousand
harps and
voices"*

Then along that river, a thousand miles,   *With grow-*
The vine-snared trees fell down in files.   *ing delibera-*
                                                     tion and joy
Pioneer angels cleared the way
For a Congo paradise, for babes at play,
For sacred capitals, for temples clean.
Gone where the skull-faced witch-men lean;
There, where the wild ghost-gods had wailed,   *In a rather*
A million boats of the angels sailed   *high key—as*
                                                     delicately as
With oars of silver, and prows of blue,   *possible*
And silken pennants that the sun shone through.
'Twas a land transfigured, 'twas a new creation.
Oh, a singing wind swept the Negro nation,
And on through the backwoods clearing flew:—   *To the tune*
"Mumbo-Jumbo is dead in the jungle.   *of "Hark,*
                                                     ten thousand
Never again will he hoo-doo you.   *harps and*
Never again will he hoo-doo you."   *voices"*

Redeemed were the forests, the beasts and the men,
And only the vulture dared again
By the far lone mountains of the moon
To cry, in the silence, the Congo tune: *Dying down*
                                                     into a pene-
"Mumbo-Jumbo will hoo-doo you,   *trating,*
Mumbo-Jumbo will hoo-doo you.   *terrified*
                                                     whisper
Mumbo . . . Jumbo . . . will . . . hoo-doo . . . you."

HOW SAMSON BORE AWAY THE GATES OF GAZA
A Negro Sermon

Once, in a night as black as ink,
She drove him out when he would not drink.
Round the house there were men in wait
Asleep in rows by the Gaza gate.
But the Holy Spirit was in this man.
Like a gentle wind he crept and ran.
("It is midnight," said the big town clock.)

He lifted the gates up, post and lock,
The hole in the wall was high and wide
When he bore away old Gaza's pride
Into the deep of the night:

The bold Jack-Johnson Israelite—
Samson, the Judge, the Nazarite.

The air was black, like the smoke of a dragon.
Samson's heart was as big as a wagon.
He sang like a shining golden fountain;
He sweated up to the top of the mountain.
He threw down the gates with a noise like judgment.
And the quails all ran with the big arousement.

But he wept: "I must not love tough queens,
And spend on them my hard-earned means.
I told that girl I would drink no more.
Therefore she drove me from her door.
Oh, sorrow,

Sorrow,
I cannot hide!
O Lord, look down from your chariot side!
You made me Judge, and I am not wise;
I am weak as a sheep for all my size."

> *Let Samson*
> *Be coming*
> *Into your mind.*

The moon shone out, the stars were gay—
He saw the foxes run and play.
He rent his garments, he rolled around
In deep repentance on the ground.

Then he felt a honey in his soul;
Grace abounding made him whole.
Then he saw the Lord in a chariot blue.
The gorgeous stallions whinnied and flew;
The iron wheels hummed an old hymn-tune
And crunched in thunder over the moon.
And Samson shouted to the sky:
"My Lord, my Lord is riding high."

Like a steed, he pawed the gates with his hoof;
He rattled the gates like rocks on the roof,

And danced in the night
On the mountain-top;
Danced in the deep of the night—
The Judge, the holy Nazarite,
Whom ropes and chains could never bind.

> *Let Samson*
> *Be coming*
> *Into your mind.*

Whirling his arms, like a top he sped;
His long black hair flew around his head
Like an outstretched net of silky cord,
Like a wheel of the chariot of the Lord.

> *Let Samson*
> *Be coming*
> *Into your mind.*

Samson saw the sun anew.
He left the gates in the grass and dew.
He went to a county-seat a-nigh,
Found a harlot proud and high,
Philistine that no man could tame—
Delilah was her lady-name.
Oh, sorrow,
Sorrow—
She was too wise!
She cut off his hair,
She put out his eyes.

> *Let Samson*
> *Be coming*
> *Into your mind.*

JOHN BROWN

(To be sung by a leader and chorus, the leader singing the body of the poem while the chorus interrupts with the question.)

I've been to Palestine.
    What did you see in Palestine?
I saw the Ark of Noah—
It was made of pitch and pine;
I saw old Father Noah
Asleep beneath his vine;
I saw Shem, Ham and Japhet
Standing in a line;
I saw the tower of Babel
In a gorgeous sunrise shine—
By a weeping-willow tree
Beside the Dead Sea.

I've been to Palestine.
    What did you see in Palestine?
I saw abominations
And Gadarene swine;
I saw the sinful Canaanites
Upon the shewbread dine,
And spoil the temple vessels
And drink the temple wine;
I saw Lot's wife, a pillar of salt
Standing in the brine—
By a weeping-willow tree
Beside the Dead Sea.

I've been to Palestine.
    What did you see in Palestine?
Cedars on Mount Lebanon,
Gold in Ophir's mine,
And a wicked generation
Seeking for a sign;
And Baal's howling worshippers
Their god with leaves entwine.

And . . .
I SAW THE WAR-HORSE RAMPING
AND SHAKE HIS FORELOCK FINE—
By a weeping-willow tree
Beside the Dead Sea.

I've been to Palestine.
  What did you see in Palestine?
Old John Brown,
Old John Brown.
I saw his gracious wife
Dressed in a homespun gown.
I saw his seven sons
Before his feet bow down.
And he marched with his seven sons,
His wagons and goods and guns,
To his campfire by the sea,
By the waves of Galilee.

I've been to Palestine.
  What did you see in Palestine?
I saw the harp and psaltery
Played for Old John Brown.
I heard the Ram's horn blow,
Blow for Old John Brown.
I saw the Bulls of Bashan—
They cheered for Old John Brown.
I saw the big Behemoth—
He cheered for Old John Brown.
I saw the big Leviathan,
He cheered for Old John Brown.
I saw the Angel Gabriel
Great power to him assign.
I saw him fight the Canaanites
And set God's Israel free.
I saw him when the war was done
In his rustic chair recline—
By his camp-fire by the sea,
By the waves of Galilee.

I've been to Palestine.
> *What did you see in Palestine?*

Old John Brown,
Old John Brown.
And there he sits
To judge the world.
His hunting-dogs
At his feet are curled.
His eyes half-closed,
But John Brown sees
The ends of the earth,
The Day of Doom.
AND HIS SHOT-GUN LIES
ACROSS HIS KNEES—
Old John Brown,
Old John Brown.

ALADDIN AND THE JINN

"Bring me soft song," said Aladdin;
  "This tailor-shop sings not at all.
Chant me a word of the twilight,
  Of roses that mourn in the fall.
Bring me a song like hashish
  That will comfort the stale and the sad,
For I would be mending my spirit,
  Forgetting these days that are bad:
Forgetting companions too shallow,
  Their quarrels and arguments thin;
Forgetting the shouting muezzin."
  "*I am your slave*," said the Jinn.

"Bring me old wines," said Aladdin,
  "I have been a starved pauper too long.
Serve them in vessels of jade and of shell,
  Serve them with fruit and with song:
Wines of pre-Adamite Sultans
  Digged from beneath the black seas,

New-gathered dew from the heavens
  Dripped down from heaven's sweet trees,
Cups from the angels' pale tables
  That will make me both handsome and wise;
For I have beheld her, the Princess—
  Firelight and starlight her eyes!
Pauper I am—I would woo her.
  And . . . let me drink wine to begin,
Though the Koran expressly forbids it."
  "*I am your slave,*" said the Jinn.

"Plan me a dome," said Aladdin,
  "That is drawn like the dawn of the moon,
When the sphere seems to rest on the mountains
  Half-hidden, yet full-risen soon.
Build me a dome," said Aladdin,
  "That shall cause all young lovers to sigh—
The fulness of life and of beauty,
  Peace beyond peace to the eye;
A palace of foam and of opal,
  Pure moonlight without and within,
Where I may enthrone my sweet lady."
  "*I am your slave,*" said the Jinn.

THE CHINESE NIGHTINGALE

A Song in Chinese Tapestries
Dedicated to S. T. F.

"How, how," he said. "Friend Chang," I said,
"San Francisco sleeps as the dead—
Ended license, lust and play:
Why do you iron the night away?
Your big clock speaks with a deadly sound,
With a tick and a wail till dawn comes round.
While the monster shadows glower and creep,
What can be better for man than sleep?"

"I will tell you a secret," Chang replied;
"My breast with vision is satisfied,

And I see green trees and fluttering wings,
And my deathless bird from Shanghai sings."
Then he lit five fire-crackers in a pan.
"Pop, pop!" said the fire-crackers, "cra-cra-crack!"
He lit a joss-stick long and black.
Then the proud gray joss in the corner stirred;
On his wrist appeared a gray small bird,
And this was the song of the gray small bird:

"Where is the princess, loved forever,
Who made Chang first of the kings of men?"

And the joss in the corner stirred again;
And the carved dog, curled in his arms, awoke,
Barked forth a smoke-cloud that whirled and broke.
It piled in a maze round the ironing-place,
And there on the snowy table wide
Stood a Chinese lady of high degree,
With a scornful, witching, tea-rose face . . .
Yet she put away all form and pride,
And laid her glimmering veil aside
With a childlike smile for Chang and for me.

The walls fell back, night was aflower,
The table gleamed in a moonlit bower,
While Chang, with a countenance carved of stone,
Ironed and ironed, all alone.
And thus she sang to the busy man Chang:
"Have you forgotten . . .
Deep in the ages, long, long ago,
I was your sweetheart, there on the sand—
Storm-worn beach of the Chinese land?
We sold our grain in the peacock town
Built on the edge of the sea-sands brown—
Built on the edge of the sea-lands brown . . .

"When all the world was drinking blood
From the skulls of men and bulls,
And all the world had swords and clubs of stone,
We drank our tea in China beneath the sacred spice-trees,
And heard the curled waves of the harbor moan.

And this gray bird, in Love's first spring,
With a bright-bronze breast and a bronze-brown wing,
Captured the world with his carolling.
Do you remember, ages after,
At last the world we were born to own?
You were the heir of the yellow throne—
The world was the field of the Chinese man
And we were the pride of the sons of Han.
We copied deep books, and we carved in jade,
And wove white silks in the mulberry shade." . . .

"I remember, I remember
That Spring came on forever,
That Spring came on forever,"
Said the Chinese nightingale.

My heart was filled with marvel and dream,
Though I saw the western street-lamps gleam,
Though dawn was bringing the western day,
Though Chang was a laundryman ironing away . . .
Mingled there with the streets and alleys,
The railroad-yard, and the clock-tower bright,
Demon-clouds crossed ancient valleys;
Across wide lotus-ponds of light
I marked a giant firefly's flight.

And the lady, rosy-red,
Opened her fan, closed her fan,
Stretched her hand toward Chang, and said:
"Do you remember,
Ages after,
Our palace of heart-red stone?
Do you remember
The little doll-faced children
With their lanterns full of moon-fire,
That came from all the empire
Honoring the throne?—
The loveliest fête and carnival
Our world had ever known?
The sages sat about us

With their heads bowed in their beards,
With proper meditation on the sight.
Confucius was not born;
We lived in those great days
Confucius later said were lived aright . . .
And this gray bird, on that day of spring,
With a bright-bronze breast and a bronze-brown wing,
Captured the world with his carolling.
Late at night his tune was spent.
Peasants,
Sages,
Children,
Homeward went,
And then the bronze bird sang for you and me.
We walked alone, our hearts were high and free.
I had a silvery name, I had a silvery name,
I had a silvery name—do you remember
The name you cried beside the tumbling sea?"

Chang turned not to the lady slim—
He bent to his work, ironing away;
But she was arch and knowing and glowing.
And the bird on his shoulder spoke for him.

"Darling . . . darling . . . darling . . . darling . . . "
Said the Chinese nightingale.

.   .   .   .

The great gray joss on a rustic shelf,
Rakish and shrewd, with his collar awry,
Sang impolitely, as though by himself,
Drowning with his bellowing the nightingale's cry:
"Back through a hundred, hundred years
Hear the waves as they climb the piers,
Hear the howl of the silver seas,
Hear the thunder!
Hear the gongs of holy China
How the waves and tunes combine
In a rhythmic clashing wonder,
Incantation old and fine:

'Dragons, dragons, Chinese dragons;
  Red fire-crackers, and green fire-crackers,
  And dragons, dragons, Chinese dragons.'"

Then the lady, rosy-red,
Turned to her lover Chang and said:
"Dare you forget that turquoise dawn
When we stood in our mist-hung velvet lawn,
And worked a spell this great joss taught
Till a God of the Dragons was charmed and caught?
From the flag high over our palace-home
He flew to our feet in rainbow-foam—
A king of beauty and tempest and thunder
Panting to tear our sorrows asunder,
A dragon of fair adventure and wonder.
We mounted the back of that royal slave
With thoughts of desire that were noble and grave.
We swam down the shore of the dragon-mountains,
We whirled to the peaks and the fiery fountains.
To our secret ivory house we were borne.
We looked down the wonderful wing-filled regions
Where the dragons darted in glimmering legions.
Right by my breast the nightingale sang;
The old rhymes rang in the sunlit mist
That we this hour regain—
Song-fire for the brain . . .
When my hands and my hair and my feet you kissed,
When you cried for your heart's new pain,
What was my name in the dragon-mist,
In the rings of rainbowed rain?"

  "Sorrow and love, glory and love,"
  Said the Chinese nightingale.
  "Sorrow and love, glory and love,"
  Said the Chinese nightingale.

And now the joss broke in with his song:
"Dying ember, bird of Chang,
Soul of Chang, do you remember?—
Ere you returned to the shining harbor

There were pirates by ten thousand
Descended on the town
In vessels mountain-high and red and brown,
Moon-ships that climbed the storms and cut the skies.
On their prows were painted terrible bright eyes.
But I was then a wizard and a scholar and a priest;
I stood upon the sand;
With lifted hand I looked upon them
And sunk their vessels with my wizard eyes,
And the stately lacquer-gate made safe again.
Deep, deep below the bay, the sea-weed and the spray,
Embalmed in amber every pirate lies,
Embalmed in amber every pirate lies."

Then this did the noble lady say:
"Bird, do you dream of our home-coming day
When you flew like a courier on before
From the dragon-peak to our palace-door,
And we drove the steed in your singing path—
The ramping dragon of laughter and wrath;
And found our city all aglow,
And knighted this joss that decked it so?
There were golden fishes in the purple river
And silver fishes and rainbow fishes.
There were golden junks in the laughing river,
And silver junks and rainbow junks.
There were golden lilies by the bay and river,
And silver lilies and tiger-lilies;
And tinkling wind-bells in the gardens of the town
By the black-lacquer gate
Where walked in state
The kind king Chang
And his sweet-heart mate . . .
With· his flag-born dragon
And his crown of pearl . . . and . . . jade;
And his nightingale reigning in the mulberry shade,
And sailors and soldiers on the sea-sands brown,
And priests who bowed them down to your song—
By the city called Han, the peacock town,

By the city called Han, the nightingale town,
The nightingale town."

Then sang the bird, so strangely gay,
Fluttering, fluttering, ghostly and gray,
A vague, unravelling, answering tune,
Like a long unwinding silk cocoon;
Sang as though for the soul of him
Who ironed away in that bower dim:

"I have forgotten
Your dragons great,
Merry and mad and friendly and bold.
Dim is your proud lost palace-gate.
I vaguely know
There were heroes of old,
Troubles more than the heart could hold.
There were wolves in the woods
Yet lambs in the fold,
Nests in the top of the almond tree . . .
The evergreen tree . . . and the mulberry tree . . .
Life and hurry and joy forgotten,
Years on years I but half-remember . . .
Man is a torch, then ashes soon,
May and June, then dead December,
Dead December, then again June.
Who shall end my dream's confusion?
Life is a loom, weaving illusion . . .
I remember, I remember
There were ghostly veils and laces
In the shadowy, bowery places . . .
With lovers' ardent faces
Bending to one another,
Speaking each his part.
They infinitely echo
In the red cave of my heart.
'Sweetheart, sweetheart, sweetheart!'
They said to one another.
They spoke, I think, of perils past.
They spoke. I think, of peace at last.

One thing I remember:
Spring came on forever,
Spring came on forever,"
Said the Chinese nightingale.

THE LEADEN–EYED

Let not young souls be smothered out before
They do quaint deeds and fully flaunt their pride.
It is the world's one crime its babes grow dull,
Its poor are ox-like, limp and leaden-eyed.
Not that they starve, but starve so dreamlessly;
Not that they sow, but that they seldom reap;
Not that they serve, but have no gods to serve;
Not that they die, but that they die like sheep.

THE EAGLE THAT IS FORGOTTEN

John P. Altgeld: Dec. 30, 1847–March 12, 1902

Sleep softly . . . eagle forgotten . . . under the stone.
Time has its way with you there, and the clay has its own.

"We have buried him now," thought your foes, and in secret
    rejoiced.
They made a brave show of their mourning, their hatred un-
    voiced.
They had snarled at you, barked at you, foamed at you day after
    day;
Now you were ended. They praised you . . . and laid you
    away.

The others that mourned you in silence and terror and truth—
The widow bereft of her crust, and the boy without youth,
The mocked and the scorned and the wounded, the lame and
    the poor,
That should have remembered forever . . . remember no more

Where are those lovers of yours, on what name do they call—
The lost, that in armies wept over your funeral pall?

They call on the names of a hundred high-valiant ones;
A hundred white eagles have risen, the sons of your sons.
The zeal in their wings is a zeal that your dreaming began,
The valor that wore out your soul in the service of man.

Sleep softly . . . eagle forgotten . . . under the stone.
Time has its way with you there, and the clay has its own.
Sleep on, O brave-hearted, O wise man, that kindled the flame—
To live in mankind is far more than to live in a name;
To live in mankind, far, far more . . . than to live in a name.

ABRAHAM LINCOLN WALKS AT MIDNIGHT

In Springfield, Illinois

It is portentous, and a thing of state
That here at midnight in our little town,
A mourning figure walks, and will not rest,
Near the old court-house pacing up and down.

Or by his homestead, or in shadowed yards,
He lingers where his children used to play;
Or through the market, on the well-worn stones,
He stalks until the dawn-stars burn away.

A bronzed lank man! His suit of ancient black,
A famous high top-hat and plain worn shawl,
Make his the quaint great figure that men love,
The prairie lawyer, master of us all.

He cannot sleep upon his hillside now.
He is among us—as in times before!
And we who toss and lie awake for long
Breathe deep, and start, to see him pass the door.

His head is bowed. He thinks on men and kings.
Yea, when the sick world cries, how can he sleep?
Too many peasants fight, they know not why;
Too many homesteads in black terror weep.

The sins of all the war-lords burn his heart.
He sees the dreadnaughts scouring every main.

He carries on his shawl-wrapped shoulders now
The bitterness, the folly and the pain.

He cannot rest until a spirit-dawn
Shall come—the shining hope of Europe free:
The league of sober folk, the Workers' Earth,
Bringing long peace to Cornland, Alp and Sea.

It breaks his heart that kings must murder still,
That all his hours of travail here for men
Seem yet in vain.   And who will bring white peace
That he may sleep upon his hill again?

THE VIRGINIANS ARE COMING AGAIN

Babbitt, your tribe is passing away.
This is the end of your infamous day.
The Virginians are coming again.

With your neat little safety-vault boxes,
With your faces like geese and foxes,
You
Short-legged, short-armed, short-minded men,
Your short-sighted days are over—
Your habits of strutting through clover,
Your movie-thugs killing off souls and dreams,
Your magazines drying up healing streams,
Your newspapers blasting truth and splendor,
Your shysters ruining progress and glory.
Babbitt, your story is passing away—
The Virginians are coming again.

All set for the victory, calling the raid,
I see them, the next generation,
Gentlemen, hard-riding, long-legged men,
With horse-whip, dog-whip, gauntlet and braid,
Mutineers, musketeers,
In command
Unafraid:
Great-grandsons of tide-water, and the bark-cabins,

Bards of the Blue-ridge, in buckskin and boots,
Up from the proudest war-path we have known
The Virginians are coming again.

The sons of ward-heelers
Threw out the ward-heelers,
The sons of bartenders
Threw out the bartenders,
And made our streets trick-boxes all in a day,
Kicked out the old pests in a virtuous way.
The new tribe sold kerosene, gasoline, paraffine.
Babbitt sold Judas. Babbitt sold Christ.
Babbitt sold everything under the sun.
The Moon-proud consider a trader a hog.
The Moon-proud are coming again.

Bartenders were gnomes,
Foreigners, tyrants, hairy baboons.
But you are no better with saxophone tunes,
Phonograph tunes, radio tunes,
Water-power tunes, gasoline tunes, dynamo tunes;
And pitiful souls like your pitiful tunes,
And crawling old insolence blocking the road.
So, Babbitt, your racket is passing away.
Your sons will be changelings, and burn down your world—
Fire-eaters, troubadours, conquistadors.
Your sons will be born refusing your load,
Thin-skinned scholars, hard-riding men,
Poets unharnessed, the moon their abode,
With the statesman's code, the gentleman's code,
With Jefferson's code, Washington's code,
With Powhatan's code!
From your own loins, for your fearful defeat,
The Virginians are coming again.

Our first Virginians were peasants' children
But the power of Powhatan reddened their blood,
Up from the sod came splendor and flood.
Eating the maize made them more than men,
Potomac fountains made gods of men.

In your tottering age, not so long from you now
The terror will blast, the armies will whirl,
Cavalier boy beside cavalier girl
In the glory of pride, not the pride of the rich,
In the glory of statesmanship, not of the ditch.
The old grand manner, lost no longer:
Exquisite art born with heart-bleeding song
Will make you die horribly, raving at wrong.
You will not know your sons who are true to this soil,
For Babbitt could never count much beyond ten,
For Babbitt could never quite comprehend men.
You will die in your shame, understanding not day—
Out of your loins, to your utmost confusion
The Virginians are coming again.

Do you think boys and girls that I pass on the street
More strong than their fathers, more fair than their fathers,
More clean than their fathers, more wild than their fathers,
More in love than their fathers, deep in thought not their
    fathers',
Are meat for your schemes diabolically neat?
Do you think that all youth is but grist to your mill,
And what you dare plan for them boys will fulfil?
The next generation is free. You are gone.
Out of your loins, to your utmost confusion,
The Virginians are coming again.

Rouse the reader to read it right.
Find a good hill by the full-moon light,
Gather the boys and chant all night—
"The Virginians are coming again."
Put in rhetoric, whisper, and hint;
Put in shadow, murmur, and glint;
Jingle and jangle this song like a spur.
Sweep over each tottering bridge with a whirr,
Clearer and faster up main street and pike
Till sparks flare up from the flints that strike.
Leap metrical ditches with bridle let loose.
This song is a way, with an iron-shod use.

Let no musician, with blotter and pad
Scribble his pot-hooks to make the song sad.
Find
Your own rhythms
When Robert E. Lee
Gallops once more to the plain from the sea.
Give the rebel yell every river they gain.
Hear Lee's light cavalry rhyme with rain.
In the star-proud natural fury of men
The Virginians are coming again.

Haniel Long

THE HERD BOY

The night I brought the cows home
  Blue mist was in the air,
And in my heart was heaven
  And on my lips a prayer.

I raised my arms above me,
  I stretched them wide apart,
And all the world was pressing
  In beauty on my heart.

The lane led by a river
  Along an ancient wood,
And ancient thoughts came softly
  As with the leaves they should.

I hung the cows with garlands,
  And proud they walked before;
While mother-naked after
  A laurel branch I bore.

DEAD MEN TELL NO TALES

They say that dead men tell no tales!

Except of barges with red sails,
And sailors mad for nightingales;

Except of jongleurs stretched at ease
Beside old highways through the trees;

Except of dying moons that break
The hearts of lads who lie awake;

Except of fortresses in shade,
And heroes crumbled and betrayed.

But dead men tell no tales, they say!

Except old tales that burn away
The stifling tapestries of day:

Old tales of life, of love and hate,
Of time and space, and will, and fate.

THE CAUSE OF THIS I KNOW NOT

The cause of this I know not,
    Whither they went, nor why;
But I still remember the laughter
    And the bright eyes flashing by—
The day the girls were kissing
    The boys who had to die.

I search in vain for the reason—
    What does a poet know?—
Only that youth is lovely,
    Only that youth must go;
And hearts are made to be broken,
    And love is always woe.

HIS DEATHS

He bore the brunt of it so long,
And carried it off with wine and song,
The neighbors paused and raised an eye
At hearing he had learned to die.

'Twas on a Friday that he died,
But Easter day his neighbors spied
His usual figure on the streets,
And one and all were white as sheets.

"I died," said he, "on Good Friday,
And someone rolled the stone away;
And I come back to you alive
To die tonight at half past five.

"Monday at Babylon I fall,
And Tuesday on the Chinese wall;
Wednesday I die on the Thracian plain,
And Thursday evening at Compiègne.

"Saturday, Sunday, Monday too,
I die, and come to life anew;
Neighbors like Thomas look and touch,
Amazed that I can live so much."

Amy Lowell

PATTERNS

I walk down the garden paths,
And all the daffodils
Are blowing, and the bright blue squills.
I walk down the patterned garden paths
In my stiff brocaded gown.
With my powdered hair and jewelled fan,
I too am a rare
Pattern, as I wander down
The garden paths.

My dress is richly figured,
And the train
Makes a pink and silver stain
On the gravel, and the thrift
Of the borders.
Just a plate of current fashion,
Tripping by in high-heeled, ribboned shoes.
Not a softness anywhere about me,
Only whale-bone and brocade.
And I sink on a seat in the shade
Of a lime tree. For my passion
Wars against the stiff brocade.
The daffodils and squills
Flutter in the breeze
As they please.
And I weep;
For the lime tree is in blossom
And one small flower has dropped upon my bosom.

And the plashing of waterdrops
In the marble fountain
Comes down the garden paths.
The dripping never stops.
Underneath my stiffened gown
Is the softness of a woman bathing in a marble basin,
A basin in the midst of hedges grown
So thick, she cannot see her lover hiding.
But she guesses he is near,
And the sliding of the water
Seems the stroking of a dear
Hand upon her.
What is summer in a fine brocaded gown!
I should like to see it lying in a heap upon the ground.
All the pink and silver crumpled up on the ground.

I would be the pink and silver as I ran along the paths,
And he would stumble after,
Bewildered by my laughter.
I should see the sun flashing from his sword hilt and the buckles
    on his shoes.

I would choose
To lead him in a maze along the patterned paths,
A bright and laughing maze for my heavy-booted lover,
Till he caught me in the shade,
And the buttons of his waistcoat bruised my body as he clasped
    me,
Aching, melting, unafraid.
With the shadows of the leaves and the sundrops,
And the plopping of the waterdrops,
All about us in the open afternoon—
I am very like to swoon
With the weight of this brocade,
For the sun sifts through the shade.

Underneath the fallen blossom
In my bosom
Is a letter I have hid.
It was brought to me this morning by a rider from the Duke.
"Madam, we regret to inform you that Lord Hartwell
Died in action Thursday se'nnight."
As I read it in the white morning sunlight,
The letters squirmed like snakes.
"Any answer, Madam?" said my footman.
"No," I told him.
"See that the messenger takes some refreshment.
No, no answer."

And I walked into the garden,
Up and down the patterned paths,
In my stiff, correct brocade.
The blue and yellow flowers stood up proudly in the sun,
Each one.
I stood upright too,
Held rigid to the pattern
By the stiffness of my gown.
Up and down I walked,
Up and down.

In a month he would have been my husband.
In a month, here, underneath this lime,

We would have broke the pattern;
He for me, and I for him,
He as Colonel, I as Lady,
On this shady seat.
He had a whim
That sunlight carried blessing.
And I answered, "It shall be as you have said."
Now he is dead.

In summer and in winter I shall walk
Up and down
The patterned garden paths
In my stiff brocaded gown.
The squills and daffodils
Will give place to pillared roses, and to asters, and to snow.
I shall go
Up and down,
In my gown,
Gorgeously arrayed,
Boned and stayed.
And the softness of my body will be guarded from embrace
By each button, hook, and lace.
For the man who should loose me is dead,
Fighting with the Duke in Flanders,
In a pattern called a war.
Christ! What are patterns for?

THE TRUMPET-VINE ARBOR

1777

The throats of the little red trumpet-flowers are wide open,
And the clangor of brass beats against the hot sunlight.
They bray and blare at the burning sky.
Red! Red! Coarse notes of red,
Trumpeted at the blue sky.
In long streaks of sound, molten metal,
The vine declares itself.
Clang!—from its red and yellow trumpets.
Clang!—from its long, nasal trumpets,
Splitting the sunlight into ribbons, tattered and shot with noise.

I sit in the cool arbor, in a green and gold twilight.
It is very still, for I cannot hear the trumpets;
I only know that they are red and open,
And that the sun above the arbor shakes with heat.
My quill is newly mended,
And makes fine-drawn lines with its point.
Down the long white paper it makes little lines,
Just lines—up—down—criss-cross.
My heart is strained out at the pin-point of my quill;
It is thin and writhing like the marks of the pen.
My hand marches to a squeaky tune,
It marches down the paper to a squealing of fifes.
My pen and the trumpet-flowers,
And Washington's armies away over the smoke-tree to the
  southwest.
Yankee Doodle, my darling! It is you against the British,
Marching in your ragged shoes to batter down King George.
What have you got in your hat? Not a feather, I wager.
Just a hay-straw, for it is the harvest you are fighting for.
Hay in your hat, and the whites of their eyes for a target!
Like Bunker Hill, two years ago, when I watched all day from the
  housetop,
Through father's spy-glass—
The red city, and the blue, bright water,
And puffs of smoke which you made.
Twenty miles away,
Round my Cambridge, or over the Neck,
But the smoke was white—white!
Today the trumpet-flowers are red—red—
And I cannot see you fighting;
But old Mr. Dimond has fled to Canada,
And Myra sings *Yankee Doodle* at her milking.

The red throats of the trumpets bray and clang in the sunshine,
And the smoke-tree puffs dun blossoms into the blue air.

VENUS TRANSIENS

Tell me,
Was Venus more beautiful
Than you are,
When she topped
The crinkled waves,
Drifting shoreward
On her plaited shell?
Was Botticelli's vision
Fairer than mine;
And were the painted rosebuds
He tossed his lady
Of better worth
Than the words I blow about you
To cover your too great loveliness
As with a gauze
Of misted silver?

For me,
You stand poised
In the blue and buoyant air,
Cinctured by bright winds,
Treading the sunlight.
And the waves which precede you
Ripple and stir
The sands at my feet.

A LADY

You are beautiful and faded,
Like an old opera tune
Played upon a harpsichord;
Or like the sun-flooded silks
Of an eighteenth-century boudoir.
In your eyes
Smoulder the fallen roses of outlived minutes,
And the perfume of your soul
Is vague and suffusing,

With the pungence of sealed spice jars.
Your half-tones delight me,
And I grow mad with gazing
At your blent colors.

My vigor is a new-minted penny,
Which I cast at your feet.
Gather it up from the dust,
That its sparkle may amuse you.

CHINOISERIES

REFLECTIONS

When I looked into your eyes,
I saw a garden
With peonies, and tinkling pagodas,
And round-arched bridges
Over still lakes.
A woman sat beside the water
In a rain-blue, silken garment.
She reached through the water
To pluck the crimson peonies
Beneath the surface,
But as she grasped the stems,
They jarred and broke into white-green ripples;
And as she drew out her hand,
The water-drops dripping from it
Stained her rain-blue dress like tears.

FALLING SNOW

The snow whispers about me,
And my wooden clogs
Leave holes behind me in the snow.
But no one will pass this way
Seeking my footsteps,
And when the temple bell rings again
They will be covered and gone.

HOAR-FROST

In the cloud-gray mornings
I heard the herons flying;
And when I came into my garden,
My silken outer-garment
Trailed over withered leaves.
A dried leaf crumbles at a touch,
But I have seen many autumns
With herons blowing like smoke
Across the sky.

SOLITAIRE

When night drifts along the streets of the city,
And sifts down between the uneven roofs,
My mind begins to peek and peer.
It plays at ball in old blue Chinese gardens,
And shakes wrought dice-cups in Pagan temples,
Amid the broken flutings of white pillars.
It dances with purple and yellow crocuses in its hair,
And its feet shine as they flutter over drenched grasses.
How light and laughing my mind is,
When all the good folk have put out their bed-room candles,
And the city is still!

RED SLIPPERS

Red slippers in a shop-window; and outside the street, flaws
of gray, windy sleet!

Behind the polished glass the slippers hang in long threads of
red, festooning from the ceiling like stalactites of blood, flooding the eyes of passers-by with dripping color, jamming their
crimson reflections against the windows of cabs and tram-cars,
screaming their claret and salmon into the teeth of the sleet,
plopping their little round maroon lights upon the tops of umbrellas.

The row of white, sparkling shop-fronts is gashed and bleeding, it bleeds red slippers. They spout under the electric light,
fluid and fluctuating, a hot rain—and freeze again to red slippers, myriadly multiplied in the mirror side of the window.

They balance upon arched insteps like springing bridges of
crimson lacquer; they swing up over curved heels like whirling
tanagers sucked in a wind-pocket; they flatten out, heelless,
like July ponds, flared and burnished by red rockets.

Snap, snap, they are cracker sparks of scarlet in the white,
monotonous block of shops.

They plunge the clangor of billions of vermilion trumpets into
the crowd outside, and echo in faint rose over the pavement.

People hurry by, for these are only shoes, and in a window farther down is a big lotus bud of cardboard, whose petals open
every few minutes and reveal a wax doll, with staring bead eyes
and flaxen hair, lolling awkwardly in its flower chair.

One has often seen shoes, but whoever saw a cardboard lotus
bud before?

The flaws of gray, windy sleet beat on the shop-window where
there are only red slippers.

A GIFT

See! I give myself to you, Beloved!
My words are little jars
For you to take and put upon a shelf.
Their shapes are quaint and beautiful,
And they have many pleasant colors and lustres
To recommend them.
Also the scent from them fills the room
With sweetness of flowers and crushed grasses.

When I shall have given you the last one
You will have the whole of me,
But I shall be dead.

APOLOGY

Be not angry with me that I bear
    Your colors everywhere,
    All through each crowded street,
        And meet
    The wonder-light in every eye,
        As I go by.

Each plodding wayfarer looks up to gaze,
    Blinded by rainbow-haze,
    The stuff of happiness,
        No less,
    Which wraps me in its glad-hued folds
        Of peacock golds.

Before my feet the dusty rough-paved way
    Flushes beneath its gray.
    My steps fall ringed with light,
        So bright
    It seems a myriad suns are strown
        About the town.

Around me is the sound of steepled bells,
    And rich perfumed smells
    Hang like a wind-forgotten cloud,
        And shroud
    Me from close contact with the world.
        I dwell, impearled.

You blazon me with jewelled insignia.
    A flaming nebula
    Rims in my life. And yet
        You set
    The word upon me, unconfessed,
        To go unguessed.

MEETING–HOUSE HILL

I must be mad, or very tired,
When the curve of a blue bay beyond a railroad track
Is shrill and sweet to me like the sudden springing of a tune,
And the sight of a white church above thin trees in a city square
Amazes my eyes as though it were the Parthenon.
Clear, reticent, superbly final,
With the pillars of its portico refined to a cautious elegance,
It dominates the weak trees,
And the shot of its spire
Is cool, and candid,
Rising into an unresisting sky.
Strange meeting-house
Pausing a moment upon a squalid hill-top.
I watch the spire sweeping the sky,
I am dizzy with the movement of the sky,
I might be watching a mast
With its royals set full
Straining before a two-reef breeze.
I might be sighting a tea-clipper,
Tacking into the blue bay,
Just back from Canton
With her hold full of green and blue porcelain
And a Chinese coolie leaning over the rail
Gazing at the white spire
With dull, sea-spent eyes.

OMBRE CHINOISE

Red foxgloves against a yellow wall streaked with plum-colored
        shadows;
A lady with a blue and red sunshade;
The slow dash of waves upon a parapet.
That is all.
Non-existent—immortal—
As solid as the centre of a ring of fine gold.

NIGHT CLOUDS

The white mares of the moon rush along the sky
Beating their golden hoofs upon the glass heavens;
The white mares of the moon are all standing on their hind legs
Pawing at the green porcelain doors of the remote heavens.
Fly, mares!
Strain your utmost,
Scatter the milky dust of stars,
Or the tiger sun will leap upon you and destroy you
With one lick of his vermilion tongue.

THE GARDEN BY MOONLIGHT

A black cat among roses,
Phlox, lilac-misted under a first-quarter moon,
The sweet smells of heliotrope and night-scented stock.
The garden is very still;
It is dazed with moonlight,

Contented with perfume,
Dreaming the opium dreams of its folded poppies.
Firefly lights open and vanish,
High as the tip buds of the golden glow,
Low as the sweet alyssum flowers at my feet.
Moon-shimmer on leaves and trellises,
Moon-spikes shafting through the snow-ball bush,
Only the little faces of the ladies' delight are alert and staring;
Only the cat, padding between the roses,
Shakes a branch and breaks the chequered pattern
As water is broken by the falling of a leaf.
Then you come,
And you are quiet like the garden,
And white like the alyssum flowers,
And beautiful as the silent sparks of the fireflies.
Ah, Beloved, do you see those orange lilies?
They knew my mother.
But who belonging to me will they know
When I am gone?

FOUR SIDES TO A HOUSE

Peter, Peter, along the ground,
Is it wind I hear, or your shoes' sound?
Peter, Peter, across the air,
Do dead leaves fall, or is it your hair?
Peter, Peter, North and South,
They have stopped your mouth
With water, Peter.

The long road runs, and the long road runs,
   Who comes over the long road, Peter?
Who knocks at the door in the cold twilight,
And begs a heap of straw for the night,
And a bit of a sup, and a bit of a bite—
   Do you know the face, Peter?

He lays him down on the floor and sleeps.
   Must you wind the clock, Peter?
It will strike and strike the dark night through.
He will sleep past one, he will sleep past two,
But when it strikes three what will he do?
   He will rise and kill you, Peter.

He will open the door to one without.
   Do you hear that voice, Peter?
Two men prying and poking about—
Is it here, is it there, is it in, is it out?
Cover his staring eyes with a clout.
   But you're dead, dead, Peter.

They have ripped up the boards, they have pried up the stones,
   They have found your gold, dead Peter.
Ripe red coins to itch a thief's hand,
But you drip ripe red on the floor's white sand,
You burn their eyes like a firebrand.
   They must quench you, Peter.

It is dark in the North, it is dark in the South.
   The wind blows your white hair, Peter.
One at your feet and one at your head.

A soft bed, a smooth bed,
Scarcely a splash, you sink like lead.
 Sweet water in your well, Peter.

Along the road and along the road,
 The next house, Peter.
Four-square to the bright and the shade of the moon.
The North winds shuffle, the South winds croon,
Water with white hair over-strewn.
 The door, the door, Peter!
Water seeps under the door.

They have risen up in the morning grey.
 What will they give to Peter?
The sorrel horse with the tail of gold,
Fastest pacer ever was foaled.
Shoot him, skin him, blanch his bones,
Nail up his skull with a silver nail
Over the door, it will not fail.
No ghostly thing can ever prevail
 Against a horse's skull, Peter.

Over the lilacs, gazing down,
 Is a window, Peter.
The north winds call, and the south winds cry.
Silver white hair in a bitter blowing,
Eel-green water washing by,
A red mouth floating and flowing.
 Do you come, Peter?

They rose as the last star sank and set.
 One more for Peter.
They slew the black mare at the flush of the sun,
And nailed her skull to the window-stone.
In the light of the moon how white it shone—
 And your breathing mouth, Peter!

Around the house, and around the house,
With a wind that is North, and a wind that is South,
 Peter, Peter.
Mud and ooze and a dead man's wrist

Wrenching the shutters apart, like mist
The mud and the ooze and the dead man twist.
   They are praying, Peter.

Three in stable a week ago.
   This is the last, Peter.
"My strawberry roan in the morning clear,
Lady heart and attentive ear,
Foot like a kitten, nose like a deer,
But the fear! The fear!"
   Three skulls, Peter.

The sun goes down, and the night draws in.
   Toward the hills, Peter.
What lies so stiff on the hill-room floor,
When the gusty wind claps to the door?
They have paid three horses and two men more.
   Gather your gold, Peter.

Softly, softly, along the ground
Lest your shoes sound.
Gently, gently, across the air
Lest it stream, your hair.
North and South
For your aching mouth.
But the moon is old, Peter,
And death is long, and the well is deep.
Can you sleep, sleep, Peter?

ON LOOKING AT A COPY OF ALICE MEYNELL'S
POEMS GIVEN ME YEARS AGO BY A FRIEND

     Upon this greying page you wrote
     A whispered greeting, long ago.
     Faint pencil-marks run to and fro
     Scoring the lines I loved to quote.

     A sea-shore of white shoaling sand,
     Blue creeks zigzagging through marsh-grasses,

Sandpipers, and a wind which passes
Cloudily silent up the land.

Upon the high edge of the sea
A great four-master sleeps; three hours
Her bowsprit has not cleared those flowers.
I read and look alternately.

It all comes back again, but dim
As pictures on a winking wall,
Hidden save when the dark clouds fall
Or crack to show the moon's bright rim.

I well remember what I was,
And what I wanted. You, unwise
With sore unwisdom, had no eyes
For what was patently the cause.

So are we sport of others' blindness,
We who could see right well alone.
What were you made of—wood or stone?
Yet I remember you with kindness.

You gave this book to me to ease
The smart in me you could not heal.
Your gift a mirror—woe or weal.
We sat beneath the apple-trees.

And I remember how they rang,
These words, like bronze cathedral bells
Down ancient lawns, or citadels
Thundering with gongs where choirs sang.

Silent the sea, the earth, the sky,
And in my heart a silent weeping.
Who has not sown can know no reaping!
Bitter conclusion and no lie.

O heart that sorrows, heart that bleeds,
Heart that was never mine, your words
Were like the pecking autumn birds
Stealing away my garnered seeds.

No future where there is no past!
O cherishing grief which laid me bare,
I wrapped you like a wintry air
About me. Poor enthusiast!

How strange that tumult, looking back.
The ink is pale, the letters fade.
The verses seem to be well made,
But I have lived the almanac.

And you are dead these drifted years,
How many I forget. And she
Who wrote the book, her tragedy
Long since dried up its scalding tears.

I read of her death yesterday,
Frail lady whom I never knew
And knew so well. Would I could strew
Her grave with pansies, blue and grey.

Would I could stand a little space
Under a blowing brightening sky,
And watch the sad leaves fall and lie
Gently upon that lonely place.

So cried her heart, a feverish thing.
But clay is still, and clay is cold,
And I was young, and I am old,
And in December what birds sing!

Go, wistful book, go back again
Upon your shelf and gather dust.
I've seen the glitter through the rust
Of old long years; I've known the pain.

I've recollected both of you,
But I shall recollect no more.
Between us I must shut the door.
The living have so much to do.

Archibald MacLeish

ARS POETICA

A poem should be palpable and mute
As a globed fruit;

Dumb
As old medallions to the thumb;

Silent as the sleeve-worn stone
Of casement ledges where the moss has grown—

A poem should be wordless
As the flight of birds.

.   .   .   .

A poem should be motionless in time
As the moon climbs,

Leaving, as the moon releases
Twig by twig the night-entangled trees,

Leaving, as the moon behind the winter leaves,
Memory by memory the mind.

A poem should be motionless in time
As the moon climbs.

.   .   .   .

A poem should be equal to:
Not true.

For all the history of grief
An empty doorway and a maple leaf;

For love
The leaning grasses and two lights above the sea—

A poem should not mean
But be.

IMMORTAL AUTUMN

I speak this poem now with grave and level voice
In praise of autumn of the far-horn-winding fall
I praise the flower-barren fields the clouds the tall
Unanswering branches where the wind makes sullen noise

I praise the fall it is the human season
                              now
No more the foreign sun does meddle at our earth
Enforce the green and bring the fallow land to birth
Nor winter yet weigh all with silence the pine bough

But now in autumn with the black and outcast crows
Share we the spacious world the whispering year is gone
There is more room to live now the once secret dawn
Comes late by daylight and the dark unguarded goes

Between the mutinous brave burning of the leaves
And winter's covering of our hearts with his deep snow
We are alone there are no evening birds we know
The naked moon the tame stars circle at our eaves

It is the human season on this sterile air
Do words outcarry breath the sound goes on and on
I hear a dead man's cry from autumn long since gone

I cry to you beyond upon this bitter air

MEN

On a phrase of Apollinaire

Our history is grave noble and tragic
We trusted the look of the sun on the green leaves
We built our towns of stone with enduring ornaments
We worked the hard flint for basins of water

We believed in the feel of the earth under us
We planted corn grapes apple-trees rhubarb
Nevertheless we knew others had died
Everything we have done has been faithful and dangerous

We believed in the promises made by the brows of women
We begot children at night in the warm wool
We comforted those who wept in fear on our shoulders
Those who comforted us had themselves vanished

We fought at the dikes in the bright sun for the pride of it
We beat drums and marched with music and laughter
We were drunk and lay with our fine dreams in the straw
We saw the stars through the hair of lewd women

Our history is grave noble and tragic
Many of us have died and are not remembered
Many cities are gone and their channels broken
We have lived a long time in this land and with honor.

L'AN TRENTIESME DE MON EAGE

And I have come upon this place
By lost ways, by a nod, by words,
By faces, by an old man's face
At Morlaix lifted to the birds,

By hands upon the tablecloth
At Aldebori's, by the thin
Child's hands that opened to the moth
And let the flutter of the moonlight in,

By hands, by voices, by the voice
Of Mrs. Husman on the stair,
By Margaret's "If we had the choice
To choose or not—" through her thick hair,

By voices, by the creak and fall
Of footsteps on the upper floor,
By silence waiting in the hall
Between the doorbell and the door,

By words, by voices, a lost way—
And here above the chimney stack
The unknown constellations sway—
And by what way shall I go back?

THE END OF THE WORLD

Quite unexpectedly as Vasserot
The armless ambidextrian was lighting
A match between his great and second toe,
And Ralph the lion was engaged in biting
The neck of Madame Sossman while the drum
Pointed, and Teeny was about to cough
In waltz-time swinging Jocko by the thumb—
Quite unexpectedly the top blew off:

And there, there overhead, there, there, hung over
Those thousands of white faces, those dazed eyes,
There in the starless dark the poise, the hover,
There with vast wings across the cancelled skies,
There in the sudden blackness the black pall
Of nothing, nothing, nothing—nothing at all.

YOU, ANDREW MARVEL

And here face down beneath the sun
And here upon earth's noonward height
To feel the always coming on
The always rising of the night

To feel creep up, the curving east
The earthy chill of dusk and slow
Upon those under lands the vast
And ever climbing shadow grow

And strange at Ecbatab the trees
Take leaf by leaf the evening strange
Take flooding dark about their knees
The mountains over Persia change

And now at Kermanshah the gate
Dark empty and the withered grass
And through the twilight now the late
Few travellers in the westward pass

And Baghdad darken and the bridge
Across the silent river gone
And through Arabia the edge
Of evening widen and steal on

And deepen on Palmyra's street
The wheel rut in the ruined stone
And Lebanon fade out and Crete
High through the clouds and overblown

And over Sicily the air
Still flashing with the landward gulls
And loom and slowly disappear
The sails above the shadowy hulls

And Spain go under and the shore
Of Africa the gilded sand
And evening vanish and no more
The low pale light across that land

Nor now the long light on the sea

And here face downward in the sun
To feel how swift how secretly
The shadow of the night comes on . . .

Joseph Gordon Macleod

SAGITTARIUS OR THE ARCHER

As a corpse face in shadow of a shrub
Would gleam, pale, bruised, and half invisible,
So hangs the moon, gibbous, and no more subdivisible.
We go no farther thus.
                  But come with me,
Old Berkeley, join our Lion-Scales-Virginity
In search without extension of triangularity.
News is, in Space-Time Einstein got
Two simultaneous events and unconnected
Which, he discovered, one pure triangle erected.

Is this our quest? We know that it is not.
Come, for the sky is crisp with crystal prisms,
The ground is bouldered o'er with cataclysms.
Knee-high the air is dense with ghostly hills
And ghostly parapets and plains too cool,
Flat bulky floors of cottonwool
And gaps in space that spatial fluid fills.
This grey-white city grown of pendent curves
Whose corners fold, whose copingstones are domes,
Bulging façades with pores like honeycombs
And every wall as womb to neighbor serves,
Tramp we, our calves nakedly its foundations
Piercing, as the keelskins of canoes.
On not a fathom's half of lucid air
Opaque the clustered floatages do cruise
Each saturating, bumping, drifting everywhere.
As our cold feet the empty bottom tread,
So above rounded roofs our triple head
Counts unobstructed glintings in the sky:
Silver Orion watching angrily
The quiet spinning of the Pleiades
Like nuns at home; while in the Western seas
Her blue hull Vega steers without farewell.
Resolute Sirius at the warrior's feet
Stares his loud wealth, which from a higher street
Procyon copies: caught in his own spell
The wizard Algol dying on the hill
With weakened grip has fallen from his net,
But one strand stretches to suspend him yet.
The mists float liquid, but the sky is still,
A city on a city laid. We come
Resignedly, and reverently, dumb
Our quarry in its sanctuary to find.

Tauten our mind.
Our quarry in its sanctuary sleeps
As yet; as yet no raping daylight creeps
Brutally on its quest: nor stops the owl
Dashing destroyer-like with foghorn howl.

We bruise our feet because no vision is,
And shut our eyes along the precipice.
The pools we plunge in through the ground mist splash
Spurting in stars that vanish as they flash:
The molehills lift us under the thick sheet:
And if in spaces we may clearings meet
They serve but to disclose a further fog.
Night is the end, and mist the epilogue.

Rhyming our pathway falters. On the banks
Of pale wool widen flanks of paler waves
Like moonlit headstones over moonlit graves,
And purpose gathers on those widening flanks.
Up in the citadel the windows cease
To glint metallic: in the darker west
Where Vega on the horizon long has pressed,
Glimmer the far departing Pleiades,
And wan Orion bows too to depart.
The eastern constellations like a hart
Seen mottles betwixt leaves of forest trees,
Dappling fade into the siccate sky,
But white and stedfast as they pass him by
His destined note the Morning Planet frees.

Come let us draw our bows. The quarry springs
Alarmed from cover: at whose noisy break
A thousand pigeons swift on squeaky wings
Flood, like the firmament become awake,
Across this glade. Magpies and startled rails
Squawk: and the rabbits ricochet their tails
White-tufted. Suddenly and far away
Not dawn-dumb yet the bittern in the marsh
Booms: and the corbies make the morning harsh.
In the mute suburbs at the dawn of day
Bird bands in garden bandstands make all gay,
Misselthrush, throstle, blackbird, and redbreast;
And ladies to newspapers write to say
Which of the pretty songsters they like best,
When in their soft beds, proud to be awake,
They hear sweet nature from her slumber break.

But here there is no comfort and no light.
A dull expansion, dawn makes our earth bare
Of cover. We have trodden down the night,
Now its successor fronts us. The white air
Shudders. Nothing is still. Contempt
Echoes from rocks. Aye, for our cowardice
Us from the blame who would not hold exempt,
Who alone braved the fog-made precipice?
What though we shut our eyes? Come, let us draw.
That little triple speck of dark you saw
Flung like a petal from the blossoming east,
That be our mark. Aim at the Morning Star,
Aim at the mists that yet too thick are pierced,
Aim where you will, so you stand where you are.
For thus, for thus . . .
                              But Dawn comes meaningless.
Of all this purpose can we make nought wise?
Will nothing follow nights of nothingness?
Mists take the bird. The archer none the less
Shoots, and the arrow flies.

Frederic Manning

SACRIFICE

Love suffereth all things.
And we,
Out of the travail and pain of our striving,
Bring unto Thee the perfect prayer:
For the heart of no man uttereth love,
Suffering even for love's sake.

For us no splendid apparel of pageantry—
Burnished breast-plates, scarlet banners, and trumpets
Sounding exultantly.
But the mean things of the earth hast Thou chosen,
Decked them with suffering;
Made them beautiful with the passion for rightness,
Strong with the pride of love.

Yea, though our praise of Thee slayeth us,
Yet love shall exalt us beside Thee triumphant,
Dying, that these live;
And the earth again be beautiful with orchards,
Yellow with wheatfields;
And the lips of others praise Thee, though our lips
Be stopped with earth, and songless.

But we shall have brought Thee their praises,
Brought unto Thee the perfect prayer:
For the lips of no man utter love,
Suffering even for love's sake.

O God of sorrows,
Whose feet come softly through the dews,
Stoop Thou unto us,
For we die so Thou livest,
Our hearts the cups of Thy vintage:
And the lips of no man utter love,
Suffering even for love's sake.

AT EVEN

Hush ye! Hush ye! My babe is sleeping.
Hush, ye winds, that are full of sorrow!
Hush, ye rains, from your weary weeping!
Give him slumber until to-morrow.

Hush ye, yet! In the years hereafter,
Surely sorrow is all his reaping;
Tears shall be in the place of laughter,
Give him peace for a while in sleeping.

Hush ye, hush! he is weak and ailing:
Send his mother his share of weeping.
Hush ye, winds, from your endless wailing;
Hush ye, hush ye, my babe is sleeping!

THE SIGN

From the trenches

We are here in a wood of little beeches;
And the leaves are like black lace
Against a sky of nacre.

One bough of clear promise
Across the moon.

It is in this wise that God speaketh unto me.
He layeth hands of healing upon my flesh,
Stilling it in an eternal peace;
Until my soul reaches out myriad and infinite hands
Toward him,
And is eased of its hunger.

And I know that this passes—
This implacable fury and torment of men—
As a thing insensate and vain.
And the stillness hath said unto me,
Over the tumult of sounds and shaken flame,
Out of the terrible beauty of wrath,
I alone am eternal.

One bough of clear promise
Across the moon.

John Masefield

SHIPS

I cannot tell their wonder nor make known
Magic that once thrilled through me to the bone;
But all men praise some beauty, tell some tale,
Vent a high mood which makes the rest seem pale,
Pour their heart's blood to flourish one green leaf,
Follow some Helen for her gift of grief,

And fail in what they mean, whate'er they do:
You should have seen, man cannot tell to you
The beauty of the ships of that my city.
That beauty now is spoiled by the sea's pity;
For one may haunt the pier a score of times,
Hearing St. Nicholas bells ring out the chimes,
Yet never see those proud ones swaying home
With mainyards backed and bows a cream of foam,
Those bows so lovely-curving, cut so fine,
Those coulters of the many-bubbled brine—
As once, long since, when all the docks were filled
With that sea-beauty man has ceased to build.

Yet, though their splendor may have ceased to be,
Each played her sovereign part in making me;
Now I return my thanks with heart and lips
For the great queenliness of all those ships.

And first the first bright memory, still so clear,
An autumn evening in a golden year,
When in the last lit moments before dark
The *Chepica*, a steel-gray lovely barque,
Came to an anchor near us on the flood,
Her trucks aloft in sun-glow red as blood.

Then come so many ships that I could fill
Three docks with their fair hulls remembered still,
Each with her special memory's special grace,
Riding the sea, making the waves give place
To delicate high beauty; man's best strength,
Noble in every line in all their length.
Ailsa, *Genista*, ships with long jibbooms,
The *Wanderer* with great beauty and strange dooms,
Liverpool (mightiest then) superb, sublime,
The *California* huge, as slow as time.
The *Copley* swift, the perfect *J. T. North*,
The loveliest barque my city has sent forth,
Dainty *John Lockett* well remembered yet,
The splendid *Argus* with her skysail set,
Stalwart *Drumcliff*, white-blocked, majestic *Sierras*,

Divine bright ships, the water's standard-bearers;
Melpomene, Euphrosyne, and their sweet
Sea-troubling sisters of the Fernie fleet;
Corunna (in whom my friend died) and the old
Long since loved *Esmeralda* long since sold.
Centurion passed in Rio, *Glaucus* spoken,
Aladdin burnt, the *Bidston* water-broken,
Yola, in whom my friend sailed, *Dawpool* trim,
Fierce-bowed *Egeria* plunging to the swim,
Stanmore wide-sterned, sweet *Cupica,* tall *Bard,*
Queen in all harbors with her moon-sail yard.

Though I tell many, there must still be others,
McVickar Marshall's ships and Fernie Brothers',
Lochs, Counties, Shires, Drums, the countless lines
Whose house-flags all were once familiar signs
At high main-trucks on Mersey's windy ways
When sunlight made the wind-white water blaze.
Their names bring back old mornings, when the docks
Shone with their house-flags and their painted blocks,
Their raking masts below the Custom House
And all the marvellous beauty of their bows.

Familiar steamers, too, majestic steamers,
Shearing Atlantic roller-tops to streamers,
Umbria, Etruria, noble, still at sea,
The grandest, then, that man had brought to be.
Majestic, City of Paris, City of Rome,
Forever, jealous racers, out and home.
The *Alfred Holt's* blue smoke-stacks down the stream,
The fair *Loanda* with her bows a-cream.
Booth liners, Anchor liners, Red Star liners,
The marks and styles of countless ship-designers,
The *Magdalena, Puno, Potosi,*
Lost *Cotopaxi,* all well known to me.

These splendid ships, each with her grace, her glory,
Her memory of old song or comrade's story,
Still in my mind the image of life's need,
Beauty in hardest action, beauty indeed.

"They built great ships and sailed them" sounds most brave,
Whatever arts we have or fail to have.
I touch my country's mind, I come to grips
With half her purpose, thinking of these ships:
That art untouched by softness, all that line
Drawn ringing hard to stand the test of brine;
That nobleness and grandeur, all that beauty
Born of a manly life and bitter duty;
That splendor of fine bows which yet could stand
The shock of rollers never checked by land;
That art of masts, sail-crowded, fit to break,
Yet stayed to strength and backstayed into rake;
The life demanded by that art, the keen
Eye-puckered, hard-case seamen, silent, lean.
They are grander things than all the art of towns;
Their tests are tempests and the sea that drowns.
They are my country's line, her great art done
By strong brains laboring on the thought unwon.
They mark our passage as a race of men—
Earth will not see such ships as those again.

CARGOES

Quinquireme of Nineveh from distant Ophir,
Rowing home to haven in sunny Palestine,
With a cargo of ivory,
And apes and peacocks,
Sandalwood, cedarwood, and sweet white wine.

Stately Spanish galleon coming from the Isthmus,
Dipping through the Tropics by the palm-green shores,
With a cargo of diamonds,
Emeralds, amethysts,
Topazes, and cinnamon, and gold moidores.

Dirty British coaster with a salt-caked smoke-stack,
Butting through the Channel in the mad March days,
With a cargo of Tyne coal,
Road-rails, pig-lead,
Firewood, iron-ware, and cheap tin trays.

WATCHING BY A SICK-BED

I heard the wind all day,
And what it was trying to say.
I heard the wind all night
Rave as it ran to fight;
After the wind the rain,
And then the wind again
Running across the hill
As it runs still.

And all day long the sea
Would not let the land be,
But all night heaped her sand
On to the land.
I saw her glimmer white
All through the night,
Tossing the horrid hair
Still tossing there.

And all day long the stone
Felt how the wind was blown;
And all night long the rock
Stood the sea's shock;
While, from the window, I
Looked out, and wondered why,
Why at such length
Such force should fight such strength.

WHAT AM I, LIFE?

What am I, life? A thing of watery salt
Held in cohesion by unresting cells,
Which work they know not why, which never halt,
Myself unwitting where their Master dwells.
I do not bid them, yet they toil, they spin
A world which uses me as I use them;
Nor do I know which end or which begin
Nor which to praise, which pamper, which condemn.

So, like a marvel in a marvel set,
I answer to the vast, as wave by wave
The sea of air goes over, dry or wet,
Or the full moon comes swimming from her cave,
Or the great sun comes forth: this myriad I
Tingles, not knowing how, yet wondering why.

THE PASSING STRANGE

Out of the earth to rest or range
Perpetual in perpetual change—
The unknown passing through the strange.

Water and saltness held together
To tread the dust and stand the weather
And plough the field and stretch the tether.

To pass the wine-cup and be witty,
Water the sands and build the city,
Slaughter like devils and have pity;

Be red with rage and pale with lust,
Make beauty come, make peace, make trust—
Water and saltness mixed with dust;

Drive over earth, swim under sea,
Fly in the eagle's secrecy,
Guess where the hidden comets be;

Know all the deathy seeds that still
Queen Helen's beauty, Cæsar's will,
And slay them even as they kill;

Fashion an altar for a rood,
Defile a continent with blood,
And watch a brother starve for food;

Love like a madman, shaking, blind,
Till self is burnt into a kind
Possession of another mind;

Brood upon beauty till the grace
Of beauty with the holy face
Brings peace into the bitter place;

Probe in the lifeless granites, scan
The stars for hope, for guide, for plan;
Live as a woman or a man;

Fasten to lover or to friend
Until the heart-break at the end,
The break of death that cannot mend;

Then to lie useless, helpless, still;
Down in the earth, in dark, to fill
The roots of grass or daffodil.

Down in the earth, in dark, alone,
A mockery of the ghost in bone,
The strangeness passing the unknown.

Time will go by, that outlasts clocks,
Dawn in the thorps will rouse the cocks,
Sunset be glory on the rocks;

But it, the thing, will never heed
Even the rootling from the seed
Thrusting to suck it for its need.

Since moons decay and suns decline
How else should end this life of mine?
Water and saltness are not wine.

But in the darkest hour of night,
When even the foxes peer for sight,
The byre-cock crows; he feels the light.

So, in this water mixed with dust,
The byre-cock spirit crows from trust
That death will change because it must.

For all things change—the darkness changes,
The wandering spirits change their ranges,
The corn is gathered to the granges.

The corn is sown again, it grows;
The stars burn out, the darkness goes.
The rhythms change, they do not close.

They change; and we, who pass like foam,
Like dust blown through the streets of Rome,
Change ever too; we have no home,

Only a beauty, only a power,
Sad in the fruit, bright in the flower,
Endlessly erring for its hour,

But gathering, as we stray, a sense
Of Life, so lovely and intense,
It lingers when we wander hence,

That those who follow feel behind
Their backs, when all before is blind,
Our joy, a rampart to the mind.

THE FRONTIER

Persons: Cotta, Lucius, their Chief

Cotta.   Would God the route would come for home.
My God—this place, day after day,
A month of heavy march from Rome!
This camp, the troopers' huts of clay,
The horses tugging at their pins,
The roaring brook, and then the whins,
And nothing new to do or say.
    Lucius.   They say the tribes are up.
    Cotta.   Who knows?
    Lucius.   Our scouts say that they saw their fires.
    Cotta.   Well, if we fight it's only blows,
And bogging horses in the mires.
    Lucius.   Their raiders crossed the line last night,
Eastward from this, to raid the stud.
They stole our old chief's stallion, Kite.
He's in pursuit.
    Cotta.   That looks like blood.

Lucius.   Well, better that than dicing here
Beside this everlasting stream.
   Cotta.   My God! I was in Rome last year,
Under the sun—it seems a dream.
   Lucius.   Things are not going well in Rome;
This frontier war is wasting men
Like water, and the Tartars come
In hordes.
   Cotta.   We beat them back again.
   Lucius.   So far we have, and yet I feel
The Empire is too wide a bow
For one land's strength.
   Cotta.   The stuff's good steel.
   Lucius.   Too great a strain may snap it though.
If we were ordered home . . .
   Cotta.   Good Lord . . .
   Lucius.   If . . . then our friends, the tribesmen there
Would have glad days.
   Cotta.   This town would flare
To warm old Foxfoot and his horde.
   Lucius.   We have not been forethoughtful here.
Pressing the men to fill the ranks,
Centurions sweep the province clear.
   Cotta.   Rightly.
   Lucius.   Perhaps.
   Cotta.   We get no thanks.
   Lucius.   We strip the men for troops abroad,
And leave the women and the slaves
For merchants and their kind. The graves
Of half each province line the road.
These people could not stand a day
Against the tribes, with us away.
   Cotta.   Rightly.
   Lucius.   Perhaps.
   Cotta.   Here comes the Chief.
   Lucius.   Sir, did your riders catch the thief?
   Chief.   No, he got clear and keeps the horse.
But bad news always comes with worse:
The frontier's fallen, we're recalled,

Our army's broken, Rome's appalled—
My God, the whole world's in a blaze!
So now we've done with idle days,
Fooling on frontiers. Boot and start.
It gives a strange feel in the heart
To think that this, that Rome has made,
Is done with. Yes, the stock's decayed.
We march at once. You mark my words—
We're done, we're crumbled into sherds,
We shall not see this place again
When once we go.
   Lucius.   Do none remain?
 Chief. No, none, all march. Here ends the play.
March, and burn camp. The order's gone—
Your men have sent your baggage on.
  Cotta. My God, hark how the trumpets bray!
  Chief. They do. You see the end of things.
The power of a thousand kings
Helped us to this, and now the power
Is so much hay that was a flower.
  Lucius. We have been very great and strong.
  Chief. That's over now.
  Lucius.   It will be long
Before the world will see our like.
  Chief. We've kept these thieves beyond the dyke
A good long time, here on the Wall.
  Lucius. Colonel, we ought to sound a call
To mark the end of this.
  Chief.   We ought.
Look—there's the hill-top where we fought
Old Foxfoot. Look—there in the whin.
Old ruffian knave! Come on. Fall in.

Edgar Lee Masters

SPOON RIVER ANTHOLOGY

THE HILL

Where are Elmer, Herman, Bert, Tom and Charley,
The weak of will, the strong of arm, the clown, the boozer, the fighter?
All, all, are sleeping on the hill.

One passed in a fever,
One was burned in a mine,
One was killed in a brawl,
One died in a jail,
One fell from a bridge toiling for children and wife—
All, all are sleeping, sleeping, sleeping on the hill.
Where are Ella, Kate, Mag, Lizzie and Edith,
The tender heart, the simple soul, the loud, the proud, the happy
* one?—*
All, all, are sleeping on the hill.

One died in shameful child-birth,
One of a thwarted love,
One at the hands of a brute in a brothel,
One of a broken pride, in the search for her heart's desire,
One after life in far-away London and Paris
Was brought to her little space by Ella and Kate and Mag—
All, all are sleeping, sleeping, sleeping on the hill.

Where are Uncle Isaac and Aunt Emily,
And old Towny Kincaid and Sevigne Houghton,
And Major Walker who had talked
With venerable men of the revolution—
All, all, are sleeping on the hill.

They brought them dead sons from the war,
And daughters whom life had crushed,
And their children fatherless, crying—
All, all are sleeping, sleeping, sleeping on the hill.

Where is Old Fiddler Jones
Who played with life all his ninety years,
Braving the sleet with bared breast,
Drinking, rioting, thinking neither of wife nor kin,
Nor gold, nor love, nor heaven?
Lo! he babbles of the fish-frys of long ago,
Of the horse-races of long ago at Clary's Grove,
Of what Abe Lincoln said
One time at Springfield.

MOLLIE McGEE

Have you seen walking through the village
A man with downcast eyes and haggard face?
That is my husband who, by secret cruelty
Never to be told, robbed me of my youth and my beauty;
Till at last, wrinkled and with yellow teeth,
And with broken pride and shameful humility,
I sank into the grave.
But what think you gnaws at my husband's heart?
The face of what I was, the face of what he made me!
These are driving him to the place where I lie.
In death, therefore, I am avenged.

DAISY FRASER

Did you ever hear of Editor Whedon
Giving to the public treasury any of the money he received
For supporting candidates for office?
Or for writing up the canning factory
To get people to invest?
Or for suppressing the facts about the bank,
When it was rotten and ready to break?
Did you ever hear of the Circuit Judge
Helping anyone except the "Q" railroad,
Or the bankers? Or did Rev. Peet or Rev. Sibley
Give any part of their salary, earned by keeping still
Or speaking out as the leaders wished them to do,
To the building of the water works?
But I—Daisy Fraser, who always passed
Along the streets through rows of nods and smiles,

And coughs and words such as "there she goes,"
Never was taken before Justice Arnett
Without contributing ten dollars and costs
To the school fund of Spoon River!

DOC HILL

I went up and down the streets
Here and there by day and night,
Through all hours of the night caring for the poor who were
sick.
Do you know why?
My wife hated me, my son went to the dogs.
And I turned to the people and poured out my love to them.
Sweet it was to see the crowds about the lawns on the day of my
funeral,
And hear them murmur their love and sorrow.
But oh, dear God, my soul trembled, scarcely able
To hold to the railing of the new life
When I saw Em Stanton behind the oak tree
At the grave,
Hiding herself, and her grief!

FIDDLER JONES

The earth keeps some vibration going
There in your heart, and that is you.
And if the people find you can fiddle,
Why, fiddle you must, for all your life.
What do you see, a harvest of clover?
Or a meadow to walk through to the river?
The wind's in the corn; you rub your hands
For beeves hereafter ready for market;
Or else you hear the rustle of skirts
Like the girls when dancing at Little Grove.
To Cooney Potter a pillar of dust
Or whirling leaves meant ruinous drouth;
They looked to me like Red-head Sammy
Stepping it off, to "Toor-a-Loor."
How could I till my forty acres,
Not to speak of getting more,

With a medley of horns, bassoons and piccolos
Stirred in my brain by crows and robins
And the creak of a wind-mill—only these?
And I never started to plow in my life
That some one did not stop in the road
And take me away to a dance or picnic.
I ended up with forty acres;
I ended up with a broken fiddle—
And a broken laugh, and a thousand memories,
And not a single regret.

THOMAS RHODES

Very well, you liberals,
And navigators into realms intellectual,
You sailors through heights imaginative,
Blown about by erratic currents, tumbling into air pockets,
You Margaret Fuller Slacks, Petits,
And Tennessee Claflin Shopes—
You found with all your boasted wisdom
How hard at the last it is
To keep the soul from splitting into cellular atoms.
While we, seekers of earth's treasures,
Getters and hoarders of gold,
Are self-contained, compact, harmonized,
Even to the end.

EDITOR WHEDON

To be able to see every side of every question;
To be on every side, to be everything, to be nothing long;
To pervert truth, to ride it for a purpose,
To use great feelings and passions of the human family
For base designs, for cunning ends,
To wear a mask like the Greek actors—
Your eight-page paper—behind which you huddle,
Bawling through the megaphone of big type:
"This is I, the giant."
Thereby also living the life of a sneak-thief,
Poisoned with the anonymous words
Of your clandestine soul.

To scratch dirt over scandal for money,
And exhume it to the winds for revenge,
Or to sell papers
Crushing reputations, or bodies, if need be,
To win at any cost, save your own life.
To glory in demoniac power, ditching civilization,
As a paranoiac boy puts a log on the track
And derails the express train.
To be an editor, as I was—
Then to lie here close by the river over the place
Where the sewage flows from the village,
And the empty cans and garbage are dumped,
And abortions are hidden.

SETH COMPTON

When I died, the circulating library
Which I built up for Spoon River,
And managed for the good in inquiring minds,
Was sold at auction on the public square,
As if to destroy the last vestige
Of my memory and influence.
For those of you who could not see the virtue
Of knowing Volney's *Ruins* as well as Butler's *Analogy*
And *Faust* as well as *Evangeline*,
Were really the power in the village,
And often you asked me,
"What is the use of knowing the evil in the world?"
I am out of your way now, Spoon River—
Choose your own good and call it good.
For I could never make you see
That no one knows what is good
Who knows not what is evil;
And no one knows what is true
Who knows not what is false.

HENRY C. CALHOUN

I reached the highest place in Spoon River,
But through what bitterness of spirit!
The face of my father, sitting speechless,

Child-like, watching his canaries,
And looking at the court-house window
Of the county judge's room,
And his admonitions to me to seek
My own life, and punish Spoon River
To avenge the wrong the people did him,
Filled me with furious energy
To seek for wealth and seek for power.
But what did he do but send me along
The path that leads to the grove of the Furies?
I followed the path and I tell you this:
On the way to the grove you'll pass the Fates,
Shadow-eyed, bent over their weaving.
Stop for a moment, and if you see
The thread of revenge leap out of the shuttle
Then quickly snatch from Atropos
The shears and cut it, lest your sons,
And the children of them and their children
Wear the envenomed robe.

PERRY ZOLL

My thanks, friends of the County Scientific Association,
For this modest boulder,
And its little tablet of bronze.
Twice I tried to join your honored body,
And was rejected,
And when my little brochure
On the intelligence of plants
Began to attract attention
You almost voted me in.
After that I grew beyond the need of you
And your recognition.
Yet I do not reject your memorial stone,
Seeing that I should, in so doing,
Deprive you of honor to yourself.

ARCHIBALD HIGBIE

I loathed you, Spoon River. I tried to rise above you,
I was ashamed of you. I despised you

As the place of my nativity.
And there in Rome, among the artists,
Speaking Italian, speaking French,
I seemed to myself at times to be free
Of every trace of my origin.
I seemed to be reaching the heights of art
And to breathe the air that the masters breathed,
And to see the world with their eyes.
But still they'd pass my work and say:
"What are you driving at, my friend?
Sometimes the face looks like Apollo's,
At others it has a trace of Lincoln's."
There was no culture, you know, in Spoon River,
And I burned with shame and held my peace.
And what could I do, all covered over
And weighted down with western soil,
Except aspire, and pray for another
Birth in the world, with all of Spoon River
Rooted out of my soul?

FATHER MALLOY

You are over there, Father Malloy,
Where holy ground is, and the cross marks every grave,
Not here with us on the hill—
Us of wavering faith, and clouded vision
And drifting hope, and unforgiven sins.
You were so human, Father Malloy,
Taking a friendly glass sometimes with us,
Siding with us who would rescue Spoon River
From the coldness and the dreariness of village morality
You were like a traveler who brings a little box of sand
From the wastes about the pyramids
And makes them real and Egypt real.
You were a part of and related to a great past,
And yet you were so close to many of us.
You believed in the joy of life.
You did not seem to be ashamed of the flesh.
You faced life as it is,
And as it changes.

Some of us almost came to you, Father Malloy,
Seeing how your church had divined the heart,
And provided for it,
Through Peter the Flame,
Peter the Rock.

LUCINDA MATLOCK

I went to the dances at Chandlerville,
And played snap-out at Winchester.
One time we changed partners,
Driving home in the moonlight of middle June,
And then I found Davis.
We were married and lived together for seventy years,
Enjoying, working, raising the twelve children,
Eight of whom we lost
Ere I had reached the age of sixty.
I spun, I wove, I kept the house, I nursed the sick,
I made the garden, and for holiday
Rambled over the fields where sang the larks,
And by Spoon River gathering many a shell,
And many a flower and medicinal weed—
Shouting to the wooded hills, singing to the green valleys.
At ninety-six I had lived enough, that is all,
And passed to a sweet repose.
What is this I hear of sorrow and weariness,
Anger, discontent and drooping hopes?
Degenerate sons and daughters,
Life is too strong for you—
It takes life to love Life.

ANNE RUTLEDGE

Out of me unworthy and unknown
The vibrations of deathless music—
"With malice toward none, with charity for all."
Out of me the forgiveness of millions toward millions,
And the beneficent face of a nation
Shining with justice and truth.
I am Anne Rutledge who sleep beneath these weeds,
Beloved in life of Abraham Lincoln,

Wedded to him, not through union,
But through separation.
Bloom forever, O Republic,
From the dust of my bosom!

WILLIAM H. HERNDON

There by the window in the old house
Perched on the bluff, overlooking miles of valley,
My days of labor closed, sitting out life's decline,
Day by day did I look in my memory,
As one who gazes in an enchantress' crystal globe.
And I saw the figures of the past,
As if in a pageant glassed by a shining dream,
Move through the incredible sphere of time.
And I saw a man arise from the soil like a fabled giant
And throw himself over a deathless destiny,
Master of great armies, head of the republic,
Bringing together into a dithyramb of recreative song
The epic hopes of a people;
At the same time Vulcan of sovereign fires,
Where imperishable shields and swords were beaten out
From spirits tempered in heaven.
Look in the crystal! See how he hastens on
To the place where his path comes up to the path
Of a child of Plutarch and Shakespeare.
O Lincoln, actor indeed, playing well your part,
And Booth, who strode in a mimic play within the play,
Often and often I saw you,
As the cawing crows winged their way to the wood
Over my house-top at solemn sunsets,
There by my window,
Alone.

RUTHERFORD McDOWELL

They brought me ambrotypes
Of the old pioneers to enlarge.
And sometimes one sat for me—
Someone who was in being
When giant hands from the womb of the world

Tore the republic.
What was it in their eyes?—
For I could never fathom
That mystical pathos of drooped eyelids,
And the serene sorrow of their eyes.
It was like a pool of water,
Amid oak trees at the edge of a forest,
Where the leaves fall,
As you hear the crow of a cock
From a far-off farm house, seen near the hills
Where the third generation lives, and the strong men
And the strong women are gone and forgotten.
And these grand-children and great-grand-children
Of the pioneers!—
Truly did my camera record their faces, too,
With so much of the old strength gone,
And the old faith gone,
And the old mastery of life gone,
And the old courage gone,
Which labors and loves and suffers and sings
Under the sun!

ARLO WILL

Did you ever see an alligator
Come up to the air from the mud,
Staring blindly under the full glare of noon?
Have you seen the stabled horses at night
Tremble and start back at the sight of a lantern?
Have you ever walked in darkness
When an unknown door was open before you
And you stood, it seemed, in the light of a thousand candles
Of delicate wax?
Have you walked with the wind in your ears
And the sunlight about you,
And found it suddenly shine with an inner splendor?
Out of the mud many times,
Before many doors of light,
Through many fields of splendor,
Where around your steps a soundless glory scatters

Like new-fallen snow,
Will you go through earth, O strong of soul,
And through unnumbered heavens
To the final flame!

AARON HATFIELD

Better than granite, Spoon River,
Is the memory-picture you keep of me
Standing before the pioneer men and women
There at Concord Church on Communion day.
Speaking in broken voice of the peasant youth
Of Galilee who went to the city
And was killed by bankers and lawyers;
My voice mingling with the June wind
That blew over wheat fields from Atterbury;
While the white stones in the burying ground
Around the Church shimmered in the summer sun.
And there, though my own memories
Were too great to bear, were you, O pioneers,
With bowed heads breathing forth your sorrow
For the sons killed in battle and the daughters
And little children who vanished in life's morning,
Or at the intolerable hour of noon.
But in those moments of tragic silence,
When the wine and bread were passed,
Came the reconciliation for us—
Us the ploughmen and the hewers of wood,
Us the peasants, brothers of the peasant of Galilee—
To us came the Comforter
And the consolation of tongues of flame!

WEBSTER FORD

Do you remember, O Delphic Apollo,
The sunset hour by the river, when Mickey M'Grew
Cried, "There's a ghost," and I, "It's Delphic Apollo;"
And the son of the banker derided us, saying, "It's light
By the flags at the water's edge, you half-witted fools."
And from thence, as the wearisome years rolled on, long after
Poor Mickey fell down in the water tower to his death.

Down, down, through bellowing darkness, I carried
The vision which perished with him like a rocket which falls
And quenches its light in earth, and hid it for fear
Of the son of the banker, calling on Plutus to save me?
Avenged were you for the shame of a fearful heart,
Who left me alone till I saw you again in an hour
.When I seemed to be turned to a tree with trunk and branches
Growing indurate, turning to stone, yet burgeoning
In laurel leaves, in hosts of lambent laurel,
Quivering, fluttering, shrinking, fighting the numbness
Creeping into their veins from the dying trunk and branches!
'Tis vain, O youth, to fly the call of Apollo.
Fling yourselves in the fire, die with a song of spring,
If die you must in the spring. For none shall look
On the face of Apollo and live, and choose you must
'Twixt death in the flame and death after years of sorrow,
Rooted fast in the earth, feeling the grisly hand,
Not so much in the trunk as in the terrible numbness
Creeping up to the laurel leaves that never cease
To flourish until you fall. O leaves of me
Too sere for coronal wreaths, and fit alone
For urns of memory, treasured, perhaps, as themes
For hearts heroic, fearless singers and livers—
Delphic Apollo!

SILENCE

I have known the silence of the stars and of the sea,
And the silence of the city when it pauses,
And the silence of a man and a maid,
And the silence of the sick
When their eyes roam about the room.
And I ask: For the depths
Of what use is language?
A beast of the field moans a few times
When death takes its young.
And we are voiceless in the presence of realities—
We cannot speak.

A curious boy asks an old soldier
Sitting in front of the grocery store,
"How did you lose your leg?"
And the old soldier is struck with silence,
Or his mind flies away
Because he cannot concentrate it on Gettysburg.
It comes back jocosely
And he says, "A bear bit it off."
And the boy wonders, while the old soldier
Dumbly, feebly lives over
The flashes of guns, the thunder of cannon,
The shrieks of the slain,
And himself lying on the ground,
And the hospital surgeons, the knives,
And the long days in bed.
But if he could describe it all
He would be an artist.
But if he were an artist there would be deeper wounds
Which he could not describe.

There is the silence of a great hatred,
And the silence of a great love,
And the silence of an embittered friendship.
There is the silence of a spiritual crisis,
Through which your soul, exquisitely tortured,
Comes with visions not to be uttered
Into a realm of higher life.
There is the silence of defeat.
There is the silence of those unjustly punished;
And the silence of the dying whose hand
Suddenly grips yours.
There is the silence between father and son,
When the father cannot explain his life,
Even though he be misunderstood for it.

There is the silence that comes between husband and wife.
There is the silence of those who have failed;
And the vast silence that covers
Broken nations and vanquished leaders.

There is the silence of Lincoln,
Thinking of the poverty of his youth.
And the silence of Napoleon
After Waterloo.
And the silence of Jeanne d'Arc
Saying amid the flames, "Blessed Jesus"—
Revealing in two words all sorrows, all hope.
And there is the silence of age,
Too full of wisdom for the tongue to utter it
In words intelligible to those who have not lived
The great range of life.

And there is the silence of the dead.
If we who are in life cannot speak
Of profound experiences,
Why do you marvel that the dead
Do not tell you of death?
Their silence shall be interpreted
As we approach them.

THE GARDEN

I do not like my garden, but I love
The trees I planted and the flowers thereof.
How does one choose his garden? Oh with eyes
O'er which a passion or illusion lies.
Perhaps it wakens memories of a lawn
You knew before somewhere. Or you are drawn
By an old urn, a little gate, a roof
Which soars into a blue sky, clear, aloof.
One buys a garden gladly. Even the worst
Seems tolerable or beautiful at first.
Their very faults give loving labor scope—
One can correct, adorn; 'tis sweet to hope
For beauty to emerge out of your toil,
To build the walks and fertilize the soil.
Before I knew my garden, or awoke
To its banality, I set an oak
At one end for a life-long husbandry,

A white syringa and a lilac tree
Close to one side to hide a crumbling wall
Which was my neighbor's, held in several
Title and beyond my right to mend—
One cannot with an ancient time contend.

Some houses shadowed me. I did not dream
The sun would never look over them and gleam,
Save at the earliest hour. So all the day
One half my garden under twilight lay.
Another soul had overlooked the shade:
I found the boundaries of a bed he made
For tulips. Well, I had a fresher trust
And spent my heart upon this sterile dust.
What thing will grow where never the sun shines?
Vainly I planted flowering stalks and vines.
What years to learn the soil? Why, even weeds
Look green and fresh. But if one concedes
Salvia will flourish not, nor palest phlox,
One might have hope left for a row of box.

Why is it that some silent places thrill
With elfin comradeship, and others fill
The heart with sickening loneliness? My breast
Seems hollow for great emptiness, unrest—
Casting my eyes about my garden where
I still must live, breathing its lifeless air.
Why should I have a garden anyway?
I have so many friends who pass the day
In streets or squares, or little barren courts.
I fancy there are gardens of all sorts,
Far worse than mine. And who has this delight?—
There's my syringa with its blooms of white!
It flourishes in my garden! In this brief
Season of blossoms and unfolding leaf
What if I like my garden not, but love
The oak tree and the lilac tree thereof,
And hide my face, lest one my rapture guess,
Amid the white syringa's loveliness?

DESOLATE SCYTHIA

When there are no distances in music,
No far-off things suggested of faery forests or celestial heights;
When nothing undiscovered stands back of the written page,
And the landscape contains nothing hidden,
And no alluring spirits of further places;
When no more in eyes shines the light of mystery,
And the thrill of discovered kinships
Has fallen into the familiar recognition
That takes all men and women
As daily associates of an accustomed world,
Then you have come to the uttermost plain of earth
Where lie the rocks of desolate Scythia.

MY LIGHT WITH YOURS

When the sea has devoured the ships,
And the spires and the towers
Have gone back to the hills,
And all the cities
Are one with the plains again,
And the beauty of bronze
And the strength of steel
Are blown over silent continents
As the desert sand is blown—
My dust with yours forever.

When folly and wisdom are no more,
And fire is no more,
Because man is no more;
When the dead world, slowly spinning,
Drifts and falls through the void—
My light with yours
In the Light of Lights forever!

SLIP-SHOE LOVEY

You're the cook's understudy,
A gentle idiot body.
You are slender like a broom,
Weaving up and down the room
With your dirt hair in a twist
And your left eye in a mist.
Never thinkin', never hopin',
With your wet mouth open.
So bewildered and so busy
As you scrape the dirty kettles,
O Slip-shoe Lizzie,
As you rattle with the pans.
There's a clatter of old metals,
O Slip-shoe Lovey,
As you clean the milk cans.
You're a greasy little dovey,
A laughing scullery daughter,
As you slop the dish water—
So abstracted and so dizzy,
O Slip-shoe Lizzie!

So mussy, little hussie,
With the china that you break.
And the kitchen in a smear
When the bread is yet to bake,
And the market things are here—
O Slip-shoe Lovey!

You are hurrying and scurrying
From the sink to the oven,
So forgetful and so sloven.
You are bustling and hustling
From the pantry to the door,
With your shoe-strings on the floor,
And your apron-strings a-draggin',
And your spattered skirt a-saggin'.

You're an angel idiot lovey—
One forgives you all this clatter
Washing dishes, beating batter.
But there is another matter
As you dream above the skin;
You're in love pitter-patter,
With the butcher-boy, I think.
And he'll get you, he has got you!
If he hasn't got you yet.

For he means to make you his,
O Slip-shoe Liz;
And your open mouth is wet
To a little boyish chatter.
You're an easy thing to flatter,
With your hank of hair a-twist,
And your left eye in a mist,
O Slip-shoe Lovey!

So hurried and so flurried,
And just a little worried,
You lean about the room
Like a mop, like a broom.
O Slip-shoe Lovey!
O Slip-shoe Lovey!

CHRISTMAS AT INDIAN POINT

Who is that calling through the night,
A wail that dies when the wind roars?
We heard it first on Shipley's Hill,
It faded out at Comingoer's.

Along five miles of wintry road
A horseman galloped with a cry,
"'Twas two o'clock," said Herman Pointer,
"When I heard clattering hoofs go by.

"I flung the winder up to listen;
I heerd him there on Gordon's Ridge;

I heerd the loose boards bump and rattle
When he went over Houghton's Bridge."

Said Roger Ragsdale: "I was doctorin'
A heifer in the barn, and then
My boy says: 'Pap, that's Billy Paris.'
'There,' says my boy, 'it is again:'

"Says I: 'That kain't be Billy Paris,
We seed 'im at the Christmas tree.
It's two o'clock,' says I, 'and Billy
I seed go home with Emily.'

" 'He is too old for galavantin'
Upon a night like this,' says I.
'Well, pap,' says he, ' I know that frosty
Good-natured huskiness in that cry.'

" 'It kain't be Billy,' says I, swabbin'
The heifer's tongue and mouth with brine;
'I never thought—it makes me shiver,
And goose-flesh up and down the spine.'"

Said Doggie Traylor: "When I heard it
I 'lowed 'twas Pin Hook's rowdy new 'uns.
Them Cashner boys was at the schoolhouse
Drinkin' there at the Christmas doin's."

Said Pete McCue: "I lit a candle
And held it up to the winder-pane;
But when I heerd again the holler
'Twere half-way down the Bowman Lane."

Said Andy Ensley: "First I knowed
I thought he'd thump the door away.
I hopped from bed, and says, 'Who is it?'
'O Emily,' I heard him say.

"And ther stood Billy Paris tremblin'—
His face so white, he looked so queer.
'O Andy'—and his voice went broken.
'Come in,' says I, 'and have a cheer.'

" 'Sit by the fire'—I kicked the logs up—
'What brings you here, I would be told?'
Says he: 'My hand just . . . happened near hers,
It teched her hand . . . and it war cold.

" 'We got back from the Christmas doin's
And went to bed, and she was sayin',
(The clock struck ten) if it keeps snowin'
Tomorrow there'll be splendid sleighin'.'

" 'My hand teched hers, the clock struck two,
And then I thought I heerd her moan,
It war the wind I guess, for Emily
War lyin' dead. . . . She's thar alone.'

"I left him then to call my woman
To tell her that her mother died.
When we came back his voice was steady,
The big tears in his eyes was dried.

"He just sot there and quiet like
Talked 'bout the fishin' times they had,
And said for her to die on Christmas
Was somethin' 'bout it made him glad.

"He grew so calm he almost skeered us.
Says he: 'It's a fine Christmas over there.'
Says he: 'She was the lovingest woman
That ever walked this vale of care.'

"Says he: 'She allus laughed and sang,
I never heerd her once complain.'
Says he: 'It's not so bad a Christmas
When she can go, and have no pain.'

"Says he: 'The Christmas's good for her.'
Says he: . . . 'Not very good for me.'
He hid his face then in his muffler,
And sobbed and sobbed, 'O Emily!' "

THE LAKE BOATS

In an old print
I see a thicket of masts on the river.
But in the prints to be
There will be lake boats,
With port holes, funnels, rows of decks,
Huddled like swans by the docks,
Under the shadows of cliffs of brick.
And who will know from the prints to be,
When the Albatross and the Golden Eagle,
The flying craft which shall carry the vision
Of impatient lovers wounded by spring
To the shaded rivers of Michigan,
That it was the Missouri, the Iowa,
And the City of Benton Harbor
Which lay huddled like swans by the docks?

You are not Lake Leman,
Walled in by Mt. Blanc.
One sees the whole world round you
And beyond you, Lake Michigan.
And when the melodious winds of March
Wrinkle you and drive on the shore
The serpent rifts of sand and snow,
And sway the giant limbs of oaks,
Longing to bud,
The boats put forth for the ports that began to stir,
With the creak of reels unwinding the nets,
And the ring of the caulking wedge.
But in the June days—
The Alabama ploughs through liquid tons
Of sapphire waves.
She sinks from hills to valleys of water,
And rises again
Like a swimming gull!
I wish a hundred years to come, and forever
All lovers could know the rapture
Of the lake boats sailing the first spring days

To coverts of hepatica,
With the whole world sphering round you,
And the whole of the sky beyond you.

I knew the Captain of the City of Grand Rapids.
He had sailed the seas as a boy.
And he stood on deck against the railing
Puffing a cigar,
Showing in his eyes the cinema flash of the sun on the waves.
It was June and life was easy. . . .
One could lie on deck and sleep,
Or sit in the sun and dream.
People were walking the decks and talking,
Children were singing.
And down on the purser's deck
A man was dancing by himself,
Whirling around like a dervish.
And this captain said to me:
"No life is better than this.
I could live forever,
And do nothing but run this boat
From the dock at Chicago to the dock at Holland
And back again."

One time I went to Grand Haven
On the Alabama with Charley Shippey.
It was dawn, but white dawn only,
Under the reign of Leucothea,
As we volplaned, so it seemed, from the lake
Past the lighthouse into the river;
And afterward, laughing and talking,
Hurried to Van Dreezer's restaurant
For breakfast.
(Charley knew him and talked of things
Unknown to me as he cooked the breakfast.)
Then we fished the mile's length of the pier
In a gale full of warmth and moisture
Which blew the gulls about like confetti,
And flapped like a flag the linen duster
Of a fisherman who paced the pier—

(Charley called him Rip Van Winkle.)
The only thing that could be better
Than this day on the pier
Would be its counterpart in heaven,
As Swedenborg would say—
Charley is fishing somewhere now, I think.

There is a grove of oaks on a bluff by the river
At Berrien Springs.
There is a cottage that eyes the lake
Between pines and silver birches
At South Haven.
There is the inviolable wonder of wooded shore
Curving for miles at Saugatuck;
And at Holland a beach like Scheveningen's;
And at Charlevoix the sudden quaintness
Of an old-world place by the sea.
There are the hills around Elk Lake
Where the blue of the sky is so still and clear
It seems it was rubbed above them
By the swipe of a giant thumb.
And beyond these the Little Traverse Bay
Where the roar of the breeze goes round
Like a roulette ball in the groove of the wheel,
Circling the bay;
And beyond these Mackinac and the Cheneaux Islands—
And beyond these a great mystery!

Neither ice floes, nor winter's palsy
Stays the tide in the river.
And under the shadows of cliffs of brick
The lake boats,
Huddled like swans,
Turn and sigh like sleepers—
They are longing for the spring!

Marjorie Meeker

WHERE MY STEP FALTERS

Where my step falters
  My fathers trod;
But I raze their altars
  For my God,

At whose cruel
  Thrust I am learning,
I am fuel
  For his burning.

My brain is humming,
  My heart is dusk
With awe at his coming.
  I am the husk

Cast away
  For his leaping higher;
I am the gray
  Ash of his fire.

No one knows,
  And little it matters
Where the husk blows
  Or the ash scatters.

PROPHECY

You will be the color of water;
Your voice will be like the wind.
You will go where the dust goes;
None will know you have sinned.

None will know you are quiet
Or fluent or bound or free.
None will care you are nothing;
You will be nothing to me

Except a scarlet remembrance—
As if, in a dream of pride,
A poppy had flaunted her petals
One day to the sun, and died.

AFTER PAIN

An old forgetting
Follows what befell,
And veiled regretting;
Yet even this is well.

The light breath flutters,
A thin sharp wing of wind.
The dark blood mutters
Old histories to the mind.

Beyond the riot
Of little pulse and breath
Again the quiet
Avenues of death

Are far and lonely.
And even this is well.
Death may be only
A lie that liars tell.

Charlotte Mew

THE FARMER'S BRIDE

Three summers since I chose a maid—
Too young maybe—but more's to do
At harvest-time than bide and woo.
   When us was wed she turned afraid
Of love and me and all things human;

Like the shut of a winter's day.
Her smile went out, and 'twasn't a woman—
　　More like a little frightened fay.
　　One night, in the fall, she runned away.

"Out 'mong the sheep, her be," they said.
Should properly have been abed;
But sure enough she wasn't there
Lying awake with her wide brown stare.
So over seven-acre field and up-along across the down
We chased her, flying like a hare
Before our lanterns.　To Church-town
All in a shiver and a scare
We caught her, fetched her home at last
And turned the key upon her, fast.

She does the work about the house
As well as most, but like a mouse:
　　Happy enough to chat and play
　　With birds and rabbits and such as they,
　　So long as men-folk keep away.
"Not near, not near!" her eyes beseech
When one of us comes within reach.
　　The women say that beasts in stall
　　Look round like children at her call.
　　I've hardly heard her speak at all.

Shy as a leveret, swift as he;
Straight and slight as a young larch tree;
Sweet as the first wild violets, she,
To her wild self.　But what to me?
The short days shorten and the oaks are brown,
　　The blue smoke rises to the low grey sky,
One leaf in the still air falls slowly down,
　　A magpie's spotted feathers lie
On the black earth spread white with rime,
The berries redden up to Christmas-time.
　　What's Christmas-time without there be
　　Some other in the house than we!

She sleeps up in the attic there
Alone, poor maid. 'Tis but a stair
Betwixt us. Oh, my God!—the down,
The soft young down of her; the brown,
The brown of her—her eyes, her hair, her hair!

BESIDE THE BED

Some one has shut the shining eyes, straightened and folded
    The wandering hands quietly covering the unquiet breast:
So, smoothed and silenced you lie, like a child, not again to be
        questioned or scolded;
    But, for you, not one of us believes that this is rest.

Not so to close the windows down can cloud and deaden
    The blue beyond; or to screen the wavering flame subdue its
        breath:
Why, if I lay my cheek to your cheek, your gray lips, like dawn,
        would quiver and redden,
    Breaking into the old odd smile at this fraud of death.

Because all night you have not turned to us or spoken
    It is time for you to wake; your dreams were never very deep:
I, for one, have seen the thin bright twisted threads of them
        dimmed suddenly and broken;
    This is only a most piteous pretence of sleep!

Alice Meynell

"RIVERS UNKNOWN TO SONG"

Wide waters in the waste; or, out of reach,
Rough Alpine falls where late a glacier hung;
Or rivers groping for the alien beach,
Through continents, unsung.

Nay, not these nameless, these remote, alone;
But all the streams from all the watersheds—

Peneus, Danube, Nile—are the unknown.
Young in their ancient beds.

Man has no tale for them. O travellers swift
From secrets to oblivion! Waters wild
That pass in act to bend a flower, or lift
The bright limbs of a child!

For they are new, they are fresh; there's no surprise
Like theirs on earth. O strange for evermore!
This moment's Tiber with his shining eyes
Never saw Rome before.

Man has no word for their eternity—
Rhine, Avon, Arno, younglings, youth uncrowned:
Ignorant, innocent, instantaneous, free,
Unwelcomed, unrenowned.

THE POET TO THE BIRDS

You bid me hold my peace,
Or so I think, you birds; you'll not forgive
My kill-joy song that makes the wild song cease,
Silent or fugitive.

Yon thrush stopt in mid-phrase
At my mere footfall; and a longer note
Took wing and fled afield, and went its ways
Within the blackbird's throat.

Hereditary song,
Illyrian lark and Paduan nightingale,
Is yours, unchangeable the ages long;
Assyria heard your tale;

Therefore you do not die.
But single, local, lonely, mortal, new,
Unlike, and thus like all my race, am I,
Preluding my adieu.

My human song must be
My human thought. Be patient till 'tis done.
I shall not hold my little peace; for me
There is no peace but one.

MATERNITY

One wept whose only child was dead
  New-born, ten years ago.
"Weep not; he is in bliss," they said.
  She answered, "Even so.

"Ten years ago was born in pain
  A child not now forlorn.
But oh, ten years ago, in vain
  A mother, a mother was born."

CHIMES

Brief on a flying night,
  From the shaken tower,
A flock of bells take flight,
  And go with the hour.

Like birds from the cote to the gales,
  Abrupt—oh, hark!—
A fleet of bells set sails,
  And go to the dark.

Sudden the cold airs swing:
  Alone, aloud,
A verse of bells takes wing
  And flies with the cloud.

Max Michelson

O BROTHER TREE

O brother tree! O brother tree! Tell to me, thy brother,
The secret of thy life,
The wonder of thy being.

My brother tree, my brother tree,
My heart is open to thee—
Reveal me all thy secrets.

Beloved tree, beloved tree,
I have shattered all my pride.
I love thee, brother, as myself.
Oh, explain to me thy wonders.

Beloved one, adored one,
I will not babble of it among fools—
I will tell it only to the unspoiled:
Reveal to me thy being.

I have watched thy leaves in sunshine,
I have heard them in the storm.
My heart drank a droplet of thy holy joy and wonder,
One drop from the ocean of thy wonder.

I am thy humble brother—I am thine own.
Reveal thy life to me,
Reveal thy calm joy to me,
Reveal to me thy serene knowledge.

THE BIRD

From a branch
The bird called:

I hold your heart!
I wash it
And scour it
With bits of song

Like pebbles;
And your doubts
And your sorrows
Fall—drip, drip, drip—
Like dirty water.
I pipe to it
In little notes
Of life clear as a pool,
And of death
Clearer still;
And I swoop with it
In the blue
And in the nest
Of a cloud.

A HYMN TO NIGHT

Come, mysterious night;
Descend and nestle to us.

Descend softly on the houses
We built with pride,
Without worship.
Fold them in your veil,
Spill your shadows.

Come over our stores and factories,
Hide our pride—our shame—
With your nebulous wings.

Come down on our cobbled streets:
Unleash your airy hounds.
Come to the sleepers, night;
Light in them your fires.

LOVE LYRIC

Stir—
Shake off sleep.
Your eyes are the soul of clear waters—

Pigeons
In a city street.

Suns now dead
Have tucked away of their gold for your hair:
My buried mouth still tastes their fires.

A tender god built your breasts—
Apples of desire;
Their whiteness slakes the throat;
Their form soothes like honey.

Wake up!
Or the song-bird in my heart
Will peck open the shell of your dreams.

.   .   .   .

Sleep, my own,
Soaring over rivers of fire.
Sleep, my own,
Wading waters of gold.

Joy is in my heart—
It flutters around in my soul.
. . . Softly—
I hear the rosy dreams . . .

Edna St. Vincent Millay

GOD'S WORLD

O world, I cannot hold thee close enough!
Thy winds, thy wide gray skies!
Thy mists, that roll and rise!
Thy woods, this autumn day, that ache and sag
And all but cry with color! That gaunt crag
To crush! To lift the lean of that black bluff!
World, world, I cannot get thee close enough!

Long have I known a glory in it all
But never knew I this.

Here such a passion is
As stretcheth me apart. Lord, I do fear
Thou'st made the world too beautiful this year.
My soul is all but out of me—let fall
No burning leaf; prithee, let no bird call.

SPRING

To what purpose, April, do you return again?
Beauty is not enough.
You can no longer quiet me with the redness
Of little leaves opening stickily.
I know what I know.
The sun is hot on my neck as I observe
The spikes of the crocus.
The smell of the earth is good.
It is apparent that there is no death.
But what does that signify?
Not only under ground are the brains of men
Eaten by maggots.
Life in itself
Is nothing—
An empty cup, a flight of uncarpeted stairs.
It is not enough that yearly, down this hill,
April
Comes like an idiot, babbling and strewing flowers!

RECUERDO

We were very tired, we were very merry—
We had gone back and forth all night on the ferry.
It was bare and bright, and smelled like a stable—
But we looked into a fire, we leaned across a table,
We lay on a hill-top underneath the moon;
And the whistles kept blowing, and the dawn came soon.

We were very tired, we were very merry—
We had gone back and forth all night on the ferry;
And you ate an apple, and I ate a pear,

From a dozen of each we had bought somewhere;
And the sky went wan, and the wind came cold,
And the sun rose dripping, a bucketful of gold.

We were very tired, we were very merry,
We had gone back and forth all night on the ferry.
We hailed, "Good-morrow, mother!" to a shawl-covered head,
And bought a morning-paper, which neither of us read;
And she wept, "God bless you!" for the apples and pears,
And we gave her all our money but our subway fares.

TRAVEL

The railroad track is miles away,
    And the day is loud with voices speaking;
Yet there isn't a train goes by all day
    But I hear its whistle shrieking.

All night there isn't a train goes by,
    Though the night is still for sleep and dreaming,
But I see its cinders red on the sky,
    And hear its engine steaming.

My heart is warm with the friends I make,
    And better friends I'll not be knowing;
Yet there isn't a train I wouldn't take,
    No matter where it's going.

FEAST

I drank at every vine.
The last was like the first.
I came upon no wine
So wonderful as thirst.

I gnawed at every root,
I ate of every plant.
I came upon no fruit
So wonderful as want.

Feed the grape and bean
To the vintner and monger;
I will lie down lean
With my thirst and my hunger.

THE BETROTHAL

Oh come, my lad, or go, my lad,
And love me if you like.
I shall not hear the door shut
Nor the knocker strike.

Oh, bring me gifts or beg me gifts,
And wed me if you will.
I'd make a man a good wife,
Sensible and still.

And why should I be cold, my lad,
And why should you repine,
Because I love a dark head
That never will be mine?

I might as well be easing you
As lie alone in bed
And waste the night in wanting
A cruel dark head.

You might as well be calling yours
What never will be his,
And one of us be happy.
There's few enough as is.

THE CURSE

Oh, lay my ashes on the wind
That blows across the sea.
And I shall meet a fisherman
Out of Capri,

And he will say, seeing me,
"What a strange thing!
Like a fish's scale or a
Butterfly's wing."

Oh, lay my ashes on the wind
That blows away the fog.
And I shall meet a farmer boy
Leaping through the bog,

And he will say, seeing me,
"What a strange thing!
Like a peat-ash or a
Butterfly's wing."

And I shall blow to your house
And, sucked against the pane,
See you take your sewing up
And lay it down again.

And you will say, seeing me,
"What a strange thing!
Like a plum petal or a
Butterfly's wing."

And none at all will know me
That knew me well before.
But I will settle at the root
That climbs about your door,

And fishermen and farmers
May see me and forget,
But I'll be a bitter berry
In your brewing yet.

ASHES OF LIFE

Love has gone and left me, and the days are all alike.
    Eat I must, and sleep I will—and would that night were here!
But ah, to lie awake and hear the slow hours strike!
    Would that it were day again, with twilight near!

Love has gone and left me, and I don't know what to do;
   This or that or what you will is all the same to me;
But all the things that I begin I leave before I'm through—
   There's little use in anything as far as I can see.

Love has gone and left me, and the neighbors knock and borrow,
   And life goes on forever like the gnawing of a mouse.
And tomorrow and tomorrow and tomorrow and tomorrow
   There's this little street and this little house.

THE SHROUD

Death, I say, my heart is bowed
   Unto thine, O mother!
This red gown will make a shroud
   Good as any other.

(I, that could not wait to wear
   My own bridal things,
In a dress dark as my hair
   Made my answerings.

I, tonight, that till he came
   Could not, could not wait,
In a gown as bright as flame
   Held for them the gate.)

Death, I say, my heart is bowed
   Unto thine, O mother!
This red gown will make a shroud
   Good as any other.

EPITAPH

Heap not on this mound
Roses that she loved so well—
Why bewilder her with roses,
That she cannot see or smell?
She is happy where she lies
With the dust upon her eyes.

PRAYER TO PERSEPHONE

Be to her, Persephone,
All the things I might not be;
Take her head upon your knee.
She that was so proud and wild,
Flippant, arrogant and free—
She that had no need of me—
Is a little lonely child
Lost in Hell. Persephone,
Take her head upon your knee;
Say to her, "My dear, my dear,
It is not so dreadful here."

CHORUS

Give away her gowns,
Give away her shoes—
She has no more use
For her fragrant gowns.
Take them all down—
Blue, green, blue,
Lilac, pink, blue—
From their padded hangers.
She will dance no more
In her narrow shoes;
Sweep her narrow shoes
From the closet floor.

THE BUCK IN THE SNOW

White sky, over the hemlocks bowed with snow,
Saw you not at the beginning of evening the antlered buck and
   his doe
Standing in the apple-orchard? I saw them. I saw them suddenly
   go,
Tails up, with long leaps lovely and slow,
Over the stone wall into the wood of hemlocks bowed with snow.

Now lies he here, his wild blood scalding the snow.

How strange a thing is death, bringing to his knees, bringing to
    his antlers,
The buck in the snow.
How strange a thing—a mile away by now, it may be,
Under the heavy hemlocks that as the moments pass
Shift their loads a little, letting fall a feather of snow—
Life, looking out attentive from the eyes of the doe.

DIRGE WITHOUT MUSIC

I am not resigned to the shutting away of loving hearts in the
    hard ground.
So it is, and so it will be, for so it has been, time out of mind:
Into the darkness they go, the wise and the lovely. Crowned
With lilies and with laurel they go; but I am not resigned.

Lovers and thinkers, into the earth with you.
Be one with the dull, the indiscriminate dust.
A fragment of what you felt, of what you knew,
A formula, a phrase remains—but the best is lost.

The answers quick and keen, the honest look, the laughter, the
    love—
They are gone. They are gone to feed the roses. Elegant and
    curled
Is the blossom. Fragrant is the blossom. I know. But I do not
    approve.
More precious was the light in your eyes than all the roses of
    the world.

Down, down, down into the darkness of the grave
Gently they go, the beautiful, the tender, the kind;
Quietly they go, the intelligent, the witty, the brave.
I know. But I do not approve. And I am not resigned.

ON HEARING A SYMPHONY OF BEETHOVEN

    Sweet sounds, O beautiful music, do not cease!
    Reject me not into the world again.

With you alone is excellence and peace,
Mankind made plausible, his purpose plain.
Enchanted in your air benign and shrewd,
With arms a-sprawl and empty faces pale,
The spiteful and the stingy and the rude
Sleep like the scullions in the fairy-tale.
This moment is the best the world can give:
The tranquil blossom on the tortured stem.
Reject me not, sweet sounds! oh, let me live,
Till Doom espy my towers and scatter them,
A city spell-bound under the aging sun,
Music my rampart, and my only one.

SONNETS

Oh, think not I am faithful to a vow!
Faithless am I save to Love's self alone.
Were you not lovely I would leave you now—
After the feet of Beauty fly my own.
Were you not still my hunger's rarest food,
And water ever to my wildest thirst,
I would desert you—think not but I would!—
And seek another, as I sought you first.
But you are mobile as the veering air,
And all your charms more changeful than the tide;
Wherefore to be inconstant is no care—
I have but to continue at your side.
So wanton, light and false, my love, are you,
I am most faithless when I most am true.

Into the golden vessel of great song
Let us pour all our passion. Breast to breast
Let other lovers lie, in love and rest;
Not we, articulate, so, but with the tongue
Of all the world: the churning blood, the long
Shuddering quiet, the desperate hot palms pressed
Sharply together upon the escaping guest,
The common soul, unguarded, and grown strong.
Longing alone is singer to the lute;

Let still on nettles in the open sigh
The minstrel, that in slumber is as mute
As any man; and love be far and high,
That else forsakes the topmost branch, a fruit
Found on the ground by every passer-by.

Not with libations, but with shouts and laughter
We drenched the altars of Love's sacred grove,
Shaking to earth green fruits, impatient after
The launching of the colored moths of Love.
Love's proper myrtle and his mother's zone
We bound about our irreligious brows,
And fettered him with garlands of our own,
And spread a banquet in his frugal house,
Not yet the god has spoken; but I fear,
Though we should break our bodies in his flame,
And pour our blood upon his altar, here
Henceforward is a grove without a name—
A pasture to the shaggy goats of Pan,
Whence flee forever a woman and a man.

Cherish you then the hope I shall forget
At length, my lord, Pieria?—put away
For your so passing sake, this mouth of clay,
These mortal bones against my body set,
For all the puny fever and frail sweat
Of human love?—renounce for these, I say,
The Singing Mountain's memory, and betray
The silent lyre that hangs upon me yet?
Ah, but indeed some day shall you awake,
Rather, from dreams of me, that at your side
So many nights, a lover and a bride,
But stern in my soul's chastity, have lain,
To walk the world forever for my sake,
And in each chamber find me gone again!

And you as well must die, beloved dust
And all your beauty stand you in no stead;
This flawless vital hand, this perfect head,
This body of flame and steel, before the gust

Of Death, or under his autumnal frost,
Shall be as any leaf, be no less dead
Than the first leaf that fell—this wonder fled,
Altered, estranged, disintegrated, lost.
Nor shall my love avail you in your hour,
In spite of all my love you will arise
Upon that day and wander down the air
Obscurely as the unattended flower,
It mattering not how beautiful you were,
Or how beloved above all else that dies.

Euclid alone has looked on Beauty bare.
Let all that prate of Beauty hold their peace,
And lay them prone upon the earth, and cease
To ponder on themselves, the while they stare
At nothing, intricately drawn nowhere
In shapes of shifting lineage. Let geese
Gabble and hiss, but heroes seek release
From dusty bondage into luminous air.
Oh, blinding hour—oh, holy terrible day—
When first the shaft into his vision shone
Of light anatomized! Euclid alone
Has looked on Beauty bare; fortunate they
Who though once only, and then but far away,
Have heard her massive sandal set on stone.

Harold Monro

GREAT CITY

When I returned at sunset,
The serving-maid was singing softly
Under the dark stairs, and in the house
Twilight had entered like a moon-ray.
Time was so dead I could not understand
The meaning of midday or of midnight,
But like falling waters—falling, hissing, falling—
Silence seemed an everlasting sound.

I sat in my dark room,
And watched sunset
And saw starlight.
I heard the tramp of homing men,
And the last call of the last child.
Then a lone bird twittered,
And suddenly, beyond the housetops,
I imagined dew in the country,
In the hay, on the buttercups;
The rising moon,
The scent of early night,
The songs, the echoes,
Dogs barking,
Day closing,
Gradual slumber,
Sweet rest.

When all the lamps were lighted in the town
I passed into the street ways and I watched,
Wakeful, almost happy,
And half the night I wandered in the street.

YOUTH IN ARMS

Happy boy, happy boy,
David the immortal-willed,
Youth a thousand thousand times
Slain, but not once killed,
Swaggering again today
In the old contemptuous way;

Leaning backward from your thigh
Up against the tinselled bar—
Dust and ashes! is it you?
Laughing, boasting, there you are!
First we hardly recognized you
In your modern avatar.

Soldier, rifle, brown khaki—
Is your blood as happy so?

Where's your sling or painted shield,
Helmet, pike or bow?
Well, you're going to the wars—
That is all you need to know.

Graybeards plotted. They were sad.
Death was in their wrinkled eyes.
At their tables, with their maps,
Plans and calculations, wise
They all seemed; for well they knew
How ungrudgingly Youth dies.

At their green official baize
They debated all the night
Plans for your adventurous days
Which you followed with delight,
Youth in all your wanderings,
David of a thousand slings.

THE STRANGE COMPANION

A Fragment

That strange companion came on shuffling feet,
Passed me, then turned, and touched my arm.

He said (and he was melancholy,
And both of us looked fretfully,
And slowly we advanced together),
He said: "I bring you your inheritance."

I watched his eyes; they were dim.
I doubted him, watched him, doubted him . . .
But, in a ceremonious way,
He said: "You are too grey:
Come, you must be merry for a day."

And I, because my heart was dumb,
Because the life in me was numb,
Cried: "I will come. I *will* come."

So, without another word,
We two jaunted on the street.
I had heard, often heard,
The shuffling of those feet of his,
The shuffle of his feet.

And he muttered in my ear
Such a wheezy jest
As a man may often hear—
Not the worst, not the best
That a man may hear.

Then he murmured in my face
Something that was true.
He said: "I have known this long, long while,
All there is to know of you."
And the light of the lamp cut a strange smile
On his face, and we muttered along the street,
Good enough friends, on the usual beat.

We lived together long, long.
We were always alone, he and I.
We never smiled with each other;
We were like brother and brother,
Dimly accustomed.
                    Can a man know
Why he must live, or where he should go?

He brought me that joke or two,
And we roared with laughter, for want of a smile.
As every man in the world might do.
He who lies all night in bed
Is a fool, and midnight will crush his head.

When he threw a glass of wine in my face
One night, I hit him, and we parted;
But in a short space
We came back to each other melancholy-hearted,
Told our pain,
Swore we would not part again.

One night we turned a table over
The body of some slain fool to cover,
And all the company clapped their hands;
So we spat in their faces,
And travelled away to other lands.

I wish for every man he find
A strange companion so
Completely to his mind
With whom he everywhere may go.

Harriet Monroe

THE HOTEL

The Waldorf-Astoria in 1908

The long resounding marble corridors, the shining parlors with shining women in them.

The French room, with its gilt and garlands under plump little tumbling painted Loves.

The Turkish room, with its jumble of many carpets and its stiffly squared un-Turkish chairs.

The English room, all heavy crimson and gold, with spreading palms lifted high in round green tubs.

The electric lights in twos and threes and hundreds, made into festoons and spirals and arabesques, a maze and magic of bright persistent radiance.

The people sitting in corners by twos and threes, and cooing together under the glare.

The long rows of silent people in chairs, watching with eyes that see not while the patient band tangles the air with music.

The bell-boys marching in with cards, and shouting names over and over into ears that do not heed.

The stout and gorgeous dowagers in lacy white and lilac, bedizened with many jewels, with smart little scarlet or azure hats on their gray-streaked hair.

The business men in trim and spotless suits, who walk in and out with eager steps, or sit at the desks and tables, or watch the shining women.

The telephone girls forever listening to far voices, with the silver band over their hair and the little black caps obliterating their ears.

The telegraph tickers sounding their perpetual chit—chit-chit from the uttermost ends of the earth.

The waiters, in black swallow-tails and white aprons, passing here and there with trays of bottles and glasses.

The quiet and sumptuous bar-room, with purplish men softly drinking in little alcoves, while the barkeeper, mixing bright liquors, is rapidly plying his bottles.

The great bedecked and gilded café, with its glitter of a thousand mirrors, with its little white tables bearing gluttonous dishes whereto bright forks, held by pampered hands, flicker daintily back and forth.

The white-tiled immaculate kitchen, with many little round blue fires, where white-clad cooks are making spiced and flavored dishes.

The cool cellars filled with meats and fruits, or layered with sealed and bottled wines mellowing softly in the darkness.

The invisible stories of furnaces and machines, burrowing deep down into the earth, where grimy workmen are heavily laboring.

The many-windowed stories of little homes and shelters and sleeping-places, reaching up into the night like some miraculous high-piled honey-comb of wax-white cells.

The clothes inside of the cells—the stuffs, the silks, the laces; the elaborate delicate disguises that wait in trunks and drawers and closets, or bedrape and conceal human flesh.

The people inside of the clothes, the bodies white and young, bodies fat and bulging, bodies wrinkled and wan, all alike veiled by fine fabrics, sheltered by walls and roofs, shut in from the sun and stars.

The souls inside of the bodies—the naked souls; souls weazen and weak, or proud and brave; all imprisoned in flesh, wrapped in woven stuffs, enclosed in thick and painted masonry, shut away with many shadows from the shining truth.

God inside of the souls, God veiled and wrapped and imprisoned
    and shadowed in fold on fold of flesh and fabrics and
    mockeries; but ever alive, struggling and rising again, seek-
    ing the light, freeing the world.

THE TURBINE

To W. S. M.

Look at her—there she sits upon her throne
As ladylike and quiet as a nun!
But if you cross her—whew! her thunderbolts
Will shake the earth! She's proud as any queen—
The beauty; knows her royal business too—
To light the world; and does it night by night
When her gay lord, the sun, gives up his job.
I am her slave; I wake and watch and run
From dark till dawn beside her: all the while
She hums there softly, purring with delight
Because men bring the riches of the earth
To feed her hungry fires. I do her will
And dare not disobey, for her right hand
Is power, her left is terror, and her anger
Is havoc. Look—if I but lay a wire
Across the terminals of yonder switch
She'll burst her windings, rip her casings off,
And shriek till envious Hell shoots up its flames,
Shattering her very throne. And all her people,
The laboring, trampling, dreaming crowds out there—
Fools and the wise who look to her for light—
Will walk in darkness through the liquid night,
Submerged.

        Sometimes I wonder why she stoops
To be my friend—oh yes, who talks to me
And sings away my loneliness; my friend,
Though I am trivial and she sublime.
Hard-hearted?—No, tender and pitiful,
As all the great are; every arrogant grief

She comforts quietly, and all my joys
Dance to her measures through the tolerant night.
She talks to me, tells me her troubles too,
Just as I tell her mine. Perhaps she feels
An ache deep down—that agonizing stab
Of grit grating her bearings; then her voice
Changes its tune, it wails and calls to me
To soothe her anguish, and I run, her slave,
Probe like a surgeon and relieve the pain.

We have our jokes too, little mockeries
That no one else in all the swarming world
Would see the point of. She will laugh at me
To show her power: maybe her carbon packings
Leak steam, and I run madly back and forth
To keep the infernal fiends from breaking loose:
Suddenly she will throttle them herself
And chuckle softly, far above me there,
At my alarms.

               But there are moments, too,
When my turn comes; her slave can be her master,
Conquering her he serves. For she's a woman,
Gets bored there on her throne, tired of herself.
Tingles with power that turns to wantonness.
Suddenly something's wrong—she laughs at me,
Bedevils the frail wires with some mad caress
That thrills blind space, calls down ten thousand lightnings
To ruin her pomp and set her spirit free.
Then with this puny hand, swift as her threat,
Must I beat back the chaos, hold in leash
Destructive furies, rescue her—even her—
From the fierce rashness of her truant mood,
And make me lord of far and near a moment,
Startling the mystery. Last night I did it—
Alone here with my hand upon her heart,
I faced the mounting fiends and whipped them down;
And never a wink from the long file of lamps
Betrayed her to the world.

So there she sits,
Mounted on all the ages, at the peak
Of time. The first man dreamed of light, and dug
The sodden ignorance away, and cursed
The darkness; young primeval races dragged
Foundation stones, and piled into the void
Rage and desire; the Greek mounted and sang
Promethean songs and lit a signal fire;
The Roman bent his iron will to forge
Deep furnaces; slow epochs riveted
With hope the secret chambers: till at last
We, you and I, this living age of ours,
A new-winged Mercury, out of the skies
Filch the wild spirit of light, and chain him there
To do her will forever.

Look, my friend,
Here is a sign! What is this crystal sphere—
This little bulb of glass I lightly lift,
This iridescent bubble a child might blow
Out of its brazen pipe to hold the sun—
What strange toy is it! In my hand it lies
Cold and inert, its puny artery—
That curling cobweb film—ashen and dead.
But now—a twist or two—let it but touch
The hem, far trailing, of my lady's robe,
And look, the burning life-blood of the stars
Leaps to its heart, and glows against the dark,
Kindling the world.

Even so I touch her garment,
Her servant through the quiet night; and thus
I lay my hand upon the Pleiades
And feel their throb of fire. Grandly she gives
To me unworthy; woman inscrutable,
Scatters her splendors through my darkness, leads me
Far out into the workshop of the worlds.
There I can feel those infinite energies
Our little earth just gnaws at through the ether,

And see the light our sunshine hides. Out there,
Close to the heart of life, I am at peace.

ON THE PORCH

As I lie roofed in, screened in,
From the pattering rain,
The summer rain—
As I lie
Snug and dry,
And hear the birds complain:

Oh, billow on billow,
Oh, roar on roar,
Over me wash
The seas of war.

Over me—down—down—
Lunges and plunges
The huge gun with its one blind eye,
The armored train,
And, swooping out of the sky,
The aëroplane.
Down—down—
The army proudly swinging
Under gay flags,
The glorious dead heaped up like rags,
A church with bronze bells ringing,
A city all towers,
Gardens of lovers and flowers,
The round world swinging
In the light of the sun:
All broken, undone,
All down—under
Black surges of thunder . . .

Oh, billow on billow
Oh, roar on roar,
Over me wash
The seas of war . . .

As I lie roofed in, screened in,
From the pattering rain,
The summer rain—
As I lie
Snug and dry,
And hear the birds complain.

THE WONDER OF IT

How wild, how witch-like weird that life should be!
That the insensate rock dared dream of me,
And take to bursting out and burgeoning—
        Oh, long ago—yo ho!—
And wearing green! How stark and strange a thing
That life should be!

Oh, mystic mad, a rigadoon of glee,
That dust should rise, and leap alive, and flee
A-foot, a-wing, and shake the deeps with cries—
        Oh, far away—yo-hay!
What moony masque, what arrogant disguise
That life should be!

THE INNER SILENCE

Noises that strive to tear
Earth's mantle soft of air
And break upon the stillness where it dwells:
The noise of battle and the noise of prayer,
The cooing noise of love that softly tells
Joy's brevity, the brazen noise of laughter—
All these affront me not, nor echo after
Through the long memories.
They may not enter the deep chamber where
Forever silence is.

Silence more soft than spring hides in the ground
Beneath her budding flowers;

Silence more rich than ever was the sound
Of harps through long warm hours.
It's like a hidden vastness, even as though
Great suns might there beat out their measures slow,
Nor break the hush mightier than they.
There do I dwell eternally,
There where no thought may follow me,
Nor stillest dreams whose pinions plume the way.

LOVE SONG

I love my life, but not too well
　　To give it to thee like a flower,
So it may pleasure thee to dwell
　　Deep in its perfume but an hour.
I love my life, but not too well.

I love my life, but not too well
　　To sing it note by note away,
So to thy soul the song may tell
　　The beauty of the desolate day.
I love my life, but not too well.

I love my life, but not too well
　　To cast it like a cloak on thine,
Against the storms that sound and swell
　　Between thy lonely heart and mine.
I love my life, but not too well.

A FAREWELL

Good-by!—no, do not grieve that it is over,
　　The perfect hour;
That the winged joy, sweet honey-loving rover,
　　Flits from the flower.

Grieve not—it is the law. Love will be flying—
　　Oh, love and all.
Glad was the living—blessed be the dying!
　　Let the leaves fall.

LULLABY

My little one, sleep softly
  Among the toys and flowers.
Sleep softly, O my first-born son,
  Through all the long dark hours.
And if you waken far away
  I shall be wandering too.
If far away you run and play
  My heart must follow you.

Sleep softly, O my baby,
  And smile down in your sleep.
Here are red rose-buds for your bed—
  Smile, and I will not weep.
We made our pledge—you did not fear
  To go—why then should I?
Though long you sleep, I shall be near;
  So hush—we must not cry.

Sleep softly, dear one, softly—
  They can not part us now;
Forever rest here on my breast,
  My kiss upon your brow.
What though they hide a little grave
  With dream-flowers false or true?
What difference? We will just be brave
  Together—I and you.

PAIN

She heard the children playing in the sun,
And through her window saw the white-stemmed trees
Sway like a film of silver in the breeze
Under the purple hills; and one by one
She noted chairs and cabinets, and spun
The pattern of her bed's pale draperies:
Yet all the while she knew that each of these
Was a dull lie, in irony begun.

For down in hell she lay, whose livid fires
Love may not quench, whose pangs death may not quell.
The round immensity of earth and sky
Shrank to a point that speared her. Loves, desires,
Darkened to torturing ministers of hell,
Whose mockery of joy deepened the lie.

Little eternities the black hours were,
That no beginning knew, that knew no end.
Day waned, and night came like a faithless friend,
Bringing no joy; till slowly over her
A numbness grew, and life became a blur,
A silence, an oblivion, a dark blend
Of dim lost agonies, whose downward trend
Led into time's eternal sepulchre.
And yet, when after æons infinite
Of dark eclipse she wakened, it was day!
The pictures hung upon the walls, each one;
Under the same rose-patterned coverlet
She lay; spring was still young, and still the play
Of happy children sounded in the sun.

THE WATER OUZEL

Little brown surf-bather of the mountains!
Spirit of foam, lover of cataracts, shaking your wings in falling
    waters!
Have you no fear of the roar and rush when Nevada plunges—
Nevada, the shapely dancer, feeling her way with slim white
    fingers?
How dare you dash at Yosemite the mighty—
Tall, white-limbed Yosemite, leaping down, down, over the cliff?
Is it not enough to lean on the blue air of mountains?
Is it not enough to rest with your mate at timber-line, in bushes
    that hug the rocks?
Must you fly through mad waters where the heaped-up granite
    breaks them?
Must you batter your wings in the torrent?
Must you plunge for life or death through the foam?

THE PINE AT TIMBER-LINE

What has bent you,
Warped and twisted you,
Torn and crippled you?—
What has embittered you,
O lonely tree?

You search the rocks for a footing,
    dragging scrawny roots;
You bare your thin breast to the storms,
    and fling out wild arms behind you;
You throw back your witch-like head,
    with wisps of hair stringing the wind.

You fight with the snows,
You rail and shriek at the tempests.
Old before your time, you challenge the cold stars.

Be still, be satisfied—
Stand straight like your brothers in the valley,
The soft green valley of summer down below.
Why front the endless winter of the peak?
Why seize the lightning in your riven hands?
Why cut the driven wind and shriek aloud?

Why tarry here?

MOUNTAIN SONG

I have not where to lay my head;
    Upon my breast no child shall lie;
For me no marriage feast is spread:
    I walk alone under the sky.

My staff and scrip I cast away—
    Light-burdened to the mountain height!
Climbing the rocky steep by day,
    Kindling my fire against the night.

The bitter hail shall flower the peak,
  The icy wind shall dry my tears.
Strong shall I be, who am but weak,
  When bright Orion spears my fears.

Under the horned moon I shall rise
  Up-swinging on the scarf of dawn.
The sun, searching with level eyes,
  Shall take my hand and lead me on.

Wide flaming pinions veil the West—
  Ah, shall I find? and shall I know?
My feet are bound upon the quest—
  Over the Great Divide I go.

MOTHER EARTH

Oh a grand old time has the earth
In the long long life she lives!
From her huge mist-shrouded birth,
When reeling from under
She tore space asunder,
And feeling her way
Through the dim first day
Rose wheeling to run
In the path of the sun—
From then till forever,
Tiring not, pausing never,
She labors and laughs and gives.

Plains and mountains
She slowly makes,
With mighty hand
Sifting the sand,
Lifting the land
Out of the soft wet clutch of the shouting sea.
At lofty fountains
Her thirst she slakes,
And over the hills
Through the dancing rills

Wide rivers she fills,
That shine and sing and leap in their joy to be free.
Cool greenness she needs
And rich odor of bloom;
And longing, believing,
Slowly conceiving,
Her germ-woof weaving,
She spawns little seeds
By the wombful, the worldful,
And laughs as the pattern grows fair at her loom.

Proudly she trails
Her flower-broidered dresses
In the sight of the sun.
Loudly she hails
Through her far-streaming tresses
His racers that run.
For her heart, ever living, grows eager for life,
Its delight and desire;
She feels the high praise of its passion and strife,
Of its rapture and fire.
There are wings and songs in her trees,
There are gleaming fish in her seas;
The brute beasts brave her
And gnaw her and crave her;
And out of the heart of these
She wrests a dream, a hope,
An arrogant plan
Of life that shall meet her,
Shall know and complete her,
That through ages shall climb and grope,
And at last be man.

Out of the bitter void she wins him—
Out of the night;
With terror and wild hope begins him,
And fierce delight.
She beats him into caves,
She starves and spurns him.
Her hills and plains are graves—

Into dust she turns him.
She teaches him war and wrath
And waste and lust and greed;
Then over his blood-red path
She scatters her fruitful seed.
With bloom of a thousand flowers,
With songs of the summer hours,
With the love of the wind for the tree,
With the dance of the sun on the sea,
She lulls and quells him—
Oh soft her caress!
And tenderly tells him
Of happiness.
Through her ages of years,
Through his toil and his tears,
At her wayward pleasure
She yields of her treasure
A gleam, a hope,
Even a day of days
When the wide heavens ope
And he loves and prays.
Then she laughs in wonder
To see him rise
Her leash from under
And brave the skies!

Oh a grand old time has the earth
In the long long life she lives!—
A grand old time at her work sublime
As she labors and laughs and gives!

SUPERNAL DIALOGUE

Two beings
Stood on the edge of things—
Their breath was space,
And their eyes were suns.

It was this way he passed—
I know the sound.

II More worlds—
     He can not forbear—

I   Look down this lane—
     It was dark till he passed.
     Do you see—anything?

II Seeds of light—glowing, whirling—
     A handful.

I   Separating now.

II Fierce fire-balls—
     So many—so many. Will he get what he wants—
     The perfect flower?

I   Flower of delight—to bloom beside his throne?
     Sometime he will.
                    [*A pause*]

I   Look—that little one—
     Burning, aching—
     Trailing its tiny orbs—

II Which one?

I   See—scarlet—oh, alive!
     Deep in that right-hand cluster near the dark.

II With tiny trailers—will it be one of them?
     That clouded one, maybe?

I   Look—it foams down.
     The clouds lift—
     There are seas—

II Lands—a creeping green—
     Sounds of air moving.

I   Hush—oh, whisper!—do you see
     Dark specks that crawl?
     And wings that flash in the air?

II Spawn—immeasurably minute.
What does he mean, the fecund one, creating without
    reason or mercy?

I He must—life is his song.
He dreams—he wills.

II Watch now—they change, those atoms.
They stand on end—they lay stone on stone—
They go clad—they utter words.

I Proud—they take their spoil.
Kings—and slaves.

II Oh queer—ingenious! They gather in towns,
They filch our fires to carry them over land and sea.

I They measure the stars—they love—they dream.

II But war—pain—obliterative war and pain.

I So brief—each one a tiny puff—and out.

II Grotesque!

I A few look up—salute us before they fall.
A few dare face him.

II Is it enough?
     [A pause]

I It cools down—their whirling world.
It is silent—cold.

II Has he lost again? Can he fail?

I Who are we to question? Though he fail again and again—

II Yes, who are we?

I He must go on—he must get the flower.

Two beings
Stood on the edge of things—
Their breath was space,
And their eyes were suns.

Marianne Moore

THAT HARP YOU PLAY SO WELL

O David, if I had
Your power, I should be glad—
    In harping, with the sling,
    In patient reasoning!

Blake, Homer, Job, and you,
Have made old wine-skins new.
    Your energies have wrought
    Stout continents of thought.

But, David, if the heart
Be brass, what boots the art
    Of exorcising wrong,
    Of harping to a song?

The sceptre and the ring
And every royal thing
    Will fail. Grief's lustiness
    Must cure the harp's distress.

TALISMAN

Under a splintered mast,
Torn from ship and cast
    Near her hull,
A stumbling shepherd found
Embedded in the ground,
    A sea-gull

Of lapis lazuli,
A scarab of the sea,
    With wings spread—
Curling its coral feet,
Parting its beak to greet
    Men long dead.

"SUN!"

Hope and Fear—those internecine fighters—accost him.

"No man may him hyde
From Deth holow-eyed;"
This, for us mortal truth, for us shall not suffice.
You are not male or female, but a plan
Deep-set within the heart of man.
Splendid with splendor hid you come, from your Arab abode,
A fiery topaz smothered in the hand of a great prince who rode
Before you, Sun—whom you outran.
Piercing his caravan.

O Sun, you shall stay
With us. Holiday
And day of wrath shall be as one, wound in a device
Of Moorish gorgeousness, round glasses spun
To flame as hemispheres of one
Great hourglass dwindling to a stem. Consume hostility;
Employ your weapon in this meeting-place of surging enmity!
Insurgent feet shall not outrun
Multiplied flames, O Sun.

A GRAVEYARD

Man, looking into the sea—
taking the view from those who have as much right to it as you
        have to it yourself—
it is human nature to stand in the middle of a thing
but you cannot stand in the middle of this:
the sea has nothing to give but a well excavated grave.
The firs stand in a procession, each with an emerald turkey-
        foot at the top;
reserved as their contours, saying nothing.
Repression, however, is not the most obvious characteristic
        of the sea;
the sea is a collector, quick to return a rapacious look.
There are others beside you who have worn that look,

whose expression is no longer a protest. The fish no longer in-
    vestigate them,
for their bones have not lasted:
men lower nets, unconscious of the fact that they are desecrat-
    ing a grave,
and row quickly away; the blades of the oars
moving together like the feet of water-spiders as if there were
    no such thing as death.
The wrinkles progress upon themselves in a phalanx, beautiful
    under networks of foam,
and fade breathlessly while the sea rustles in and out of the sea-
    weed.
The birds swim through the air at top speed, emitting cat-calls
    as heretofore;
the tortoise-shell scourges about the feet of the cliffs, in motion
    beneath them;
and the ocean, under the pulsation of light-houses and noise of
    bell-buoys,
advances as usual, looking as if it were not that ocean in which
    dropped things are bound to sink—
in which, if they turn and twist, it is neither with volition or
    consciousness.

POETRY

I too, dislike it; there are things
    that are important beyond all this fiddle. Reading it,
        however, with a perfect contempt for it,
            one discovers that there is in it, after all, a place for the
                genuine:
                hands that can grasp, eyes that can dilate, hair that
                    can rise if it must,
the bat holding on upside down,
    an elephant pushing, a tireless wolf under a tree,
        the immovable critic twitching his skin
            like a horse that feels a fly, the base-ball fan, the statis-
                tician—nor is it
                valid to discriminate against business documents,
                    school-books,

trade reports—these phenomena
  are important; but dragged into conscious oddity by
    half poets, the result is not poetry.
       This we know. In a liking for the raw material in all
          its rawness,
          and for that which is genuine, there is liking for poetry.

Merrill Moore

THE NOISE THAT TIME MAKES

The noise that Time makes in passing by
Is very slight but even you can hear it,
Having not necessarily to be near it,
Needing only the slightest will to try:

Hold the receiver of a telephone
To your ear when no one is talking on the line.
And what may at first sound to you like the whine
Of wind over distant wires is Time's own
Garments brushing against a windy cloud.

That same noise again, but not so well,
May be heard by taking a small cockle-shell
From the sand and holding it against your head;

Then you can hear Time's footsteps as they pass
Over the earth brushing the eternal grass.

THE POET TELLS ABOUT NATURE

What if the winds sang softly the whole night long
On the wet beach wandering slowly up and down,

What if the winds there sang so loud a song
That the waves were hushed, waves that were loud and strong
And older than the wind, waves stronger grown
Being closer to earth.

Winds might swing over a town,
But the face of the earth the waves would finger long
After the winds were asleep and the sun was down.

What if the winds and the waves sung? I cannot tell you
Other than that they both themselves once lulled me
To sleep in the sea-grass beside a cold salt sea

Under a sky that was brilliant with stars, and blue
With the justifiable expectation of dawn,
For the sun was a long time set and its glow was gone.

WARNING TO ONE

Death is the strongest of all living things
But when it happens do not look in the eyes
For a dead fire or a lack-lustre there,
But listen for the words that fall from lips
Or do not fall. Silence is not death;
It merely means that the one who is conserving breath
Is not concerned with tattle and small quips.

Watch the quick fingers and the way they move
During unguarded moments—words of love
And love's caresses may be cold as ice,
And cold the glitter of engagement rings.
Death is the sword that hangs on a single hair;
And that thin tenuous hair is no more than love,
And yours is the silly head it hangs above.

John G. Neihardt

PRAYER FOR PAIN

I do not pray for peace nor ease,
Nor truce from sorrow:
No suppliant on servile knees
Begs here against to-morrow!

Lean flame against lean flame we flash,
    O Fates that meet me fair;
Blue steel against blue steel we clash—
    Lay on, and I shall dare!

But Thou of deeps the awful Deep,
    Thou Breather in the clay,
Grant this my only prayer—Oh, keep
    My soul from turning gray!

For until now, whatever wrought
    Against my sweet desires,
My days were smitten harps strung taut,
    My nights were slumbrous lyres.

And howso'er the hard blow rang
    Upon my battered shield,
Some lark-like, soaring spirit sang
    Above my battle-field.

And through my soul of stormy night
    The zigzag blue flame ran.
I asked no odds—I fought my fight—
    Events against a man.

But now—at last—the gray mist chokes
    And numbs me. Leave me pain!
Oh, let me feel the biting strokes,
    That I may fight again!

ENVOI

Oh, seek me not within a tomb—
    Thou shalt not find me in the clay!
I pierce a little wall of gloom
    To mingle with the day!

I brothered with the things that pass,
    Poor giddy joy and puckered grief;
I go to brother with the grass
    And with the sunning leaf.

Not death can sheathe me in a shroud;
　　A joy-sword whetted keen with pain,
I join the armies of the cloud,
　　The lightning and the rain.

Oh, subtle in the sap athrill,
　　Athletic in the glad uplift,
A portion of the cosmic will,
　　I pierce the planet-drift.

My God and I shall interknit
　　As rain and ocean, breath and air;
And oh, the luring thought of it
　　Is prayer!

Robert Nichols

BY THE WOOD

How still the day is, and the air how bright!
　　A thrush sings and is silent in the wood;
The hillside sleeps dizzy with heat and light;
　　A rhythmic murmur fills the quietude;
A woodpecker prolongs his leisured flight,
　　Rising and falling on the solitude.

But there are those who far from yon wood lie,
　　Buried within the trench where all were found.
A weight of mold oppresses every eye,
　　Within that cabin close their limbs are bound;
And there they rot amid the long profound
　　Disastrous silence of grey earth and sky.

These once too rested where now rests but one
　　Who scarce can lift his panged and heavy head,
Who drinks in grief the hot light of the sun,
　　Whose eyes watch dully the green branches spread,
Who feels his currents ever slowlier run,
　　Whose lips repeat a silent . . . "Dead! all dead!"

Oh, youths to come shall drink air warm and bright,
  Shall hear the bird cry in the sunny wood.
All my Young England fell today in fight:
  That bird, that wood, was ransomed by our blood!
I pray you, when the drum rolls let your mood
  Be worthy of our deaths and your delight.

NEARER

Nearer and ever nearer . . .
  My body, tired but tense,
Hovers 'twixt vague pleasure
  And tremulous confidence.

Arms to have and to use them,
  And a soul to be made
Worthy, if not worthy;
  If afraid, unafraid.

To endure for a little,
  To endure and have done:
Men I love about me,
  Over me the sun!

And should at last suddenly
  Fly the speeding death,
The four great quarters of heaven
  Receive this little breath.

Yone Noguchi

THE POET

Out of the deep and the dark,
A sparkling mystery, a shape,
Something perfect,
Comes like the stir of the day:
One whose breath is an odor,
Whose eyes show the road to stars,

The breeze in his face,
The glory of heaven on his back.
He steps like a vision hung in air,
Diffusing the passion of eternity;
His abode is the sunlight of morn,
The music of eve his speech:
In his sight,
One shall turn from the dust of the grave,
And move upward to the woodland.

I HAVE CAST THE WORLD

I have cast the world,
       and think me as nothing.
Yet I feel cold on snow-falling day,
And happy on flower day.

HOKKU

Bits of song—what else?
I, a rider of the stream,
Lone between the clouds.

LINES

When I am lost in the deep body of the mist on a hill,
The universe seems built with me as its pillar.
Am I the god upon the face of the deep—nay, deepless deepness
    in the beginning?

Jessica Nelson North

HIBERNALIA

I can survive on ears the huskers leave
In stubbled cornfields when their day is finished.
I can retrieve

Roots from deserted gardens after frost.
I thrive on all things thwarted and diminished,
Abandoned and lost.

But you are sleeker than your sleekest dove,
Your eyes affront me with their eagerness.
Temper your love
For me with meagreness.

You would not spread a dinner in the sun
To tempt the hidden rabbit from his burrow,
Who after dark
Explores the beauty of the frosted furrow,
Nibbles the frugal bark:

But leave outside your door in negligence
Some tidbit of your passion if you will,
And I will creep, charmed by indifference,
Quivering to your sill.

TO DUNCAN

Death stood beside us on your night of birth
With no black accident or grim abyss.
He brought a gray pervading quietness,
A moist aroma of the summer earth.

No silver invitation sought my bed,
Nor winding of the thin celestial horn.
He offered me, beneath the friendly corn,
A dreamless pillow for a drowsy head.

Insistent were his overtures, and sweet;
But somewhere still my flesh denial made,
And so with fainting insolence I laid
My warm and wailing challenge at his feet.

O little son, assume your enterprise:
Now to the years in which we have no part
Carry your father's dark endearing eyes,
And my unquiet heart.

TRUTH

The world is hollow like a pumpkin-shell—
We know it well—
And warm and full of true delightful things,
Hop-o'-my-thumbs and flittermice with wings,
And frequent beanstalks reaching to the sky,
And giants nine feet high.

When with your button nose against the pane
You say, watching the rain,
"The clouds are elephants with ears like sails
And trunks to match their tails"—
Oh that is true, oh that is very true!
I see them too.

Now stop your little ears with both your thumbs,
For here the Doubter comes;
And up and down he shortly will declare
The world is dirt and skies are made of air.

Never believe him though he looks so wise.
I marvel that his skies,
Like Chicken Little's, do not tumble down
And crash upon his crown.

A YOUNG BOY

Let him alone, and when he is one year older
We will send him away to school.
This year he is twelve. His eyes are colder
Than stars in a rainy pool.

Cold and clear. He bends his graceful head
Not to our sorrow nor to any other.
Perhaps, we think, he would have loved his mother,
But his mother is dead.

His round cheek is like a sun-sweetened apple
And his brown throat is bare.

Is there any sorrow with which he must grapple
We would not die to share?

He will not help us. He puts his thoughts behind him,
And not of these will he speak.
He is like the waters out of Nameless Creek,
Dark and still. There you may seek and find him.

There he dives like the gull, with the mill-sluice races,
His curving arm dappled with shade and sun,
Rises and dips, but he comes not back for our praises
When his race is done.

A child is harder to win than any lover.
Let him alone, there is nothing more to say.
He is young now, but when a year is over
We will send him away.

RAINY MORNING

The wet leaves fall in a pattern of rusty yellows.
The first rains of autumn seethe in a turbulent brew.
The women patter to work in a sea of umbrellas,
Crimson and green and blue.

The women are strangely glorified by these
Gay moons of silk that blossom under the rain,
As if impossible flowers should fall from trees
Never to bloom again.

As if in autumn hearts the folded passions
Should wake in calyx and be wide unfurled,
Crimson and green and blue, after their fashions,
To flame in a wet world.

The clouds break, a wavering sunlight shines,
A few leaves spatter the rainbow throng,
The brave convolvulus folds on its whispering vines,
And the women patter along.

MATHEMATICAL

With what contentment in its ordered ways
The rhomboid goes, with what assurance fine
The parallelopiped stands on space,
Fixed and definitive in every line!
Here is security, precise and sweet,
Since lines drawn parallel can never meet.

Curves are the road of change. The humblest peach,
That ripens now and in a week decays,
Hangs like the moon as round and out of reach.
Something eludes us even while we gaze.
And common hearts get strangely out of hand,
Running on curves no compass ever planned.

Grace Fallow Norton

ALLEGRA AGONISTES

A gleam of gold in gloom and gray,
A call from out a fairer day.
O pang at heart and ebbing blood!
(Hush, bread and salt should be thy mood,
Stern woman of the Brotherhood.)

Clamor of golden tones and tunes,
Hunt of faint horns, breath of bassoons;
They wound my soul again; I lie
Face earthward in fresh agony.
Oh, give me joy before I die!

World, world, I could have danced for thee,
And I had tales and minstrelsy;
Kept fairer, I had been more good.
(Hush, bread and salt should be thy mood,
Soul of the breadless Brotherhood.)

Some thou hast formed to play thy part,
The bold, the cold, the hard of heart.
Thy rue upon my lips I toss.
Rose was my right. O world, the loss,
When Greek limbs writhe upon the cross!

MAKE NO VOWS

I made a vow once, one only.
I was young and I was lonely.
When I grew strong I said: "This vow
Is too narrow for me now.
Who am I to be bound by old oaths?
I will change them as I change my clothes!"

But that ancient outworn vow
Was like fetters upon me now.
It was hard to break, hard to break;
Hard to shake from me, hard to shake.

I broke it by day, but it closed upon me at night.
He is not free who is free only in the sunlight.
He is not free who bears fetters in his dreams,
Nor he who laughs only by dark dream-fed streams.

Oh, it costs much bright coin of strength to live!
Watch, then, where all your strength you give!
For I, who would be so wild and wondrous now,
Must give, give, to break a burdening bitter vow.

I GIVE THANKS

There's one that I once loved so much
    I am no more the same.
I give thanks for that transforming touch.
    I tell you not his name.

He has become a sign to me
    For flowers and for fire.

For song he is a sign to me
  And for the broken lyre,

And I have known him in a book
  And never touched his hand.
And he is dead—I need not look
  For him through his green land.

Heaven may not be. I have no faith,
  But this desire I have—
To take my soul on my last breath,
  To lift it like a wave,

And surge unto his star and say,
  His friendship had been heaven;
And pray, for clouds that closed his day
  May light at last be given!

And say, he shone at noon so bright
  I learned to run and rejoice!
And beg him for one last delight—
  The true sound of his voice.

There's one that once moved me so much
  I am no more the same;
And I pray I too, I too, may touch
  Some heart with singing flame.

Elder Olson

ESSAY ON DEITY

God's body is all space.
He is the shifting land
And the lifting seas.
He is the turning wind.
Like waters all his strange
Substance suffers change
Forever, yet is known
Forever to be one.

Though water dress as blue
Wave or mist or dew
Or ice at the world's end,
It is one element.
Even as waters he
Takes shape of cloud and tree:
I see his essence plain
In transparent rain
And blowing mist; I know
His presence in the snow.

How then, embittered dust
But hostaged unto death,
Thought you to refuse
Your substance to his use?
To every glint of dust,
To every spark of frost,
To every grain of sand,
He set his shining hand,
He breathed his shining breath.
How thought you to withstand,
Narrow heart, this power
That touches dimmest star,
That pierces finest seed?
Narrow brain, how thought
Your thinking to shut out
The undimensional mind?
And you, most narrow sight,
You glass set in the skull,
Reflecting the least leaf,
The littlest flake to fall,
How thought you to lie blind
To the absolute light?

Yet since he everywhere,
In water, land and air,
Moves as everything—
The gull on stony wing,
The sliding rock, the fish
In the sea's dim mesh,

Then, minute breast of bone,
Behold how all unknown
You drew him home as breath
In crystal lapse and flood.
Heart that refuses God,
You bear him for your blood;
Obdurate mouth, he is
The food that fed your hunger.
Deny him then no longer—
You took him for your bread.
Behold how, unaware,
In breathing the wild air,
In seeing, being fed,
In knowing even now
These words, this mist and snow,
These birds at the earth's rim,
Whether you will or no,
You have accepted him.

WATERS

The waters of the world in their cold chasm
Move with slow silver muscles, glide beneath
A tenuous green sheath,
Unfurl to massy folds, or march in mountains.
Rivers and fountains
And waterfalls in ravelling ropes of smoke
Feed the green chasm.
The waters of the world conceive cold slow
Insinuating fish, that ghost and glow
Suspended in steep streams or glossy mountains.

The marble thews of earth are washed with waters.
The rivers of earth in twisted silver trees
Root within twinkling seas.
Steely rain
Trembles in taut blue wires. The grey ocean,
Sliding with rugged hackles in slow wind,
Moves with an inextinguishable motion.

Only we transient, we besieged by death,
We doomed to the tall winds in their cold commotion,
To the wind in the hemlocks breaking, the wind in the pines,
Cry truce, now, with all lovely fury of motion.

Wherefore, O waters, we, being with one breath
Troubled intolerably, being at length no more
Than various waters moving to one end—
Many and mutable, to one end only
Of utter darkness and invading wind—
It is as waters then, as waters bound
To stern surrender of their trivial guise,
We yield, who were intransigent and lonely,
Fearing no ultimate darkness, having found
Night comes like the slow closing of tired eyes.

George O'Neil

FABLE

I led him on into the frosted wood.
Stamping our feet, beneath a larch we stood,
Breathing white edifices on the air;
And nothing else was moving there.

The branches hung as if they had not known
A day when any little wind had blown.
The snow above our heads wrought wondrously
A thousand gargoyles on a tree.

Freezing, we waited by the frozen brook . . .
"Listen!" I said, and hardly dared to look.
A drift slid suddenly across the ice,
A frigid hawthorne trembled twice . . .

Then slowly through the brambles, marble-veined,
A hoof, a haunch, a heavy shoulder, strained;
A head swung down into a glassy heap
And smashed it with a sideward sweep.

I could not hold my tongue: "You see the horn!
That twisted golden bone . . . the Unicorn!"
I could not hold it back. And as I spoke
A splintered universe awoke.

The thing was gone. "You saw!" I spun around
To read his eyes. He kicked a knotted mound,
And all the gargoyles tumbled on his head.
"I'm numb, I'm going home," he said.

ADAM'S WONDER

The amber morning floats a tree.
This is insoluble to me—
That boughs bear apples, bronzen, clear,
There, in the shimmer of the year.

Reason for this I have not found—
That seeds pulled sunward in the ground,
Pressing the dark with airy shoots,
Should whirl up iron from burning roots.

What mind, in witnessing, perceives
The golden purpose of the leaves
When feathered arrows spring and pass
To whip the morning from the grass?

No man that speaks can lay for me
In thought's most staunch suspensory
The high bewilderment I know
To see an orchard shining so,
To watch a pendent apple stare
At stranger substance in the air—
A figure moving toward a tree,
An arm uplifted, radiantly.

A WOMAN PASSES A DOOR

I was astonished by no grace,
No signal beauty in your face,
As quickly, quietly, you went,
Ineffable astonishment.

You were a figure through a door,
And then unutterably more.

"I know I shall not see her dead,
Though she is hurrying . . ." I said.
And silently I saw you go,
And you were music, you were snow.

James Oppenheim

THE SLAVE

They set the slave free, striking off his chains . . .
Then he was as much of a slave as ever.

He was still chained to servility,
He was still manacled to indolence and sloth,
He was still bound by fear and superstition,
By ignorance, suspicion, and savagery . . .
His slavery was not in the chains,
But in himself. . . .

They can only set free men free . . .
And there is no need of that:
Free men set themselves free.

THE LONELY CHILD

Do you think, my boy, when I put my arms around you
To still your fears,
That it is I who conquer the dark and the lonely night?

My arms seem to wrap love about you,
As your little heart fluttering at my breast
Throbs love through me . . .

But, dear one, it is not your father:
Other arms are about you, drawing you near,
And drawing the earth near, and the night near,
And your father near. . . .

Some day you shall lie alone at nights,
As now your father lies;
And in those arms, as a leaf fallen on a tranquil stream,
Drift into dreams and healing sleep.

NOT OVERLOOKED

Though I am little as all little things,
Though the stars that pass over my tininess are as the sands of
    the sea,
Though the garment of the night was made for a sky-giant and
    does not fit me,
Though even in a city of men I am as nothing,
Yet at times the gift of life is almost more than I can bear. . . .
I laugh with joyousness, the morning is a blithe holiday;
And in the overrunning of my hardy bliss praise rises for the
    very breath I breathe.

How soaked the universe is with life—
Not a cranny but is drenched!
Ah, not even I was overlooked!

THE RUNNER IN THE SKIES

Who is the runner in the skies—
With her blowing scarf of stars,
And our earth and sun hovering like bees about her blossoming
    heart!
Her feet are on the winds where space is deep;
Her eyes are nebulous and veiled;
She hurries through the night to a far lover.

Patrick Orr

ANNIE SHORE AND JOHNNIE DOON

Annie Shore, 'twas, sang last night
    Down in South End saloon;
A tawdry creature in the light—
Painted cheeks, eyes over-bright,
    Singing a dance-hall tune.

I'd be forgetting Annie's singing—
    I'd not have thought again—
But for the thing that cried and fluttered
    Through all the shrill refrain:
Youth crying above foul words, cheap music,
    And innocence in pain.

    They sentenced Johnnie Doon today
        For murder, stark and grim;
    Death's none too dear a price, they say,
    For such-like men as him to pay;
        No need to pity him!

And Johnnie Doon I'd not be pitying—
    I could forget him now—
But for the childish look of trouble
    That fell across his brow,
For the twisting hands he looked at dumbly
    As if they'd sinned, he knew not how.

IN THE MOHAVE

As I rode down the arroyo through yuccas belled with bloom,
    I saw a last year's stalk lift dried hands to the light;
Like age at prayer for death within a careless room,
    Like one by day o'ertaken, whose sick desire is night.

And as I rode I saw a lean coyote lying
    All perfect as in life upon a silver dune,
Save that his feet no more could flee the harsh light's spying,
    Save that no more his shadow would cleave the sinking moon.

O cruel land, where form endures, the spirit fled!
  You chill the sun for me with your gray sphinx's smile,
Brooding in the bright silence above your captive dead,
  Where beat the heart of life so brief, so brief a while!

Seumas O'Sullivan

MY SORROW

My sorrow that I am not by the little dun,
By the lake of the starlings at Rosse's under the hill—
And the larks there, singing over the fields of dew,
Or evening there, and the sedges still!
For plain I see now the length of the yellow sand,
And Lissadell far off and its leafy ways,
And the holy mountain whose mighty heart
Gathers into it all the colored days.
My sorrow that I am not by the little dun,
By the lake of the starlings at evening when all is still—
And still in whispering sedges the herons stand.
'Tis there I would nestle at rest till the quivering moon
Uprose in the golden quiet over the hill.

SPLENDID AND TERRIBLE

Splendid and terrible your love.
The searing pinions of its flight
Flamed but a moment's space above
The place where ancient memories keep
Their quiet; and the dreaming deep
Moved inly with a troubled light,
And that old passion woke and stirred
Out of its sleep.

Splendid and terrible your love.
I hold it to me like a flame;
I hold it like a flame above
The empty anguish of my breast.

There let it stay, there let it rest—
Deep in the heart whereto it came
Of old as some wind-wearied bird
Drops to its nest.

THE OTHERS

From our hidden places,
    By a secret path,
We come in the moonlight
    To the side of the green rath.

There the night through
    We take our pleasure,
Dancing to such a measure
    As earth never knew.

To dance and lilt
    And song without a name,
So sweetly chanted
    'Twould put a bird to shame.

And many a maiden
    Is there, of mortal birth,
Her young eyes laden
    With dreams of earth.

Music so piercing wild
    And forest-sweet would bring
Silence on blackbirds singing
    Their best in the ear of spring.

And many a youth entrancèd
    Moves slow in the dreamy round,
His brave lost feet enchanted
    With the rhythm of faëry sound.

Oh, many a thrush and blackbird
    Would fall to the dewy ground,
And pine away in silence
    For envy of such a sound.

So the night through,
     In our sad pleasure,
We dance to many a measure
     That earth never knew.

Wilfred Owen

STRANGE MEETING

It seemed that out of the battle I escaped
Down some profound dull tunnel, long since scooped
Through granites which Titanic wars had groined.
Yet also there encumbered sleepers groaned,
Too fast in thought or death to be bestirred.
Then, as I probed them, one sprang up and stared
With piteous recognition in fixed eyes,
Lifting distressful hands as if to bless.
And by his smile I knew that sullen hall:
With a thousand fears that vision's face was grained;
Yet no blood reached there from the upper ground,
And no guns thumped, or down the flues made moan.
"Strange friend," I said, "here is no cause to mourn."
"None," said the other, "save the undone years,
The hopelessness. Whatever hope is yours
Was my life also; I went hunting wild
After the wildest beauty in the world,
Which lies not calm in eyes, or braided hair,
But mocks the steady running of the hour,
And if it grieves, grieves richlier than here.
For by my glee might many men have laughed,
And of my weeping something has been left
Which must die now. I mean the truth untold,
The pity of war, the pity war distilled.
Now men will go content with what we spoiled,
Or, discontent, boil bloody, and be spilled.
They will be swift with swiftness of the tigress,
None will break ranks, though nations trek from progress.
Courage was mine, and I had mystery;

Wisdom was mine, and I had mastery;
To miss the march of this retreating world
Into vain citadels that are not walled.
Then, when much blood had clogged their chariot-wheels,
I would go up and wash them from sweet wells,
Even with truths that lie too deep for taint.
I would have poured my spirit without stint,
But not through wounds; not on the cess of war.
Foreheads of men have bled where no wounds were.
I am the enemy you killed, my friend.
I knew you in this dark; for so you frowned
Yesterday through me as you jabbed and killed.
I parried; but my hands were loath and cold.
Let us sleep now . . ."

ARMS AND THE BOY

Let the boy try along this bayonet-blade
How cold steel is, and keen with hunger of blood;
Blue with all malice, like a madman's flash;
And thinly drawn with famishing for flesh.

Lend him to stroke these blind blunt bullet-heads
Which long to muzzle in the hearts of lads.
Or give him cartridges of fine zinc teeth,
Sharp with the sharpness of grief and death.

For his teeth seem for laughing round an apple.
There lurk no claws behind his fingers supple;
And God will grow no talons at his heels,
Nor antlers through the thickness of his curls.

THE ANTHEM FOR DOOMED YOUTH

What passing-bells for these who die as cattle?
Only the monstrous anger of the guns.
Only the stuttering rifles' rapid rattle
Can patter out their hasty orisons.

No mockeries for them; no prayers nor bells,
Nor any voice of mourning save the choirs—
The shrill demented choirs of wailing shells;
And bugles calling for them from sad shires.

What candles may be held to speed them all?
Not in the hands of boys, but in their eyes
Shall shine the holy glimmers of good-byes.
The pallor of girls' brows shall be their pall;
Their flowers the tenderness of patient minds,
And each slow dusk a drawing-down of blinds.

APOLOGIA PRO POEMATE MEO

I too saw God through mud—
　　The mud that cracked on cheeks when wretches smiled.
　　War brought more glory to their eyes than blood,
　　And gave their laughs more glee than shakes a child.

Merry it was to laugh there—
　　Where death becomes absurd and life absurder.
　　For power was on us as we slashed bones bare
　　Not to feel sickness or remorse of murder.

I too have dropped off fear—
　　Behind the barrage, dead as my platoon;
　　And sailed my spirit surging, light and clear,
　　Past the entanglement where hopes lay strewn;

And witnessed exultation—
　　Faces that used to curse me, scowl for scowl,
　　Shine and light up with passion of oblation—
　　Seraphic for an hour; though they were foul.

I have made fellowships—
　　Untold of happy lovers in old song.
　　For love is not the binding of fair lips
　　With the soft silk of eyes that look and long,

By Joy, whose ribbon slips:
　　But wound with war's hard wire whose stakes are strong;

Bound with the bandage of the arm that drips;
Knit in the welding of the rifle-thong.

I have perceived much beauty
    In the hoarse oaths that kept our courage straight;
    Heard music in the silentness of duty;
    Found peace where shell-storms spouted reddest spate.

Nevertheless, except you share
    With them in hell the sorrowful dark of hell,
    Whose world is but the trembling of a flare,
    And heaven but as the highway for a shell,

You shall not hear their mirth:
    You shall not come to think them well content
    By any jest of mine. These men are worth
    Your tears; you are not worth their merriment.

November, 1917

Josephine Preston Peabody

CRADLE SONG

I

Lord Gabriel, wilt thou not rejoice
When at last a little boy's
    Cheek lies heavy as a rose,
    And his eyelids close?

Gabriel, when that hush may be,
This sweet hand all heedfully
    I'll undo, for thee alone,
    From his mother's own.

Then the far blue highways, paven
With the burning stars of heaven,
    He shall gladden with the sweet
    Hasting of his feet—

Feet so brightly bare and cool,
Leaping, as from pool to pool;
From a little laughing boy
Splashing rainbow joy!

Gabriel, wilt thou understand
How to keep his hovering hand—
Never shut, as in a bond,
From the bright beyond?

Nay, but though it cling and close
Tightly as a clinging rose,
Clasp it only so—aright,
Lest his heart take fright.

(*Dormi, dormi, tu;*
The dusk is hung with blue.)

II

Lord Michael, wilt not thou rejoice
When at last a little boy's
Heart, a shut-in murmuring bee,
Turns him into thee?

Wilt thou heed thine armor well—
To take his hand from Gabriel,
So his radiant cup of dream
May not spill a gleam?

He will take thy heart in thrall,
Telling o'er thy breastplate, all
Colors, in his bubbling speech,
With his hand to each.

(*Dormi, dormi, tu,*
Sapphire is the blue;
Pearl and beryl, they are called,
Chrysoprase and emerald,
Sard and amethyst.
Numbered so, and kissed.)

Ah, but find some angel-word
For thy sharp, subduing sword!
  Yea, Lord Michael, make no doubt
  He will find it out:

(*Dormi, dormi, tu!*)
His eyes will look at you.

III

Last, a little morning space,
Lead him to that leafy place
  Where Our Lady sits awake,
  For all mothers' sake.

Bosomed with the Blessèd One,
He shall mind her of her Son,
  Once so folded from all harms,
  In her shrining arms.

(*In her veil of blue,*
Dormi, dormi, tu.)

  So—and fare thee well.
  Softly—Gabriel . . .
When the first faint red shall come,
Bid the Day-star lead him home—
  For the bright world's sake—
  To my heart, awake.

A SONG OF SOLOMON

King Solomon was the wisest man
  Of all that have been kings.
He built an House unto the Lord;
  And he sang of creeping things.

Of creeping things, of things that fly,
  Or swim within the seas;
Of the little weed along the wall,
  And of the cedar-trees.

And happier he, without mistake,
Than all men since alive.
God's House he built; and he did make
A thousand songs and five.

Padraic Pearse

IDEAL

Naked I saw thee,
O beauty of beauty!
And I blinded my eyes
For fear I should fail.

I heard thy music,
O melody of melody!
And I closed my ears
For fear I should falter.

I kissed thy mouth,
O sweetness of sweetness!
And I hardened my heart
For fear of my slaying.

I blinded my eyes,
And I closed my ears.
I hardened my heart
And I smothered my desire.

I turned my back
On the vision I had shaped,
And to this road before me
I turned my face.

I have turned my face
To this road before me,
To the deed that I see,
To the death I shall die.

LULLABY OF A WOMAN OF THE MOUNTAIN

O little head of gold! O candle of my house!
Thou will be a guide to all who travel this country.

Be quiet, O house! And O little grey mice,
Stay at home tonight in your hidden lairs!

O moths on the window, fold your wings!
Cease your droning, O little black chafers!

O plover and O curlew, over my house do not travel!
Speak not, O barnacle-goose going over the mountain here!

O creatures of the mountain, that wake so early,
Stir not tonight till the sun whitens over you!

(Translated from the Irish by Thomas MacDonagh)

A RANN I MADE

A rann I made within my heart
To the rider, to the high king,
A rann I made to my love,
To the king of kings, ancient Death.

Brighter to me than light of day
The dark of thy house, though black clay;
Sweeter to me than the music of trumpets
The quiet of thy house and its eternal silence.

Josephine Pinckney

PHYLLIS AND THE PHILOSOPHER

It was maybe eight o'clock
When we passed the roosting cock,

The out-buildings that slept aloof,
The dairy with a pointed roof;

Moonlight on the white-washed farm
Lay like milk, new-spilt and warm.

(It was very long ago
That we strolled together so.)

Down the row we scuffed to where
The careless plowman's idle share

Broke the middle of the field,
With a furrow half unreeled
And hoof-marks where the mule had wheeled.

I mounted to the plowman's seat,
The new-cut ground was dark and sweet,

And the gentle air came over
With the strong smell of bruised clover.

I was young and not afraid,
I laughed like any dairy maid—

Laughed with stupid happy laughter
For love with joy forever after.

You said, "Spring winds will always bring
This same sorrow of the spring,

"Longing always unappeased
For something lost—something unseized . . ."

You looked a white affrighted ghost,
I said, "If you have love, what's lost?"

You said, "Oh, I do not know . . ."
And fled me down the gaping row.
This was very long ago.

PEGGY CONSIDERS HER GRANDMOTHERS

The haycocks stand along the fence
Like grandmothers in rows;
They rasp my temper with their tense
And disciplined repose.

Tight-bosomed bodies, tiny of waist
Above their petticoats,

Are bustled and billowing with a chaste
Denial of legs and throats.

Majestically they decree
Deportment for a maid;
"Be meek," they say, "be womanly,
Be always boned and stayed."

My body is straight as any sheaf's,
My breasts are like a boy's;
They hide my inconsolable griefs
And little doubtful joys.

If I should lose my iron pride
And cast a look their way—
"Who gave me this hard flesh to hide,
You—haycocks!" I would say.

IN THE BARN

The sun, in wanton pride,
Drenches the country-side
With spilt gold from his old autumnal store.
But Scipio sits within the barn's thick gloom,
The merest crack of light coming in the door—
Sits and husks the corn long after working hours.
Vainly for him the autumn bloom
Is on the flowers.
The inside of the barn is velvet black
Except where a gold thread runs along a crack;
And the inquisitive sun thrusts points of light
Through chink and cranny, piercing the midnight.
The dry husks rattle, and his shuffling feet
Keep time to what he sings—an elusive tune,
Husky and monotonous and sweet,
Scarce audible, so softly does he croon
To keep away the evil eye:
> *Everybody*
> *Who is livin'*
> *Got to die.*

Across the evening fields the setting sun
Richly intones toil done.
The home-bound negroes idle in the lanes,
Gossiping as they go; coarse laughter falls
On the resonant air; from a far field cat-calls
Float over, and a banjo's strains.
Shucking corn in the darkness, Scipio in reply
Sits and sings his mournful husky stave:

> *Wid a silver spade*
> *You kin dig my grave;*
> *Everybody*
> *Who is livin'*
> *Got to die.*

Ezra Pound

Δώρια

Be in me as the eternal moods
    of the bleak wind, and not
As transient things are—
    gaiety of flowers.
Have me in the strong loneliness
    of sunless cliffs
And of gray waters.
      Let the gods speak softly of us
In days hereafter—
    the shadowy flowers of Orcus
Remember thee.

THE RETURN

See, they return; ah, see the tentative
Movements, and the slow feet,
The trouble in the pace and the uncertain
Wavering!

See, they return, one, and by one,
With fear, as half-awakened;
As if the snow should hesitate
And murmur in the wind,
                and half turn back;
These were the "Wing'd-with-Awe,"
                inviolable.

Gods of the wingéd shoe!
With them the silver hounds,
                sniffing the trace of air!

Haie! Haie!
        These were the swift to harry;
These the keen-scented;
These were the souls of blood.

Slow on the leash,
                pallid the leash-men!

N. Y.

My City, my beloved, my white!
    Ah, slender,
Listen! Listen to me, and I will breathe into thee a soul.
Delicately upon the reed, attend me!

Now do I know that I am mad,
For here are a million people surly with traffic;
This is no maid.
Neither could I play upon any reed if I had one.

My City, my beloved,
Thou art a maid with no breasts,
Thou art slender as a silver reed.
Listen to me, attend me!
And I will breathe into thee a soul,
And thou shalt live for ever.

THE COMING OF WAR: ACTÆON

An image of Lethe,
  and the fields
Full of faint light
  but golden,
Gray cliffs,
  and beneath them
A sea
Harsher than granite,
  unstill, never ceasing;

High forms
  with the movement of gods,
Perilous aspect.
  And one said:
"This is Actæon."
  Actæon of golden greaves!

Over fair meadows,
Over the cool face of that field,
Unstill, ever moving,
Hosts of an ancient people,
The silent cortège.

THE GARDEN

En robe de parade.
SAMAIN

Like a skein of loose silk blown against a wall
She walks by the railing of a path in Kensington Gardens,
And she is dying piece-meal
  of a sort of emotional anemia.

And round about there is a rabble
Of the filthy, sturdy, unkillable infants of the very poor.
They shall inherit the earth.

In her is the end of breeding.
Her boredom is exquisite and excessive.

She would like someone to speak to her,
And is almost afraid that I
            will commit that indiscretion.

ORTUS

How have I labored?
How have I not labored
To bring her soul to birth,
To give these elements a name and a centre!
She is beautiful as the sunlight, and as fluid.
She has no name, and no place.
How have I labored to bring her soul into separation;
To give her a name and her being!

Surely you are bound and entwined,
You are mingled with the elements unborn;
I have loved a stream and a shadow.

I beseech you enter your life.
I beseech you learn to say "I"
When I question you:
For you are no part, but a whole;
No portion, but a being.

THE GARRET

Come let us pity those who are better off than we are.
Come, my friend, and remember
            that the rich have butlers and no friends,
And we have friends and no butlers.
Come let us pity the married and the unmarried.

Dawn enters with little feet
            like a gilded Pavlova,
And I am near my desire.
Nor has life in it aught better
Than this hour of clear coolness,
            the hour of waking together.

DANCE FIGURE

For the Marriage in Cana of Galilee

Dark-eyed,
O woman of my dreams,
Ivory-sandaled,
There is none like thee among the dancers,
None with swift feet.

I have not found thee in the tents,
In the broken darkness.
I have not found thee at the well-head
Among the women with pitchers.

Thine arms are as a young sapling under the bark;
Thy face as a river with lights.

White as an almond are thy shoulders;
As new almonds stripped from the husk.

They guard thee not with eunuchs;
Not with bars of copper.
Gilt turquoise and silver are in the place of thy rest.
A brown robe, with threads of gold woven in patterns,
          hast thou gathered about thee,
O Nathat-Ikanaie, "Tree-at-the-river."

As a rillet among the sedge are thy hands upon me;
Thy fingers a frosted stream.

Thy maidens are white like pebbles;
Their music about thee—

There is none like thee among the dancers;
None with swift feet.

FROM *NEAR PÉRIGORD*

Ed eran due in uno, ed uno in due.
Inferno, XXVIII, 125

I loved a woman. The stars fell from heaven.
And always our two natures were in strife.
Bewildering spring, and by the Auvezère
Poppies and day's eyes in the green émail
Rose over us; and we knew all that stream,
And our two horses had traced out the valleys;
Knew the low flooded lands squared out with poplars,
In the young days when the deep sky befriended.

And great wings beat above us in the twilight,
And the great wheels in heaven
Bore us together . . . surging . . . and apart . . .
Believing we should meet with lips and hands.

High, high and sure . . . and then the counterthrust:
"Why do you love me? Will you always love me?
But I am like the grass, I can not love you."
Or, "Love, and I love and love you,
And hate your mind, not *you*, your soul, your hands."

So to this last estrangement, Tairiran!

There shut up in his castle, Tairiran's,
She who had nor ears nor tongue save in her hands,
Gone—ah, gone—untouched, unreachable!
She who could never live save through one person,
She who could never speak save to one person,
And all the rest of her a shifting change,
A broken bundle of mirrors . . .!

THE STUDY IN ÆSTHETICS

The very small children in patched clothing,
Being smitten with an unusual wisdom,
Stopped in their play as she passed them
And cried up from their cobbles:
　　　　Guarda! Ahi, guarda! ch'e be'a!

But three years after this
I heard the young Dante, whose last name I do not know—
For there are, in Sirmoine, twenty-eight young Dantes and
    thirty-four Catulli;
And there had been a great catch of sardines,
And his elders
Were packing them in the great wooden boxes
For the market in Brescia, and he
Leapt about, snatching at the bright fish
And getting in both of their ways;
And in vain they commanded him to *sta fermo!*
And when they would not let him arrange
The fish in the boxes
He stroked those which were already arranged,
Murmuring for his own satisfaction
This identical phrase:
        Ch'e be'a.

And at this I was mildly abashed.

FURTHER INSTRUCTIONS

Come, my songs, let us express our baser passions.
Let us express our envy for the man with a steady job
    and no worry about the future.

You are very idle, my songs;
I fear you will come to a bad end.

You stand about the streets.
You loiter at the corners and bus-stops,
You do next to nothing at all.
You do not even express our inner nobilities;
You will come to a very bad end.

And I? I have gone half cracked.
I have talked to you so much
    that I almost see you about me,
Insolent little beasts! Shameless! Devoid of clothing!

But you, newest song of the lot,
You are not old enough to have done much mischief.
I will get you a green coat out of China
With dragons worked upon it.
I will get you the scarlet silk trousers
From the statue of the infant Christ at Santa Maria Novella;
Lest they say we are lacking in taste,
Or that there is no caste in this family.

VILLANELLE: THE PSYCHOLOGICAL HOUR

I

I had over-prepared the event—
      that much was ominous.
With middle-aging care
      I had laid out just the right books,
I had almost turned down the pages.

      Beauty is so rare a thing . . .
      So few drink of my fountain.

So much barren regret!
So many hours wasted!
And now I watch from the window
      the rain, the wandering busses.

"Their little cosmos is shaken"—
      the air is alive with that fact.
In their parts of the city
      they are played on by diverse forces;
How do I know?
      Oh, I know well enough—
For them there is something afoot.

      As for me,
I had over-prepared the event—

      Beauty is so rare a thing . . .
      So few drink of my fountain.

Two friends: a breath of the forest . . .
Friends? Are people less friends
   because one has just, at last, found them?
Twice they promised to come.

  "Between the night and morning?"

Beauty would drink of my mind.
Youth would awhile forget
   my youth is gone from me.

II

("Speak up! You have danced so stiffly?
Someone admired your works,
And said so frankly.

"Did you talk like a fool,
The first night?
The second evening?"

"*But* they promised again:
   'Tomorrow at tea-time.'")

III

Now the third day is here—
   no word from either;
No word from her nor him,
Only another man's note:
   "Dear Pound, I am leaving England."

BALLAD OF THE GOODLY FERE

Simon Zelotes speaketh it somewhile after the Crucifixion.

Ha' we lost the goodliest fere o' all
For the priests and the gallows tree?
Aye lover he was of brawny men,
O' ships and the open sea.

When they came wi' a host to take Our Man
His smile was good to see,

"First let these go!" quo' our Goodly Fere,
"Or I'll see ye damned," says he.

Aye he sent us out through the crossed high spears
And the scorn of his laugh rang free,
"Why took ye not me when I walked about
Alone in the town?" says he.

Oh we drunk his "Hale" in the good red wine
When we last made company.
No capon priest was the Goodly Fere,
But a man o' men was he.

I ha' seen him drive a hundred men
Wi' a bundle o' cords swung free,
That they took the high and holy house
For their pawn and treasury.

They'll no' get him a' in a book, I think,
Though they write it cunningly;
No mouse of the scrolls was the Goodly Fere
But aye loved the open sea.

If they think they ha' snared our Goodly Fere
They are fools to the last degree.
"I'll go to the feast," quo' our Goodly Fere,
"Though I go to the gallows tree."

"Ye ha' seen me heal the lame and blind,
And wake the dead," says he.
"Ye shall see one thing to master all:
'Tis how a brave man dies on the tree."

A son of God was the Goodly Fere
That bade us his brothers be.
I ha' seen him cow a thousand men.
I have seen him upon the tree.

He cried no cry when they drave the nails
And the blood gushed hot and free.
The hounds of the crimson sky gave tongue,
But never a cry cried he.

I ha' seen him cow a thousand men
On the hills o' Galilee.
They whined as he walked out calm between,
Wi' his eyes like the gray o' the sea.

Like the sea that brooks no voyaging,
With the winds unleashed and free,
Like the sea that he cowed at Genseret
Wi' twey words spoke suddently.

A master of men was the Goodly Fere,
A mate of the wind and sea.
If they think they ha' slain our Goodly Fere
They are fools eternally.

I ha' seen him eat o' the honey-comb
Sin' they nailed him to the tree.

LA FRAISNE

Scene: The Ash Wood of Malvern

For I was a gaunt grave councillor,
Being in all things wise, and very old;
But I have put aside this folly and the cold
That old age weareth for a cloak.

I was quite strong—at least they said so—
The young men at the sword-play;
But I have put aside this folly, being gay
In another fashion that more suiteth me.

I have curled mid the boles of the ash wood,
I have hidden my face where the oak
Spread his leaves over me, and the yoke
Of the old ways of men have I cast aside.

By the still pool of Mar-nan-otha
Have I found me a bride
That was a dog-wood tree some syne.
She hath called me from mine old ways;
She hath hushed my rancor of council,

Bidding me praise
Naught but the wind that flutters in the leaves.

She hath drawn me from mine old ways,
Till men say that I am mad;
But I have seen the sorrow of men, and am glad,
For I know that the wailing and bitterness are a folly.
And I? I have put aside all folly and all grief.
I wrapped my tears in an ellum leaf
And left them under a stone;
And now men call me mad because I have thrown
All folly from me, putting it aside
To leave the old barren ways of men,
Because my bride
Is a pool of the wood; and
Though all men say that I am mad
It is only that I am glad—
Very glad, for my bride hath toward me a great love
That is sweeter than the love of women
That plague and burn and drive one away.

Aie-e! 'Tis true that I am gay,
    Quite gay, for I have her alone here
    And no man troubleth us.

Once when I was among the young men . . .
And they said I was quite strong, among the young men . . .
Once there was a woman . . .
. . . but I forget . . . she was . . .
. . . I hope she will not come again.

. . . I do not remember . . .

I think she hurt me once, but . . .
That was very long ago.

I do not like to remember things any more.

I like one little band of winds that blow
In the ash trees here:
For we are quite alone,
Here 'mid the ash trees.

THE RIVER–MERCHANT'S WIFE: A LETTER
From the Chinese of Li Po

While my hair was still cut straight across my forehead
I played about the front gate, pulling flowers.
You came by on bamboo stilts, playing horse;
You walked about my seat, playing with blue plums.
And we went on living in the village of Chokan:
Two small people, without dislike or suspicion.

At fourteen I married My Lord you.
I never laughed, being bashful.
Lowering my head, I looked at the wall.
Called to, a thousand times, I never looked back.

At fifteen I stopped scowling;
I desired my dust to be mingled with yours
Forever and forever and forever.
Why should I climb the look-out?

At sixteen you departed,
You went into far Ku-to-Yen, by the river of swirling eddies,
And you have been gone five months.
The monkeys make sorrowful noise overhead.
You dragged your feet when you went out.
By the gate now the moss is grown, the different mosses,
Too deep to clear them away!
The leaves fall early this autumn, in wind.
The paired butterflies are already yellow with August
Over the grass in the west garden—
They hurt me. I grow older.
If you are coming down through the narrows of the river Kiang,
Please let me know beforehand,
And I will come out to meet you,
    As far as Cho-fu-Sa.

EXILE'S LETTER

From the Chinese of Li Po; written by him while in exile about 760 A. D., to the Hereditary War Councillor of Sho, "recollecting former companionship."

To So-Kin of Rakuho, ancient friend, Chancellor of Gen.
Now I remember that you built me a special tavern,
By the south side of the bridge at Ten-Shin.
With yellow gold and white jewels we paid for songs and laughter,
And we were drunk for month on month, forgetting the kings
    and princes.
Intelligent men came drifting in, from the sea and from the west
    border,
And with them, and with you especially,
There was nothing at cross-purpose;
And they made nothing of sea-crossing or of mountain-crossing,
If only they could be of that fellowship.
And we all spoke out our hearts and minds, and without regret.

And then I was sent off to South Wei, smothered in laurel groves,
And you to the north of Raku-hoku,
Till we had nothing but thoughts and memories in common.
And then, when separation had come to its worst,
We met, and travelled together into Sen-Go
Through all the thirty-six folds of the turning and twisting
    waters;
Into a valley of a thousand bright flowers . . .
That was the first valley,
And into ten thousand valleys, full of voices and pine-winds.
And with silver harness and reins of gold,
Out came the East-of-Kan foreman and his company;
And there came also the "True-man" of Shi-yo to meet me,
Playing on a jeweled mouth-organ.
In the storied houses of San-Ko they gave us more Sennin music;
Many instruments, like the sound of young phœnix broods.
And the foreman of Kan-Chu, drunk, danced
Because his long sleeves wouldn't keep still
With that music playing.

And I, wrapped in brocade, went to sleep with my head on his
    lap,
And my spirit so high it was all over the heavens.

And before the end of the day we were scattered like stars or rain.
I had to be off to So, far away over the waters,
You back to your river-bridge.

And your father, who was brave as a leopard,
Was governor in Hei Shu and put down the barbarian rabble.
And one May he had you send for me, despite the long distance;
And what with broken wheels and so on, I won't say it wasn't
    hard going . . .
Over roads twisted like sheep's guts.
And I was still going, late in the year, in the cutting wind from
    the north,
And thinking how little you cared for the cost . . . and you
    caring enough to pay it.
Then what a reception!
Red jade cups, food well set on a blue jeweled table;
And I was drunk, and had no thought of returning;
And you would walk out with me to the western corner of the
    castle,
To the dynastic temple, with water about it clear as blue jade,
With boats floating, and the sound of mouth-organs and drums,
With ripples like dragon-scales going grass-green on the water;
Pleasure lasting, with courtezans going and coming without
    hindrance,
With the willow-flakes falling like snow,
And the vermilioned girls getting drunk about sunset,
And the water a hundred feet deep reflecting green eye-brows—
Eyebrows painted green are a fine sight in young moonlight,
Gracefully painted—and the girls singing back at each other,
Dancing in transparent brocade,
And the wind lifting the song, and interrupting it,
Tossing it up under the clouds.

               And all this comes to an end,
               And is not again to be met with.

I went up to the court for examination,
Tried Layu's luck, offered the Choyu song,
And got no promotion,
And went back to the East Mountains white-headed.

And once again, later, we met at the south bridge-head.
And then the crowd broke up—you went north to San palace.
And if you ask how I regret that parting:
It is like the flowers falling at spring's end, confused, whirled
    in a tangle.
What is the use of talking! And there is no end of talking—
There is no end of things in the heart.
I call in the boy,
Have him sit on his knees here to seal this,
And I send it a thousand miles, thinking.

> (*Translated by E. P. from the notes of the late Ernest Fenol-
> losa and the deciphering of the Professors Mori and Araga.*)

FROM THE *MAUBERLEY POEMS*
First Series—No. IV

These fought in any case,
And some believing—
                    pro domo, in any case . . .

Some quick to arm,
Some for adventure,
Some from fear of weakness,
Some from fear of censure,
Some for love of slaughter, in imagination,
Learning later . . .
Some in fear, learning love of slaughter.

Died some, pro patria,
                    non "dulce" non "et decor" . . .
Walked eye-deep in hell
Believing in old men's lies, then unbelieving
Came home, home to a lie,
Home to many deceits,

Home to old lies and new infamy;
Usury age-old and age-thick
And liars in public places.

Daring as never before, wastage as never before.
Young blood and high blood,
Fair cheeks, and fine bodies;

Fortitude as never before,

Frankness as never before,
Disillusions as never told in the old days,
Hysterias, trench confessions,
Laughter out of dead bellies.

. . . .

There died a myriad,
And of the best, among them,
For an old bitch gone in the teeth,
For a botched civilization.

Charm, smiling at the good mouth,
Quick eyes gone under earth's lid,

For two gross of broken statues,
For a few thousand battered books.

MAUBERLEY, 1920

*"Qu'est ce qu'ils savent de l'amour, et
qu'est-ce qu'ils peuvent comprendre?
S'ils ne comprennent pas la poésie, s'ils ne sentent pas la
musique, qu'est-ce qu'ils peuvent comprendre de cette passion en comparaison avec laquelle la rose est grossière et
le parfum des violettes un tonnerre?"*   CAID ALI

For three years, diabolus in the scale,
He drank ambrosia,
All passes, ANANGKE prevails,
Came end, at last, to that Arcadia.

He had moved amid her phantasmagoria,
Amid her galaxies,
NUKTIS 'AGALMA

. . . .

Drifted . . . drifted precipitate,
Asking time to be rid of . . .
Of his bewilderment; to designate
His new-found orchid. . . .

To be certain . . . certain . . .
(Amid aërial flowers) . . . time for arrangements—
Drifted on
To the final estrangement;

Unable in the supervening blankness
To sift TO AGATHON from the chaff
Until he found his sieve . . .
Ultimately, his seismograph:
—Given that is his "fundamental passion,"
This urge to convey the relation
Of eye-lid and cheek-bone
By verbal manifestations;

To present the series
Of curious heads in medallion—

He had passed, inconscient, full gaze,
The wide-banded irides
And botticellian sprays implied
In their diastasis;

Which anæthesis, noted a year late,
And weighed, revealed his great effect,
(Orchid), mandate
Of Eros, a retrospect.

. . . .

Mouths biting empty air,
The still stone dogs,
Caught in metamorphosis, were
Left him as epilogues.

CANTO XIII

Kung walked
        by the dynastic temple
And into the cedar grove,
        and then out by the lower river,
And with him Khieu Tchi
        and Tian the low speaking.
And "We are unknown," said Kung,
"You will take up charioteering?
        Then you will become known,
Or perhaps I should take up charioteering, or archery?
Or the practice of public speaking?"
And Tseu-lou said, "I would put the defences in order."
And Khieu said, "If I were lord of a province
I would put it in better order than this is."
And Tchi said, "I would prefer a small mountain temple,
With order in the observances,
        with a suitable performance of the ritual."
And Tian said, with his hand on the strings of his lute,
The low sounds continuing
        after his hand left the strings—
And the sound went up like smoke, under the leaves,
And he looked after the sound:
        "The old swimming hole,
And the boys flopping off the planks,
Or sitting in the underbrush playing mandolins."
        And Kung smiled upon all of them equally.
And Thseng-sie desired to know
        which had answered correctly.
And Kung said, "They have all answered correctly,
That is to say, each in his nature."
And Kung raised his cane against Yuan Jang,
        Yuan Jang being his elder,
For Yuan Jang sat by the roadside pretending to
        be receiving wisdom.
And Kung said,
        "You old fool, come out of it,
Get up and do something useful."

And Kung said,
"Respect a child's faculties
From the moment it inhales the clear air,
But a man of fifty who knows nothing
     Is worthy of no respect."
And, "When the prince has gathered about him
All the savants and artists, his riches will be fully employed."
And Kung said, and wrote on the bo leaves:
     "If a man have not order within him
He can not spread order about him;
And if a man have not order within him
His family will not act with due order;
     And if the prince have not order within him
He can not put order in his dominions.
And Kung gave the words "order"
And "brotherly deference"
And said nothing of the "life after death."
And he said,
     "Anyone can run to excesses,
It is easy to shoot past the mark,
It is hard to stand firm in the middle."

And they said: "If a man commit murder
     Should his father protect him, and hide him?"
And Kung said:
     "He should hide him."

And Kung gave his daughter to Kong-Tchang
     Although Kong-Tchang was in prison.
And he gave his niece to Nan-Young
     Although Nan-Young was out of office.

And Kung said, "Wang ruled with moderation,
     In his day the State was well kept,
And even I can remember
A day when the historians left blanks in their writings,
I mean for things they didn't know,
But that time seems to be passing.

And Kung said, "Without character you will
　　　　Be unable to play on that instrument
Or to execute the music fit for the Odes.
The blossoms of the apricot
　　　　Blow from the east to the west,
And I have tried to keep them from falling."

John Crowe Ransom

BELLS FOR JOHN WHITESIDES' DAUGHTER

There was such speed in her little body,
And such lightness in her footfall,
It is no wonder that her brown study
Astonishes us all.

Her wars were bruited in our high window,
We looked among orchard trees and beyond,
Where she took arms against her shadow,
Or harried unto the pond

The lazy geese, like a snow cloud
Dripping their snow on the green grass,
Tricking and stopping, sleepy and proud,
Who cried in goose, Alas,

For the tireless heart within the little
Lady with rod that made them rise
From their noon apple dreams, and scuttle
Goose-fashion under the skies!

But now go the bells, and we are ready;
In one house we are sternly stopped
To say we are vexed at her brown study,
Lying so primly propped.

PARTING, WITHOUT SEQUEL

She has finished and sealed the letter
At last, which he so richly has deserved,
With characters venomous and hatefully curved,
And nothing could be better.

But even as she gave it,
Saying to the blue-capped functioner of doom,
"Into his hands," she hoped the leering groom
Might somewhere lose and leave it.

Then all the blood
Forsook the face. She was too pale for tears,
Observing the ruin of her younger years.
She went and stood

Under her father's vaunting oak
Who kept his peace in wind and sun, and glistened
Stoical in the rain; to whom she listened
If he spoke.

And now the agitation of the rain
Rasped his sere leaves, and he talked low and gentle,
Reproaching the wan daughter by the lintel;
Ceasing, and beginning again.

Away went the messenger's bicycle,
His serpent's track went up the hill forever,
And all the time she stood there hot as fever
And cold as any icicle.

BLUE GIRLS

Twirling your blue skirts, travelling the sward
Under the towers of your seminary,
Go listen to your teachers old and contrary
Without believing a word.

Tie the white fillets then about your lustrous hair
And think no more of what will come to pass

Than bluebirds that go walking on the grass
And chattering on the air.

Practice your beauty, blue girls, before it fail;
And I will cry with my loud lips and publish
Beauty which all our power shall never establish,
It is so frail.

For I could tell you a story which is true:
I know a lady with a terrible tongue,
Blear eyes fallen from blue,
All her perfections tarnished—and yet it is not long
Since she was lovelier than any of you.

John Reed

SANGAR

To Lincoln Steffens

Somewhere I read a strange old rusty tale
Smelling of war; most curiously named
The Mad Recreant Knight of the West.
Once, you have read, the round world brimmed with hate,
Stirred and revolted, flashed unceasingly
Facets of cruel splendor. And the strong
Harried the weak . . .

                Long past, long past, praise God,
In these fair, peaceful, happy days.

The Tale:

    Eastward the Huns break border,
        Surf on a rotten dyke;
    They have murdered the Eastern Warder
        (His head on a pike).
    "Arm thee, arm thee, my father!
        Swift rides the Goddes-bane,
    And the high nobles gather
        On the plain!"

"O blind world-wrath!" cried Sangar,
　"Greatly I killed in youth;
I dreamed men had done with anger
　Through Goddes truth!"
Smiled the boy then in faint scorn,
　Hard with the battle-thrill;
"Arm thee, loud calls the war-horn
　And shrill!"

He has bowed to the voice stentorian,
　Sick with thought of the grave;
He has called for his battered morion
　And his scarred glaive.
On the boy's helm a glove
　Of the Duke's daughter—
In his eyes splendor of love
　And slaughter.

Hideous the Hun advances
　Like a sea-tide on sand;
Unyielding, the haughty lances
　Make dauntless stand.
And ever amid the clangor,
　Butchering Hun and Hun,
With sorrowful face rides Sangar
　And his son. . . .

Broken is the wild invader
　(Sullied, the whole world's fountains);
They have penned the murderous raider
　With his back to the mountains.
Yet though what had been mead
　Is now a bloody lake,
Still drink swords where men bleed,
　Nor slake.

Now leaps one into the press,
　The hell 'twixt front and front—
Sangar, bloody and torn of dress
　(He has borne the brunt).

"Hold!" cries, "Peace! God's peace!
　　Heed ye what Christus says—"
And the wild battle gave surcease
　　In amaze.

"When will ye cast out hate?
　　Brothers—my mad, mad brothers—
Mercy, ere it be too late,
　　These are sons of your mothers.
For sake of Him who died on Tree,
　　Who of all creatures, loved the least—"
"Blasphemer! God of Battles, He!"
　　Cried a priest.

"Peace!" and with his two hands
　　Has broken in twain his glaive.
Weaponless, smiling he stands—
　　(Coward or brave?)
"Traitor!" howls one rank, "Think ye
　　The Hun be our brother?"
And "Fear we to die, craven, think ye?"
　　The other.

Then sprang his son to his side—
　　His lips with slaver were wet,
For he had felt how men died
　　And was lustful yet;
(On his bent helm a glove
　　Of the Duke's daughter,
In his eyes splendor of love
　　And slaughter)—

Shouting, "Father no more of mine—
　　Shameful old man—abhorr'd
First traitor of all our line!"
　　Up the two-handed sword.
He smote—fell Sangar—and then
　　Screaming, red, the boy ran
Straight at the foe, and again
　　Hell began. . . .

Oh, there was joy in Heaven when Sangar came.
Sweet Mary wept, and bathed and bound his wounds,
And God the Father healed him of despair,
And Jesus gripped his hand, and laughed and laughed. . . .

PROUD NEW YORK

By proud New York and its man-piled Matterhorns,
The hard blue sky overhead and the west wind blowing,
Steam-plumes waving from sun-glittering pinnacles,
And deep streets shaking to the million-river:

> Manhattan, zoned with ships, the cruel
> Youngest of all the world's great towns,
> Thy bodice bright with many a jewel,
> Imperially crowned with crowns . . .

> Who that has known thee but shall burn
> In exile till he come again
> To do thy bitter will, O stern
> Moon of the tides of men!

Lizette Woodworth Reese

THE COMMON LOT

I am so little that the gods go by,
And leave me to my house, my garden plot,
My clump of jonquils in a windy spot.
I tend the herbs; I look up at the sky.
As great a thing am I as e'er drew breath—
The grey hushed steps of them that bore from here
My lovely ones still sound within mine ear—
Yea, great enough to have been hurt by Death!
Nothing I reckon of the pomps of men;
I am too little for a sword, a crown,
Or any purples that the kings begirt;
Out in the spring my jonquils blow again,

Yellow and windy as the lights of town—
But I would die, I am so hurt, so hurt!

WOMEN

Some women herd such little things—a box
Oval and glossy in its gilt and red;
Or square of satin, or a high dark bed.
But when love comes, they drive to it all their flocks,
Yield up their crooks, take little, gain for fold
And pasture each a small forgotten grave.
When they are gone, then lesser women crave
And squander their sad hoards, their shepherd's gold.
Some gather life like fagots in a wood,
And crouch its blaze, without a thought at all
Past warming their pinched selves, to the last spark.
And women, as a whole, are swift and good;
In humor scarce, their measure being small,
They plunge; they leap, yet somehow miss the dark.

SCARCITY

Scarcity saves the world,
    And by that is it fed:
Then give it hunger, God,
    Not bread.

Scarce things are comely things;
    In little there is power;
November measures best
    Each vanishing flower.

If you dig a well,
    If you sing a song,
By what you do without,
    You make it strong.

And life as well as art,
  By scarceness grows,
Not surfeit. Theirs must be
  The hunger of the rose.

A PURITAN LADY

Wild Carthage held her, Rome,
  Sidon. She stared to tears
Tall golden Helen, wearying
  Behind the Trojan spears.

Towered Antwerp knew her well;
  She wore her quiet gown
In some hushed house in Oxford grass,
  Or lane in Salem town.

Humble and high in one,
  Cool, certain, different,
She lasts; scarce saint, yet half a child,
  As hard, as innocent.

What grave long afternoons,
  What caged airs round her blown,
Stripped her of humor, left her bare
  As cloud, or wayside stone?

Made her as clear a thing,
  In this slack world as plain,
As a white flower on a grave,
  Or sleet sharp at a pane?

THRIFT

A star proves never traitor, and a weed—
Even that vetch obscurely purple there—
Can hoard such loyalties against your need,
You may go rich, though all the world go bare.
A blackbird's whistle over the young grass,
Is but another wealth; so are these, too—

The old rememberings that start and pass
At its short music, when the year is new.
If stars you love, and all their like, then know
Your love will be a thrift to set you clear
Of beggary, and whining at a door.
You change, life changes; it is ever so;
But these last on from whirling year to year:
Learn God of them, and add Him to your store.

WRITTEN IN A SONG–BOOK

A song is such a curious thing,
To last beyond a day in spring;
It comes from low, it comes from high;
Is all of earth, and all of sky.

From Laughter set at tavern door,
Round, rosy, with his cranks of yore;
From Grief, struck down upon the clod,
Crying his wild heart out to God.

Like hawthorn whitening in the grass,
To haunt the folk that by it pass;
Like sheep-bells tinkling small and clear
In star-lit fields at end of year;
Like dust-pink silks, like Tyrian gold,
A little verse remembered, old.

And while you polish line by line—
For though so frail, it must be fine—
Ere it turns lovely, as it must,
A hundred towns tumble to dust!

Charles Reznikoff

A GROUP OF VERSE

I

The stars are hidden,
The lights are out;
The tall black houses
Are ranked about.

I beat my fists
On the stout doors,
No answering steps
Come down the floors.

I have walked until
I am faint and numb;
From one dark street
To another I come.

The comforting
Winds are still.

This is a chaos
Through which I stumble,
Till I reach the void
And down I tumble.

The star will then
Be out forever;
The fist unclenched,
The feet walk never,

And all I say
Blown by the wind
Away.

II

I met in a merchant's place
Diana:
Lithe body and flowerlike face.

Through the woods I had looked for her
And beside the waves.

III

How shall we mourn you who are killed and wasted,
Sure that you would not die with your work unended.
As if the iron scythe in the grass stops for a flower?

IV

From where she lay she could see the snow crossing the darkness
    slowly,
Thick about the arc-lights like moths in summer.
She could just move her head. She had been lying so for months.

Her son was growing tall and broad-shouldered, his face becom-
    ing like that of her father,
Dead now for years.

She lay under the bed-clothes as if she too were covered with
    snow,
Calm, facing the blackness of night,
Through which the snow fell in the crowded movement of stars.

.   .   .   .

Dead, nailed in a box, her son was being sent to her,
Through fields and cities cold and white with snow.

V

Hour after hour in a rocking-chair on the porch,
Hearing the wind in the shade trees.

At times a storm comes up and the dust is blown in long curves
    along the street,
Over the carts driven slowly, drivers and horses nodding.

Years are thrown away as if I were immortal,
The nights spent in talking
Shining words, sometimes, like fireflies in the darkness—
Lighting and going out, and after all no light.

VI—A SUNNY DAY

The curved leaves of the little tree are shining;
The bushes across the street are purple with flowers.

A man with a red beard talks to a woman with yellow hair;
She laughs like the clash of brass cymbals.

Two negresses are coming down the street;
They munch lettuce
And pull the leaves slowly out of a bag.

The pigeons wheel in the bright air;
Now white, now the grey backs showing,
They settle down upon a roof;
The children shout, the owner swings his bamboo.

Ernest Rhys

DAGONET'S CANZONET

A queen lived in the South;
And music was her mouth,
And sunshine was her hair.
By day, and all the night
The drowsy embers there
Remembered still the light.
    My soul, was she not fair!

But for her eyes—they made
An iron man afraid;
Like sky-blue pools they were,
Watching the sky that knew
Itself transmuted there
Light blue, or deeper blue.
    My soul, was she not fair!

The lifting of her hands
Made laughter in the lands
Where the sun is, in the South:
But my soul learnt sorrow there
In the secrets of her mouth,
Her eyes, her hands, her hair.
    O soul, was she not fair!

A SONG OF HAPPINESS

Ah, Happiness:
Who called you "Earandel"?
(Winter-star, I think, that is);
And who can tell the lovely curve
By which you seem to come, then swerve
Before you reach the middle-earth?
And who is there can hold your wing,
Or bind you in your mirth,
Or win you with a least caress,
Or tear, or kiss, or anything—
Insensate Happiness?

Once I thought to have you
Fast there in a child:
All her heart she gave you,
Yet you would not stay.
Cruel, and careless,
Not half reconciled,
Pain you cannot bear.
When her yellow hair
Lay matted, every tress;
When those looks of hers
Were no longer hers,
You went—in a day
She wept you all away.

Once I thought to give
You, plighted holily—
No more fugitive,
Returning like the sea.
But they that share so well
Heaven must portion Hell
In their copartnery:
Care, ill fate, ill health,
Came we know not how
And broke our commonwealth.
Neither has you now.

Some wait you on the road,
Some in an open door
Look for the face you showed
Once there—no more.
You never wear the dress
You danced in yesterday;
Yet, seeming gone, you stay,
And come at no man's call.
Yet, laid for burial,
You lift up from the dead
Your laughing spangled head.

Yes, once I did pursue
You, unpursuable;
Loved, longed for, hoped for you,
Blue-eyed and morning-brow'd.
Ah, lovely Happiness!
Now that I know you well,
I dare not speak aloud
Your fond name in a crowd;
Nor conjure you by night,
Nor pray at morning light,
Nor count at all on you.

But, at a stroke, a breath—
After the fear of death,
Or bent beneath a load;
Yes, ragged in the dress
And houseless on the road,
I might surprise you there.
Yes, who of us shall say
When you will come, or where?
Ask children at their play,
The leaves upon the tree,
The ships upon the sea,
Or old men who survived,
And lived, and loved, and wived—
As sorrow to confess
Your sweet improvidence,

And prodigal expense
And cold economy,
Ah, lovely Happiness!

Lola Ridge

THE SONG

That day, in the slipping of torsos and straining flanks
On the bloodied ooze of fields plowed by the iron,
And the smoke, bluish near earth and bronze in the sunshine,
Floating like cotton-down;
And the harsh and terrible screaming,
And that strange vibration at the roots of us . . .
Desire, fierce like a song . . .
And we heard—do you remember?—
All the Red Cross bands on Fifth Avenue,
And bugles in little home towns,
And children's harmonicas bleating
AMERICA!

And after . . .
(Do you remember?)
The drollery of the wind on our faces,
And horizons reeling,
And the terror of the plain,
Heaving like a gaunt pelvis to the sun
Under us—threshing and twanging
Torn-up roots of the song?

IRON WINE

The ore in the crucible is pungent, smelling like acrid wine.
It is dusky red like the ebb of poppies,
And purple like the blood of elderberries.
Surely it is a strong wine—juice distilled of the fierce iron.
I am drunk of its fumes;
I feel its fiery flux

Diffusing, permeating,
Working some strange alchemy.
So that I turn aside from the goodly board,
So that I look askance upon the common cup,
And from the mouths of crucibles
Suck forth the acrid sap.

ALTITUDE

I wonder
How it would be here with you,
Where the wind,
That has shaken off its dust in low valleys,
Touches one cleanly
As with a new-washed hand;
And pain
Is as the remote hunger of droning things;
And anger
But a little silence
Sinking into the great silence.

TO E. A. R.

Centuries shall not deflect
Nor many suns
Absorb your stream,
Flowing immune and cold
Between the banks of snow;
Nor any wind
Carry the dust of cities
To your high waters,
That arise out of the peaks
And return again into the mountain,
And never descend.

DÉBRIS

I love those spirits
That men stand off and point at,
Or shudder and hood up their souls—
Those ruined ones,
Where Liberty has lodged an hour
And passed like flame,
Bursting asunder the too small house.

THE EDGE

I thought to die that night in the solitude
    where they would never find me . . .
But there was time . . .
And I lay quietly on the drawn knees of the mountain
    staring into the abyss.

I do not know how long . . .
I could not count the hours, they ran so fast—
Like little bare-foot urchins—shaking my hands away.
But I remember
Somewhere water trickled like a thin severed vein . . .
And a wind came out of the grass,
Touching me gently, tentatively, like a paw.

As the night grew
The gray cloud that had covered the sky-line sackcloth
Fell in ashen folds about the hills,
Like hooded virgins pulling their cloaks about them . . .
There must have been a spent moon,
For the Tall One's veil held a shimmer of silver. . . .

That too I remember,
And the tenderly rocking mountain.
Silence,
And beating stars. . . .

Dawn
Lay like a waxen hand upon the world,

And folded hills
Broke into a sudden wonder of peaks, stemming clear and cold,
Till the Tall One bloomed like a lily,
Flecked with sun
Fine as a golden pollen.
It seemed a wind might blow it from the snow.

I smelled the raw sweet essences of things,
And heard spiders in the leaves,
And ticking of little feet
As tiny creatures came out of their doors
To see God pouring light into his star.

It seemed life held
No future and no past but this.

And I too got up stiffly from the earth
And held my heart up like a cup.

Elizabeth Madox Roberts

THE PILASTER

The church has pieces jutting out
   Where corners of the walls begin.
I have one for my little house,
   And I can feel myself go in.

I feel myself go in the bricks,
   And I can see myself in there.
I'm always waiting all alone,
   I'm sitting on a little chair.

And I am sitting very still,
   And I am waiting on and on
For something that is never there,
   For something that is gone.

WATER NOISES

When I am playing by myself,
  And all the boys are lost around,
Then I can hear the water go—
  It makes a little talking sound.

Along the rocks below the tree,
  I see it ripple up and wink;
And I can hear it saying on,
  "And do you think? and do you think?"

A bug shoots by that snaps and ticks,
  And a bird flies up beside the tree
To go into the sky to sing.
  I hear it say, "Killdee, killdee!"

Or else a yellow cow comes down
  To splash a while and have a drink.
But when she goes I still can hear
  The water say, "And do you think?"

STRANGE TREE

Away beyond the Jarboe house
  I saw a different kind of tree.
Its trunk was old and large and bent,
  And I could feel it look at me.

The road was going on and on
  Beyond, to reach some other place.
I saw a tree that looked at me,
  And yet it did not have a face.

It looked at me with all its limbs;
  It looked at me with all its bark.
The yellow wrinkles on its sides
  Were bent and dark.

And then I ran to get away,
  But when I stopped and turned to see,
The tree was bending to the side
  And leaning out to look at me.

MY HEART

My heart is beating up and down,
  Is walking like some heavy feet.
My heart is going every day,
  And I can hear it jump and beat.

At night before I go to sleep
  I feel it beating in my head;
I hear it jumping in my neck
  And in the pillow on my bed.

And then I make some little words
  To go along and say with it—
    The men are sailing home from Troy,
    And all the lamps are lit.

    The men are sailing home from Troy,
    And all the lamps are lit.

A BALLET SONG OF MARY

Her smock was of the holland fine,
  Skinkled with colors three;
Her shawl was of the velvet blue,
  The Queen of Galilee.

Her hair was yellow like the wex,
  Like the silken floss fine-spun;
The girdle for her golden cloak
  Was all in gold bedone.

She sat her down in her own bower place
  And dressed herself her hair.
Her gold kemb in her braid she laid,
  And a sound fell on the door.

He came within her own bower room
  "Hail, Mary, hail!" says he,
"A goodly grace is on your head,
  For the Lord is now with thee."

She folded down her little white hands
  When Gabriel spoke again.
She set her shawl, the corners right,
  For ceremony then.

"And the God will overshadow thee
  And bring a holy sweven.
Fear not, fear not," then Gabriel said,
  "It's the God of the good high heaven.

"And what must be born it will heal the sick;
  It will make a goodly lear;
It will fettle men for christentie
  And to keep holy gear."

Then up then rose this little maid
  When Gabriel's word was said,
And out of the bower she ran in haste,
  And out of the hall she is sped.

She is running far to Zachary's house;
  "Is this the way?" says she.
"A little maid in haste," they said,
  "Has gone to the hills of Judee."

And what will be born it will ope their eyes;
  It will hearten men in their stear;
It will fettle men for christentie
  And to have holy gear.

It will scourge with a thong when those make gain
  Where a humble man should be;
It will cast the witches from out of his saule
  And drown them into the sea.

It will give men drink from the horn of the wind,
  And give men meat from the song of a bird;

Their cloak they will get from the sheen of the grass,
  And a roof from a singen word.

And when they come to the Brig o' Dread,
  And they cry, "I fall! I'm afear!"
It will close their eyes and give them sleep
  To heal them outen their lonesome cheer,
When they come to the Brig o' Dread.

Edwin Arlington Robinson

THE MASTER

Lincoln as he appeared to one soon after the Civil War

A flying word from here and there
Had sown the name at which we sneered,
But soon the name was everywhere,
To be reviled and then revered:
A presence to be loved and feared—
We cannot hide it, or deny
That we, the gentlemen who jeered,
May be forgotten by and by.

He came when days were perilous
And hearts of men were sore beguiled,
And having made his note of us,
He pondered and was reconciled.
Was ever master yet so mild
As he, and so untamable?
We doubted, even when he smiled,
Not knowing what he knew so well.

He knew that undeceiving fate
Would shame us whom he served unsought;
He knew that he must wince and wait—
The jest of those for whom he fought;
He knew devoutly what he thought
Of us and of our ridicule;
He knew that we must all be taught
Like little children in a school.

We gave a glamour to the task
That he encountered and saw through;
But little of us did he ask,
And little did we ever do.
And what appears if we review
The season when we railed and chaffed?—
It is the face of one who knew
That we were learning while we laughed.

The face that in our vision feels
Again the venom that we flung,
Transfigured to the world reveals
The vigilance to which we clung.
Shrewd, hallowed, harassed, and among
The mysteries that are untold—
The face we see was never young,
Nor could it wholly have been old.

For he, to whom we had applied
Our shopman's test of age and worth,
Was elemental when he died,
As he was ancient at his birth:
The saddest among kings of earth,
Bowed with a galling crown, this man
Met rancor with a cryptic mirth,
Laconic—and Olympian.

The love, the grandeur, and the fame
Are bounded by the world alone;
The calm, the smouldering, and the flame
Of awful patience were his own:
With him they are forever flown
Past all our fond self-shadowings,
Wherewith we cumber the Unknown
As with inept Icarian wings.

For we were not as other men:
'Twas ours to soar and his to see.
But we are coming down again,
And we shall come down pleasantly;

Nor shall we longer disagree
On what it is to be sublime,
But flourish in our perigee
And have one Titan at a time.

JOHN GORHAM

"Tell me what you're doing over here, John Gorham—
Sighing hard and seeming to be sorry when you're not.
Make me laugh or let me go now, for long faces in the moonlight
Are a sign for me to say again a word that you forgot."

"I'm over here to tell you what the moon already
May have said or maybe shouted ever since a year ago;
I'm over here to tell you what you are, Jane Wayland,
And to make you rather sorry, I should say, for being so."

"Tell me what you're saying to me now, John Gorham,
Or you'll never see as much of me as ribbons any more;
I'll vanish in as many ways as I have toes and fingers,
And you'll not follow far for one where flocks have been before."

"I'm sorry now you never saw the flocks, Jane Wayland;
But you're the one to make of them as many as you need.
And then about the vanishing: it's I who mean to vanish;
And when I'm here no longer you'll be done with me indeed."

"That's a way to tell me what I am, John Gorham!
How am I to know myself until I make you smile?
Try to look as if the moon were making faces at you,
And a little more as if you meant to stay a little while."

"You are what it is that over rose-blown gardens
Makes a pretty flutter for a season in the sun.
You are what it is that with a mouse, Jane Wayland,
Catches him and lets him go and eats him up for fun."

"Sure I never took you for a mouse, John Gorham.
All you say is easy, but so far from being true

That I wish you wouldn't ever be again the one to think so;
For it isn't cats and butterflies that I would be to you."

"All your little animals are in one picture—
One I've had before me since a year ago tonight;
And the picture where they live will be of you, Jane Wayland,
Till you find a way to kill them or to keep them out of sight."

"Won't you ever see me as I am, John Gorham,
Leaving out the foolishness and all I never meant?
Somewhere in me there's a woman, if you know the way to find
    her—
Will you like me any better if I prove it and repent?"

"I doubt if I shall ever have the time, Jane Wayland;
And I dare say all this moonlight lying round us might as well
Fall for nothing on the shards of broken urns that are forgotten,
As on two that have no longer much of anything to tell."

RICHARD CORY

Whenever Richard Cory went down town,
    We people on the pavement looked at him:
He was a gentleman from sole to crown,
    Clean favored, and imperially slim.

And he was always quietly arrayed,
    And he was always human when he talked;
But still he fluttered pulses when he said,
    "Good-morning," and he glittered when he walked.

And he was rich—yes, richer than a king,
    And admirably schooled in every grace:
In fine, we thought that he was everything
    To make us wish that we were in his place.

So on we worked, and waited for the light,
    And went without the meat, and cursed the bread;
And Richard Cory, one calm summer night,
    Went home and put a bullet through his head.

THE GROWTH OF LORRAINE

I

While I stood listening, discreetly dumb,
Lorraine was having the last word with me:
"I know," she said, "I know it, but you see
Some creatures are born fortunate, and some
Are born to be found out and overcome—
Born to be slaves, to let the rest go free;
And if I'm one of them (and I must be)
You may as well forget me and go home.

"You tell me not to say these things, I know,
But I should never try to be content:
I've gone too far; the life would be too slow.
Some could have done it—some girls have the stuff;
But I can't do it—I don't know enough.
I'm going to the devil." And she went.

II

I did not half believe her when she said
That I should never hear from her again;
Nor when I found a letter from Lorraine,
Was I surprised or grieved at what I read:
"Dear friend, when you find this, I shall be dead.
You are too far away to make me stop.
They say that one drop—think of it, one drop!—
Will be enough; but I'll take five instead.

"You do not frown because I call you friend;
For I would have you glad that I still keep
Your memory, and even at the end—
Impenitent, sick, shattered—cannot curse
The love that flings, for better or for worse,
This worn-out, cast-out flesh of mine to sleep."

CASSANDRA

I heard one who said: "Verily,
   What word have I for children here?
Your Dollar is only your Word,
   The wrath of it your only fear.

"You build it altars tall enough
   To make you see, but you are blind;
You cannot leave it long enough
   To look before you or behind.

"When Reason beckons you to pause,
   You laugh and say that you know best;
But what it is you know, you keep
   As dark as ingots in a chest.

"You laugh and answer, 'We are young;
   Oh, leave us now, and let us grow:'
Not asking how much more of this
   Will Time endure or Fate bestow.

"Because a few complacent years
   Have made your peril of your pride,
Think you that you are to go on
   Forever pampered and untried?

"What lost eclipse of history,
   What bivouac of the marching stars,
Has given the sign for you to see
   Millenniums and last great wars?

"What unrecorded overthrow
   Of all the world has ever known,
Or ever been, has made itself
   So plain to you, and you alone?

"Your Dollar, Dove and Eagle make
   A Trinity that even you
Rate higher than you rate yourselves;
   It pays, it flatters, and it's new.

"And though your very flesh and blood
    Be what your Eagle eats and drinks,
You'll praise him for the best of birds,
    Not knowing what the Eagle thinks.

"The power is yours, but not the sight;
    You see not upon what you tread;
You have the ages for your guide,
    But not the wisdom to be led.

"Think you to tread forever down
    The merciless old verities?
And are you never to have eyes
    To see the world for what it is?

"Are you to pay for what you have
    With all you are?"—No other word
We caught, but with a laughing crowd
    Moved on. None heeded, and few heard.

DEMOS

I

All you that are enamored of my name
And least intent on what most I require,
Beware; for my design and your desire,
Deplorably, are not as yet the same.
Beware, I say, the failure and the shame
Of losing that for which you now aspire
So blindly, and of hazarding entire
The gift that I was bringing when I came.

Give as I will, I cannot give you sight
Whereby to see that with you there are some
To lead you, and be led. But they are dumb
Before the wrangling and the shrill delight
Of your deliverance, that has not come,
And shall not, if I fail you—as I might.

II

So little have you seen of what awaits
Your fevered glimpse of a democracy
Confused and foiled with an equality
Not equal to the envy it creates,
That you see not how near you are the gates
Of an old king who listens fearfully
To you that are outside and are to be
The noisy lords of imminent estates.

Rather be then your prayer that you shall have
Your kingdom undishonored. Having all,
See not the great among you for the small
But hear their silence; for the few shall save
The many, or the many are to fall—
Still to be wrangling in a noisy grave.

MINIVER CHEEVY

Miniver Cheevy, child of scorn,
  Grew lean while he assailed the seasons;
He wept that he was ever born,
  And he had reasons.

Miniver loved the days of old
  When swords were bright and steeds were prancing;
The vision of a warrior bold
  Would set him dancing.

Miniver sighed for what was not,
  And dreamed, and rested from his labors;
He dreamed of Thebes and Camelot,
  And Priam's neighbors.

Miniver mourned the ripe renown
  That made so many a name so fragrant:
He mourned Romance, now on the town,
  And Art, a vagrant.

Miniver loved the Medici,
   Albeit he had never seen one;
He would have sinned incessantly
   Could he have been one.

Miniver cursed the commonplace
   And eyed a khaki suit with loathing;
He missed the mediæval grace
   Of iron clothing.

Miniver scorned the gold he sought,
   But sore annoyed was he without it;
Miniver thought, and thought, and thought,
   And thought about it.

Miniver Cheevy, born too late,
   Scratched his head and kept on thinking:
Miniver coughed, and called it fate,
   And kept on drinking.

EROS TURANNOS

She fears him, and will always ask
   What fated her to choose him;
She meets in his engaging mask
   All reasons to refuse him;
But what she meets and what she fears
Are less than are the downward years,
Drawn slowly to the foamless weirs
   Of age, were she to lose him.

Between a blurred sagacity
   That once had power to sound him,
And love, that will not let him be
   The seeker that she found him,
Her pride assuages her, almost,
As if it were alone the cost.
He sees that he will not be lost,
   And waits, and looks around him.

A sense of ocean and old trees
    Envelops and allures him;
Tradition, touching all he sees,
    Beguiles and reassures him;
And all her doubts of what he says
Are dimmed with what she knows of days,
Till even prejudice delays,
    And fades—and she secures him.

The falling leaf inaugurates
    The reign of her confusion;
The pounding wave reverberates
    The crash of her illusion;
And home, where passion lived and died,
Becomes a place where she can hide—
While all the town and harbor-side
    Vibrate with her seclusion.

We tell you, tapping on our brows,
    The story as it should be,
As if the story of a house
    Were told, or ever could be.
We'll have no kindly veil between
Her visions and those we have seen—
As if we guessed what hers have been,
    Or what they are, or would be.

Meanwhile, we do no harm; for they
    That with a god have striven,
Not hearing much of what we say,
    Take what the god has given;
Though like waves breaking it may be,
Or like a changed familiar tree,
Or like a stairway to the sea,
    Where down the blind are driven.

FIRELIGHT

Ten years together without yet a cloud,
They seek each other's eyes at intervals

Of gratefulness to firelight and four walls
For love's obliteration of the crowd.
Serenely and perennially endowed
And bowered as few may be, their joy recalls
No snake, no sword; and over them there falls
The blessing of what neither says aloud.

Wiser for silence, they were not so glad
Were she to read the graven tale of lines
On the wan face of one somewhere alone;
Nor were they more content could he have had
Her thoughts a moment since of one who shines
Apart, and would be hers if he had known.

CAPUT MORTUUM

Not even if with a wizard force I might
Have summoned whomsoever I would name,
Should anyone else have come than he who came,
Uncalled, to share with me my fire that night;
For though I should have said that all was right,
Or right enough, nothing had been the same
As when I found him there before the flame,
Always a welcome and a useful sight.

Unfailing and exuberant all the time,
Having no gold, he paid with golden rhyme
Of older coinage than his old defeat—
A debt that like himself was obsolete
In Art's long hazard, where no man may choose
Whether he play to win or toil to lose.

THE NEW TENANTS

The day was here when it was his to know
How fared the barriers he had built between
His triumph and his enemies unseen,
For them to undermine and overthrow;

And it was his no longer to forego
The sight of them, insidious and serene,
Where they were delving always, and had been
Left always to be vicious and to grow.

And there were the new tenants who had come,
By doors that were left open unawares,
Into his house, and were so much at home
There now that he would hardly have to guess,
By the slow guile of their vindictiveness,
What ultimate insolence would soon be theirs.

MR. FLOOD'S PARTY

Old Eben Flood, climbing alone one night
Over the hill between the town below
And the forsaken upland hermitage
That held as much as he should ever know
On earth again of home, paused warily.
The road was his with not a native near;
And Eben, having leisure, said aloud,
For no man else in Tilbury Town to hear:

"Well, Mr. Flood, we have the harvest moon
Again, and we may not have many more;
The bird is on the wing, the poet says,
And you and I have said it here before.
Drink to the bird." He raised up to the light
The jug that he had gone so far to fill,
And answered huskily: "Well, Mr. Flood,
Since you propose it, I believe I will."

Alone, as if enduring to the end
A valiant armor of scarred hopes outworn,
He stood there in the middle of the road
Like Roland's ghost winding a silent horn.
Below him, in the town among the trees,
Where friends of other days had honored him,
A phantom salutation of the dead
Rang thinly till old Eben's eyes were dim.

Then, as a mother lays her sleeping child
Down tenderly, fearing it may awake,
He set the jug down slowly at his feet
With trembling care, knowing that most things break;
And only when assured that on firm earth
It stood, as the uncertain lives of men
Assuredly did not, he paced away,
And with his hand extended paused again:

"Well, Mr. Flood, we have not met like this
In a long time; and many a change has come
To both of us, I fear, since last it was
We had a drop together. Welcome home!"
Convivially returning with himself,
Again he raised the jug up to the light;
And with an acquiescent quaver said:
"Well, Mr. Flood, if you insist, I might.

"Only a very little, Mr. Flood—
For auld lang syne. No more, sir; that will do."
So, for the time, apparently it did,
And Eben evidently thought so too;
For soon amid the silver loneliness
Of night he lifted up his voice and sang,
Secure, with only two moons listening,
Until the whole harmonious landscape rang—

"For auld lang syne." The weary throat gave out,
The last word wavered; and the song being done,
He raised again the jug regretfully,
And shook his head, and was again alone.
There was not much that was ahead of him,
And there was nothing in the town below—
Where strangers would have shut the many doors
That many friends had opened long ago.

Carl Sandburg

CHICAGO

Hog-butcher for the world,
Tool-maker, Stacker of Wheat,
Player with Railroads and the Nation's Freight-handler;
Stormy, husky, brawling,
City of the Big Shoulders:

They tell me you are wicked and I believe them, for I have seen
    your painted women under the gas lamps luring the farm
    boys.
And they tell me you are crooked, and I answer: Yes, it is
    true I have seen the gunman kill and go free to kill
    again.
And they tell me you are brutal and my reply is: On the faces
    of women and children I have seen the marks of wanton
    hunger.
And having answered so I turn once more to those who sneer at
    this my city, and I give them back the sneer and say to
    them:
Come and show me another city with lifted head singing
    so proud to be alive and coarse and strong and cun-
    ning.
Flinging magnetic curses amid the toil of piling job on job,
    here is a tall bold slugger set vivid against the little soft
    cities;
Fierce as a dog with tongue lapping for action, cunning as a
    savage pitted against the wilderness,
    Bareheaded,
    Shoveling,
    Wrecking,
    Planning,
    Building, breaking, rebuilding,
Under the smoke, dust all over his mouth, laughing with white
    teeth,
Under the terrible burden of destiny laughing as a young man
    laughs,

Laughing even as an ignorant fighter laughs who has never lost
    a battle,
Bragging and laughing that under his wrist is the pulse, and
    under his ribs the heart of the people.
               Laughing!
Laughing the stormy, husky, brawling laughter of youth; half-
    naked, sweating, proud to be Hog-butcher, Tool-maker,
    Stacker of Wheat, Player with Railroads, and Freight-
    handler to the Nation.

THE HARBOR

Passing through huddled and ugly walls,
By doorways where women
Looked from their hunger-deep eyes,
Haunted with shadows of hunger-hands,
Out from the huddled and ugly walls,
I came sudden, at the city's edge,
On a blue burst of lake—
Long lake waves breaking under the sun
On a spray-flung curve of shore;
And a fluttering storm of gulls,
Masses of great gray wings
And flying white bellies
Veering and wheeling free in the open.

SKETCH

The shadows of the ships
Rock on the crest
In the low blue lustre
Of the tardy and the soft inrolling tide.

A long brown bar at the dip of the sky
Puts an arm of sand in the span of salt.
The lucid and endless wrinkles
Draw in, lapse and withdraw.

Wavelets crumble and white spent bubbles
Wash on the floor of the beach.

Rocking on the crest
In the low blue lustre
Are the shadows of the ships.

LOST

Desolate and lone
All night long on the lake
Where fog trails and mist creeps,
The whistle of a boat
Calls and cries unendingly,
Like some lost child
In tears and trouble
Hunting the harbor's breast
And the harbor's eyes.

JAN KUBELIK

Your bow swept over a string, and a long low note quivered to
the air.
(A mother of Bohemia sobs over a new child, perfect, learning to
suck milk.)

Your bow ran fast over all the high strings fluttering and
wild.
(All the girls in Bohemia are laughing on a Sunday afternoon in
the hills with their lovers.)

AT A WINDOW

Give me hunger,
O you gods that sit and give
The world its orders.
Give me hunger, pain and want;
Shut me out with shame and failure

From your doors of gold and fame,
Give me your shabbiest, weariest hunger.

But leave me a little love,
A voice to speak to me in the day end,
A hand to touch me in the dark room
Breaking the long loneliness.
In the dusk of day-shapes
Blurring the sunset,
One little wandering western star
Thrust out from the changing shores of shadow.
Let me go to the window,
Watch there the day-shapes of dusk,
And wait and know the coming
Of a little love.

THE POOR

Among the mountains I wandered and saw blue haze and red
    crag and was amazed;
On the beach where the long push under the endless tide maneu-
    vers, I stood silent;
Under the stars on the prairie watching the Dipper slant over
    the horizon's grass, I was full of thoughts.
Great men, pageants of war and labor, soldiers and workers,
    mothers lifting their children—these all I touched, and felt
    the solemn thrill of them.
And then one day I got a true look at the Poor, millions of the
    Poor, patient and toiling; more patient than crags, tides,
    and stars; innumerable, patient as the darkness of night—
    and all broken humble ruins of nations.

THE ROAD AND THE END

I shall foot it
Down the roadway in the dusk,
Where shapes of hunger wander
And the fugitives of pain go by.

I shall foot it
In the silence of the morning,
See the night slur into dawn,
Hear the slow great winds arise
Where tall trees flank the way
And shoulder toward the sky.

The broken boulders by the road
Shall not commemorate my ruin.
Regret shall be the gravel under foot.
I shall watch for
Slim birds swift of wing
That go where wind and ranks of thunder
Drive the wild processionals of rain.

The dust of the traveled road
Shall touch my hands and face.

KILLERS

I am singing to you
Soft as a man with a dead child speaks;
Hard as a man in handcuffs,
Held where he can not move;

Under the sun
Are sixteen million men,
Chosen for shining teeth,
Sharp eyes, hard legs,
And a running of young warm blood in their wrists.

And a red juice runs on the green grass;
And a red juice soaks the dark soil.
And the sixteen million are killing . . . and killing and killing.
I never forget them day or night:
They beat on my head for memory of them;
They pound on my heart and I cry back to them,
To their homes and women, dreams and games.
I wake in the night and smell the trenches,
And hear the low stir of sleepers in lines—

Sixteen million sleepers and pickets in the dark:
Some of them long sleepers for always,
Some of them tumbling to sleep tomorrow for always,
Fixed in the drag of the world's heartbreak,
Eating and drinking, toiling . . . on a long job of killing.

Sixteen million men.

NOCTURNE IN A DESERTED BRICKYARD

Stuff of the moon
Runs on the lapping sand
Out to the longest shadows.
Under the curving willows,
And round the creep of the wave line,
Fluxions of yellow and dusk on the waters
Make a wide dreaming pansy of an old pond in the night.

HANDFULS

Blossoms of babies
Blinking their stories
Come soft
On the dusk and the babble;
Little red gamblers,
Handfuls that slept in the dust.

Summers of rain,
Winters of drift,
Tell off the years;
And they go back
Who came soft—
Back to the sod,
To silence and dust;
Gray gamblers,
Handfuls again.

UNDER THE HARVEST MOON

Under the harvest moon,
When the soft silver
Drips shimmering
Over the garden nights,
Death, the gray mocker,
Comes and whispers to you
As a beautiful friend
Who remembers.

Under the summer roses,
When the flagrant crimson
Lurks in the dusk
Of the wild red leaves,
Love, with little hands,
Comes and touches you
With a thousand memories,
And asks you
Beautiful unanswerable questions.

CHOOSE

The single clenched fist lifted and ready,
Or the open asking hand held out and waiting.
Choose:
For we meet by one or the other.

KIN

Brother, I am fire
Surging under the ocean floor.
I shall never meet you, brother—
Not for years, anyhow;
Maybe thousands of years, brother.
Then I will warm you,
Hold you close, wrap you in circles,
Use you and change you—
Maybe thousands of years, brother.

PLACES

Roses and gold
For you today,
And the flash of flying flags.

I will have
Ashes,
Dust in my hair,
Crushes of hoofs.

Your name
Fills the mouth
Of rich man and poor.
Women bring
Armfuls of flowers
And throw on you.

I go hungry
Down in dreams
And loneliness,
Across the rain
To slashed hills
Where men wait and hope for me.

JOY

Let a joy keep you.
Reach out your hands
And take it when it runs by,
As the Apache dancer
Clutches his woman.
I have seen them
Live long and laugh loud,
Sent on singing, singing,
Smashed to the heart
Under the ribs
With a terrible love.

Joy always,
Joy everywhere—
Let joy kill you!
Keep away from the little deaths.

THE GREAT HUNT

I can not tell you now;
    When the wind's drive and whirl
      Blow me along no longer,
    And the wind's a whisper at last—
Maybe I'll tell you then—
                  some other time.

    When the rose's flash to the sunset
    Reels to the wrack and the twist,
    And the rose is a red bygone,
    When the face I love is going
    And the gate to the end shall clang,
    And it's no use to beckon or say, "So long"—
Maybe I'll tell you then—
                  some other time.

I never knew any more beautiful than you:
    I have hunted you under my thoughts,
    I have broken down under the wind
    And into the roses looking for you.
    I shall never find any
              greater than you.

OUR PRAYER OF THANKS

For the gladness here where the sun is shining at evening on the
    weeds at the river,
    Our prayer of thanks.

For the laughter of children who tumble barefooted and bare-
    headed in the summer grass,
    Our prayer of thanks.

For the sunset and the stars, the women and their white arms
    that hold us,
  Our prayer of thanks.

  God,
If you are deaf and blind, if this is all lost to you,
God, if the dead in their coffins amid the silver handles on the
    edge of town, or the reckless dead of war days thrown un-
    known in pits, if these dead are forever deaf and blind and
    lost,
  Our prayer of thanks.

  God,
The game is all your way, the secrets and the signals and the
    system; and so, for the break of the game and the first play
    and the last,
  Our prayer of thanks.

HELGA

The wishes on this child's mouth
Came like snow on marsh cranberries;
The tamarack kept something for her;
The wind is ready to help her shoes.

The North has loved her; she will be
A grandmother feeding geese on frosty
Mornings; she will understand
Early snow on the cranberries
Better and better then.

GONE

Everybody loved Chick Lorimer in our town.
        Far off
      Everybody loved her.
So we all love a wild girl keeping a hold
      On a dream she wants.
Nobody knows now where Chick Lorimer went.

Nobody knows why she packed her trunk . . . a few old things
And is gone,
      Gone with her little chin
      Thrust ahead of her,
      And her soft hair blowing careless
      From under a wide hat—
Dancer, singer, a laughing passionate lover.

Were there ten men or a hundred hunting Chick?
Were there five men or fifty with aching hearts?
      Everybody loved Chick Lorimer.
      Nobody knows where she's gone.

FIRE–LOGS

Nancy Hanks dreams by the fire;
Dreams, and the logs sputter,
And the yellow tongues climb.
Red lines lick their way in flickers.

Oh, sputter, logs.
      Oh, dream, Nancy.
Time now for a beautiful child.
Time now for a tall man to come.

REPETITIONS

They are crying salt tears
Over the beautiful beloved body
Of Inez Milholland,
Because they are glad she lived,
Because she loved open-armed,
Throwing love for a cheap thing
Belonging to everybody—
Cheap as sunlight,
And morning air.

CALLS

Because I have called to you
As the flame flamingo calls,
Or the want of a spotted hawk
Is called—
        Because in the dusk
The warblers shoot the running
Waters of short songs to the
Homecoming warblers—
              Because
The cry here is wing to wing
And song to song—

    I am waiting,
Waiting with the flame flamingo,
The spotted hawk, the running water
Warbler—
        Waiting for you.

EVENING WATERFALL

What was the name you called me?—
And why did you go so soon?

The crows lift their caw on the wind,
And the wind changed and was lonely.

The warblers cry their sleepy-songs
Across the valley gloaming,
Across the cattle-horns of early stars.

Feathers and people in the crotch of a treetop
Throw an evening waterfall of sleepy-songs.

What was the name you called me?—
And why did you go so soon?

LOSERS

If I should pass the tomb of Jonah
I would stop there and sit for awhile;
Because I was swallowed one time deep in the dark
And came out alive after all.

If I pass the burial spot of Nero
I shall say to the wind, "Well, well!"—
I who have fiddled in a world on fire,
I who have done so many stunts not worth doing.

I am looking for the grave of Sinbad too.
I want to shake his ghost-hand and say,
"Neither of us died very early, did we?"

And the last sleeping-place of Nebuchadnezzar—
When I arrive there I shall tell the wind:
"You ate grass; I have eaten crow—
Who is better off now or next year?"

Jack Cade, John Brown, Jesse James,
There too I could sit down and stop for awhile.
I think I could tell their headstones:
"God, let me remember all good losers."

I could ask people to throw ashes on their heads
In the name of that sergeant at Belleau Woods,
Walking into the drumfires, calling his men,
"Come on, you——! Do you want to live forever?"

OLD TIMERS

I am an ancient reluctant conscript.

On the soup wagons of Xerxes I was a cleaner of pans.

On the march of Miltiades' phalanx I had a haft and head;
I had a bristling gleaming spear-handle.

Red-headed Cæsar picked me for a teamster.
He said, "Go to work, you Tuscan bastard!
Rome calls for a man who can drive horses."

The units of conquest led by Charles the Twelfth,
The whirling whimsical Napoleonic columns:
They saw me one of the horseshoers.
I trimmed the feet of a white horse Bonaparte swept the night
    stars with.

Lincoln said, "Get into the game; your nation takes you."
And I drove a wagon and team, and I had my arm shot off
At Spottsylvania Court House.

I am an ancient reluctant conscript.

NIGHT STUFF

Listen awhile—the moon is a lovely woman, a lonely woman,
    lost in a silver dress, lost in a circus-rider's silver dress.

Listen awhile—the lake by night is a lonely woman, a lovely
    woman, circled with birches and pines mixing their green
    and white among stars shattered in spray clear nights.

I know the moon and the lake have twisted the roots under my
    heart—the same as a lonely woman, a lovely woman, in a
    silver dress, in a circus-rider's silver dress.

FALLTIME

Gold of a ripe oat straw, gold of a southwest moon,
Canada-thistle blue and flimmering larkspur blue,
Tomatoes shining in the October sun with red hearts,
Shining five and six in a row on a wooden fence,
Why do you keep wishes on your faces all day long,
Wishes like women with half-forgotten lovers going to new cities?
What is there for you in the birds, the birds, the birds, crying
    down on the north wind in September—acres of birds spot-
    ting the air going south?

Is there something finished? And some new beginning on the
    way?

AUTUMN MOVEMENT

I cried over beautiful things, knowing no beautiful thing lasts.

The field of cornflower yellow is a scarf at the neck of the copper
sunburned woman, the mother of the year, the taker of
seeds.

The northwest wind comes and the yellow is torn full of holes,
new beautiful things come in the first spit of snow on the
northwest wind, and the old things go, not one lasts.

PRAIRIE

Finale—a fragment

O prairie mother, I am one of your boys.
I have loved the prairie as a man with a heart shot full of pain
over love.
Here I know I will hanker after nothing so much as one more
sunrise, or a sky moon of fire doubled to a river moon of
water.

I speak of new cities and new people.
I tell you the past is a bucket of ashes.
I tell you yesterday is a wind gone down,
            A sun dropped in the west.
I tell you there is nothing in the world
            Only an ocean of tomorrows,
            A sky of tomorrows.

I am a brother of the cornhuskers who say at sundown:
            Tomorrow is a day.

PRAYERS OF STEEL

Lay me on an anvil, O God!
Beat me and hammer me into a crowbar.
Let me pry loose old walls;
Let me lift and loosen old foundations.

Lay me on an anvil, O God!
Beat me and hammer me into a steel spike.
Drive me into the girders that hold a skyscraper together.
Take red-hot rivets and fasten me into the central girders.
Let me be the great nail holding a skyscraper through blue nights
    into white stars.

GRASS

Pile the bodies high at Austerlitz and Waterloo.
Shovel them under and let me work:
    I am the grass; I cover all.

And pile them high at Gettysburg,
And pile them high at Ypres and Verdun.
Shovel them under and let me work.
Two years, ten years, and passengers ask the conductor:
    What place is this?
    Where are we now?

    I am the grass.
    Let me work.

BRINGERS

Cover me over
In dusk and dust and dreams.

Cover me over
And leave me alone.

Cover me over,
You tireless, great.

Hear me and cover me,
Bringers of dusk and dust and dreams.

COOL TOMBS

When Abraham Lincoln was shoveled into the tombs, he forgot
the copperheads and the assassin . . . in the dust, in the
cool tombs.

And Ulysses Grant lost all thought of con men and Wall Street,
cash and collateral turned ashes . . . in the dust, in the
cool tombs.

Pocahontas' body, lovely as a poplar, sweet as a red haw in
November or a pawpaw in May—did she wonder? does
she remember? . . . in the dust, in the cool tombs?

Take any streetful of people buying clothes and groceries, cheering a hero or throwing confetti and blowing tin horns . . .
tell me if the lovers are losers . . . tell me if any get more
than the lovers . . . in the dust . . . in the cool tombs.

FOUR PRELUDES ON PLAYTHINGS OF THE WIND
"The past is a bucket of ashes."

I

The woman named Tomorrow
Sits with a hairpin in her teeth
And takes her time,
And does her hair the way she wants it,
And fastens at last the last braid and coil,
And puts the hairpin where it belongs,
And turns and drawls: "Well, what of it?
My grandmother, Yesterday, is gone.
What of it? Let the dead be dead."

II

The doors were cedar
And the panels strips of gold;
And the girls were golden girls,
And the panels read and the girls chanted:
    "We are the greatest city,
    the greatest nation;
    nothing like us ever was."

The doors are twisted on broken hinges.
Sheets of rain swish through on the wind
      where the golden girls ran and the panels read:
      "We are the greatest city,
      the greatest nation;
      nothing like us ever was."

III

It has happened before.
Strong men put up a city and got
      a nation together,
And paid singers to sing and women
      to warble: "We are the greatest city,
      the greatest nation;
      nothing like us ever was."

And while the singers sang,
And the strong men listened
And paid the singers well
And felt good about it all,
      there were rats and lizards who listened . . .
      and the only listeners left now . . .
      are . . . the rats . . . and the lizards.

And there are black crows
Crying, "Caw, caw,"
Bringing mud and sticks,
Building a nest
Over the words carved
On the doors where the panels were cedar
And the strips on the panels were gold,
And the golden girls came singing:
      "We are the greatest city,
      the greatest nation:
      nothing like us ever was."

The only singers now are crows crying, "Caw, caw;"
And the sheets of rain whine in the wind and doorways.
And the only listeners now are . . . the rats . . . and the
    lizards.

IV

The feet of the rats
Scribble on the door-sills;
The hieroglyphs of the rat footprints
Chatter the pedigrees of the rats,
And babble of the blood
And gabble of the breed
Of the grandfathers and the great-grandfathers
Of the rats.

And the wind shifts,
And the dust on the door-sill shifts,
And even the writing of the rat footprints
Tells us nothing, nothing at all
About the greatest city, the greatest nation,
Where the strong men listened
And the women warbled: "Nothing like us ever was."

Lew Sarett

THE BLUE DUCK
A Chippewa Medicine Dance

Hi′! Hi! Hi′! Hi!
Hi′! Hi! Hi′! Hi!
Heé′-ya! Hoi-ya!
Heé′-ya! Hoi-ya!
Keetch′-ie Má-ni-dó, Má-ni-dó,
The hunter-moon is chipping at his flints,
At his dripping bloody flints,
He is rising for the hunt,
And his face is red with blood
From the spears of many spruces,
And his blood is on the leaves that flutter down.
The winter-maker, Beé-bo-an′,
Is walking in the sky,
And his windy blanket rustles in the trees.

To be read with a vigorous lilt emphasizing the drum-beats

He is blazing out the trail
Through the fields of nodding rice
For the swift and whistling wings
Of his She-shé-be,
For the worn and weary wings
Of many duck—
Ho! plenty duck! plenty duck!
Ho! plenty, plenty duck!

Hi′! Hi!   *More slowly and quietly,*
Hi′! Hi!   *verging on a chant*
Hoy-eeeeé! Ya!
Hoy-eeeeé! Ya!
Keetch′-ie Má-ni-dó, Má-ni-dó,
The seasons have been barren.
In the moon of flowers and grass,
From the blighted berry patches
And the maple-sugar bush,
The hands of all my children
Came home empty, came home clean.
And the big rain of Nee-bín, the summer-maker,
Washed away the many little pa'tridge.
And even Ad-ik-kum′-aig, sweetest white-fish,
Went sulking all the summer moon,
Hiding in the deepest waters,
Silver belly in the mud;
And he would not walk into my nets. Ugh!
Thus the skin-sacks and the mo′kuks
Hang within my teepee empty.

Soon the winter moon will come,   *Slower—chant rising to a*
Slipping through the silent timber,   *wail*
Walking on the silent snow,
Stalking on the frozen lake.
Lean-bellied,
Squatting with his rump upon the ice,
The phantom wolf will fling his wailings to the stars.
Then Wéen-di-go, the Devil-spirit,
Whining through the lodge-poles,

Will clutch and shake my teepee,
Calling,
Calling,

Melancholy wailing from this point on—higher and higher in pitch

Calling as he sifts into my lodge;
And ghostly little shadow-arms
Will float out through the smoke-hole, in the night—
Leaping, tossing shadow-arms,
Little arms of little children,
Hungry hands of shadow-arms,
Clutching,
Clutching,
Clutching at the breast that is not there . . .
Shadow-arms and shadow-breasts,
Twisting,
Twisting,
Twisting in and twisting out,
On the ghastly clouds of smoke . . .
Riding on the whistling wind . . .
Riding on the whistling wind . . .
Riding on the whistling wind . . .
Starward.
Blow, blow, blow, Kee-wáy-din, North-wind,
Warm and gentle on my children,
Cold and swift upon the wild She-shé-be!
Ha-a-ah-eeeee-oooooooooo . . . Plenty duck . . .
Ha-a-a-ah-eeeeeee-ooooooooooo . . . Plenty duck . . .

Hi'! Hi! Hi'! Hi!
Hi'! Hi! Hi'! Hi!

Faster, with a lilt. Dancing rhythm

Keetch'-ie Má-ni-dó, Má-ni-dó,
Blow on Ah-bi-tee'-bi many wings:
Wings of teal and wings of mallard,
Wings of green and blue.
My little lake lies waiting,
Singing for her blust'ry lover;
Dancing on the golden-stranded shore
With many little moccasins,
Pretty little moccasins,
Beaded with her silver sands,

And with her golden pebbles.
And upon her gentle bosom
Lies Mah-no'-min, sweetest wild-rice,
Green and yellow,
Rustling blade and rippling blossom.
Hi-yee! Hi-yee! Blow on Ah-bi-tee'-bi plenty duck!
Ho! Plenty duck! Ho! Plenty duck!

Hi'! Hi! Hi'! Hi! Hi'! Hi! Hi'! Hi!   *Faster and louder—with*
                                              abandon
Hee'-ya! Hoi'-ya! Hee'-ya! Hoi'-ya!
Keetch'-ie, Má-ni-dó, Má-ni-dó,
I place this pretty duck upon your hand;
Upon its sunny palm and in its windy fingers.
Hi-yee! Blue and beautiful is he, beautifully blue;
Carved from sleeping cedar
When the stars like silver fishes
Were a-quiver in the rivers of the sky;
Carved from dripping cedar
When the Koo'-koo-koo' dashed hooting
At the furtive feet that rustled in the leaves,
And seasoned many moons, many moons!—
Ho! seasoned many, many, many sleeps!
Hi-yee! Blue and beautiful is he, beautifully blue.
Though his throat is choked with timber,
And he honks not on his pole,
And his wings are weak with hunger,
Yet his heart is plenty good!
Hi-yee! Hi-yee! His heart is plenty good, plenty good!
Hi-yee! Hi-yee! Hi-yee! His heart is good!

My heart like his is good!

Ugh! My tongue is straight!

Ho!

Ho!

BEAT AGAINST ME NO LONGER

Ai-yee! My yellow-bird-woman,
My ne-ne-moosh, ai-yee! my loved-one,
Be not afraid of my eyes!
Beat against me no longer!
Come! Come with a yielding of limbs!
Ai-yee! Woman, woman,
Trembling there in the teepee
Like the doe in the season of mating,
Why foolishly fearest thou me?
Cast the strange doubts from thy bosom—
Be not afraid of my eyes!
Be not as the flat-breasted squaw-sich
Who feels the first womanly yearnings
And hides, by the law of our people,
Alone three sleeps in the forest;
Be not as that brooding young maiden
Who wanders forlorn in the cedars,
And slumbers with troubled dreams,
To awaken suddenly, fearing
The hot throbbing blood in her bosom,
The strange eager life in her limbs.
Ai-yee! Foolish one, woman,
Cast the strange fears from thy heart—
Wash the red shame from thy face.
Be not afraid of my glances—
Be as the young silver birch
In the moon-of-the-green-growing-flowers,
Who sings with the thrill of the sap
As it leaps to the south-wind's caresses;
Who yields her rain-swollen buds
To the kiss of the sun with glad dancing.
Be as the cool tranquil moon
Who flings off her silver-blue blanket
To bare her white breast to the pine;
Who walks through the many-eyed night
In her gleaming white nudeness
With proud eyes that will not look down.

Be as the sun in her glory,
Who dances across the blue day
And flings her red soul, fierce-burning,
Into the arms of the twilight.
Ai-yee! Foolish one, woman,
Be as the sun and the moon!
Cast the strange doubts from thy bosom—
Wash the red shame from thy face!
Thou art a woman, a woman—
Beat against me no longer!
Be not afraid of my eyes!

TO A WILD GOOSE OVER DECOYS

O lonely trumpeter, coasting down the sky,
Like a winter leaf blown from the bur-oak tree
By whipping winds, and flapping silverly
Against the sun—I know your lonely cry.

I know the worn wild heart that bends your flight
And circles you above this beckoning lake,
Eager of neck, to find the honking drake
Who speaks of reedy refuge for the night.

I know the sudden rapture that you fling
In answer to our friendly gander's call—
Halloo! Beware decoys!—or you will fall
With a silver bullet whistling in your wing!

Beat on your weary flight across the blue!
Beware, O traveller, of our gabbling geese!
Beware this weedy counterfeit of peace!—
Oh, I was once a passing bird like you.

BLACKTAIL DEER

The blacktail held his tawny marble pose,
With every supple muscle set to spring,
Nosing the tainted air—his slender limbs
And sinews like corded copper quivering.

Ponderous the minutes, while his smoldering eyes
Went burning over me, and searching mine;
His heart ticked off each moment as he stood
Waiting an ominous word, a sound, a sign.

I tossed a friendly gesture! The sinews snapped
And flung his bulk of rippled tawny stone
Over an alder, as when a bended pine,
Released from pressure, catapults a cone.

Bending an arch above the alder-crown,
In a stream of whistling wind the great buck went,
Flirting his tail in exclamation marks
To punctuate his vast astonishment.

WAILING LYNX

What cry—from out the moonlit blue of wood—
That lays the jagged crimson of a scar
Upon the face of this dark solitude
     And stabs each pallid star!

What eerie terror this, that starts and spills
Its tones from out the mountain's naked heart—
Whose echoes ricochet among the hills
     And cleave the sky apart!

FOUR LITTLE FOXES

Speak gently, Spring, and make no sudden sound;
For in my windy valley yesterday I found
New-born foxes squirming on the ground—
          Speak gently.

Walk softly, March, forbear the bitter blow;
Her feet within a trap, her blood upon the snow,
The four little foxes saw their mother go—
          Walk softly.

Go lightly, Spring—oh, give them no alarm;
When I covered them with boughs to shelter them from
    harm,
The thin blue foxes suckled at my arm—
        Go lightly.

Step softly, March, with your rampant hurricane;
Nuzzling one another, and whimpering with pain,
The new little foxes are shivering in the rain—
        Step softly.

FEATHER

High in the noon's bright bowl of blue
I saw an idling eagle tilt
His suave white wings. As smooth he flew
    As water flows on silt.

He wheeled; a feather from his wing
Fluttered from out the clean clear dome
And sank on the grassy carpeting,
    Soft as a moth on foam.

In the eerie hour before the dawn,
I heard, out of the starry height,
The gentle ghost of one long gone
    Whisper across the night.

The tender fragment of a call
Fell soft as the down of any bird.
And none but I saw the feather fall;
    And no man caught the word.

Siegfried Sassoon

THE KISS

To these I turn, in these I trust;
Brother Lead and Sister Steel.
To his blind power I make appeal;
I guard her beauty clean from rust.

He spins and burns and loves the air,
And splits a skull to win my praise;
But up the nobly marching days
She glitters naked, cold and fair.

Sweet sister, grant your soldier this;
That in good fury he may feel
The body where he sets his heel
Quail from your downward darting kiss.

A MYSTIC AS SOLDIER

I lived my days apart,
Dreaming fair songs for God,
By the glory in my heart
Covered and crowned and shod.

Now God is in the strife,
And I must seek Him there,
Where death outnumbers life,
And fury smites the air.

I walk the secret way
With anger in my brain.
O music through my clay,
When will you sound again?

AUTUMN

October's bellowing anger breaks and cleaves
The bronzed battalions of the stricken wood
In whose lament I hear a voice that grieves
For battle's fruitless harvest, and the feud
Of outraged men. Their lives are like the leaves
Scattered in flocks of ruin, tossed and blown
Along the westering furnace flaring red.
O martyred youth and manhood overthrown,
The burden of your wrongs is on my head.

DOES IT MATTER?

Does it matter—losing your legs? . . .
For people will always be kind,
And you need not show that you mind
When the others come in after hunting
To gobble their muffins and eggs.

Does it matter—losing your sight? . . .
There's such splendid work for the blind;
And people will always be kind,
As you sit on the terrace remembering
And turning your face to the light.

Do they matter—those dreams from the pit? . . .
You can drink and forget and be glad,
And people won't say that you're mad;
For they'll know that you've fought for your country,
And no one will worry a bit.

SICK LEAVE

When I'm asleep, dreaming and lulled and warm,
They come, the homeless ones, the noiseless dead.
While the dim charging breakers of the storm
Bellow and drone and rumble overhead,
Out of the gloom they gather about my bed.

They whisper to my heart; their thoughts are mine.
"Why are you here with all your watches ended?
From Ypres to Frise we sought you in the Line."
In bitter safety I awake, unfriended;
And while the dawn begins with slashing rain
I think of the Battalion in the mud.
"When are you going out to them again?
Are they not still your brothers through our blood?"

EVERYONE SANG

Armistice Day

Everyone suddenly burst out singing;
And I was filled with such delight
As prisoned birds must find in freedom,
Winging wildly across the white
Orchards and dark-green fields; on—on—and out of sight.

Everyone's voice was suddenly lifted,
And beauty came like the setting sun.
My heart was shaken with tears; and horror
Drifted away. . . . Oh, but everyone
Was a bird; and the song was wordless—the singing will never
    be done.

Alan Seeger

I HAVE A RENDEZVOUS WITH DEATH

I have a rendezvous with Death
At some disputed barricade
When spring comes back with rustling shade
And apple-blossoms fill the air.
I have a rendezvous with Death
When spring brings back blue days and fair.

It may be he shall take my hand
And lead me into his dark land

And close my eyes and quench my breath.
It may be I shall pass him, still
I have a rendezvous with Death
On some scarred slope of battered hill
When spring comes 'round again this year
And the first meadow-flowers appear.

God knows 'twere better to be deep
Pillowed in silk and scented down,
Where love throbs out in blissful sleep,
Pulse nigh to pulse, and breath to breath,
Where hushed awakenings are dear. . . .
But I've a rendezvous with Death
At midnight in some flaming town,
When spring trips north again this year.
And I to my pledged word am true—
I shall not fail that rendezvous.

Marjorie Allen Seiffert

THE OLD WOMAN
A Morality Play in Two Parts

I

Doctor	There is an old woman Who ought to die—
Deacon	And nobody knows But what she's dead—
Doctor	The air will be cleaner When she's gone—
Deacon	But we dare not bury her Till she's dead.
Landlady	Come, young doctor From the first floor front, Come, dusty deacon

From the fourth floor back.
You take her heels
And I'll take her head—

Doctor and   We'll carry her
Deacon   And bury her—
If she's dead!

House   They roll her up
In her old red quilt,
They carry her down
At a horizontal tilt.
She doesn't say, "Yes!"
And she doesn't say, "No!"
She doesn't say, "Gentlemen,
Where do we go?"

Doctor   Out in the lot
Where the ash-cans die,
There, old woman,
There shall you lie!

Deacon   Let's hurry away,
And never look behind
To see if her eyes
Are dead and blind,
To see if the quilt
Lies over her face.
Perhaps she'll groan,
Or move in her place—

House   The room is empty
Where the old woman lay,
And I no longer
Smell like a tomb—

Landlady   Doctor, deacon,
Can you say
Who'll pay the rent
For the old woman's room?

II

House
> The room is empty
> Down the hall;
> There are mice in the closet,
> Ghosts in the wall.
> A pretty little lady
> Comes to see—

Woman
> Oh, what a dark room!
> Not for me!

Landlady
> The room is large
> And the rent is low;
> There's a deacon above,
> And a doctor below.

Deacon
> When the little mice squeak
> I will pray—

Doctor
> I'll psycho-analyze
> The ghosts away.

Landlady
> The bed is large
> And the mattress deep;
> Wrapped in a featherbed
> You shall sleep—

Woman
> But here's the door
> Without a key—
> An unlocked room
> Won't do for me!

Doctor
> Here's a bolt—

Deacon
> And here's a bar—

Landlady
> You'll sleep safely
> Where you are!

Woman
> Good-night, gentlemen,
> It's growing late.
> Good-night, landlady,
> Pray don't wait!

I'm going to bed—
I'll bolt the door
And sleep more soundly
Than ever before!

Deacon   Good-night, madam,
I'll steal away—

Doctor   Glad a pretty lady
Has come to stay!

House   She lights a candle—
What do I see?
That cloak looks like
A quilt to me!
She climbs into bed
Where long she's lain;
She's come back home—
She won't leave again.
She's found once more
Her rightful place—
Same old lady
With a pretty new face.
Let the deacon pray
And the doctor talk—
The mice will squeak
And the ghosts will walk.
There's a crafty smile
On the landlady's face—
The old woman's gone
And she's filled her place!

Landlady   It's nothing to me
If the old woman's dead—
I've somebody sleeping
In every bed!

A JAPANESE VASE WROUGHT IN METALS

Five harsh black birds shining in bronze come crying
Into a silver sky.
Piercing and jubilant is the shape of their flying;
Their beaks are pointed with delight,
Curved sharply with desire.
The passionate direction of their flight,
Clear and high,
Stretches their bodies taut like humming wire.
The cold wind blows into angry patterns the jet-bright
Feathers of their wings;
Their claws curl loosely, safely, about nothingness—
They clasp no things.
Direction and desire they possess,
By which in sharp unswerving flight they hold
Across an iron sea to the golden beach
Whereon lies carrion, their feast: a shore of gold
That birds wrought on a vase can never reach.

LORENZO'S BAS–RELIEF FOR A FLORENTINE CHEST

Lust is the oldest lion of them all,
And he shall have first place;
With a malignant growl satirical
To curve in foliations prodigal
Round and around his face,
Extending till the echoes interlace
With Pride and Prudence, two cranes gaunt and tall.

Four lesser lions crouch and malign the cranes.
Cursing and gossiping, they shake their manes,
While from their long tongues leak
Drops of thin venom as they speak.
The cranes, unmoved, peck grapes and grains
From a huge cornucopia, which rains
A plenteous meal from its antique
Interior—a note quite curiously Greek.

And nine long serpents twist
And twine, twist and twine—
A riotously beautiful design
Whose elements consist
Of eloquent spirals, fair and fine,
Embracing cranes and lions, who exist
Seemingly free, yet tangled in that living vine.

And in this chest shall be
Two cubic metres of space—
Enough to hold all memory
Of you and me. . . .
And this shall be the place
Where silence shall embrace
Our bodies, and obliterate the trace
Our souls made on the purity
Of night. . . .
    Now lock the chest, for we
Are dead, and lose the key!

INTERIOR

Words curl like fragrant smoke-wreaths in the room
From the majestic beard of an old man
Who props his shabby feet upon the stove
Recalling ancient sorrows. In the gloom
Beyond the lamp a woman thinks of love,
Her round arms wrapped in her apron, her dark head
Drooping. She has a bitter thing to learn.
His words drift over her . . . uncomforted
Her pain whirls up and twists like a scarlet thread
Among his words. He rises, shoves his chair
Back from the stove, pauses beside her there;
Shuffles irresolutely off to bed.

A BALLAD OF RIDING

I'll gallop away to market town
And get me a girl in a crimson gown—

A girl with innocent sidelong eyes
To hide that her heart is bitterly wise;

A girl with a neck so slender and sweet
You can see the thin blue pulses beat;

And a body to give no comfort, no rest,
But curl like a small white snake at your breast.

For my heart is bare as a china dish,
And nothing is left to hope or wish,

Because in the spring, because in the fall,
The world can offer me nothing at all—

Till my eyes turn hard, and my heart turns dumb,
To think of the years that come, and come.

It's better to get you a wicked wench
Than sit all day on a sunny bench;

It's better to drink from a poisoned spring
Than not to be thirsty for anything;

It's better to curse your gods and die
Than look up into an empty sky.

I'll gallop away to the market-place
And get me a girl with a three-cornered face,

A girl with a singular sidelong smile
Whose tongue is scarlet and smooth with guile,

Whose heart is twisted with bitter hate,
Who might have loved, but I come too late.

For the round empty world shows me nothing at all
But leaves that are budding, and leaves that fall,

And the year rolls around like a wheel in the dust
Whose axle is ancient and creaks with rust.

IRON FARE

Let courage stiffen
  Neck and chin
When the first nail
  Bites through the skin;

And let pride paint
  With a lasting varnish
The quivering face
  That tears would tarnish.

Press in the nail,
  And hold aloft
A metal smile
  On lips too soft.

Let nobody see
  A wound that bleeds;
Iron's a tonic
  The spirit needs.

Let acid reason
  And healthy blood
Corrode the nail
  And find it good.

Hold wide the eyes
  So frost may cover
The pain beneath
  From friend and lover;

For hearts that feed
  On iron fare
Dispense with pity
  And mock despair.

Frances Shaw

WHO LOVES THE RAIN

Who loves the rain
And loves his home,
And looks on life with quiet eyes,
  Him will I follow through the storm,
  And at his hearth-fire keep me warm.
Nor hell nor heaven shall that soul surprise,
  Who loves the rain,
  And loves his home,
And looks on life with quiet eyes.

THE HARP OF THE WIND

My house stands high—
Where the harp of the wind
Plays all day,
Plays all night;
And the city light
Is far away.

Where hangs the harp that the winds play?—
High in the air—
Over the sea?

The long straight streets of the far-away town,
Where the lines of light go sweeping down,
Are the strings of its minstrelsy.

And the harp of the wind
Gives to the wind
A song of the city's tears;
Thin and faint, the cry of a child,
Plaint of the soul unreconciled,
A song of the passing years.

THE RAGPICKER

The Ragpicker sits and sorts her rags:
    Silk and homespun and threads of gold
She plucks to pieces and marks with tags;
    And her eyes are ice and her fingers cold.

The Ragpicker sits in the back of my brain;
    Keenly she looks me through and through.
One flaming shred I have hidden away—
    She shall not have my love for you.

COLOGNE CATHEDRAL

The little white prayers
    Of Elspeth Fry
Float up the arches
    Into the sky.

A little black bird
    On the belfry high
Pecks at them
    As they go by.

STAR THOUGHT

I shall see a star tonight
From a distant mountain height;
From a city you will see
The same star that shines on me.

'Tis not of the firmament
On a solar journey bent;
Fixed it is through time and weather—
'Tis a thought we hold together.

THE CHILD'S QUEST

My mother twines me roses wet with dew;
Oft have I sought the garden through and through;

I cannot find the tree whereon
My mother's roses grew.
> Seek not, O child, the tree whereon
> Thy mother's roses grew.

My mother tells me tales of noble deeds;
Oft have I sought her book when no one heeds;
I cannot find the page, alas,
From which my mother reads.
> Seek not, O child, to find the page
> From which thy mother reads.

My mother croons me songs all soft and low,
Through the white night where little breezes blow;
Yet never when the morning dawns
My mother's songs I know.
> Seek not, O child, at dawn of day
> Thy mother's songs to know.

LITTLE PAGAN RAIN SONG

In the dark and peace of my final bed,
The wet grass waving above my head,
At rest from love, at rest from pain,
I lie and listen to the rain.

> Falling, softly falling,
>   Song of my soul that is free;
> Song of my soul that has not forgot
>   The sleeping body of me.

When quiet and calm and straight I lie,
High in the air my soul rides by.
Shall I await thee, soul, in vain?
Hark to the answer in the rain.

> Falling, softly falling,
>   Song of my soul that is free;
> Song of my soul that will not forget
>   The sleeping body of me.

THE LAST GUEST

Why have you lit so bright a fire
    For chatterers to sit about,
While wistful at the door,
And lonely at the door,
    One waits without?

Why have you spread so rich a feast
    For careless and insatiate,
While eager at the door,
And wanly at the door,
    Waits one most delicate?

When the night deepens, and the guests
Have passed to some new clamorous goal,
Let in the quiet one,
Let in the longing one;
Close to the last red embers draw
    Your welcome soul.

William H. Simpson

IN ARIZONA

HOPI GHOSTS

Ghosts of the early earth!
The sly coyote knows you,
And the timid deer.
I asked the eagle, circling skyward,
And saw your twin shadows.
The fox looks everywhere
And calls you brother.

Was it your whisper,
Your mocking whisper,
Among the twisted cedars?

Or only the tired winds,
Cuddling on the cool breasts of evening?

BURDENS

Burden of water jars,
Borne up steep trails;
Burden of babies,
Asleep in thronged cradles.

And a heaped-up load of loving,
Carried lightly
Over all the trails
To the end of them.

BAREBACK

The winds ride bareback,
Swinging lassos.

Their reins hang loose,
Their knees cling tight.

The trees bend down—
Behind rides the rain.

TREES

You root deep,
And reach skyward.

Something you say to me
That is under the earth.
Something you say to me
That is over the earth.

What it is,
Perhaps the closed eyes know.
What it is,
Maybe the folded wings know.

PITY NOT

Pity not the dead;
They are comforted.

Should they wake not,
All is forgot.

If they rise again,
Love folds them then.

Edith Sitwell

PANOPE
Fragment from Metamorphosis

Though lovely are the tombs of the dead nymphs
On the heroic shore, the glittering plinths
Of jacynth, hyacinthine waves profound
Sigh of the beauty out of sight and sound.

And many a golden foot that pressed the sand,
The panoply of suns on distant strand,
Panòpe walking like the pomp of waves
With plumaged helmet near the fountain caves

Is only now an arena for the worm;
Her golden flesh lies in the dust's frail storm

And beauty water-bright for long is laid
Deep in the empire of eternal shade.

Only the sighing waves know now the plinth
Of those deep tombs that were of hyacinth.

Still echoes of that helmeted bright hair
Are like the pomp of tropic suns, the blare

That from the inaccessible horizon runs,
The eternal music of heroic suns
When their strong youth comes freshened from deep seas,
And the first music heard among the trees.

THE PEACH TREE

Between the amber portals of the sea
The gilded fleece of heat hangs on my tree.
My skin is bright as this . . .
Come, wind, and smooth my skin, bright as your kiss.

Less bright, less bright than Fatima's gold skin
My gilded fleece that sighs,

"She is the glittering dew born of the heat,
She is that young gazelle, the leaping Sun of Paradise."

Come, Nubian shade, smooth the gilt fleece's curl
Until your long dark fluid hands unfold
My peach, that cloud of gold,
Its kernel, crackling amber water-cold.

Shine, Fatima, my Sun, show your gold face
Through panached ostrich plumes of leaves, then from above
My ripening fruits will feel the bright dew fall apace
Till at your feet I pour my golden love.

AUBADE

Jane, Jane,
Tall as a crane,
The morning light creaks down again.

Comb your cockscomb-ragged hair,
Jane, Jane, come down the stair.

Each dull blunt wooden stalactite
Of rain creaks, hardened by the light,

Sounding like an overtone
From some lonely world unknown.

But the creaking empty light
Will never harden into sight,

Will never penetrate your brain
With overtones like the blunt rain.

The light would show (if it could harden)
Eternities of kitchen garden,

Cockscomb flowers that none will pluck,
And wooden flowers that 'gin to cluck.

In the kitchen you must light
Flames as staring, red and white,

As carrots or as turnips, shining
Where the cold dawn light lies whining.

Cockscomb hair on the cold wind
Hangs limp, turns the milk's weak mind . . .

Jane, Jane,
Tall as a crane,
The morning light creaks down again!

SONG

"A coral neck and a little song, so very extra, so very Susie."
GERTRUDE STEIN

In summer when the rose-bushes
Have names like all the sweetest hushes
In a bird's song—Susan, Hannah,
Martha, Harriet, and Rosannah—
My coral neck
And my little song
Are very extra
And very Susie;
A little kiss like a gold bee stings
My childish life so sweet and rosy . . .
Like country clouds of clouted cream
The round and flaxen blond leaves seem,
And dew in trills
And dew in pearls
Falls from every gardener's posy.
Marguerites, roses,
A flaxen lily
Water-chilly,
Buttercups where the dew reposes,
In fact each flower young and silly,
The gardener ties in childish posies.

NIGHT PIECE

The cold hours pass.
As blue as glass
The beads of the frost
On the boughs are lost,

And over the empty plain of snow
King James' ghost is dragging slow.

The maids say "Ah!"
The maids say "Oh!"
Like tall fir-trees
They stand in a row;

As tall as ghosts they glimmer bright
Like the lily stars so tall and white.

But I am brave, like a fairy churn
The milk in the dairy; cream I turn

To butter pats like gold moidores. . . .
Outside in the snow, across the floors,

In at the window came King James,
Pointing at me his finger-flames. . . .

"My bones are changed to cinnamon,
Cold as stones, 'neath the wintry moon,

For cold is the golf-kernelled berry
On the sweet cornelian cherry

Tree" . . . then over the plain of snow
No sight of the King, or high or low!

Only the blue glass beads of the frost,
In the furry boughs where King James is lost,

And the maids that fall
Down in a swoon,
One by one
'Neath the wintry moon!

Constance Lindsay Skinner

SONGS OF THE COAST–DWELLERS

THE CHIEF'S PRAYER AFTER THE SALMON CATCH

O Kia-Kunæ, praise!
Thou hast opened thy hand among the stars,
And sprinkled the sea with food;
The catch is great; thy children will live.
See, on the roofs of the villages, the red meat drying;
Another year thou hast encompassed us with life.
Praise! Praise! Kunæ!
O Father, we have waited with shut mouths,
With hearts silent, and hands quiet,
Waited the time of prayer;
Lest with fears we should beset thee,
And pray the unholy prayer of asking.
We waited silently; and thou gavest life.

Oh, praise! Praise! Praise!

Open the silent mouths, the shut hearts, my tribe:
Sing high the prayer of Thanksgiving,
The prayer He taught in the beginning to the Kwakiutl—
The good rejoicing prayer of thanks.
As the sea sings on the wet shore, when the ice thunders back,
And the blue water floats again, warm, shining, living,
So break thy ice-bound heart, and the cold lip's silence—
Praise Kunæ for life, as wings up-flying, as eagles to the sun.
Praise! Praise! Praise!

SONG OF WHIP-PLAITING

In the dawn I gathered cedar-boughs
For the plaiting of thy whip.
They were wet with sweet drops;
They still thought of the night.

All alone I shredded cedar-boughs,
Green boughs in the pale light,
Where the morning meets the sea,
And the great mountain stops.

Earth was very still.

I heard no sound but the whisper of my knife,
My black flint knife.
It whispered among the white strands of the cedar,
Whispered in parting the sweet cords for thy whip.
O sweet-smelling juice of cedar—
Life-ooze of love!
My knife drips:
Its whisper is the only sound in all the world!

Finer than young sea-lions' hairs
Are my cedar-strands:
They are fine as little roots deep down.
(O little roots of cedar
Far, far under the bosom of Tsa-Kumts!—
They have plaited her through with love.)
Now, into my love-gift
Closely. strongly, I will weave them—
Little strands of pain!
Since I saw thee
Standing with thy torch in my doorway,
Their little roots are deep in me.

In the dawn I gathered cedar-boughs:
Sweet, sweet was their odor,
They were wet with tears—
The sweetness will not leave my hands,
No, not in salt sea-washings.
Tears will not wash away sweetness.
I shall have sweet hands for thy service.

(Ah—sometimes— thou wilt be gentle?
Little roots of pain are deep, deep in me
Since I saw thee standing in my doorway.)

I have quenched thy torch—
I have plaited thy whip.
I am thy Woman!

Leonora Speyer

MARY MAGDALENE

I think that Mary Magdalene
Was just a woman who went to dine;
And her jewels covered her empty heart,
And her gown was the color of wine.

I think that Mary Magdalene
Sat by a stranger with shining head:
"Haven't we met somewhere?" she asked.
"Magdalene! Mary!" he said.

I think that Mary Magdalene
Fell at his feet and called his name;
Sat at his feet and wept her woe,
And rose up clean of shame.

Nobody knew but Magdalene—
Mary the woman who went to dine—
Nobody saw how he broke the bread
And poured for her peace the wine.

This is the story of Magdalene—
It isn't the tale the Apostles tell,
But I know the woman it happened to,
I know the woman well.

MEASURE ME, SKY!

Measure me, sky!
Tell me I reach by a song
Nearer the stars:
I have been little so long.

Weigh me, high wind!
What will your wild scales record?
Profit of pain,
Joy by the weight of a word.

Horizon, reach out!
Catch at my hands, stretch me taut,
Rim of the world:
Widen my eyes by a thought.

Sky, be my depth;
Wind, be my width and my height;
World, my heart's span:
Loneliness, wings for my flight!

THE HEART LOOKS ON

I urged my mind against my will.
My will shook like a rocking wall
But did not fall;
My mind was like a wind-swept tree;
And neither knew the victory.

I dashed my mind against my will.
They did not break or bend or spill;
But in my heart the songs grew still.

WORDS TO SLEEP UPON

There are words that wait
With the night,
Soft as a pillow
And white,
Cool as a rose in the rain,
Deep as disdain.

My pillow is smooth
To my face,
And its words are like
Whispering lace,

Made of a wingèd design
That is weaving of mine.

But under my pillow
I hide
A song with a singing
Inside—
A locket that hangs on a chain
Of finely-wrought pain.

James Stephens

WHAT TOMAS AN BUILE SAID IN A PUB

I saw God. Do you doubt it?
Do you dare to doubt it?
I saw the Almighty Man. His hand
Was resting on a mountain, and
He looked upon the World and all about it:
I saw Him plainer than you see me now,
You mustn't doubt it.

He was not satisfied;
His look was all dissatisfied.
His beard swung on a wind far out of sight
Behind the world's curve, and there was light
Most fearful from His forehead, and He sighed,
"That star went always wrong, and from the start
I was dissatisfied."

He lifted up His hand—
I say He heaved a dreadful hand
Over the spinning Earth, then I said: "Stay—
You must not strike it, God; I'm in the way;
And I will never move from where I stand."
He said, "Dear child, I feared that you were dead,"
And stayed His hand.

BESSIE BOBTAIL

As down the street she wambled slow,
She had not got a place to go:
She had not got a place to fall
And rest herself—no place at all.
She stumped along, and wagged her pate,
And said a thing was desperate.

Her face was screwed and wrinkled tight
Just like a nut—and, left and right,
On either side she wagged her head
And said a thing; and what she said
Was desperate as any word
That ever yet a person heard.

I walked behind her for a while
And watched the people nudge and smile.
But ever as she went she said,
As left and right she swung her head,
—"Oh, God He knows," and "God He knows."
And surely God Almighty knows.

HATE

My enemy came high,
And I
Stared fiercely in his face.
My lips went writhing back in a grimace,
And stern I watched him with a narrow eye.
Then, as I turned away, my enemy,
That bitter heart and savage, said to me:
"Some day, when this is past,
When all the arrows that we have are cast,
We may ask one another why we hate,
And fail to find a story to relate.
It may seem to us then a mystery
That we could hate each other."

Thus said he,
And did not turn away,
Waiting to hear what I might have to say.
But I fled quickly, fearing if I stayed
I might have kissed him as I would a maid.

THE WASTE PLACES

I

As a naked man I go
  Through the desert sore afraid,
Holding up my head although
  I'm as frightened as a maid.

The couching lion there I saw
  From barren rocks lift up his eye;
He parts the cactus with his paw,
  He stares at me as I go by.

He would follow on my trace
  If he knew I was afraid,
If he knew my hardy face
  Hides the terrors of a maid.

In the night he rises and
  He stretches forth, he snuffs the air;
He roars and leaps along the sand,
  He creeps and watches everywhere.

His burning eyes, his eyes of bale,
  Through the darkness I can see;
He lashes fiercely with his tail,
  He would love to spring at me.

I am the lion in his lair;
  I am the fear that frightens me;
I am the desert of despair
  And the nights of agony.

Night or day, whate'er befall,
  I must walk that desert land,
Until I can dare to call
  The lion out to lick my hand.

II

As a naked man I tread
  The gloomy forests, ring on ring,
Where the sun that's overhead
  Cannot see what's happening.

There I go: the deepest shade,
  The deepest silence pressing me;
And my heart is more afraid
  Than a maiden's heart would be.

Every day I have to run
  Underneath the demon tree,
Where the ancient wrong is done
  While I shrink in agony.

There the demon held a maid
  In his arms, and as she, daft,
Screamed again in fear, he laid
  His lips upon her lips and laughed.

And she beckoned me to run,
  And she called for help to me,
And the ancient wrong was done
  Which is done eternally.

I am the maiden and the fear;
  I am the sunless shade, the strife;
I the demon lips, the sneer
  Showing under every life.

I must tread that gloomy way
  Until I shall dare to run
And bear the demon with his prey
  From the forest to the sun.

HAWKS

And as we walked the grass was faintly stirred;
  We did not speak—there was no need to speak.
Above our heads there flew a little bird,
  A silent one who feared that we might seek
    Her hard-hid nest.

Poor little frightened one!
  If we had found your nest that sunny day
We would have passed it by; we would have gone
  And never looked or frightened you away.

O little bird! there's many have a nest,
  A hard-found, open place, with many a foe;
And hunger and despair and little rest,
  And more to fear than you can know.

      Shield the nests where'er they be,
      On the ground or on the tree;
      Guard the poor from treachery.

DARK WINGS

Sing while you may, O bird upon the tree!
  Although on high, wide-winged above the day,
Chill evening broadens to immensity,
  Sing while you may.

On thee, wide-hovering too, intent to slay,
  The hawk's slant pinion buoys him terribly—
Thus near the end is of thy happy lay.

The day and thou and miserable me
  Dark wings shall cover up and hide away
Where no songs stirs of bird or memory:
  Sing while you may.

George Sterling

A LEGEND OF THE DOVE

Soft from the linden's bough,
Unmoved against the tranquil afternoon,
   Eve's dove laments her now:
"Ah, gone! long gone! shall not I find thee soon?"

   That yearning in his voice
Told not to Paradise a sorrow's tale:
   As other birds rejoice
He sang, a brother to the nightingale.

   By twilight on her breast
He saw the flower sleep, the star awake;
   And calling her from rest,
Made all the dawn melodious for her sake.

   And then the Tempter's breath,
The sword of exile and the mortal chain—
   The heritage of death
That gave her heart to dust, his own to pain. . . .

   In Eden desolate
The seraph heard his lonely music swoon,
   As now, reiterate;
"Ah, gone! long gone! shall not I find thee soon?"

KINDRED

Musing, between the sunset and the dark,
As Twilight in unhesitating hands
Bore from the faint horizon's underlands,
Silvern and chill, the moon's phantasmal ark,
I heard the sea, and far away could mark
Where that unalterable waste expands
In sevenfold sapphire from the mournful sands,
And saw beyond the deep a vibrant spark.

There sank the sun Arcturus, and I thought:
Star, by an ocean on a world of thine,
May not a being, born like me to die,
Confront a little the eternal Naught
And watch our isolated sun decline—
Sad for his evanescence, even as I?

OMNIA EXEUNT IN MYSTERIUM

The stranger in my gates—lo! that am I,
And what my land of birth I do not know,
Nor yet the hidden land to which I go.
One may be lord of many ere he die,
And tell of many sorrows in one sigh,
But know himself he shall not, nor his woe,
Nor to what sea the tears of wisdom flow;
Nor why one star is taken from the sky.

An urging is upon him evermore,
And though he bide, his soul is wanderer,
Scanning the shadows with a sense of haste—
Where fade the tracks of all who went before:
A dim and solitary traveler
On ways that end in evening and the waste.

THE LAST DAYS

The russet leaves of the sycamore
Lie at last on the valley floor—
By the autumn wind swept to and fro
Like ghosts in a tale of long ago.
Shallow and clear the Carmel glides
Where the willows droop on its vine-walled sides.

The bracken-rust is red on the hill;
The pines stand brooding, sombre and still;
Gray are the cliffs, and the waters gray,
Where the seagulls dip to the sea-born spray.

Sad November, lady of rain,
Sends the goose-wedge over again.

Wilder now, for the verdure's birth,
Falls the sunlight over the earth;
Kildees call from the fields where now
The banding blackbirds follow the plow;
Rustling poplar and brittle weed
Whisper low to the river-reed.

Days departing linger and sigh:
Stars come soon to the quiet sky;
Buried voices, intimate, strange,
Cry to body and soul of change;
Beauty, eternal fugitive,
Seeks the home that we cannot give.

THE BLACK VULTURE

Aloof within the day's enormous dome,
He holds unshared the silence of the sky.
Far down his bleak relentless eyes descry
The eagle's empire and the falcon's home—
Far down the galleons of sunset roam.
His hazards on the sea of morning lie;
Serene, he hears the broken tempest sigh
Where cold sierras gleam like scattered foam.

And least of all he holds the human swarm—
Unwitting now that envious men prepare
To make their dream and its fulfilment one,
When, poised above the cauldrons of the storm,
Their hearts, contemptuous of death, shall dare
His roads between the thunder and the sun.

Wallace Stevens

PETER QUINCE AT THE CLAVIER

I

Just as my fingers on these keys
Make music, so the self-same sounds
On my spirit make a music too

Music is feeling then, not sound;
And thus it is that what I feel,
Here in this room, desiring you,

Thinking of your blue-shadowed silk,
Is music. It is like the strain
Waked in the elders by Susanna:

Of a green evening, clear and warm,
She bathed in her still garden, while
The red-eyed elders, watching, felt

The basses of their being throb
In witching chords, and their thin blood
Pulse pizzicati of Hosanna.

II

In the green water, clear and warm,
Susanna lay.
She searched
The touch of springs,
And found
Concealed imaginings.
She sighed
For so much melody.

Upon the bank she stood
In the cool
Of spent emotions.
She felt, among the leaves,
The dew
Of old devotions.

She walked upon the grass,
Still quavering.
The winds were like her maids,
On timid feet,
Fetching her woven scarves,
Yet wavering.

A breath upon her hand
Muted the night.
She turned—
A cymbal crashed,
And roaring horns.

III

Soon, with a noise like tambourines,
Came her attendant Byzantines.

They wondered why Susanna cried
Against the elders by her side:

And as they whispered, the refrain
Was like a willow swept by rain.

Anon, their lamps' uplifted flame
Revealed Susanna and her shame.

And then the simpering Byzantines,
Fled, with a noise like tambourines.

IV

Beauty is momentary in the mind—
The fitful tracing of a portal;
But in the flesh it is immortal.

The body dies; the body's beauty lives.
So evenings die, in their green going,
A wave, interminably flowing.

So gardens die, their meek breath scenting
The cowl of winter, done repenting.
So maidens die, to the auroral
Celebration of a maiden's choral.

Susanna's music touched the bawdy strings
Of those white elders; but, escaping,
Left only Death's ironic scraping.
Now, in its immortality, it plays
On the clear viol of her memory,
And makes a constant sacrament of praise.

IN BATTLE

Death's nobility again
Beautified the simplest men.
Fallen Winkle felt the pride
Of Agamemnon
When he died.

What could London's
Work and waste
Give him—
To that salty, sacrificial taste?

What could London's
Sorrow bring—
To that short, triumphant sting?

SUNDAY MORNING

I

Complacencies of the peignoir, and late
Coffee and oranges in a sunny chair,
And the green freedom of a cockatoo
Upon a rug, mingle to dissipate
The holy hush of ancient sacrifice.
She dreams a little, and she feels the dark
Encroachment of that old catastrophe,
As a calm darkens among water-lights.
The pungent oranges and bright green wings
Seem things in some procession of the dead,

Winding across wide water without sound.
The day is like wide water without sound,
Stilled for the passing of her dreaming feet
Over the seas to silent Palestine,
Dominion of the blood and sepulchre.

II

Why should she give her bounty to the dead?
What is divinity if it can come
Only in silent shadows and in dreams?
Shall she not find in comforts of the sun,
In pungent fruit and bright green wings, or else
In any balm or beauty of the earth,
Things to be cherished like the thought of heaven?
Divinity must live within herself:
Passions of rain, or moods in falling snow;
Grievings in loneliness, or unsubdued
Elations when the forest blooms; gusty
Emotions on wet roads on autumn nights;
All pleasures and all pains, remembering
The bough of summer and the winter branch.
These are the measures destined for her soul.

III

Jove in the clouds had his inhuman birth.
No mother suckled him, no sweet land gave
Large-mannered motions to his mythy mind.
He moved among us as a muttering king,
Magnificent, would move among his hinds,
Until our blood, commingling virginal
With heaven, brought such requital to desire
The very hinds discerned it, in a star.
Shall our blood fail? Or shall it come to be
The blood of paradise? And shall the earth
Seem all of paradise that we shall know?
The sky will be much friendlier then than now,
A part of labor and a part of pain
And next in glory to enduring love,
Not this dividing and indifferent blue.

IV

She says: "I am content when wakened birds,
Before they fly, test the reality
Of misty fields by their sweet questionings;
But when the birds are gone, and their warm fields
Return no more, where then is paradise?"
There is not any haunt of prophecy,
Nor any old chimera of the grave,
Neither the golden underground, nor isle
Melodious, where spirits gat them home,
Nor visionary South, nor cloudy palm
Remote on heaven's hill, that has endured
As April's green endures; or will endure
Like her remembrance of awakened birds,
Or her desire for June and evening, tipped
By the consummation of the swallow's wings.

V

She says, "But in contentment I still feel
The need of some imperishable bliss."
Death is the mother of beauty; hence from her
Alone shall come fulfilment to our dreams
And our desires. Although she strews the leaves
Of sure obliteration on our paths—
The path sick sorrow took, the many paths
Where triumph rang its brassy phrase, or love
Whispered a little out of tenderness—
She makes the willow shiver in the sun
For maidens who were wont to sit and gaze
Upon the grass, relinquished to their feet.
She causes boys to pile new plums and pears
On disregarded plate. The maidens taste
And stray impassioned in the littering leaves.

VI

Is there no change of death in paradise?
Does ripe fruit never fall? Or do the boughs
Hang always heavy in that perfect sky?
Unchanging, yet so like our perishing earth,

With rivers like our own that seek for seas
They never find, the same receding shores
That never touch with inarticulate pang?
Why set the pear upon those river-banks
Or spice the shores with odors of the plum?
Alas, that they should wear our colors there,
The silken weavings of our afternoons,
And pick the strings of our insipid lutes!
Death is the mother of beauty, mystical,
Within whose burning bosom we devise
Our earthly mothers waiting, sleeplessly.

VII

Supple and turbulent, a ring of men
Shall chant in orgy on a summer morn
Their boisterous devotion to the sun—
Not as a god, but as a god might be,
Naked among them, like a savage source.
Their chant shall be a chant of paradise,
Out of their blood, returning to the sky;
And in their chant shall enter, voice by voice,
The windy lake wherein their lord delights,
The trees, like seraphim, and echoing hills,
That choir among themselves long afterward.
They shall know well the heavenly fellowship
Of men that perish and of summer morn—
And whence they came and whither they shall go
The dew upon their feet shall manifest.

VIII

She hears, upon that water without sound,
A voice that cries: "The tomb in Palestine
Is not the porch of spirits lingering;
It is the grave of Jesus, where he lay."
We live in an old chaos of the sun,
Or old dependency of day and night,
Or island solitude, unsponsored, free,
Of that wide water, inescapable.
Deer walk upon our mountains, and the quail

Whistle about us their spontaneous cries;
Sweet berries ripen in the wilderness;
And in the isolation of the sky,
At evening, casual flocks of pigeons make
Ambiguous undulations as they sink
Downward to darkness on extended wings.

BOWL

For what emperor
Was this bowl of Earth designed?
Here are more things
Than on any bowl of the Sungs,
Even the rarest:
Vines that take
The various obscurities of the moon,
Approaching rain,
And leaves that would be loose upon the wind;
Pears on pointed trees,
The dresses of women,
Oxen . . .
I never tire
To think of this.

TATTOO

The light is like a spider:
It crawls over the water;
It crawls over the edges of the snow;
It crawls under your eyelids
And spreads its webs there—
Its two webs.
The webs of your eyes
Are fastened
To the flesh and bones of you
As to rafters or grass.

There are filaments of your eyes
On the surface of the water
And in the edges of the snow.

THE WORMS AT HEAVEN'S GATES

Out of the tomb we bring Badroulbadour
Within our bellies—we her chariot.
Here is an eye; and here are, one by one,
The lashes of that eye and its white lid.

Here is the cheek on which that lid declined,
And, finger after finger, here the hand,
The genius of that cheek. Here are the lips,
The bundle of the body, and the feet.

.   .   .   .

Out of the tomb we bring Badroulbadour.

FABLIAU OF FLORIDA

Barque of phosphor
On the palmy beach,

Move outward into heaven,
Into the alabasters
And night blues.

Foam and cloud are one.
Sultry moon-monsters
Are dissolving.

Fill your black hull
With white moonlight.

There will never be an end
To this droning of the surf.

PETER PARASOL

*Aux taureaux Dieu cornes donne
Et sabots durs aux chevaux . . .*

Why are not women fair,
All, as Andromache—
Having, each one, most praisable
Ears, eyes, soul, skin, hair?

Good God! That all beasts should have
The tusks of the elephant,
Or be beautiful
As large ferocious tigers are.

It is not so with women.
I wish they were all fair,
And walked in fine clothes,
With parasols, in the afternoon air.

OF THE SURFACE OF THINGS

I

In my room, the world is beyond my understanding;
But when I walk I see that it consists of three or four hills and
a cloud.

II

From my balcony, I survey the yellow air,
Reading where I have written,
"The spring is like a belle undressing."

THE PLACE OF THE SOLITAIRES

Let the place of the solitaires
Be a place of perpetual undulation.
Whether it be in mid-sea
On the dark green water-wheel,
Or on the beaches,
There must be no cessation
Of motion, or of the noise of motion,
The renewal of noise
And manifold continuation;

And, most, of the motion of thought
And its restless iteration,

In the place of the solitaires,
Which is to be a place of perpetual undulation.

THE PALTRY NUDE STARTS ON A SPRING VOYAGE

But not on a shell, she starts,
Archaic, for the sea.
But on the first-found weed
She scuds the glitters,
Noiselessly, like one more wave.

She too is discontent
And would have purple stuff upon her arms,
Tired of the salty harbors,
Eager for the brine and bellowing
Of the high interiors of the sea.

The wind speeds her,
Blowing upon her hands
And watery back.
She touches the clouds, where she goes,
In the circle of her traverse of the sea.

Yet this is meagre play
In the scurry and water-shine,
As her heels foam—
Not as when the goldener nude
Of a later day

Will go, like the centre of sea-green pomp,
In an intenser calm,
Scullion of fate,
Across the spick torrent, ceaselessly,
Upon her irretrievable way.

THE SNOW MAN

One must have a mind of winter
To regard the frost and the boughs
Of the pine-trees crusted with snow;

And have been cold a long time
To behold the junipers shagged with ice,
The spruces rough in the distant glitter

Of the January sun; and not to think
Of any misery in the sound of the wind,
In the sound of a few leaves,

Which is the sound of the land
Full of the same wind
That is blowing in the same bare place

For the listener, who listens in the snow,
And, nothing himself, beholds
Nothing that is not there and the nothing that is.

TEA AT THE PALAZ OF HOON

Not less because in purple I descended
The western day through what you called
The loneliest air, not less was I myself.

What was the ointment sprinkled on my beard?
What were the hymns that buzzed beside my ears?
What was the sea whose tide swept through me there?

Out of my mind the golden ointment rained,
And my ears made the blowing hymns they heard.
I was myself the compass of that sea:

I was the world in which I walked, and what I saw
Or heard or felt came not but from myself;
And there I found myself more truly and more strange.

ANOTHER WEEPING WOMAN

Pour the unhappiness out
From your too bitter heart,
Which grieving will not sweeten.

Poison grows in this dark.
It is in the water of tears
Its black blooms rise.

The magnificent cause of being—
The imagination, the one reality
In this imagined world—

Leaves you
With him for whom no fantasy moves,
And you are pierced by a death.

THE LOAD OF SUGAR-CANE

The going of the glade-boat
Is like water flowing;

Like water flowing
Through the green saw-grass,
Under the rainbows;

Under the rainbows
That are like birds,
Turning, bedizened,

While the wind still whistles
As kildeer do,

When they rise
At the red turban
Of the boatmen.

HIBISCUS ON THE SLEEPING SHORES

I say now, Fernando, that on that day
The mind roamed as a moth roams,
Among the blooms beyond the open sand;

And that whatever noise the motion of the waves
Made on the sea-weeds and the covered stones
Disturbed not even the most idle ear.

Then it was that that monstered moth
Which had lain folded against the blue
And the colored purple of the lazy sea,

And which had drowsed along the bony shores,
Shut to the blather that the water made,
Rose up besprent and sought the flaming red

Dabbled with yellow pollen—red as red
As the flag above the old café—
And roamed there all the stupid afternoon.

LE MONOCLE DE MON ONCLE

I

"Mother of heaven, regina of the clouds,
O sceptre of the sun, crown of the moon,
There is not nothing, no, no, never nothing,
Like the clashed edges of two words that kill."
And so I mocked her in magnificent measure.
Or was it that I mocked myself alone?
I wish that I might be a thinking stone.
The sea of spuming thought foists up again
The radiant bubble that she was. And then
A deep up-pouring from some saltier well,
Within me, bursts its watery syllable.

II

A red bird flies across the golden floor.
It is a red bird that seeks out his choir
Among the choirs of wind and wet and wing.
A torrent will fall from him when he finds.
Shall I uncrumple this much-crumpled thing?
I am a man of fortune greeting heirs;
For it has come that thus I greet the spring.
These choirs of welcome choir for me farewell.
No spring can follow past meridian.
Yet you persist with anecdotal bliss
To make believe a starry *connaissance*.

III

Is it for nothing, then, that old Chinese
Sat tittivating by their mountain pools
Or in the Yangtse studied out their beards?
I shall not play the flat historic scale.
You know how Utamaro's beauties sought
The end of love in their all-speaking braids.
You know the mountainous coiffures of Bath.
Alas! Have all the barbers lived in vain,
That not one curl in nature has survived?
Why, without pity on these studious ghosts,
Do you come dripping in your hair from sleep?

IV

This luscious and impeccable fruit of life
Falls, it appears, of its own weight to earth.
When you were Eve, its acrid juice was sweet,
Untasted, in its heavenly orchard air.
An apple serves as well as any skull
To be the book in which to read a round,
And is as excellent, in that it is composed
Of what, like skulls, comes rotting back to ground.
But it excels in this, that as the fruit
Of love, it is a book too mad to read
Before one merely reads to pass the time.

V

In the high west there burns a furious star.
It is for fiery boys that star was set
And for sweet-smelling virgins close to them.
The measure of the intensity of love
Is measure, also, of the verve of earth.
For me, the firefly's quick electric stroke
Ticks tediously the time of one more year.
And you? Remember how the crickets came
Out of their mother grass, like little kin . . .
In the pale nights, when your first imagery
Found inklings of your bond to all that dust.

VI

If men at forty will be painting lakes,
The ephemeral blues must merge for them in one,
The basic slate, the universal hue.
There is a substance in us that prevails.
But in our amours amorists discern
Such fluctuations that their scrivening
Is breathless to attend each quirky turn.
When amorists grow bald, then amours shrink
Into the compass and curriculum
Of introspective exiles, lecturing.
It is a theme for Hyacinth alone.

VII

The mules that angels ride come slowly down
The blazing passes, from beyond the sun.
Descensions of their tinkling bells arrive.
These muleteers are dainty of their way.
Meantime, centurions guffaw and beat
Their shrilling tankards on the table-boards.
This parable, in sense, amounts to this:
The honey of heaven may or may not come,
But that of earth both comes and goes at once.
Suppose these couriers brought amid their train
A damsel heightened by eternal bloom.

VIII

Like a dull scholar I behold, in love,
An ancient aspect touching a new mind.
It comes, it blooms, it bears its fruit and dies.
This trivial trope reveals a way of truth.
Our bloom is gone. We are the fruit thereof.
Two golden gourds distended on our vines,
We hang like warty squashes, streaked and rayed,
Into the autumn weather, splashed with frost—
Distorted by hale fatness, turned grotesque.
The laughing sky will see the two of us
Washed into rinds by rotting winter rains.

IX

In verses wild with motion, full of din,
Loudened by cries, by clashes, quick and sure
As the deadly thought of men accomplishing
Their curious fates in war, come, celebrate
The faith of forty, ward of Cupido.
Most venerable heart, the lustiest conceit
Is not too lusty for your broadening.
I quiz all sounds, all thoughts, all everything
For the music and manner of the paladins
To make oblation fit. Where shall I find
Bravura adequate to this great hymn?

X

The fops of fancy in their poems leave
Memorabilia of the mystic spouts,
Spontaneously watering their gritty soils.
I am a yeoman, as such fellows go.
I know no magic trees, no balmy boughs,
No silver-ruddy, gold-vermilion fruits.
But, after all, I know a tree that bears
A semblance to the thing I have in mind.
It stands gigantic, with a certain tip
To which all birds come sometime in their time.
But when they go that tip still tips the tree.

XI

If sex were all, then every trembling hand
Could make us squeak, like dolls, the wished-for words.
But note the unconscionable treachery of fate,
That makes us weep, laugh, grunt and groan, and shout
Doleful heroics, pinching gestures forth
From madness or delight, without regard
To that first foremost law. Anguishing hour!
Last night we sat beside a pool of pink,
Clippered with lilies scudding the bright chromes,
Keen to the point of starlight, while a frog
Boomed from his very belly odious chords.

XII

A blue pigeon it is that circles the blue sky,
On side-long wing, around and round and round.
A white pigeon it is that flutters to the ground,
Grown tired of flight. Like a dark rabbi, I
Observed, when young, the nature of mankind,
In lordly study. Every day I found
Man proved a gobbet in my mincing world.
Like a rose rabbi, later, I pursued,
And still pursue, the origin and course
Of love, but until now I never knew
That fluttering things have so distinct a shade.

Marion Strobel

LOST CITY

We shall build it again though it caves in,
And the ramparts fall where the moss is,
And the draw-bridge no horseman crosses
Lets the dusk and the wind and the waves in.

We shall build it with hills and with hollows,
And small slopes where vineyards are sprawling,
And a wall that crumbles in falling,
And a river nobody follows.

Through the gateways we'll see to the centre
Where fountains are playing, and flowers
Run a flame up the twilit towers
Of the city we never shall enter.

And the wind will die down in the streamers,
And the spires will fall with the night-fall;
But a door will open—a light fall
On a street that is peopled with dreamers.

PASTORAL

The hill was flowing with sheep,
The stream was shadowed and blown,
But love was so much our own
We loosed it and went to sleep.

We loosed it in sleep, and still
In the windlessness of a dream
The sheep flowed over the hill,
The shadows blew over the stream.

DOG OVER SNOW

The greyhound skims the boulevard.
The night comes down. The lamps are lit.
The snow is starred.
A silver bit
Is pencilled on a passing horse.
Now dimly, as the twilight dims
Crossing his course,
The greyhound skims.

And winter, going, does not go;
And nights, in passing, still leave night.
And over the snow
A dog in flight.

WE HAVE A DAY

We have a day, we have a night
Which have been made for our delight!

Shall we run, and run, and run
Up the path of the rising sun?

Shall we roll down every hill,
Or lie still
Listening while the whispering leaves
Promise what no one believes?

The hours poise, breathless for flight, and bright.

Only a night, only a day—
We must not let them get away;

Don a foolish cap and bell,
For all is well and all is well.

Dance through woods a purple-blue!
Dance into
Lanes that are a hidden stem
Beneath the beauty over them.

The hours lift their shadow-form, are warm.

Why do you still stand mute and white?
The day is passed, but there is night.

Turn your head, give me your lips—
The darkness slips! The darkness slips.

We could make it hushed and still.
If you will
We could hear, close to the ground
Life—the one authentic sound.

The hours, as a startled faun, are gone.

LITTLE THINGS

Little things I'll give to you—
Till your fingers learn to press
Gently
On a loveliness;

Little things and new—
Till your fingers learn to hold
Love that's fragile,
Love that's old.

DAILY PRAYER

And at last when I go
Will it be so?
Shall I find you behind
The rude platitude of death?

I kneel within the certainty
That you are near to me:
Each day I pray
That I may follow through
To you.
Each day I pray.

EIGHT MONTHS OLD

Eight months ago, when you were born,
You were a tiny thing and light.
I was afraid to touch you much,
Or hold you very tight.

And then quite suddenly you grew
Fast as a little willow sprig.
And I was reassured—within
My arms you felt so big.

But oh, today you laughed at me,
And stood alone and did not fall.
And oh, I am afraid again—
You are so small—so small!

A GOD FOR YOU

I am making songs for you,
Soon you will be asking me
With your solemn baby stare—
Soon I'll have to answer you
When you ask me, "What is God?"

God is where you want to go
When we reach the river's head
Where the branches are too low—
And we go home instead.

God is everything that you
Have not done and want to do.

God is all those shiny bright
Stories that I say I'll keep
To tell to you another night—
If you will go to sleep.

God is every lovely word
You want to hear and haven't heard.

And if you should need a place,
After searching everywhere,
To hide a secret, or your face—
You could hide it there.

God is much the safest place
To hide a secret—or your face.

TO MY CHILDREN

Believe! And if, while standing under a shower
That bursts in April from a yellow sun,
And roughens softened earth, and leaves a flower;

And if, while breathing rain and petals growing,
It is enough that petals have begun—
Then let it be enough, when skies are snowing,

When frost has come: like a perennial thing
Keep the faith sheltered in yourself till spring.

Believe! And if, like many a girl before,
Love is your hidden faith, then let it be!
The immaterial man whom you adore,

Who is no higher than a man is high,
Who walks along, or stands indefinitely,
Be all the earth to you, be all the sky,

Be foreign countries you were dreaming of:
If love should be your faith, let it be love!

Or if, with shimmering streets of sun outside,
A well-worn door solicits and you falter,
Stepping at last through pillars that divide

Shadow and coolness; if, like those who came
Bearing tall candles to an ancient altar,
You kneel on flagstones, and you cry God's name

As they did—when you journey out afar
Cry it as well, and kneel where candles are.

But if you find, wherever you make your search,
No loss of love enough for you to grieve in,
No yellow flowers and no ivied church

Enough to stir your faith, let it be stirred
If only by some twaddle you believe in,
If only by a dream, a transient word,

A hopelessness you have some hope in still—
However it can be, or however it will.

Muriel Stuart

MAN AND HIS MAKERS

I am one of the wind's stories,
I am a poem of the rain—
A memory of the high moon's glories,
A hint the sunset had of pain.

They dreamed me, as they dreamed all other.
Hawthorn and I, I and the grass,

With sister shade and phantom brother,
Across their slumber glide and pass.

Twilight is in my blood, my being
Mingles with trees and ferns and stones,
Thunder and stars my lips are freeing,
And there is sea-rack in my bones.

Those that have dreamed me shall outwake me,
Though I go hence with flowers and weeds;
I am no more to those who make me
Than other falling fruit and seeds.

And though I love them, mourn to leave them,—
Sea, earth and sunset, stars and streams,
My tears, my passing do not grieve them . . .
Others dreams have they, other dreams.

THE SEED–SHOP

Here in a quiet and dusty room they lie,
Faded as crumbled stone and shifting sand,
Forlorn as ashes, shrivelled, scentless, dry—
Meadows and gardens running through my hand.

Dead that shall quicken at the trump of spring,
Sleepers to stir beneath June's morning kiss;
Though bees pass over, unremembering,
And no bird seeks here bowers that were his.

In this brown husk a dale of hawthorn dreams;
A cedar in this narrow cell is thrust
That will drink deeply of a century's streams;
These lilies shall make summer on my dust.

Here in their safe and simple house of death,
Sealed in their shells, a million roses leap;
Here I can blow a garden with my breath,
And in my hand a forest lies asleep.

IN THE ORCHARD

"I thought you loved me." "No, it was only fun."
"When we stood there, closer than all?" . . . "Well, the har-
      vest moon
Was shining and queer in your hair, and it turned my head."
"That made you?" "Yes." "Just the moon and the light it
      made
Under the tree?" "Well, your mouth too . . ." "Yes, my
      mouth?"
"And the quiet there that sang like the drum in the booth.
You shouldn't have danced like that." "Like what?" "So
      close,
With your head turned up, and the flower in your hair, a
      rose
That smelt all warm." "I loved you. I thought you knew
I wouldn't have danced like that with any but you."
"I didn't know. I thought you knew it was fun."
"I thought it was love you meant." "Well, it's done." "Yes,
      it's done.
I've seen boys stone a blackbird, and watched them drown
A kitten . . . it clawed at the reeds, and they pushed it down
Into the pool while it screamed. Is that fun, too?"
"Well, boys are like that . . . your brothers . . ." "Yes, I
      know.
But you, so lovely and strong! Not you! Not you!"
"They don't understand it's cruel. It's only a game."
"And are girls fun, too?" "No, still in a way it's the same.
It's queer and lovely to have a girl . . ." "Go on."
"It makes you mad for a bit to feel she's your own,
And you laugh and kiss her, and maybe you give her a ring;
But it's only in fun." "But I gave you everything."
"Well, you shouldn't have done it—you know what a fellow
      thinks
When a girl does that." "Yes, he talks of her over his
      drinks
And calls her a—" "Stop that, now—I thought you knew."
"But it wasn't with anyone else—it was only you."
"How did I know? I thought you wanted it too—

I thought you were like the rest. Well, what's to be done?"
"To be done?" "Is it all right?" "Yes." "Sure?" "Yes, but
    why?"
"I don't know—I thought you were going to cry—
You said you had something to tell me." "Yes, I know.
It wasn't anything really . . . I think I'll go."
"Yes, it's late. There's thunder about, a drop of rain
Fell on my hand in the dark. I'll see you again
At the dance next week. You're sure that everything's right?'
"Yes." "Well, I'll be going." "Kiss me . . .", "Good night
   . . ." "Good night."

Ajan Syrian

THE SYRIAN LOVER IN EXILE REMEMBERS
THEE, LIGHT OF MY LAND

Rose and amber was the sunset on the river,
Red-rose the hills about Bingariz.
High upon their brows, the black tree-branches
Spread wide across the turquoise sky.
I saw the parrots fly—
A cloud of rising green from the long green grasses,
A mist of gold and green winging fast
Into the gray shadow-silence of the tamarisks.
Pearl-white and wild was the flood below the ford.
I ran down the long hot road to thy door;
Thy door shone—a white flower in the dusk lingering to close.
The stars rose and stood above thy casement.
I cast my cloak and climbed to thee,
To thee, Makhir Subatu!

.   .   .   .

Naked she stood and glistening like the stars over her—
Her hair trailed about her like clouds about the moon—
Naked as the soul seeking love,
As the soul that waits for death.
White with benediction, pendulous, unfolding from the dark

As the crystal sky of morning, she waited,
And leaned her light above the earth of my desire.
Like a world that spins from the hand of Infinity,
Up from the night I leaped—
To thee, Makhir Subatu!

. . . .

Pearl-bright and wild, a flood without a ford,
The River of Love flowed on.
Her eyes were gleaming sails in a storm,
Dipping, swooning, beckoning.
The dawn came and trampled over her;
Gay-arched and wide, the sanctuary of light descended.
It was the altar where I lay;
And I lifted my face at last, praying.
I saw the first glow fall about her,
Like marble pillars coming forth from the shadow.
I raised my hands, thanking the gods
That in love I had grown so tall
I could touch the two lamps in heaven,
The sun and moon hanging in the low heaven beneath her face.
How great through love had I grown
To breathe my flame into the two lamps of heaven!

O eyes of the eagle and the dove,
Eyes red-starred and white-starred,
Eyes that have too much seen, too much confessed,
Close, close, beneath my kisses!
Tell me no more, demand me no more—it is day.
I see the gold-green rain of parrot-wings
Sparkling athwart the gray and rose-gold morning.
I go from thy closed door down the long lone road
To the ricefields beyond the river,
Beyond the river that has a ford.

. . . .

I came to thee with hope, with desire. I have them no longer.
Sleep, sleep; I am locked in thee.

. . . .

Thus the exile lover remembers thee, Makhir Subatu!

Genevieve Taggard

FOR EAGER LOVERS

I understand what you were running for,
Slim naked boy, and why from far inland
You came between dark hills. I know the roar
The sea makes in some ears. I understand.

I understand why you were running now,
And how you heard the sea resound, and how
You leaped and left your valley for the long
Brown road. I understand the song

You chanted with your running, with your feet
Marking the measure of your high heart's beat.
Now you are broken. Seeing your wide brow,
I see your dreams. I understand you now.

Since I have run like you, I understand
The throat's long wish, the breath that comes so quick,
The heart's light leap, the heels that drag so sick,
And warped heat wrinkles, lengthening the sand. . . .

Now you are broken. Seeing your wide brow
I see your dreams, understanding now
The cry, the certainty, wide arms—and then
The way rude ocean rises and descends. . . .

I saw you stretched and wounded where tide ends.
I do not want to walk that way again.

THE ENAMEL GIRL

Fearful of beauty, I always went
Timidly indifferent;

Dainty, hesitant, taking in
Just what was tiniest and thin;

Careful not to care
For burning beauty in blue air;

Wanting what my hand could touch—
That not too much;

Looking not to left nor right
On a honey-silent night;

Fond of arts and trinkets, if,
Imperishable and stiff,

They never played me false, nor fell
Into fine dust. They lasted well.

They lasted till you came, and then
When you went sufficed again.

But for you, they had been quite
All I needed for my sight.

You faded. I never knew
How to unfold as flowers do,

Or how to nourish anything
To make it grow. I wound a wing

With one caress, with one kiss
Break most fragile ecstasies. . . .

Now terror touches me when I
Dream I am touching a butterfly.

THE QUIET WOMAN

I will defy you down until my death
With cold body, indrawn breath;
Terrible and cruel I will move with you
Like a surly tiger. If you knew
Why I am shaken, if fond you could see
All the caged arrogance in me,
You would not lean so boyishly, so bold,
To kiss my body, quivering and cold.

SEA–CHANGE

You are no more, but sunken in a sea
Sheer into dream ten thousand leagues you fell;
And now you lie green-golden, while a bell
Swings with the tide, my heart. And all is well
Till I look down, and, wavering, the spell—
Your loveliness—returns. There in the sea,
Where you lie amber-pale and coral-cool,
You are most loved, most lost, most beautiful.

TROPICAL GIRL TO HER GARDEN

Withhold your breath!
Heavy in noon and sleepy as slow death,
Garden of sweets and sours,
The cluster of my body hangs
Odorous with flowers:
Stamen serpent fangs,
Sultry, in showers.

Withhold your hand!
My boughs are bent with gold, my face is fanned
With wings of bees that, thirsting, curve and kiss.
Under green leaves green tendrils coil and hiss;
Gloom-laden branches bear me down too much.
My yellow fruit will fall without a touch
From hanging long in sultriness like this.

Rabindranath Tagore

FROM *GITANJALI*

I

Thou hast made me known to friends whom I knew not. Thou
hast given me seats in homes not my own. Thou hast
brought the distant near and made a brother of the stranger.

I am uneasy at heart when I have to leave my accustomed shelter; I forgot that there abides the old in the new, and that there also thou abidest.

Through birth and death, in this world or in others, wherever thou leadest me it is thou, the same, the one companion of my endless life who ever linkest my heart with bonds of joy to the unfamiliar. When one knows thee, then alien there is none, then no door is shut. Oh, grant me my prayer that I may never lose the bliss of the touch of the One in the play of the many.

II

No more noisy, loud words from me, such is my master's will. Henceforth I deal in whispers. The speech of my heart will be carried on in murmurings of a song.

Men hasten to the King's market. All the buyers and sellers are there. But I have my untimely leave in the middle of the day, in the thick of work.

Let then the flowers come out in my garden, though it is not their time, and let the midday bees strike up their lazy hum.

Full many an hour have I spent in the strife of the good and the evil, but now it is the pleasure of my playmate of the empty days to draw my heart on to him, and I know not why is this sudden call to what useless inconsequence!

III

On the day when the lotus bloomed, alas, my mind was straying, and I knew it not. My basket was empty and the flower remained unheeded.

Only now and again a sadness fell upon me, and I started up from my dream and felt a sweet trace of a strange smell in the south wind.

That vague fragrance made my heart ache with longing, and it seemed to me that it was the eager breath of the summer seeking for its completion.

I knew not then that it was so near, that it was mine, and this perfect sweetness had blossomed in the depth of my own heart.

IV

By all means they try to hold me secure who love me in this world. But it is otherwise with thy love, which is greater than theirs, and thou keepest me free. Lest I forget them they never venture to leave me alone. But day passes by after day and thou art not seen.

If I call not thee in my prayers, if I keep not thee in my heart— thy love for me still waits for my love.

V

I was not aware of the moment when I first crossed the threshold of this life. What was the power that made me open out into this vast mystery like a bud in the forest at midnight? When in the morning I looked upon the light I felt in a moment that I was no stranger in this world, that the inscrutable without name and form had taken me in its arms in the form of my own mother. Even so, in death the same unknown will appear as ever known to me. And because I love this life, I know I shall love death as well. The child cries out when from the right breast the mother takes it away, to find in the very next moment its consolation in the left one.

VI

Thou art the sky and thou art the nest as well. O thou beautiful, there in the nest it is thy love that encloses the soul with colors and sounds and odors. There comes the morning, with the golden basket in her right hand, bearing the wreath of beauty, silently to crown the earth. And there comes the evening over the lonely meadows deserted by herds, through trackless paths, carrying cool draughts of peace in her golden pitcher from the western ocean of rest.

But there, where spreads the infinite sky for the soul to take her flight in, reigns the stainless white radiance. There is no day nor night, nor form nor color, and never never a word.

FROM *THE GARDENER*

I

Over the green and yellow rice-fields sweep the shadows of the
autumn clouds, followed by the swift-chasing sun.

The bees forget to sip their honey—drunken with the light they
foolishly hum and hover; and the ducks in the sandy riverbank clamor in joy for mere nothing.

None shall go back home, brothers, this morning, none shall go
to work.

We will take the blue sky by storm and plunder the space as we
run.

Laughters fly floating in the air like foams in the flood.

Brothers, we shall squander our morning in futile songs.

II

Keep me fully glad with nothing. Only take my hand in your
hand.

In the gloom of the deepening night take up my heart and play
with it as you list. Bind me close to you with nothing.

I will spread myself out at your feet and lie still. Under this
clouded sky I will meet silence with silence. I will become
one with the night, clasping the earth in my breast.

Make my life glad with nothing.

The rains sweep the sky from end to end. Jasmines in the wet
untamable wind revel in their own perfume. The cloud-
hidden stars thrill in secret. Let me fill to the full of my
heart with nothing but my own depth of joy.

III

My soul is alight with your infinitude of stars. Your world has
broken upon me like a flood. The flowers of your garden
blossom in my body. The joy of life that is everywhere
burns like an incense in my heart. And the breath of all
things plays on my life as on a pipe of reeds.

IV

Leave off your works, bride. Listen, the guest has come.

Do you hear, he is gently shaking the fastening chain of the door?

Let not your anklets be loud, and your steps be too hurried to
meet him.
Leave off your works, bride; the guest has come, in the evening.
No, it is not the wind, bride. Do not be frightened.
It is the full-moon night of April, shadows are pale in the court-
yard, the sky overhead is bright.
Draw your veil over your face if you must, take the lamp from
your room if you fear.
No, it is not the wind, bride; do not be frightened.

Have no word with him if you are shy, stand aside by the door
when you meet him.
If he asks you questions, lower your eyes in silence if you wish.
Do not let your bracelets jingle, when, lamp in hand, you lead
him in.
Have no word with him if you are shy.

Have you not finished your works yet, bride? Listen, the guest
has come.
Have you not lit the lamp in the cowshed?
Have you not got ready the offering basket for the evening service?
Have you not put the auspicious red mark at the parting of your
hair, and done your toilet for the night?
O bride, do you hear, the guest has come?
Have you not finished your works yet?

V

Come as you are, tarry not over your toilet.
If your braiding has come loose, if the parting of your hair be
not straight, if the ribbons of your bodice be not fastened,
do not mind.
Come as you are, tarry not over your toilet.

Come with quick steps over the grass.
If your feet are pale with the dew, if your anklets slacken, if
pearls drop out of your chain, do not mind.
Come with quick steps over the grass.

Do you see the clouds wrapping the sky?
Flocks of cranes fly up from the further riverbank, and fitful
gusts of wind rush over the heath.

The anxious cattle run to their stalls in the village.
Do you see the clouds wrapping the sky?

In vain you light your toilet lamp; it flickers and goes out in
    the wind.
Surely, who would know that with lamp-black your eyelids are
    not touched? For your eyes are darker than rain clouds.
In vain you light your toilet lamp; it goes out.

Come as you are, tarry not over your toilet.
If the wreath is not woven, who cares? If the wrist-chain has
    not been tied, leave it by.
The sky is overcast with clouds; it is late.
Come as you are, tarry not over your toilet.

VI

Lest I should know you too easily, you play with me.
You blind me with flashes of laughter to hide your tears.
I know, I know your art;
You never say the word you would.

Lest I should prize you not, you elude me in a thousand ways.
Lest I should mix you with the crowd, you stand aside.
I know, I know your art;
Your never walk the path you would.

Your claim is more than others; that is why you are silent.
With a playful carelessness you avoid my gifts.
I know, I know your art;
You never accept what you would.

VII

Amidst the rush and roar of life, O Beauty carved in stone, you
    stand mute and still, alone and aloof.
Great Time sits enamoured at your feet and repeats to you:
"Speak, speak to me, my love; speak, my mute bride!"
But your speech is shut up in stone, O you immovably fair!

VIII

Tell me if this is all true, my lover—tell me if it is true?
When the eyes of me flash their lightning on you,
    dark clouds in your breast make stormy answer;

Is it then true
 that the dew-drops fall from the night when I am seen,
 and the morning light is glad when it wraps my body?

Is it true, is it true, that your love
 travelled alone through ages and worlds in search of me?
 that when you found me at last, your age-long desire
 found utter peace in my gentle speech, and my eyes and
  lips and flowing hair?

Is it then true
 that the mystery of the Infinite is written on this little brow
  of mine?
Tell me, my lover, if all this is true?

IX

With a glance of your eyes you could plunder all the wealth of
 songs struck from poets' harps, fair woman!
But for their praises you have no ear; therefore do I come to
 praise you.
You could humble at your feet the proudest heads of all the
 world;
But it is your loved ones, unknown to fame, whom you choose
 to worship; therefore I worship you.
Your perfect arms would add glory to kingly splendor with their
 touch;
But you use them to sweep away the dust, and to make clean
 your humble home; therefore I am filled with awe.

Allen Tate

ODE TO THE CONFEDERATE DEAD

Row after row with strict impunity
The headstones yield their names to the element,
The wind whirs without recollection;
In the riven troughs the splayed leaves
Pile up, of nature the casual sacrament
To the seasonal eternity of death,

Then driven by the fierce scrutiny
Of heaven to their business in the vast breath,
They sough the rumor of mortality.

Autumn is desolation in the plot
Of a thousand acres, where these memories grow
From the inexhaustible bodies that are not
Dead, but feed the grass row after rich row:
Remember now the autumns that have gone—
Ambitious November with the humors of the year,
With a particular zeal for every slab,
Staining the uncomfortable angels that rot
On the slabs, a wing chipped here, an arm there:
The brute curiosity of an angel's stare
Turns you like them to stone,
Transforms the heaving air,
Till plunged to a heavier world below
You shift your sea-space blindly,
Heaving, turning like the blind crab.

    Dazed by the wind, only the wind
    The leaves flying, plunge

You know who have waited by the wall
The twilit certainty of an animal;
Those midnight restitutions of the blood
You know—the immitigable pines, the smoky frieze
Of the sky, the sudden call; you know the rage—
The cold pool left by the mounting flood—
The rage of Zeno and Parmenides.
You who have waited for the angry resolution
Of those desires that should be yours tomorrow,
You know the unimportant shrift of death
And praise the vision
And praise the arrogant circumstance
Of those who fall
Rank upon rank, hurried beyond decision—
Here by the sagging gate, stopped by the wall.

    Seeing, seeing only the leaves
    Flying, plunge and expire

Turn your eyes to the immoderate past,
Turn to the inscrutable infantry rising
Demons out of the earth—they will not last.
Stonewall, Stonewall—and the sunken fields of hemp—
Shiloh, Antietam, Malvern Hill, Bull Run.
Lost in that orient of the thick and fast
You will curse the setting sun.

Cursing only the leaves crying
Like an old man in a storm

You hear the shout—the crazy hemlocks point
With troubled fingers to the silence which
Smothers you, a mummy, in time.   The hound bitch
Toothless and dying, in a musty cellar
Hears the wind only.

Now that the salt of their blood
Stiffens the saltier oblivion of the sea,
Seals the malignant purity of the flood,
What shall we, who count our days and bow
Our heads with a commemorial woe,
In the ribboned coats of grim felicity,
What shall we say of the bones, unclean—
Their verdurous anonymity will grow—
The ragged arms, the ragged heads and eyes
Lost in these acres of the insane green?
The grey lean spiders come; they come and go;
In a tangle of willows without light
The singular screech-owl's bright
Invisible lyric seeds the mind
To the furious murmur of their chivalry.

We shall say only, the leaves
Flying, plunge and expire

We shall say only, the leaves whispering
In the improbable mist of nightfall
That flies on multiple wing:
Night is the beginning and the end,

And in between the ends of distraction
Waits mute speculation, the patient curse
That stones the eyes, or like the jaguar leaps
For his own image in a jungle pool, his victim.

What shall we say who have knowledge
Carried to the heart? Shall we take the act
To the grave? Shall we, more hopeful, set up the grave
In the house? The ravenous grave?

                              Leave now
The turnstile and the old stone wall:
The gentle serpent, green in the mulberry bush,
Riots with his tongue through the hush—
Sentinel of the grave who counts us all!

Sara Teasdale

LEAVES

One by one, like leaves from a tree,
All my faiths have forsaken me;
But the stars above my head
Burn in white and delicate red,
And beneath my feet the earth
Brings the sturdy grass to birth.
I who was content to be
But a silken-singing tree,
But a rustle of delight
In the wistful heart of night,
I have lost the leaves that knew
Touch of rain and weight of dew.
Blinded by a leafy crown
I looked neither up nor down—
But the little leaves that die
Have left me room to see the sky;
Now for the first time I know
Stars above and earth below.

MORNING

I went out on an April morning
  All alone, for my heart was high.
I was a child of the shining meadow,
  I was a sister of the sky.

There in the windy flood of morning
  Longing lifted its weight from me,
Lost as a sob in the midst of cheering,
  Swept as a sea-bird out to sea.

THE FLIGHT

Look back with longing eyes and know that I will follow,
Lift me up in your love as a light wind lifts a swallow,
Let our flight be far in sun or windy rain—
But what if I heard my first love calling me again?

Hold me on your heart as the brave sea holds the foam,
Take me far away to the hills that hide your home;
Peace shall thatch the roof and love shall latch the door—
But what if I heard my first love calling me once more?

OVER THE ROOFS

I said, "I have shut my heart,
  As one shuts an open door,
That Love may starve therein
  And trouble me no more."

But over the roofs there came
  The wet new wind of May,
And a tune blew up from the curb
  Where the street-pianos play.

My room was white with the sun
  And Love cried out in me,
"I am strong, I will break your heart
  Unless you set me free."

DEBT

What do I owe to you
    Who loved me deep and long?
You never gave my spirit wings
    Or gave my heart a song.

But oh, to him I loved
    Who loved me not at all,
I owe the little gate
    That led through heaven's wall.

THE ANSWER

When I go back to earth
And all my joyous body
Puts off the red and white
That once had been so proud,
If men should pass above
With false and feeble pity,
My dust will find a voice
To answer them aloud:

"Be still, I am content,
Take back your poor compassion!—
Joy was a flame in me
Too steady to destroy.
Lithe as a bending reed
Loving the storm that sways her,
I found more joy in sorrow
Than you could find in joy."

BLUE SQUILLS

How many million Aprils came
    Before I ever knew
How white a cherry bough could be,
    A bed of squills how blue—

And many a dancing April,
　　When life is done with me,
Will lift the blue flame of the flower
　　And the white flame of the tree.

Oh, burn me with your beauty then—
　　Oh, hurt me, tree and flower,
Lest in the end death try to take
　　Even this glistening hour.

O shaken flowers, O shimmering trees,
　　O sunlit white and blue,
Wound me, that I through endless sleep
　　May bear the scar of you!

WHAT DO I CARE?

What do I care, in the dreams and the languor of spring,
　　That my songs do not show me at all?
For they are a fragrance, and I am a flint and a fire;
　　I am an answer, they are only a call.

But what do I care—for love will be over so soon—
　　Let my heart have its say and my mind stand idly by,
For my mind is proud, and strong enough to be silent—
　　It is my heart that makes my songs, not I.

ON THE DUNES

If there is any life when death is over,
　　These tawny beaches will know much of me;
I shall come back, as constant and as changeful
　　As the unchanging many-colored sea.

If life was small, if it has made me scornful,
　　Forgive me—I shall straighten like a flame
In the great calm of death, and if you want me
　　Stand on the seaward dunes and call my name.

THERE WILL COME SOFT RAINS

War Time

There will come soft rains and the smell of the ground,
And swallows circling with their shimmering sound;

And frogs in the pools singing at night,
And wild plum-trees in tremulous white.

Robins will wear their feathery fire
Whistling their whims on a low fence-wire;

And not one will know of the war, not one
Will care at last when it is done.

Not one would mind, neither bird nor tree,
If mankind perished utterly;

And Spring herself, when she woke at dawn,
Would scarcely know that we were gone.

MY HEART IS HEAVY

My heart is heavy with many a song,
  Like ripe fruit bearing down the tree;
And I can never give you one—
  My songs do not belong to me.

Yet in the evening, in the dusk
  When moths go to and fro,
In the gray hour if the fruit has fallen,
  Take it—no one will know.

IT IS NOT A WORD

It is not a word spoken—
  Few words are said,
Nor even a look of the eyes,
  Nor a bend of the head;

But only a hush of the heart
That has too much to keep,
Only memories waking
That sleep so light a sleep.

LET IT BE FORGOTTEN

Let it be forgotten, as a flower is forgotten,
  Forgotten as a fire that once was singing gold.
Let it be forgotten for ever and ever—
  Time is a kind friend, he will make us old.

If anyone asks, say it was forgotten
  Long and long ago—
As a flower, as a fire, as a hushed footfall
  In a long forgotten snow.

STARS

Alone in the night
  On a dark hill
With pines around me
  Spicy and still,

And a heaven full of stars
  Over my head,
White and topaz
  And misty red—

Myriads with beating
  Hearts of fire
That æons
  Cannot vex or tire—

Up the dome of heaven
  Like a great hill,
I watch them marching
  Stately and still;

And I know that I
Am honored to be
Witness
Of so much majesty.

EFFIGY OF A NUN

Sixteenth Century

Infinite gentleness, infinite irony
  Are in this face with fast-sealed eyes,
And round this mouth that learned in loneliness
  How useless their wisdom is to the wise.

In her nun's habit carved, patiently, lovingly,
  By one who knew the ways of womankind,
This woman's face still keeps, in its cold wistful calm,
  All of the subtle pride of her mind.

These long patrician hands, clasping the crucifix,
  Show she had weighed the world, her will was set;
These pale curved lips of hers, holding their hidden smile,
  Once having made their choice, knew no regret.

She was of those who hoard their own thoughts carefully,
  Feeling them far too dear to give away,
Content to look at life with the high, insolent
  Air of an audience watching a play.

If she was curious, if she was passionate,
  She must have told herself that love was great,
But that the lacking it might be as great a thing
  If she held fast to it, challenging fate.

She who so loved herself and her own warring thoughts,
  Watching their humorous, tragic rebound,
In her thick habit's fold, sleeping, sleeping,
  Is she amused at dreams she has found?

Infinite tenderness, infinite irony
  Are hidden forever in her closed eyes,
Who must have learned too well in her long loneliness
  How empty wisdom is, even to the wise.

ARCTURUS IN AUTUMN

When, in the gold October dusk, I saw you near to setting,
    Arcturus, bringer of spring,
Lord of the summer nights, leaving us now in autumn,
    Having no pity on our withering;

Oh then I knew at last that my own autumn was upon me
    I felt it in my blood,
Restless as dwindling streams that still remember
    The music of their flood.

There in the thickening dark a wind-bent tree above me
    Loosed its last leaves in flight—
I saw you sink and vanish, pitiless Arcturus,
    You will not stay to share our lengthening night.

ON THE SUSSEX DOWNS

Over the downs there were birds flying,
    Far off glittered the sea,
And toward the north the weald of Sussex
    Lay like a kingdom under me.

I was happier than the larks
    That nest on the downs and sing to the sky,
Over the downs the birds flying
    Were not so happy as I.

It was not you, though you were near,
    Though you were good to hear and see,
It was not earth, it was not heaven,
    It was myself that sang in me.

BEAUTIFUL PROUD SEA

Careless forever, beautiful proud sea,
    You laugh in happy thunder all alone,
You fold upon yourself, you dance your dance
    Impartially on drift-weed, sand or stone.

You make us believe that we can outlive death,
　You make us, for an instant, for your sake,
Burn, like stretched silver of a wave,
　Not breaking, but about to break.

SWALLOW FLIGHT

I love my hour of wind and light,
　I love men's faces and their eyes;
I love my spirit's veering flight,
　Like swallows under evening skies.

Edward Thomas

THERE'S NOTHING LIKE THE SUN

There's nothing like the sun as the year dies;
Kind as it can be, this world being made so,
To stones and men and beasts and birds and flies—
To all things that it touches except snow,
Whether on mountain side or street or town.
The south wall warms me: November has begun,
Yet never shone the sun as fair as now
While the sweet last-left damsons from the bough
With spangles of the morning's storm drop down
Because the starling shakes it, whistling what
Once swallows sang. But I have not forgot
That there is nothing, too, like March's sun,
Like April's, or July's, or June's, or May's,
Or January's or February's—great days;
And August, September, October, and December
Have equal days, all different from November.
No day of any month but I have said—
Or, if I could live long enough, should say—
"There's nothing like the sun that shines to-day."
There's nothing like the sun till we are dead.

THE WORD

There are so many things I have forgot,
That once were much to me, or that were not—
All lost, as is a childless woman's child
And its child's children, in the undefiled
Abyss of what can never be again.
I have forgot, too, names of the mighty men
That fought and lost or won in the old wars;
Of kings and fiends and gods, and most of the stars.
Some things I have forgot that I forget.
But lesser things there are, remembered yet,
Than all the others. One name that I have not—
Though 'tis an empty thingless name—forgot
Never can die because spring after spring
Some thrushes learn to say it as they sing.
There is always one at midday saying it clear
And tart—the name, only the name I hear.
While perhaps I am thinking of the elder scent
That is like food; or while I am content
With the wild-rose scent that is like memory,
This name suddenly is cried out to me
From somewhere in the bushes by a bird
Over and over again, a pure thrush word.

SOWING

It was a perfect day
For sowing; just
As sweet and dry was the ground
As tobacco-dust.

I tasted deep the hour
Between the far
Owl's chuckling first soft cry
And the first star.

A long stretched hour it was;
Nothing undone

Remained; the early seeds
All safely sown.

And now, hark at the rain,
Windless and light,
Half a kiss, half a tear,
Saying good-night.

ADLESTROP

Yes, I remember Adlestrop—
The name—because one afternoon
Of heat the express-train drew up there
Unwontedly. It was late June.

The steam hissed. Someone cleared his throat.
No one left and no one came
On the bare platform. What I saw
Was Adlestrop—only the name—

And willows, willow-herb, and grass,
And meadowsweet, and haycocks dry;
No whit less still and lonely fair
Than the high cloudlets in the sky.

And for that minute a blackbird sang
Close by, and round him, mistier,
Farther and farther, all the birds
Of Oxfordshire and Gloucestershire.

THE MANOR FARM

The rock-like mud unfroze a little, and rills
Ran and sparkled down each side of the road
Under the catkins wagging in the hedge.
But earth would have her sleep out, spite of the sun;
Nor did I value that thin gliding beam
More than a pretty February thing
Till I came down to the old Manor Farm,

And church and yew-tree opposite, in age
Its equals and in size. The church and yew
And farmhouse slept in a Sunday silentness.
The air raised not a straw. The steep farm roof,
With tiles duskily glowing, entertained
The mid-day sun; and up and down the roof
White pigeons nestled. There was no sound but one.
Three cart-horses were looking over a gate
Drowsily through their forelocks, swishing their tails
Against a fly, a solitary fly.
The winter's cheek flushed as if he had drained
Spring, summer, and autumn at a draught
And smiled quietly. But 'twas not winter—
Rather a season of bliss unchangeable,
Awakened from farm and church where it had lain
Safe under tile and thatch for ages since
This England, Old already; was called Merry.

BEAUTY

What does it mean? Tired, angry, and ill at ease,
No man, woman, or child alive could please
Me now. And yet I almost dare to laugh
Because I sit and frame an epitaph—
"Here lies all that no one loved of him
And that loved no one." Then in a trice that whim
Has wearied. But, though I am like a river
At fall of evening when it seems that never
Has the sun lighted it or warmed it, while
Cross breezes cut the surface to a file,
This heart, some fraction of me, happily
Floats through the window even now to a tree
Down in the misting, dim-lit, quiet vale;
Not like a pewit that returns to wail
For something it has lost, but like a dove
That slants unswerving to its home and love.
There I find my rest, and through the dusk air
Flies what yet lives in me. Beauty is there.

Eunice Tietjens

THE BACCHANTE TO HER BABE

Scherzo

Come, sprite, and dance! The sun is up,
The wind runs laughing down the sky
That brims with morning like a cup.
Sprite, we must race him,
We must chase him—
You and I!
And skim across the fuzzy heather—
You and joy and I together
Whirling by!

You merry little roll of fat!—
Made warm to kiss, and smooth to pat,
And round to toy with, like a cub;
To put one's nozzle in and rub
And breathe you in like breath of kine,
Like juice of vine,
That sets my morning heart a-tingling,
Dancing, jingling,
All the glad abandon mingling
Of wind and wine!

Sprite, you are love, and you are joy,
A happiness, a dream, a toy,
A god to laugh with,
Love to chaff with,
The sun come down in tangled gold,
The moon to kiss, and spring to hold.

There was a time once, long ago,
Long—oh, long since . . . I scarcely know.
Almost I had forgot . . .
There was a time when you were not,
You merry sprite, save as a strain,
The strange dull pain

607

Of green buds swelling
In warm straight dwelling
That must burst to the April rain.
A little heavy I was then,
And dull—and glad to rest. And when
The travail came
In searing flame . . .
But, sprite, that was so long ago!—
A century!—I scarcely know.
Almost I had forgot
When you were not.

So, little sprite, come dance with me!
The sun is up, the wind is free!
Come now and trip it,
Romp and skip it,
Earth is young and so are we.
Sprite, you and I will dance together
On the heather;
Glad with all the procreant earth,
With all the fruitage of the trees,
And golden pollen on the breeze,
With plants that bring the grain to birth,
With beast and bird
Feathered and furred,
With youth and hope and life and love,
And joy thereof—
While we are part of all, we two—
For my glad burgeoning in you!

So, merry little roll of fat,
Made warm to kiss and smooth to pat
And round to toy with, like a cub,
To put one's nozzle in and rub,
My god to laugh with,
Love to chaff with,
Come and dance beneath the sky,
You and I!
Look out with those round wondering eyes,
And squirm, and gurgle—and grow wise!

THE STEAM SHOVEL

Beneath my window in a city street
A monster lairs, a creature huge and grim
And only half believed: the strength of him—
Steel-strung and fit to meet
The strength of earth—
Is mighty as men's dreams that conquer force.
Steam belches from him. He is the new birth
Of old Behemoth, late-sprung from the source
Whence Grendel sprang, and all the monster clan
Dead for an age, now born again of man.

The iron head,
Set on a monstrous jointed neck,
Glides here and there, lifts, settles on the red
Moist floor, with nose dropped in the dirt, at beck
Of some incredible control.
He snorts, and pauses couchant for a space;
Then slowly lifts, and tears the gaping hole
Yet deeper in earth's flank. A sudden race
Of loosened earth and pebbles trickles there
Like blood-drops in a wound.
But he, the monster, swings his load around—
Weightless it seems as air.
His mammoth jaw
Drops widely open with a rasping sound,
And all the red earth vomits from his maw.

O thwarted monster, born at man's decree,
A lap-dog dragon, eating from his hand
And doomed to fetch and carry at command,
Have you no longing ever to be free?
In warm electric days to run a-muck,
Ranging like some mad dinosaur,
Your fiery heart at war
With this strange world, the city's restless ruck,
Where all drab things that toil, save you alone,
Have life;
And you the semblance only, and the strife?

Do you not yearn to rip the roots of stone
Of these great piles men build,
And hurl them down with shriek of shattered steel,
Scorning your own sure doom, so you may feel,
You too, the lust with which your fathers killed?
Or is your soul in very deed so tame,
The blood of Grendel watered to a gruel,
That you are well content
With heart of flame
Thus placidly to chew your cud of fuel
And toil in peace for man's aggrandizement?

Poor helpless creature of a half-grown god,
Blind of yourself and impotent!
At night,
When your forerunners, sprung from quicker sod,
Would range through primal woods, hot on the scent,
Or wake the stars with amorous delight,
You stand, a soiled unwieldy mass of steel,
Black in the arc-light, modern as your name,
Dead and unsouled and trite;
Till I must feel
A quick creator's pity for your shame:
That man, who made you and who gave so much,
Yet cannot give the last transforming touch;
That with the work he cannot give the wage—
For day, no joy of night,
For toil, no ecstasy of primal rage.

THE GREAT MAN

I cannot always feel his greatness.
Sometimes he walks beside me, step by step,
And paces slowly in the ways—
The simple wingless ways
That my thoughts tread. He gossips with me then,
And finds it good;
Not as an eagle might, his great wings folded, be content
To walk a little, knowing it his choice,

But as a simple man,
My friend.
And I forget.

Then suddenly a call floats down
From the clear airy spaces,
The great keen lonely heights of being.
And he who was my comrade hears the call
And rises from my side, and soars,
Deep-chanting, to the heights.
Then I remember.
And my upward gaze goes with him, and I see
Far off against the sky
The glint of golden sunlight on his wings.

COMPLETION

My heart has fed today.
My heart, like hind at play,
Has grazed in fields of love, and washed in streams
Of quick imperishable dreams.

In moth-white beauty shimmering,
Lovely as birches in the moon glimmering,
From coigns of sleep my eyes
Saw dawn and love arise.

And like a bird at rest,
Steady in a swinging nest,
My heart at peace lay gloriously
While winds of ecstasy
Beat round me and above.

I am fulfilled of love.

ON THE HEIGHT

The foothills called us, green and sweet;
    We dallied, but we might not stay,
And all day long we set our feet
    In the wind's way.

We climbed with him the wandering trail
   Up to the last keen lonely height—
Where snow-peaks clustered, sharp and frail,
   Swimming in light.

Sheer on the edge of heaven we dwelt
   And laughed above the blue abyss,
While on my happy lips I felt
   Your windy kiss.

You were the spirit of the height,
   The breath of sun and air.
A bird dipped wing, and, swift and white,
   Peace brooded there.

PARTING AFTER A QUARREL

You looked at me with eyes grown bright with pain,
   Like some trapped thing's. And then you moved your head
Slowly from side to side, as though the strain
   Ached in your throat with anger and with dread.

And then you turned and left me, and I stood
   With a queer sense of deadness over me,
And only wondered dully that you could
   Fasten your trench-coat up so carefully—

Till you were gone. Then all the air was quick
   With my last words, that seemed to leap and quiver;
And in my heart I heard the little click
   Of a door that closes—quietly, forever.

MY MOTHER'S HOUSE

"It's strange," my mother said, "to think
Of the old house where we were born.
I can remember every chink
And every board our feet had worn.

"It's gone now. Many years ago
They tore it down. It was too old,
And none too grand as houses go,
Not like a new house, bought or sold.

"And so they tore it down. But we
Could talk about it still, and say
'Just so the kitchen used to be,
And the stairs turned in such a way.'

"But we're gone too now. Everyone
Who knew the house is dead and buried.
And I'll not last so long alone
With all my children grown and married.

"There's not a living soul can tell,
Except myself, just how the grass
Grew round the pathway to the well,
Or where the china-cupboard was.

"Yet while I live you cannot say
That the old house is quite, quite dead.
It still exists in some dim way
While I remember it," she said.

OLD FRIENDSHIP

Beautiful and rich is an old friendship,
Grateful to the touch as ancient ivory,
Smooth as aged wine, or sheen of tapestry
Where light has lingered, intimate and long.

Full of tears and warm is an old friendship.
That asks no longer deeds of gallantry,
Or any deed at all—save that the friend shall be
Alive and breathing somewhere, like a song.

THE CITY WALL
Wusih, China

About the city where I dwell, guarding it close, runs an embattled wall.

It was not new, I think, when Arthur was a king, and plumed knights before a British wall made brave clangor of trumpets, that Launcelot came forth.

It was not new, I think, and now not it but chivalry is old:

Without, the wall is brick, with slots for firing; and it drops straightway into the evil moat, where offal floats and nameless things are thrown.

Within, the wall is earth; it slants more gently down, covered with grass and stubby with cut weeds. Below it in straw lairs the beggars herd, patiently whining, stretching out their sores.

And on the top a path runs.

As I walk, lifted above the squalor and the dirt, the timeless miracle of sunset mantles in the west,

The blue dusk gathers close

And beauty moves immortal through the land.

And I walk quickly, praying in my heart that beauty will defend me, will heal up the too great wounds of China.

I will not look—tonight I will not look—where at my feet the little coffins are,

The boxes where the beggar children lie, unburied and unwatched.

I will not look again, for once I saw how one was broken, torn by the sharp teeth of dogs. A little tattered dress was there, and some crunched bones. . . .

I need not look. What can it help to look?

Ah, I am past!

And still the sunset glows.

The tall pagoda, like a velvet flower, blossoms against the sky; the Sacred Mountain fades, and in the town a child laughs suddenly.

I will hold fast to beauty! Who am I, that I should die for these?

I will go down. I am too sorely hurt, here on the city wall.

THE MOST-SACRED MOUNTAIN

Space, and the twelve clean winds of heaven,
And this sharp exultation, like a cry, after the slow six thousand
    steps of climbing!
This is Tai Shan, the beautiful, the most holy.

Below my feet the foot-hills nestle, brown with flecks of green;
    and lower down the flat brown plain, the floor of earth,
    stretches away to blue infinity.
Beside me in this airy space the temple roofs cut their slow curves
    against the sky,
And one black bird circles above the void.

Space, and the twelve clean winds are here;
And with them broods eternity—a swift white peace, a presence
    manifest.
The rhythm ceases here. Time has no place. This is the end
    that has no end.

Here, when Confucius came, a half a thousand years before the
    Nazarene, he stepped, with me, thus into timelessness.
The stone beside us waxes old, the carven stone that says: "On
    this spot once Confucius stood and felt the smallness of the
    world below."
The stone grows old:
Eternity is not for stones.

But I shall go down from this airy space, this swift white peace,
    this stinging exultation.
And time will close about me, and my soul stir to the rhythm of
    the daily round.
Yet, having known, life will not press so close, and always I shall
    feel time ravel thin about me;
For once I stood
In the white windy presence of eternity.

Ridgely Torrence

THE BIRD AND THE TREE

Blackbird, blackbird in the cage,
There's something wrong tonight.
Far off the sheriff's footfall dies,
The minutes crawl like last year's flies
Between the bars, and like an age
The hours are long tonight.

The sky is like a heavy lid
Out here beyond the door tonight.
What's that? A mutter down the street.
What's that? The sound of yells and feet.
For what you didn't do or did
You'll pay the score tonight.

No use to reek with reddened sweat,
No use to whimper and to sweat.
They've got the rope; they've got the guns,
They've got the courage and the guns;
And that's the reason why tonight
No use to ask them any more.
They'll fire the answer through the door—
You're out to die tonight.

There where the lonely cross-road lies,
There is no place to make replies;
But silence, inch by inch, is there,
And the right limb for a lynch is there;
And a lean daw waits for both your eyes,
Blackbird.

Perhaps you'll meet again some place.
Look for the mask upon the face:
That's the way you'll know them there—
A white mask to hide the face.
And you can halt and show them there
The things that they are deaf to now,
And they can tell you what they meant—

To wash the blood with blood. But how
If you are innocent?

Blackbird singer, blackbird mute,
They choked the seed you might have found.
Out of a thorny field you go—
For you it may be better so—
And leave the sowers of the ground
To eat the harvest of the fruit,
Blackbird.

THE SON

Southern Ohio Market Town

I heard an old farm-wife,
    Selling some barley,
Mingle her life with life
    And the name "Charley."

Saying: "The crop's all in,
    We're about through now;
Long nights will soon begin,
    We're just us two now.

"Twelve bushel at sixty cents,
    It's all I carried—
He sickened making fence;
    He was to be married.

"It feels like frost was near—
    His hair was curly.
The spring was late that year,
    But the harvest early."

INVITATION

Arvia, east of the morning,
Before the daylight grayed,
I heard a night song's warning:
"This bubble-world shall fade."

"The daytime with its fire-flower,"
It sang, "shall fail and stray;
And beauty, like a brier-flower,
Shall pass—shall pass away."

Then soon the faint and far light
Would fade beyond a beam,
And we'd lie down without starlight
And there would be no dream.

But now, when the moon is bluest,
Like a shell that murmurs all,
I see this world is the truest
Of any I recall.

The sky's wild birds are glancing,
The sea's long waves are slow;
It's all a place for dancing—
But no one seems to know.

Come with me to the meadows—
We'll dance your secret name,
With an outside dance in shadows
And an inside dance in flame.

The songs and the wings have slanted
And blow with a golden sound;
Life burns like a peak enchanted,
Oh wild, enchanted, crowned!

All day, while songs from the height fall,
We'll dance the valleys bright,
But we'll be on the hills at nightfall
In the lovely lonely light.

> *Let's play we are a tune,*
> *And make a kind of song*
> *About the sun and moon*
> *Before the stars were born.*
> *You be the breath, I'll be the horn,*
> *It will not take us long.*

THREE O'CLOCK—MORNING

The jewel-blue electric flowers
Are cold upon their iron trees.
Upraised, the deadly harp of rails
Whines for its interval of ease.
The stones keep all their daily speech
Buried, but can no more forget
Than would a water-vacant beach
The hour when it was wet.

A whitened few wane out like moons,
Ghastly from some torn edge of shade;
A drowning one, a reeling one,
And one still loitering after trade.
On high the candor of a clock
Portions the dark with solemn sound.
The burden of the bitten rock
Moans up from underground.

Far down the street a shutting door
Echoes the yesterday that fled
Among the days that should have been
Which people cities of the dead.
The banners of the steam unfold
Upon the towers to meet the day;
The lights go out in red and gold,
But time goes out in gray.

Mark Turbyfill

STRANGERS

I shall tell you:
I am seeing and seeing strangers
Who are not strangers,
For there is something in their eyes,
And about their faces
That whispers to me

(But so low
That I can never quite hear)
Of the lost half of myself
Which I have been seeking since the beginning of earth;
And I could follow them to the end of the world,
Would they but lean nearer, nearer,
And tell me. . . .

THINGS NOT SEEN

The sea-gull poises
In the charged, expectant air.

The sea-gull poises
With delicate resistance.

Its sheer conscious being
Is cause to strike creation
Out of all this emptiness.

The sea-gull waits,
Wavering slightly
Against this mighty immanence.

So does my heart wait
For the release of a substance
Not yet seen.

PRAYER FOR SOPHISTICATION

Close all open things, O God!
Close the rose,
The throats of flutes and birds.
Close all eyes
To tears not yet fallen.
Close my heart.
Close all open things, O God!

A SONG FOR SOULS UNDER FIRE

Lo, that doves
Should soften
These surging streets!

I found him talking simply and gladly of God,
In the unmoved city of granite
And noise.

Thought kindled in his cheek,
And his white faith
Was the tree in spring
To look upon.

He whispered me he knew the God of Daniel
In the lions' den;
The faith of Joan of Arc
On parapets.

He will walk, a spirit
Of unguessed power,
Into battle.

He will walk unreached
Into fire!

SHAPES

Let us deliberately sit into design,
With these elephant ears
Stretched from the glazed pot
Into green wax consciousness.

Let us exert
Our unused selves
Into other static
Sharpnesses.

In what fleet gestures
Have you found eternity?

His amber-painted torso
A Persian dancer
Has conceived into a leaf-line,
The head inclined.

BENEDICTION

Let no blasphemer till the sacred earth
Or scatter seed upon it,
Lest fruit should fail
And weed-scars sting its fineness.

Send him here who loves its beauty
And its brownness.

He will plow the earth
As a dancer dances—
Ecstatically.

Let no blasphemer till the sacred earth
Or scatter seed upon it.

APOLLO ALONE APPROVES

Severely now will we dance
In these deserted stretches,
No ground but the words beneath us.

Swiftness and slowness—themselves—
Come and move with us.

With posture like a bronze pear
I anchor knees and fold feet under.
On urgent points you come running;
You sway like a brittle flower,
Swiftly to fall with little sharp knees
Upon the oblique and tempered thighs.

Angular and singular our attitude,
But its beauty pleases us.
Your glazed surfaces shine.

There is no objection and no applause
As I exit with you upon my arm,
Drawing your bright satin points after us
Like a blade across this intangible ground.

Jean Starr Untermeyer

LAKE SONG

The lapping of lake water
Is like the weeping of women,
The weeping of ancient women
Who grieved without rebellion.

The lake falls over the shore
Like tears on their curven bosoms.
Here is languid luxurious wailing,
The wailing of kings' daughters.

So do we ever cry,
A soft unmutinous crying,
When we know ourselves each a princess
Locked fast within her tower.

The lapping of lake water
Is like the weeping of women,
The fertile tears of women
That water the dreams of men.

CLAY HILLS

It is easy to mold the yielding clay,
And many shapes grow into beauty
Under the facile hand.
But forms of clay are lightly broken;
They will lie shattered and forgotten in a dingy corner.

But underneath the slipping clay
Is rock. . . .
I would rather work in stubborn rock
All the years of my life,

And make one strong thing;
And set it in a high clean place
To recall the granite strength of my desire.

SINFONIA DOMESTICA

When the white wave of a glory that is hardly I
Breaks through my mind and washes it clean,
I know at last the meaning of my ecstasy,
And know at last my wish and what it can mean.

To have sped out of life that night—to have vanished
Not as a vision, but as something touched, yet grown
Radiant as the moonlight, circling my naked shoulder;
Wrapped in a dream of beauty, longed for, but never known.

Louis Untermeyer

"FEUERZAUBER"

I never knew the earth had so much gold—
    The fields run over with it, and this hill
Hoary and old,
    Is young with buoyant blooms that flame and thrill.

Such golden fires, such yellow—lo, how good
    This spendthrift world, and what a lavish God!
This fringe of wood,
    Blazing with buttercup and goldenrod.

You too, beloved, are changed. Again I see
    Your face grow mystical, as on that night
You turned to me,
    And all the trembling world—and you—were white.

Aye, you are touched; your singing lips grow dumb;
    The fields absorb you, color you entire . . .
And you become
    A goddess standing in a world of fire!

IRONY

Why are the things that have no death
The ones with neither sight nor breath!
Eternity is thrust upon
A bit of earth, a senseless stone.
A grain of dust, a casual clod
Receives the greatest gift of God.
A pebble in the roadway lies—
            It never dies.

The grass our fathers cut away
Is growing on their graves today;
The tiniest brooks that scarcely flow
Eternally will come and go.
There is no kind of death to kill
The sands that lie so meek and still. . . .
But Man is great and strong and wise—
            And so he dies.

INFIDELITY

You have not conquered me—it is the surge
    Of love itself that beats against my will;
It is the sting of conflict, the old urge
    That calls me still.

It is not you I love—it is the form
    And shadow of all lovers who have died
That gives you all the freshness of a warm
    And unfamiliar bride.

It is your name I breathe, your hands I seek;
    It will be you when you are gone.
And yet the dream, the name I never speak,
    Is that that lures me on.

It is the golden summons, the bright wave
    Of banners calling me anew;
It is all beauty, perilous and grave—
    It is not you.

Allen Upward

SCENTED LEAVES FROM A CHINESE JAR

THE ACACIA LEAVES

The aged man, when he beheld winter approaching, counted the leaves as they lapsed from the acacia trees; while his son was talking of the spring.

THE BITTER PURPLE WILLOWS

Meditating on the glory of illustrious lineage, I lifted up my eyes and beheld the bitter purple willows growing round the tombs of the exalted Mings.

THE ESTUARY

Some one complained to the Master, "After many lessons I do not fully understand your doctrine." In response the Master pointed to the tide in the mouth of the river, and asked, "How wide is the sea in this place?"

THE INTOXICATED POET

A poet, having taken the bridle off his tongue, spoke thus: "More fragrant than the heliotrope, which blooms all the year round, better than vermilion letters on tablets of sandal, are thy kisses, thou shy one!"

THE JONQUILS

I have heard that a certain princess, when she found that she had been married by a demon, wove a wreath of jonquils and sent it to the lover of former days.

THE MARIGOLD

Even as the seed of the marigold, carried by the wind, lodges on the roofs of palaces, and lights the air with flame-colored blossoms, so may the child-like words of the insignificant poet confer honor on lofty and disdainful mandarins.

THE MERMAID

The sailor boy who leant over the side of the Junk of Many Pearls, and combed the green tresses of the sea with his ivory fingers, believing that he had heard the voice of a mermaid, cast his body down between the waves.

THE MIDDLE KINGDOM

The emperors of fourteen dynasties, clad in robes of yellow silk embroidered with the Dragon, wearing gold diadems set with pearls and rubies, and seated on thrones of incomparable ivory, have ruled over the Middle Kingdom for four thousand years.

THE MILKY WAY

My mother taught me that every night a procession of junks carrying lanterns moves silently across the sky, and the water sprinkled from their paddles falls to the earth in the form of dew. I no longer believe that the stars are junks carrying lanterns, no longer that the dew is shaken from their oars.

THE STUPID KITE

A kite, while devouring a skylark, complained, "Had I known that thy flesh was no sweeter than that of a sparrow I should have listened longer to thy delicious notes."

THE WINDMILL

The exquisite painter Ko-tsu was often reproached by an industrious friend for his fits of idleness. At last he excused himself by saying, "You are a watermill—a windmill can grind only when the wind blows."

THE WORD

The first time the emperor Han heard a certain Word he said, "It is strange." The second time he said, "It is divine." The third time he said, "Let the speaker be put to death."

John V. A. Weaver

DRUG STORE

Pardon me, lady, but I wanta ast you,
For God's sake, stop that tappin'! I'll go nuts,
Plain bug-house if I hear that tap-tap-tap
Much longer!
              Now I went and used such language,
I got to tell you why . . . Well, in the first place,
My business is all shot. Now drugs theirselves
Don't pay much, and the extra stuff, like candy,
Cigars and stationery and et cetery,
Don't make their keep. And that damn soda-fountain—
Excuse me, lady, but I just can't help it! . . .

Some day I'm gointa catch the guy I bought it off—
I'm losin' money every day it's here.
And soda-jerkers—now I can't get none
For love or money, so myself I got to
Mess with them malted milks, banana splits,
And slop like that. And just as doggone sure
As I start workin' on some fine prescription,
The kind I love to mix—got to be careful,
The weights is hittin' on that perfect balance—
Why, then some fool wants a marshmallow sundæ,
And tap-tap-tap he starts in on the show-case,
And taps and taps till I come runnin' out,
Leavin' the drugs half-done.
                 And that ain't all;
Here's the big trouble— I can't talk good grammar.
People don't think a man that mixes drugs
Can do it right and talk the way I do.
It makes me sick—why have I got to sound
Like a school-teacher? Why, I know my stuff:
"Registered Pharmacist"—see? I taught myself,
Workin' at night whiles I was four years clerkin';
And then I took three months down at the U,
And passed a fine exam. But here's the thing:

I quit the public school in seventh grade,
And never paid no attention to my talk.
So it's the way I tell you—they're suspicious
Because I use such slang. I try to stop,
But it's too late now. I found out too late . . .

I got a dream of what I'll do some day:
I want to quit this drug stuff altogether,
Have a nice office, with a big oak desk,
And sell just real estate. I'd like to bet
I'd make a clean-up at it. It'd be swell,
That office . . .
                        But this life is killin' me.
It's the fool questions they keep askin' me!
You see that clock there? Well, just on a guess
Three times an hour some silly fish comes in here
And calls me out, and asts me, "Is that right?—
Is your clock right?" Honest to Heaven, lady,
One day I got so sore I took a hammer
And smashed the face in. And it cost twelve dollars
To fix it. But I had peace for a week.
Oh, gosh, my nerves! . . . But that's the way it is.
I'm sorry I spoke so rough about that tappin',
But when I get to sellin' real estate,
They'll be no place where folks can take a coin
And tap, and tap, till I come runnin' out.
That's a man's business! . . .
                        If I ever get it . . .

NOCTURNE

"Nothin' or everythin' it's got to be,"
You says, and hides your face down on my arm.
"If it meant nothin', 'twouldn't do no harm,
Or either everythin'—but this way—see? . . .

I feel your tremblin' heart against my coat,
An' the big arc-light moon grins down so cool,
"Go on!" I think it says, "you softie fool!" . . .
I love you so it hurts me in my throat . . .

"Don't make me kiss you; sure, I know you could,"
You're pleadin', "an' we gone too far for play;
I care a lot . . . but yet not so's to say
I love you yet . . . Aw, help me to be good!" . . .

O darlin', darlin', can't you let it be
Nothin' to you, an' everythin' to me?

TWO WAYS

Oncet in the museum
    We seen a little rose
In a jar of alcohol—
    You turns up your nose:
"That's the way people think
    Love ought to be—
Last forever! Pickled roses!—
    None o' that for me!"

That night was fireworks
    Out to Riverview—
Gold and red and purple
    Bustin' over you.
"Beautiful!" you says then,
    "That's how love should be!
Burn wild and die quick—
    That's the love for me!"

Now you're gone for good . . . say,
Wasn't they no other way?

Winifred Welles

TRINKET

Now that it is moonlight I must be mournful,
    Darken my eyes and whiten my face;
    Wander by myself with a lonely lily grace.
And here are lovely tears, a whole silver hornful!—
    Blow them like beads upon the velvet of this place.

Forget my blue sash and my gallant yellow ruffle—
I am now a statue, I am stone-gowned.
So when you blow that silver, mind that you muffle
The silver sound of blowing; even tears on the ground,
Falling and pooling, must make no sound.

Just for this moonlight, I think that I shall borrow
One shiny grief no greater than a star—
(Someone might be fickle, or everyone afar!)
So that I can sit in silence saying, "Sorrow, Sorrow!—
My very own sorrow, how adorable you are."

LANGUAGE

I made new speech for you—a secret tongue,
Dearest and best of all in book or scroll.
To hear it spoken was to hear it sung—
I copied all of it upon my soul.
There were those leafy letters, wreathed like vines—
Such trellises of words as Sappho spoke;
Heavy as silver flagons of old wines
Some Latin phrases carved by stately folk.
I could not find a sound for leave-takings
Slower, more sorrowful than Spanish is,
And the French names with flower-dusty wings
Flew in and out among the sentences.
So, with my heart a voice made musical,
I went to you, and did not speak at all.

THE LAST NIGHT OF WINTER

Whose whips are those cracking up the river
Till the long shudder of sound,
Half a sharp cry and half ecstatic shiver,
Clutches through the snow at the still ground?

I cannot sleep, so I will light my candle,
I will lead my shadow down the long stair.
At the far door where someone tries the handle,
Each of us will whisper, "Who goes there?"

And wood will whimper and stone be shaken—
　While, locked like a heart, the old house grieves,
Rocking in its sleep and yearning to waken
　Warm tears in the silver eaves.

When clouds collapse, when the darkness releases
　A trickle of stars, this house at one bound
Will burst like a bulb and fall to pieces,
　Floor and door one dust on the ground.

Let the windows crackle and curl like paper,
　The rafters slide and the beams fly—
I shall be off on the end of this taper,
　Out through the roof and up through the sky:

Straight as a rocket I shall shoot through the shadow;
　All out of breath and blinking I shall land
In a green gown in a green meadow—
　A crocus, not a candle, in my hand.

A DOG WHO ATE A POND LILY

Tired of being my dog, and with grave anger
That there were only ivory bones to eat,
He left me for the pond, filled with a hunger,
Half memory, for some immaculate meat
To lay on his bright tongue—I saw him linger,
Fastidiously nose the shimmering heat,
And, as if suddenly grown brisker, younger,
Snap up a lily, living, flushed and sweet.

Like one frail sound the summer, softly muted,
Buzzed in his silky ear. A long, long while
He stood in reeds and godlike trance fast-rooted.
The taste of lotos made him strangely smile—
No more my humble dog, sad-eyed, four-footed,
He was Anubis wading in the Nile.

BOY

Does no one see that in your wood
The season is not spring but winter?
You are too proud to wear a hood,
You love to drive a crystal splinter
Through your bare hands, your naked feet.
White nuts, snow berries you will eat,
If wild birds bring them, on your tongue
The taste of ice is piercing sweet.
Will no one say that being young
Is being hurt, is being bled,
Enduring dagger-thirsts, wolf-hungers,
Is being self-raised from the dead
More times than boys have toes and fingers?

Does no one know the unicorn
Kneels down to you as to your sister?
If with his single cryptic horn
He has crept close and sharply kissed her,
He is no less your animal;
He will run with you till befall
Your freshet, flower and furrowed mold.
Will no one say that growing tall
Is crouching down and feeling cold
Outside dark windows starred with frost?
That being innocent is only
Being locked out, alone and lost,
White as the snow, as still, as lonely?

THE HEART OF LIGHT

Once, on a cliff, I saw perfection happen—
The full gold moon was balanced on the sea,
Just as the red sun rested on the moor.
The summer evening ripened and fell open;
And people walking through that fruit's rich core
Were suddenly what they were meant to be,
Quiet and happy, softly moving, lovely,

With still, translucent faces and clear eyes,
And all their heads and bodies brightly rimmed
With delicate gold; so radiantly, so gravely,
These people walked, so crowned, so golden-limbed,
The cliff seemed like an edge of Paradise.

Glenway Wescott

THE POET AT NIGHT-FALL

I see no equivalents
For that which I see,
Among words.

And sounds are nowhere repeated,
Vowel for vocal wind
Or shaking leaf.

Ah me, beauty does not enclose life,
But blows through it—
Like that idea, the wind,

Which is unseen and useless,
Even superseded upon
The scarred sea;

Which goes and comes
Altering every aspect—
The poplar, the splashing crest—

Altering all, in that moment
When it is not
Because we see it not.

But who would hang
Like a wind-bell
On a porch where no wind ever blows?

WITHOUT SLEEP

He earns the oblivion of book and shelf
Who will have for muse a Beatrice
Sitting content by the hearth
To whisper his history and thought.

Poet uncuckolded, he hears
No mad ethereal crying
For merciless cloud and ridge
Tormented by the golden horn.

Ah, she will never lift
Her intolerant head like a stag
And scorn him, thinking of wind
And naked hunter and his hallooing hound.

THESE ARE THE SUBTLE RHYTHMS

These are the subtle rhythms, rhythms of sloth:

Mountains which fall in the green swirls
Of twilight as petals, fallen and languid,
Bud in the dawn, and fall again
In the green swirls of twilight, a little
Nearer the stars and the flickering final fires.

These are the rhythms of sloth:
Mountains, my feet on the trails.

I, IN MY PITIFUL FLESH

I, in my pitiful flesh
Transfigured, have woven
Music of wilderness.

And now that my old fear is flung
Aside, I will hold
In my hands what hunger has sung.

From all the roads where I go
Shame like a red mist vanishes.
On—oh . . .

The desert is shaken with cries:
"Come, and I will be kind."
I am the lover with frightened eyes.

John Hall Wheelock

SUNDAY EVENING IN THE COMMON

Look—on the topmost branches of the world
    The blossoms of the myriad stars are thick.
    Over the huddled rows of stone and brick
A few sad wisps of empty smoke are curled
    Like ghosts, languid and sick.

One breathless moment now the city's moaning
    Fades, and the endless streets seem vague and dim.
    There is no sound around the whole world's rim,
Save in the distance a small band is droning
    Some desolate old hymn.

Van Wyck, how often have we been together
    When this same moment made all mysteries clear—
    The infinite stars that brood above us here,
And the gray city in the soft June weather,
    So tawdry and so dear!

LIKE MUSIC

Your body's motion is like music;
    Her stride ecstatical and bright
Moves to the rhythm of dumb music,
    The unheard music of delight.

The silent splendor of the creation
    Speaks through your body's stately strength,

And the lithe harmony of beauty
   Undulates through its lovely length.

And rhythmically your bosom's arches,
   Alternately, with every breath
Lift lifeward in long lines of beauty,
   And lapse along the slopes of death.

THE THUNDER–SHOWER

The lightning flashed, and lifted
   The lids of heaven apart,
The fiery thunder rolled you
   All night long through my heart.

From dreams of you at dawn
   I rose to the window ledge:
The storm had passed away,
   The lake lapped on the sedge.

The lyre of heaven trembled
   Still with the thought of you,
The twilight on the waters,
   And all my spirit too.

SONG

All my love for my sweet
   I bared one day to her.
Carelessly she took it,
   And like a conqueror.
She bowed the neck of my soul
   To fit it to her yoke,
And bridled the lips of Song.
   Fear within me awoke,
But Love cried: "Swiftly, swiftly
   Bear her along the road;
Beautiful is the goal
   And beauty is the goad."

TRIUMPH OF THE SINGER

I shake my hair in the wind of morning
  For the joy within me that knows no bounds.
I echo backward the vibrant beauty
  Wherewith heaven's hollow lute resounds.

I shed my song on the feet of all men,
  On the feet of all shed out like wine;
On the whole and the hurt I shed my bounty,
  The beauty within me that is not mine.

Turn not away from my song, nor scorn me
  Who bear the secret that holds the sky
And the stars together; but know within me
  There speaks another more wise than I.

Nor spurn me here from your heart to hate me,
  Yet hate me here if you will.   Not so
Myself you hate, but the love within me
  That loves you whether you would or no.

Here love returns with love to the lover
  And beauty unto the heart thereof,
And hatred unto the heart of the hater,
  Whether he would or no, with love!

NIRVANA

Sleep on—I lie at heaven's high oriels,
  Over the stars that murmur as they go
  Lighting your lattice-window far below.
And every star some of the glory spells
  Whereof I know.

I have forgotten you, long long ago;
  Like the sweet silver singing of thin bells
Vanished, or music fading faint and low.
  Sleep on—I lie at heaven's high oriels,
Who loved you so.

ONCE IN A LONELY HOUR

Upon my breast,
  Once in a lonely hour your head was laid,
And you had rest
  From much that troubled you—you were no longer afraid.

But now, even here
  No refuge is; you shall not ever lie
As once, in my heart's shelter here,
  Poor heart, while the great hounds of Time go roaring by.

Vain was the strength
  You leaned on in that hour, you did not guess
How vain the strength
  Whereon you propped your ignorant lovingness.

And yet—what more
  Has life to offer life, here in the lone
Tumult? A little rest, no more—
  Upon a heart as troubled as its own.

THE VICTORY

I shall take flight from Death on sudden wings
  In some swift song, he shall not have me here—
For all his cunning, all his snares and slings.
  I shall escape him whom I fear.

Then, though he wander through all woods and ways,
  He will not reach to *me*, out of the strong
Net of these tangled nights and days
  Escaped forever in a song.

But now my wings are broken and I hide
  In this tall grass, to hear his foot go by
  Stealthily, stealthily—
Searching the field on either side.

Heal me, O Time, and I will rise again
  On swifter wings and for a surer flight,
    Remembering this pain!
So, when he comes, he shall not find me here
  By day or night—
    But search forever, and in vain.

Anna Wickham

THE SINGER

If I had peace to sit and sing,
Then I could make a lovely thing;
But I am stung with goads and whips,
So I build songs like iron ships.

Let it be something for my song,
If it is sometimes swift and strong.

GIFT TO A JADE

For love he offered me his perfect world.
This world was so constricted, and so small,
It had no sort of loveliness at all,
And I flung back the little silly ball.
At that cold moralist I hotly hurled
His perfect, pure, symmetrical, small world.

THE CONTEMPLATIVE QUARRY

My love is male and properman
And what he'd have he'd get by chase,
So I must cheat as women can
And keep my love from off my face.
'Tis folly to my dawning thrifty thought
That I must run, who in the end am caught.

THE SILENCE

When I meet you, I greet you with a stare;
Like a poor shy child at a fair.
I will not let you love me, yet am I weak:
I love you so intensely that I cannot speak.
When you are gone, I stand apart
And whisper to your image in my heart.

THE TIRED MAN

I am a quiet gentleman,
And I would sit and dream;
But my wife is on the hillside,
Wild as a hill-stream.

I am a quiet gentleman,
And I would sit and think;
But my wife is walking the whirlwind
Through night as black as ink.

Oh, give me a woman of my race
As well controlled as I,
And let us sit by the fire,
Patient till we die!

THE RECOMPENSE

Of every step I took in pain
I had some gain.
Of every night of blind excess
I had reward of half-dead idleness.
Back to the lone road
With the old load!
But rest at night is sweet
To wounded feet;
And when the day is long
There is miraculous reward of song.

Margaret Widdemer

THE BEGGARS

The little pitiful, worn, laughing faces,
Begging of life for joy!

I saw the little daughters of the poor,
Tense from the long day's working, strident, gay,
Hurrying to the picture-place. There curled
A hideous flushed beggar at the door,
Trading upon his horror, eyeless, maimed,
Complacent in his profitable mask.
They mocked his horror, but they gave to him
From the brief wealth of pay-night, and went in
To the cheap laughter and the tawdry thoughts
Thrown on the screen; in to the seeking hand
Covered by darkness, to the luring voice
Of Horror, boy-masked, whispering of rings,
Of silks, of feathers, bought—so cheap!—with just
Their slender starved child-bodies palpitant
For beauty, laughter, passion—that are life:
(A frock of satin for an hour's shame,
A coat of fur for two days' servitude;
"And the clothes last," the thought runs on, within
The poor warped girl-minds drugged with changeless days;
"Who cares or knows after the hour is done?")—
Poor little beggars at life's door for joy!

The old man crouched there, eyeless, horrible,
Complacent in the marketable mask
That earned his comforts—and they gave to him!

But ah, the little painted wistful faces
Questioning life for joy!

TERESINA'S FACE

He saw it last of all before they herded in the steerage,
  Dark against the sunset where he lingered by the hold—
The tear-stained dusk-rose face of her, the little Teresina,
  Sailing out to lands of gold.

Ah, his days were long, long days, still toiling in the vineyard,
  Working for the gold to set him free to go to her,
Where gay it glowed, the flower-face of little Teresina,
  Where all joy and riches were.

Hard to find one rose-face where the dark rose-faces cluster,
  Where the outland laws are strange and outland voices hum—
Only one lad's hoping, and the word of Teresina,
  Who would wait for him to come!

  . . . .

God grant he may not find her, since he may not win her freedom,
  Nor yet be great enough to love, in such marred captive guise,
The patient painted face of her, the little Teresina,
  With its cowed all-knowing eyes!

GREEK FOLK SONG

Under dusky laurel leaf,
  Scarlet leaf of rose,
I lie prone, who have known
  All a woman knows.

Love and grief and motherhood,
  Fame and mirth and scorn—
These are all shall befall
  Any woman born.

Jewel-laden are my hands,
  Tall my stone above—
Do not weep that I sleep,
  Who was wise in love.

Where I walk, a shadow gray,
Through gray asphodel,
I am glad, who have had
All that life can tell.

Marguerite Wilkinson

A WOMAN'S BELOVED

A Psalm

To what shall a woman liken her beloved,
And with what shall she compare him to do him honor?
He is like the close-folded new leaves of the woodbine, odorless
　　but sweet,
Flushed with a new and swiftly rising life,
Strong to grow and give glad shade in summer.
Even thus should a woman's beloved shelter her in her time of
　　anguish.

And he is like the young robin, eager to try his wings,
For within soft-stirring wings of the spirit has she cherished
　　him,
And with the love of the mother bird shall she embolden him,
　　that his flight may avail.

A woman's beloved is to her as the roots of the willow,
Long strong white roots, bedded lovingly in the dark.
Into the depths of her have gone the roots of his strength and
　　of his pride,
That she may nourish him well and become his fulfilment.
None may tear him from the broad fields where he is planted!

A woman's beloved is like the sun rising upon the waters, mak-
　　ing the dark places light;
And like the morning melody of the pine trees.
Truly, she thinks the roses die joyously
If they are crushed beneath his feet.

A woman's beloved is to her a great void that she may illumine,
A great king that she may crown, a great soul that she may re-
    deem.
And he is also the perfecting of life,
Flowers for the altar, bread for the lips, wine for the chalice.

You that have known passion, think not that you have fathomed
    love—
It may be that you have never seen love's face.
For love thrusts aside storm-clouds of passion to unveil the
    heavens,
And, in the heart of a woman, only then is love born.

To what shall I liken a woman's beloved,
And with what shall I compare him to do him honor?
He is a flower, a song, a struggle, a wild storm;
And, at the last, he is redemption, power, joy, fulfilment and
    perfect peace.

AN INCANTATION

O great sun of heaven, harm not my love;
Sear him not with your flame, blind him not with your beauty,
Shine for his pleasure!

O gray rains of heaven, harm not my love;
Drown not in your torrent the song of his heart,
Lave and caress him.

O swift winds of heaven, harm not my love;
Bruise not nor buffet him with your rough humor,
Sing you his prowess!

O mighty triad, strong ones of heaven,
Sun, rain, and wind, be gentle, I charge you!
For your mad mood of wrath have me—I am ready—
But spare him, my lover, most proud and most dear,
O sun, rain and wind, strong ones of heaven!

William Carlos Williams

PEACE ON EARTH

The Archer is wake!
The Swan is flying!
Gold against blue
An Arrow is lying.
There is hunting in heaven—
Sleep safe till tomorrow.

The Bears are abroad!
The Eagle is screaming!
Gold against blue
Their eyes are gleaming!
Sleep!
Sleep safe till tomorrow.

The Sisters lie
With their arms intertwining;
Gold against blue
Their hair is shining!
The Serpent writhes!
Orion is listening!

Gold against blue
His sword is glistening!
Sleep!
There is hunting in heaven—
Sleep safe till tomorrow.

THE SHADOW

Soft as the bed in the earth
Where a stone has lain—
So soft, so smooth and so cool,
Spring closes me in
With her arms and her hands.

Rich as the smell
Of new earth on a stone,
That has lain, breathing
The damp through its pores—
Spring closes me in
With her blossomy hair;
Brings dark to my eyes.

METRIC FIGURE

There is a bird in the poplars—
It is the sun!
The leaves are little yellow fish
Swimming in the river;
The bird skims above them—
Day is on his wings.
Phœnix!
It is he that is making
The great gleam among the poplars.
It is his singing
Outshines the noise
Of leaves clashing in the wind.

SUB TERRA

Where shall I find you—
You, my grotesque fellows
That I seek everywhere
To make up my band?
None, not one
With the earthy tastes I require:
The burrowing pride that rises
Subtly as on a bush in May.

Where are you this day—
You, my seven-year locusts
With cased wings?
Ah, my beauties, how I long!

That harvest
That shall be your advent—
Thrusting up through the grass,
Up under the weeds,
Answering me—
That shall be satisfying!
The light shall leap and snap
That day as with a million lashes!

Oh, I have you!
Yes, you are about me in a sense,
Playing under the blue pools
That are my windows.
But they shut you out still
There in the half light—
For the simple truth is
That though I see you clear enough . .
You are not there.

It is not that—it is you,
You I want, my companions!
God! if I could only fathom
The guts of shadows!—
You to come with me
Poking into Negro houses
With their gloom and smell!
In among children
Leaping around a dead dog!
Mimicking
Onto the lawns of the rich!
You!
To go with me a-tip-toe
Head down under heaven,
Nostrils lipping the wind!

SLOW MOVEMENT

All those treasures that lie in the little bolted box whose tiny
   space is
Mightier than the room of the stars, being secret and filled with
   dreams:
All those treasures—I hold them in my hand—are straining
   continually
Against the sides and the lid and the two ends of the little box in
   which I guard them;
Crying that there is no sun come among them this great while
   and that they weary of shining;
Calling me to fold back the lid of the little box and to give them
   sleep finally.

But the night I am hiding from them, dear friend, is far more
   desperate than their night!
And so I take pity on them and pretend to have lost the key to
   the little house of my treasures;
For they would die of weariness were I to open it, and not be
   merely faint and sleepy
As they are now.

POSTLUDE

Now that I have cooled to you
Let there be gold of tarnished masonry,
Temples soothed by the sun to ruin,
That sleep utterly.
Give me hand for the dances,
Ripples at Philæ, in and out;
And lips, my Lesbian,
Wallflowers that once were flame.

Your hair is my Carthage
And my arms the bow,
And our words arrows
To shoot the stars
Who from that misty sea
Swarm to destroy us.

But you there beside me—
Oh, how shall I defy you,
Who wound me in the night
With breasts shining
Like Venus and like Mars?
The night that is shouting Jason
When the loud eaves rattle
As with waves above me
Blue at the prow of my desire.

LOVE SONG

What have I to say to you
When we shall meet?
Yet—
I lie here thinking of you.

The stain of love
Is upon the world.
Yellow, yellow, yellow,
It eats into the leaves,
Smears with saffron
The horned branches that lean
Heavily
Against a smooth purple sky.

There is no light—
Only a honey-thick stain
That drips from leaf to leaf
And limb to limb,
Spoiling the colors
Of the whole world.

I am alone.
The weight of love
Has buoyed me up
Till my head
Knocks against the sky.

See me!
My hair is dripping with nectar—
Starlings carry it
On their black wings.
See, at last
My arms and my hands
Are lying idle.

How can I tell
If I shall ever love you again
As I do now?

MAN IN A ROOM

Here, no woman, nor man besides,
Nor child, nor dog, nor bird, nor wasp,
Nor ditch pool, nor green thing. Color of flower,
Blood-bright berry none, nor flame-rust
On leaf, nor pink gall-sting on stem, nor
Staring stone. *Ay de mí!*
No hawthorn's white thorn-tree here, nor lawn
Of buttercups, nor any counterpart:

Bed, book-backs, walls, floor,
Flat pictures, desk, clothes-box, litter
Of paper scrawls. So sit I here,
So stand, so walk about. Beside
The flower-white tree not so lonely I:
Torn petals, dew-wet, blotched yellow my bare instep.

WILLOW POEM

It is a willow when summer is over,
a willow by the river
from which no leaf has fallen nor,
bitten by the sun,
turned orange or crimson.
The leaves cling and grow paler,

swing and grow paler
over the swirling waters of the river
as if loth to let go;
they are so cool, so drunk with
the swirl of the wind and of the river—
oblivious to winter,
the last to let go and fall
into the water and on the ground.

WINTER TREES

All the complicated details
of the attiring and
the disattiring are completed!
A liquid moon
moves gently among
the long branches.
Thus having prepared their buds
against a sure winter,
the wise trees
stand sleeping in the cold.

JANUARY

Again I reply to the triple winds
running chromatic fifths of derision
outside my window:
                    Play louder.
You will not succeed. I am
bound more to my sentences
the more you batter at me
to follow you.
                    And the wind,
as before, fingers perfectly
its derisive music.

THE WIDOW'S LAMENT IN SPRINGTIME

Sorrow in my own yard
where the new grass
flames as it has flamed
often before, but not
with the cold fire
that closes round me this year.
Thirty-five years
I lived with my husband.
The plum tree is white today
with masses of flowers.
Masses of flowers
load the cherry branches
and color some bushes
yellow and some red,
but the grief in my heart
is stronger than they;
for though they were my joy
formerly, today I notice them
and turn away forgetting.
Today my son told me
that in the meadows,
at the edge of the heavy woods
in the distance, he saw
trees of white flowers.
I feel that I would like
to go there
and fall into those flowers
and sink into the marsh near them.

THE BOTTICELLIAN TREES

The alphabet of
the trees

is fading in the
song of the leaves

the crossing
bars of the thin

letters that spelled
winter

and the cold
have been illumined

with
pointed green

by the rain and sun
the strict simple

principles of
straight branches

are being modified
by pinched out

ifs of color, devout
conditions

the smiles of love

    .   .   .   .   .

until the stript
sentences

move as a woman's
limbs under cloth

and praise from secrecy
with hot ardor

love's ascendancy
in summer —

in summer the song
sings itself

above the muffled words—

Yvor Winters

TWO SONGS OF ADVENT

I

On the desert, between pale mountains, our cries;
Far whispers creeping through an ancient shell.

II

Coyote, on delicate mocking feet,
Hovers down the canyon, among the mountains,
His voice running wild in the wind's valleys.

Listen! listen! for I enter now your thought.

THE WALKER

A leaf turns—
The mind burns.

Thin and clear
Deaths stands here.

His lips bend
For Time's end.

Over all
My feet fall.

THE IMMOBILE WIND

Blue waves within the stone
Turn like deft wrists interweaving.

Emotion, undulant, alone.
Curled wings flow beyond perceiving.

Swift points of sight,
    mystic and amorous little hands,
The wind has drunk
    as water swallows sifting sands.

The wings of a butterfly
Feel of the wind
Tentatively; as men die
In thought, that have not sinned.

THE PRIESTHOOD

We stand apart
That men may see
The lines about our eyes.

We perish, we
Who die in art,
With that surprise

Of one who speaks
To us and knows
Wherein he lies.

DEATH GOES BEFORE ME

Death goes before me on his hands and knees,
And we go down among the bending trees.

Weeping I go, and no man gives me ease—
I am that strange thing that each strange eye sees.

Eyes of the silence, and all life an eye,
Turn in the wind; and always I walk by.

Too still I go, and all things go from me—
As down far autumn beaches a man runs to the sea.

My hands are cold, my lips are thin and dumb.
Stillness is like the beating of a drum.

Humbert Wolfe

THE WATERS OF LIFE

When, hardly moving, you decorate night's hush
  with the slim pencil of your grace, retrieving
the clean flat stroke of some old Grecian brush
  that painted dancers fair beyond believing;

when, leaning back the harvest of your hair
  under the moon with beauty as still as hers,
your body's wonder writes upon the air
  the perfect cadence of consummate verse,

I think, if this upon the air be shaken,
  brief as a falling blossom, it can but be
that Time records, by beauty overtaken,
  in one gold instant, immortality,

and that the patterns you weave upon the night
  have such swift passion, such essential heat,
that all the painter sees, the poet can write,
  are but pale shadows of your dancing feet.

THE WHITE DRESS

Some evening, when you are sitting alone
  by your high window, motionless and white—
I shall come, by the way that none but I have known,
  into the quiet room out of the night.

You will know I have come, without turning your head,
  because of the way the air will lie quite still,
as though it waited for something to be said
  that no man has ever said, and no man will.

But you will be wiser than the air. You know
  that for the thing we feel there is no word—
and you will not move even when I turn to go,
  even when the sound of my footsteps is no longer heard.

657

ENDYMION

Then I'll say this—life is so still
  without your love, that when I wake,
at night, I hear over the hill
  (you know my hill) the moon's heart break.

She's dreaming of her shepherd lover—
  ah, skyey wanton!—he is gone
this thousand years, and love is over
  for us and for Endymion.

TULIP

Clean as a lady,
cool as glass,
fresh without fragrance
the tulip was.

The craftsman, who carved her
of metal, prayed:
"Live, O thou lovely!"
Half metal she stayed.

THE ROSE

Why should a man,
though six foot tall,
think he matters
at all, at all?

and though he live
for seventy years,
does he suppose that
anyone cares?

Rather let me
to him propose
the flushed example
of the rose,

who, with her dazzling
inch of scent,
a summer's day
weighs imminent

upon the spirit
entranced, and goes
richer with that
than he with those.

Charles Erskine Scott Wood

THE POET IN THE DESERT

Extracts from the Prologue

I have come into the desert because my soul is athirst as the
    desert is athirst;
My soul which is the soul of all; universal, not different.
We are athirst for the waters which make beautiful the path
And entice the grass, the willows and poplars,
So that in the heat of the day we may lie in a cool shadow,
Soothed as by the hands of quiet women, listening to the dis-
    course of running waters as the voices of women, exchanging
    the confidences of love.

.   .   .   .

The mountains afar girdle the desert as a zone of amethyst;
Pale translucent walls of opal,
Girdling the desert as life is girt by eternity.
They lift their heads high above our tribulation
Into the azure vault of Time;
Theirs are the airy castles which are set upon foundations of
    sapphire.
My soul goes out to them as the bird to her secret nest.
They are the abode of peace.

The flowers bloom in the desert joyously—
They do not weary themselves with questioning;
They are careless whether they be seen, or praised.

They blossom unto life perfectly and unto death perfectly,
  leaving nothing unsaid.
They spread a voluptuous carpet for the feet of the wind,
And to the frolic breezes which overleap them they whisper:
"Stay a moment, brother; plunder us of our passion;
Our day is short, but our beauty is eternal."

Never have I found a place, or a season, without beauty.
Neither the sea, where the white stallions champ their bits and
  rear against their bridles,
Nor the desert, bride of the sun, which sits scornful, apart,
Like an unwooed princess, careless, indifferent.
She spreads her garments, wonderful beyond estimation,
And embroiders continually her mantle.
She is a queen, seated on a throne of gold
In the hall of silence.

          .   .   .   .

She is a courtesan, wearing jewels,
Enticing, smiling a bold smile;
Adjusting her brilliant raiment negligently,
Lying brooding upon her floor which is richly carpeted;
Her brown thighs beautiful and naked.
She toys with the dazzelry of her diadems,
Smiling inscrutably.
She is a nun, withdrawing behind her veil;
Gray, subdued, silent, mysterious, meditative; unapproach-
  able.
She is fair as a goddess sitting beneath a flowering peach-tree,
  beside a clear river.
Her body is tawny with the eagerness of the sun
And her eyes are like pools which shine in deep canyons.
She is beautiful as a swart woman, with opals at her throat,
Rubies on her wrists and topaz about her ankles.
Her breasts are like the evening and the day stars;
She sits upon her throne of light, proud and silent, indifferent to
  her wooers.
The sun is her servitor, the stars are her attendants, running
  before her.
She sings a song unto her own ears, solitary, but it is sufficient—

It is the song of her being. Oh, if I may sing the song of my being
    it will be sufficient.
She is like a jeweled dancer, dancing upon a pavement of gold;
Dazzling, so that the eyes must be shaded.
She wears the stars upon her bosom and braids her hair with the
    constellations.

I know the desert is beautiful, for I have lain in her arms and she
    has kissed me.
I have come to her, that I may know freedom;
That I may lie upon the breast of the Mother and breathe the
    air of primal conditions.
I have come out from the haunts of men;
From the struggle of wolves upon a carcass,
To be melted in Creation's crucible and be made clean;
To know that the law of Nature is freedom.

Edith Wyatt

ON THE GREAT PLATEAU

In the Santa Clara Valley, far away and far away,
Cool-breathed waters dip and dally, linger towards another
    day—
Far and far away—far away.
Slow their floating step, but tireless, terraced down the Great
    Plateau.
Towards our ways of steam and wireless, silver-paced the brook-
    beds go.
Past the ladder-walled pueblos, past the orchards, pear and
    quince,
Where the back-locked river's ebb flows, miles and miles the
    valley glints,
Shining backwards, singing downwards, towards horizons blue
    and bay.
All the roofs the roads ensconce so dream of visions far away—
Santa Cruz and Ildefonso, Santa Clara, Santa Fé.
Ancient sacred fears and faiths, ancient sacred faiths and
    fears—

Some were real, some were wraiths—Indian, Franciscan years,
Built the kivas, swung the bells; while the wind sang plain and
    free,
"Turn your eyes from visioned hells!—look as far as you can
    see!"
In the Santa Clara Valley, far away and far away,
Dying dreams divide and dally, crystal-terraced waters sally—
Linger towards another day, far and far away—far away.

As you follow where you find them, up along the high plateau,
In the hollows left behind them Spanish chapels fade below—
Shaded court and low corrals. In the vale the goat-herd browses.
Hollyhocks are seneschals by the little buff-walled houses.
Over grassy swale and alley have you ever seen it so—
Up the Santa Clara Valley, riding on the Great Plateau?
Past the ladder-walled pueblos, past the orchards, pear and
    quince,
Where the trenchèd waters' ebb flows, miles and miles the
    valley glints,
Shining backwards, singing downwards towards horizons blue
    and bay.
All the haunts the bluffs ensconce so breathe of visions far away,
As you ride near Ildefonso back again to Santa Fé.
Pecos, mellow with the years, tall-walled Taos—who can know
Half the storied faiths and fears haunting green New Mexico?
Only from her open places down arroyos blue and bay,
One wild grace of many graces dallies towards another day.
Where her yellow tufa crumbles, something stars and grasses
    know,
Something true, that crowns and humbles, shimmers from the
    Great Plateau:
Blows where cool-paced waters dally from the stillness of Puyé,
Down the Santa Clara Valley through the world from far away—
Far and far away—far away.

TO F. W.

You are my companion—
Down the silver road,

Still and many-changing,
Infinitely changing.
You are my companion.
Something sings in lives—
Days of walking on and on,
Deep beyond all singing,
Wonderful past singing.

Wonderful our road,
Long and many-changing,
Infinitely changing.
This, more wonderful—
We are here together,
You and I together,
I am your companion;
You are my companion,
My own true companion.

Let the road-side fade:
Morning on the mountain-top,
Hours along the valley,
Days of walking on and on,
Pulse away in silence,
In eternal silence.
Let the world all fade,
Break and pass away;
Yet will this remain,
Deep beyond all singing,
My own true companion,
Beautiful past singing:
We were here together—
I was your companion,
You were my companion,
My own true companion.

A CITY AFTERNOON

Green afternoon serene and bright, along my street you sail
    away
Sun-dappled like a ship of light that glints upon a rippled bay.

Afar, freight-engines call and toll; the sprays flash on the fragrant
 grass;
The children and the nurses stroll; the charging motors plunge
 and pass.
Invisibly the shadows grow, empurpling in a rising tide
The walks where light-gowned women go, white curb, gray
 asphalt iris-dyed.
A jolting trolley shrills afar; nasturtiums blow, and ivy vines;
Wet scents of turf and black-smoothed tar float down the roof-
 trees' vergent lines.
Where will you go, my afternoon, that glints so still and swift
 away,
Blue-shaded like a ship of light bound outward from a wimpled
 bay?
Oh—thrilling, pulsing, dark and bright, shall you, your work,
 your pain, your mirth,
Fly into the immortal night and silence of our mother
 earth?
She bore all Eden's green and dew, and Persia's scented wine
 and rose,
And, flowering white against the blue, acanthus leaf and mar-
 bled pose.
And deep the Maenad's choric dance, Crusader's cross, and
 heathen crest
Lie sunk with rose and song and lance all veiled and vanished
 in her breast.

And all those afternoons once danced and sparkled in the sapphire light
And iris shade as you have glanced, green afternoon, in vibrant
 flight.
As down dim vistas echoing, dead afternoons entreat our
 days,
What breath of beauty will you sing to souls unseen and unknown
 ways?
How close and how unanswering, green afternoon, you pulse
 away,
So little and so great a thing—deep towards the bourne of every
 day.

Elinor Wylie

BEAUTY

Say not of Beauty she is good,
Or aught but beautiful,
Or sleek to doves' wings of the wood
Her wild wings of a gull.

Call her not wicked—that word's touch
Consumes her like a curse;
But love her not too much, too much,
For that is even worse.

Oh, she is neither good nor bad,
But innocent and wild!
Enshrine her and she dies, who had
The hard heart of a child.

THE EAGLE AND THE MOLE

Avoid the reeking herd,
Shun the polluted flock,
Live like that stoic bird,
The eagle of the rock.

The huddled warmth of crowds
Begets and fosters hate;
He keeps, above the clouds,
His cliff inviolate.

When flocks are folded warm
And herds to shelter run,
He sails above the storm,
He stares into the sun.

If in the eagle's track
Your sinews cannot leap,
Avoid the lathered pack,
Turn from the steaming sheep.

If you would keep your soul
From spotted sight or sound,
Live like the velvet mole;
Go burrow underground.

And there hold intercourse
With roots of trees and stones,
With rivers at their source
And disembodied bones.

VELVET SHOES

Let us walk in the white snow
In a soundless space;
With footsteps quiet and slow,
At a tranquil pace,
Under veils of white lace.

I shall go shod in silk,
And you in wool,
White as a white cow's milk,
More beautiful
Than the breast of a gull.

We shall walk through the still town
In a windless peace;
We shall step upon white down,
Upon silver fleece,
Upon softer than these.

We shall walk in velvet shoes:
Wherever we go
Silence will fall like dews
On white silence below.
We shall walk in the snow.

ATAVISM

I always was afraid of Somes's Pond:
Not the little pond, by which the willow stands,

Where laughing boys catch alewives in their hands
In brown bright shallows; but the one beyond.
There, when the frost makes all the birches burn
Yellow as cow-lilies, and the pale sky shines
Like a polished shell between black spruce and pines,
Some strange thing tracks us, turning where we turn.

You'll say I dream it, being the true daughter
Of those who in old times endured this dread.
Look! Where the lily-stems are showing red
A silent paddle moves below the water.
A sliding shape has stirred them like a breath;
Tall plumes surmount a painted mask of Death.

HYMN TO EARTH

Farewell, incomparable element,
Whence man arose, where he shall not return;
And hail, imperfect urn
Of his last ashes, and his firstborn fruit;
Farewell, the long pursuit,
And all the adventures of his discontent;
The voyages which sent
His heart averse from home:
Metal of clay, permit him that he come
To thy slow-burning fire as to a hearth;
Accept him as a particle of earth.

Fire, being divided from the other three,
It lives removed, or secret at the core;
Most subtle of the four,
When air flies not, nor water flows,
It disembodied goes,
Being light, elixir of the first decree,
More volatile than he;
With strength and power to pass
Through space, where never his least atom was:
He has no part in it, save as his eyes
Have drawn its emanation from the skies.

A wingless creature heavier than air,
He is rejected of its quintessence;
Coming and going hence,
In the twin minutes of his birth and death,
He may inhale as breath,
As breath relinquish heaven's atmosphere,
Yet in it have no share,
Nor can survive therein
Where its outer edge is filtered pure and thin:
It doth but lend its crystal to his lungs
For his early crying, and his final songs.

The element of water has denied
Its child; it is no more his element;
It never will relent;
Its silver harvests are more sparsely given
Than the rewards of heaven,
And he shall drink cold comfort at its side.
The water is too wide:
The seamew and the gull
Feather a nest made soft and pitiful
Upon its foam; he has not any part
In the long swell of sorrow at its heart.

Hail and farewell, beloved element,
Whence he departed, and his parent once;
See where thy spirit runs
Which for so long hath had the moon to wife;
Shall this support his life
Until the arches of the waves be bent
And grow shallow and spent?
Wisely it cast him forth
With his dead weight of burdens nothing worth,
Leaving him, for the universal years,
A little seawater to make his tears.

Hail, element of earth, receive thy own,
And cherish, at thy charitable breast,
This man, this mongrel beast:

He plows the sand, and, at his hardest need,
He sows himself for seed;
He plows the furrow, and in this lies down
Before the corn is grown;
Between the apple bloom
And the ripe apple is sufficient room
In time, and matter, to consume his love
And make him parcel of a cypress grove.

Receive him as thy lover for an hour
Who will not weary, by a longer stay,
The kind embrace of clay;
Even within thine arms he is dispersed
To nothing, as at first;
The air flings downward from its four-quartered tower
Him whom the flames devour;
At the full tide, at the flood,
The sea is mingled with his salty blood:
The traveler dust, although the dust be vile,
Sleeps as thy lover for a little while.

SONNETS FROM *ONE PERSON*

O love, how utterly am I bereaved
By Time, who sucks the honey of our days,
Sets sickle to our Aprils, and betrays
To killing winter all the sun achieved!
Our parted spirits are perplexed and grieved,
Severed by cold, and change that never stays;
And what the clock, and what the season says
Is rumor neither valued nor believed.

Thus absence chills us to apparent death
And withers up our virtue, but together
We grow beyond vagaries of the weather
And make a summer of our mingled breath
Wherein we flourish, and forget to know
We must lie murdered by predestined snow.

. . . .

When I perceive the sable of your hair
Silvered, and deep within those caverns are
Your eye-sockets, a double-imaged star,
And your fine substance fretted down by care,
Then do I marvel that a woman dare
Prattle of mortal matters near and far
To one so wounded in demonic war
Against some prince of Sirius or Altair.

How is it possible that this hand of clay,
Though white as porcelain, can contrive a touch
So delicate it shall not hurt too much?
What voice can my invention find to say
So soft, precise, and scrupulous a word
You shall not take it for another sword?

.   .   .   .

My honored lord, forgive the unruly tongue
That utters blasphemy; forgive the brain
Born on a whirlwind of unhallowed pain:
Remember only the intrepid song;
The flag defended and the gauntlet flung;
The love that speech can never render plain;
The mind's resolve to turn and strive again;
The fortitude that has endured so long.

My cherished lord, in charity forgive
A starveling hope that may at times desire
To warm its frozen fingers at your fire;
'Tis by such trifles that your lovers live,
And so rise up, and in the starlight cold
Frighten the foxes from your loneliest fold.

.   .   .   .

I hereby swear that to uphold your house
I would lay my bones in quick destroying lime
Or turn my flesh to timber for all time;
Cut down my womanhood; lop off the boughs
Of that perpetual ecstasy that grows
From the heart's core; condemn it as a crime

If it be broader than a beam, or climb
Above the stature that your roof allows.

I am not the hearthstone nor the cornerstone
Within this noble fabric you have builded;
Not by my beauty was its cornice gilded;
Not on my courage were its arches thrown:
My lord, adjudge my strength, and set me where
I bear a little more than I can bear.

. . . .

Upon your heart, which is the heart of all
My late discovered earth and early sky,
Give me the dearest privilege to die:
Your pity for the velvet of my pall;
Your patience for my grave's inviolate wall;
And for my passing bell, in passing by,
Your voice itself, diminished to a sigh
Above all other sounds made musical.

Meanwhile I swear to you I am content
To live without a sorrow to my name;
To live triumphant, and to die the same,
Upon the fringes of this continent,
This map of paradise, this scrap of earth
Whereon you burn like flame upon a hearth.

William Butler Yeats

THE WILD SWANS AT COOLE

The trees are in their autumn beauty,
The woodland paths are dry;
Under the October twilight the water
Mirrors a still sky.
Upon the brimming water among the stones
Are nine and fifty swans.

The nineteenth autumn has come upon me
Since I first made my count.

I saw, before I had well finished,
All suddenly mount
And scatter wheeling in great broken rings
Upon their clamorous wings.

I have looked upon those brilliant creatures,
And now my heart is sore.
All's changed since I, hearing at twilight,
The first time on this shore,
The bell-beat of their wings above my head,
Trod with a lighter tread.

Unwearied still, lover by lover,
They paddle in the cold
Companionable streams, or climb the air.
Their hearts have grown old;
Passion or conquest, wander where they will,
Attend upon them still.

But now they drift on the still water
Mysterious, beautiful.
Among what rushes will they build,
By what lake's edge or pool
Delight men's eyes, when I awake some day
To find they have flown away?

THE COLD HEAVEN

Suddenly I saw the cold and rook-delighting Heaven
That seemed as though ice burned and was but the more ice;
And thereupon imagination and heart were driven
So wild that every casual thought of that and this
Vanished, and left but memories, that should be out of season
With the hot blood of youth, of love crossed long ago.
And I took all the blame out of all sense and reason,
Until I cried and trembled and rocked to and fro,
Riddled with light. Ah! when the ghost begins to quicken,
Confusion of the death-bed over, is it sent
Out naked on the roads, as the books say, and stricken
By the injustice of the skies for punishment?

THAT THE NIGHT COME

She lived in storm and strife;
Her soul had such desire
For what proud death may bring
That it could not endure
The common good of life,
But lived as 'twere a king
That packed his marriage day
With banneret and pennon,
Trumpet and kettledrum,
And the outrageous cannon,
To bundle time away
That the night come.

NO SECOND TROY

Why should I blame her that she filled my days
With misery, or that she would of late
Have taught to ignorant men most violent ways,
Or hurled the little streets upon the great,
Had they but courage equal to desire?
What could have made her peaceful with a mind
That nobleness made simple as a fire,
With beauty like a tightened bow, a kind
That is not natural in an age like this,
Being high and solitary and most stern?
Why, what could she have done being what she is?—
Was there another Troy for her to burn?

TO A FRIEND WHOSE WORK HAS COME TO NOTHING

Now all the truth is out,
Be secret and take defeat
From any brazen throat.
For how can you compete,
Being honor-bred, with one

Who, were it proved he lies,
Were neither shamed in his own
Nor in his neighbors' eyes?
Bred to a harder thing
Than triumph, turn away
And, like a laughing string
Whereon mad fingers play
Amid a place of stone,
Be secret and exult,
Because of all things known
That is most difficult.

THE COLLAR-BONE OF A HARE

Would I could cast a sail on the water
Where many a king has gone
And many a king's daughter,
And alight at the comely trees and the lawn,
The playing upon pipes and the dancing,
And learn that the best thing is
To change my loves while dancing
And pay but a kiss for a kiss.

I would find by the edge of that water
The collar-bone of a hare
Worn thin by the lapping of water,
And pierce it through with a gimlet, and stare
At the old bitter world where they marry in churches;
And laugh over the untroubled water
At all who marry in churches
Through the white thin bone of a hare.

THE DAWN

I would be ignorant as the dawn,
That has looked down
On that old queen measuring a town
With the pin of a brooch,
Or on the withered men that saw

From their pedantic Babylon
The careless planets in their courses,
The stars fade out where the moon comes,
And took their tablets and did sums.
I would be ignorant as the dawn,
That merely stood, rocking the glittering coach
Above the cloudy shoulders of the horses.
I would be—for no knowledge is worth a straw—
Ignorant and wanton as the dawn.

THE MAGI

Now as at all times I can see in the mind's eye,
In their stiff painted clothes, the pale unsatisfied ones
Appear and disappear in the blue depth of the sky—
With all their ancient faces like rain-beaten stones,
And all their helms of silver hovering side by side,
And all their eyes still fixed, hoping to find once more,
Being by Calvary's turbulence unsatisfied,
The uncontrollable mystery on the bestial floor.

THE FISHERMAN

Although I can see him still,
The freckled man who goes
To a grey place on a hill
In grey Connemara clothes
At dawn to cast his flies,
It's long since I began
To call up to the eyes
This wise and simple man.
All day I'd looked in the face
What I had hoped 'twould be
To write for my own race
And the reality:
The living men that I hate,
The dead man that I loved,
The craven man in his seat,
The insolent unreproved—

And no knave brought to book
Who has won a drunken cheer,
The witty man and his joke
Aimed at the commonest ear,
The clever man who cries
The catch-cries of the clown,
The beating down of the wise
And great Art beaten down.
Maybe a twelvemonth since
Suddenly I began,
In scorn of this audience,
Imagining a man,
And his sun-freckled face
And grey Connemara cloth,
Climbing up to a place
Where stone is dark under froth,
And the down turn of his wrist
When the flies drop in the stream—
A man who does not exist,
A man who is but a dream;
And cried, "Before I am old
I shall have written him one
Poem maybe as cold
And passionate as the dawn."

EGO DOMINUS TUUS

Hic
On the grey sand beside the shallow stream,
Under your old wind-beaten tower, where still
A lamp burns on beside the open book
That Michael Robartes left, you walk in the moon;
And though you have passed the best of life, still trace,
Enthralled by the unconquerable delusion,
Magical shapes.

Ille   By the help of an image
I call to my own opposite, summon all
That I have handled least, least looked upon.

Hic
> And I would find myself and not an image.

Ille
> That is our modern hope, and by its light
> We have lit upon the gentle, sensitive mind
> And lost the old nonchalance of the hand.
> Whether we have chosen chisel, pen or brush
> We are but critics, or but half create,
> Timid, entangled, empty and abashed,
> Lacking the countenance of our friends.

Hic   And yet
> The chief imagination of christendom,
> Dante Aligieri, so utterly found himself
> That he has made that hollow face of his
> More plain to the mind's eye than any face
> But that of Christ.

Ille   And did he find himself,
> Or was the hunger that had made it hollow
> A hunger for the apple on the bough
> Most out of reach? and is that spectral image
> The man that Lapo and that Guido knew?
> I think he fashioned from his opposite
> An image that might have been a stony face,
> Staring upon a bedouin's horse-hair roof
> From doored and windowed cliff, or half upturned
> Among the coarse grass and the camel dung.
> He set his chisel to the hardest stone.
> Being mocked by Guido for his lecherous life,
> Derided and deriding, driven out
> To climb that stair and eat that bitter bread,
> He found the unpersuadable justice, he found
> The most exalted lady loved by a man.

Hic
> Yet surely there are men who have made their art
> Out of no tragic war—lovers of life,
> Impulsive men that look for happiness
> And sing when they have found it.

Ille   No, not sing;
  For those that love the world serve it in action,
  Grow rich, popular and full of influence,
  And should they paint or write still it is action:
  The struggle of the fly in marmalade.
  The rhetorician would deceive his neighbors,
  The sentimentalist himself; while art
  Is but a vision of reality.
  What portion in the world can the artist have
  Who has awakened from the common dream,
  But dissipation and despair?

Hic   And yet
  No one denies to Keats love of the world.
  Remember his deliberate happiness.

Ille
  His art is happy, but who knows his mind?
  I see a school-boy when I think of him,
  With face and nose pressed to a sweet-shop window.
  For certainly he sank into his grave
  His senses and his heart unsatisfied,
  And made—being poor, ailing and ignorant,
  Shut out from all the luxury of the world,
  The ill-bred son of a livery-stable keeper—
  Luxuriant song.

Hic   Why should you leave the lamp
  Burning alone beside an open book,
  And trace these characters upon the sands?
  A style is found by sedentary toil
  And by the imitation of great masters.

Ille
  Because I seek an image not a book,
  Those men that in their writings are most wise
  Own nothing but their blind stupified hearts.
  I call to the mysterious one who yet
  Shall walk the wet sands by the edge of the stream
  And look most like me, being indeed my double,
  And prove if all imaginable things

The most unlike, begin my anti-self,
And standing by these characters disclose
All that I seek; and whisper it as though
He were afraid the birds, who cry aloud
Their momentary cries before it is dawn,
Would carry it away to blasphemous men.

Morton Dauwen Zabel

TEUFELSDRÖCKH MINOR

The lucid instant comes upon
A day when light goes up and up,
Imprisoned like a breathless dawn
Within the sky's tremendous cup;

When every fish in still suspense
Is guiltless of a waving fin,
And on the city's iron tents
Leans an arrested cloud of din;

And in the air's transcending span
Hangs weightless the bewildered bird,
While dumb is every tongue in man
And silence is a crystal word;

When millions of the quick are slain
To give a sudden life to one
Who walks a moment free of pain
Alone beneath a waiting sun.

So in the eyelid's interval
May strike a triumph or a curse,
When wisdom rises tall and tall
To hypnotize the universe.

HERAKLES ARCHER

A tense and whittled thundershaft he pulls
Within his supple crescent,
To send the bolt of death among the gulls
Or drop the pheasant.

The padding fox has heard the leather sing
Against his restless hand,
The swallow bends a slow and cautious wing
Above the hunter's land.

The stag with horny trees upon his brow
Has seen the arrow gleam,
The otter plunges to elude the bow
Under the stream.

For he alone is brave who bends the branch
And draws the fatal dart
To send a fire no blood can ever quench
Into the innocent heart.

THE NETTLE, THE FLOWER

Fair brow in the strict cold shrine,
Helen, smothered by dust,
The sword unstiffened by flame
Cracks early in the frost.

The heart held beyond challenge,
Guarded when dangers shout,
Festers like the wound of scorn
Fed by veins of doubt.

Turn beauty toward the sun;
Her eyes are not dismayed,
Her brow retains the leaves
Dew nourished in the shade.

Drive honor over flames;
His sinews never flinch,

Even while the fiery knives
Pare down the vital inch.

Send love across the wastes
Of winter; he will bend
To shield his blown frail wick
From the wind's wrath.

THE TRAITORS

A cry of ruin strides the sky
Tonight above our burdened fields
That lift the weight of summer high
Like trophy on their glittering shields.

Wings tread night's silent noon, and words
Of peril fall from straining bills,
Where loud with prophecy the birds
Call startled sleepers to their sills,

While windows swing, and iron chains
Strangle the hound's uproarious throat,
To see on farms and silver skeins
Of brooks the moon-live shadows float.

The geese bear windward to the south
Arousing panic as they ride,
Their treachery the first, their mouth
The first to shake earth's drowsing pride,

Till fear assails the eyes that scan
The troubled night whose breath the frost
Will stiffen, and the bravest man
Cries ruin and the world is lost.

For treason threads the lakes and groves
Whose swallows hear wild cries, and stir
Till summer waits alone, but loves
The thief who comes to plunder her.

THE STORM AT NIGHTFALL

From whose white summits was this wind released
To lift the dust's impalpable grey shroud?
Whose sword of lightning in the troubled East
Severed the gusty cloud

Wherein these coursers of the sky were bred—
Invisible cold hounds that never pant
In weariness until their foes are dead
After the stormy hunt?

The heart pursues them on their crying flight,
The tongue halloes the swift relentless pack
Before the wide and drifting hems of night
Cover their silver track.

In the high towers of the mind their omen
Endures as long as winding horns may blow,
Until the roundsman of the moon will summon
Back to their lairs of snow

The ruthless dogs whose cold pursuit has routed
Adventure from the coverts of the heart,
Bravery from thickets of a soul who doubted
That any wind could start.

SCÈNE À FAIRE

The silent moment comes at last;
It is not met with loud surprise;
We know and nod, perceiving past
The troubled wisdom of the eyes.

Gone are the doubts that made us pause,
Gone is the tongue's uncertainty.
Forgotten are earth's transient laws,
Convention's obvious courtesy.

Now love is proud, and scorns the crude
Contention by the sword and kiss.
Our dubious words shall not intrude
Upon surrender stern as this.

So stop before the harsh embrace,
The meeting of the finger-tips.
Let distance consecrate your face
And silence dedicate your lips.

HOMAGE TO MÜRREN

Who hail us from the hill
Above the steep valley,
Lifting their sudden shrill
Young voices? Their unruly
Hair blows wide on the sky.
White dresses whip their knees.
Lifting free hands high
They are no enemies.

We see them above us, struck
By the shafts of the sun,
Clear on the windy rock,
Fearing no one,
Their salutation flying
Across the spilling lake,
And over the mountains, trying
To cry the dead awake.

Our hot brows flash a banner
Across the narrowing gulf.
Courage starts like a runner
Outleaguing the god himself.
Bravery flowers in the staff.
The pall of shadow is furled.
Three stand high on the cliff
Hailing the world.

Marya Zaturensky

SONG OF A FACTORY GIRL

It's hard to breathe in a tenement hall,
So I ran to the little park,
As a lover runs from a crowded ball
To the moonlit dark.

I drank in clear air as one will
Who is doomed to die,
Wistfully watching from a hill
The unmarred sky.

And the great trees bowed in their gold and red
Till my heart caught flame;
And my soul, that I thought was crushed or dead,
Uttered a name.

I hadn't called the name of God
For a long time;
But it stirred in me as the seed in sod,
Or a broken rhyme.

AN OLD TALE

What shall we say of her,
Who went the path we knew of? She is dead—
What shall we say of her?

Men who are very old
Still speak of her. They say
That she was far too beautiful; they say
Her beauty wrought her ruin. But they
Are very old.

The old wives break their threads, they shake their heads.
They shake their heads when men will speak of her;
They say she was too beautiful.

I must not think of her, I must
Not speak of her! My mother says
One should not think of her.

She went the path we knew of; she is dead.
They say few knew her truly while she lived,
Though men will speak of her.

It really does not matter she is dead—
One need not think of her. Although one night
Folks heard her weeping, yet beside a pool
One moonlit springtime I could swear she sang!

But she is dead—one must not think of her.

THE ELEGY OF THE KREMLIN BELLS

For John Reed

Peace to the quiet dead
And the unquiet soul—
Great peace from feet to head
While floods of time shall roll!

Far from your shouting West,
Here shall this sorrowed land
Take you to her dreaming breast,
And love and understand.

Let the old bells toll,
That long have tolled for sorrow,
Peace to your lonely soul
And Russia's glad tomorrow!

Chorus

"Place over him a stone
And write with a soft sigh,
*For people not my own
I laid me down to die.*"

CHORALE FOR AUTUMN

The leaves of autumn burning through the grey—
Are you dark head, stilled blood, and perilous tongue?
Burn, O thin trees, and in small gardens scatter
Your leaves that on reluctant branches stray.

How many seasons has this tamed heart known
Lashing the hounds of fall to the bare hills,
Hallooing among the shadows of a dream,
The bright leaves lying where the flowers have grown!

Gather the chilled days in, let the calm house
Of peace entreat, enclose, and comfort them.
The days burn cold and high, the sheaves are in—
Prepare, O Death, to hold your last carouse.

The world grows cool as crystal, and as clear.
That which is dark grows light; the daylight stands
Obscure as anguish, worn out by sharp time.
As a leaf in its season falls the year.

BIOGRAPHICAL NOTES WITH
BIBLIOGRAPHIES

In preparing the following biographical sketches, the editor has tried to be accurate in stating dates and facts. In the brief critical estimates, she has quoted frequently, sometimes without quotation marks, from her own essays and reviews, published either in *Poetry: A Magazine of Verse*, or in her book, *Poets and Their Art*, or both. When she has quoted from other writers, she has been careful to give proper credit.

In the bibliographical appendices, the effort has been made to list all the books of verse, or books about poetry, thus far printed by the poets quoted in this anthology; and then to refer the reader to certain magazines which have published these poets, and to some of the anthologies which have included the quoted poems. Credit has been given especially to those periodicals which make a specialty of poetry.

It has been attempted to include in this bibliography all books published previous to June 1st, 1932.

An asterisk (*) indicates a book from which poems in this anthology have been borrowed.

LÉONIE ADAMS

Born in Brooklyn in 1899, educated in local schools and Barnard College, Miss Adams first appeared as a poet about 1921 in *The New Republic*, but made few further contributions to periodicals. Her first book being well received in 1925, a Guggenheim Fellowship enabled her to live abroad for a year and a half in 1928–29, and soon after her return her second book was published.

Miss Adams has been listed, by those who love the precision of groups and catalogues, in the "metaphysical school" of modern poets, and obviously her imagination is excited by the secret violence of thought rather than the common emotional drama of human experience. She seems to derive, in certain poems, from Donne and Vaughan, with leanings also toward the intricate rhythms of Sir Thomas Browne; and then again certain of her lyrics have an unmistakable Elizabethan, or post-Elizabethan melody, reminding us of Campion and Herrick and Crashaw. Her motive is intensely spiritual—austerely ascetic if you will, though the ascetic, however frugal within, is robed in splendor—in a rich fabric of embroidered phrases and jewelled metaphors.

In a sense more or less true of every authentic poet, Miss Adams' art is singularly her own; singularly the expression of a shy and sensitive spirit, keenly aroused by soft tunes, colors, perfumes of beauty which would escape a grosser mind. Edward Sapir, reviewing her first book in *Poetry*, while regretting the common abuse of the word *beautiful*, said:

"Her poetry is beautiful in a pre-eminent degree and in every sense of the word. It is beautiful in diction, beautiful in its highly sophisticated rhythms, beautiful above all in the quality of its feeling and in the movement of its thought, at once sensuous and mystical. . . . In essence her style is never precious, never a thing of technique, but always the subtle, even tortured, embodiment of a spirit that is at least as subtle and as tortured. . . . It is the charming paradox of her finest poetry that it creates an utterly fresh and breathless beauty out of materials that are almost worn with loveliness."

Those Not Elect..............................Robert M. McBride & Co., N. Y.: 1925
* High Falcon and Other Poems......................The John Day Co., N. Y.: 1929
In *Poetry:* March 1927 (Vol. XXIX).

CONRAD AIKEN

Conrad Aiken was born in Savannah, Georgia, in 1889, was graduated from Harvard in 1912, and after three years of travel, lived for a few years in South Yarmouth, Massachusetts. About 1921 he took his family to the Sussex coast of England, choosing an ancient house at Rye for his residence.

Mr. Aiken was a long time finding his own style. "The unquiet ghosts of Masefield and Gibson, Frost and Masters, stalk behind" his first two books. With *The Jig of Forslin* he began to develop his own form and mood, deliberately attempting to parallel the musical symphony. Helen Hoyt, reviewing it in *Poetry* in 1917, said:

"We have had other symphonies in verse, but none of them gives the effect of music, evokes so nearly the same kind of emotion music evokes, as this book does. . . . The parts are bound together not as the parts of a story, but as the movements of a symphony, with repetition of phrase and theme, moods and motives, which appear and reappear, are joined and again dispersed, in no logical pattern, but fluctuating and flowing.

"In it you may know what it is you are thinking when you are not thinking, see the procession of dream and memory and desire as it goes sliding by in the mind, when the mind is numbed or drifts, resting from its obvious actual life, and experience merges with the experience outside."

This book and *The Charnel Rose* mark the climax of this over-melodious symphonic dreaming, expressed too expansively in orthodox lyric measures. *Senlin's Morning Song* is typical, perhaps the peak of Mr. Aiken's reach in presenting the conflict between modern facts and the poet's consciousness of inexplicable life and human inadequacies. Owing something, no doubt, to T. S. Eliot's *Prufrock*, this monologue yet quivers with a sincere personal emotion, even though the tone is, as the author confesses, "acid, humorous, ironic."

With *Punch: The Immortal Liar* there is a more emphatic acceptance of the "acid ironic" mood. Eunice Tietjens calls *What Punch Told Them* a "masterpiece of bragging—the good old robust bragging of burlier days, with a big sweep of imagination, a dash of Rabelais and a fine abandon."

Houston Peterson, in his book on Aiken, *The Melody of Chaos*, says: "Others have discussed the 'Lost Provinces' of God, Truth, Beauty, and Goodness, but Aiken discusses the loss of the ego itself. That is the final skepticism."

Earth Triumphant......................................Macmillan Co., N. Y.: 1914
Turns and Movies................................Houghton Mifflin Co., Boston: 1916
The Jig of Forslin......................................Four Seas Co., Boston: 1916
Nocturne of Remembered Spring.................................Four Seas Co.: 1917
* The Charnel Rose: Senlin, a Biography ....Four Seas Co.: 1918

* The House of Dust...Four Seas Co., 1920
* Punch, The Immortal Liar..........Alf. A. Knopf, N. Y.; Martin Secker, London: 1921
Priapus and the Fool.........................Dunster House, Cambridge, Mass.: 1922
The Jig of Forslin (revised)..Martin Secker: 1922
Nocturne of Remembered Spring (revised).......................Martin Secker: 1922
The Pilgrimage of Festus...Martin Secker: 1924
Selected Poems.................................Charles Scribner's Sons, N. Y.: 1929
John Deth and Other Poems...........Charles Scribner's Sons, N. Y. and London: 1930
* Preludes for Memnon....................................Charles Scribner's Sons: 1931
The Coming Forth by Day of Osiris Jones................Charles Scribner's Sons: 1931
Scepticisms: Notes on Contemporary Poetry...................Alf. A. Knopf: 1919
In *Poetry:* Sept. 1915 (Vol. VI); Aug. 1919 (XIV); Sept. 1925 (XXVI); July 1927 (XXX); Sept. 1930 (XXXVI); June 1931 (XXXVIII).

ZOË AKINS

Born in Missouri in 1886, educated chiefly in St. Louis, Miss Akins was "discovered," like so many other writers, by the late William Marion Reedy, of *Reedy's Mirror*. Since the appearance of her book of poems in 1912, she has devoted herself mostly to the writing of plays, of which a number have been successfully produced.

* Interpretations..Grant Richards, London: 1912
* Interpretations..Mitchell Kennerley, N. Y.: 1914
In *Poetry:* Jan. 1915 (Vol. V); Sept. 1918 (XII).

RICHARD ALDINGTON

Richard Aldington, English-born in 1892 and a graduate of London University, was the first of the "imagist" group to get into print, when his *Choricos* appeared in the second number of *Poetry*—November, 1912. This poem, one of the finest death songs in the language—"of a beauty pure and sculpturesque, whitely carved in marble," is youth's glamorous vision of death, beautiful under its mask of terror. It was an ironic destiny which led this poet-youth, soon after, into the front-line trenches of the world's worst war, and changed the glamour into horrible realism. It was a long way, a bitterly cruel way, the poet had to travel—reluctantly, protestingly—from *Choricos* to *The Blood of the Young Men*. The reaction to war was cynicism— bitter disbelief in life, its values and its gods. The *Images of War* are images of utter horror and disaster, that eat up souls as well as bodies. The *Images of Desire* are an absent soldier-lover's mind-pictures of his beloved, and *From Exile* is perhaps the bitterest war poem of all.

Finally we have, in *A Fool in the Forest*, the mature poet's sardonic re- action to all this violent experience of life and death. This poem has been catalogued with *The Waste Land* as a revelation of civilization defeating itself and destroying with its own excess the spirit of man.

Except for a score or less of brief metrical lyrics, done more recently in the filigree fashion of two centuries ago, Mr. Aldington's instrument is free verse of a more or less imagistic pattern. In certain poems and passages his keen instinct for rhythm and tone and word-music achieves an effect of beauty rare in modern poetry. On the whole, he has followed with fair consistency the stern principles under which he and the other imagists began their revolution in 1912.

* Images, Old and New................................Poetry Bookshop, London: 1915
* Images, Old and New.................................Four Seas Co., Boston: 1916
Reverie (ed. of 50)....................................Clerk's Press, Cleveland: 1917

War and Love...Four Seas Co.: 1919
Images of War...Beaumont Press, London: 1919
Medallions in Clay..Alf. A. Knopf, N. Y.: 1921
Exile and Other Poems........Allen & Unwin, London: 1923; Four Seas Co., Boston: 1924
Collected Poems.........................Covici, Friede, N. Y.: 1928; Allen & Unwin: 1929
Mystery of the Nativity (trans. by R. A.).........................Allen & Unwin: 1924
Fifty Romance Lyric Poems (trans. by R. A.)..............Random House, N. Y.: 1928
A Dream of the Luxembourg.........................Chatto & Windus, London: 1930
Love and the Luxembourg........................Covici, Friede, Inc., New York: 1930
The Eaten Heart...Hours Press, Paris: 1930
Also translation from Greek and Latin in Poets' Translation Series: Egoist Press, London.
In *Poetry:* Nov. 1912 (Vol. I); Jan. 1914 (III); Nov. 1914 (V); Oct. 1915 (VII); Nov. 1918
    (XIII); July 1919 (XIV); June 1923 (XXII); June 1931 (XXXVIII).
In *Des Imagistes*.................................Albert & Chas. Boni, New York: 1914
In *Some Imagist Poets:* I–III........................Houghton Mifflin Co.: 1915–16–17

MARY ALDIS

Mary Aldis is a Kentuckian by birth, but since her marriage to Arthur Aldis she has lived mostly in Chicago, or its suburb, Lake Forest. She at first wrote plays, trained a company of her friends, and was a progressive influence in the drama, giving many plays, her own included, in a made-over barn of her country home. When *Poetry* began in 1912, she was much interested in the imagistic movement, and her book of verse is somewhat in that mode.

* Flashlights...Duffield & Co., N. Y.: 1916
In *Poetry:* May 1915 (Vol. VI); May 1916 (VIII); Oct. 1918 (XIII); Jan. 1921 (XVII); Jan.
    1923 (XXI); Jan. 1924 (XXIII).
In *Others: An Anthology of the New Verse*....................Alf. A. Knopf, N. Y.: 1916

SHERWOOD ANDERSON

Sherwood Anderson, born in Ohio in 1876, is better known as a novelist and short-story writer than as a poet, though his group of *Mid-American Songs*, published by *Poetry* in 1917, are an early date in his literary history. In these, reprinted soon after in his first book of poems, he has followed the Whitman tradition with a series of strongly emotional dithyrambic chants in free verse expressive of the feelings of common men in laborious contact with the earth, machines, people. Mrs. Henderson, reviewing his book, said:

"What he gives us is the cry of the singer under the burden of industrialism, the dust of the cities against the clean green life of the corn-fields, the strident need for song above the clatter of the machines. And through it all is conveyed also a certain love of this thing that we call our civilization— the dust, the weariness, the undercurrent of remembrance."

* Mid-American Chants..................................John Lane Co., N. Y.: 1918
* Mid-American Chants.................................B. W. Huebsch, N. Y.: 1921
A New Testament.....................................Boni & Liveright, N. Y.: 1927
In *Poetry:* Sept. 1917 (Vol. X).

JOSEPH AUSLANDER

Joseph Auslander, born in Philadelphia in 1897 of Spanish and Russian parentage, educated there, at Harvard and the Sorbonne, became an instructor at Harvard in 1922.

His first two books are loaded with the fervor of youth, expressed in a lush and liquid lyricism. He loves words, and whips them into tunes with too much facility; but occasionally carries off a song with true concentrated emotion, expressed as if in a tenor voice of fine quality. In the *Letters to Women* he rather unwisely drops his lyric mood, and becomes analytic and sententious; and in *Hell in Harness* he attempts a monologue narrative done in the rough-stuff English of prize-fighters and their kind.

George Dillon, in a review of *Cyclop's Eye* in *Poetry*, credits this poet with "a Keatsian opulence, a Spenserian preciosity, and a peculiar music apparently contrived by setting sonorous delicately recalcitrant rhythms against swift metres."

```
* Sunrise Trumpets.......................................Harper & Bros., N. Y.: 1924
* Cyclops' Eye..............................................Harper & Bros.: 1926
Letters to Women..........................................Harper & Bros.: 1929
Hell in Harness............................Doubleday, Doran & Co., Inc., N. Y.: 1929
The Winged Horse: The Story of the Poets and Their Poetry, by Jos. Auslander and
    Frank E. Hill...................................Doubleday, Page & Co., N. Y.: 1927
In Poetry: May 1922 (Vol. XX); March 1924 (XXIII).
```

MARY AUSTIN

Mary Austin, born in Illinois in 1868 and living mostly in California and New Mexico, has made a life-long study of American-Indian, or "Amerindian" songs and rhythms. Most of her work in verse is based on that study, and is interpretive of aboriginal life. A number of prose books—stories, essays, plays—record further her love of the West, and *The American Rhythm* is a study of aboriginal influences on our life, speech, and literature. Her early book of poems for children, mostly on western subjects, has unusual charm.

```
The Children Sing in the Far West........................Houghton Mifflin Co.: 1928
In Poetry: Feb. 1917 (Vol. IX); Jan. 1920 (XV); Jan. 1921 (XVII); April 1923 (XXII); June
    1928 (XXXII); Nov. 1930 (XXXVII).
```

JOSEPH WARREN BEACH

Born in 1880 in Gloversville, New York, and taking degrees at the University of Minnesota and Harvard, Mr. Beach has been, since 1907, in the English department of his western *alma mater*. An early volume of poems, certain literary essays, and a novel have recorded his literary career.

```
Sonnets of the Head and Heart.......................Richard G. Badger, Boston: 1903
In Poetry: May 1915 (Vol. VI); Dec. 1916 (IX).
```

STEPHEN VINCENT BENÉT

Stephen Vincent Benét, born in Pennsylvania in 1898 of old colonial stock, was graduated from Yale in 1919. His first book, published at seventeen, shows a youthful talent for rhymed eloquence shaping monologues from the mouths of Roman heroes. *Young Adventure* also consists mostly of "weedy rhymes," as the poet confesses in the dedicatory poem, but expended upon a more generous choice of subjects. In much of *Heavens and Earth* he is still preoccupied with classic and mediæval romance, but *The Walkers* and other

New York sketches show him awaking to the poetic suggestiveness of modern life. *King David*, which took the *Nation Prize* in 1923, is mere practice work in biblical narrative, and *Tiger Joy* contained little to enhance its author's reputation, though *The Ballad of William Sycamore* offered promise of a swift and vigorous narrative style.

In 1926 a Guggenheim Fellowship gave Mr. Benét the leisure to complete his long poem of the American Civil War, *John Brown's Body;* and its publication in 1928 made the poet famous and the book a best seller. Reviewing it under the title *A Cinema Epic* in *Poetry* for November, 1928, the editor said: Here is a rousing American verse-tale, a kind of cinema epic, brilliantly flashing an hundred different aspects of American character and history on the silver screen of an unobtrusively fluent and responsive style. The scene-shiftings are sometimes jerky, not always adroit; occasionally the scenario is faulty or the camera-work slipshod, conceding a too "happy ending," for example, in at least one detail of the enormous scheme; and one is forced to admit that the poem, like most epics, falls off somewhat toward the end—*Books VII* and *VIII* do not quite keep up the gallant stride with which the poem began.

But these are minor blemishes, to be admitted but not dwelt upon when there is so much to praise. Mr. Benét has held his reins well in hand, and kept to the straight road of his subject, riding lightly and gracefully a Pegasus which has more paces than a gaited horse. Most of the narrative passages run in a loosely-syllabled variously rhymed three-time pentameter; but one never has a chance to tire of this measure, for suddenly, with a change of mood or subject in the story, the lines will trot into tetrameters, or scuffle into free verse, or, as at the opening of *Book VII*, march solemnly into four-time hexameters. And the lyrics, which happily interrupt the narrative at intervals, are set to different song-measures, from the hymn-tune of *John Brown's Prayer* to the sapphics of Sally Dupré's lament for her wounded lover. In short, the technique shows admirable variety, with fewer lapses into dullness or prosiness than one would expect in so long a poem.

The characterization of some of the historic characters is vivid, the leading actors in the drama—Grant, Lee, Davis, especially—standing out in full stature and color. And in certain episodes there is icy satire. On the whole, it is "a book which reaches out over this broad America, and looks not only backward but forward."

Five Men and Pompey............................The Four Seas Co., Boston: 1915
Young Adventure................................Yale Univ. Press, New Haven: 1918
Heavens and Earth...................................Henry Holt & Co., N. Y.: 1920
King David...Henry Holt & Co.: 1923
Tiger Joy.......................................George H. Doran Co., N. Y.: 1925
* John Brown's Body.......................Doubleday, Doran & Co., Inc., N. Y.: 1928
* Ballads and Poems, 1915–1930..................Doubleday, Doran & Co., Inc.: 1931

WILLIAM ROSE BENÉT

Born in 1886 at Fort Hamilton, in the harbor of New York, a graduate of Yale in 1907, Mr. Benét engaged in literary journalism, was an officer in the air service during the War, and is now one of the editors of the *Saturday Review of Literature*, and an adviser of the publishing firm, Brewer and Warren.

In poetry, fantastic balladry is Mr. Benét's specialty, done with much gusto in swift facile measures. In this field he celebrates a great variety of subjects—oriental, wild-western, sea-faring, besides brief tales of modern people in cities, and purely imaginary episodes of dream-life. One of his books, *Perpetual Light*, is a sheaf of poems written to or about his first wife; and *Man Possessed* contains a group *To E. W.*, his second wife having been the distinguished poet, Elinor Wylie.

Merchants from Cathay.....................................Century Co., N. Y.: 1913
* The Falconer of God......................Yale Univ. Press, New Haven, Conn.: 1914
The Great White Wall...Yale Univ. Press: 1916
The Burglar of the Zodiac.....................................Yale Univ. Press: 1918
Perpetual Light..Yale Univ. Press: 1919
Moons of Grandeur...............................George H. Doran Co., N. Y.: 1920
* Man Possessed: Selected Poems.......................George H. Doran Co.: 1927
In *Poetry:* June 1914 (Vol. IV); Aug. 1915 (VI); April 1916 (VIII); Aug. 1917 (X); Oct. 1917
   (XI); May 1919 (XIV).

MacKNIGHT BLACK (*Died 1931*)

MacKnight Black was born on Christmas day, 1897, and educated at Lafayette and Harvard. Through the War he served in the Navy, and by 1924 he had been "a sailor, newspaper reporter and advertising writer," and a contributor to magazines.

"Machines," said this young poet, "are the most beautiful and moving things I know," and he was stirred as well by the skyscraper architecture of great cities. A critic has complained that his vocabulary and figures of speech have not been enriched by the new words and ideas so plentiful in machine technique, that his love of these evidences of man's power is that of an observer rather than a machinist or engineer. Still, he has borne testimony, so to speak, to the vibrant grandeur of these modern miracles which have aroused so few poets, and one is compelled to grant the splendor of his subject and the validity of his emotion. "Machinery deserves at least one passionate champion" who has no doubt of the benefits to be derived from a mechanized civilization.

The sudden lamentable death of this young poet in August, 1931, prevented his finishing the narrative poem which entitles his second book, in which he tries with renewed ardor "to fit his rhythms to the song of steel."

* Machinery...Horace Liveright, N. Y.: 1929
Thrust at the Sky and Other Poems....................Simon & Schuster, N. Y.: 1932
In *Poetry:* Aug. 1925 (Vol. XXVI).

MAXWELL BODENHEIM

Maxwell Bodenheim, born in Natchez, Mississippi, in 1892, enlisted in the army at eighteen, and after serving a full term of three years, turned up in Chicago and began writing poems about the time *Poetry* was founded.

His first group, appearing in the summer of 1914, showed him a witty student of the imagist technique, deft in the invention of figures and the manipulation of words. His first books developed this manner, decorating with it motives of intricate emotion or sardonic irony.

In later books Mr. Bodenheim has used rhyme in more or less conventional patterns for some of his poems, and the ironic mood is more definitely stressed. Monologue and dialogue forms he has carved fancifully into appropriate frames for his satirical or whimsical reflections upon the shortcomings of humanity, which are lit by a somewhat sardonic gleam.

Reviewing *Returning to Emotion* in *The New Republic*, Conrad Aiken said: "Consciously or not, Mr. Bodenheim's approach to the writing of verse is studiously cerebral. . . . In his simpler and less pretentious things, when he merely indulges his fancy, as in *Chinese Gifts*, he can be charming. Here the verbalist and the cerebralist momentarily surrender, the colder processes are in abeyance, and the result is a poetry slight but fragrant. But for the rest, one finds Mr. Bodenheim a little bit wordy and prosy. One feels that he works too hard and plays too little; or that when he plays, he plays too solemnly and heavily."

In *The King of Spain* he tells a story of melodramatic intrigue which reminds one of Browning's *Dramatic Idyls*. But the rest of this volume returns to his usual manner. One tires sometimes of his elaborate and self-conscious egoism and of his eager sword-play with words; but his attack upon modern abuses and discomforts is keen and relentless. He emphasizes this attack more definitely in a number of novels.

* Minna and Myself.....................................Pagan Pub. Co., N. Y.: 1918
Advice...Alf. A. Knopf, N. Y.: 1920
* Introducing Irony...................................Boni & Liveright, N. Y.: 1922
The Sardonic Arm.....................................Covici-McGee, Chicago: 1923
Returning To Emotion.................................Boni & Liveright: 1927
The King of Spain: A Book of Poems...................Boni & Liveright: 1928
Bringing Jazz..Horace Liveright, N. Y.: 1930
In *Poetry:* Aug. 1914 (Vol. IV); Nov. 1914 (V); Nov. 1915 (VII); May 1916 (VIII); May & Sept. 1919 (XIV); May 1921 (XVIII); Sept. 1923 (XXII); Oct. 1924 (XXV); March 1926 (XXVII); Dec. 1928 (XXXIII).
In *Others: An Anthology of the New Verse*......................Alf. A. Knopf: 1916–17

LOUISE BOGAN

Louise Bogan was born in Maine in 1897, educated in country schools and in Boston, and she has lived mostly in New York. A few months in Europe, and later a season in Santa Fe with her husband, Raymond Holden, had little effect on her art, which uses externals merely as imagery to point the inner accuracies of emotion. Profound feeling, at work with a brooding mind, have resulted in lyrics spare, stark, impassioned, and often of a tragic bitterness. Her art is most expert in these personal poems, which are, as it were, dragged out of a severe discipline of suffering, "a refusal to take life on easy terms," and which disdain to employ a technical method less firmly controlled.

Mr. M. D. Zabel, reviewing *Dark Summer* in *Poetry*, says: "With a creative patience rivaled by that of few other living poets, she has brought her verse to a state of ripe completeness; it does not seek its reward through stylistic variety or the diversity of its ideas and pictures, but rather in the fine unity of purpose and craftsmanship it achieves. Miss Bogan usually restricts herself to a kind of lyric poetry in which her mastery is sure and undisputed. Signs of this mastery are abundant, the delicate use of imagery being probably first among them. Instead of employing irrelevant pictorial devises or garnishing a poem with elaborate ornaments and decorations, she carves the image out of the concept with scrupulous care. The poem finds its substance in the mind, and its shape around the symbol which the mind selects from experience."

And Yvor Winters, always an exacting critic, wrote in *The New Republic:* "She suffers no diminution by comparison with the best of the English lyricists, . . . and she is beyond doubt one of the principal ornaments of contemporary American poetry."

* Body of This Death.........................Robert M. McBride & Co., N. Y.: 1923
* Dark Summer...................................Charles Scribner's Sons, N. Y.: 1929
In *Poetry:* Aug. 1922 (Vol. XX); March 1928 (XXXI); Oct. 1931 (XXXIX).

GORDON BOTTOMLEY

Gordon Bottomley, born at Keighly, England, in 1874, and educated there, is better known as a playwright than as a lyric poet. His blank verse plays, *King Lear's Wife* and *Gruach*, actually seem youthful portraits of Shakespeare's more mature figures of Goneril and Lady Macbeth. Something of the dramatic fervor so manifest in his plays is to be found in certain of his shorter poems.

* Chambers of Imagery: Series I–II.......................Elkin Mathews, London. 1912
Laodice and Danaë...Four Seas Co., Boston: 1916
Poems of Thirty Years................................Constable & Co., London: 1922
Poems (Augustan Books)...........................Ernest Benn, Ltd., London: 1928
Scenes and Plays...............................Macmillan Co., N. Y. & London: 1929
In *Poetry:* Jan. 1917 (Vol. IX).
In *Georgian Poetry:* I–IV...........................Poetry Bookshop, London: 1912–19

POLLY CHASE BOYDEN

Polly Chase was born in Chicago in 1898, educated locally and at Bryn Mawr, married Preston Boyden in 1918, and in 1930 secured a divorce and the custody of her children.

Her first entry in *Poetry*, in 1924, introduced a poet of keen emotional integrity whose feminine intuitions were imaginatively expressed with a searching intensity of phrase. Her first book shows rigid selection and a strictly disciplined art, interpreting a rich emotional experience.

* Toward Equilibrium.....................................Covici, Friede, N. Y.: 1930
In *Poetry:* Oct. 1924 (Vol. XXV); April 1926 (XXVIII); July 1927 (XXX); Dec. 1929
   (XXXV).

RUPERT BROOKE (*Died 1915*)

This poet, one of the Georgian group, was born in 1884 at Rugby, where his father was assistant master, and died of sun-stroke or blood-poisoning at Skyros, April 23, 1915, during the ill-fated British naval expedition to the Dardanelles. The early death of this beautiful youth and gifted poet has become a symbol and proof of the waste and futility of war.

Contradictory moods inspired his earlier work. An athlete, a traveller, a lover of life at one moment, he turned with disgust at the next from

> "half-men, and their dirty songs and dreary,
> And all the little emptiness of love."

Returning from Tahiti in 1913 or early 1914 and pausing a moment in Chicago, he expressed some doubt as to his next move. But the War soon seized him, and changed his romantic quests and disillusions to an equally romantic acceptance of war's heroic glamour. He found a new meaning in life, and sent his war sonnets to *Poetry* in the first flush of his exaltation. At least one of them, *The Soldier*, expresses with passionate sincerity this high heroic mood, and must remain in men's memories as a tragic picture of youth going singing to the sacrifice.

* The Collected Poems of Rupert Brooke.........John Lane Co., London and N. Y.: 1915
Selected Poems.....................................Sidgwick & Jackson, London: 1917
Rupert Brooke, a Memoir, by Edward Marsh......................John Lane Co.: 1918
In *Poetry:* Oct. 1914 (Vol. V); April 1915 (VI).
In *New Numbers*...................................Privately printed, London: 1914–15
In *Georgian Poetry:* I–II.........................Poetry Bookshop, London: 1912, 1915

WITTER BYNNER

Mr. Bynner, though born in Brooklyn (in 1881), and a graduate of Harvard, has become a transplanted product of down-east culture. He has broken away from the Harvard tradition which threatened at one time to enslave him, and avoiding the European refuge of so many of our intelligentsia, has travelled, mind and body, in the orient, and has made Santa Fe and our south-western wonderland, leading into Mexico, his permanent home, not only in terms of real-estate and residence, but in the loyalties and wistful ardors of his spirit.

A cosmopolite and a traveller, Mr. Bynner testifies in his books to his widely varied interests in the world's literature and life. Lyrics, meditative poems, blank verse plays, burlesques, satires, translations of Vildrac's love-poems and (in collaboration with Kiang Kang-Hu) of old Chinese lyrics, interpretations of aboriginal rituals in New Mexico pueblos—all these prove the resources of his mind and the quality of his imagination, his scholarship, and poetic insight.

But it is as a lyric poet that Mr. Bynner makes his highest claim to remembrance. In such poems as the series *To Celia* a grave emotion is expressed in softly flowing low-toned melodies. Some of the later *Chapala Poems*, which are done mostly in octaves, show the influence of the strict poetry of China—its lyric spontaneity and stark simplicity. They are delightfully unaffected and unencumbered, with no excess weight of adjectives or figures of speech or eloquence.

An undertone of lament runs through *Indian Earth*, a soft basic strain noting the impermanence of life against the solidity of rocks and mountains. In private life one of the most friendly of boon companions, this poet loves the far spaces and high places for the closer intercourse of solitude.

An Ode to Harvard and Other Poems..............Small, Maynard & Co., Boston: 1907
Tiger....................................Mitchell Kennerley, New York: 1913
The Little King...Mitchell Kennerley: 1914
* The New World...Mitchell Kennerley: 1915
Iphigenia in Tauris....................................Mitchell Kennerley: 1916
* Grenstone Poems...Fred A. Stokes Co.: 1917
A Canticle of Praise (ltd. ed.)..Privately printed by John Henry Nash, San Francisco: 1919
* The Beloved Stranger...................................Alf. A. Knopf, N. Y.: 1919
Spectra, by Anne Knish (Arthur Davison Ficke), Emanuel Morgan
    (Witter Bynner), and Elijah Hay (Marjorie Seiffert).......Mitchell Kennerley: 1916
Pins for Wings, by Emanuel Morgan......................Sunwise Turn, N. Y.: 1920
* A Canticle of Pan...Alf. A. Knopf: 1920
A Book of Plays (in verse)...................................Alf. A. Knopf: 1922
    (In 1921 Alf. A. Knopf, N. Y., became the publisher of all Mr. Bynner's books except the "Emanuel Morgan" ones.)
A Book of Love, trans. from the French of Charles Vildrac....E. P. Dutton & Co., N. Y.: 1923
Young Harvard...Alf. A. Knopf: 1925
Caravan..Alf. A. Knopf: 1929
* Indian Earth...Alf. A. Knopf: 1929
The Jade Mountain, trans. in collaboration with Dr. Kiang-Kang-Hu.. Alf. A. Knopf: 1929

JOSEPH CAMPBELL (*Seosamh MacCathmhaoil*)

Joseph Campbell (in Gaelic, Seosamh MacCathmhaoil) was born in
Belfast in 1879, and educated in its schools. He has served as an officer of
the Irish Literary Society and Irish Texts of London, has lectured on Irish
literature and history on both sides of the Atlantic, and is well known as one
of the foremost scholars in this field.

Mr. Campbell's poetry is loyally and typically Celtic in its origins and
rhythms. It records his intense love of his country and its customs, and of
the early Gaelic literature which he has done so much to restore to modern
knowledge and usage.

NANCY CAMPBELL

The wife of Joseph Campbell is almost as Celtic as he, but her mood, in
the little books which record her poetic talent, is less serious, more whimsical
than his. She also is steeped in the Gaelic tradition and literature.

EMANUEL CARNEVALI

Emanuel Carnevali was born in Florence, Italy, in 1897. When he was ten
his mother died, and at sixteen he decided to emigrate to America. Landing
in New York almost penniless and ignorant of English, he found a job as
waiter in an Italian *table d'hote*—fifteen hours a day, thirty dollars a month.

In 1917 he began to write poems, mostly in free rhythms, which were
printed in *Poetry* and afterwards in *The Seven Arts*. A little later he left
New York for Chicago, and there, about 1921 he was stricken with a disease
afterwards diagnosed as sleeping-sickness. His father sent for him, and for
some years he has been an invalid in the village of Bazzano, near Bologna.

His poetry has been, from first to last, a powerfully realistic recital of his
emotional rebellion against the conditions of his life, and that of the poor in
great cities. To his plaint he brings a certain Latin directness and sense of
style, and a vigorous instinct for word-values and free-swinging rhythms.

Mr. Carnevali wrote once in a letter: "I have no convictions—I have moments; these moments are the begetters of my poems."

His prose stories, published abroad, with his poems, in a volume called *A Hurried Man*, have attracted some attention from expert critics. Like his verse, they have a rude power.

* A Hurried Man...................................Contact Editions, Paris: 1925
In *Poetry:* March 1918 (Vol. XI); May & Sept. 1919 (XIV); Dec. 1921 (XIX); May 1924 (XXIV); July 1928 (XXXII); Feb. 1930 (XXXV); Feb. 1931 (XXXVII); Aug. 1931 (XXXVIII).
In *Others: An Anthology of the New Verse*.....................N. L. Brown, N. Y.: 1920

WILLA CATHER

Miss Cather was born in Winchester, Virginia, in 1876, had journalistic experience in her youth, and was for six years—1906–12—editor of *McClure's Magazine*.

She is much better known as a novelist than as a poet, such books as *My Antonia* and *Death Comes to the Archbishop* having been widely read, and highly praised by the best critics. However, her one book of verse contains a few much-quoted poems, such as those we offer and *Grandmither*.

Though Miss Cather was born in Virginia and now lives mostly in or near New York, she has spent much of her life in the West, and her novels celebrate mostly the life of its pioneers.

April Twilights.............Richard G. Badger, Boston: 1903; Alf. A. Knopf, N. Y.: 1923
In *McClure's Magazine:* June 1909 (Vol. XXXIII); June 1912 (XXXIX).

PADRAIC COLUM

Padraic Colum, born in 1881, is Irish by birth, breeding, and innate racial loyalties, although since 1915 he has lived mostly in New York and New England, with extensive travels for lectures and readings. Around 1900 he helped to start Dublin's famous Abbey Theatre, and later wrote three or four plays. Since coming to America he has written many books for children, retelling with charm and delight not only old Celtic legends but also the stories of Odysseus and heroes of other lands and ages.

Reviewing *Dramatic Legends* in *Poetry* for July, 1923, the editor wrote: "This book is rich with personality, not only of an individual but of a race. One feels in it that touch of Celtic madness which civilization cannot conquer, which keeps intact Mr. Colum's faith in fairies throughout a seven-years' contact with New York. . . . His songs have an easy spontaneity; one would no more think of questioning their sincerity than of challenging his mountain thrush. And their lyric quality is quite frank and fearless, full of tune-shifts old and new but apparently never sought for. . . . A book full of light winds—from Erin sometimes, but often from nowhere at all."

* Wild Earth...................................Maunsel & Co., Ltd., Dublin: 1910 (*cir.*)
* Wild Earth and Other Poems.........................Henry Holt & Co., N. Y.: 1916
* Dramatic Legends and Other Poems......................Macmillan Co., N. Y.: 1922
* Creatures..Macmillan Co.: 1927
Old Pastures..Macmillan Co.: 1930
* Poems...Macmillan Co.: 1932
In *Poetry:* March 1914 (Vol. III); April 1915 (VI); July 1915 (VI); July 1919 (XIV); Jan. 1921 (XVII).

GRACE HAZARD CONKLING

Mrs. Conkling was born in New York City in 1878. After graduating from Smith College, she studied music abroad for two years. Returning, she was absorbed by marriage, life in Mexico, and the birth of two daughters. In 1914 she returned to her *alma mater* to teach English and stir up an appreciation of poetry; and she still holds this position.

Mrs. Conkling's verse shows her love of color-luxuries, of crowding images, a love not held in check with enough sternness. One finds a confusing richness of fancy and lack of emphasis. But a few poems "rise slim and straight, with enchanting movement, like the flying fish of her book's title."

* Afternoons of April..............................Houghton Mifflin Co., Boston: 1915
* Wilderness Songs.................................Henry Holt & Co., N. Y.: 1920
Variations on a Theme.........................Carolina Press, Charleston, S. C.: 1922
Ship's Log.......................................Alf. A. Knopf, N. Y.: 1924
* Flying Fish.....................................Alf. A. Knopf: 1926
Witch and Other Poems...........................Alf. A. Knopf: 1929
In *Poetry:* Oct. 1912 (Vol. I); June 1914 (IV); Nov. 1915 (VII); April 1917 (X); Dec. 1917 (XI); Sept. 1920 (XVI); June 1921 (XVIII); Sept. 1924 (XXIV); June 1926 (XXVIII).

HILDA CONKLING

Hilda Conkling, the second child of Grace Hazard Conkling, was that phenomenon commoner in musical art than poetic, a wonder-child. She was born in October, 1910, and from the age of four she began to speak her thoughts to her mother with perfect simplicity and sincerity; and her utterance was always imaginative and rhythmical, a beautiful and very original expression of childish feeling. At that time *Poetry* ran a child section every July for poets under ten, and Hilda at once became its star; the poems here quoted, with many others, appeared first there.

In her preface to Hilda's first book, Amy Lowell said: "I know of no other instance in which such really beautiful poetry has been written by a child."

* Poems by a Little Girl................................Fred. A. Stokes Co., N. Y.: 1920
Shoes of the Wind...................................Fred. A. Stokes Co.: 1922
In *Poetry:* July 1916 (Vol. VIII); July 1917 (X); July 1918 (XII); July 1919 (XIV); July 1920 (XVI); Aug. 1922 (XX); Aug. 1923 (XXII).

HAROLD LEWIS COOK

Harold Lewis Cook, born in 1898, was living in Albany, New York, when *Poetry*, in 1921, first printed his poems. For some years he taught in a school for Americans in France, but in 1930 he returned to America to accept a post in Avon, Connecticut.

As a poet, he uses traditional forms in a closely studied technique, attaining a delicate tonal quality. He seems to play softly a wood-wind instrument.

In *Poetry:* Jan. 1921 (Vol. XVII); Dec. 1922 (XXI); June 1928 (XXXII); Sept. 1929 (XXXIV); Sept. 1931 (XXXVIII).

ALICE CORBIN (*Mrs. William Penhallow Henderson*)

Alice Corbin, born in St. Louis, Missouri, in 1881, spent her childhood and youth in Virginia and Chicago, studied for a time at the University of Chicago, and married the painter, William P. Henderson. She was the first associate editor of *Poetry* (1912–1916), and she assisted in preparing the 1917 edition of *The New Poetry*. In 1916 she and her family removed to Santa Fé, where they still reside.

Her work seems to fall into two divisions: *First*, a deep-rooted sense of the soil and of folk-feeling in *Red Earth* and in poems influenced by her Virginia childhood. *Second*, lyric poems, with a quality akin to Elizabethan and seventeenth-century poets. She was briefly influenced by the Celtic poetry revival, but her natural expression belongs more to earth and the reality of personal experience.

She is represented in American, French and Italian anthologies. André Spire translated a group of her poems for *Le Monde Nouveau*.

In a review of *Red Earth* in *The New Republic*, Padraic Colum said: "Amongst American books of verse, Alice Corbin's is the nearest to a collection of folk-songs that I know of. The poems are concerned with very simple and quite fundamental themes; many of them are in traditional forms and behind them one feels the life of a community that is conscious of having been many generations in a particular environment. The poems too have an impressive landscape. . . .

"She has put into a book of poems a community that has a spiritual life of its own. She lets us not only see but know men and women at the edge of the desert, and the people she tells us of belong to the earth she writes about. With its landscape, its men and women, its poems that have the guitar-measure of the Spanish folk-song or the dull chant of the Indian ceremony, there is much life between the red-and-black covers of *Red Earth*."

Adam's Dream, and Two Other Miracle Plays for Children. . Chas. Scribner's Sons, N. Y.: 1907
* The Spinning Woman of the Sky . . . . Ralph Fletcher Seymour, Chicago: 1912
* Red Earth. . . . . Ralph Fletcher Seymour: 1920
In *Poetry:* Dec. 1912 (Vol. I); Nov. & Dec. 1914 (V); Jan. 1916 (VII); Feb. 1917 (IX); July 1917 (X); Nov. 1917 (XI); Jan. 1919 (XIII); April & Aug. 1920 (XVI); Sept. 1924 (XXIV).

HOWARD McKINLEY CORNING

Howard McKinley Corning was born in 1896 on a farm near Lincoln, Nebraska. He lived and went to school in Ohio until the family moved to Oregon in 1919; since then he has been a florist living near Portland. He has taken a keen interest in local poets, who have gathered into an interested group under his leadership.

Corning loves the Northwest, and his best poems express his feeling for the mountains and other wild places of his region. His technique is a disciplined instrument.

These People. . . . . Harold Vinal, N. Y.: 1926
The Mountain in the Sky. . . . . Metropolitan Press, Portland, Oregon: 1930
In *Poetry:* Oct. 1926 (Vol. XXIX); March 1928 (XXXI); May 1930 (XXXVI).

MALCOLM COWLEY

Malcolm Cowley, born in Pennsylvania, 1898, was educated in Pittsburgh schools, at Harvard, and later in the 700-year-old University of

Montpellier. After some war experience in France, he worked as a journalist, and made some excellent translations from Paul Valéry and others. He returned to his own country about 1925, and since then has lived in or near New York.

His first appearance in *Poetry*, in November, 1919, was with rural character sketches done in loose pentameters, a rough imitation of the Masters type of homely realistic narrative. In 1923 a group, coming from France, shows him escaping from this mood, but following a slow development. By 1926 he was publishing poems more arresting, and in 1929 the appearance of his book convinced the critics of his powerful masculine mind and vibrant voice.

This volume, *Blue Juniata*, has been called "a log-book of literary youth in America during the ten years which followed the War, and which came just after the first fruits of our modern literary revival had been harvested." If its earlier poems show the influence of Sandburg, Masters, and some of the foreign radicals, gradually the poet escapes them and asserts his own personality and style.

In this book one seems to feel a strong arm striking musically something hard. There is nothing facile about Mr. Cowley—he beats his poems out of iron, or sometimes bronze, and hammers them into a sturdily beautiful shape, that bears his own impress. In his rhythms is something forbidding—they don't ripple along in traditional tunes. Yet one follows them with ever-increasing accord; they make a modern music, setting the talk of farmers and brokers, or of the poet himself, to a kind of stern and broken song. And his familiars are very ordinary people. He makes this person or that whom he has observed or known glow with an inner fire, quiver with intensity of life. And he feels, as perhaps no other poet has felt, the beauty and lyric agony of New York with its burden of skyscrapers.

We find a thinker in this book, and a man who lives profoundly to the depths of his being. We find also a singer who feels the value of harshness and discords to emphasize his harmonies.

* Blue Juniata..........................Jonathan Cape & Harrison Smith, N. Y.: 1929
In *Poetry:* Nov. 1919 (Vol. XV); Feb. 1923 (XXI); Nov. 1926 (XXIX).

HART CRANE (*Died 1932*)

Hart Crane, born in Ohio in 1899, and educated there in the public schools, worked later at advertising in New York and other cities, and drifted to the Pacific coast, the West Indies, Mexico, and elsewhere. He early began writing poetry of a difficult, sometimes almost cryptic utterance, but shot through with startling gleams of beauty.

Yvor Winters, reviewing *White Buildings* in *Poetry* for April, 1927, said: "The poems suggest here and there, slightly, T. S. Eliot and Wallace Stevens, but the greater part of them are more or less imagistic. The imagism, however, is of the more fragile variety, calling to mind the brittle Parnassianism of H. D. or the thin symbolic flame of Ezra Pound's shorter poems, rather than the packed vitality of a Williams or a Mina Loy. His faults appear to me to be an occasional tendency to slip into rather vague rhetoric and an attempt to construct poems of a series of perceptions so minute and so thoroughly insulated from each other that little unifying force or outline results."

And Morton Dauwen Zabel, reviewing *The Bridge* in *The Commonweal*, calls Hart Crane "one of the few authentic poets now writing in English," and continues: "By means of a symbol drawn from the long steel leap whereby Brooklyn Bridge spans one of the vital waterways of the continent, coupling the populations of two crowded islands, Mr. Crane has tried to describe America herself as a bridge between the past and the future. His theme is, virtually, the complete history and destiny of the American people. By its very scope and grandeur, it seems to entail the defeat of its exponents. Doubtless Mr. Crane has failed to realize its essential implications and its final significance. But meanwhile he has done three things: he has attempted to bring to some actual artistic issue the basic philosophy of American life, he has presented a symbol wherein that philosophy may be embodied, and he has created a language of profound energy and vitality, one of the most searching of poetic styles. His poetry makes every possible demand on the insight and perceptions of the reader. But it is compact of dynamic energy."

Early in 1931 Hart Crane received a Guggenheim Fellowship, and went to Mexico for his foreign year, living mostly in the city of Mexico, where the altitude may have affected his naturally nervous temperament. On the voyage back to New York from Vera Cruz he was seriously distraught, and on April 28th he ran arcoss the deck of the Orizaba and leapt into the sea.

* White Buildings...Boni & Liveright, N. Y.: 1926
The Bridge (lim. ed.)...................................Black Sun Press, Paris: 1930
* The Bridge..Horace Liveright, N. Y.: 1930
In *Poetry:* Oct. 1927 (Vol. XXIX); Oct. 1927 (XXXI); April 1930 (XXXVI).

ADELAIDE CRAPSEY (*Died 1914*)

Adelaide Crapsey was born in Rochester, New York, in September, 1878, and died of tuberculosis at Saranac in October, 1914. Between these two dates she went to school, was graduated at Vassar, studied in the school of archæology in Rome, became instructor in poetics at Smith, was obliged to retreat to Saranac because of failing health, and there, during a year of illness, wrote the tiny volume of fine poems which serves to perpetuate her memory.

The five-line form which she called *cinquain* seems to have been her own invention, doubtless suggested by those Japanese brevities, the *hokku* and *tanka*. She used it with a skill far superior to any of her imitators, breathing it out with extraordinary delicacy of rhythmic utterance.

* Verse...................................The Manas Press, Rochester, N. Y.: 1915
* Verse..Alf. A. Knopf, N. Y.: 1922
A Study in English Metrics.......................................Alf. A. Knopf: 1918
In *Others: An Anthology of the New Verse*........................Alf. A. Knopf: 1916

GLADYS CROMWELL (*Died 1919*)

Gladys Cromwell and her twin sister Dorothea led a protected life of intense family affection, in a luxurious environment. Born in Brooklyn in 1885, they travelled much and were interested in problems of social adjustment, so it was natural that, their parents being dead, they should volunteer for war work in France in 1918. For eight months they served the Red Cross at the Front, but the experience was too nerve-shattering, and on the evening when they had boarded a steamer to sail for home the two sisters leapt overboard, January 24, 1919.

Miss Cromwell, from her first appearances in *Poetry* in 1917–18, showed a style carefully molded to grave beauty. Her poems have the austerity of sculpture—they are severely cut in marble. In them the zeal and beauty of an ardent life is composed and patterned and held in level planes, as in a firm and tautly designed bas-relief. There is no facility, no playing with emotion; it must be strong and deep enough to endure thought, and command hard reluctant materials. Without parade of suffering they express that tragedy of inadequacy which seems to have haunted this woman's mind and caused her too early death. We have in these expressive poems the confession of inexpressiveness.

The Gates of Utterance and Other Poems..........Sherman French & Co., Boston: 1915
* Poems...Macmillan Co., N. Y.: 1919
In *Poetry:* April 1917 (Vol. X); March 1918 (XI).

COUNTEE CULLEN

Countee Cullen was born in New York into a Negro minister's family in 1903, and educated in local schools until his graduation from the New York University in 1925, the year his first book gathered together youthful lyrics which already had been widely published. Some of these are marred by a rhetorical style and too lofty diction, but others are stripped bare of ornament. In later books, the defects of youth are less manifest.

George Dillon, writing of Cullen's best lyrics, said: "Poems like these have a kind of mysterious simplicity, a note which Mr. Cullen has struck untutored. Here, translated into poetry, is freshness and severity of vision toward the profound commonplaces of life and death. . . . In reading such poems, one is aware of a tender and sensitive soul commanding language of ingenuous sweetness and accuracy."

The racial flavor is not so rich as in certain other Negro poets, but the lyric dexterity and tunefulness are characteristic of the race.

* Color..Harper & Bros., N. Y.: 1925
* Copper Sun...Harper & Bros.: 1927
The Ballad of the Brown Girl........................Harper & Bros.: 1927
The Black Christ and Other Poems....................Harper & Bros.: 1929
In *Poetry:* May 1924 (Vol. XXIV); May 1925 (XXVI); July 1925 (XXVI); Nov. 1926 (XXIX).

E. E. CUMMINGS

Edward Estlin Cummings was born in Cambridge, Massachusetts, in 1896, and educated in this country. While he was serving in the A. E. F., an official error caused his arrest and imprisonment, an experience which he has graphically described in *The Enormous Room*.

A few years after his return, he began publishing poems in *The Dial*, using an eccentric typography which is still associated with his style. In spite of this peculiarity, however, the mind behind the queerly printed lines is not unconventional, and we find the poet using the sonnet and other traditional forms in an exuberance of mood not unsuggestive of adolescence.

Reviewing his first book in *Poetry* in January, 1924, the editor said: "Mr. Cummings opens with a fanfare—there is a flourish of trumpets and a crash of cymbals in the resounding music of *Epithalamion*, a certain splendor of sound carried just to that point of blare which should match an exaggerated and half-satiric magnificence of mood. 'Go to, ye classic bards,' he seems to say, 'I will show you what I can do with iambic pentameter, and a rhyme-patterned stanza, with high-sounding processional adjectives, long simile-embroidered sentences, and *O-thou* invocations of all the gods!'

"In a more or less grandiloquent mood the poet swaggers and riots through his book, carrying off Beauty in his arms as tempestuously as ever Petruchio his shrew. The important thing, of course, is that he does capture her—she is recognizable even when the poet, like Petruchio, laughs at her, tumbles her up-to-date raiment, sometimes almost murders her as he sweeps her along."

This mood of exuberance continues more or less through his later books. Some poems guffaw into grotesques leering with tragic or comic significance. The poet is often too nimble—he tires the reader with intricate acrobatics which scarcely repay one for puzzling out their motive over the slippery typographical stepping-stones. He is as agile and outrageous as a faun, and as full of delight over the beauties and monstrosities of this brilliant and grimy old planet. There is gusto in him, and that is rare enough to be welcomed.

Close analysis does not unearth a profoundly original intellectual basis for the gusto. Mr. Cummings is like a mettlesome high-spirited colt who paws the ground and exhibits new and lively paces over well-trodden paths.

* Tulips and Chimneys.....................................Thomas Seltzer, N. Y.: 1923
* XLI Poems...Dial Press, N. Y.: 1925
Is Five..Boni & Liveright, N. Y.: 1926
Him (A Play)...Boni & Liveright: 1927
Viva (Seventy New Poems).................................Horace Liveright: 1931

H. D. (*Hilda Doolittle Aldington*)

Hilda Doolittle was a Pennsylvanian by birth and breeding. Her father was director of the Flower Observatory through most of her childhood, and her college was Bryn Mawr. In 1911, when twenty-five years old, she went abroad, fell in with Ezra Pound whom she had known when both were students, and helped him gather together a small group of poets who called themselves Imagists.

The first fruits of their new and revolutionary growth were published in *Poetry's* first numbers in 1912–13, and in March *A Few Don't's by an Imagist* announced their creed. H. D. was its most perfect exponent, and her art, so still a small voice when it first appeared, became in two or three years a subject of loud controversy. Its delicate beauty persisted, however, beyond the uproar, and the principles followed by her and Aldington (whom she married before the War), by Pound and Flint and the others, shook the Victorian tradition and discarded its excesses.

The amazing thing about H. D.'s poetry is the wildness of it. She is as wild as deer on the mountain, as hepaticas under the wet mulsh of spring, as a dryad racing nude through the wood. She is never indoors, never even in a tent. Her feet know the harsh rocks, but never the ordered hardness of pavements. Her breath is drawn from bright breezes and bold winds, but never from the walled-in atmosphere of rooms. She is, in a sense, one of the most civilized, most ultra-refined, of poets; and yet never was a poet more unaware of civilization, more independent of its thralls. She doesn't talk about nature, doesn't praise or patronize or condescend to it; but she is, quite unconsciously, a lithe, hard, bright-winged spirit of nature to whom humanity is but an incident.

Thus she carries English poetry back to the Greeks more instinctively than any other poet who has ever written in our language. Studying Greek poetry, she finds herself at home there, and quite simply expresses the kinship in her art. For the Greeks, like all singers of primitive races, were never indoors, and their gods were effluences of nature, personifications of her forces.

Her technique, like her spiritual motive, is lithe and nude. The free-verse forms she chooses are not even clothing, so innocent are they of any trace of artificiality; they are as much a part of her spirit, they complete it as essentially, as harmoniously, as the skin which encloses and outlines the flesh of a human body.

There is a bold and trained athleticism in her poetry. Its lines are simple in their strict firmness, but their simplicity is the result, not of instinct alone, but of right instinct sternly educated and disciplined.

* Sea-Garden: Imagist Poems
Constable & Co., Ltd., London; Houghton Mifflin Co., Boston: 1916
* Hymen. . . . . Henry Holt & Co., N. Y.: 1921
* Collected Poems. . . . . Boni & Liveright, N. Y.: 1925
Red Roses for Bronze. . . . . Houghton Mifflin Co.: 1931
Also translations from Greek and Latin in *Poets' Translation Series:* Egoist Press, London: 1919
In *Poetry:* Jan. 1913 (Vol. I); Feb. 1914 (III); March 1915 (V); Dec. 1919 (XV); Oct. 1921
    (XIX); May 1923 (XXVII); June 1926 (XXX); Dec. 1928 (XXXIII).
In *Des Imagistes*. . . . . Albert & Chas. Boni, N. Y.: 1914
In *Some Imagist Poets:* I–III. . . . . Houghton Mifflin Co.: 1915–16–17

H. L. DAVIS

Harold Lenoir Davis was born in Oregon in 1896 of Tennessee parents. His education was casual, but he managed to pick up a knowledge of two or three languages, including Greek. His knowledge of life is founded on extensive experience, and wide acquaintance with all kinds of people; for he has "followed the professions of printer, farm-hand, range rider, country newspaper editor, surveyor, deputy sheriff and bank clerk."

Davis was introduced by *Poetry* with a group which attracted wide attention because of the feeling of great spaces in the poems, and of human beings as part of the fundamental life of the earth. The swinging rhythms of his long lines seemed to belong to the subject and the place, and in a very special sense to belong to the man. This group brought to the poet the Levinson Prize.

Davis has been in no hurry to publish a book of verse, but one is due soon. Meantime he contributes stories and articles to the *American Mercury* and other magazines. In 1932 he received a Guggenheim Fellowship to enable him to complete a narrative poem of pioneer life in the West.

In *Poetry:* April 1919 (Vol. XIV); June 1920 (XVI); Oct. 1922 (XXI); March 1925 (XXV); Jan. 1927 (XXIX); Sept. 1928 (XXXII).

WALTER DE LA MARE

Walter de la Mare, born in Kent, England's southeasternmost county, in 1873, made his first appearance as a poet in 1902 with *Songs of Childhood*, and some of his best-known lyrics (in *Peacock Pie* especially) have been keyed to childish ears. However, *The Listeners*, with its eerie fade-out motive and its unusual four-time rhythmic pattern, is one of the magical lyrics of our time, and a few other poems in his various books approach its beauty.

Essentially Mr. de la Mare is a romanticist. His poetry is an escape from his age and place—touched with fantasy, adventuring toward the supernatural; and he uses a technique more or less orthodox, but lifted often with very personal twists and turns. His style is as fragile as it is delicate, and in working out his effects he is sometimes impeded by inherited formulæ. But if many of his poems are rococo vases of an eighteenth-century artificiality, a few are memorable and perfect lyrics.

Mr. de la Mare has written also novels and tales.

Songs of Childhood........................Longmans, Green & Co., London: 1902, 1916
Poems...John Murray, London: 1906
A Child's Day.................................Constable & Co., Ltd., London: 1912
Peacock Pie..Constable & Co., Ltd.: 1913
* The Listeners...Constable & Co., Ltd.: 1912
* The Listeners...................................Henry Holt & Co., New York: 1915
The Sunken Garden and Other Poems (ltd. ed.)............Beaumont Press, London: 1917
Peacock Pie...Henry Holt & Co.: 1917
* Motley and Other Poems...................Constable & Co.; Henry Holt & Co.: 1918
* Collected Poems (2 vols.)...................Constable & Co.; Henry Holt & Co.: 1920
The Veil...................................Constable & Co.; Henry Holt & Co.: 1922
Down-adown Derry.........................Constable & Co.; Henry Holt & Co.: 1922
Thus Her Tale..................................Porpoise Press, Edinburgh: 1923
A Ballad of Christmas.............................Selwyn & Blount, London: 1924
Ding Dong Bell.......................Selwyn & Blount; Alf. A. Knopf, N. Y.: 1924
Selected Poems...Henry Holt & Co.: 1927
Stuff and Nonsense.....................Constable & Co., Ltd.; Henry Holt & Co.: 1927
The Listeners and Other Poems...........................Constable & Co., Ltd.: 1927
Motley and Other Poems...............................Constable & Co., Ltd.: 1927
Alone...Faber & Guyer, London: 1927
Captive and Other Poems......................................Rudge, London: 1930
Self to Self, A Snowdrop, News (Ariel Poems)...........Faber & Faber, London: 1928–1930
Poems for Children.......................................Constable & Co., Ltd.: 1930
In *Poetry:* April 1917 (Vol. X); Dec. 1921 (XIX).
In *Georgian Poetry:* I–IV..........................Poetry Bookshop, London: 1912–19

GEORGE DILLON

George Dillon was born November 12th, 1907, in Jacksonville, Florida. The family soon moved to Kentucky and he went to local schools there and in St. Louis, until at sixteen he was brought to Chicago and entered its University, taking his B. A. degree in 1927. While an undergraduate, he was president of the University of Chicago Poetry Club, was awarded the Fiske Prize by the University and the Young Poet's Prize by *Poetry*. After this latter award, he served—1925–27—as associate editor of *Poetry*, resigning at graduation to enter the advertising business, from which he definitely retired in 1930. In the spring of 1932 a Guggenheim Fellowship enabled him to go abroad for a year of travel and work at his art. At the same time *The Flowering Stone* received the Pulitzer Poetry Prize for the year 1931.

His earliest poems—a group in *The Forge*, a students' magazine, and six *Preludes* in *Poetry*—showed a rare lyric gift, a compact emotional utterance, and a disciplined and finished technique. His first book, *Boy in the Wind*, appearing during his twentieth year, seems indeed the singing voice of youth, expressing youth's awe and wonder over the mysterious emergence of life from nowhere, the emotional intensity of love, the strange overhanging threat of death. The second book shows increasing intellectual power, with perhaps an even more profoundly inspired lyricism.

* Boy in the Wind...Viking Press, N. Y.: 1927
* The Flowering Stone..Viking Press: 1931
In *Poetry:* Aug. 1925 (Vol. XXVI); Aug. 1926 (XXVIII); Feb. 1927 (XXXIV); Aug. 1929 (XXXIV); Oct. 1930 (XXXVII); June 1931 (XXXVIII).

GLENN WARD DRESBACH

Glenn Ward Dresbach, born on a farm near Lanark, Illinois, in 1889, and a graduate of the University of Wisconsin, began his verse-apprenticeship while filling a government clerkship in the Canal Zone, during the construction of the Panama Canal. Later he was in business in Tyrone, New Mexico, and served through the War, emerging as Captain in the United States Army. Since then he has been an efficiency expert in commercial employ, living chiefly in Chicago, with long sojourns among western plains and mountains.

Mr. Dresbach's numerous books show him preoccupied with the regional beauty of nature and episodes of human and animal emotion. Among his many poems, too similar and often too slight in motive and texture, one finds him achieving now and then a beautiful lyric, and certain of his western poems are keenly descriptive.

The Road to Everywhere....................................Four Seas Co., Boston: 1916
In the Paths of the Wind.......................................Four Seas Co.: 1917
* Morning, Noon and Night.......................................Four Seas Co.: 1920
In Colors of the West....................................Henry Holt & Co., N. Y.: 1922
The Enchanted Mesa and Other Poems........................Henry Holt & Co.: 1924
Cliff Dwellings and Other Poems...........................Harold Vinal, N. Y.: 1926
* Star-Dust and Stone.........................P. L. Turner Co., Dallas, Texas: 1928
The Wind in the Cedars..................................Henry Holt & Co.: 1930
* Selected Poems..Henry Holt & Co.: 1931
In *Poetry:* Nov. 1915 (Vol. VII); June 1917 (X); July 1919 (XIV); June 1920 (XVI); Oct. 1920 (XVII); Jan. 1922 (XIX); May 1922 (XX); March 1924 (XXIII); May 1925 (XXVI); Jan. 1927 (XXIX); Jan. 1928 (XXXI); Oct. 1928 (XXXIII); Aug. 1930 (XXXVI).

JOHN DRINKWATER

John Drinkwater, English-born in 1882, went to the Oxford high school, and later into the insurance business. His first book of verse was published at twenty-one, and in youth he became interested in the theatre, and was connected with Miss Hourniman's company in Birmingham.

Drinkwater's various books of verse prove his loyalty to the Victorian tradition. But the success of his historic drama, *Abraham Lincoln*, turned his attention chiefly to the theatre. It was followed by *Oliver Cromwell* and other plays in the same genre, as well as one or two charming comedies.

Poems of Men and Hours..................................David Nutt, London: 1911
Cophetua..David Nutt: 1912
Poems of Love and Earth...David Nutt: 1913
Rebellion...David Nutt: 1914
* Swords and Ploughshares......................Sidgwick & Jackson, London: 1915
Olton Pools..Sidgwick & Jackson: 1916
Poems: 1908–1914...Sidgwick & Jackson: 1917
Pawns: Three Poetic Plays................................Sidgwick & Jackson: 1917
Tides...Sidgwick & Jackson: 1917
Loyalties...Sidgwick & Jackson: 1919
* Poems 1908–1919...........................Houghton Mifflin Co., Boston: 1919
Seeds of Time..Houghton Mifflin Co.: 1922
Pawns: Four Poetic Plays.............................Houghton Mifflin Co.: 1920
Selected Poems..Sidgwick & Jackson: 1922
Collected Poems...Sidgwick & Jackson: 1923
Preludes 1921–1922..............Sidgwick & Jackson: 1922; Houghton Mifflin Co.: 1923
New Poems..Houghton Mifflin Co.: 1925
Poems (Augustan Books)...Benn, London: 1925
Persephone..Rudge, London: 1927
All about Me (Child Poems)................Collins, London; Houghton Mifflin Co.: 1928
More About Me...............................Collins: 1929; Houghton Mifflin Co.: 1930
In *Poetry:* Dec. 1915 (Vol. VII); Sept. 1916 (VIII); Nov. 1917 (XI); Dec. 1920 (XVII).
In *Georgian Poetry:* I–IV...........................Poetry Bookshop, London: 1912–19

LOUISE DRISCOLL

Louise Driscoll was born in the Hudson valley and has spent all her life there, living of late in Catskill, New York. She has published stories as well as verse. She was deeply moved by the War, and her brief tragedy, *Metal Checks*, here quoted, won the prize as the best poem submitted for *Poetry's* War Number—November, 1914.

The Garden of the West.................................Macmillan Co., N. Y.: 1922
Garden Grace...Macmillan Co.: 1924
In *Poetry:* Nov. 1913 (Vol. III); Nov. 1914 (V); May 1915 (VI); Feb. 1918 (XI); Dec. 1918
    (XIII); Nov. 1919 (XV); Oct. 1921 (XIX); June 1923 (XXII); July 1924 (XXIV); July
    1925(XXVI); July 1926 (XXVIII); July 1928 (XXXII); Jan. 1929 (XXXIII).

HELEN DUDLEY

Helen Dudley, who was born in Chicago, one of four brilliant sisters, is a poet of a single poem, too poignant to be omitted from this collection.

In *Poetry:* Oct. 1912 (Vol. I); Aug. 1914 (IV); Dec. 1917 (XI); May 1920 (XVI).

T. S. ELIOT

Thomas Stearns Eliot was born in 1888 in St. Louis, Missouri; received his A. B. from Harvard in 1909 and A. M. in 1910; studied at the Sorbonne in Paris and at Merton College, Oxford; became successively a lecturer, editor, and banker in London after taking up residence there in 1914; founded and became the editor of *The Criterion* in 1923; and has finally become an English citizen and one of the most influential critics of present-day London.

For the following brief essay the editor is indebted to Morton Dauwen Zabel:

Eliot's poetry was regarded for over ten years as the typical expression of the problems of the modern consciousness. Informed with a witty symbolism and an extreme satiric penetration, it voiced in perfect accents the disillusionment and terrifying frustration which the nineteenth-century pessimists—Arnold, James Thomson, Gissing, Housman, and Hardy—left to their twentieth-century inheritors. In *The Love-song of J. Alfred Prufrock* (which appeared in *Poetry* in 1915, the first of Eliot's poems to be printed); in the series of satires constructed around the absurd and tragic figure of Sweeney, Eliot's character of the average man; in the spiritual cowardice which produced the tragedies in *Portrait of a Lady* and *La Figlia che Piange;* and finally in the dry defeat of premature senility expressed in *Gerontion,* Eliot gave classic utterance to the spiritual bankruptcy of the contemporary world. The nineteenth-century Englishmen, however, were not Eliot's immediate tutors. His sensibility had been enriched by exhaustive study of the Elizabethan dramatists—Chapman, Webster, Kyd, Marlowe, and Jonson—who, with Dante, enlivened in Eliot's consciousness the grandeur of a heroic past which only served to emphasize the sterility of the present. His intelligence had been tutored by the analytical dexterity of Donne and the metaphysical poets of the seventeenth century. His technical tutelage, as well as his lessons in symbolism, came largely from the more intellectual of the French symbolists—Corbière, Rimbaud, Laforgue, and Tailhade. With this wide literary acquaintance supporting his native subtlety and refinement of style, Eliot was prepared to write the master-piece which *The Dial* printed in 1922, *The Waste Land*. This poem, elabo-rately documented with literary and anthropological motives, forms a centre for the poetic achievement of the first quarter of the present century. Of brilliant design, and unfailingly accurate in metaphorical reference, it sums up and closes the age of skepticism and tortured intellectual doubt. In the desolate waste land, where no rain falls to revive the parched and with-ered spirit of man, Eliot found a symbol of disillusionment which is the sum-mary of all the lesser creations of modern poets and novelists. Compact of derivations and confusion influences, varying in its stylistic resources from splendid blank verse to meretricious parody, and at times lifted above its inherent emptiness only by the firm integrity of Eliot's conception, *The Waste Land* must under any circumstances stand as a clue and a summary to much of the creative history of our time.

Eliot's influence, already unmistakable, now became acknowledged every-where. His readers and disciples never questioned the fact which Ezra Pound (foremost among Eliot's friends and perhaps the first to recognize his genius fully) had declared: that he was one of the few modern poets to discover a personal idiom and rhythm for his verse. They were left to won-der, however, where Eliot would lead them next. They were scarcely pre-pared for a reversion (announced as fully achieved in the preface to his book of essays of 1929, *For Launcelot Andrewes*) to the moral absolutism of which the *Hippopotamus* was an inverted parody, the *Sunday Morning Service* a social indictment, *Gerontion* a broken and pathetic echo, and the chorus of *The Hollow Men* a derisive denial. What had long been implicit in Eliot's work was at length fully disclosed: he never had succeeded in cutting the roots of native puritanism which bound him to the soil of Christianity. His nostalgia for the heroic and sanctified glories of the past, when man's rôle in the universe was less equivocal and his destiny mystically shrouded by the doctrine of redemption, had finally led him to the affirmations of faith. Yet his conversion might have been forecast. The very finality of his despairing self-scrutiny had implied a reserve of idealism to which, escaping suicide, he must some day fly for recourse. "The eagles and the trumpets" might be "buried beneath some snow-deep Alps," but the pos-sibility of digging them out remained. "The old man in a dry month, being read to by a boy, waiting for rain" did not release his last hope of a reviving shower, even where, across the parched acres of the waste land, it failed to fall. The straw-stuffed men in their idiotic dance around the prickly pear, waiting for the world to end "not with a bang but a whimper," could not forget the phrases of a liturgy promising the resurrection and the life.

The Hollow Men of 1925 led the way, through a series of short poems—*Animula, Journey of the Magi, Song for Simeon,* and *Marina*—toward *Ash Wednesday* (1930), the poem wherein Eliot's spiritual recovery is finally assured. No one who mistrusts the method of Eliot's recovery, or who marks a recognizable lessening of stylistic acuteness in the later poems, will be able to deny that they are still distinguished by unpredictable stylistic subtleties, and find their place in a remarkable personal document which contains some of the finest poetry in modern literature.

Eliot's brilliant essays have appeared in many magazines; some of the best are collected in two volumes, *The Sacred Wood* (1921), and *For Launcelot Andrewes* (1929). He has likewise written studies of seventeenth-century poets under the title *Homage to John Dryden* (1924) and an essay on *Dante* (1930). His editorship of *The Criterion* has made that quarterly the single English magazine to keep closely in line with the intellectual and creative activity of the Continent and America, and through its pages Eliot still exercises a wide and unmistakable influence on younger poets and critics. In any history of twentieth-century literature, his importance will remain preëminent, if merely because his work has expressed at its best the ordeal of the mind in an age of spiritual strife and moral adjustment.

* Prufrock and Other Observations.....................The Egoist, Ltd., London: 1917
Ara Vus Prec..Ovid Press, London: 1919
* Poems...Alf. A. Knopf, N. Y.: 1920
The Waste Land......................................Boni & Liveright, N. Y.: 1922
Poems 1909–1925....................................Faber & Gwyer, London: 1926
Poems...Alf. A. Knopf: 1929
Ash Wednesday...............Faber & Faber, London; G. P. Putnam's Sons, N. Y.: 1930
Journey of the Magi, A Song for Simeon, Animula, * Marina, Triumphal March
   (Ariel Poems).....................................Faber & Faber, Ltd.: 1928–31
Ezra Pound, his Metric and Poetry.....................Alf. A. Knopf, New York: 1917
Homage to John Dryden..............................Hogarth Press, London: 1924
For Launcelot Andrewes (essays)......................Faber & Faber, Ltd.: 1928
The Sacred Wood (essays)..........Methuen & Co., London; Alf. A. Knopf, N. Y.: 1928
Dante..Faber & Faber, Ltd.: 1929
In *Poetry:* June 1915 (Vol. VI); Oct. 1915 (VII); Sept. 1916 (VIII).

WILLIAM CLOSSON EMORY

William Closson Emory was born in Fitchburg, Massachusetts, in 1894, but between the ages of three and twenty he lived in Honolulu. He is now assistant sales manager of a steel corporation, residing in Detroit or Buffalo.

In 1917 he volunteered for the War, and served at the French front, an experience which his poem commemorates. He came out of the War a "militant pacifist." As a poet he has usually preferred a radical technique, though some of his poems are in rhymed form.

* Be Still..Lotus Press, Detroit, Mich.: 1929
In *Poetry:* Aug. 1928 (Vol. XXXII); Nov. 1928 (XXXIII); May 1930 (XXXVI).

ABBIE HUSTON EVANS

Abbie Huston Evans was born in New Hampshire and is a graduate of Radcliffe. After serving overseas with the A. E. F., she did settlement work in a coal camp in the Rockies and the steel district of Pittsburgh. She is now living in Philadelphia.

Miss Evans' poetry is an assertion of strength, a quiet declaration of unity and completeness. There is no shouting, no strain or pose, but there is a deep satisfaction, a lyric joy in being one with nature and her processes. We hear details of this harmony, asserted always with a close compactness in figures that surprise and delight with their keen accuracy—like the *solder* simile in the sonnet *Hill-born*. It is faith in life that moves her, in the earth and the sky, in day and night and trees and rocks and all primal things; and her adequate art expresses this firm delight as freshly as if the song had never been sung before.

But nature is not this poet's only subject; the same sturdiness, strength of fibre, is manifest in her poems of personal experience and emotion. There is a disciplined sternness in her artistic theory as in her character, and her work becomes a revelation of delight in a spirit absolute and sincere.

Outcrop...Harper & Bros., N. Y.: 1928
In *Poetry:* June 1923 (Vol. XXII); Nov. 1923 (XXIII); Feb. 1927 (XXIX); Sept. 1929
   (XXXIV); Sept. 1930 (XXXVI).

DONALD EVANS (*Died 1921*)

Donald Evans was born in 1884 and died in 1921. His mature years were passed mostly in New York, where for some time he was the musical critic of *The Globe*.

He began as an adept writer of sophisticated satirical verse, but the War sobered him, and *Vie de Bordeaux* is in praise of the gallant attitude of his beloved France. Other later poems also, however wittily phrased and pointed, show his own sympathetic gallantry of spirit.

Discords..Brown Brothers, Philadelphia: 1912
Two Deaths in the Bronx..........................Nich. L. Brown, Philadelphia: 1915
Nine Poems from a Valetudinarian...........................Nich. L. Brown: 1916
* Sonnets from the Patagonian.................................Nich. L. Brown: 1918
Ironica...Nich. L. Brown: 1919

ARTHUR DAVISON FICKE

Arthur Davison Ficke was born in Davenport, Iowa, in 1883, educated there and at Harvard, was admitted to the bar in 1908 and practiced law at home until the War took him to France. Returning to America in 1919, he gave up the law for literature, and has lived mostly in or near New York, with intervals of oriental travel and a health-sojourn in Santa Fe.

His books introduce a lyric poet whose sad song, done in conventional measures, complains of life's futility, of the inadequate and temporary joys, the bitter sorrows, the fierce and fleeting emotions accorded to the questioning human spirit. He arrives at no solution—with him it is the passion of perfection fevering the blood to madness, the quest of the unattainable leading the soul into the void. We find here the dark struggle, the brooding mystery; but somehow the note is of frantic restlessness rather than tragic agony, as if modern man were not strong enough to swim in deep waters.

In *Twelve Japanese Painters*, a connoisseur celebrates his love of Japanese art. Even here his preference for regular metrics and accepted stanzaic forms is manifest. When the imagists were fighting their free-verse campaign, Mr. Ficke, in 1915-16 joined with Witter Bynner and Marjorie Seiffert in a satiric hoax labelled *Spectra*, which out-played the innovators at their own game, and deceived most of the critics of the time.

From the Isles.........................Samurai Press, Cranleigh and London: 1907
The Happy Princess and Other Poems............Small, Maynard & Co., Boston: 1907
The Earth Passion...Samurai Press: 1908
The Breaking of Bonds.............................Mitchell Kennerley, N. Y.: 1910
Twelve Japanese Painters.........................R. F. Seymour Co., Chicago: 1913
Mr. Faust...Mitchell Kennerley: 1913
* Sonnets of a Portrait Painter.................................Mitchell Kennerley: 1914
* The Man on the Hilltop...Mitchell Kennerley: 1915
An April Elegy..Mitchell Kennerley: 1917
* Sonnets of a Portrait Painter (revised) and Other Sonnets......Mitchell Kennerley: 1922
Out of Silence and Other Poems.............................Alf. A. Knopf, N. Y.: 1924
Mountain against Mountain.....................Doubleday, Doran & Co., N. Y.: 1929
In *Poetry:* Feb. 1913 (Vol. I); March 1915 (V); June 1915 (VI); Nov. 1916 (IX); April & May
    1921 (XVIII); Aug. 1923 (XXII); Sept. 1923 (XXII).

HILDEGARDE FLANNER (*Mrs. Frederick Monhoff*)

When Hildegarde Flanner went from her native Indiana to study in the University of California, she joined Witter Bynner's class in verse-writing and her group of poems, *Young Girl*, received the Cook Prize and a beautiful *edition de luxe* black-red-and-gold dress done by the Crocker Company.

Although Miss Flanner's "maturity as a craftsman is still far from complete," she has achieved, in poems of personal experience and more or less religious quest, a few conspicuous successes, such as one or two elegies, and some of the quaint *Sonnets in Quaker Language*.

* Young Girl.....................................H. S. Crocker Co., San Francisco: 1920
* This Morning...Frank Shay, N. Y.: 1921
* Time's Profile...Macmillan Co., N. Y.: 1929
In *Poetry:* Feb. 1921 (Vol. XVII); March 1924 (XXIII); Sept. 1927 (XXX); June 1929 (XXXIV); Nov. 1931 (XXXIX).

JOHN GOULD FLETCHER

John Gould Fletcher was born January 3d, 1886, in Little Rock, Arkansas, where he attended school until he was sent to Andover and afterwards Harvard. He left Harvard in his senior year, already an inveterate traveller, sailed to Europe in 1908, and the next year settled in London. Later he went to the orient to confirm and develop his love of Japanese art.

Fletcher's literary career began with the publication of five small books of verse in 1913. This brought him into contact with Ezra Pound and the imagists, and in December, 1913, his *Irradiations* were published in *Poetry*. At that time he called himself "a vers-librist but not an imagist," and indeed his artistic theory and technique have never been strictly according to the imagistic creed; but in 1915–16–17 he was included in the three *Some Imagists* annuals which were sponsored by Amy Lowell.

Mr. Fletcher has been called a landscape poet because of his emotional delight in scenic beauty and his power of vivid presentation. City scenes moved him as well as rural, and his range extended from the rainy streets and silvery lawns of London to the deserts of Arizona. His *Symphonies*—one for each color of the rainbow—celebrate as lovingly as a painter might the rich spectacle of color offered to human eyes.

Of late he has turned his eyes inward in the quest of spiritual truth. "*In The Black Rock*," says M. D. Zabel in a *Poetry* review, "we get an account of a world crowded with conflict and distress, calling every moment upon the poet for sympathy and succor. Here 'man is the cracked beggarman of the stars,' growing bitter with his twisted longing. He climbs toward the summits of his hope only to find them sheathed in relentless ice. The towers he finally builds stand lonely and unvisited. . . .

"Such themes carry an ackowledgment of profound responsibility not only toward man but toward the larger spirit which shapes his destiny. Mr. Fletcher wrestles with that burden and tries to probe his painful world for a clue to its purpose. What he finds is told in the final poem, *To the Unknown God*. Strife may fail, and even where it succeeds it may prove profitless, but in the striving a life of new power and advancing beauty is shaped. Our salvation is born not of our triumphs but of our agony.

"*The Black Rock* lacks the rhythmic and descriptive charm of Mr. Fletcher's earlier books, but it possesses a tougher substance."

Fire and Wine..Grant Richards, London: 1913
Fool's Gold..Max Goschen, Ltd., London: 1913
The Dominant City.....................................Max Goschen, Ltd.: 1913
The Book of Nature............................Constable & Co., Ltd., London: 1913
Visions of the Evening............................Erskine McDonald, London: 1913
* Irradiations...................................Houghton Mifflin Co., Boston: 1916

F. S. FLINT

Francis Stewart Flint, born in 1885, and spending most of his life in London, has educated himself in a number of languages while earning his living, and published, besides his own verse, excellent translations of French and mediæval Latin poets.

From the first Mr. Flint preferred to write in "unrhymed cadence," a form which he called, in his preface to *Otherworld* in 1920, "the real tradition of English poetry," quoting Chaucer and Cynewulf to support him; and arguing that "rhyme and metre are artificial and external additions to poetry." His first little book, published in 1909, had shown him a pioneer in the use of his chosen form, so it was natural that he should join the imagist group two or three years later, and send his poems to *Poetry,* which introduced him to America in July, 1913.

Richard Aldington, in *Poetry* for October, 1920, found in *Otherworld:* "Melancholy, sometimes a little bitter, sometimes mellowed by reflection; an eager love of beauty which is often thwarted and disappointed; an essential sweetness, loneliness and good sense; above all, an instinctive gusto for ordinary human life in spite of the weakness and folly and sordidness."

FORD MADOX (*Hueffer*) FORD

Ford Madox Ford—born Hueffer in 1873, a grandson of Ford Madox Brown of the pre-Raphaelite group—was educated in London and abroad. As founder and editor of *The English Review,* he is credited with many discoveries of writers now famous. Among these he introduced Joseph Conrad, and collaborated with him in certain early novels. Also he has written many novels of his own, and other prose works.

His *Collected Poems* of 1914 gather together earlier very casual publications. Soon after, he was caught up by the modern movement, and *On Heaven,* a 500-line poem published in *Poetry* in June, 1914, showed a power and tenderness, and an easy command of a free-flowing measure, altogether new in his poetic style. A few later poems gave side-long glimpses of his war service at the front, a service more completely suggested in the four Tietjens novels. Indeed, poetry has been something of a side-issue in Mr. Ford's crowded life, although his fitful service of the muse has produced a few very human and beautiful poems. One of these, *A House*, a fanciful dialogue too long to quote, took a *Poetry* prize in 1921.

Collected Poems......................................Max Goschen, London: 1914
Antwerp...Poetry Bookshop, London: 1915
* On Heaven and Poems Written on Active Service..John Lane Co., London & N. Y.: 1918
In *Poetry:* June 1914 (Vol. IV); March 1917 (IX); April 1918 (XII); March 1921 (XVII); June 1923 (XXII); Feb. 1932 (XXXIX).

MOIREEN FOX (*a Cheavasa*)

Moireen Fox has been steeped in the Celtic tradition ever since her birth in Ireland. Most of her subjects are taken from Irish legend.

* Liadain and Curithir...........................B. H. Blackwell, Oxford, Eng.: 1917
Midyir and Etain...................................Candle Press, Dublin: 1918
In *Poetry:* March 1915 (Vol. V); May 1917 (X); Jan. 1921 (XVII).

FLORENCE KIPER FRANK

Florence Kiper, Mrs. Jerome Frank, a member of a prominent Jewish family of Chicago, has stressed the racial point of view in her work, her first appearance having been with the sonnet *A Jew to Jesus* in *The Century*. Since her book was published, she has been diverted a good deal from poetry to play-writing.

Cinderelline...Dramatic Publ. Co., Chicago: 1913
* The Jew to Jesus and Other Poems..................Mitchell Kennerley, N. Y.: 1915
In *Poetry:* Oct. 1914 (Vol. V); Dec. 1917 (XI); Nov. 1920 (XVII); Nov. 1922 (XXI); Jan. 1926 (XXVII); June 1927 (XXX).

ROBERT FROST

Robert Frost, although a New Englander by family tradition and instinctive sympathy, was born, March 26th, 1875, in San Francisco, whither his parents had removed. His mother returning east after his father's death, the boy went to the Lawrence high school, later for a short time to Dartmouth College, and, after his early marriage, to Harvard for two years, followed by some years of teaching, farming, and other struggles to make a living.

Although he began in boyhood to write, and even publish, poems, the editors were slow to appreciate them; and so he decided on a complete change, sold his farm and sailed for England in September, 1912. Here he soon found himself among controversial literary groups, made friends with English poets, secured a publisher for his first book, and met Ezra Pound, who sent to *Poetry The Code*, which, appearing in February, 1914, was practically Frost's introduction to his own country. The next year he returned to New Hampshire, and since then has lived there and in Vermont, with seasons of a kind of honorary professorship at Amherst College and the University of Michigan.

This poet, however loyally local, is bigger than his environment; and his art, plunging beneath surfaces and accidents, seizes upon the essential, the typical, in the relations of men and women with each other and with the earth, the sky, and all that lives and moves between them. Such art passes local boundaries as lightly as an airplane, and swings out into wider circles of time and space.

Mr. Frost has never been in a hurry. He was almost forty when his first book was published in 1913, and the title of that book was *A Boy's Will*, as if he had just got around to the business of growing up. I doubt if he ever moved before he was ready; but, unlike some slow-stepping philosophers, he has always known when he was ready and has not hesitated when the moment arrived.

If Mr. Frost was working at his art during that score of formative years, I think he was studying chiefly the rhythms of speech. He felt, no doubt, that if he could satisfy himself that his verse presented the musical essence of his neighbors' talk, all the rest—subject, emotional motive, dexterity of technique—would be added unto him. At any rate he did not publish until his poems had caught those slow and simple, but elusive and difficult, rhythms. He transmutes them almost always into a freely moving iambic measure, usually blank verse in the longer poems, and in the shorter ones rhyming couplets or stanzas. His metrical patterns are according to precedent—he tries no free-verse experiments; but there is a subtle originality, a very personal style, in his weaving of cadences over the basic metre. The music has more variety than one would admit at first. The blank verse of *New Hampshire*, for example, goes swinging familiarly along in a loose stride, while that of *Snow* rises to symphonic eloquence in suggesting the preacher's duel with the blizzard. And the quatrains of *The Hill Wife* play a very different tune from those of *Brown's Descent*. Yet in each case there is no mere facile music-making—the speech-rhythms are intensified, patterned if you will into melody, but not artificialized.

Perhaps no poet in our history has put the best of the Yankee spirit into a book so completely, so happily, as Robert Frost. The poems of nature and of farm life all express delight, and some are ecstatic. The poet knows what he is talking about, and loves the country and the life. He gets a thrill out of birches in the sun, a cow running cider-wild (such real animals in these poems!), out of mending stony walls, planting seed, etc. His touch upon these subjects is sure and individual, the loving touch of a specialist—we know he knows. And in the character pieces we feel just as sure of him.

When it comes to personal confession—to autobiography, so to speak— Mr. Frost refuses to take himself seriously. He has to laugh—or rather, he has to smile in that whimsical observant side-long way of his. This mood greets us most characteristically in *New Hampshire*, the long poem, which, in painting a portrait, so to speak, of his state, establishes a sympathetic relation with himself, and paints, more or less consciously, his own portrait. New Hampshire and her poet both have character, as well as a penetrating, humorous and sympathetic quality of genius. They face the half-glance of the world, and the huge laughter of destiny, with pride and grit, and without egotism.

* A Boy's Will..David Nutt, London: 1913
* A Boy's Will..Henry Holt & Co., N. Y.: 1915
* North of Boston..David Nutt: 1914
* North of Boston..Henry Holt & Co.: 1915
* Mountain Interval..Henry Holt & Co.: 1916
(In 1922 William Heinemann took over the publication of Mr. Frost's books in England.)

* New Hampshire...Henry Holt & Co.: 1923
* West-running Brook.......................................Henry Holt & Co.: 1928
Selected Poems...Henry Holt & Co.: 1928
In *Poetry:* Feb. 1914 (Vol. III); Nov. 1916 (IX); Jan. 1922 (XIX); Aug. 1923 (XXII).

WILFRID WILSON GIBSON

Wilfrid Gibson (his latest book drops the "Wilson") was born in Northumberland in 1880, and achieved a rather frugal education. In his early twenties he was already the author of five small books, containing five romantically imitative plays. With *Daily Bread* in 1910, he became a realist, a poet interested in his neighbors of the countryside. His frail health prevented his being accepted as a soldier in 1914, but some of his war poems present briefly and vividly episodes of a common man's service at the front.

Gibson's work presents a conflict between the old manner and the new— he cannot quite forget the one or completely accept the other. His style is pedestrian, but in his best poems, those from 1912 to 1920, he resists an instinctive facility and expresses the obscure and reticent emotions of inexpressive lives.

The Golden Helm......................................Elkin Mathews, London: 1903
The Nets of Love...Elkin Mathews: 1905
On the Threshold............................Samurai Press, Cranleigh & London: 1907
The Stonefolds...Samurai Press: 1907
The Web of Life..Samurai Press: 1908
Fires I–II...Elkin Mathews: 1912
Daily Bread..................Elkin Mathews, London: 1913; Macmillan Co., N. Y.: 1923
Womenkind......................................Adams & Black, London: 1913
Womenkind..Macmillan Co., N. Y.: 1912
* Borderlands..Elkin Mathews: 1914
* Thoroughfares..Elkin Mathews: 1914
* Borderlands and Thoroughfares......................Macmillan Co., N. Y.: 1914
* Battle and Other Poems...........Elkin Mathews, London; Macmillan Co., N. Y.: 1916
Daily Bread..Macmillan Co.: 1916
Fires...Macmillan Co., 1916
Livelihood...................................Macmillan Co., N. Y. & London: 1917
* Poems 1904–1917............................Macmillan Co., N. Y. & London: 1917
Hill Tracks..................................Macmillan Co., N. Y. & London: 1918
Neighbors...................................Macmillan Co., N. Y. & London: 1920
I Heard a Sailor.................................Macmillan & Co., London: 1925
Collected Poems, 1905–1925........Macmillan & Co., London, Macmillan Co., N. Y.: 1929
The Golden Room and Other Poems..........Macmillan Co., Ltd., N. Y. & London: 1928
Hazards...Macmillan Co., Ltd., N. Y. & London: 1930
In *Poetry:* June 1914 (Vol. IV); April 1915 (VI); Aug. 1915 (VI); March 1916 (VII); Jan. 1917 (IX).
In *Georgian Poetry:* I–IV...........................Poetry Bookshop, London: 1912–19

HORACE GREGORY

Horace Gregory was born in Milwaukee in 1898, and educated there at the German-English Academy and the Milwaukee School of Fine Arts. In 1923 he took a degree at the University of Wisconsin, and since then has lived in or near New York City. In 1925 he married the poet Marya Zaturensky.

Gregory may be grouped among the more radical technicians. Also he prefers subjects of intensely modern interest.

* Chelsea Rooming House...............................Covici-Friede, Inc., N. Y.: 1930
The Poems of Catullus (trans. from Latin)....................Covici-Friede, Inc.: 1931
In *Poetry:* Jan. 1926 (Vol. XXVII); Oct. 1927 (XXXI); Feb. 1930 (XXXV); March 1931 (XXXVII).

HAZEL HALL (*Died 1924*)

Hazel Hall, born in St. Paul, Minnesota, in 1886, was taken in childhood to Portland, Oregon, where she lived until her death in 1924. From the age of twelve she was paralyzed and confined to a wheeled chair, though otherwise in good health, and she partly supported herself by delicate needle-work. When past thirty, she discovered her talent for writing verse, and her earlier poems speak for countless generations of women by using the needle as their figurative subject.

Being unable to walk, she followed imaginatively the procession of foot-steps outside her window, and this becomes the central theme of her second, and perhaps her strongest book. Her work showed increasing spirituality until the end, and the posthumous volume gives evidence that the meaning of life and death were absorbing her imagination.

*Curtains................John Lane Co., N. Y.; 1921; Dodd, Mead & Co., N. Y.: 1922
*Walkers...Dodd, Mead & Co.: 1923
*Cry of Time...E. P. Dutton & Co., N. Y.: 1928
In *Poetry:* July 1918 (Vol. XII); April 1920 (XVI); May 1921 (XVIII); Jan. 1923 (XXI); July 1924 (XXIV).

THOMAS HARDY (*Died 1928*)

Thomas Hardy was born June 2d, 1840, in Upper Bockhampton, Wessex, the son of a stonemason. His schooling was casual, and at sixteen he was apprenticed to an architect. Later he worked in London and in 1863 won a prize offered by the Royal Institute of Architects. In 1871 he gave up archi-tecture for literature, and published his first novel anonymously. His sec-ond was a success, and from that time he was famous as a novelist.

But the poems in certain of his books are dated as early as the eighteen-sixties, reminding us that Hardy's long career as a man of letters began with the writing of verse. To poetry he returned in the late 'nineties, when hostile criticism of *Tess* and *Jude the Obscure* made him decide to abandon his career as a novelist after writing at least five novels which must rank among the greatest of their time. Thus between 1899, when the *Wessex Poems* appeared, and 1929, when *Winter Words* was published posthumously, he achieved a great body of poems which carry over from the novels those qualities of austere, unflinching intellectual integrity which are the un-failing marks of Hardy's genius. These poems are, like the novels, rich in drama and earthy incident, in studies of man moving against the dark background of his mysterious destiny, and in the authentic accents of com-mon speech which always make Hardy's work, even at its most philo-sophical and speculative, adhere to its origins in the common life of man. In 1907 appeared *The Dynasts*, a huge and spectacular epic of the Napoleonic Wars, wherein Hardy threw the persistent philosophical doubt and tragic intuition, which motivates even the least of his lyrics, against the wide panorama of a war-torn world. The implication of a final hope which he expressed in the last lines of this tragic poem was perhaps an incident, rather than an essential aspect, of his thought. For just as he brought to its most tragic expression the fundamental doubt of scientific and philosophical inquiry in the nineteenth century, so he persisted in his tragic but ennobling agnosticism to the end. His work formed an epilogue to one great age of speculation, but by the freshness and constantly renewed vigor of his poetic genius he lived to become part of a new age,—one of the most honored, and most formidable, rivals of the new poets who appeared in England and America during and after the War. His shorter poems—whether written as dialogues or dramas, reflections or occasional lyric songs—are an integral part of his personality, and give brief insight into an intellectual experience which bridged two centuries.

Wessex Poems, and Other Verses........................Macmillan & Co., London: 1899
Wessex Poems, and Other Verses.........................Harper & Bros., N. Y.: 1899
Poems of the Past and the Present......................Macmillan & Co., London: 1901
Poems of the Past and the Present..............................Harper & Bros.: 1901
The Dynasts: a Drama in Three Parts............Macmillan Co., London & N. Y.: 1904
* Time's Laughing-stocks...........................Macmillan & Co., London: 1909
* Satires of Circumstance.....................................Macmillan & Co.: 1914
Selected Poems..Macmillan & Co.: 1916
* Moments of Vision and Miscellaneous Verses.................Macmillan & Co.: 1917
* Collected Poems..................................Macmillan Co., N. Y.: 1919
Selected Poems..Medici Society: 1922
Late Lyrics and Earlier....................................Macmillan & Co.: 1922, 1926
Human Shows, Far Phantasies, Songs and Trifles...........Macmillan Co., N. Y.: 1925
Yuletide in a Younger World (Ariel Poems)...............Faber & Gwyer, London: 1927
Winter Words in Various Moods and Metres.....................Macmillan Co.: 1928

DUBOSE HEYWARD

DuBose Heyward was born in Charleston, South Carolina, in August, 1885, and educated in the state. As a poet, his interests have been regional. With his friend Hervey Allen he versified some of the local legends of white and Negro people, and his own book celebrated chiefly the hardy life of the mountaineers.

Of late he has studied chiefly the Negroes of the low country, and presented authentic pictures of their customs and superstitions in novels and the successful and beautiful play, *Porgy*.

Carolina Chansons (with Hervey Allen)....................Macmillan Co., N. Y.: 1922
* Skylines and Horizons...Macmillan Co.: 1924
In *Poetry:* July 1920 (Vol. XVI); Aug. 1921 (XVIII); April 1922 (XX); Dec. 1923 & March 1924 (XXIII).

RALPH HODGSON

Ralph Hodgson, born in Yorkshire in 1872, has been a draughtsman, an editor, a breeder of dogs; has lived chiefly in England, but for a time in America; and for two or three years in Japan as a lecturer on English literature in Sendai University.

He began writing lyrics early in the century, printing them in his first book, and later in broadsides and chapbooks. His method is traditional, but he brings spontaneity and a sunlit freshness to his delight in human characters and animals. He has never been a prolific poet, and has been very reticent in regard to his art.

The Last Blackbird and Other Lines.........George Allen & Unwin, Ltd., London: 1907
* Eve...Flying Fame, London: 1913
The Bull..Flying Fame: 1913
* The Mystery...Flying Fame: 1913
The Song of Honour...Flying Fame: 1913
Seven Broadsides (Decorated by Lovat Fraser)...........................Flying Fame: 1913
    All the above reissued by the Poetry Bookshop, London: 1914.
* Poems...Macmillan Co., N. Y.: 1917
The Last Blackbird and Other Lines..............................Macmillan Co.: 1917
In *Georgian Poetry:* II–III.........................Poetry Bookshop, London: 1915–17

HELEN HOYT (*Mrs. W. W. Lyman*)

Helen Hoyt was of New England parentage, but she came west in child-hood and in 1912 she was doing office work in Chicago. Her first appearance as a poet was in *Poetry* for August, 1913, with the much quoted *Ellis Park*, and from that time she contributed poems frequently to the more progressive magazines. In 1918–19 she was associate editor of *Poetry*, until the wanderlust carried her to California, where she married and remained.

From the first Helen Hoyt has expressed her emotional life in a very personal rhythm and with a delightful freshness. Rhyme, when she uses it, comes as it were inadvertently, and her measures, like the ideas they express, seem unpremeditated and artless. She has been in no hurry to publish, and some of her best work is not yet in book form.

* Apples Here in My Basket. . . . . .Harcourt, Brace & Co., N. Y.: 1924
Leaves of Wild Grape. . . . . .Harcourt, Brace & Co., N. Y.: 1929
The Name of a Rose. . . . . .Privately printed, San Francisco: 1931
In *Poetry:* Aug. 1913 (Vol. II); Aug. 1914 (IV); Aug. 1915 (VI); March 1917 (IX); Dec. 1918
    (XIII); March 1920 (XV); Oct. 1923 (XXIII); Aug. 1928 (XXXII); Sept. 1929
    (XXXIV); March 1931 (XXXVII).
In *Masses:* Dec. 1915 (Vol. VIII).
In *Others: An Anthology of the New Verse*. . . . . .Alf. A. Knopf, N. Y.: 1916–17

LANGSTON HUGHES

Langston Hughes was born in 1902 in Joplin, Missouri, of Negro parents, and educated in the Middle West. Being of an adventurous disposition, he travelled much with or without money—studied at Columbia, taught in Mexico, took ship as a sailor, worked his way through Spain, France, and Italy, and was a busboy in a Washington hotel when Vachel Lindsay discovered his talent and read some of his poems to an audience he was addressing there.

Hughes' first poems were written "after the manner of the Negro folk-songs known as blues," and his haunting melodies enrich the form with that strange combination of pathos and laughter so characteristic of the racial mind. And some of his poems present the weariness of labor, as primitive minds feel it.

Julia Peterkin, reviewing his second book in *Poetry*, said: "Stark, fierce, tragic bits of life fall into simple words which keep up an insistent rhythmic beating. No matter what the mood is, each one of these poems has that definite swing or cadence which is the sign of an unfailing musical sense."

The Weary Blues. . . . . .Alf. A. Knopf, N. Y.: 1926
* Fine Clothes to the Jew. . . . . .Alf. A. Knopf: 1927
In *Poetry:* Nov. 1926 (Vol. XXIX); Oct. 1931 (XXXIX).

ROBINSON JEFFERS

Robinson Jeffers was born in Pittsburgh in 1887, and was "carried about Europe a good deal" until his family came home and moved to California. Far-western colleges and the University of Zurich failed to detach him from his chief interest, poetry. In 1913 he married, and the next year was prevented by the War from going to England. So he and his bride discovered the beauty of the Coast, and have lived ever since at Carmel, on the granite rocks above the Pacific.

Jeffers' first two books were practice work, but in *Tamar*, which was poorly printed by an obscure publisher, he began to show his hand. James Daly, who picked it up by accident, wholly ignorant of the unknown author, told the New York critics about his find and wrote about it as follows in *Poetry* for August, 1925: "Before I had read a page I was tense with excitement. Here was writing that seemed to spring from genius of a deep poetic compulsion, writing that had what one rarely finds in contemporary poetry—genuine passion. Here was a nuggeted ruggedness of imagery. Here was magnificent rhythm, responsive to the spur and rein of the thought riding it. And here were a beauty and vigor and objective immediacy of phrase—prolific, seemingly unpremeditated, yet restrained."

The long slow line is Jeffers' method, a deep pulsing rhythm which suggests the majesty of classic hexameters. Indeed, a profound study of Greek measures underlies Jeffers' technique, and in *The Tower Beyond Tragedy* and other poems he essays Greek subjects.

Jeffers' philosophical motive is nihilistic—the hero, typifying the race, unable to find a solution or a goal, raging through crime and agony to destruction. In *Cawdor* and *The Women of Point Sur* the poet carries this theme to the extreme of horror—the bottomless pit is opened. But one feels an unabashed sincerity in the man—his despair is nobly pitched, and in the strain and tragedy of unfulfilled hope he recognizes the doom of the race.

The critical chorus of praise for this poet has not been without dissenting voices. Yvor Winters, in reviewing *Dear Judas*, calls him an incurable romanticist guilty of "sentimental misanthropy," and finds his technique "loose, turgid and careless." Of his general theme Winters says: "Self-repetition has been the inevitable effect of anti-intellectualist doctrine on all of its supporters. If life is valued, explored, subdivided, and defined, poetic themes are infinite in number; if life is denied, the only theme is the rather sterile and monotonous one of the denial."

M. D. Zabel wrote, in March, 1929: "Mr. Jeffers' obsession for heroic violence and the grand passion of the Greeks furnishes him with wild and massive themes. . . . The very factors which make it possible for him to stand apart from huge cities, political warfare and industrial vanity allow him to indulge in a kind of oracular aloofness. The disclosures of science have armed him with a seer-like omnipotence from which to look down on the swarming efforts of man."

Flagons and Apples...............................Grafton Pub. Co., Los Angeles: 1912
Californians...Macmillan Co., N. Y.: 1916
Tamar and Other Poems..................................Peter G. Boyle, N. Y.: 1924
* Roan Stallion, Tamar and Other Poems.................Boni & Liveright, N. Y.: 1925
The Women at Point Sur.....................................Boni & Liveright: 1927
* Cawdor...Horace Liveright, N. Y.: 1928
Poems.............................The Book Club of California, San Francisco: 1928
Dear Judas..Horace Liveright: 1929
Descent to the Dead...............................Random House, Inc., N. Y.: 1931
Thurso's Landing and Other Poems............................Liveright, Inc.: 1932
In *Poetry:* Jan. 1928 (Vol. XXXI).

ORRICK JOHNS

Orrick Johns was born in St. Louis in 1887, and spent most of his youth there. His first appearance as a poet was in the *Lyric Year* competition, in which his *Second Avenue* won the first prize over Miss Millay's *Renascence* and many other poems. In February, 1914, he burst out in *Poetry* with

Songs of Deliverance, a flare-up of youth's rebellion against the preceding generation.

This sequence was in free verse, following the mood of the time, but Johns' best poems are in pure lyric forms. They celebrate, to the point of ecstasy, his delight in natural beauty and in animal life, as well as in more personal experiences.

```
* Asphalt and Other Poems................................Alf. A. Knopf, N. Y.: 1917
Black Branches....................................Pagan Publishing Co., N. Y.: 1920
* Wild Plum...........................................Macmillan Co., N. Y.: 1926
In Poetry: Feb. 1914 (Vol. V); March 1917 (IX); May 1918 (XII); Jan. 1931 (XXXVII);
    Dec. 1931 (XXXIX).
In Others: An Anthology of the New Verse.........................Alf. A. Knopf: 1916
```

FENTON JOHNSON

Fenton Johnson, a young journalist, founder and editor of *The Champion,* a magazine for Negroes, was born in Chicago in 1888, and was still living there thirty years later, working for the benefit of his race. Since his removal to New York, the editor has lost track of him.

```
A Little Dreaming...........................Peterson Linotyping Co., Chicago: 1913
Visions of the Dusk..............................Printed by the Author, N. Y.: 1915
Songs of the Soil................................Printed by the Author, N. Y.: 1916
In Poetry: June 1918 (Vol. XII); Dec. 1921 (XIX).
In Others for 1919........................................Nich. L. Brown, N. Y.: 1919
```

JAMES WELDON JOHNSON

James Weldon Johnson was born in Jacksonville, Florida, in 1871, and educated at Atlanta and later Columbia University. He became a vaudeville and musical-comedy artist, and served seven years as U. S. Consul in Venezuela.

Johnson has become the leader of his race in literature, not only because of his own work but also his encouragement of all excellence among Negroes, which is expressed especially in his well-edited anthology, *The Book of American Negro Poetry.* His own poetry is often too facile, but he has made admirable use of old folk-poetry, improvised long ago and handed down, much of it on religious subjects, like the one we quote. *God's Trombones,* his best work, gathers together such narratives.

```
Fifty Years and Other Poems..................................................
* God's Trombones......................................Viking Press, N. Y.: 1927
```

JAMES JOYCE

James Joyce was born in Dublin in February, 1882, and educated at a Jesuit school and the Royal University. Medicine, professional singing, and teaching were professions he discarded before turning whole-heartedly to literature. His first book was verse, always traditional in form, and in 1917 he sent his *Penyeach* group of beautiful lyrics to *Poetry.* But fiction diverted him from the sister art, and *The Dubliners, A Portrait of an Artist as a Young Man*, and especially the revolutionary *Ulysses* lifted his fame to great heights and exerted a strong influence on the art of novel-writing. Mr. Joyce has lived on the continent for many years, mostly in Paris.

* Chamber Music.................Elkin Mathews, London; B. W. Huebsch, N. Y.: 1918
* Chamber Music......................................Egoist Press, London: 1922
* Pomes Penyeach......................................Shakespeare & Co., Paris: 1927
In *Poetry:* May 1917 (Vol. X); Nov. 1917 (XI).

ALINE KILMER

Aline Murray was born in Norfolk, Virginia, in 1888. In 1909 she married Joyce Kilmer, who about four years later began to be known as a poet. After his death in the War, she began to write poems of exquisitely feminine significance, illustrating the contrarieties of a woman's temperament with pathos or whimsical grace. Out of bitter knowledge she reminds us that passion is unreasonable, inconsequent, ephemeral, and that perhaps only a woman's children find something in her that is steadfast. Such a poem as *The Heart Knoweth Its Own Bitterness* digs under the dead leaves of convention. Indeed, the tenor of Mrs. Kilmer's poetry is an accusation—of herself primarily, and thence of all these pitiable human souls who long so ineffectually for light and power and joy. And the least of her songs records, in its delicate ever-moving gleam and rhythm, the beauty of a spirit which demands too much of itself—of life.

* Candles That Burn.............................George H. Doran Co., N. Y.: 1919
* Vigils..George H. Doran Co.: 1921
The Poor King's Daughter..............................George H. Doran Co.: 1925
Selected Poems.........................Doubleday, Doran & Co., N. Y.: 1929
In *Poetry:* May 1921 (Vol. XVIII); Oct. 1922 (XXI); Oct. 1924 (XXV).

JOYCE KILMER (*Died 1918*)

Joyce Kilmer was born in New Brunswick, New Jersey, December 6th, 1886. He was graduated from Columbia in 1908, taught English and Latin for a year in the Morristown High School, and then moved to New York and became one of the editors of the *Standard Dictionary* and *The Literary Digest*. Soon after his marriage in 1909, he and his wife become converts to Roman Catholicism.

When the United States entered the War he volunteered at once, although over draft age and the father of four children. He asked to be transferred to the Rainbow Division, and on August 1st, 1918, he was killed in action near the Ourcq.

Kilmer wrote only about thirty lyrics, all in simple measures, but one of them, *Trees*, is sure of immortality. Considering the fact that for some years its motto-card royalties brought $1500 a year to his publisher and family, it may be interesting to quote a sentence from his letter of May 26th, 1913, to the editor of *Poetry:* "Six dollars will satisfy me for *Trees*." Probably this is the most quoted poem *Poetry* ever published.

Summer of Love.................................Doubleday Page & Co., N. Y.: 1911
* Trees and Other Poems.........................George H. Doran Co., N. Y.: 1914
Main Street and Other Poems............................George H. Doran Co.: 1917
Joyce Kilmer: Poems, Essays and Letters; with a Memoir by Robert Coates Holliday
George H. Doran Co.: 1918
In *Poetry:* Aug 1913 (Vol. II); April 1914 (IV); Mar. 1917 (IX).

ALFRED KREYMBORG

Alfred Kreymborg was born December 10th, 1883, in the East Side of New York, and his education was fitfully gained. He was a wonder-child at chess, and until he gave it up at twenty-five, the game partly supported him through teaching and exhibitions. For a time music was his keenest interest, and he was music critic of a New York daily. When the "new movement" in poetry began in 1912, he turned to that art and later to the experimental theatre.

In these arts, Kreymborg has been a progressive to the point of radicalism. As an organ of the radical group, he started in 1915, without a cent of capital, the clever little magazine, *Others*, which ran precariously for a year or more under his valiant editorship. Since then his literary career has been continuously adventurous and varied. He has written novels, memoirs, freeverse lyrics and dialogs, and many plays which have been produced far and wide in the "little theatres."

* Mushrooms..............................John Marshall Co., Ltd., New York: 1916
Plays for Poem-mimes............................The Others Press, New York: 1918
* Blood of Things...............................Nich. L. Brown, Philadelphia: 1920
Plays for Merry Andrews................................Sunwise Turn, N. Y.: 1920
Less Lonely.....................................Harcourt, Brace & Co., N. Y.: 1923
Scarlet and Mellow..................................Boni & Liveright, N. Y.: 1926
Manhattan Men.......................................Coward-McCann, N. Y.: 1929
In *Poetry:* Feb. 1916 (Vol. VII); April 1917 (X); March 1918 (XI); Jan. 1920 (XV); July 1922 (XX); June 1923 (XXII); Sept. 1923 (XXII); Nov. 1924 (XXV); Feb. 1926 (XXVII); Aug. 1927 (XXX); July 1928 (XXXII).
In *Others: An Anthology of the New Verse*.................Alf. A. Knopf, N. Y.: 1916–17

STANLEY J. KUNITZ

Stanley J. Kunitz was born July 29th, 1905, in Worcester, Massachusetts, and educated in local public schools and at Harvard. Since graduation he has done newspaper work in New York. *The Nation* printed his first poem in the summer of 1928, *Poetry* followed the next year with an 8-poem group, and other magazines soon recognized his keen poetic intelligence.

The title of *Intellectual Things* offers a hint of the poet's interests. William Rose Benét, reviewing it in *The Saturday Review of Literature* in July, 1930, said: "There is a new poet; his first book is an event. Here is a man immediately asserting his own fresh utterance, modern and yet very old, intricate and metaphysical and yet undeniably full of the sagacity of the true seer. . . . One quality of his commands our admiration, his spiritual discipline."

Kunitz's technique is not always so well disciplined as his mind. M. D. Zabel finds "verbal gymnastics, odd unnatural symbols and a strained attitude" in his less successful poems. But he credits him with possessing "a melodic gift—a special ability to define and sustain fluently the verbal and tonal pattern on which his poem is built."

* Intellectual Things.................Doubleday, Doran & Co., Garden City, N. Y.: 1930
In *Poetry:* July 1929 (Vol. XXXIV).

D. H. LAWRENCE (*Died 1930*)

David Herbert Lawrence was born September 17th, 1885, in the coal-mining region of Nottinghamshire. Though the son of a poor miner, he won a high-school scholarship and in youth tried teaching, but soon gave it up for literature.

His early verse, in *Love Poems and Others* (1913), and his first novel, *Sons and Lovers*, showed his remarkable literary gift and the trend of his mind toward the analysis of sexual emotion. This subject became an obsession with him; his novels pursue it to the point of propaganda, like a Puritan preacher bent on reforming the world.

Though primarily a novelist, Lawrence gave himself a wider range of interests in his poems. His first group in *Poetry*—his American introduction in January, 1914—showed him moved by color, the wind, roses, a woman's sorrow over the death of her husband or the departure of her sons. And when the War made havoc everywhere, his poems stressed phases of that agony, and *Resurrection* moves with solemn splendor, like an orchestral dirge.

But he was a very careless technician. Never was poet more casual than D. H. Lawrence; fitful, temperamental, never twice of the same mind as to details of his art, trying out and trying again one reading after another of his poems and often spoiling them in the revision; clinging only to the main trend of intimate revelation—the unveiling of human souls, the souls of men and women in all the contradictory stresses and counter-stresses of love, with its corollaries of hate and indifference; or in stresses of war, and other experiences of agony or ecstasy. Many of his poems are so personal that, in their fragmentary fashion, they make up a biography of an emotional inner life. These personal poems are sex-explorative mostly, for the poet's philosophy is founded upon sex as life's fundamental inescapable motive. He pursues his inquiries even into the animal world. His revelation of the love-affair of a pair of tortoises is a masterpiece of grim, tremendous, respectful humor. Being almost a satyr himself, he is marvellously sympathetic with beasts, birds, even reptiles.

Lawrence was always frail, more or less tuberculous. In quest of health, he lived, for years at a time, in the Mediterranean countries, New Mexico, and Mexico, centering his tales and novels in all these regions. He was said to be planning for Arizona when death overtook him in Venice, near Nice, March 2, 1930.

Love Poems and Others................................Duckworth, London: 1913
* Amores................................Duckworth, London; B. W. Huebsch, N. Y.: 1916
* Look! We have Come Through......................Chatto & Windus, London: 1917
* Look! We have Come Through................................B. W. Huebsch: 1918
New Poems................................Martin Secker, London: 1918
Bay................................Cyril W. Beaumont, Manchester, Eng.: 1919
Tortoises................................Thomas Seltzer, N. Y.: 1921
Pansies................................Alf. A. Knopf, N. Y.: 1929
* Collected Poems (2 vols.)................Jonathan Cape & Harrison Smith, N. Y.: 1929
In *Poetry*: Jan. 1914 (Vol. III); Dec. 1914 (V); June 1917 (X); July 1918 (XII); Feb. 1919 (XIII); July 1919 (XIV); Nov. 1922 (XXI); April 1923(XXII).
In *Some Imagist Poets*: I–III................................Houghton Mifflin Co.: 1915–16–17
In *Georgian Poetry*: I–IV................................Poetry Bookshop, London: 1912–19

AGNES LEE (*Mrs. Otto Freer*)

Agnes Rand was born in Chicago, but spent eight years of her childhood in Switzerland and Germany. She married F. W. Lee and lived in Boston, until in 1911 her second marriage, to Dr. Otto Freer, brought her to Chicago, where she still lives.

She began as a writer for children, contributing verse and prose to *St. Nicholas*. The translation of French poems revealed an original talent and soon she was contributing her own poems to magazines.

Agnes Lee is instinctively observant and dramatic. Hers is the questing mind that delves into strange places for blooms no other would suspect. "Faces and open doors" lead her within them; some little thing startles her to emotion which tugs at her heart and brain, and we have a poem piteous, wistful, whimsical according to the kind of sympathy which inspired it, but recording imaginative rather than personal experience. She is absorbed, to the point of intense emotion, in the emotions of other people; and the only personal utterances one finds in her books are quiet reflections like *Numbers* or *At Dawn*.

Verses for Children.................................Copeland and Day, Boston: 1898
Verses for Children............................Small, Maynard & Co., Boston: 1901
The Border of the Lake..........................Sherman, French & Co., Boston: 1910
* The Sharing....................................Sherman, French & Co.: 1914
* Faces and Open Doors.......................Ralph Fletcher Seymour, Chicago: 1922
New Lyrics and a Few Old Ones.........................Ralph Fletcher Seymour: 1930
Théophile Gautier's Émaux et Camées (translation)...........George D. Sproul, N. Y.: 1903
Fernand Gregh's La Maison de l'Enfance (translation)......Dodd, Mead & Co., N. Y.: 1907
In *Poetry*: March 1913 (Vol. I); Dec. 1913 (III); Oct. 1914 (V); Sept. 1915 (VI); Feb. 1916
    (VII); April 1916 (VIII); May 1917 (X); May 1918 (XII); Dec. 1918 (XIII); Jan. 1919
    (XIII); June 1920 (XVI); Nov. 1921 (XIX); Aug. 1924 (XXIV); Dec. 1925 (XXVII);
    July 1926 (XXVIII); Dec. 1926 (XXIX); Oct. 1927 (XXXI); Sept. 1929 (XXXIV);
    July 1930 (XXXVI); Nov. 1930 (XXXVII); Dec. 1931 (XXXIX).

MUNA LEE (*Mrs. Luiz Muñoz-Marin*)

Muna Lee was born in Mississippi in 1895, and was taken to Oklahoma in 1902. She attended the Universities of Oklahoma and Mississippi. During the War she translated Spanish in the secret-service bureau of the government, and when it was over she married a Porto Rican, and has lived mostly on the island. She became Director of the Bureau of International Relations of its University, and she has represented the women of the island in Pan-American affairs in Washington. Also, for two years she has directed there the affairs of the National Woman's Party.

As a poet, she has written lyrics exclusively, always in simple measures. Some of these, in translation, have had much currency in Latin America. And in return she has translated into English many Latin-American poems.

* Sea-change..Macmillan Co., N. Y.: 1923
In *Poetry*: Jan. 1916 (Vol. VII); Aug. 1917 (X); Aug. 1922 (XX); June 1923 (XXII); June 1925
    (XXVI); March 1930 (XXXV).

WILLIAM ELLERY LEONARD

William Ellery Leonard was born in Plainfield, New Jersey, January 25th, 1876. From sixteen to eighteen, when he was preparing himself for college, he lived in a Massachusetts village where his father was a Unitarian minister. He was class poet at Boston University, where he was graduated in 1898, studying later in Germany. Since 1906 he has been in the English department of the University of Wisconsin.

Leonard is almost a one-poem poet, for *Two Lives* is by far his most important work. Here we have man's nobility in modern attire, set against a modern city and landscape, but contending, like Œdipus of old, with fates whose malignity began before he was born. The story—of a marriage destroyed by madness and suicide—would be full of pitfalls for an unwary artist. The slightest touch of insincerity or sentimentality, the slightest lapse from a simple straightforward narrative style, would spoil the tragic dignity of the poem. That Mr. Leonard has avoided such pitfalls, that he has told his bitter story without a hint of cheapness or melodrama, without once slipping out of tone or key, and carried it moreover on a majestically rising tide to a powerful climax, proves him a poet of noble inspiration and quite exceptional quality of style.

The story is told in about two hundred stanzas of fourteen lines: sonnets, if you will, but with much variety in the arrangement of rhymes and a wilful disloyalty to certain other conventions of the form. This free-flowing movement of cadences and consonances as variable as water saves the form from monotony, and carries the reader along with unconscious attention to the story.

Leonard's shorter poems—lyrical, satirical, fabulous, all more or less autobiographical—are much more casual and careless. *Indian Summer,* quoted in this book, is the finale of *Two Lives.*

The Vaunt of Man and Other Poems......................B. W. Huebsch, N. Y.: 1913
The Lynching Bee and Other Poems...........................B. W. Huebsch: 1920
Tutankhamen and After......................................B. W. Huebsch: 1924
* Two Lives...................Viking Press, N. Y.; Wm. Heinemann, Ltd., London: 1925
A Son of Earth (Collected Poems)..........................Viking Press, N. Y.: 1928
This Midland City..Lotus Press, Detroit: 1930
Fragments of Empedocles, trans. into English verse....Open Court Pub. Co., Chicago: 1908
Æsop and Hyssop (fables in verse).........................Open Court Pub. Co.: 1912
Of the Nature of Things, by Lucretius, translated into blank verse
            J. M. Dent & Sons, London; E. P. Dutton & Co., New York: 1916
In *Poetry:* Oct. 1913 (Vol. III); Jan. 1924 (XXIII).

MAURICE LESEMANN

Maurice Lesemann, born in Chicago at the very end of 1899, was educated there, graduating in 1920 from its university, where he had served as president of its well-disciplined students' Poetry Club. His poems, appearing in *Poetry* from 1920, received that year the Young Poet's Prize and in 1927 the Levinson Prize. Those here quoted recall his two or three years' residence in New Mexico and his sympathetic study of the habits and emotions of the more primitive members of the three races who live in the state's high spaces of plain, desert, and mountains.

Lesemann has been in no hurry to publish a book. He is now preparing a novel and a book of poems, under contract to a well-known publisher.

In *Poetry:* April 1920 (Vol. XVI); Aug. 1923 (XXII); Oct. 1926 (XXIX); June 1929 (XXXIV); Apr. 1932 (XL).

VACHEL LINDSAY (*Died 1931*)

Nicholas Vachel Lindsay was born in 1879 in Springfield, Illinois, where his father was a physician, and his mother a leader of church societies, a domineering civic worker and speaker. The boy was sent to local schools and to Hiram College, and his parents were much disappointed when he refused to study medicine and showed an obstinate preference for art.

It was a long formative period with this youth. In Hiram College for three years from 1897, in the Art Institute of Chicago until 1903, and for five years under Chase and Henri in New York, he was doggedly studying the wrong art, while supporting himself as a museum instructor and guide. His rhyme-making seems to have begun during long tramps through southern and western states, when he offered at farmers' doors his thin-paper pamphlet, *Rhymes to Be Traded for Bread*, in exchange for a supper and a night's lodging, and it was during one of these tramps from somewhere in the Far West, that he sent to *Poetry*, in response to an invitation from the editor, *General William Booth Enters into Heaven*.

This poem, published in January, 1913, was the definite beginning of Lindsay's literary career. It attracted attention, received a prize, and in March, 1914, at *Poetry's* first banquet, given for William Butler Yeats, was accorded public praise by the Irish poet, who welcomed the young American to the guild of poets. Lindsay responded by reciting *The Congo*, the earliest of his Negro interpretations, beating out its rhythms with that resonant chant which at once associated its tune inextricably with the poem.

From that time Lindsay's story is legible in seven or eight books of verse and prose, and especially in the *Collected Poems*. It is a consistent story; it has admirable unity. From the first this poet has been led by certain sacred and impassioned articles of faith—faith in beauty, in goodness (even human goodness), in the splendor of common things and common experiences; faith so sure, so living, that it has fed rapturously upon the present and never sought refuge in the past. Indeed, Lindsay is a modern knight-errant, the Don Quixote of our so-called unbelieving, unromantic age. To say this is not scorn but praise, for Don Quixote's figure looms heroically tall in perspective, and his quests, however immediately futile, become triumphant in the final account. Lindsay's whimsical imagination, even as the madder fancy of Cervantes' hero, cuts the light into seven colors like a prism, so that facts become glamorous before our eyes. Booth strides, full-haloed, into a Salvation Army heaven; fat black bucks of South State Street dance along a mystical glorified Congo; motor-cars on a Kansas road are chariots from now to forever; Bryan "sketches a silver Zion"; Johnny Appleseed is a wandering god of the soil, as mythical as Ceres; our yellow neighbor the Chinese laundryman is a son of Confucius, and his nightingale utters deathless beauty. Lindsay links up the electric sign with the stars, and sometimes, not always, he does this so effectively that we believe him. For his art, at its best, is adequate; Rosinante becomes Pegasus and soars beyond the moon.

Lindsay's sense of humor is true to type in its extreme variety; a faint and wistful smile, yearning for elusive and everlasting beauty, in *The Chinese Nightingale*, it becomes a sly grin in *So Much the Worse for Boston*, a tenderly sympathetic laugh in *Bryan, Bryan*, a louder laugh in *The Santa Fe Trail* or *The Kallyope Yell*, and a real guffaw in *Samson*. But the laugh, whether whispered or loud, is always genial, is never a satiric cackle. Often there is pathos in it, the trace of those tears which spring from the same bubbling fountain of human sympathy. Like the Chinese philosopher squinting at the cataract, Lindsay feels the tragedy—he is aware of the littleness of man. And to know man's littleness is to know also his greatness, for the point of the cosmic joke lies in the contrast.

Lindsay imparts a new flare of whimsical and colorful beauty to this American scene, and presents its extraordinary variety of emotion and mood. And his tonal reading of his poems suggests a veritable troubadour sympathy between poetry and song as a possibility of this modern age.

Lindsay's technique makes a generous use of the chant and the refrain. Sometimes his rhythms beat like a trip-hammer, again they move as softly as a ghost-dance. He has tried to marry poetry with music, to hark back to the old Greek days when the two were one. Yet of all our poets of rank, he is doubtless the most distinctively and unmistakably American.

Probably *The Chinese Nightingale* will remain his most ambitious interpretation of the spirit of man facing with humility and humor, with pride and wonder, his place in this mysterious and magnificent universe.

Sudden death closed the career of Vachel Lindsay on December 5th, 1931, in his fifty-third year. He died in his beloved city of Springfield, in the ancestral home where he was born.

Rhymes to Be Traded for Bread.................Privately printed, Springfield, Ill.: 1912
The Village Magazine.........................Privately printed, Springfield, Ill.: 1912
* General William Booth Enters into Heaven and Other Poems
                        Mitchell Kennerley, N. Y., 1913; Macmillan Co., N. Y.: 1916
* The Congo and Other Poems.....................................Macmillan Co.: 1915
* The Chinese Nightingale and Other Poems.....................Macmillan Co.: 1917
The Golden Whales of California...............................Macmillan Co.: 1920
* Collected Poems..Macmillan Co.: 1923 & 1925
Going-to-the-Sun................................D. Appleton & Co.: N. Y.: 1923
The Candle in the Cabin..................................D. Appleton & Co.: 1926
Going-to-the-Stars.......................................D. Appleton & Co.: 1926
Every Soul Is a Circus.......................................Macmillan Co.: 1929
Selected Poems...Macmillan Co.: 1931
In *Poetry:* Jan. 1913 (Vol. I); July 1913 (II); April and July 1914 (IV); Feb. 1915 (V); June 1916 (VIII); July 1917 (X); Oct. 1917 (XI); Sept. 1918 (XII); Aug. 1919 (XIV); Aug. 1923 (XXII); April 1926 (XXVIII); April 1928 (XXXII); July 1932 (XL).

HANIEL LONG

Haniel Long was born in Rangoon, Burma, in 1888, but in spite of this oriental origin he has lived mostly in the United States, and he was for some years Professor of English in the School of Design of the Carnegie Institute at Pittsburgh. He spent a few years at Santa Fe, where he became much interested in the pueblo tribes and their arts, and after another sojourn in Pittsburgh, returned there to live.

Mr. Long's poems are mostly lyrics in simple measures. Some of them show how deeply he was moved by the War.

* Poems..Moffat, Yard & Co., N. Y.: 1920
In *Poetry:* May 1918 (Vol. XVII); Oct. 1923 (XXIII).

AMY LOWELL (*Died 1925*)

Amy Lowell was born in Brookline, February 9th, 1874, and she died in the same ancestral mansion, May 12th, 1925. A member of a historic family, she carried on with magnificent authority its aristocratic traditions. She was a stately figure in her spacious library, book-lined to the ceiling, and loved to talk there with one or more congenial friends until almost the crack of dawn—for she always inverted day and night. Though handicapped by her heavy physique and deeply attached to her own place, she travelled much, always with a veritable retinue, going abroad often, and in her later life giving readings in many of our cities.

Miss Lowell was twenty-eight when she began to write, and after a ten-year apprenticeship her first quite conventional book of poems appeared in 1912. From that time until her death she wrote ten more books of verse and three important and lengthy critical works in prose, until her health broke under the strain of her conscientious literary and typographical exactitudes in putting her life of Keats through the press.

In her 1912 book, Miss Lowell followed Victorian fashions, but it was no sooner out than the Imagists began their bombardment and she soon became a fighter in their campaign. The poems she offered to *Poetry* during a Chicago visit in the winter of 1913–14 were distinctly in the newer manner, and a trip to London that summer, when she met Messrs. Pound, Fletcher, Flint, and others of the group, confirmed her revolutionary enthusiasm. The Declaration of War at the end of July suddenly sent her home, and the following spring the first of the three *Some Imagists* annuals, which were due to her initiative, signalized her break with Pound, both being too dominant to play together.

The imagistic discipline sharpened her technique but did not enslave it. Her study of French poetry was another enrichment. The range of subjects and methods in her poetry shows great variety; lyrics in rhyme or free verse, narratives ditto, character monologues in Yankee dialect, historic episodes in explosive "polyphonic prose" with its repetitions and internal rhymes—these were a few facets of her many-sided mind; and from each and all the world caught brilliant reflections. Her poetry is more visual than emotional—or rather, her emotions were excited by visual impressions. Many of her poems are decorative paintings, and she keeps her planes intact, and holds her vivid tones to the key and the pattern. The only trouble is, she is tempted to become too much involved with her decorative scheme. Her form, whether it is rhythm-royal or polyphonic prose, sometimes becomes too formal, holding not only the characters of the story, but the poet herself, in too tight a mesh. It is a relief when the heroine of *Patterns*, the most humanly poignant of all these picture-poems, cuts the mesh with the sword of tragedy.

In her New England narratives and monologues in dialect she presents queer characters and weird episodes—revelations of left-overs, chiefly, among her neighbors who had stayed in their own place, deserted by the more adventurous members of their families. In poems like *Lilacs* she gives us another phase of her attachment to New England. Always the notes she strikes are hard and clear—brilliant colors that flash and sparkle with a vivid glaze. She rarely softens to the confession of personal emotion; the Mrs. Meynell poem quoted in this book is a rare exception.

An extract from the editor's review of one of Amy Lowell's posthumous books may be quoted in conclusion:

She "might have been a queen"—perhaps in that direction lay her major talent. For she was magnificently dominant, she loved to rule; and in most of life's contacts she succeeded in imposing her will on those around her. . . .

She "might have been a poet": well, of that talent, in the high and mighty sense she meant by the word—of that talent one does not feel so sure. She set out deliberately to be a poet, and succeeded far enough to achieve distinction and influence in the art. Her keen intelligence and vivid imagination, her sense of human character, her love of color in nature and life, and sometimes her own innermost feelings of disappointment and pain—all found free play and rich expression in it. And she delighted in its audacious handling of words, in its varied metres and cadences; she experimented to the limit in the forms it offered, both new and old. But she lacked that last magic which the poet must be born with, which even the most explosive adventure will hardly impart. As we have said before, she had everything but genius.

She was a great woman; she will live among the rich, flavorous, idiosyncratic personalities of our time.

* A Dome of Many-coloured Glass.................Houghton Mifflin Co., Boston: 1912
* A Dome of Many-coloured Glass.......................Macmillan Co., N. Y.: 1914

* Sword Blades and Poppy Seed...............................Macmillan Co.: 1914
Men, Women and Ghosts.......................................Macmillan Co.: 1916
Can Grande's Castle...Macmillan Co.: 1918
* Pictures of the Floating World.............................Macmillan Co.: 1919
Six French Poets..Macmillan Co.: 1915
Tendencies in Modern American Poetry........................Macmillan Co.: 1917
    (In 1921 the Houghton Mifflin Co. took over the publication of all above books by
    Miss Lowell.)
* Legends...Houghton Mifflin Co.: 1921
Fir-flower Tablets, Translated from the Chinese by Florence Ayscough, English Versions by
    Amy Lowell..Houghton Mifflin Co.: 1921
A Critical Fable...Houghton Mifflin Co.: 1922
What's O'Clock...Houghton Mifflin Co.: 1925
East Wind..Houghton Mifflin Co.: 1926
Ballads for Sale...Houghton Mifflin Co.: 1927
John Keats (in 2 vols.)....................................Houghton Mifflin Co.: 1925
Poetry and Poets (essays)..................................Houghton Mifflin Co.: 1930
In *Poetry:* July 1913 (Vol. II); April 1914 (IV); Nov. 1914 (V); April & Sept. 1915 (VI); May
    & Aug. 1916 (VIII); March 1917 (IX); Jan. 1918 (XI); Aug. 1918 (XII); Feb. 1919
    (XIII); Sept. 1919 (XIV); Nov. 1920 (XVII); Dec. 1922 (XXI); June 1921 (XVIII);
    Aug. 1923 (XXII); Oct. 1923 (XXIII); Dec. 1925 (XXVII).

ARCHIBALD MACLEISH

Archibald MacLeish was born in Glencoe, a Chicago suburb, in May, 1892, and educated in local schools, Yale, and the Harvard Law School. He married, served in the Field Artillery of the A. E. F. in France, was re-called to train young artillerymen, and when the War was over accepted a law-partnership in Boston. After three years of practice he gave up the law at the thrill of a new resolution, took his family to France to emphasize the break, and from that time devoted himself to poetry, living partly near Paris but most of the year on a farm in Massachusetts.

MacLeish's first book, put out by a friendly publisher as he left for France in 1917, was the mere practice work of a young amateur. Seven or eight years later his next two books were the first-fruits of his new passion. They are "tone-poems" played with muted strings; played in the half-light or the half-dark when rapture and anguish, however real, become sus-pect of dreams. What we all fear, the poet sees come to pass—life blurs and dissolves before his eyes; lovely concords are hushed; beauty that is too beautiful perishes of its own fragility, like a soap-bubble vanishing with its flicker of iridescence.

All this is not expressly said, any more than in music. In the earlier book we have indeed the delicate raptures of a happy marriage; but the poet, singing the changes of joy, feels how perishable is joy in this vibrating, dis-solving world. And he knows that the soul cannot be bound, but must beat away from the closest contacts. . . .

In *The Pot of Earth* we find the poet's instinct for rhythms and tone-values developed almost to virtuosity. A certain relation to *The Waste Land* is obvious. Mr. MacLeish, either consciously or unconsciously, has set him-self to study Mr. Eliot's wavering variable rhythms, his way of neither beginning nor ending, of leaping backward and forward, and somehow reach-ing his goal by wayward paths no other poet could travel.

From this book to *Streets in the Moon* was a long leap. In a year the poet had gained firmer ground to stand on, and though we still hear echoes of Eliot, and both hear and see reminders of the *transition* experimenters with rhythm and typography, the poet is developing his own style and using it to express his own personality. The book contains such modernistic meditations as *Einstein*, such self-questionings as *L'an trentiesme de mon œge* and the beautiful *Signature for Tempo*, such grotesques as *March* and *Man!;* and everywhere the expert touch, the delicate manipulation of rhythms, the fine, sometimes almost-too-studied phrasing. In the later book, *New Found Land*, we find a further development of these qualities: poems of rare and usually melancholy beauty, like *Immortal Autumn* and *Epistle to Be Left in the Earth*—a beauty marred only by eccentric typography and troublesome lack of punctuation.

Through all these books the poet's philosophy of life—or perhaps one should say the instinctive feeling about life which becomes the underlying motive of his art—is less hard in texture and brazen in tone than most of the Parisian-American group could sympathize with; there is room for human pity in it, and even for human love—that love of the race which, implying the merging of the individual in the mass, may be the democratic, or at least the communistic, ideal—an ideal difficult, perhaps inaccessible to the poet, who is always by instinct an individualist.

We find this instinct of human pity underlying the self-analysis presented as the artistic motive of *The Hamlet of A. MacLeish.* Here the Elizabethan doubter shrinks into the modern agonist, and "the King his father's ghost," revisiting the glimpses of the moon, becomes the symbol of the world's irrevocable past, of dead generations and their dreams.

MacLeish's latest poem takes the conquest of Mexico for its subject—a bigger, sterner and more dramatic theme than he had as yet attempted. One of the greatest stories in American history is adequately told at last. In *Conquistador*, an epic set to an adroit *terza rima* of assonances, the poet follows the fortunes of a common soldier of Cortez' army, as it marches through "that good land" magnificent in beauty, even to Montezuma's capital, and overthrows his throne. This poem's quality lies in something beyond details of subject or technique; it springs from a mind capable of fusing these into a grandly molded work of art, wherein each unobtrusive detail counts toward the symmetry of the whole.

Tower of Ivory.....................................Yale Univ. Press, New Haven: 1917
The Happy Marriage...........................Houghton Mifflin Co., Boston: 1924
The Pot of Earth.......................................Houghton Mifflin Co.: 1925
* Streets in the Moon...................................Houghton Mifflin Co.: 1926
The Hamlet of A. MacLeish.............................Houghton Mifflin Co.: 1929
* New Found Land.....................................Houghton Mifflin Co.: 1930
Conquistador...Houghton Mifflin Co.: 1932
In *Poetry:* June 1926 (Vol. XXVIII); Jan. 1930 (XXXIII).

JOSEPH GORDON MACLEOD

Joseph Gordon Macleod is a young English poet, living partly in Cambridge, and partly in Hemingford, Huntingdonshire. His long poem in twelve sections, *The Ecliptic*, is his first publication. The grandeur of its theme, and the originality of the conception and the rhythmic treatment, have aroused keen interest among authoritative critics.

* The Ecliptic.......................................Faber & Faber, Ltd., London: 1910
Beauty and the Beast: an Essay.............................Viking Press, N. Y.: 1929
In *Poetry:* Feb. 1932 (Vol. XXXIX).

FREDERIC MANNING

Frederic Manning was born in Sydney, Australia, in July, 1884, and his adult life has been passed in England. He served as a private in the trenches during the World War, and some of the most poignant poems in *Eidola* record the reactions of a man whose previous poems, chiefly of love and beauty, had been of an extreme delicacy.

Richard Aldington, reviewing this book, calls its war poems "the cries and consolations of a tortured soul . . . poetry stern and true, yet beautiful."

The Vigil of Brunhilde....................................John Murray, London: 1905
Poems...John Murray: 1908
* Eidola......................John Murray, London; E. P. Dutton & Co., N. Y.: 1917
In *Poetry:* June 1913 (Vol. II); July 1916 (VIII); Jan. 1917 (IX).

JOHN MASEFIELD

John Masefield was born in Herefordshire, June 1st, 1878, the son of a lawyer. While still in his teens, he went to sea and earned a meagre living from time to time in various ports—in 1895 as a barkeeper in New York. Returning to England in 1897, he formed the friendship with Synge which he has beautifully commemorated in *John M. Synge; A Few Personal Recollections.* In 1912 he received a prize for poetry from the Royal Society of Literature. After the death of Robert Bridges he was appointed, in 1930, Poet Laureate. For many years he has lived in Oxford, but during the War he served with the Red Cross in France, and made a tour of America, giving lectures and readings in a manner superlatively simple, with a voice deeply pitched "that has in it all the sorrows of the world."

His earlier books are chiefly sea poems, and *Dauber* is a kind of sea epic with a common sailor for its hero; and with a long powerful intimate description of a storm which is perhaps the best poem Masefield ever wrote. A year before it appeared the poet had been widely acclaimed, and since 1912 his audience has been large on both sides of the Atlantic.

He has a sweeping forward-marching narrative style, and he chooses, through instinctive sympathy, subjects of common life. In *Reynard the Fox* he celebrates a great national sport with the delight of a person who loves the whole thing—fox, hounds, horses, and riders.

Masefield's style is too facile, and his subjects and mental attitude are usually conventional. "He is headlong and rough and not profound, but he keeps on telling stories"—stories which move the reader without straining his intellect. And there is a rush of movement and sound in some of his briefer poems, especially those about ships and the sea. Also his meditative poems have an engaging modesty and simplicity.

* Salt Water Ballads....................................Grant Richards, London: 1902
Ballads (out of print)....................................Elkin Mathews, London: 1903
Ballads and Poems...Elkin Mathews: 1910
The Everlasting Mercy............................Sidgwick & Jackson, London: 1911
The Widow in the Bye Street..............................Sidgwick & Jackson: 1912
The Everlasting Mercy and the Widow in the Bye Street.....Macmillan Co., N. Y.: 1912
The Story of a Round-house and Other Poems (including Dauber)....Macmillan Co.: 1912
The Daffodil Fields..............Wm. Heinemann, London; Macmillan Co., N. Y.: 1913
Dauber...Wm. Heinemann, London: 1914
Philip the King and Other Poems..............................Macmillan Co.: 1914
Philip the King...Wm. Heinemann: 1914
John M. Synge: A Few Personal Recollections (Edition limited to 500).Macmillan Co.: 1915
Good Friday and Other Poems.....Wm. Heinemann, London; Macmillan Co., N. Y.: 1916
* Sonnets..Macmillan Co.: 1916
* Salt-water Poems and Ballads (reprint).........................Macmillan Co.: 1916
* Lollingdon Downs and Other Poems
                    Wm. Heinemann, London; Macmillan Co., N. Y.: 1917
Rosas (autographed ed.)..Macmillan Co.: 1917

* Poems and Plays (collected, 2 vols.)............................Macmillan Co.: 1918
A Poem and Two Plays..Wm. Heinemann: 1919
Reynard the Fox...Macmillan Co.: 1919
* Enslaved and Other Poems..................................Macmillan Co.: 1920
Right Royal...Macmillan Co.: 1922
The Dream (illustrated).....................................Macmillan Co.: 1922
Esther and Berenice (2 plays tr'd from the French)................Macmillan Co.: 1922
Selected Poems..Wm. Heinemann: 1922
Selected Poems.......................................Macmillan Co., N. Y.: 1925
Collected Poems...Wm. Heinemann: 1923
King Cole and Other Poems........Wm. Heinemann, London; Macmillan Co., N. Y.: 1923
A King's Daughter, a Tragedy in Verse
                      Wm. Heinemann, London; Macmillan Co., N. Y.: 1923
A Sailor's Garland..............................Methuen & Co., Ltd., London: 1924
Tristan and Isolt.............Wm. Heinemann, London; Macmillan Co., N. Y.: 1927
Midsummer Night.............Wm. Heinemann, London; Macmillan Co., N. Y.: 1928
The Coming of Christ..Macmillan Co.: 1928
Poems (new complete edition)................................Macmillan Co.: 1929
The Wanderer of Liverpool...........................Macmillan Co., N. Y.: 1931
Minnie Maylow's Story and Other Tales and Scenes.........Macmillan Co., N. Y.: 1931
In *Georgian Poetry:* I–III......................Poetry Bookshop, London: 1912–15–17

EDGAR LEE MASTERS

Edgar Lee Masters was born in Garrett, Kansas, August 23d, 1869. The family moved to Illinois in his boyhood, and after an irregular education he studied law in his father's office at Lewiston, going later to Chicago to practice his profession.

But he was always attracted to literature, and during fifteen years or more, from 1895, he wrote little books of serious and academic poems and plays, and published them under various pseudonyms. No one paid any attention to these, and even his old friend Bill Reedy refused the classic poems he sent to *Reedy's Mirror* and urged him to write on modern subjects. At forty-four Masters was a failure as a poet, and in danger of becoming embittered; for he could contrast the silence around him with the réclame which was beginning to salute the Imagists and other free-versifiers during 1913.

One can almost see the satiric smile with which he said to himself, "If that's what they want, I'll give it to them!" But *Spoon River*, begun as a more or less satirical challenge to "the new movement," soon caught him up and carried him out to the depths. For the first time he found a theme which drew upon his humor as well as his knowledge and fervor and sympathy; and a form which disciplined his loose technique, made him forget old-fashioned prejudices, and thereby freed his art. By the time the world found him he had found himself. And it was a big discovery.

Spoon River, with its humors and tragedies and common-places, its strange interweavings of destiny, is precisely central Illinois, the very heart of Middle-West America; yet Lucretius or Omar or Li Po would recognize its types and incidents, and probably the poets of the twenty-fifth century will still pronounce it true. And the form of those terse little epitaphs is not only a perfect fit but that triumphant completion and fulfillment which marks the masterpieces of all the arts.

Spoon River classed its author as essentially an epic poet—that is, a poet whose chief urge is to tell the tale of the tribe. And although Masters has written fine lyrics, most of his best poems emphasize the epic quality of his vision. Although each of his numerous volumes needs weeding out, each contains a few essential and memorable poems which help to symmetrize and complete this poet's record of our time and place.

Throughout one is swept along by the man's impassioned quest of truth. In this quest he is sincere and uncompromising; yet, though he admits humanity's crimes, and lashes our smug and faulty civilization with laughter or even fury, one feels the warmth of a big-hearted wistful sympathy with all God's sorely tried and tempted creatures as they move about among illusions and are ignorantly stirred by appearances and dreams. He is the attorney for the defense before the bar of ultimate justice, admitting the strong case against his client but pleading the sadness and bitter irony of man's endless struggle between good and evil, between beauty and sordidness.

The desecration of life—that is the unpardonable sin which he lashes in countless poems. The magnificence of the opportunity and the insignificance of our response to it—that is the gods' food for laughter, and the poet's stuff of satire.

If this poet is fundamentally epic in the sweep of his vision, his prolific art indulges also other moods. Certain fine poems of more or less cosmic motive are epic corollaries, no doubt—such things as *The Loom, The Star, Silence, Worlds*. And many poems about real or typical characters—*William Marion Reedy, Cato Braden, Widow La Rue, Emily Brosseau,* and others— as well as out-door poems like *Grand River Marshes, The Landscape,* and the supremely joyous *Lake Boats,* may be classed as details of that story of his place and people which is his chief legacy to art. Even the poet's technique, so often slipshod, has nobilities of its own at ecstatic moments. Perhaps the great thing about him is that he is *capable* of ecstasy, that he lives hard and deep, and knows the extremes, the agonies.

Edgar Lee Masters, whatever else one may say of him, has size. He bulks large and it may be that in that "next age," to which we accord the ultimate accounting, he will make a number of other figures now conspicuous look small. He has, not unnaturally, the faults that go with size—careless technique, uncritical sanctionings, indelicacies of emotional excess, far-sightedness which misses obvious imperfections of detail. The world will sift out and throw away many poems in his numerous books of verse; and much of his prose—not all—will go into the discard. But when hurrying time has done its worst, enough will remain to prove a giant's stature and other attributes of power in this Illinois lawyer-poet of a changing age.

A Book of Verses...................................Way & Williams, Chicago: 1898
Maximilian, a Tragedy in Blank Verse.................Richard G. Badger, Boston: 1902
The Blood of the Prophets, by Dexter Wallace................Rooks Press, Chicago: 1905
Songs and Sonnets, by Webster Ford................................Rooks Press: 1910
* Spoon River Anthology.. ..Macmillan Co., N. Y., 1915; T. Werner Laurie, London: 1917
* Songs and Satires.......................................Macmillan Co., N. Y.: 1916
* The Great Valley..Macmillan Co.: 1916
Spoon River Anthology (with additions)...........................Macmillan Co.: 1916
* Toward the Gulf..Macmillan Co.: 1918
* Starved Rock..Macmillan Co.: 1919
    (Spoon River Anthology, Songs and Satires, The Great Valley, and Works have been pub-
    lished in England by T. Werner Laurie, London.)
The Domesday Book......Macmillan Co., N. Y.: 1920; Eveleigh Nash, Ltd., London: 1921
* The Open Sea...Macmillan Co.: 1921
The New Spoon River..................................Boni & Liveright, N. Y.: 1924
Selected Poems..Macmillan Co.: 1925
Lee, a Dramatic Poem......................................Macmillan Co.: 1926
Jack Kelso...D. Appleton & Co., N. Y.: 1928
Lichee Nuts...Horace Liveright, N. Y.: 1930
In *Reedy's Mirror:* 1914.
In *Poetry:* Feb. 1915 (Vol. V); Nov. 1915 & Mar. 1916 (VII); July 1916 (VIII); Oct. 1917 (XI); April & June 1919 (XIV); Jan. 1921 (XVII); Oct. 1922 (XXI); Aug. 1923 (XXII); Sept. 1023 (XXII); Feb. 1924 (XXIII); June 1928 (XXXII); Sept. 1928 (XXXII).

MARJORIE MEEKER (*Mrs. Vivian Collins*)

Marjorie Meeker was born in Bradford, England, but was brought to the United States as a child. She attended Bryn Mawr for three years, living mostly in Columbus, Ohio. Since her marriage to General Collins, of the U. S. Army, she has been residing in St. Augustine, Florida.

Miss Meeker is a writer of lyrics expressing in carefully modulated tones feminine reactions to the beauty of nature and human experience. Her work has a supple strength in spite of its delicacy.

* Color of Water...Brentano's, N. Y.: 1928
In *Poetry:* May 1919 (Vol. XIV); Jan. 1922 (XIX); June 1923 (XXII); Feb. 1924 (XXIII); Feb. 1925 (XXV); Nov. 1927 (XXXI).

CHARLOTTE MEW (*Died 1928*)

Charlotte Mew was born in 1870. Her father dying soon after, her life was a succession of adversities and sorrows, until finally the death of her mother and sister left her a lonely recluse in London. She died in 1928.

Miss Mew began to write verse during the 'nineties—one may find her name in *The Yellow Book*. But she published little and destroyed much, being an exacting critic. John Gould Fletcher, reviewing *Saturday Market* in *The Freeman*, compares her to Emily Dickinson, saying: "Each of these two poets owns the same power of quick feminine apprehension; each is haunted by the shadow of a great renunciation; each is tortured by the same subliminal consciousness of a life beyond; and each makes use of the same devastating simplicity of statement."

* The Farmer's Bride.................................Poetry Bookshop, London: 1916
* Saturday Market.....................................Macmillan Co., N. Y.: 1921

ALICE MEYNELL (*Died 1922*)

Alice Thompson was born in 1850, and educated mostly by her father, spending much of her early life in Italy. In 1877 she married Wilfred Meynell, and from that time they lived in London chiefly, and seven children were born to them. Much of the time her husband was editor of a Catholic weekly, and she contributed countless brief, wise, finely written essays to that and other papers; a few of these being now accessible in book form. The Meynells befriended Francis Thompson, and tried to restore him to health and literature.

As a poet, Alice Meynell was always fastidious, and a stern self-critic. She published little, but whatever she gave the world has a superfine delicacy of color and line and workmanship. Sometimes her quest of an austere beauty is carried too far toward preciosity, but often she attains without effort a severe clarity and precision of tone and form.

Our selection in this book is from her later poems.

Poems........................John Lane Co., London; Copeland & Day, Boston: 1896
* Later Poems................................John Lane Co., London and N. Y.: 1902
* Poems (including above)..........................Charles Scribner's Sons, N. Y.: 1913
* The Poems of Alice Meynell (complete ed.)...............Charles Scribner's Sons: 1923
In *Poetry:* March 1913 (Vol. I).

MAX MICHELSON

Max Michelson was a young furrier of Russian extraction at the time *Poetry* began in 1912, a man of the finest fibre and most sensitive taste. He used to haunt the office and help the editor in various ways, and his delicate poems saw the light chiefly in the magazine. Later the family moved to Seattle, and mental illness overtook the poet.

In *Poetry:* July 1915 (Vol. VI); May 1916 (VIII); Mar. 1917 (IX); Feb. 1918 (XI); Nov. 1918 (XIII); Feb. 1921 (XVII).

EDNA ST. VINCENT MILLAY

Edna St. Vincent Millay was born February 22d, 1892, in Rockland, Maine, and her childhood was passed along its rocky coast. She entered Vassar, was graduated in 1917, and supported herself afterwards in New York's Greenwich Village by writing pot-boilers, translating, and by acting and directing with the Provincetown Players. She went to Europe some years after the War, and returning, married Eugen Boissevain, a Belgian American. Their present home is in New York state, an hour or two north of the metropolis.

Miss Millay's literary début was the publication of *Renascence* in *The Lyric Year*, a volume financed by Ferdinand Earle, who intended it to be the first number of an annual. At that time, 1912, Miss Millay was utterly unknown, and she received none of the book's three prizes, Mr. Earle being the only one of the three judges who gave her a vote (his highest). The editor of *Poetry*, reviewing *The Lyric Year* in January, 1913, said of *Renascence:* "One poem outranks the rest and ennobles the book. It is the daring flight of a wide-winged imagination, and the art of it is strong enough to carry us through keen emotions of joy and agony to a climax of spiritual serenity."

Others also acclaimed this poem, yet a dilatory publisher held back Miss Millay's first book until 1918. The editor said of it, in December of that year: "One would have to go back a long way in literary history to find a young lyric poet singing so freely and musically in such a big world." Three years later appeared *Second April*, a small volume of perfect lyrics, full of the triumphant passion of youth—youth's delight in life, and its agony and dark surprise at the intrusion of death.

Later, the War furnished another stimulus; the poet was powerfully moved by the contrast between its tragic futilities and the gay little pleas-antries of Greenwich-Village life, between youth wounded and killed to order, and youth eating, gossiping, and making love so irresponsibly around her. In *Aria da Capo* she was able to lift this savage motive into the realm of tragic beauty, of satire profound and unendurable, choked with dark laughter and dry weeping. In this brief, swiftly moving, symbolic Pierrot play she was able to strike the hardest blow at the War-god which has ever been dealt him by any poet of our language—and this, paradoxically, with the lightest possible touch.

The Euclid sonnet is a still stranger evidence of emotion seizing upon a sheerly intellectual motive and making it blaze with poetic fire. Our language has been rich in poets, many of them college-trained in the calculus; but no man of them all has felt the icy beauty of the higher mathematics like this girl fresh out of Vassar—at least, it remained for her to express that beauty in a sonnet which attains grandeur.

So her work goes on—in many moods, but always moods of power and praise for life, never of disillusion or frustration. *Figs From Thistles* are playful and mischievous, the love sonnets in various books are something new in feminine history, for they hold inviolate the "soul's chastity" through all the veering flames of passion.

The sonnet has been Miss Millay's favorite instrument. She has used both forms, Petrarchan and Shakespearian; but more often the latter, in which she has attained a mastery of cadence and phrasing worthy of Shakespeare himself. In her latest sequence, *Fatal Interview*, the form is Shakespearian, and Allen Tate has called attention to her extraordinary skill with "that difficult final couplet." This series exhibits a mood less haughtily independent than that of her youth, more capable of despair when the "fatal interview" turns love to disaster. In these sonnets the poet plays with words like a virtuoso, yet with never an effect of virtuosity, in expressing the lift and fall, the infinite byplay of emotion, between lovers haunted always by the dread of love's brevity. Here we find more complete absorption in the experience than in those love-sonnets of her youth which were first published in *Reedy's Mirror*; we miss a certain wood-nymph wildness which held aloof from passion even while yielding to it, but we find instead a poet sure of her love's endurance. In the early sequence, lovers' partings, however cruel, had an element of high comedy; in this later one the tragic emotion is relieved only by the beauty of its utterance, which reaches a triumphant climax in the final sonnet.

* Renascence and Other Poems......................Mitchell Kennerley, N. Y.: 1917
* Second April...Mitchell Kennerley: 1921
Aria Da Capo...Mitchell Kennerley: 1921
* A Few Figs from Thistles.................................Frank Shay, N. Y.: 1921
The Lamp and the Bell..Frank Shay: 1921
* The Harp-Weaver and Other Poems....................Harper & Bros., N. Y.: 1923
Three Plays...Harper & Bros.: 1926
The King's Henchman.......................................Harper & Bros.: 1927
* The Buck in the Snow.......................................Harper & Bros.: 1928
Fatal Interview...Harper & Bros.: 1931
In *Poetry:* Aug. 1917 (Vol. X); June 1918 (XII); May 1919 (XIV); May 1920 (XVI); May 1923 (XXII); Oct. 1930 (XXXVII).

HAROLD MONRO (*Died 1932*)

Harold Monro was born in 1879 in Brussels, and his university life was at Cambridge. In 1912 he started the Poetry Bookshop in London, and began the publication of *Poetry and the Drama*, which ran for a year as a monthly and later briefly as a quarterly. He became the publisher of most of the younger poets, and his shop was a literary centre where poetry readings were given weekly in an attic hall. In 1919 he began publication of *The Chapbook*, a monthly beautifully printed and illustrated, which, for the few years it continued, was the chief organ of the art in England. He was instrumental also in putting out the *Georgian Anthologies*, though not their editor.

To Harold Monro, the world of illusion is more real than so-called realities, and inanimate objects have a thrilling life of their own. He is full of nerve-emotions that tingle his flesh, but do not quite reach his heart. He is shrinkingly sensitive to the questionings of chairs and tables, the agonies of a deserted house. His beloved, be she alive or dead, inhabits inextricably a certain mansion in a certain street, haunting these like a ghost. Rarely are poems so full of a bitterly melancholy shrinking from life as some of those in *The Earth for Sale*. It is as though the poet's spirit were flayed; surface agonies are so intense that the deeper sources of feeling are benumbed. Sudden death closed this poet's career in March, 1932.

Judas..Sampson Low, London: 1908
Before Dawn....................................Constable & Co., Ltd., London: 1911
* Children of Love....................................Poetry Bookshop, London: 1914
Trees...Poetry Bookshop: 1915
Strange Meetings...Poetry Bookshop: 1917
Real Property..................Poetry Bookshop, London; Macmillan Co., N. Y.: 1922
The Earth for Sale..................Poetry Bookshop, London; Dial Press, N. Y.: 1928
Some Contemporary Poets...........................Leonard Parsons, London: 1920
In *Poetry:* Sept. 1916 (Vol. VIII); March 1920 (XV); Feb. 1921 (XVII); Feb. 1922 (XIX); May 1928 (XXXII).
In *Georgian Poetry:* I–IV...........................Poetry Bookshop, London: 1912–19

HARRIET MONROE

Harriet Monroe was born in Chicago in December, 1860, and educated in local schools and, for the final two years, in the Visitation Convent at Georgetown, D. C., although she has never been a Roman Catholic. She earned her living in journalism—as art critic chiefly—and by writing for magazines. Because of some local success as a poet, she was invited by the Committee on Ceremonies of the World's Columbian Exposition to write a poem for the Dedication of Buildings, an occasion which was to celebrate the 400th anniversary of the Discovery of America a half-year before the actual opening of the Fair. She accepted the commission and her *Columbian Ode* was read and sung (parts of it) October 21st, 1892, before an audience of 125,000 persons in the great hall which afterwards housed the exhibition of Manufactures and Liberal Arts.

The following twenty years were "hard sledding" for poets, a period when the magazines were inhospitable and the public indifferent. Impatience at this situation led Miss Monroe to project a magazine to be devoted exclusively to poetry. Advised by Hobart C. Chatfield-Taylor, she secured five-year pledges of $50 a year from over one hundred Chicago men and women interested in the art and the project. She then wrote to poets of standing, and to those who had contributed interesting verse to the magazines of the previous five years, and received from many of them effective co-operation and generous help.

The first number of *Poetry* appeared in October, 1912, and from that day to the present it has been published every month. It struck the psychological moment, for the "new movement" began at that time, and its early numbers contained names like Ezra Pound, Vachel Lindsay, Rabindranath Tagore, H. D., Richard Aldington, Amy Lowell, John Gould Fletcher, Carl Sandburg, Robert Frost, Edgar Lee Masters, Arthur Ficke, Witter Bynner, Carlos Williams, Wallace Stevens—many others—a large number of whom the magazine had the honor of introducing.

Miss Monroe's poems, from the first, showed the variety of her intensely modern sympathies. The *Columbian Ode* drew upon no classic symbols or models. *The Hotel*, first printed in *The Atlantic* in 1907, was a pioneer in free verse, for it appeared five or six years before the Imagists and their trail of vers-librists began their revolution. *The Turbine, The Telephone, The Ocean Liner*, etc., showed that she was interested in machinery, which few poets have been inspired by; and her sketches of painters *At the Prado* are a poetic by-product of her experience as an art critic. Her poems of the West celebrate tramping trips and other travels in Arizona, New Mexico, and California. While she has written much free verse, the greater part of her work is in rhymed forms.

Valeria and Other Poems...........................Privately printed, New York: 1892
Valeria and Other Poems...........................A. C. McClurg & Co., Chicago: 1893
Columbian Ode (decorations by Will. H. Bradley).....W. Irving Way & Co., Chicago: 1893
The Passing Show: Five Modern Plays in Verse..............Houghton Mifflin Co.: 1903
* You and I..Macmillan Co., N. Y.: 1914
* The Difference and Other Poems.............................Macmillan Co.: 1924
Poets and Their Art (essays)....................................Macmillan Co.: 1926
In *Poetry:* Nov. 1912 (Vol. I); Feb. 1914 (III); Sept. 1914 (IV); Aug. 1915 (VI); Nov. 1916
   & Jan. 1917 (IX); March 1918 (XI); April 1918 (XII); Dec. 1918 (XIII); Dec. 1921
   (XIX); July 1922 (XX); Jan. 1923 (XXI); June 1923 (XXII); Jan. 1924 (XXIII); March
   1924 (XXIII); March 1928 (XXXI); Oct. 1929 (XXXV); March 1931 (XXXVII); Jan.
   1932 (XXXIX).

MARIANNE MOORE

Marianne Moore was born in St. Louis, Missouri, in 1887. After graduation from Bryn Mawr, she taught at the United States Indian School at Carlisle, Pennsylvania, for a few years, left for service in the New York Public Library, and was editor of *The Dial* from 1925 until it ceased in 1929.

Miss Moore's first appearance as a poet was in *Poetry* for May, 1915. From the first her style was closely knit, keenly intellectualized, with a sharp and pungent flavor, and a persistent rhythmic beat not unlike certain phases of oriental music.

Some critics find her work crabbed and puzzling, full of "jagged clauses, barbed quotations," and scornful and sophisticated satire. Others more sympathetic praise her richly ironic wit and her elliptic word-arrangements. Yvor Winters, reviewing *Observations* in *Poetry* (April, 1925), refers to her "extraordinary magnificence of phraseology, often coincident with intentions purely satirical." The comedy of animal life has a special appeal for her. From elephants to unicorns she tricks them out in vivid words, as "one phase of the painfully sharp observation with which she scrutinizes everything—animals, persons and ideas."

* Poems..Egoist Press, London: 1921
Observations...Dial Press, N. Y.: 1924
In *Poetry:* May 1915 (Vol. VI); June 1932 (XL).
In *Others: An Anthology of the New Verse*.................Nich. L. Brown, N. Y.: 1916–17

MERRILL MOORE

Merrill Moore was born of southern stock in Columbia, Tennessee, in 1903. He went to school in Nashville, and after graduation from Vanderbilt University he studied and practiced medicine. His work as a poet began with the group of young poets contributing to *The Fugitive*, the verse-magazine published in Nashville from April, 1922, to December, 1925.

At twenty-five Dr. Moore is said to have already written some 2000 sonnets, and his book is entirely made up of hasty 14-line hybrids roughly measured into this form. They have a strong American accent, and they talk about familiar experiences and everyday characters in a rhythm accepting good-naturedly enough all kinds of syllabic and metric irregularities.

* The Noise That Time Makes....................Harcourt, Brace & Co., New York: 1929
In *Poetry:* May 1929 (Vol. XXXIV); May 1932 (XL).

JOHN G. NEIHARDT

John Gneisenau Neihardt was born in Sharpsburg, Illinois, in 1881. After a scientific course at the Nebraska Normal College, he lived for six years among the Omaha Indians, studying their customs and folk-lore. This experience was useful to him later in the writing of his epic-trilogy of pioneer times in the West.

Neihardt's style is Victorian and rhetorical, and his trilogy gives us trappers and Indians robed as it were in classic togas. He has been an earnest student, but without the imagination to accept pioneer life on its own rough terms, or the creative power to design a fit poetic medium. However, if one grants his premise of the heroic couplet and a heroic style, one gets an interesting development of pioneer legend and history.

The Divine Enchantment.....................James T. White & Co., N. Y.: 1900 (cir.)
A Bundle of Myrrh..Outing Co., N. Y.: 1907
* Man-Song..Mitchell Kennerley, N. Y.: 1909
The Stranger at the Gate.................................Mitchell Kennerley: 1912
The Song of Hugh Glass.................................Macmillan Co., N. Y.: 1915
* The Quest (Collected Lyrics)................................Macmillan Co.: 1916
The Song of Three Friends....................................Macmillan Co.: 1919
The Song of the Indian Wars.................................Macmillan Co.: 1925
Collected Poems...Macmillan Co.: 1926
In Poetry: May 1913 (Vol. II).

ROBERT NICHOLS

Robert Nichols was born on the Isle of Wight in 1893. While still an undergraduate at Oxford, he volunteered for the World War, but suffered shell-shock after a year of artillery service. Soon after the War, he made a lecture tour of the United States, and sojourned for a year or two in a Japanese university as a teacher of English.

His poems follow traditional lines in subject and method. A few have enriched the war anthologies. Of late he has been writing fantastic novels and plays. Wings over Europe, done in collaboration with Maurice Browne, made a recent theatrical success on both sides of the Atlantic.

Invocation and Other War Poems.....................Chatto & Windus, London: 1915
* Ardours and Endurances........................Frederick A. Stokes Co., N. Y.: 1917
The Assault and Other Poems.............................Chatto & Windus: 1918
Aurelia and Other Poems..........................E. P. Dutton & Co., N. Y.: 1920
In Poetry: July 1919 (Vol. XIV); Nov. 1919 (XV).

YONE NOGUCHI

Yone Noguchi was born at Tsuchima, Japan, in 1875. At eighteen he crossed the Pacific and remained ten years in California, spending three years with Joaquin Miller. He has also visited China and England, lecturing in Oxford on Japanese poetry by invitation of Robert Bridges—the course afterwards published by John Murray. In 1921 he interrupted his professorship of English literature in the Keio College at Tokyo to make a lecture trip in the United States.

Noguchi's two small books in free verse—English adaptations of the Japanese mood and manner—published in California in 1897-98, were "the first poetry of an oriental expressed in English," and they may be cited as one of the oriental influences tending to modify our poetic practice. Since his return to Japan he has continued to write at intervals in English and our selections are from these later poems.

From the Eastern Sea: Privately printed, London: 1906; Elkin Mathews, London: 1910
Japan Press, Tokio: 1910
* The Pilgrimage......The Valley Press, Kamakura, Japan: 1908; Elkin Mathews, London
Mitchell Kennerley, N. Y.: 1912
Spirit of Japanese Poetry.............................E. P. Dutton & Co., N. Y.: 1914
Japanese Hokkus...Four Seas Co., Boston: 1920
Seen and Unseen...Orientalia, N. Y.: 1920
Selected Poems...Four Seas Co.: 1921
* Collected Poems...Four Seas Co.: 1921
In *Poetry:* Nov. 1919 (Vol. XV); Aug. 1926 (XXVIII).

JESSICA NORTH (*Mrs. R. I. MacDonald*)

Jessica North was born in Madison, Wisconsin, and lived in that state until 1919, when she came to Chicago to study in the university and serve as private secretary to its president. She was married in 1922, and from 1927 to 1929 she was associate editor of *Poetry.*

Her poems are essentially feminine. Few poets have shown in their work such a tang of woman's wisdom and woman's humor, or such intimate understanding of children. She rhymes easily, but not with dangerous facility, and the form of her poem follows its mood with keen and concentrated precision.

A Prayer Rug...Will Ransom, Chicago: 1922
* The Long Leash................................Houghton Mifflin Co., Boston: 1928
In *Poetry:* Nov. 1921 (Vol. XIX); Aug. 1922 (XX); April 1923 (XXII); Sept. 1923 (XXII);
Feb. 1925 (XXV); Dec. 1926 (XXIX); July 1928 (XXXII); Nov. 1930 (XXXVII).

GRACE FALLOW NORTON (*Mrs. George Macrum*)

Grace Fallow Norton was born in Northfield, Minnesota, in 1876. The quiet delicately flavored poems in her various books are the only personal confession which she offers to the public.

Little Gray Songs from St. Joseph's...................Houghton Mifflin Co., Boston: 1912
* The Sister of the Wind................................Houghton Mifflin Co.: 1914
Roads..Houghton Mifflin Co.: 1916
What is Your Legion?....................................Houghton Mifflin Co.: 1916
The Miller's Youngest Daughter..........................Houghton Mifflin Co.: 1924
In *Poetry:* Jan. 1914 (Vol. III); Dec. 1915 (VII); Feb. 1920 (XV); Jan. 1922 (XIX); July 1923
(XXII); July 1924 (XXIV); Aug. 1929 (XXXIV).

ELDER OLSON

Elder Olson was born in Chicago in 1910, and educated in local schools and the University of Chicago, where he has been of late president of its Poetry Club. He is a trained pianist as well as a poet. For two years he was in the employ of the Commonwealth Edison Company, an occupation interrupted by a trip to Europe in the summer of 1931.

Olson's mood is usually imaginatively contemplative, but a few poems show a whimsically satiric drift in his temperament.

In *Poetry:* May 1928 (Vol. XXXII); July 1930 (XXXVI); Oct. 1931 (XXXIX).

GEORGE O'NEIL

George O'Neil was born in St. Louis, Missouri, in 1898. With intervals of travel, he has lived there and in New York or its New England neighborhood.

His first book showed a lyric talent and a taste for delicate fantasy which have developed and grown more adept in the later volumes.

George Dillon, reviewing *The White Rooster* in *Poetry* for May, 1927, said: "Mr. O'Neil can be simple with sincerity. He is a romantic and his world is accordingly transfigured—the color is more intense, the pattern swifter. Most of his poems achieve a synthesis: fantastic conceptions are supported by the results of minute observation."

M. D. Zabel, three years later, finds danger of exhaustion in this "steady coinage of brilliant images. . . . O'Neil's imagination has served him both well and badly. Upon its more complete discipline by the serious qualities of the mind his future development will depend."

The Cobbler in Willow Street..........................Boni & Liveright, N. Y.: 1919
* The White Rooster..Boni & Liveright: 1927
* God-beguiled..Horace Liveright: 1929
In *Poetry:* May 1919 (Vol. XIV); Dec. 1925 (XXVII); April 1928 (XXXII).

JAMES OPPENHEIM (*Died 1932*)

James Oppenheim, born in St. Paul, Minnesota, in 1882, was brought to New York in infancy and has always lived there. Local schools, courses at Columbia, settlement work, and teaching on the East Side, gave him material for a book of stories and another of poems (both 1909).

His real beginning as a poet, however, dates from his 1914 book, *Songs for the New Age*, poems of Whitmanic eloquence founded on social and racial distinctions of modern life. There is a strong biblical tune in his rhythmic chants—one hears a modern prophet warning the present age. Oppenheim's war poems and autobiographical poems are further exhibits of a spirit by turns depressed and exalted—a spirit mystically akin to the prophets of his Hebraic ancestry.

The death of this poet in August is announced as we go to press.

Monday Morning and Other Poems..................Sturgis & Walton Co., N. Y.: 1909
The Pioneers..B. W. Huebsch, N. Y.: 1910
* Songs for the New Age....................................Century Co., N. Y.: 1914
War and Laughter..Century Co.: 1916
The Book of Self..Alf. A. Knopf, N. Y.: 1917
The Solitary..B. W. Huebsch, N. Y.: 1919
The Mystic Warrior..Alf. A. Knopf: 1921
The Sea..Alf. A. Knopf: 1924

PATRICK ORR

"Patrick Orr" is the pseudonym used in the literary partnership of a California woman poet and a wandering young Irishman who was afterwards killed in the War. We retain these poems in the present edition because of their intrinsic charm.

In *Poetry:* Jan. 1915 (Vol. V).

SEUMAS O'SULLIVAN

James Starkey, who uses the above pseudonym, was born in Dublin in 1878. He was introduced as a poet by "A. E" (George Russell), and his work has been consistently in the Celtic tradition. He is now editor of *The Dublin Magazine: A Quarterly Review.*

New Songs (in collaboration)..............................O'Donoghue, Dublin: 1904
The Twilight People..Whaley, Dublin: 1905
Verses Sacred and Profane.........................Maunsel & Co., Ltd., Dublin: 1908
The Earth Lover...................................New Nation Press, Dublin: 1909
Selected Lyrics...............................Thos. B. Mosher, Portland, Maine: 1910
Poems..Maunsel & Co., Ltd.: 1912
An Epilogue and Other Poems............................Maunsel & Co., Ltd.: 1914
Requiem and Other Poems...........................Privately printed, Dublin: 1917
* The Rosses and Other Poems...........................Maunsel & Co., Ltd.: 1918
Poems..B. J. Brimmer Co., Boston: 1923
In *Poetry:* Dec. 1914 (Vol. V).

WILFRED OWEN (*Died 1918*)

Wilfred Owen was one of the most costly of the War's sacrifices. He was born in 1893 at Oswestry, educated at London University, was a private tutor in France for two years, and volunteered for war service in spite of frail health. He received the Military Cross for gallantry a month before the Armistice, and was killed November 4th, 1918.

Siegfried Sassoon, sponsoring the posthumous volume which presented his friend's poems to the world, says in his introduction: "He was a man of absolute integrity of mind; . . . he pitied others, he did not pity himself." And most critics have pronounced him the most distinguished poet of the War.

Alice Corbin Henderson, reviewing his books in *Poetry* for August, 1921, said: "The trouble with these poems, if one considers them as propaganda, is that they do not propagandize. . . . But when it comes to the slow horror of such a poem as *The Show,* or the subtle satire of *Arms and the Boy,* or the pitiful hopelessness of *Strange Meeting,* there you have the deep personal experience and revelation which is the only sort of propaganda (and one might say of poetry) that counts. . . . Such poems are fine also in sheer poetic quality; with a certain seventeenth-century perfection like George Herbert or Donne."

* Poems.......................Chatto & Windus, London; B. W. Huebsch, N. Y.: 1912
* The Poems of Wilfred Owen (Memoir by Edmund Blunden)....Viking Press, N. Y.: 1931

JOSEPHINE PRESTON PEABODY (*Mrs. Lionel S. Marks—Died 1922*)

Josephine Preston Peabody was born in New York City in 1874. When eight years old she was taken to Boston and educated there at a private school and Radcliffe College. In 1906 she married Lionel Marks, then an instructor at Wellesley. Her later years were spent in Cambridge.

In her youth she wrote many poems, three or four blank verse plays and a choric idyl for music. One of the plays, *The Piper,* received in 1909 the Stratford-on-Avon prize and was produced in the Shakespeare theatre, the author being present.

Mrs. Marks died in December, 1922.

The Wayfarers...................................Copeland & Day, Boston: 1898
Marlowe, A Drama...........................Houghton Mifflin Co., Boston: 1901
The Singing Leaves.................................Houghton Mifflin Co.: 1903
The Book of the Little Past.........................Houghton Mifflin Co.: 1908
Fortune and Men's Eyes............................Houghton Mifflin Co.: 1909
* The Singing Man..................................Houghton Mifflin Co.: 1911
The Piper..Houghton Mifflin Co.: 1911
The Wolf of Gubbio................................Houghton Mifflin Co.: 1914
* Harvest Moon...................................Houghton Mifflin Co.: 1916

PADRAIC PEARSE (*Died 1916*)

Padraic Pearse was born in Ireland, and throughout his life he was a
devoted patriot, becoming one of the founders of the Gaelic League, which
strove to introduce the ancient language into the schools. To learn it he lived
months at a time in West Connacht. He translated poems of the old bards,
and wrote many of his own in Gaelic.

In the effort to free his country from British rule, he took up arms like his
mythical hero Cuchullain, and joined the group, mostly poets, who brought
on the Easter rebellion in 1916. He was one of the three poets executed for
this spasmodic outbreak.

The Singer and Other Poems......................Maunsel & Co., Ltd., Dublin: 1919
* Collected Poems.................................Fred. A. Stokes Co., N. Y.: 1919

JOSEPHINE PINCKNEY

Josephine Pinckney was born early in the century in Legari Street,
Charleston, S. C., which, according to a saying current in the Old South,
makes her an inheritor of the Kingdom of Heaven. She was educated in
local schools and through travel, and began in youth the writing of verse.
With DuBose Heyward and others, she was instrumental in founding the
Poetry Society of South Carolina.

The title of her book indicates her love of her own region, and its contents
give vivid pictures of the life, both black and white, around her.

* Sea-drinking Cities.................................Harper & Bros., N. Y.: 1927
In *Poetry:* July 1921 (Vol. XVIII); April 1922 (XX); April 1925 (XXVI); Sept. 1927 (XXX);
May 1932 (XL).

EZRA POUND

Ezra Pound was born in Idaho, October 30, 1885, spent most of his boyhood
in Minnesota, and entered the University of Pennsylvania at fifteen. The
next year he began his life-long study of comparative literature, continued
it as a special student there and at Hamilton College, became an "instructor
with professorial functions" at the age of twenty at Pennsylvania, and taught
for four months at Wabash College, Crawfordsville, Indiana, until a clash
with the faculty unfortunately brought to a close the pedagogical career of a
great teacher. Pound then went abroad, lived in London for some years on
little or nothing, later moved to Paris; and more recently, a confirmed
cosmopolite, he resides during most of the year in Rapallo, Italy.

Elkin Mathews, Pound's first publisher, called his early poems "pure
poetry," and their simple diction and haunting Debussy-like music certainly
struck a blow at the Victorian tradition. Between 1910 and 1912 Pound

gathered around him a group of young enthusiasts—Fletcher, Flint, H. D., Aldington, the mythical Hulme—and the Imagist movement began, fortified by his code of rules, or rather "Don'ts," which aimed to lop off certain redundancies, archaisms, and rhetorical excesses of the very recent past. *Poetry*, in far-away Chicago, became their organ, and the "Don'ts" were printed in its sixth number. A still small voice at first, the movement gradually became famous and developed enormous influence. Pound then passed on to Vorticism, which soon died in the War, he being a confirmed revolutionist whose stormy energies must have an outlet. As Carl Sandburg put it in a study of him in *Poetry*, "Pound has done most of living men to incite new impulses in poetry." In the pugilistic sense of utter prowess, he called Pound "the best man writing poetry today," for he not only wrote it but made it effective and powerful by ramming it, and his artistic credo as well, down people's throats.

The strange wavering music of *Personæ* was somewhat a twelfth-century revival. Pound's early poems, after the rich orchestration of centuries of English poetry, sound to our inner ear like Palestrina after Wagner, Schubert, Beethoven. Their wayward cadences owe something, of course, to the Provençal poets whom he had so closely studied, something to Villon, something to Yeats. They recapture primitive simplicities and discard efficient regularities. They play with rhyme or not, they keep time with metrics or not, but always they follow their own wilful way and ride the changing winds of mood as lightly as a swallow.

The same wayward beauty inspires many of the songs in *Lustra*. The motive here is more audacious, indeed often satiric; the music more emphatic for either gay or serious emotion, with less of the Provençal plaintiveness.

Pound has translated, or rather adapted, from Provençal, Italian, Anglo-Saxon, Latin and Greek poets, and even Chinese. And he has helped Anthiel explore new domains for modern music. His latest poems, the thirty *Cantos*, are provocative and stimulating even when most difficult and obscure. They make use of quotations and phrases from numerous languages, they trail elusive rhythms, and some of them strain the limits of decorum. The magic which they undoubtedly possess escapes some readers, and controversy rages as to whether they are a mass of doggerel or the greatest poem of the century.

A Lume Spento (ed. of 100)............................Autonelli, Venice, Italy: 1908
A Quinzaine for this Yule.......Pollock, London (100); Elkin Mathews, London (100): 1908
* Personæ..Elkin Mathews, London: 1909
* Exultations...Elkin Mathews: 1909
Provença.................................Small, Maynard & Co., Boston: 1910
Canzoni...Elkin Mathews: 1911
* Ripostes................................Stephen Swift & Co., Ltd., London: 1912
Sonnets and Ballate of Guido Cavalcanti
    Small, Maynard & Co., Boston; Stephen Swift & Co., Ltd., London: 1912
* Poems (Vols. I–II)......................................Elkin Mathews: 1913
* Cathay...Elkin Mathews: 1915
* Lustra...Elkin Mathews: 1916
* Lustra, with Earlier Poems...........................Alf. A. Knopf, New York: 1917
Certain Noble Plays of Japan, trans. by Ernest Fenollosa and Ezra Pound
    Cuala Press, Dundrum, Ireland: 1916
* Umbra..Elkin Mathews: 1920
* Poems, 1918–1921................................Boni & Liveright, N. Y.: 1921
* Personæ, The Collected Poems of Ezra Pound.................Boni & Liveright: 1926
* A Draft of XXX Cantos................................Hours Press, Paris: 1930
Guido Cavalcanti—Rime (translation and essay)....................Milan, Italy: 1931
The Spirit of Romance.............................J. M. Dent & Co., London: 1911
Noh, or Accomplishment: a Study of the Classical Stage of Japan with translations of 15 plays
    by E. F. & E. P.........Macmillan & Co., Ltd., London; Alf. A. Knopf, N. Y.: 1917
Pavannes and Divisions (prose essays).............................Alf. A. Knopf: 1918

Quia Pauper Amavi.....................................Egoist Press, London: 191ç
Instigations...Boni & Liveright, N. Y.: 1921
Irritations..Three Mountains Press, Paris: 1923
Antheil and Treatise on Harmony Three Mountains Press, Paris; Pascal Covici, Chicago: 1925
How to Read...................................Desmond Harmsworth, London: 1931
In *Poetry:* Oct. 1912 (Vol. I); April 1913 (II); Nov. 1913 (III); Aug. 1914 (IV); March 1915
   (V); Dec. 1915 (VII); Sept. 1916 (VIII); June July & Aug. 1917 (X); March 1919 (XIII).
In *Others: An Anthology of the New Verse*.......................Alf. A. Knopf, N. Y.: 1919

JOHN CROWE RANSOM

John Crowe Ransom was born in 1888 in Pulaski, Tennessee, the son of a minister. Some years after graduation from Vanderbilt University he became a Rhodes Scholar at Oxford, taking his B. A. degree in the classical course in 1923. Between these two college courses, he had taught at Vanderbilt and spent two years in the War with the A. E. F. In 1922 he combined with Allen Tate and others to found *The Fugitive*, the stimulating southern poetry magazine published at Nashville; but already, three years earlier, he had published his first rather ineffectual book.

His second book, *Chills and Fever*, was a mature and finished product. One finds in it, and in *Two Gentlemen in Bonds*, something of the cavalier attitude; he is the gentleman satirist, half-laughing, half-serious, and always the perfection of finish and good manners. His style has a light touch, and his mood is never unsympathetic or bitter, even though his keen mind is quite aware of human vanities. Ransom is capable of elegance; he can wear his twentieth-century tweeds with the grace and charm of velvet and lace. And whatever fabric his poems are woven in, it is of the finest quality and its cut and colors are in perfect taste.

Poems about God.....................................Henry Holt & Co., N. Y.: 1919
* Chills and Fever...Alf. A. Knopf, N. Y.: 1924
* Two Gentlemen in Bonds.......................................Alf. A. Knopf: 1927
In *Poetry:* May 1932 (Vol. XL).

JOHN REED (*Died 1920*)

John Reed was born in Portland, Oregon, October 22d, 1887, and died in Russia October 17th, 1920. Between those two dates rises a varied and adventurous career, for Reed was a communist and a born fighter, who had to be in every labor war and every other war for which he could find or manufacture a communist excuse, like even Villa's in Mexico. Of course the Russian revolution called him, and in the midst of it he died of typhus in Moscow, where his tomb in the Kremlin has become a place of pilgrimage.

Reed was by profession a journalist. Though poetry was but one facet of his many-sided mind, it was perhaps the most intense and highly colored of all. His finest poem, *Sangar*, published in *Poetry's* third number, December, 1912, was dedicated to his friend Lincoln Steffens, and symbolized what Reed called his "magnificent try for peace during the trial of the Mc-Namaras."

* Sangar.....................................Privately printed, Riverside, Conn.: 1912
The Day in Bohemia.......................Privately printed, Riverside, Conn.: 1913
Tamburlaine and Other Poems.................Fred. C. Bursch, Riverside, Conn.: 191ƒ
In *Poetry:* Dec. 1912 (Vol. I); Apr. 1914 (IV); Aug. 1917 (X); Apr. 1919 (XIV).

LIZETTE WOODWORTH REESE

Lizette Woodworth Reese was born in Baltimore in 1856, and educated in public and private schools. For many years she taught in the Western High School at Baltimore, until her retirement in 1921.

Miss Reese began in youth to write her spare, closely concentrated lyrics. Her forms are traditional and simple, and her subjects are those of a keen observer much interested in nature's phenomena of beauty, and in the joys and sorrows of her neighbors. *Little Henrietta* is a sequence of forty numbers commemorating the short life of a little child.

A Wayside Lute.............................Thomas B. Mosher, Portland, Me.: 1909
A Branch of May (First ed. 1887)...........................Thomas B. Mosher: 1912
A Handful of Lavender (First ed. 1891)......................Thomas B. Mosher: 1915
A Quiet Road (First ed. 1896).............................Thomas B. Mosher: 1916
* Spicewood...............................Norman Remington Co., Baltimore: 1920
* Wild Cherry.......................................Norman Remington Co.: 1923
The Selected Poems................................George H. Doran Co., N. Y.: 1926
Little Henrietta..George H. Doran Co.: 1927
* White April...................................Farrar & Rinehart, Inc., N. Y.: 1930
In *Poetry:* May 1932 (Vol. XL).

CHARLES REZNIKOFF

Charles Reznikoff was born in Brooklyn in 1894. For a time in 1910 he conducted a column of verse and comment in the *University Missourian* at Columbia, Missouri; later he practiced law in New York.

He may be grouped among the more radical technicians. He has printed his poems mostly on his own hand press, and issued them in small pamphlets. He has also written novels.

Poems...Samuel Roth, N. Y.: 1918
Uriel Acosta, and a Fourth Group of Verse................Privately printed, N. Y.: 1920
Chatterton, The Black Death, & Meriweather Lewis, Three Plays
Privately printed, N. Y.: 1922
* Five Groups of Verse..................................Charles Reznikoff, N. Y.: 1927
In *Poetry:* Feb. 1931 (Vol. XXXVII).

ERNEST RHYS

Ernest Rhys was born in London of Welsh ancestry in July, 1859. He has published books of verse, ballads, romances, plays; and has edited *Everyman's Library* and other literary series.

Mr. Rhys has lived chiefly in London, but has travelled much in America, his first visit having been a lecture trip in 1887–88.

The Great Cockney Tragedy............................T. Fisher Unwin, London: 1891
A London Rose and Other Rhymes..........................John Lane, London: 1894
Welsh Ballads..David Nutt, London: 1898
Guenevere................................J. M. Dent & Sons, Ltd., London: 1905
Lays of the Round Table..............................J. M. Dent & Sons, Ltd.: 1905
Enid..J. M. Dent & Sons, Ltd.: 1908
The Masque of the Grail..............................Elkin Mathews, London: 1908
The Leaf-burners.....................................J. M. Dent & Sons, Ltd.: 1916
In *Poetry:* Jan. 1913 (Vol. I); Sept. 1913 (II); Apr. 1916 (VIII).

LOLA RIDGE

Lola Ridge was born in Dublin, spent her childhood and youth mostly in Australia, and left there for the United States in 1907 to put an end to an unsatisfactory marriage. For ten years she earned a precarious living by writing, drawing, working in a factory, etc. In 1918 *The New Republic* introduced her as a poet with her long episodic poem of tenement and factory life in New York, *The Ghetto*, a poem of fiery attack on the social system and poignant sympathy with those who suffer from it.

Sun-up is a poem of personal experience, and *Red Flag*, as its title indicates, emphasizes still further *The Ghetto's* subject. *Firehead* is a narrative of the Crucifixion, or rather a series of monologues by John, Peter, the two Marys, etc., describing the tragedy from different angles.

```
* The Ghetto and Other Poems...........................B. W. Huebsch, N. Y.: 1919
* Sun-up.....................................................B. W. Huebsch: 1920
Red Flag....................................................Viking Press, N. Y.: 1927
Firehead...........................................Payson & Clarke, Ltd., N. Y.: 1929
In Poetry: Oct. 1918 (Vol. XIII); Sept. 1920 (XVI); July 1922 (XX); March 1923 (XXI);
    March 1924 (XXIII).
In Others for 1919.........................................Nich. L. Brown, N. Y.: 1919
```

ELIZABETH MADOX ROBERTS

Elizabeth Madox Roberts was born in 1885 near Springfield, Kentucky. Her education was episodic until a small legacy enabled her to enter the University of Chicago in 1921. She won the Fiske prize there with a group of poems written with exquisite simplicity from a child's point of view. These soon after became the basis of a group in *Poetry* and of her first book. In these a delicate satirical spirit is veiled under the naïve diction.

Miss Roberts has studied profoundly the lives and dialects of her Kentucky neighbors, and her two novels, *The Time of Man* and *The Great Meadow*, make an almost epic use of this material.

```
* Under the Tree.........................................B. W. Huebsch, N. Y.: 1922
Under the Tree (illustrated)...............................Viking Press, N. Y.: 1931
In Poetry: July 1921 (Vol. XVIII); Aug. 1922 (XX); July 1924 (XXIV); Dec. 1927 (XXXI).
```

EDWIN ARLINGTON ROBINSON

Edwin Arlington Robinson was born in a Maine village December 22d, 1869, and passed his childhood in Gardiner, the *Tilbury Town* of his early poems. He spent two years (1891–93) in Harvard, printed his first two little books privately in 1896–97, and soon after tried in various ways to make a living in New York while never sacrificing his more important vocation. In 1902 *Captain Craig*, a closely knit narrative of a down-and-out old lovable codger, aroused some attention, and caused President Roosevelt to give the poet a clerkship in the New York Custom House, a post he held from 1905 to 1910. By this time critics were beginning to remark Robinson's departure from the Victorian tradition—his clean, hard, simple, unrhetorical style and his homely neighborhood themes. A few years later they began to call him the beginning of the "new movement"; in his stern stript austerities they found the heredity of Robert Frost, Edgar Lee Masters, and other poets of modern life.

A few extracts may be quoted from the editor's essay on this poet in *Poets and Their Art:*

In reading Robinson's *Collected Poems* in chronological order, one notes a gradual and sure development. It begins with *The Children of the Night,* poems of 1890–97. Here one finds no juvenilia—neither immature thinking nor faulty workmanship. To be sure, the poet tries ballades and villanelles, though hardly in the gay tempo of the Austin-Dobson fashion of the hour. And he offers many sonnets—a more enduring fashion, always with a firm touch on the form and with an eye for

The perfect word that is the poet's wand.

With sonnet-like compactness he writes *Richard Cory,* one of the first, and still one of the best, of his numerous studies of tragic incongruities in human character. And in a number of poems he sounds the key-note of his austere philosophy.

No facile faith could satisfy this poet—it is a stern spiritual discipline which he has accepted through the years, one not always relieved even by that remote vision of "the coming glory of the Light." But though the Puritan God of his fathers is never personally in evidence, we feel in Robinson's make-up something akin to him—an outreaching toward his implacable austerity and blinding majesty through orbit on orbit of modern discovery and thought.

If the psychology of failure, or of that uncertain middle ground between spiritual success and failure, is Robinson's recurrent motive, it may be interesting to study his attitude and his methods in presenting that motive in art. It is heroic, not ignoble, struggle that engages him, or if not heroic, at least the struggle of highly strung sensitive souls to fulfil their manifest destiny; ending either in acceptance of compromise, or in tragic spiritual revolt that induces some kind of dark eclipse. The form is usually narrative, with the poet as the narrator, under some assumption of friendship or at least neighborliness; but in the longer poems we have, as a rule, monologue and dialogue, the characters unfolding their perplexities, or recording their action upon each other, in long speeches which are not talk, as talk actually ever was or could be, but which are talk intensified into an extra-luminous self-revelation; as if an X-ray, turned into the suffering soul, made clear its hidden structural mysteries.

Sometimes he uses his method with bitter brevity, as in *Richard Cory, John Gorham, Another Dark Lady, Lorraine, Clavering,* and certain sonnets of marital discord; but brevity which heightens the dramatic effect. Again he pushes it to the other extreme of too detailed analysis in speeches of too great length. Perhaps the temptation to excess is strongest in the three legendary poems *Merlin, Lancelot,* and *Tristram;* here it is emphasized by the academic traditions of conventionalized archaistic speech.

Of the soul-biographies of his New England neighbors, *The Man Who Died Twice* may be cited as typical and one of Robinson's best poems in that kind. It is the record of a great soul, self-ruined and self-betrayed. Fernando Nash, born to be of the line of Bach and Beethoven, the man of genius who never fulfilled his genius, is a grand figure in his ruin, and in honor of his tragic agony the poet tolls deep bells and beats muffled drums. The solemn fall of the lines strikes on the heart like the slow march of a regiment passing with dirges to a hero's burial. It is quite wonderful what the poet has done with his simple instrument of blank verse, piling up splendid chords that seem to reverberate through cathedral aisles as he records disaster.

A few years ago we were all congratulating Mr. Robinson on his jubilee. The tribute of Edgar Lee Masters ended as follows:

"As a craftsman he is a master, as a thinker he is subtle and original, as an artist he has kept the faith. The poets of America look to him, now that he is at the meridian of his career, to fight on in the war of spiritualizing America, since he has inherited this day of hope after a beginning that did not bring adequate reward."

Somewhat shy and aloof, haughtily austere in thought and manner of life, imaginatively observant, impassioned like tempered steel, Mr. Robinson stands today, as in his more obscure yesterdays, adequate, uncompromising, a big man, a thorough and keen-visioned artist.

Someone has called him "the proudest figure in American letters." At least he led the modern procession for his countrymen; wilful and self-advised, he struck his own path, and found, no doubt with surprise, that he had blazed a trail for others.

The Torrent and the Night Before . . . . Privately printed, Gardiner, Me.: 1896
The Children of the Night . . . . Richard G. Badger: 1897
Captain Craig . . . . Houghton Mifflin Co.: 1902
* The Children of the Night . . . . Chas. Scribner's Sons, N. Y.: 1905
* The Town down the River . . . . Chas. Scribner's Sons: 1910
* Captain Craig . . . . Macmillan Co., N. Y.: 1915
* The Man against the Sky . . . . Macmillan Co.: 1916
Merlin . . . . Macmillan Co.: 1917
Lancelot . . . . Thomas Seltzer, N. Y.: 1920
* The Three Taverns . . . . Macmillan Co.: 1920
Avon's Harvest . . . . Macmillan Co.: 1921
* Collected Poems . . . . Macmillan Co.: 1921
Roman Bartholow . . . . Macmillan Co.: 1923
Sonnets . . . . Macmillan Co.: 1928
Tristram . . . . Macmillan Co.: 1928
Cavender's House . . . . Macmillan Co.: 1929
Collected Poems . . . . Macmillan Co.: 1929
The Glory of the Nightingales . . . . Macmillan Co.: 1930
Matthias at the Door . . . . Macmillan Co.: 1931
Nicodemus . . . . Macmillan Co.: 1932
In *Poetry:* March 1914 (Vol. III); Sept. 1915 (VI); Oct. 1922 (XXI); Oct. 1922 (XXI); Aug. 1923 (XXII).

CARL SANDBURG

Carl Sandburg was born at Galesburg, Illinois, January 6th, 1878, the son of Swedish immigrants who had bought a farm. After casual schooling, he began at thirteen to earn his living as porter, scene-shifter, pottery apprentice, harvest hand, etc., and at twenty he enlisted for the war with Spain, and was sent to Porto Rico.

Returning with his pay saved up and a budding interest in literature, he entered Lombard College in his home town. After college, he earned his living in various ways, chiefly more or less journalistic, and in 1904 he testified to his interest in poetry by putting out a tiny pamphlet of twenty-three poems, mostly in free rhythms somewhat reminiscent of Whitman, and suggestive of his own future style.

However, ten years passed before he was heard of as a poet. In March, 1914, a group of his *Chicago Poems* appeared in *Poetry*, and the following November this group received the Levinson Prize, then awarded for the first time. The award aroused a tempest of satirical protest and a few voices of praise, and through the noise it became evident that the new poet had arrived.

A few passages may be quoted from the editor's reviews and essays. Of *Chicago Poems*, Sandburg's first book, published in 1916, she wrote:

Carl Sandburg has the unassailable and immovable earthbound strength of a great granite rock which shows a weather-worn surface above the soil. Like such a rock, he has a tender and intimate love of all soft growing things —grasses, lichens, flowers, children, suffering human lives. One would no more question his sincerity than that of the wind and rain. His book, whether you like it or not, whether you call it poetry or not, is fundamental in the same majestic sense—it is a man speaking with his own voice, authoritatively like any other force of nature. It is speech torn out of the heart because the loveliness of "yellow dust on a bumble-bee's wing," of "worn wayfaring men," of ships at night, of a fog coming "on little cat feet"—the incommunicable loveliness of the earth, of life—is too keen to be borne; or because the pain of "the poor, patient and toiling," of children behind mill-doors, of soldiers bleeding in the trenches—all the unnecessary human anguish—is too bitter for any human being, poet or not, to endure in silence.

Mr. Sandburg knows his Chicago, and the book as a whole gives us the city in a masterpiece of portraiture.

The free-verse rhythms which this poet prefers are as personal as his slow speech or his massive gait; always a reverent beating-out of his subject. They are rugged enough at times—as when he salutes Chicago, "stormy, husky, brawling," and sets her high among cities. Or again, under softer inspiration, his touch becomes exquisitely delicate. Indeed, there is orchestral richness in his music; he plays divers instruments. Such lyrics as *The Great Hunt*, *Under*, *Beachy*, *At a Window*, *The Road and the End*, have a primal fundamental beauty, a sound and swing as of tides or bending grain.

Chicago Poems is an urban book—the subjects are a city and its people, including of course the author; also the War, which was killing men overseas. *Cornhuskers* goes back to the western-Illinois country where the poet was born, and to the railroads he rode on, the taverns he stopped in, and the laborers and hoboes, the children, women, horses, he got acquainted with while earning a living at rough jobs. *Smoke and Steel* carries the tale into the shops and factories, taking for its special motive man-made machines and machine-made men. In a sense all three books are epic—that is, they give us the tale of the tribe in a strongly centralized locale. But the method is lyric rather than epic. The story is presented by flashes; it is revealed by strongly lit details, emotions, episodes, rather than told by chapters which knit together into a shaped and ordered whole.

Sandburg's technique is less radical and more metrical than it seems at the first glance. What he does is not, as some students seem to infer, the complete sweeping-away of the metrical pattern. There is an underlying three-time or four-time beat in each poem, his preference leaning, oftener than with most poets, to four-time, which admits that generous use of spondees—sometimes four long syllables in succession—from which he gets some of his most telling effects. But in his underlying pattern Sandburg permits himself more variety than the prosodic laws have allowed for, especially in the number of syllables to a bar, and in a free use of rests. On these patterns, like all poets but more skilfully than most of them, he swings the larger tides of his cadences.

Another element of his art—his vocabulary—may call for comment. It is enough to say that any writer who can use the common speech of the people for beauty thereby enriches and revivifies the language. A static language is half dead—the "well of English undefiled" will dry up unless fresh waters out of the common earth continually fill it.

This use of so-called vulgar speech—of slang—is often in the service of his rich and whimsical humor, a humor that jokes with the earth, and with time and fate, and other slow-moving obstinate obstacles. And again he takes off his hat to these enemies: some of his finest lyrics are salutations of death—*The Road and the End, Grass, Loam,* and especially *Cool Tombs.*

A biography of Lincoln, of which *The Prairie Years* has been published in two volumes, has occupied most of Mr. Sandburg's time for the past six or eight years.

```
* Chicago Poems......................................Henry Holt & Co., N. Y.: 1916
* Cornhuskers.............................................Henry Holt & Co.: 1918
* Smoke and Steel..............................Harcourt, Brace & Co., N. Y.: 1920
Slabs of the Sunburnt West...........................Harcourt, Brace & Co.: 1922
Selected Poems.......................................Harcourt, Brace & Co.: 1926
Good Morning America................................Harcourt, Brace & Co.: 1928
Early Moon..........................................Harcourt, Brace & Co.: 1930
```
In *Poetry:* March 1914 (Vol. III); June 1914 (IV); Nov. 1914 (V); Oct. 1915 (VII); April 1917 (X); Nov. 1917 (XI); July 1918 (XII); Oct. 1918 (XIII); Feb. 1920 (XV); March 1922 (XIX).
In *Others: An Anthology of the New Verse*....................Alf. A. Knopf, N. Y : 1916–17

LEW SARETT

Lew Sarett was born in Chicago, May 16th, 1888, but a childhood passed chiefly out-of-doors in Michigan and the wilds of northern Wisconsin ill prepared him to return as a youth to the city and try to earn a living and support his mother in its slums. So he became a guide in the Chippewa country, serving hunters and fishermen for nine seasons, and earning enough to pay for a college education in Beloit and the University of Illinois.

In 1918, when Sarett was an instructor in the English department of the University of Illinois, the editor heard him give Indian chants to his own piano accompaniment, and urged him to translate these songs in free verse, or otherwise use his rich material to interpret aboriginal life. The result was the appearance of *The Blue Duck* and the *Chippewa Flute Song* in *Poetry* for November, 1918.

Sarett's first book presented these and other phases of his wilderness experience. Not only is he the most sympathetic imaginative interpreter of aboriginal feeling and rhythms, but he brings to us, in many poems, a stronger suggestion of the true spirit of the pioneers than those poets who have more directly undertaken to tell the epic story of their conquest of the West; for he reveals with finer art the love of adventurous men for the wilderness, their delight in animals and birds, in forests, plains, mountains, and all free spaces.

Alice Corbin Henderson, reviewing this book in December, 1920, said: "Sarett has attempted a difficult thing, to write Indian poems with the beat of Indian music. This is an almost impossible thing to do, and I think he has come closer to it, in *The Blue Duck*, than any other poet who has attempted it. It is extremely difficult for the trained musician to catch the intervals of Indian music both in pitch and time, and when the poet tries to catch the accent of Indian song, he usually resorts to the expedient of *mentioning* the accompanying drumbeats or gourd rattles, or of imitating them by onomatopœic methods, usually not successful. Mr. Sarett has come closer than the others to achieving the Indian accent in the *ictus* of his verse itself, although he too sometimes reverts to the more imitative and descriptive methods, as in the *Squaw Dance.* Indian symbolism, with the image as employed by the Indian, is to my mind the most fruitful and translatable contribution that Indian poetry can make to our own."

Sarett, as a lover of all wild things, has sought wilderness experience. In his work as guide and forest ranger, he has known simple hard-working men. It is their spiritual attitude which his *Box of God* presents—not statedly and consciously, but by a larger and more absolute implication than he may be aware of. This poem is an out-door man's profession of faith—the creed of the pioneer, of the explorer, the discoverer, the inventor in whatever field; of the man who sees something beckoning ahead, and who must follow it, wherever it leads; of the hero with the future in his keeping, who, though called by different names in different ages, is always the same type. Mr. Sarett makes an Indian guide his spokesman—one who rebels against confinement in that ritualistic "box of God," the little church in the mountains in which his "conversion" had been registered. The poem is an out-door man's protest against in-door creeds.

The feel of the West is in all Lew Sarett's books—intimate knowledge of the wilderness and the people and animals to be found there.

```
* Many Many Moons....................................Henry Holt & Co., N. Y.: 1920
The Box of God...........................................Henry Holt & Co.: 1922
* Slow Smoke.............................................Henry Holt & Co.: 1925
* Wings Against the Moon.................................Henry Holt & Co.: 1931
In Poetry: Nov. 1918 (Vol. XIII); Nov. 1919 (XV); April 1921 (XVIII); Nov. 1924 (XXV);
    Sept. 1925 (XXVI); Jan. 1929 (XXXIII); May 1931 (XXXVIII).
```

SIEGFRIED SASSOON

Siegfried Sassoon was born in 1886, and educated at Marlborough and Oxford University. During the War he was a captain in the Royal Welsh Fusiliers, served in France and Palestine, winning the Military Cross for valor.

Sassoon's literary career began mildly with lyrics and Masefieldian narratives, and continued fiercely with some of the bitterest, most sardonic war poems which the universal tragedy called forth. His friend and fellow poet Robert Nichols quotes Sassoon as saying: "Let no one ever from henceforth say a word in any way countenancing war. . . . For war is hell, and those who institute it are criminals." It is in this mood that Sassoon's war poems of personal feeling and experience were written.

Sassoon is an enthusiastic fox-hunter, as *The Old Huntsman* and other poems, also recent books in prose, testify.

```
* The Old Huntsman............Wm. Heinemann, London; E. P. Dutton & Co., N. Y.: 1917
* Counter-Attack..........................Wm. Heinemann; E. P. Dutton & Co.: 1918
* Picture Show............................Wm. Heinemann; E. P. Dutton & Co.: 1919
Selected Poems..................................................Wm. Heinemann: 1925
Satirical Poems.................................................Wm. Heinemann: 1926
Poems (Augustan Books)........................Ernest Benn, Ltd., London: 1926
The Heart's Journey.....................Wm. Heinemann: 1928; Harper & Bros.: 1929
Nativity, To My Mother, In Sicily (Ariel Poems)........Faber & Faber, London: 1928-30
```

ALAN SEEGER (*Died 1916*)

Alan Seeger was born in New York, June 22d, 1888, and passed his childhood and early youth in Staten Island and Mexico. Harvard in 1906, New York again in 1910, and Paris with vague literary ambitions in 1913.

In 1914, during the first month of the War, Seeger enlisted in the Foreign Legion of France, and for almost two years was in active service on various fronts. On July 1st, 1916, the Legion was ordered to clear the enemy out of the village of Belloy-en-Santerre. On the Fourth of July Seeger was killed in an early morning rush, with most of his company, by ambushed machine-gun fire.

His literary career begins and ends with the poem we quote; except for that, his book records promise rather than achievement.

* Poems..Charles Scribner's Sons, N. Y.: 1917

MARJORIE ALLEN SEIFFERT

Marjorie Allen was born in Moline, Illinois, her family having been pioneers in the manufacture of agricultural machines. At Smith College her chief interest was musical composition, but after graduation, marriage to Otto Seiffert, and maternity, she turned to poetry as more directly expressive and less exacting in its demands upon time and place.

It was a well endowed mind which proceeded to practice a new technique to a point of rare sensitiveness and expertness; and it was a keenly emotional spirit which used it, but one saved from solemnity and egoism by an unfailing and altogether delightful whimsicality. In Mrs. Seiffert was that rare phenomenon, a poet capable of wit, not wit superficial, concerned only with turns of phrase and tricks of humorous observation, but wit profoundly inherent in the subject and in the philosophical attitude of the poet's mind. This kind of wit is rare in English poetry; it is much more Gallic than Anglo-Saxon. In her "modern morality play" *The Old Woman*, a *Poetry* prize-winner, and in *Noah's Ark*—two rhymed dialogues written a few years apart, we find what may rank almost as masterpieces in that particular genre. In these the poet draws lightly, easily, and with gay audacity a full circle of deep and serious meaning.

Her wit served her in the *Spectrist* hoax inaugurated by her friends Witter Bynner and Arthur Ficke to satirize the Imagists, she being the "Elijah Hay" of that riotous trio.

Such poems as the crisp and metallic *Japanese Vase* testify to the richness and variety of this poet's culture. She has travelled far and wide, not only physically but mentally, and she feels, sympathetically and instinctively, the art of other races. There are, however, in her books many lyrics of simple human experience—love, motherhood, friendship, emotional illusions and disillusions. *Maura* is a fine sequence of half-fulfilled half-frustrated love, a sequence which tells not quite the whole story. Her ballads are mostly modern allegories disguised in fantastic garments, and her long narrative, *The King with Three Faces*, is a more ambitious design of the same kind.

* A Woman of Thirty...................................Alf. A. Knopf, N. Y.: 1919
* Ballads of the Singing Bowl......................Charles Scribner's Sons, N. Y.: 1927
The King with Three Faces................................Charles Scribner's Sons: 1929
In *Poetry*: Dec. 1916 (Vol. IX); Nov. 1917 (XI); April 1918 (XII); Jan. 1919 (XIII); Oct. 1919 (XV); July 1921 (XVIII); Feb. 1923 (XXI); June, 1923 (XXII); Sept. 1923 (XXII); June 1924 (XXIV); Oct. 1925 (XXVII); Feb. 1927 (XXIX); April 1928 and Sept. 1928, (XXXII); July 1929 (XXXIV); March 1931 (XXXVII); July 1932 (XL).
In *Others for 1919*..Nich. L. Brown, N. Y.: 1919

FRANCES SHAW

Frances Wells was born in 1872 in Chicago, and educated in local schools and Farmington, Connecticut. At twenty she married Howard Van Doren Shaw, who became distinguished as an architect.

Mrs. Shaw's literary career has been episodic—occasional poems and plays expressive of an exploring mind, sensitive, picturesquely imaginative and somewhat whimsical. Her brief lyrics are as casual and delicate as the notes of a finch on a bough.

Ragdale Book of Verse.........................Privately printed, Lake Forest, Ill.: 1911
Songs of a Baby's Day.............................A. C. McClurg & Co., Chicago: 1917
In *Poetry:* March 1914 (Vol. III); July 1915 (VI); May 1917 (X); Mar. 1919 (XIII); Feb 1921
    (XVII); March 1923 (XXI); Oct. 1923 (XXIII); May 1925 (XXVI);. Oct. 1926 (XXIX).

WILLIAM HASKELL SIMPSON (*Died 1933*)

William Haskell Simpson was born in Lawrence, Kansas, in January, 1858. His college was the University of Kansas, but before graduation he took a job on the *Kansas City Journal.* Since 1881 he has been in the employ of the Santa Fe Railway, from 1900 in charge of that company's advertising. Much travelling through its area has familiarized him with aboriginal life and song, and more than half of his poetry is a lyric interpretation of the pueblo tribes and the Mexican inhabitants of Arizona and New Mexico.

* Along Old Trails...Houghton Mifflin Co.: 1929
In *Poetry:* May 1919 (Vol. XIV); Jan. 1920 (XV); May 1922 (XX); Oct. 1925 (XXVII).

EDITH SITWELL

Edith Sitwell, the daughter of a baronet and granddaughter of an earl, was born in Yorkshire in 1887. She was privately educated, and since 1914 she has lived in London.

In 1916 she began to edit *Wheels* for Basil Blackwell in Oxford. Its modernism was a shock to the Georgians and certain critics, but she further emphasized the direction of her taste by offering, in rapid succession, four or five small volumes of her own verse.

Miss Sitwell is a poet of the baroque. She makes poetry with the aid of intricate devices metrical, fanciful, intellectual. She fabricates it like a fashionable couturier, out of patterned silks tucked and pleated and ruffled; trimmed with ribbons and beads and laces, the whole folded and draped over hoops and corsets. Perhaps there is a human form under the framework, invisible under the enormous skirts, but almost discernible behind the painted mask and the scarlet wig. Indeed, we behold it pacing in elaborate measures, curving, dancing, pirouetting over the drawing-room floor of life. Now and then it opens a window on the queer impossible scrambling world; and then, quickly shutting out the view again, makes a pattern of horrors out of what it imagines it has seen.

All this is authentic art, as skilful as the rococo decorations of Louis the Fifteenth's palaces, though less valid as an expression of its period.

Occasionally some poem takes a shape of more personal beauty, like the first of the *Six Songs* and parts of the long and complicated *Metamorphosis;* for Miss Sitwell cannot always hold her art within restrictive bounds. And under her artificialities is a certain hard harsh brazen motive of satire which with slight strain might be taken as an indictment of her time, her uppercrust world, and herself.

The Wooden Pegasus..............................Basil Blackwell, Oxford, Eng.: 1920
* Bucolic Comedies.......................Gerald Duckworth & Co., Ltd., London: 1923
The Sleeping Beauty...Gerald Duckworth & Co., Ltd., London: Alf. A. Knopf, N. Y.: 1924

* Troy Park.............................Gerald Duckworth & Co., Ltd., London: 1925
Elegy on Dead Fashion...................Gerald Duckworth & Co., Ltd., London: 1926
Poems (Augustan Books)................................Ernest Benn, Ltd., London: 1926
Rustic Elegies...............Gerald Duckworth & Co., Ltd., London; Alf. A. Knopf: 1927
Popular Song (Ariel Poems)...............................Faber & Gwyer, London: 1928
Edith Sitwell (Pamphlet Poets)..................................Stokes, London: 1929
* Gold Coast Customs
            Gerald Duckworth & Co., Ltd., London; Houghton Mifflin Co., Boston: 1929
* Collected Poems.....Gerald Duckworth & Co., Ltd., London; Houghton Mifflin Co.: 1930
Poetry and Criticism........Hogarth Press, London: 1925; Henry Holt & Co., N. Y.: 1926

CONSTANCE LINDSAY SKINNER

Constance Lindsay Skinner was born "in the Canadian Far North," and much of her childhood and youth was passed in close contact with the British-Columbian Indian tribes, whereby she learned much of their customs, feelings, and speech-rhythms. Of late she has lived in New York.

She began as a journalist, and has written plays, novels, tales for children, and sketches of Northwest pioneer history, as well as poems. Her poems are mostly interpretations of aboriginal life and feeling.

* Songs of the Coast Dwellers.......................Coward-McCann, Inc., N. Y.: 1930
In *Poetry:* Oct. 1914 (Vol. V); Jan. 1915 (VII); Feb. 1917 (IX); Feb. 1922 (XIX); Feb. 1925
    (XXV).

LEONORA SPEYER

Leonora von Stosch was born in Washington, D. C., in 1872, the daughter of a Prussian nobleman who had fought for the Union, become a citizen and married a New England girl. Leonora began her career as a violinist, playing solos with the leading orchestras. On marrying Sir Edgar Speyer, she retired from the concert stage and resided in England, where her husband was a prominent banker until the War made the situation difficult for people of German blood.

On coming to live in New York in 1915, Mrs. Speyer became interested in writing verse. Her apprenticeship was uncertain, but her first book (1921) contained some interesting poems in both rhyme and free verse. Her second showed distinctly a studiously developed talent and received the Pulitzer Prize in 1927. The principal poem in her third book, *Monk and Lady,* too long to quote here, is one of the most exact examples of *terza rima* in English, following the Italian model even to the very frequent use of two-syllable rhymes.

A Canopic Jar.......................................E. P. Dutton & Co., N. Y.: 1921
* Fiddler's Farewell......................................Alf. A. Knopf, N. Y.: 1926
Naked Heel..Alf. A. Knopf: 1931
In *Poetry:* July 1920 (Vol. XVI); Feb. 1922 (XIX); Sept. 1922 (XX); Oct. 1924 (XXV);
    Jan. 1926 (XXVII); Dec. 1927 (XXXI).

JAMES STEPHENS

James Stephens was born in 1882 in Dublin, where he had a hard time to get an education and earn his living. Like so many others in Ireland, he owed his literary initiation to "A. E." (George Russell) and his inspiration to Gaelic poetry and legend. His first book showed the lyric trend of his talent, and his first and best novel, if one may so classify it (*The Crock of Gold*, 1912) showed his fantastic imagination and his love of figurative and poetic prose.

In his poetry one finds a singular variety of mood. There is the boyish irresponsible gay vagabond, lover of the road and of animals. Then there is the pure lyrist, the sad singer of *Dark Wings;* or the quaint satirist, casting sidelong glances at human weakness. And lastly, we find a searching human soul, eager in the quest of truth.

Stephens has given lectures and readings in the United States. He is an eloquent platform orator, and his reading of his verse is a beautiful intoned rhythmic chant, not speech at all.

* Insurrections.....................................Maunsel & Co., Ltd., Dublin: 1909
* Insurrections..Macmillan Co., N. Y.: 1912
The Hill of Vision.....................Maunsel & Co., Ltd.; Macmillan Co.: 1912
* Songs from the Clay..Macmillan Co.: 1914
* The Adventures of Seumas Beg.................Macmillan & Co., Ltd., London: 1915
* The Rocky Road to Dublin (same contents as Seumas Beg)........Macmillan Co.: 1915
Green Branches........................Maunsel & Co., Dublin; Macmillan Co.: 1916
Reincarnations...Macmillan Co.: 1917
Little Things.....................................Privately printed, W. M. Hill: 1924
* Collected Poems.........................Macmillan Co., London: 1924; N. Y.: 1926
A Poetry Recital...........................Macmillan Co., London: 1925; N. Y.: 1926
Theme and Variations.........Cayme Press, Toulmin: 1930; Random House, N. Y.: 1930
Strict Joy..Macmillan Co.: 1931
In *Poetry:* Aug. 1914 (Vol. IV).
In *Georgian Poetry:* I–III......................Poetry Bookshop, London: 1912-15-17

GEORGE STERLING (*Died 1926*)

George Sterling was born in Sag Harbor, New York, December 1st, 1869, and educated in local schools and at St. Charles College, Ellicott City, Maryland. At about twenty-five he moved to the West, and lived mostly in San Francisco until his tragic death by suicide November 17th, 1926. In his youth he was remarkably handsome, athletic, a strong swimmer; and a very popular good companion and man about town. Also, in more intimate relations, he was always a most loyal friend. But the drink habit got possession of him and conspired with other weaknesses to ravage his career.

He found a sympathetic publisher in A. M. Robertson, and his early books show unmistakable genius marred by dangerous facility and rhetorical eloquence. His brilliant but too facile craftsmanship was tempted by the worst excesses of the Tennysonian tradition: he never *thinks*—he *deems;* he does not *ask*, but *crave;* he is *fain* for this and that; he deals in *emperies* and *auguries* and *antiphons*, in *casual throes* and *lethal voids*—in many other things of tinsel and fustian, the frippery of a by-gone fashion. However, toward the end of his life he succeeded in disciplining his style; he was "continually dropping off little things;" as he expressed it, and his later poems are of a much stronger texture and less ornate pattern than the exuberant work of his youth.

The Testimony of the Suns......................A. M. Robertson, San Francisco: 1903
A Wine of Wizardry..A. M. Robertson: 1909
The House of Orchids...A. M. Robertson: 1911
* Beyond the Breakers..A. M. Robertson: 1914
Yosemite...A. M. Robertson: 1915
The Evanescent City...A. M. Robertson: 1915
Ode on Opening of Panama Pacific Exposition.....................A. M. Robertson: 1915
The Caged Eagle..A. M. Robertson: 1916

WALLACE STEVENS

Wallace Stevens was born in Reading, Pennsylvania, in 1880, was educated locally and at Harvard, and he is now living in Hartford, Connecticut, being on the legal staff of one of the large insurance companies there located. His introduction as a poet was in *Poetry's* War Number in November, 1917, and two prizes have been awarded to him through that magazine: one for *Three Travellers Watch a Sunrise*, the best one-act play submitted in a competition and printed in July, 1916; and the Levinson Prize for the *Pecksniffiana* group in 1920.

The editor's essay on this poet, written in March, 1924, may be quoted in part:

The delight which one breathes like a perfume from the poetry of Wallace Stevens is the natural effluence of his own clear and untroubled and humorously philosophical delight in the beauty of things as they are. Others may criticize and complain, may long for more perfect worlds or search subliminal mysteries—for him it is enough to watch the iridescent fall of sunlight on blue sea-water and pink parasols, and meditate on the blessed incongruities which break into rainbow colors this earth of ours and the beings who people it. To him the whole grand spectacle is so amazing that no melodramatic upheaval of destiny could possibly increase his sense of awe and wonder, or disturb his philosophic calm. He is content to live profoundly in the beauty of a universe whose lightest, most transient phenomena are sufficient evidence, to a mind in tune with it, of harmonies magnificent to infinity.

For this reason his poems, even those which seem slight, become hints of this immutable perfection. Like a Japanese carver discovering a god in a bit of ivory, Wallace Stevens, in such a poem as the *Paltry Nude* or *Peter Quince at the Clavier* presents the ineffable serenity of beauty.

Man's interference with this serenity—an interference ineffectual in any ultimate sense—is the central theme of his longer poems. In the one-act play *Three Travellers Watch a Sunrise* this interference brings about tragedy; but even tragedy is shown as ineffectual to contradict beauty, whose processional march of splendor demands agony along with joy. In *The Comedian as the Letter C* the interference brings the more bewildering frustration of comedy; but even this falls whimsically into the scheme, for beauty invincible and immortal accepts frustration just as music accepts discord, and the symphony moves on enriched. The hero of *Carlos among the Candles* may be confused and amazed, but he goes on lighting the candles and illuminating with beams from the human imagination the inexhaustible beauty of the world.

Wallace Stevens is a past master of word-magic, and his rhythms have orchestral range, from the piccolo precision of *Peter Parasol* to the rich roll of chorded harmonies in *The Worms at Heaven's Gate*, or the pomp of color and sound in *Le Monocle de mon Oncle*. Like a super-sensitized plate, he is aware of color-subtleties and sound-vibrations which most of us do not detect, and of happiness in fine degrees which most of us do not attain. He derives, so far as one may trace the less obvious origins, from no one;

but like Napoleon he may say, "*Je suis ancêtre!*" for shoals of young poets have derived from him. Quite free of literary allegiances to period or place, he distils into a pure essence the beauty of his own world.

```
* Harmonium................................................Alf. A. Knopf, N. Y.: 1923
* Harmonium (with new poems)................................Alf. A. Knopf: 1931
In Poetry: Nov. 1914 (Vol. V); Nov. 1915 (VII); July 1916 (VIII); Dec. 1917 (XI); May
    1918 (XII); Oct. 1919 (XV); Oct. 1921 (XIX).
In Others: An Anthology of the New Verse.................Alf. A. Knopf, N. Y.: 1916-17
```

MARION STROBEL (*Mrs. James H. Mitchell*)

Marion Strobel was born in Chicago and educated in local schools and St. Timothy's School, Catonsville, Maryland. From 1920 for nearly five years she was associate editor of *Poetry*. In 1923 she married Dr. James Herbert Mitchell, and she continues to live in Chicago.

Marion Strobel's books give us the modern young woman—the various rainbow colors of her prismatic emotional experience, registered in a technique audaciously personal and felicitous. Her flirtations are here, in all their ephemeral intensity; her friendships, even her athletics; also her observation of characters and situations, presented with irony, compassion, or reverence, but always with a keen sense of drama. We have her whole vivid and varied experience of life, an experience unusually fortunate, ending with the charming *Songs to Sally* and other poems of the nursery, a fresh and fair revelation of young motherhood. There is exquisite tenderness in such poems about her friends as *A Bride, Pitiful in Your Bravery*—indeed, all the *Seven Brave Women* sequence.

Marion Strobel has also written two novels and a number of comedies.

```
* Once in a Blue Moon...........................Harcourt, Brace & Co., N. Y.: 1925
* Lost City.................................Houghton Mifflin Co., Boston: 1928
In Poetry: March 1920 (Vol. XV); Feb. 1921 (XVII); March 1922 (XIX); March 1923 (XXI);
    May 1924 (XXIV); Dec. 1924 (XXV); Sept. 1926 (XXVIII); Feb. 1928 (XXXI); Nov.
    1929 (XXXV); Aug. 1932 (XL).
```

MURIEL STUART

Muriel Stuart, an English poet, made her literary début in 1915 in the *English Review* with *Christ at Carnival*, a long poem later published in book form. Later books have emphasized her lyric talent and her dramatic feeling for human character in crises of emotion.

```
The Cockpit of Idols..............................Methuen & Co., Ltd., London: 1918
Poems...............................................Wm. Heinemann, London: 1922
* New Poems and Old.................Edwin Valentine Mitchell, Hartford, Conn.: 1926
Selected Poems.......................................Jonathan Cape, London: 1927
In Poetry: May 1917 (Vol. X); Nov. 1922 (XXI); Oct. 1925 (XXVII); Nov. 1930 (XXXVII).
```

AJAN SYRIAN

"Ajan Syrian" is the literary name of an Armenian rug-dealer long resident in the United States. The poem here quoted, though not a translation, is suggestive, in feeling and manner, of lyrics by poets of his native country.

In *Poetry:* June 1915 (Vol. VI); Aug. 1918 (XII).

GENEVIEVE TAGGARD

Genevieve Taggard was born in 1894 in the state of Washington, but in infancy she was taken to Hawaii, where she remained until the age of twenty. In 1919 she was graduated from the University of California, and soon after she went to New York and became one of the editors of *The Measure*, an excellent monthly magazine of poetry which continued a few years.

Miss Taggard's poems are mostly personal lyrics, though two or three of the best, like *Ice Age*, are reflective and imaginative evocations of conditions outside her experience. A certain hardness, an enamel finish in her technique, is confessed in one of her titles, and one feels in her work the dominance of a sternly trained mind. This trend is indicated by her editorship of the anthology of metaphysical verse, *Circumference*.

In 1931 she was awarded a Guggenheim Fellowship for study in Europe.

```
* For Eager Lovers............................Thomas Seltzer, New York: 1922
Hawaiian Hilltop (Flight I)....................Wyckoff & Gelber, San Francisco: 1923
Words for the Chisel..........................Alf. A. Knopf, N. Y.: 1926
* Travelling Standing Still.....................Alf. A. Knopf: 1928
In Poetry: June 1920 (Vol. XVI); Feb. 1921 (XVII); June 1921 (XVIII); April 1925 (XXVI);
    Feb. 1926 (XXVII); Sept. 1927 (XXX); Aug. 1928 (XXXII).
```

RABINDRANATH TAGORE

Rabindranath Tagore was born in Bengal in 1859, and educated bilingually in India and England. He was the author of lyrics, poetic plays and novels, and was already famous in his own country, when he made a visit to England in 1912, fell in with Ezra Pound and other poets, as well as publishers, and was persuaded to translate into English some of his poems and plays. The first publication of these was a group of the *Gitanjali* in *Poetry* for December, 1912, followed soon by the private *edition de luxe* done by the India Society of London. At this time the poet was visiting his son, then a student in the University of Illinois, and during that winter he made frequent visits to Chicago.

A year later the Nobel Prize for literature made Tagore internationally famous, and since then he has published in English a number of books of his verse and prose, and has given readings and lectures both as a poet and as an ardent Indian nationalist. His lyrics, whether of devotion as in the Gitanjali, or of love and other personal themes as in *The Gardener*, are exquisitely tender in feeling and expert in tonal quality. By using free verse, he avoids the well-nigh impossible task of rendering the intricate Bengali metrical patterns.

```
Gitanjali..........................Privately printed by the India Society, London: 1912
* Gitanjali..................Macmillan & Co., Ltd., London; Macmillan Co., N. Y.: 1913
* The Gardener..............................Macmillan Co., N. Y. and London: 1913
Chitra...............................................India Society, London: 1913
Chitra........................................Macmillan Co., N. Y. and London: 1913
Songs of Kabir (translation)..............................India Society, London: 1914
Songs of Kabir............................Macmillan Co., N. Y. and London: 1914
The Crescent Moon.........................Macmillan Co., N. Y. and London: 1914
The Post-office............................Macmillan Co., N. Y. and London: 1914
The King of the Dark Chamber.................Macmillan Co., N. Y. and London: 1914
Fruit-gathering...........................Macmillan Co., N. Y. and London: 1916
Stray Birds...............................Macmillan Co., N. Y. and London: 1916
The Cycle of Spring.......................Macmillan Co., N. Y. and London: 1917
Gitanjali and Fruit-gathering (1 vol., illustrated)..................Macmillan Co: 1918
Lover's Gift and Crossing.....................Macmillan Co., N. Y. and London: 1918
Gitanjali (popular ed.)....................................Four Seas Co., Boston: 1919
```

Works (Bolpur ed., 10 vols.)...................................Macmillan Co.: 1919
The Fugitive...Macmillan Co.: 1921
Fireflies..Macmillan Co.: 1928
Sheaves...Macmillan Co.: 1932
In *Poetry:* Dec. 1912 (Vol. I); June 1913 (II); Dec. 1913 (III); Sept. 1916 (VIII).

ALLEN TATE

Allen Tate was born November 19th, 1899, in Clarke County, Kentucky, and was brought up and educated in the adjoining states of Kentucky and Tennessee, taking his degree from Vanderbilt University in 1922. That year he joined with John Crowe Ransom, Donald Davidson, Stanley Johnson, and others to found *The Fugitive,* a monthly magazine which for four years did very effective work in presenting to a wider audience the poetry of this southern group. After three years in New York, he went abroad as a Guggenheim Fellow, staying chiefly in Paris from 1928 to 1930. Returning, he settled in the Cumberland Valley of Tennessee to carry out his conviction that only by the rebirth of a lively regional consciousness would the cultural and agrarian regeneration of the South be effected. Besides his book of poems he has written biographical studies of Stonewall Jackson and Jefferson Davis. And he contributes critical articles to the literary reviews.

Tate's poetry is the product of an untiring intellectual curiosity, applied alike to the contemporary world and the cultural history of the past. His earlier poems are too often consumed by their own brilliance, frequently a brilliance merely of allusion and outline, not of intuition. Written less on its own impulse than to give recreation to metaphysical ideas, his work has frequently sagged into the rhetoric of a derivative Elizabethanism. But Tate has never suffered from the skimpy background, the defeating emotional softness, of many contemporary lyrists; his poems are integrated and symmetrically constructed. The beautiful solemnity of the *Ode to the Confederate Dead;* the clairvoyance of *Mr. Pope* and *Mother and Son;* the wit of his historical epigrams; and the fine symbolism of recent poems on Biblical themes all point to the authority of his talent.

* Mr. Pope and Other Poems.........................Minton, Balch & Co., N. Y.: 1928
* Poems: 1928-1931..............................Chas. Scribner's Sons, N. Y.: 1932
In *Poetry:* Nov. 1931 (Vol. XXXIX); May, 1932 (XL).

SARA TEASDALE (*Mrs. S. T. Filsinger: Died 1933*)

Sara Teasdale was born in Saint Louis, Missouri, August 8th, 1884, and her schooling there was supplemented by European travel. Since her marriage to Ernst Filsinger in 1916 she has resided in New York.

In her early books one found a girlish softness—dream "crushes," imaginary love-affairs, tremors of woe and delight; but in *Rivers to the Sea* (1916) one noted the beginning of a hardening process which was shaping her enthusiastic outpourings into poems—poems of a finished and delicate, if narrow technique. In some of the poems in *Love Songs,* of 1917, and in the more austere and mature *Flame and Shadow,* of 1920, a fully developed fine spirit expresses its sensitive reactions to life with an economy of phrase and a simple lyric intensity that show also matured art.

Sara Teasdale's study has been to express emotion in the simplest forms of English lyric verse. Two or three quatrains of three- or four-footed iambic lines, each quatrain emphasized by a single rhyme, form usually the metrical structure of her songs. Miss Teasdale builds upon this simple structure subtle variants of rhythm and melody that weave to a climax expressing fitly some keen emotion. Her instrument is not rich and powerful, capable of chords; and it has more the aching quality of a violin than the plangent triumphant tone of a harp—a violin played with soft tenseness by feminine hands at twilight. One comes upon her music unexpectedly, so to speak, and when she is in her best mood the reward is singularly pure and fine.

Sonnets to Duse...Poet-lore Co., Boston: 1907
Helen of Troy and Other Poems.....................G. P. Putnam's Sons, N. Y.: 1911
Helen of Troy and Other Poems (revised ed.).............Macmillan Co., N. Y.: 1922
* Rivers to the Sea...Macmillan Co.: 1915
* Love Songs...Macmillan Co.: 1917
* Flame and Shadow..Macmillan Co.: 1921
Flame and Shadow (revised ed.)........................Jonathan Cape, London: 1924
* Dark of the Moon...Macmillan Co.: 1926
* Stars Tonight (for Boys and Girls)............................Macmillan Co.: 1930
Strange Victory..Macmillan Co.: 1933
In Poetry: March 1914 (Vol. III); Oct. 1915 (VII); June 1917 (X); April 1918 (XII); Sept. 1919
    (XIV); Aug. 1923 (XXII); Apr. 1924 (XXIV).

EDWARD THOMAS (Died 1916)

Edward Thomas was born in 1878 and educated at Oxford. For years he earned his living by various kinds of work in prose, never discovering his true field until a close friendship with Robert Frost, from 1912 to 1914, led to his attempting verse. He first used the pseudonym Edward Eastaway; a group of his poems was so signed in Poetry in February, 1917. In April of the same year he was killed on the French front.

Thomas' theme, like that of so many English poets—from Cowper and Thomson and John Clare to Edmund Blunden—was the local countryside, rural England. With this school, nature and animals are never wild, always domesticated; and every little detail of quiet country life is poetized with heartfelt loyalty. Thomas did this with more spontaneity and grace than any of his more recent competitors in that field; and certain of his poems are full of an emotional reverence, expressed with quiet simplicity and beauty.

* Poems..Henry Holt & Co., N. Y.: 1917
* Last Poems.......................................Selwyn & Blount, London: 1918
* Collected Poems.......................................Thomas Seltzer, N. Y.: 1921
In Poetry: Feb. 1917 (Vol. IX).

EUNICE TIETJENS (Mrs. Cloyd Head)

Eunice Hammond was born in Chicago in 1884. Her education was cosmopolitan; from fourteen to twenty-one she was in Europe, studying under tutors and at the University of Geneva and the Sorbonne. After her first marriage—to Paul Tietjens, composer of The Wizard of Oz, etc.—she lived in Germany for some years, and took the full course of the Froebel Kindergarten Institute in Dresden. Returning to Chicago, she became a member of the staff of Poetry, resigning her associate editorship to go first to China for a year, and later to France for journalistic war service. In 1920 she married Cloyd Head, and with him has resided, for brief intervals, in Tunis, Tahiti, Italy, New York, and Chicago. She still serves Poetry as a member of its advisory committee.

Amy Lowell, reviewing the Profiles from China in Poetry for September,

1917, found in it a persistent charm—"that charm of something new, sincere, an original thought expressed personally and vividly. . . . As interpretations of Chinese character, these poems are of only the slightest interest; it is as pictures of the fundamental antagonism of the East and the West that they are important. The poet makes no pretence at an esoteric sympathy which she does not possess. . . . In this age of adulation of all things oriental, it is well to meet so fearless an observer as Mrs. Tietjens. . . . There is not a word too much in these poems. They are sharp and beautiful, and extraordinarily satisfying."

And the editor said of the *Profiles from Home* eight years later: "Her loosely patterned free verse, with its rhythms swinging on the borderland between poetry and prose, suits admirably these realistic studies of an observant and uncompromising mind. . . . In the form she has chosen they achieve the maximum of emphasis, whether for beauty or a kind of grimly humorous wisdom."

Mrs. Tietjens' work in rhyme gives further evidence of a rich personality and a wide range of emotional and cosmopolitan experience. Her lyrics are in simple forms.

* Profiles from China.....................................R. F. Seymour, Chicago: 1917
* Profiles from China.......................................Alf. A. Knopf, N. Y.: 1919
* Body and Raiment...Alf. A. Knopf: 1919
Profiles from Home..Alf. A. Knopf: 1925
* Leaves in Windy Weather.......................................Alf. A. Knopf: 1929
In *Poetry:* Sept. 1914 (Vol. IV); Dec. 1914 & Mar. 1915 (V); Dec. 1916 (IX); Aug. 1919 (XIV); Nov. 1920 (XVII); Feb. 1922 (XIX); July & Aug. 1923 (XXII); Jan. 1925 (XXV); April 1927 (XXX); July 1928 (XXXII); June 1929 (XXXIV); Oct. 1930 (XXXVII).

RIDGELY TORRENCE

Ridgely Torrence was born in 1875 at Xenia, Ohio, and was educated at Miami and Princeton. At the turn of the century he was librarian of the Astor Library in New York, later editor of a popular magazine and he is now poetry editor of *The New Republic*. Until the death of William Vaughn Moody in 1908, Torrence, Moody, and Robinson enjoyed a close three-cornered friendship.

Torrence has never been prolific—twenty-five years elapsed between his first small experimental volume and his second and latest, *Hesperides*. Always reticent, sparingly creative, he weaves his mystical patterns in threads of filigree silver, drawn as it were from sky-roving clouds.

Mr. Torrence's art is extremely sensitive; it retreats from the workaday world, not neglectful of experience but yearning for escape into beauty disembodied and eternal. His mysticism bears no relation, however, to established religious systems or creeds; indeed, it works out a ritual of its own, to be used by the unchurchly for the ceremonies of child-naming, burial, etc.—a ritual fine in poetic reverence, but hardly simple enough for its intended purpose.

His poems are singularly confessional—the poet lives more than half in dreams, and most of the book presents phases of the dream in a technique delicately responsive and finished. But sometimes his text comes from everyday people or affairs. In *Eye-Witness* it is a tramp, "homeless reaper of the wind," who carries the poet along to the heights. Again, the motive is suggested by a death, as in *The Son;* or a lynching, as in *The Bird and the Tree;* or even by a city dawn, as in *Three O'Clock*. But always the poet brings us back to the dream, to a sense of the unreality of life and all its seeming-solid ephemera; capturing as he goes bubbles of beauty in poems that gleam with shifting colors.

The House of a Hundred Lights...................Small, Maynard & Co., Boston: 1900
El Dorado: A Tragedy.....................................John Lane Co., N. Y.: 1903
Abelard and Heloise................................Chas. Scribner's Sons, N. Y.: 1907
* Hesperides..Macmillan Co., N. Y.: 1925
In *Poetry:* Dec. 1912 (Vol. I); April 1915 (VI); Jan. 1917 (IX).

MARK TURBYFILL

Mark Turbyfill was born in Oklahoma in 1896, and educated in local schools and a high school in Chicago, where he has lived since he was fourteen. He has followed two arts, dancing and poetry. For some years he was a member of Adolf Bolm's ballet in Chicago, doing second parts to his chief and teaching in the Bolm school. His early poems, here quoted, are somewhat in the Imagist manner, but of late he has written a sequence of satires in free verse, one of them celebrating with laughter the American crowd-crazes for Valentino, Gertude Ederle, Krishnamurti, and other heroes of the hour.

A Marriage with Space is Turbyfill's most ambitious work—a long metaphysical, indeed mystical poem interpreting ecstatically, and often with a fine upward swing of beauty, the mystery of the universe. This poem, which required a whole issue of *Poetry* in June, 1926, won for its author the Levinson Prize.

Turbyfill is dance critic of *The Chicagoan*, and Chicago correspondent of *The Dance.*

* The Living Frieze..............................Monroe Wheeler, Evanston, Ill.: 1921
A Marriage with Space................................Pascal Covici, Chicago: 1927
Evaporation: a Symposium (poems and prose, with Samuel Putnam)
                                   Modern Review, Winchester, Mass.: 1923
In *Poetry:* May 1917 (Vol. X); Aug. 1918 (XII); Oct. 1919 (XV); June 1921 (XVIII); June 1924 (XXIV); Feb. 1926 (XXVII); May 1928 (XXXII); Sept. 1931 (XXXVIII).

JEAN STARR UNTERMEYER

Jean Starr was born in 1886 at Zanesville, Ohio, and educated in local schools and Columbia University. In 1907 she married Louis Untermeyer. She has practiced two arts with success, music and poetry. Her books reveal a rich womanly temperament and an exacting taste in crises of feminine emotion, as well as in more commonplace encounters with ordinary affairs. Her lyric style, studiously trained and developed, is wholly simple and unconscious in her best poems.

Growing Pains...B. W. Huebsch, N. Y.: 1918
* Dreams out of Darkness....................................B. W. Huebsch: 1921
Steep Ascent..Macmillan Co., N. Y.: 1927
In *Poetry:* Jan. 1917 (Vol. IX); Sept. 1918 (XII); Nov. 1921 (XIX); June 1929 (XXXIV).

LOUIS UNTERMEYER

Louis Untermeyer was born in New York in 1885, and he calls himself "the least educated writer in America." He became a designer of jewelry in his father's manufactory, and he was vice-president of the concern when he resigned in 1923 to devote himself to literature. Besides his books of serious verse, he has written a thick volume of parodies and has translated Heine's poems. He has issued also compilations and critical studies in prose for students of the art, and a number of anthologies, of which *Modern American Poetry* and *Modern British Poetry* are the most important.

The Younger Quire................................The Moods Publishing Co.: 1911
First Love......................................Sherman, French & Co., Boston: 1911
* Challenge...Century Co., N. Y.: 1914
". . . and Other Poets"..............................Henry Holt & Co., N. Y.: 1916
These Times...Henry Holt & Co.: 1917
Poems of Heinrich Heine (trans.)...........................Henry Holt & Co.: 1917
* The New Adam.................................Harcourt, Brace & Co., N. Y.: 1920
Heavens...Harcourt, Brace & Co.: 1922
Roast Leviathan..................Jonathan Cape, London; Harcourt, Brace & Co.: 1923
Burning Bush.......................................Harcourt, Brace & Co.: 1928
Food and Drink.....................................Harcourt, Brace & Co.: 1932
The New Era in American Poetry...........................Henry Holt & Co.: 1919
In *Poetry:* June 1916 (Vol. VIII); Sept. 1916 (VIII); May 1919 (XIV); March 1922 (XIX); March 1928 (XXXI); Nov. 1930 (XXXVII).

ALLEN UPWARD (*Died 1926*)

Allen Upward was born in 1863 in Worcester, England, and educated at Great Yarmouth grammar school and the Royal University of Ireland. He practiced as a barrister in both islands, volunteered in the Greek Army, and took part in its invasion of Turkey in 1897. During the twenty years from 1890 he wrote numerous romances and other works in prose, but his poems were rejected by editors and publishers.

Poetry's publication of his *Scented Leaves* in 1913 seemed to their author almost the dawn of a new day. They were widely copied, and Ezra Pound and others hailed him as an involuntary Imagist and included him in their group anthology. He called these *Leaves* "not translations, but recollections of Chinese literature in the sense that flowers are recollections of rain." They were a confession of the increasing oriental influence in occidental poetry, and were definitely in "the new movement." But unfortunately he was unable to continue on this basis, and his poems of later publication were academic and undistinguished.

Upward, working in isolation, had developed an exaggerated egoism, and neglect ended in heartbreak. On November 18th, 1926, he committed suicide in Paris.

In *Poetry:* Sept. 1913 (Vol. II); May 1916 (VIII).

JOHN VAN ALSTYNE WEAVER

John Van Alstyne Weaver was born in 1893 in Charlotte, North Carolina, and was brought to Chicago as a child and educated in local schools, followed by brief attendance at Hamilton College and Harvard. He was working for the Chicago *Daily News* when the War began, and he became a second lieutenant in the service. Since 1920 he has been literary editor of the Brooklyn *Daily Eagle*, with intervals of cinema work in Hollywood.

Weaver's three books of verse are written almost entirely in "the American language." They give us the everyday adventures of everyday city people in the slangy jargon with which they disguise the English of Oxford and Boston. In Mr. Weaver's books there is no vulgarity; for no dialect that passes through human lips is vulgar *per se*, however snobs may call it so in Piccadilly or Park Avenue. These poems in "the American language" are lifted above vulgarity by the genuine human emotion in them, the authentic characterization, the unexpected little turns of pathos, tenderness, or humor. Sometimes the monologues—of a "bar-keep" perhaps, or a drug-store man—seem harsh in their bald realism; but in each case the poet gives us a hint of the man's dream, shows us the special queer glint that lights his life. They have vitality and convincing truth.

```
* In American..............................................Alf. A. Knopf, N. Y.: 1921
* Finders......................................................Alf. A. Knopf: 1923
Turning Point.................................................Alf. A. Knopf: 1930
In Poetry: May 1918 (Vol. XII); Feb. 1920 (XV); Nov. 1922 (XXI).
```

WINIFRED WELLES (*Mrs. Harold H. Shearer*)

Winifred Welles was born in Norwich Town, Connecticut, in 1893, and educated in the neighborhood. Since her marriage to Harold H. Shearer she has lived in New York.

The editor's review of her second book, in *Poetry* for January, 1930, may be quoted in part as applicable to all her work:

These are exquisite poems, as delicately and beautifully made as a cobweb or a bit of old point lace. Their music is like a lute or a harp, their figures take one by surprise. They touch human emotion, and animal emotion also, with fine finger-tips. . . . The only trouble is, one longs, amid all this beauty, for a few strokes of strong color, a few stiff black lines. . . . Perhaps the poet comes nearest to escaping her limitations in such intimate character studies as *Boy*, which is a searching and loving picture of adolescent innocence.

```
* The Hesitant Heart....................................B. W. Huebsch, N. Y.: 1920
* This Delicate Love....................................Viking Press, N. Y.: 1929
Skipping Along Alone..................................Macmillan Co., N. Y.: 1931
In Poetry: May 1922 (Vol. XX); July 1929 (XXXIV).
```

GLENWAY WESCOTT

Glenway Wescott was born about 1900 on a farm in western Wisconsin. He was educated meagrely in the neighborhood, but managed to attend the University of Chicago, where he was elected President of its Poetry Club, organized the year before by students who wished to write verse. He trained himself and them in the precise technique of the Imagists, and the poems here quoted are in that manner. A year or two in Santa Fe after graduation explains some of their subjects.

Wescott has been living abroad mostly since about 1922, and has written two or three novels which have had a distinguished success.

```
* The Bitterns....................................Monroe Wheeler, Evanston, Ill.: 1920
Natives of Rock....................................Francesco Bianco, N. Y.: 1925
In Poetry: Sept. 1921 (Vol. XVIII); Aug. 1923 (XXII); Oct. 1923 (XXIII).
```

JOHN HALL WHEELOCK

John Hall Wheelock was born at Far Rockaway, Long Island, in 1886. In 1908 he took his B. A. at Harvard, and spent the two following years at German universities. He has lived since then in New York, working in the publishing department of Charles Scribner's Sons.

Wheelock's muse is lyric and too easily moved. His early books are lush with over-luxuriance, but among their too numerous entries are some beautiful poems, exultant songs of youth and love. His too great facility is evident in all his volumes, producing a monotony of sentiment and tune, so that the reader longs to make up and pass on to the future a thin volume of his best pieces. This would include chiefly ecstatic lyrics of youth, but a few entries of more recent work would sound a quieter, deeper chord of fervent reconciliation and acceptance. The poet's philosophy lifts him to a realm from which earthly affairs are subdued to harmony and beauty, and his best poems convey his feeling of exalted emotion.

The Human Fantasy...........................Sherman, French & Co., Boston: 1911
* The Beloved Adventure..............................Sherman, French & Co.: 1912
* Love and Liberation.................................Sherman, French & Co.: 1913
Dust and Light................................Charles Scribner's Sons, N. Y.: 1919
The Black Panther.....................................Charles Scribner's Sons: 1922
* The Bright Doom....................................Charles Scribner's Sons: 1927
In *Poetry:* Aug. 1913 (Vol. II); Nov. 1915 (VII); June 1917 (X); Sept. 1917 (X); Jan. 1921
    (XVII); July 1922 (XX); July 1926 (XXVIII); April 1927 (XXX).

ANNA WICKHAM

Anna Wickham was born in 1884 in Wimbledon, Surrey, but from six years to twenty-one she lived in Australia. Returning to study singing in Paris, she found marriage instead of an operatic engagement, and went to live in London, up the hill at Hampstead.

In her poetry, which began in a prolific outburst some years after marriage, she represents the sensitive, restless, nervous, protesting modern woman, the woman who seizes love but forever questions its manifestations. Her style is careless and often prosy, but some of her poems attain, if not beauty, a sharp and salty flavor, and a stabbing thrust toward the hidden causes of feminine aches and pains.

* The Contemplative Quarry...........................Poetry Bookshop, London: 1915
* The Man with a Hammer..................................Poetry Bookshop: 1916
The Little Old House......................................Poetry Bookshop: 1918
* The Contemplative Quarry and The Man with a Hammer
                                            Harcourt, Brace & Co., N. Y.: 1921
In *Poetry:* Jan. 1917 (Vol. IX); July 1922 (XX).

MARGARET WIDDEMER

Margaret Widdemer was born in Doylestown, Pennsylvania. Her local schooling was supplemented by a course at the Drexel Institute Library School, completed in 1909.

Her first book contains her best and most keenly inspired poems, some of which are quoted here. Since that was published, she has shown less poetic fire and energy, perhaps because of writing too much for popular magazines. Besides her books of verse, she has published a number of novels and books for girls.

* The Factories with Other Lyrics...............John C. Winston Co., Philadelphia: 1915;
                                            Henry Holt & Co., N. Y.: 1917
Old Road to Paradise......................................Henry Holt & Co.: 1918
Cross-currents....................................Harcourt, Brace & Co., N. Y.: 1922
Ballads and Lyrics.......................................Harcourt, Brace & Co.: 1925

Collected Poems.....................................Harcourt, Brace & Co.: 1928
In *Poetry:* Nov. 1912 (Vol. I); Aug. 1913 (II); Nov. 1914 & Feb. 1915 (V); Oct. 1917 (XI);
April 1923 (XXII); June 1930 (XXXVI).

MARGUERITE WILKINSON (*Died 1928*)

Marguerite Bigelow was born at Halifax, Nova Scotia, in 1883, and ed-
ucated in various schools and the Northwestern University in Evanston,
Illinois. There she met and married James G. Wilkinson, a teacher, in 1909.
They lived in Evanston, California, and finally in New York, teaching,
writing, lecturing, learning to fly, until her sudden death by drowning
January 12th, 1928.

Her early poems are mostly love lyrics, or rather chants, written in honor
of a happy marriage.

In her later years she experienced a religious exaltation which is recorded
in the sequence, *Sonnets of the New Birth*, contained in her book, *Citadels*.

* In Vivid Gardens............................Sherman, French & Co., Boston: 1911
By a Western Wayside.....................................Privately printed: 1913
Mars, a Modern Morality Play.............................Privately printed: 1915
* Bluestone...Macmillan Co., N. Y.: 1920
The Great Dream...Macmillan Co.: 1923
Citadels...Macmillan Co.: 1926
Radiant Tree...Macmillan Co.: 1927
New Voices: An Introduction to Contemporary Poetry.........Macmillan Co.: 1921, 1928
In *Poetry:* Nov. 1915 (Vol. VII); Aug. 1916 (VIII).

WILLIAM CARLOS WILLIAMS

William Carlos Williams was born in 1883 at Rutherford, New Jersey,
where he still lives as a practicing physician. His parents had recently come
to the States, his father an Englishman and his mother a Porto Rican or
Spanish race. Williams was educated locally and in Switzerland, and received his degree in medicine at the University of Pennsylvania in 1906.

Here he met Ezra Pound, and the two stimulated each other's revolutionary taste in poetry. Williams' first acceptance came from England about
1910. In May, 1913, he appeared in *Poetry* under the Imagist banner, and
from that time he has contributed to many magazines, especially of the left
wing, almost every radical group claiming his company. While many of his
experiments are sheer extravagances, his best poems have extreme beauty of
cadence and tone, and a whimsicality of motive which ranges from merriment
to a half-uttered hint of pathos. His moods and rhythms are singularly
original, unmistakably his own.

The late William Marion Reedy wrote of him: "Williams is forthright,
a hard straight bitter javelin compared to most of the staccatists. But there
is a tang of very old sherry in him, to mellow the irony; a blunt geniality
behind the harlequin. As you read him you catch in your nostrils the pungent
beauty in the wake of his 'hard stuff,' and you begin to realize how little
poetry—or prose—depends on definitions, or precedents, or forms."

The Tempers...Elkin Mathews, London: 1913
* Al Que Quiere.......................................Four Seas Co., Boston: 1917
Kora in Hell: Improvisations..................................Four Seas Co.: 1919
* Sour Grapes...Four Seas Co.: 1922
Spring and All...Contact Pub. Co., Paris: 1923
In *Poetry:* June 1913 (Vol. II); May 1915 (VI); Nov. 1916 (IX); July 1918 (XII); March 1919
(XIII); Jan. 1922 (XIX); July 1930 (XXXVI); Feb. 1931 (XXXVII).
In *Others: An Anthology of the New Verse*....................Alf. A. Knopf, N. Y.: 1916–17

YVOR WINTERS

Yvor Winters was born in Chicago in 1900. After spending most of his childhood in the West, he entered the University of Chicago, but subsequently turned West again, taking his A. B., and A. M. from the University of Colorado; living for a time in New Mexico, and at present at Palo Alto.

Winters' four volumes of verse present a personality of distinct and rigid outline. Their content extends from spare imagism to poems of larger symbolic structure, presenting an austere ethic and a counsel of rigid discipline of will in art and in conduct. The analytical introspection and self-awareness of Winters' mind has never allowed his verse to exist by its own virtue; it is overweighted with the thought to which his prose has thus far given a richer expression. His growth, however, like his thought, is organic. It proceeds from an intellectual discipline as keenly motivated as it is coherent. A reader of his verse is never allowed by its shortcomings to lose a sense of acute anticipation, or a deep confidence in the writer's esthetic responsibility. In *The Proof*, according to J. V. Cunningham, " he gave the sonnet a unique quality of hurry and excitement." In his latest book, eight fairly long poems in heroic couplets "depend on detailed descriptions and are unhurriedly calm."

* The Immobile Wind.............................Monroe Wheeler, Evanston, Ill.: 1921
The Magpie's Shadow.............................Munsterbook House, Chicago: 1922
The Bare Hills...Four Seas Co., Boston: 1928
The Proof...Coward-McCann, Inc., N. Y.: 1930
The Journey and Other Poems.......................Dragon Press, Ithaca, N. Y.: 1931
In *Poetry:* Sept. 1919 (Vol. XIV); Dec. 1920 (XVII); Sept. 1922 (XX); May 1923 (XXII); Jan. 1925 (XXV); March 1927 (XXIX).

HUMBERT WOLFE

Humbert Wolfe was born at Milan, Italy, in 1885, but in infancy he was brought to Bradford, Yorkshire, where he remained until he was nineteen. In 1909 he entered the British Civil Service.

His early verse was of little importance, but in 1919 he began to be noticed, and five years later *Kensington Gardens* became almost popular. Since then he has been much too prolific, and his numerous volumes contain many entries which would be more appropriately placed in newspaper columns.

At his best, however, he is an individualist among British poets, escaping the rural group on the one hand and the super-sophisticates on the other. His poetry, according to George Dillon, in a *Poetry* review of *Kensington Gardens*, is "very delicately articulated, or broadcast, so to speak, upon an extremely elusive wave-length." He continues:

"Indeed, he commands interest first of all as a craftsman. No one writing today has developed a more individual technique, or one more consistently loyal to his own temperament. For unless I mistake him thoroughly, the essence of Mr. Wolfe's temperament is irony; and his finest achievement as a poet has been in the direction of understatement and restraint. A part of that restraint he has achieved by adopting certain experimental devices, such as imperfect rhyme. Many stanzas are saved in this way from banality or sweetness, as when a platitude may be turned into a *bon mot* by a mere twist of inflection. Perhaps it is not too excessive to find in his combinations of a free, abandoned rhythm, set against a staccato metre, the almost symbolic expression of the poet's character—his ironical consciousness of the triviality and transience of all that underlies the most high-flown ardors and agonies."

London Sonnets...................................Basil Blackwell, Oxford: 1920
Shylock Reasons with Mr. Chesterton...........................Basil Blackwell: 1921
* The Unknown Goddess.........Harcourt, Brace & Co., N. Y.; Methuen, London: 1925
Lampoons...........Ernest Benn, Ltd., London: 1925; George H. Doran Co., N. Y.: 1927
Humoresque.........................Ernest Benn, Ltd.; Henry Holt & Co., N. Y.: 1926
Poems (Augustan Books)....................................Ernest Benn, Ltd.: 1926
* Kensington Gardens..............Ernest Benn, Ltd.: 1924; George H. Doran Co.: 1927
Requiem...............................Ernest Benn, Ltd.; George H. Doran Co.: 1927
Cursory Rhymes.........Ernest Benn, Ltd.: 1927; Doubleday Doran & Co., N. Y.: 1928
Others Abide (trans. from the Greek).........Benn: 1927; Doubleday Doran & Co.: 1928
This Blind Rose......................Gollancz, London; Doubleday Doran & Co.: 1929
Early Poems..Basil Blackwell: 1930
Uncelestial City.....................Gollancz, London; Alf. A. Knopf, N. Y.: 1930
Silver Cat and Other Poems......................William Edwin Rudge, N. Y.: 1930

CHARLES ERSKINE SCOTT WOOD

Charles Erskine Scott Wood was born in Erie, Pennsylvania, in 1852. He was graduated at West Point in 1874, and took two degrees at Columbia in 1883. While a lieutenant he engaged in the Nez Perces and Piute campaigns, and he was one of the first white men to go down the Yukon. In 1884, having resigned from the army, he was admitted to the Bar, and practiced in Portland, Oregon, becoming one of the most distinguished lawyers along the Coast. Since his retirement in 1919, he has devoted himself chiefly to literature, voicing in a number of books his protests against social tyrannies and economic injustices.

He has used both rhyme and free verse in his poems. *The Poet in the Desert*, here quoted, probably his most important poem, is in long swinging Whitmanic rhythms.

The Masque of Love......................................Walter Hill, Chicago: 1904
* The Poet in the Desert.........................Privately printed, Portland, Ore.: 1915
The Poet in the Desert (new version)...................Privately printed, Portland: 1918
Maia: a Sonnet Sequence (limited illustrated ed.)....Privately printed, Portland, Ore.: 1918
In *Poetry:* Sept. 1919 (Vol. XIV); Dec. 1920 (XVII); Feb. 1924 (XXIII).

EDITH WYATT

Edith Wyatt was born in 1873 at Tomah, Wisconsin. The family soon moved to Chicago, and Edith was educated in a local private school, followed by two years at Bryn Mawr. She has written two novels, a book of short stories, and two books of essays, besides her book of poems. In her verse she has preferred close metrical forms, sometimes with an elaborate interweaving of rhymes.

* The Wind in the Corn and Other Poems................D. Appleton & Co., N. Y.: 1917
In *Poetry:* Jan. 1915 (Vol. V); Dec. 1916 (IX); April 1931 (XXXVIII).

ELINOR WYLIE (*Died 1928*)

Elinor Hoyt was born in 1887 in New Jersey, of a family long associated, on both sides, with Pennsylvania, of which state her grandfather was governor. She lived in Washington through her girlhood and her early first marriage, but her second marriage, to Horace Wylie, took her abroad and later to New England. In 1924 she married William Rose Benét, retaining Wylie in her literary signature. They lived mostly in New York, with intervals of travel, until her sudden death in New York, December 16th, 1928, after a sojourn of several months in England.

Her first poems, like a racer's first paces, were of an instinctive yet trained precision; there was no fumbling or halting, never a stumble or a false step. To be sure, she began later than most poets, never discovering her literary gift until she was well past thirty and disciplined by a tragic experience of life. Still, waiting beyond youth for one's début in any art does not imply adequate practice in technique—a late beginning tends to make the first steps slow and painful. Not so, however, in Elinor Wylie's case; her earliest group in *Poetry*, which she called her "first acceptor," showed her a master of her tools, capable of artistry which admitted no compromise. Here we have at once that exactness of method—the true word, the balanced line, the close rhyme-scheme, in short, the skill and polish—which characterize all her work. We have also the personal significance—her own friendships, loves, joys, agonies implied but never stated, suggested but never sentimentalized.

What she seems to say in the sharp intensity of her poems is the fragility of life in its well-nigh intolerable beauty, and she says it with a sparkle of rich many-colored glazes, like eighteenth-century French porcelains. Her art, indeed, allies itself with the eighteenth-century, not so much with the poetry of that period as with those other arts, at once hard as jewels and supremely delicate, which must pass through fire to earn perfection. Like them, she protected emotion with an armor of artificiality, she glazed it with shining colors. And like those rigid old porcelains, so enduring in their fragility, her poems would seem to be protected by their quality, as faultless exhibits from our multi-varied century.

A pattern of short lines in staccato rhythm delighted her for purposes more or less satiric; we find her using it in *Peregrine*, the longest poem in her second book, and doubling it into the tetrameter lines of *Miranda's Supper* in the third book, the longest poem she ever published. The swift steps of the measure accept happily that intricate play of highly original rhymes in which she delighted; she tosses them like a juggler his balls, and catches them dangerously at the end of a line as they seem about to escape her handling. They are clever, witty, miraculously effective; but more than that, they are robust, muscular—they carry the light texture of these poems with authority and power.

But these quick-stepping staccato rhythms were not the only resource of her skilful art. From the first she used the sonnet form now and then, *Atavism* being her earliest sonnet, winning from it slow sweeping rhythms. And in the nineteen sonnets—*One Person*—of her posthumous book we have one of the notable love-sequences of the language. Here there is no trace of artificiality, none of the brittle surface to be found in much of her earlier work.

George Dillon, reviewing this book in *Poetry* for July, 1929, said:

"One reads with the consciousness that no living poet is more extraordinarily alive. The poet of the sonnet sequence and of the two magnificent longish poems, *Hymn to Earth* and *This Corruptible*, is a poet one has not known before, a poet one has never quite suspected Elinor Wylie of being. Architecturally serene, yet rooted in the very quick of emotion, these poems are at once nobler and more proficiently wrought than anything else she has written. To read them is to reckon for the first time the full stature of her genius."

*Nets to Catch the Wind...........................Harcourt, Brace & Co., N Y.: 1921
Black Armour.......George H. Doran Co., N. Y.: 1923; Martin Secker, Ltd., London: 1928

Trivial Breath...............................Alf. A. Knopf, N. Y. and London: 1928
* Angels and Earthly Creatures...................................Alf. A. Knopf: 1929
* Collected Poems...Alf. A. Knopf: 1932
In *Poetry:* April 1921 (Vol. XVIII); June 1923 (XXII); May & June 1928 (XXXII).

WILLIAM BUTLER YEATS

William Butler Yeats was born in 1865 at Sandymount, Ireland; the son of John B. Yeats, the Irish artist who passed his later years in New York. Through his childhood the boy lived in wild Sligo, imbibing fairy tales and other folk-lore as his veritable spirit food. He was educated later in London and Dublin schools.

During the 'nineties Yeats became a leader of the Irish revival, perhaps the most active and ardent leader, although his associates were such men and women of genius as J. M. Synge, Lady Gregory, George Moore, Lionel Johnson, Ernest Dowson, and others. The poet told one chapter of the story at a banquet given in his honor in Chicago by *Poetry's* staff, March 1st, 1914, saying: "When I was beginning to write in Ireland, there was all around me the rhetorical poetry of the Irish politicians. We young writers rebelled against that rhetoric; there was too much of it and to a great extent it was meaningless. When I went to London I found a group of young lyric writers who were also against rhetoric. We formed the Rhymer's Club; we used to meet and read our poems to one another, and we tried to rid them of rhetoric. . . . We wanted to get rid not only of rhetoric but of poetic diction. We tried to strip away everything that was artificial, to get a style like speech, as simple as the simplest prose, like a cry of the heart. . . . Real enjoyment of a beautiful thing is not achieved when a poet tries to teach. It is not the business of a poet to instruct his age. His business is merely to express himself, whatever that self may be."

This movement became an international influence. It definitely vetoed whatever was stilted and prosy in the Victorian tradition—volumes of rhymed eloquence and loftily worded narrative were relegated to the upper shelves of literature. Yeats himself, however, was a romantic, but he took his romance with a difference, and expressed it in Celtic folk-drama like *The Land of Heart's Desire*, or in lyrics like the lovely wistful *Lake Isle of Innisfree*. *The Wind Among the Reeds*, his volume of 1899, is frankly in the Celtic tradition, making effective use of the old heroes and symbols.

The remarkable thing about Yeats is that he was able to discipline his muse, and lead her on to more modern subjects and a sterner style. Although he remains unalterably a romantic, although he is interested in spiritism, astrology, and magic, we find in his twentieth-century work a notable change from the "iridescent brilliance" of his earlier style. As Edmund Wilson put it in the *New Republic* in April, 1925: "Those early rainbows have proved scarcely more than a romantic prelude to his more important poetry. Sometime about the beginning of the century, Mr. Yeats tells us in his autobiography, he became dissatisfied with this early work and resolved to eliminate rigorously from his style both romantic rhetoric and symbolistic vagueness. He would reduce it to something definite and hard; something both severer and more intense. . . .

"The change to his new style is seen very clearly in the collected volume of *Later Poems*. By 1912 the pre-Raphaelite growths have been completely rooted out. He has worked into a soberer and solider style from which the soap-bubble colors have vanished and left only the clear aspect of 'cold Clare rock and Galway rock and thorn.' He has become less prodigal of

symbols and names, and those symbols which he does employ have acquired
a new austerity—a new purity and precision. When he revisits the heroic
world of Irish mythology it is seen with a new homeliness of detail. And
more and more he fixes upon the imperfect in which he actually finds himself. He desires, as he says in another part of the poem about the fisherman,
'to write for my own race and for the reality.' With a boldness rewarded
by a success unequalled among his English contemporaries, he undertakes
to intensify into poetry the circumstances of his own life and the events of
the life about him. And this he does, not by vulgarizing his style, but by
dignifying his subjects—at the same time that he does not cease to deal with
them in the plainest language. He can even challenge comparison with
Dante—whom he now describes as 'the chief imagination of Christendom'—
in his ability to achieve a grand manner by sheer intensity without rhetoric."
    Mr. Wilson concludes that "Mr. Yeats is one of the few genuine masters
alive—perhaps the only poet of the first magnitude."

Mosada: A Dramatic Poem..........................Privately printed, Dublin: 1886
The Wanderings of Oisin and Other Poems......Kegan, Paul, Trench & Co., London: 1889
The Countess Kathleen and Various Legends and Lyrics....T. Fisher Unwin, London: 1892
The Land of Heart's Desire.....T. Fisher Unwin, London; Stone & Kimball, Chicago: 1894
Poems.......................T. Fisher Unwin, London; Copeland & Day, Boston: 1895
The Wind among the Reeds........John Lane, London: 1899; John Lane Co., N. Y.: 1905
The Shadowy Waters
                    Hodder & Stoughton, London: 1900; Dodd, Mead & Co., N. Y.: 1901
Plays for an Irish Theater.........A. H. Bullen, London; Maunsel & Co., Dublin: 1903–07
    (Vols. I, II, III, and V are plays by W. B. Y.)
In the Seven Woods
                    Dun Emer Press, Dundrum, Ire.; Macmillan Co., London and N. Y.: 1903
Poems 1899–1905...................A. H. Bullen, London; Maunsel & Co., Dublin: 1906
The Shadowy Waters (acting version)..............................A. H. Bullen: 1907
Collected Works in Verse and Prose (8 vols.).............Chapman & Hall, London: 1908
Poetical Works (2 vols.)..................................Macmillan Co., N. Y.: 1908
* The Green Helmet and Other Poems
                    Cuala Press, Dundrum, Ire.: 1910; Macmillan Co., N. Y.: 1921
A Selection from the Love Poetry of W. B. Y........................Cuala Press: 1913
* Responsibilities—Poems and a Play..............................Cuala Press: 1914
* Responsibilities and Other Poems........................Macmillan Co., N. Y.: 1916
* The Wild Swans at Coole, Other Verses and a Play in Verse
                    Cuala Press: 1917; Macmillan Co., N. Y.: 1919
* Per Amica Silentiæ Lunæ......................Macmillan Co., London & N. Y.: 1918
Four Plays for Dancers.........................Macmillan Co., London & N. Y.: 1921
* Selected Poems......................................Macmillan Co., N. Y.: 1921
Seven Poems and a Fragment....................................Cuala Press: 1922
Later Poems..............................Macmillan Co., London: 1922; N. Y.: 1924
Plays in Prose and Verse..Macmillan Co.: 1924
Early Poems and Stories.......................................Macmillan Co.: 1925
Works in six volumes..Macmillan Co.: 1927
The Tower..Macmillan Co.: 1928
Poems..Ernest Benn, Ltd., London: 1929
In *Poetry:* Dec. 1912 (Vol. I); April 1913 (II); Oct. 1913 (III); May 1914 (IV); Feb. 1916
    (VII); Oct. 1917 (XI); Jan. 1919 (XIII); Nov. 1919 (XV).

MORTON DAUWEN ZABEL

    Morton Dauwen Zabel was born at Minnesota Lake, Minnesota, in
1901; educated at the St. Thomas Military College, the University of Minnesota, and the University of Chicago, with briefer periods at several other
universities; has been a teacher of literature and art history; now holds a
professorship at Loyola University, Chicago; and has published extensively
in *The New Republic, The Arts, The Nation, Art and Archæology, Books,
Poetry, The London Mercury, The Commonweal, the Freeman,* and other mag-

azines. Since 1928 he has been associate editor of *Poetry: A Magazine of Verse*. He has in preparation a collection of essays on poetry, and a long study of Ingres and the classical elements in modern painting, portions of which have already been published serially.

In *Poetry:* Jan. 1928 (Vol. XXXI); Jan. 1930 (XXXV).

MARYA ZATURENSKY (*Mrs. Horace Gregory*)

Marya Zaturensky was born in Moscow in 1901, and spent her first ten years mostly in a small Russian village. After being brought to New York she attended grammar school for awhile and began work in a factory at fourteen. In 1925 she married Horace Gregory; with their two children, they live in Long Island City.

Her introduction to modern poetry was through the first edition of this book, which she read at a public library. She found the art less remote than she had thought, and began to write poems which were accepted by various editors from about 1920.

Her sequence, *Elegies over John Reed*, was awarded, in 1924, the initial John Reed Memorial Prize by *Poetry*.

In *Poetry:* April 1920 (Vol. XV); Sept. 1921 (XVIII); Aug. 1923 (XXII); March 1924 (XXIII); May 1928 (XXXII); July 1930 (XXXVI).

ANTHOLOGIES (*Chronologically listed*)

Georgian Poetry (biennials ed. by Edward Marsh)
                    Poetry Bookshop, London: 1911–12, 1913–15, 1916–17, 1918–19
The Lyric Year (ed. by Ferdinand Earle)................Mitchell Kennerley, N. Y.: 1912
Anthology of Magazine Verse (annuals, ed. by William Stanley Braithwaite)
                    B. J. Brimmer Co., Boston: 1913–1927
Des Imagistes......................................Alb. & Chas. Boni, N. Y.: 1914
Some Imagist Poets.........................Houghton Mifflin Co., Boston: 1915-16-17
Wheels: An Anthology of Verse...........................B. H. Blackwell, Oxford: 1916
Others: An Anthology of the New Verse (ed. by Alfred Kreymborg)
                    Alf. A. Knopf, N. Y.: 1916
Anthology of Irish Verse (ed. by Padraic Colum).............Macmillan Co., N. Y.: 1916
Poems of the Great War (ed. by J. W. Cunliffe)...................Macmillan Co.: 1916
An Annual of New Poetry.......................Constable & Co., Ltd., London: 1917
Christ in the (American) Poetry of Today (ed. by Martha Foote Crow)
                    Woman's Press, N. Y.: 1917
A Treasury of War Poetry (2 series, ed. by George Herbert Clarke)
                    Houghton Mifflin Co.: 1917–1919
New Paths (ed. by C. W. Beaumont & M. T. H. Sadler)...C. W. Beaumont, London: 1918
The Path on the Rainbow: Songs and Chants from Indians of North America (ed. by
        George W. Cronyn)..............................Boni & Liveright, N. Y.: 1918
Yanks: A. E. F. Verse.............................G. P. Putnam's Sons, N. Y.: 1919
Others for 1919 (ed. by Alfred Kreymborg)..............Nicholas L. Brown, N. Y.: 1920
Songs of the Cowboys (ed. by N. Howard Thorp)............Houghton Mifflin Co.: 1921
Die Neue Welt. Anthology of Recent American Lyrics (tr. into German by Claire Goll)
                    S. Fischer, Berlin: 1921
Modern American Poets (ed. by Conrad Aiken)........Martin Secker, Ltd., London: 1922
Book of American Negro Poetry (ed. by James Weldon Johnson)
                    Harcourt, Brace & Co., N. Y.: 1922, 1930
Come Hither (compiled by Walter de la Mare)
                    Constable & Co., Ltd., London: 1923; Alf. A. Knopf: 1928
The Best Poems of 1924–32 (annuals, ed. by Thomas Moult)
                    Jonathan Cape, London: Harcourt Brace & Co.: 1924–1932
The Chapbook: A Miscellany (ed. by Harold Monro)..........Poetry Bookshop: 1924–25
Continent's End, An Anthology of Contemporary California Poets (ed. by George Sterling,
        Genevieve Taggard, and James Rorty)...Book Club of California, San Francisco: 1925
Modern American Poetry (ed. by Louis Untermeyer)....Harcourt, Brace & Co.: 1925, 1930

Modern British Poetry (ed. by Louis Untermeyer)......Harcourt, Brace & Co.: 1925, 1930
The Answering Voice: Love Lyrics by Women (ed. by Sara Teasdale)
Macmillan Co.: 1926, 1930
Caroling Dusk: Anthology of Verse by Negro Poets (ed. by Countee Cullen)
Harper & Bros., N. Y.: 1927
The American Songbag (with music) (ed. by Carl Sandburg)...Harcourt, Brace & Co.: 1927
The Winged Horse (ed. by Joseph Auslander & Frank E. Hill)
Doubleday, Page & Co., N. Y.: 1927
Fugitives (the Nashville, Tenn., group).....................Harcourt, Brace & Co.: 1928
The Lyric South (ed. by Addison Hibbard)........................Macmillan Co.: 1928
The Turquoise Trail: New Mexico Poetry (ed. by Alice Corbin Henderson)
Houghton Mifflin Co.: 1928
American Poetry (compiled by Conrad Aiken).............Modern Library, N. Y.: 1929
Circumference: Varieties of Metaphysical Verse (ed. by Genevieve Taggard)
Covici, Friede, N. Y.: 1929
An Anthology of Revolutionary Poetry (ed. by Marcus Graham)............N. Y.: 1929
Twentieth Century Poetry (ed. by John Drinkwater, Henry Seidel Canby,
and Wm. Rose Benét)...................................Houghton Mifflin Co.: 1929
The Book of Sonnet Sequences (ed. by Houston Peterson)....Longmans, Green & Co.: 1929
The City Day (ed. by Eda Lou Walton)...................Ronald Press Co., N. Y.: 1929
Prize Poems 1913-29 (ed. by Charles A. Wagner)................Chas. Boni, N. Y.: 1930
The Red Harvest: The Poets' Cry for Peace (ed. by Vincent G. Burns)...Macmillan Co.: 1930
Lyric America (1630-1930) (ed. by Alfred Kreymborg)..Coward-McCann, Inc., N. Y.: 1930
Imagist Anthology 1930: New Poetry by the Imagists..................Covici, Friede: 1930
Northwest Verse (ed. by H. G. Merriam).....Caxton Printers, Ltd., Caldwell, Idaho: 1931
Younger Poets (Poems by Boys and Girls of High-school Age (ed. by Nellie B. Sergent)
D. Appleton & Co., N. Y.: 1932
Lyra Mystica (ed. by Charles Carroll Albertson)....................Macmillan Co.: 1932
A Treasury of Irish Verse (ed. by Stopford Brooke & T. W. Rolleston)
Macmillan Co.: 1932

ANTHOLOGIES OF FOREIGN VERSE TRANSLATED INTO ENGLISH

A Harvest of German Verse (tr. by Margarete Münsterberg)......D. Appleton & Co.: 1916
Songs of Ukraina, with Ruthenian Poems (tr. by Florence Randal Livesay)
J. M. Dent & Sons, Ltd., London; E. P. Dutton & Co., N. Y.: 1916
Armenian Poems (tr. by Alice Stone Blackwell)...........Robert Chambers, Boston: 1917
An Anthology of Swedish Lyrics 1750-1915 (tr. by Charles Wharton Stork)
American-Scandinavian Foundation, N. Y.: 1917
The Poets of Modern France (tr. by Ludwig Lewisohn).......B. W. Huebsch, N. Y.: 1918
Anthology of Modern Slavonic Literature (tr. by P. Selver)
Kegan Paul, Trench, Trubner & Co., Ltd., London; E. P. Dutton & Co., N. Y.: 1919
A Hundred and Seventy Chinese Poems (tr. by Arthur Waley)........Alf. A. Knopf: 1919
More Translations from the Chinese (tr. by Arthur Waley)..........Alf. A. Knopf: 1919
Anthology of Jugoslav Poetry (tr. by B. Stevenson Stanoyevich)
Rich. G. Badger, Boston: 1920
Modern Czech Poetry (tr. by P. Selver)
Kegan Paul, Trench, Trubner & Co., Ltd., London; E. P. Dutton & Co., N. Y.: 1920
Modern Russian Poetry (tr. by Babette Deutsch & Avrahm Yarmolinsky)
Harcourt, Brace & Co.: 1921
Lyric Forms from France (tr. by Helen Louise Cohen)..........Harcourt, Brace & Co.: 1922
An Anthology of Italian Poems (13th-19th Centuries) (tr. by Madame Lorna di Lucchi)
Alf. A. Knopf: 1922
Contemporary German Poetry (tr. by Babette Deutsch & Avrahm Yarmolinsky)
Harcourt, Brace & Co.: 1923
Sonnets (with Folk Songs from the Spanish) (tr. by Havelock Ellis)
Houghton Mifflin Co.: 1925
A Bouquet from France (100 French Poems: tr. by Wilfred Thorley)
Houghton Mifflin Co.: 1926
Poetry of the Orient: Classic Secular Poetry of the Major Eastern Nations
(ed. by Eunice Tietjens).......................................Alf. A. Knopf: 1928
Modern Swedish Poetry (tr. by C. D. Locock)......................Macmillan Co.: 1929
An Anthology of Czechoslovak Poetry (tr. by Clarence A. Manning)
Columbia Univ. Press, N. Y.: 1929
An Anthology of World Poetry (including English and American:
edited by Mark Van Doren).............................Alb. & Chas. Boni: 1929